Fodor's

SCOTLAND

FODOR'S
TRAVEL PUBLICATIONS

NEW YORK • TORONTO
LONDON • SYDNEY • AUCKLAND

WWW.FODORS.COM

195

CONTENTS

KEY TO SYMBOLS

- ✚ Map reference
- ✉ Address
- ☎ Telephone number
- ⊙ Opening times
- ⬝ Admission prices
- Ⓤ Underground station
- 🚌 Bus number
- 🚃 Train station
- ⛴ Ferry/boat
- ⬛ Driving directions
- ℹ Tourist office
- ⬝ Tours
- 📖 Guidebook
- 🍴 Restaurant
- ☕ Café
- 🍷 Bar
- 🏬 Shop
- ① Number of rooms
- ❄ Air conditioning
- 🏊 Swimming pool
- 🏋 Gym
- ❓ Other useful information
- ▷ Cross reference
- ★ Walk/drive start point

69

110

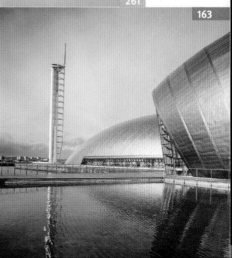

261

163

CONTENTS SCOTLAND

3

UNDERSTANDING SCOTLAND

Understanding Scotland is an introduction to the country, its geography, economy, history and its people, giving a real insight into the nation. Living Scotland gets under the skin of Scotland today, while The Story of Scotland takes you through the country's past.

Scotland is an area of northern Britain, a separate kingdom until 1707. Extending over 78,722sq km (30,414sq miles), it covers around one-third of the landmass of Britain but, with just 5 million inhabitants, has less than one-tenth of the total population. It has Britain's highest mountain, Ben Nevis (1,343m/4,406ft) and deepest lake, Loch Morar (over 305m/1,000ft). You could probably drive overland from one end to the other within 24 hours, if you wanted and weather permitting—reaching the extremities of the islands would take you a little longer. But don't be fooled by the size on a map: There's enough to explore here to take a lifetime of discovery.

GETTING PAST THE CLICHÉS

Scotland sells itself to the world as a land of misty mountains and big scenery, romantic and tragic history, tartan McHaggisry with a beating Celtic heart. Anybody who comes to these shores looking for this image is unlikely to go away disappointed—the mountains are undoubtedly majestic, the history rich and well told, and yes, some Scotsmen wear kilts.

But, of course, Scotland has a great deal to offer beyond the clichés, as any visitor who scratches the surface of this intriguing and contradictory land will soon discover. And it is the little personal discoveries—a glimpse of a hidden fairy-tale castle between the trees, the heady scent of a heather moor on a hot day, the

unexpected sight of an otter nosing along the shore, a cheery conversation with the only other walkers on a bare mountainside, a fresh-washed beach of pure shell sand in a turquoise bay, a superb meal of fresh seafood in a pub you've chanced upon in a place where you can't begin to pronounce the Gaelic name—which make any visit here memorable.

LAND AND ECONOMY

Most of the population lives around the urban centres of Edinburgh and Glasgow, Dundee and Aberdeen.

Approximately half of Scotland is covered by natural or semi-natural vegetation, which includes heather moorland, peat bog and woodland, both natural and planted. Around 11 per cent of the land is used for arable agriculture (predominantly cereals and vegetables), and slightly more for improved grazing.

The heavy manufacturing industry of the 19th and early 20th centuries (such as shipbuilding) for which Scotland was once renowned, has given way to light industry, including electronics and technology centred on Silicon Glen, the area between Glasgow and Edinburgh. Industrial production across the country includes woven textiles, brewing and distilling, and fisheries and tourism both make significant contributions. Oil and natural gas are extracted from beneath the waters of the North Sea.

RELIGION

The Protestant, Presbyterian Kirk or Church of Scotland is the established (official) religion in Scotland. Unlike the Church of England, it does not have the monarch at its head, but is governed by its General Assembly, with a leader, the Moderator, elected annually. About one third of Scottish Christians are Roman Catholics, mainly in the west of Scotland, in the Highlands and on some of the western isles.

Although Scotland, like other Eurpean nations, is becoming increasingly multi-faithed, this is most noticeable in Glasgow and Edinburgh. Islam is now the second biggest religion after Christianity, though it represents less than 1 per cent of the population—in contrast to 28 per cent who claim to have no religion at all. There are also small but important Jewish, Sikh and Hindu communities in Glasgow.

GOVERNMENT

Queen Elizabeth II is the hereditary monarch of Britain, including Scotland. The British government, based at Westminster, London, holds overall power; it is made up from the political party with the most elected Members of Parliament (MPs). The Westminster parliament, which makes the laws for Britain, includes 59 Scottish MPs.

Since 1999, Scotland has also had its own parliament, based in the capital, Edinburgh, with 129 elected members (MSPs). The Scottish government (or Scottish Executive) is made up of MSPs from the political party holding the most seats. The role of the First Minister within Scotland is approximately equivalent to the role of the Prime Minister within the whole of Britain. Powers devolved from Westminster include matters of education, health and environmental policies in Scotland; Westminster retains control of defence, fiscal policy, foreign affairs and national security.

At a more local level, Scotland is divided into 32 unitary authorities. Of these, the biggest in area is the Highland Region (2,611,906ha/6,529,765 acres, pop. 208,000), and the smallest is the City of Dundee (5,500ha/13,750 acres, pop. 145,000). The largest population falls within the City of Glasgow (pop. 612,000), the smallest in Orkney (pop. 19,810).

Opposite clockwise from left to right *The woodlands and mountains of Glen Affric in the Highlands; turreted Castle Fraser, west of Aberdeen; the modern Scottish Parliament building*

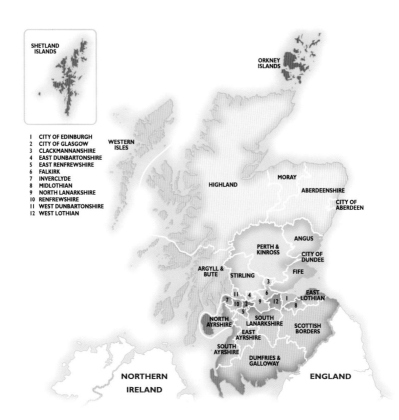

SHETLAND
ISLANDS

ORKNEY
ISLANDS

1   CITY OF EDINBURGH
2   CITY OF GLASGOW
3   CLACKMANNANSHIRE
4   EAST DUNBARTONSHIRE
5   EAST RENFREWSHIRE
6   FALKIRK
7   INVERCLYDE
8   MIDLOTHIAN
9   NORTH LANARKSHIRE
10 RENFREWSHIRE
11 WEST DUNBARTONSHIRE
12 WEST LOTHIAN

WESTERN
ISLES

MORAY

HIGHLAND

ABERDEENSHIRE

CITY OF
ABERDEEN

ANGUS

PERTH &
KINROSS

CITY OF
DUNDEE

ARGYLL &
BUTE   STIRLING

FIFE

3

11   4   6
7 10 2 9   12 1
        5   8

EAST
LOTHIAN

NORTH
AYRSHIRE

SOUTH
LANARKSHIRE

EAST
AYRSHIRE

SCOTTISH
BORDERS

SOUTH
AYRSHIRE

DUMFRIES &
GALLOWAY

NORTHERN

IRELAND

ENGLAND

SCOTLAND'S REGIONS AT A GLANCE
UNDERSTANDING THE REGIONS

To help you find your way through the information in
this book, we have divided the country into six areas.
Edinburgh and **Glasgow** have their own sections,
matching their very different identities and appeal for the
visitor, the former with a genteel, cultured, 18th-century
outlook, the latter proud of its image as a gritty Victorian
industrial city. **Southern Scotland** covers the areas of
Dumfries and Galloway, Borders and Lothians, which
are rich in rolling hills, wide green valleys, appealing
small towns and a history centred on conflict with its
English neighbours. **Central Scotland** takes in the
wooded heart of the country and extends eastward
across the fertile Perthshire farmland into Fife,
encompassing mansions and fishing villages, modern
engineering and a history of rebellion and skirmish. The
Highlands and Islands is a mantle for the wild high
country of the mainland and the stunningly beautiful
islands of the western coast, with remote fortifications,
lonely glens and Britain's last areas of wilderness. The
northern isles of **Orkney and Shetland** have an identity
that is shared as much with Scandinavia as it is with the
Highlands, which rightly earns them their own division
within the book.

EDINBURGH

Although smaller than Glasgow, Edinburgh is Scotland's
capital and home to its Parliament. The city is known for
its culture, showcased every summer in the Edinburgh
Festival. There are many fine museums and galleries,
including three national art collections. Its Victorian and
Georgian architcuture make it one of the most attractive
cities in Europe, and one that is easily explored on foot.
A walk along the Royal Mile from Holyroodhouse and the
Scottish Parliament at the eastern end, all the way up
to Edinburgh Castle at the western end, encompasses
great chunks of Scottish history.

GLASGOW

Until Glasgow was made European City of Culture in
1990, it would have been on very few lists of "must see"
European cities. The accolade opened people's eyes to
its good points, showing that behind the gritty image
was a culture and identity all its own. It continues to
grow and to bloom, but without losing any of its rugged
nature: the Glaswegian people would never allow that
to happen. This means that for most visitors Glasgow is
a pleasant surprise. Despite its industrial image, it has
over 70 parks and gardens, and some world-class art
collections. You will still find the rough-and-ready pubs,

but you will also discover chic and stylish bars and clubs, and some of Scotland's finest restaurants.

SOUTHERN SCOTLAND

The English-Scottish border runs diagonally and so there are many places in southern Scotland that are further south than parts of England. In fact, there are places on both sides of the border that, in the past, have belonged to the other country. It's what makes this part of Scotland so fascinating, as these are lands that have been fought over, lands with dramatic history. Today they are a very welcoming part of Scotland, a gentle but beautiful introduction to the country for those driving north from England. The rolling hills and the flowing rivers may not seem too different from parts of the scenery in northern England, but the Scottish culture is strong here, and there is no doubt which side of the border you are.

CENTRAL SCOTLAND

North from Edinburgh and Glasgow, Central Scotland is a good preparation for the drama and spectacle of the real highland scenery beyond. Head northeast from Edinburgh to Fife, and here you'll find yourself in heavily wooded landscape that is still know as the Kingdom of Fife within Scotland. On the coast is the golfing town of St. Andrews, and further north the equally well-known golf courses at Carnoistie, on the far side of Scotland's fourth-largest city, Dundee. Head west and you reach Perthshire, and then the grandeur of the Grampian Mountains, south of which are the wooded glens and lochs which make up the Trossachs. Central Scotland may be quite small in size, but it certainly packs a lot in.

Above *Red deer, Loch Lomond and the Trossachs National Park*

HIGHLANDS AND ISLANDS

The Scottish Highlands make up about half of the whole Scottish mainland and contain some of the most dramatic scenery in Europe. They're also the oldest mountains in Europe, dating back 3,000 million years. The area is sparsely populated, even by Scottish standards, making it the perfect place to get away from it all and see the scenery at its unspoiled best.

The islands, too, provide an escape from the modern world: of almost 800, only 130 or so are inhabited. These range from the most southerly island, Arran, which is actually further south than the English town of Berwick-upon-Tweed, to the most northerly inhabited island, which is Unst in the Shetlands (see below). It's roughly 300 miles (480km) between the two, with almost the entire Scottish mainland standing between them.

ORKNEY AND SHETLAND

These two island groups off the northeast corner of Scotland stand apart from the others, and from the mainland, even though the closest, the Orkneys, are visible from John o'Groats. To put that into perspective, the more distant Shetlands are much closer to Bergen in Norway than they are to Edinburgh. Out here the main Shetland island is called Mainland, and at 969sq km (374sq miles) it's the third-largest of the Scottish islands. Orkney's main island is also called Mainland, even though the Scottish mainland is only about 10 miles (16km) south. It's a land of farmers and fishermen, and one if its main attractions is Skara Brae, the most complete Neolithic village remaining in Europe.

THE BEST OF SCOTLAND

EDINBURGH

Edinburgh Castle (▷ 66–69) The biggest and best, an icon of Scottish history and identity that dominates the capital.

National Gallery of Scotland (▷ 76) An outstanding collection of fine art from around the world, most notably Scottish painting.

National Museum of Scotland (▷ 72–75) Scotland's striking chief national treasure house, in the heart of Edinburgh.

Restaurant Martin Wishart (▷ 102) Modern European cooking is the passion at this minuscule, minimalist restaurant in fashionable Leith.

Royal Botanic Garden (▷ 80) An accessible green oasis near the heart of the city, with glass-houses and planting for all seasons.

SOUTHERN SCOTLAND

Arran (▷ 116) Described as 'Scotland in miniature', a charming and accessible island often overlooked in the race to the Highlands.

Cosses Country House, Ballantrae (▷ 146) A country house in a woodland garden setting near the coast, in the southwest.

Culzean Castle (▷ 114) A stately 18th-century mansion in a spectacular clifftop setting in the southwest surrounded by verdant parkland.

Grey Mare's Tail (▷ 115) A waterfall is the focus of this miniature beauty in Dumfriesshire.

Lochgreen House, Troon (▷ 149) Comfort and fine food in this stylish hotel, judged the Automobile Association's Hotel of the Year for 2003–2004.

Logan Botanic Garden (▷ 118) Shelter under the natural umbrella of the giant gunneras at this exotic delight in the far southwest.

New Lanark World Heritage Site (▷ 121) An industrial village brought back to life.

Threave Garden (▷ 124) The National Trust for Scotland's teaching garden in the southwest, famous for its riot of spring bulbs.

GLASGOW

Burrell Collection (▷ 158–161) Exquisite art treasures from around the world, gathered by one extraordinary Glaswegian man.

Gallery of Modern Art (▷ 162) One of the most controversial and provocative contemporary art galleries in Britain.

One Devonshire Gardens (▷ 185) Elegant, sophisticated town-house hotel with top-class French and Scottish cuisine.

Rococo (▷ 183) Modern Scottish cuisine with French and rustic Italian influences in this popular Glasgow restaurant.

Opposite clockwise from left to right Skye's Cuillin Mountains rise up beyond the old bridge at Sligachan; Gairloch Sands, Wester Ross; prehistoric stone circle at Calanais, Lewis

The Tenement House (▷ 173) Reveals the domestic scale of life in a very ordinary Glasgow tenement.

CENTRAL SCOTLAND

Blair Castle (▷ 190) Everything you expect of a romantic castle in the heart of Scotland, with a fascinating history and its own private army.

Gleneagles Hotel, Auchterarder (▷ 226) Two convincing reasons to stay at this top hotel: the golf, and Andrew Fairlie's sublime cooking in the restaurant.

Loch Lomond and the Trossachs National Park (▷ 197) Classic landscapes of lochs and wooded hills in Scotland's first national park.

The Peat Inn, at Peat Inn (▷ 224) Top French cooking at a former coaching inn, set in the heart of Fife—an established favourite.

HIGHLANDS AND ISLANDS

The Applecross Inn, Applecross (▷ 284–285) Splendid food in an intimate coastal pub, well worth the spectacular drive over a high mountain pass to get there.

Ballachulish House, Ballachulish (▷ 290) A magnificent Highland setting for a lovely guesthouse with top-class facilities and service.

The Cairngorms (▷ 236–237) Britain's highest mountain plateau, with ancient woodlands, unusual wildlife and alpine flora.

Calanais (▷ 253) A stone circle and avenue second only to Stonehenge in importance, on Lewis.

Crarae Gardens (▷ 239) For Highland glen read Himalayan gorge in this outstanding woodland garden.

Crathes (▷ 240) Fairy-tale turrets and an outstanding garden mark out this ancient Highland beauty.

Eilean Donan (▷ 242) A picture-perfect treasure in a dream setting of loch and mountains, in the northwest.

Glen Coe (▷ 244) A dramatic valley scarred by a historic tragedy, with some of the best mountain climbing and winter sports.

Inverewe Gardens (▷ 250) A remarkable semi-tropical garden thrives on the wild northwest coast.

Islay (▷ 249) A superb museum, great birdwatching and eight distilleries in one small jewel of an island.

Isle of Eriska (▷ 291) Enjoy the luxurious facilities of this superb hotel, set on a private island off the west coast.

Kilmartin (▷ 251) A unique concentration of chambered cairns dating back to 3000BC, near the ancient capital of Dalriada.

Lewis and Harris (▷ 253) Remote beaches of white shell sand and sparkling turquoise seas reminiscent of the Caribbean (but colder!). A unique combination of ancient sites and quiet beauty on the western edge of Europe.

Skye (▷ 256–259) Spectacular mountains, scattered crofts (small farms) and a history interwoven with the flight of Bonnie Prince Charlie place Skye at the top of any visitor's list.

Sueno's Stone, Forres (▷ 243) A Pictish cross slab in the northeast, vividly carved with battle scenes.

Three Chimneys Restaurant, Colbost (▷ 289) Rustic chic and a culinary delight in the wild beauty of north Skye.

ORKNEY AND SHETLAND

Mousa Broch (▷ 305) Scotland's best preserved broch, or stone tower, on a tiny Shetland island.

Shetland (▷ 302–305) A remote group of islands quite unlike any other, with its own vibrant traditions and culture.

Skara Brae (▷ 301) A Neolithic village revealed under the shifting sands of Orkney

TOP EXPERIENCES

Take a walk—it doesn't have to be the whole of the West Highland Way, but pick something to suit your level of fitness and see some of the real Scotland (▷ 329).

Eat a top-class meal of fresh-cooked modern Scottish fare—the seafood and the beef are world-famous.

Listen to some live traditional music in a bar and see if you can stop your toes tapping to accordion and fiddle.

Climb up Calton Hill for a great view across Edinburgh (▷ 63). Also excellent views from the castle, and from Salisbury Crags.

Visit an island, and allow yourself time to slow down and enjoy the experience. Skye is so easy with its bridge, while Harris and Lewis or Shetland are more of a challenge (▷ 256–259, 253, 302–305).

Take your credit card and go shopping—the designer clothes in Glasgow and Edinburgh are beckoning you (▷ 178–179, 88–90).

See and hear a pipe band, still one of the great spectacles of Scotland. Catch them at a Highland games and other events, or satiate your senses at the World Pipe Band Championships (▷ 332).

Get lost in the National Museum of Scotland, Edinburgh. It's easily done, and you're bound to find something interesting around the next corner to illuminate the country's rich history (▷ 72–75).

Make your way to some remote extremities on the map—the Rhinns of Galloway, the Mull of Kintyre, Cape Wrath, John o'Groats, Hermaness, Fraserburgh—you'll see so much more of the real Scotland off the beaten track.

Watch a sunset over the Western Isles. You may have to share your vantage point with the midges (small insects), so come prepared (▷ 248–249).

Taste a dram or two of single malt whisky. You can add a drop of water if you like, and if you've never tried it, Cragganmore is a good one to start with (▷ 339–340).

Take a railway trip, sit back and enjoy the scenery—the West Highland route from Fort William to Mallaig is the most famous (▷ 279).

Bag a Munro peak (▷ 19), but take sensible precautions in the hills.

Party with the local people at a festival—or join in a ceilidh; the Scots know how to have a good time (▷ 331–332).

Find a sheltered spot and watch for wildlife—gannets and puffins around the cliffs, red deer and golden eagles in the hills, otters and seals on the seashore.

Look up your ancestors at a clan site, and find out if there's a tartan for you. With so many modern inventions on the books, you don't need a Scottish last name to find something suitable.

Explore Edinburgh's New Town to enjoy the splendours of the open spaces and the 18th-century architecture (▷ 77, 84–85).

Look up some Scottish art—Raeburn and Ramsay at the National Gallery, the Scottish Colourists at the Scottish National Gallery of Modern Art, the new wave at Glasgow's GoMA (▷ 76, 83, 162).

Follow the trail of a great Scot to discover the architecture of Charles Rennie Mackintosh, or the poetry of Robert Burns (▷ 168–169, 112–113).

Enjoy a traditional cup of tea in a Glasgow tea room (▷ 183).

Above *Boats at anchor silhouetted at sunset, Oban*

LIVING SCOTLAND

CLAN AND FAMILY

LIVING SCOTLAND

UNDERSTANDING

While some Scots' names are easy to spot, such as Ewan MacGregor, others reflect family origins and migrations—Magnus Magnusson (Icelandic), Robert Bruce (French), Sean Connery (Irish), Alexander Fleming (Flemish).

The Scots are by descent divided roughly fifty-fifty into Highland and Lowland, but often think of their families as more than nuclear, and claim Highland clanship. They wouldn't have done this 150 years ago, when 'teuchters' (a derogatory term for Highlanders) were low status. Modern clan gatherings and reunions can pump much needed cash into the countryside, and make the worldwide extended family more than a myth, helping to hold modern rambling and changing relationships together.

Many people have gone native in the North, from the radical playwright John McGrath to novelists Anne Fine and Kate Atkinson. And novelist William McIlvanney, playwright John Byrne, actor Sean Connery and comedian Billy Connolly emerged from the Irish communities in Scotland.

THE NEW SCOTS
More 'new Scots' have come from the overcrowded and overheated mainland of Europe, and they are a positive factor, enriching the blend. Italians came from Barga and Frosinone to sell fish and chips and ice cream (Europe's best!). They turned out commercial and cultural dynamos, from hotel magnate Lord Forte to racing driver Dario Franchitti, sculptor Eduardo Paolozzi, actors Tom Conti and Daniella Nardini, Archbishop Mario Conti and art entrepreneur Ricky Demarco. Jewish migrants brought the centenarian socialist Manny Shinwell and novelist Muriel Spark, not to speak of the legendary foul-mouthed stand-up comedian Jerry Sadowitz. And in 1997 Mohammad Sarwar, from Glasgow, became Britain's first Muslim MP.

Above clockwise from left to right Morag, a stuffed cloned sheep, looks over the shoulder of a newspaper reader in the Royal Museum in Edinburgh; alfresco dining in Glasgow's Merchant City area; John Lowrie Morrison's painting of Tobermory, Isle of Mull

RELIGION

In the 1960s the Kirk (Church of Scotland) dominated the Scottish Sabbath. In the 21st century its place has been taken by the supermarket. The Kirk likes to think of its Presbyterian structure as Scotland's true democracy, and elected its first female Moderator (leader) in 2003. Its General Assembly in May still draws headlines, and it copes with a huge amount of social work in a society proudly secular until real trouble hits. The Catholic Church grew with Irish immigration after 1800 and more recently with migrant workers from Poland. Its hierarchy is doctrinally conservative though socially radical. Pietism, encompassing the Free and Free Presbyterian Kirks, persists among the Gaels. Alternative faiths thrive, with Buddhists at Eskdalemuir and Arran and New Agers at Findhorn.

HOME AND HOUSEHOLD

Urban Scots are European-style flat-dwellers, with houses that vary from 'wally closes' (Glasgow's spectacular Victorian palazzos, so-called for their art nouveau tiled corridors) to the modern high-rises. Households are growing in number, even if the population is not: from 1.9 million in 1980 to 2.2 million in 2004. Many of these are single-person households—divorce, social mobility, falling birth rates and even the legalisation of homosexuality in the 1970s may be contributory factors—but it adds up to a lively city life. Post-1918 suburbs have bourgeois bungalows or 'cooncil hooses' (council-owned housing). But many folk still dream of escape to a 'but an' ben' (single-roomed cottage) on the land rather than the usual summer on a Spanish beach.

TOLERANCE

Do the Scots hate the English? Ignore football-tabloid prejudice, it hasn't stopped them marrying each other by the thousand. Prejudices are more about class than nation: 'He's English, but he's not a Yah.' You hear that often. A Yah is a wealthy young English person at a Scottish university with a very loud voice. So just how tolerant are the Scots? Asylum-seekers in Glasgow—the modern migrants—face mixed prospects. The new Parliament was lambasted by the late Cardinal Thomas Winning and the fundamentalist bus billionaire Brian Soutar for trying to repeal anti-gay legislation. Piety tends towards 'the divided self', illustrated by the writers who needed two voices, including Hugh MacDiarmid/Chris Grieve, Lewis Grassic Gibbon/James Leslie Mitchell, to deal with the complexity of the place.

HARD CASH

Wealth and poverty have always been here, with little material difference between the dwellings at Skara Brae (2500BC) and a 19th-century croft (small farm). In the 20th century progress avalanched in, bringing cars, phones and computers. Scotland today is developing an entrepreneurial middle class, and has 65 out of the top 1,000 of Britain's mega-rich, according to an annual poll in the *Sunday Times* newspaper. The biggest fortune is that of Sir Tom Hunter, who has made over £1,050 million in property and sports goods. In Scotland, double the UK percentage of millionaires cashed in on sport or the arts—Sean Connery, Jackie Stewart, Annie Lennox—though the mother of them all is Edinburgh-based writer J. K. Rowling: Harry Potter has earned her a cool £545 million.

LANDSCAPE AND NATURE

Look at a geological map of Europe and see it go crazy when it hits the west coast of Scotland. No wonder people come here for the scenery.

The country's complex landscape has always impinged on the lives of its people, who invented geological study in the 1780s. In the far northwest the rocks are over 3 billion years old, but it was events of 300–400 million years ago that gave Scotland many of its distinctive peaks, such as Arthur's Seat (▷ 63). The ice ages created U-shaped glaciated valleys like Glen Coe (▷ 244), and Glen Rosa on Arran. The blanket bog of the Flow Country of Caithness and Sutherland was laid down thousands of years ago, and is the largest remaining area of such peatland in Europe.

In economic terms, three quarters of the land is useless—loch, marsh, rock—but there's also the rich red earth of the Borders and Strathmore, which produced a world-changing agriculture in Perthshire, Aberdeenshire, Ayrshire and Fife. Today these areas are known for their cereal crops, and rich harvests of potatoes and raspberries.

LAND CONFLICTS
Scarcely a week goes by without an environmental flurry in the Scottish press, provoking wild words. At Lingerbay on Harris, plans by construction giant Lafarge to create a vast 'super quarry' have been abandoned after a planning appeal that lasted more than a decade. Remote Glensanda on the shores of Loch Linnhe was not so lucky: this is the largest quarry in Europe with 6,000 tonnes of granite an hour being loaded on to ships, mostly bound for European and US road schemes. Windfarms and open-cast coal mining continue to exercise rural communities and environmentalists throughout Scotland, with the usual boundary lines of jobs and money versus ecological interests often blurred by aggressive lobbying on both sides.

Above clockwise from left to right *Hill-walker near the summit of Beinn Eighe, Torridon; puffins lining up for a photo opportunity; turbines at Ardrossan wind farm, Ayrshire*

INCREASINGLY GREEN

Scots used to have a reputation as some of the world's worst recyclers. At the end of the 1990s, mined and quarried land here was being refilled with more landfill waste than any other country in Europe. However, that is rapidly changing. The rate of landfill is now down to 2.3 million tonnes (from a level of over 7 million) and over 30 per cent of waste is now being recycled. Scottish parliament targets for recycling aim for that to increase to 40 per cent by 2010 and 50 per cent by 2013.

IN THE BLOOD

The texture of Scotland—the feel of lava stone, sandstone or granite; of heather, bracken, sand and marram grass; of seaweed, sheep-cropped grass, hedges, wool—has always fed the Scottish imagination, reflected in art, design, poetry and architecture. And while peat may be despised by farmers for its acidity, it's a valuable fuel when dried, and perfumes Harris Tweed and whisky alike.

STONE-BUILT

Scotland is stone-built, so no town is like the next. Volcanic rocks like granite—grey and pink—in the north compete with sedimentaries like old red sandstone. Classical Edinburgh is built of indestructible, silver-grey Craigleith sandstone, lethal to the men who quarried and carved it. Glasgow's red Cairnpapple and creamy Dunbarton or Lanark sandstones are softer, and turn dramatically dark with time. Roofs are incredibly varied: thatch and turf for centuries, followed by tiles (originally from the Low Countries, brought as ballast in trading ships) and later slate from Ballachulish and Easdale, and corrugated iron. Harling—coating a building with a layer of small stones embedded in mortar—is a distinctive Scottish feature, from cottages to castles.

HEDGING THEIR HOGS

Since 2003, there has been an annual battle in the Western Isles over the fate of their hedgehogs. Their population has soared thanks to the abundance of birds' eggs. So bad did the problem get that Scottish Natural Heritage, the body charged with preserving the nation's wildlife, decreed that the whole hedgehog population on the Western Isles should be culled. Hedgehog preservation societies rushed from the mainland to save the Uist hedgehogs. Early attempts by SNH staff to trap and kill the creatures resulted in the deaths of around 700 hedgehogs, while preservation societies relocated a handful to the mainland for rehabilitation. The bulk of the islands' estimated 4,000-strong population remained. By 2005 SNH were proposing to hunt hedgehogs with dogs, but in 2007 they decided to try a translocation project, taking captured hedgehogs to the mainland. Preservation societies are continuing to relocate hedgehogs.

Scotland's weather is constantly varying, with a vocabulary to suit. There is no direct English translation for 'dreich', which means cold, raw, grey, damp. Be prepared: not just for rainy days, but for that sudden prospect of brilliance when you've got to get out of the city or miss the sight of a lifetime.

The need to defy the elements has partly created the landscape. Heating for homes was necessary from the start, and tree-felling by the early settlers left much of the land covered with bog. Coal mining was followed by whaling for blubber-oil, and then by William Murdoch's gas lighting and James Young's shale-derived paraffin, but it was in the 1980s—thanks to offshore oil and nuclear energy—that the Scots finally caught up with the rest of Britain on central heating.

The climate has bred a culture of hard outdoor labour, powered by drink and high-fat food, and countered by hard enjoyment: the military sports of the Highland gatherings, and dancing for men. Highland culture shows the traces of traditional hunting in fishing, deerstalking and shooting, reflecting short winter and long summer days.

PLAYING THE GAME

The Scots have been 'fitba-daft' (soccer crazy) since the 1860s, when Saturday afternoons became work-free and footballs cheap. The Glasgow Boys' Brigade ran the biggest amateur league in Europe and many players went on to local and national teams. Class and sectarian conflict still pervade the Old Firm of (Protestant) Rangers and (Catholic) Celtic, but what do bought-in European players know of such grievances? While many spectators are content to watch from the sofa at home or from the pub, tickets to the big games still sell out fast. Rugby Union was always more genteel, but a working-class sport in the Borders. The Rugby Sevens are an exciting introduction to the game. In the Highlands, shinty, a form of field hockey, prevails.

Above clockwise from left to right *Scotland's national stadium, Hampden, in Glasgow; one of Edinburgh's colourful pubs; throwing the hammer at the Highland Games*

EATING AND DRINKING

Scottish fish is legendary, and fish farms are now worth more than shipbuilding. Herring grilled in an oatmeal crust, with gooseberry sauce, is the food of the gods. And try the national dish, haggis, traditionally served with 'bashed neeps and tatties' (mashed turnips and potato). Meaty broths with barley or lentils are still served in the pubs. A few selected menus, like the great Scottish fry-up (bacon, eggs, sausages, tomatoes, mushrooms, with fried bread or potato scones) are fine if eaten once; repeated, they're a heart attack on a plate. And if whisky (▷ 339–340) is not your thing, drink the orange fizz called Irn Bru—claimed to be more popular here than Coca-Cola. It was devised to quench the thirsts of those stirring molten iron—and is also noted as a hangover cure.

SHOPPING

A recent survey put Edinburgh and Glasgow among the Top 10 happening cities of Britain—at No. 2 and No. 4, they have regularly featured in the top five, sometimes beating London for quality of life. Wander through the shopping steets and modern malls of either city and you might wonder how a country with a population of just 5 million can sustain quite so many trendy designer boutiques. Part of the answer lies with visitors, who like to shop—each year, they spend over £250 million on clothes alone. Cheap flights from Norway and Denmark have allowed a new wave of Viking invaders into the country, and Glasgow has become the unofficial shopping capital of Scandinavia.

SPORTING HEROES

While golf is viewed as an elitist game in much of Britain, in Scotland, where it was invented, golf was and is pretty democratic, with public courses readily available. At the opposite end of the scale it has become big bucks as 'corporate golf', producing heroes such as Sam Torrance and Sandy Lyle. Curling, the sliding of polished granite stones along the ice, is a peculiarly Scottish pastime that developed in the 18th century. Colder winters once saw curlers at their open-air 'bonspiels'; now it's played on indoor rinks, and is gaining a new following thanks to a gold medal performance by a Scottish women's team at the 2002 Winter Olympics, watched by millions on television. TV has also taken snooker and motor-racing, Scottish specialities, into the big time, with names such as David Coulthard.

MUNROS WITH MOBILES

Scotland has been a leisure landscape since the Victorians came north to shoot and fish. Youth hostels and Munro-bagging—climbing the peaks over 914.4m (3,000ft)—inspired worker-climbers in the 1930s into the perils and triumphs of hard rock. It's an unforgiving and little-tracked country, prone to fog and downpour, which demands warm clothes, wet-weather gear, good boots, maps and compasses and emergency rations. Twenty-eight volunteer mountain rescue teams around the country do sterling work to rescue the stranded, but it's important to remember that, no, you won't survive a Highland blizzard by taking your mobile phone. Walkers in Scotland have the right to roam in the countryside, although they are obliged to consider the rights of other land users, including farmers and gamekeepers.

PILLARS OF SOCIETY

Scotland has a proud tradition of education of the individual for the betterment of the community, and laws for the provision of free, compulsory education for all children age 5–16 have been in place since 1872. In a land where settlements may be tiny and remotely scattered, there are some very small schools indeed. The island of Canna, for instance, has a primary school with just one pupil.

The pattern of tertiary education owes more to historic links with continental Europe than with neighbouring England. While the older universities, established back in the 15th century, focus on familiar academic subjects, vocational colleges offer a diversity of practical qualifications for the 21st century. For instance, the recently formed UHI Millennium Institute, which undertakes university-level education at 15 locations across the Highlands and Islands, offers degrees relevant to local interests including Gaelic and Traditional Music, Marine Science, and Electrical Engineering with Nuclear Decommissioning, thus moving the tradition forward.

MONARCHS OF THE GLENS

Who owns Scotland? The Duke of Buccleuch, of Bowhill and Drumlanrig (▷ 111) has 81,000ha (200,000 acres). The State, through the Forestry Commission and Ministry of Defence, owns huge tracts, as do the banks and building societies who lend to home-buyers. Around 60 per cent of households rented council accommodation in 1980, a number now slashed, leaving problematic high-rises and run-down housing in the cities. Housing associations are seen as a way out for 'excluded Scots', whose situation is dramatized in the novels of James Kelman and Irvine Welsh.

Opposite clockwise from left to right *The innovative Scottish Parliament building in Edinburgh; the Kirking of the Judges Ceremony at St Giles' Cathedral, Edinburgh, marks the beginning of the legal year; fishing in Scotland is under threat from EU policies*

PARLIAMENT HOUSE

The hammerbeam hall behind St. Giles' Cathedral in Edinburgh has housed, since 1707, the Scots legal hierarchy. This runs from local Justices of the Peace (JPs) to Sheriff Courts, the High Court and Court of Session. Scottish judges wear robes with huge red crosses and are called Lord. Their principles, even after centuries of British legislation, are closer to European law than to English. If you are involved in a serious accident or a death, you will encounter the Procurator-Fiscal (an examining magistrate), who has no English counterpart. The final courts of appeal are the House of Lords and increasingly the European Court. Scotland's advocates (barristers) and writers (solicitors) have changed a lot since Sir Walter Scott's claret-fuelled day: solicitors are (unlike in England) efficient house agents and property managers.

PROVOST AND BAILIE ADIEU

Local government is increasingly less local in Scotland. The old burghs—once 175 of them, with their provosts, bailies (JPs) and councillors the great engine of local government—have now vanished under 32 multi-purpose councils. The land areas they cover range from tiny Clackmannan to Highland (bigger than Belgium), though community councils in many small towns still deal with parking, sports facilities and amenities. Despite their novelty and occasional unpopularity, the new councils have been regarded as a success story, especially for the effective way they have dealt with emergencies such as the outbreak of foot and mouth disease in 2001.

WESTMINSTER—WHO CARES?

The last Prime Minister, Tony Blair, and current leader Gordon Brown, are both Scots, as was the last leader of the Liberal Democrats, Sir Menzies Campbell. Scotland sends 59 elected representatives (MPs) south to the Wesrminster parliament (41 Labour, 11 Liberal Democrats, 6 Scottish Nationalists, 1 Conservative). While Scotland's own parliament has certain legislative powers (▷ 7), Westminster has reserved control of defence, foreign affairs, currency, economic policy and media, and the Secretary of State for Scotland continues as a role within the Cabinet. As for relations to Edinburgh's Scottish Executive? First Minister Alex Salmond says he has more dealings with the European Parliament in Brussels…

EUROPE AHOY!

Scotland's best-kept political secret is its seven Members of the European Parliament (or MEPs), elected by proportional representation on an all-Scotland list, who go to Brussels and Strasbourg. Scotland's EU record is mixed—severe setbacks in fisheries policy, envy of 'Celtic Tiger' Ireland's nifty Brussels manoeuvring for extra funds—but Scots regard themselves as more European than the rest of Britain. Since 2002 you can sail direct from Zeebrugge in Belgium to Rosyth: The trip is not cheap, nor at 18 hours as Superfast as the company name, but it is very comfortable, and makes the Forth Bridge truly the gateway to the North.

CULTURE AND THE ARTS

Scotland makes a distinct but misleading cultural impression. Only one culture? Hugh MacDiarmid exploded: 'Scotland small? Our...intricate multifold Scotland small?' An intensely regional popular culture contains far more variety than just Scots and Gaelic. The Lowland country folk have their ballads, Common Ridings, dances with fiddle and accordion bands, and exhausting strathspeys and reels (local dances are held all over the country). Scandinavian themes have influenced Orkney and Shetland from the Sagas onwards, celebrated in the stunning Orkney Festival in the great medieval cathedral at Kirkwall and in Viking Up Helly Aa festivals across Shetland.

Once denounced as 'speaking common', dialect is now being encouraged. Bizarrely, the self-appointed guardian of Scottish dialect, the Boord o' Braid Scots, is in Northern Ireland (where the Protestants demanded funding to match Gaelic resources now awarded to the Catholics). Doric, the full-strength Scottish dialect, is at its strongest in the northeast, and sounds almost like another language.

LOCAL HEROICS

Think global, act local: This really works in cultural activities that enrich communities across the country through drama, music, literature and history groups, writers in residence, craftworkers' circles, small publishers and museums. The last have gone from 150 to around 400 since the 1960s, and range from the fortress-like National Museum of Scotland (▷ 72–75) to little treasuries such as the Wick Heritage Museum (▷ 260). Schools and village halls are pressed into service for community activities that pull people together, although the competition with an evening in front of the TV may be tough. National movements tend to stress youth and nativism, but how much of this activity could survive without the input of the retired and the newcomers?

Above clockwise from left to right *Glasgow's cutting-edge SECC (Scottish Exhibition and Conference Centre); Scottish guards at the finale of the Edinburgh Military Tattoo; taking part in Edinburgh's famous Fringe Festival*

WHO WANTS ED FEST?

Not Edinburgh, at first. For long after its start in 1947 residents much preferred the excitement of the Military Tattoo at the castle, where the prancing cavalry was supplied by the Co-op's milk-float horses. Folk came around after seeing the injection of huge amounts of tourist cash and businesses drawn to the city by this annual world-famous festival. Today there are 30 or so big productions in the official Edinburgh Festival, and something close to a thousand on the Fringe, with spin-offs such as the Book Festival (▷ 96). Since being designated Europe's culture capital for 1990, Glasgow has developed its own cultural festivals, led by the fabulous folk fest, Celtic Connections, in January.

PUBLIC BUILDING

Charles Rennie Mackintosh's buildings in Glasgow (▷ 168–169) proved a hard act for architects to follow. The city's titanium-clad millennium Science Centre cost a cool £75 million (▷ 163) and suggests a new confidence in the design of public structures. And Sir Norman Foster's SECC (1997), nicknamed the Armadillo, has helped raise the profile of regeneration in the heart of the city. In Edinburgh, the Parliament building of the late Enrico Miralles at Holyrood was completed in July 2004 and is a stunner (▷ 94). Benson and Forsyth's 1999 fortress-like National Museum of Scotland (▷ 72–75) is still courting controversy, as the confusion of its interior structure is addressed.

WRITTEN FOR KIDS

Scotland has a rich tradition of storytelling for children, from the yarns of Robert Louis Stevenson to J. M. Barrie's *Peter Pan*. Modern classics include Mollie Hunter's historical fiction and Joan Lingard's haunting tales of displacement for older children. A firm favourite with youngsters, Mairi Hedderwick's beautifully illustrated Katie Morag adventures on the Isle of Struay made their first appearance in 1984, loosely based on the author's own experiences of living on the Hebridean island of Coll (▷ 249). Look, too, for her several illustrated accounts (for adults) of travelling around Scotland. Also popular is Maisie the kilted cartoon cat, who lives in an Edinburgh where even the street names and bus numbers are familiar.

GAELIC AWAKE! OR GAELIC: A WAKE?

Although the language issue marks literary politics in Wales, Scots Gaelic, with fewer than 60,000 speakers, seems headed for its deathbed. Or will projects like Gaelic pre-school playgroups and Sabhal Mór Ostaig, the Gaelic college on Skye backed by the nationalist-inclined financier Sir Iain Noble, snatch it back to life? To hear Gaelic spoken as a natural, first language in everyday use, travel to the Western Isles. Gaelic culture is celebrated each year at the Mod, a festival with competitions in writing and song, which moves from town to town. For a glimpse into the pattern and rhythm of this lyrical language, try the poetry of Skye-born Sorley MacLean (1911–96)—in translation, of course.

MUSIC

Robert Burns celebrated a contradictory power in the Calvinist psalm and the secular, often bawdy, ballad. Hamish Henderson rediscovered many of these after 1945, and singers from Jeannie Robertson to Jean Redpath, fiddlers, and folk-bands such as the Battlefield Band, have kept the tradition alive and kicking.

Contemporary music runs from the Singing Kettle for children, via an Atlantic jazz scene through to tough brassy ladies—Annie Ross, Lulu, Annie Lennox, Shirley Manson. Political pop is belted out by folk-rockers such as Runrig and the Proclaimers.

And the British pop charts are enriched by bands like Texas and Franz Ferdinand. There is a relatively thin heritage of classical and stage music, but Scotland has inspired others over the centuries, including Hector Berlioz (Waverley) and Lerner and Loewe (Brigadoon).

PAINTING…

…was almost unknown among the Scots until the 18th century, but then grew up very rapidly via Allan Ramsay, Henry Raeburn, David Wilkie, the Glasgow Boys of the 1880s and the Scottish Colourists of the 1900s, and can be seen in world-class galleries in Glasgow and Edinburgh (Scottish art schools have always looked to Europe, not to London).

Modern painting remains representational with many strong individual styles: Peter Howson, John Bellany, Stephen Campbell. Good paintings from the Royal Scottish Academy and other artist-run bodies can be bought at reasonable prices in many private galleries.

The sensationalism of Young British Artists? It's at this point you know you are in a different country: Scots don't really care. For the same daft prices you could get a D. Y. Cameron, an Elizabeth Blackadder or a Stephen Conroy. No contest.

IT'S A CRIME

Scotland's proud literary tradition includes such world-famous writers as Sir Walter Scott, Robert Burns and Robert Louis Stevenson, but it's a tradition that is very much alive and well. Harry Potter author J. K. Rowling has lived in Edinburgh since 1994, but as well as the world of fantasy, it's in the genre of crime writing that modern Scottish authors excel especially. One of the best-selling British crime writers is Ian Rankin, whose series of novels featuring Inspector John Rebus reveal a side of Edinburgh that the average visitor will only rarely glimpse. So, too, do the crime novels of Allan Guthrie, who was born on Orkney, but also now lives in Edinburgh. Guthrie's books, such as Two-way Split and Kiss Her Goodbye, have won or been nominated for several crime-writing awards. Alexander McCall Smith is another Edinburgh-based, best-selling writer, though his famous fictional character, Mma Precious Ramotswe, is a world away, solving crimes in Botswana. The connection between crime writing and Scotland's capital is nothing new, of course. Sir Arthur Coman Doyle, creator of the world's most famous detective, Sherlock Holmes, was also born in Edinburgh.

Above Runrig, Scotland's premier band, in concert at Stirling Castle

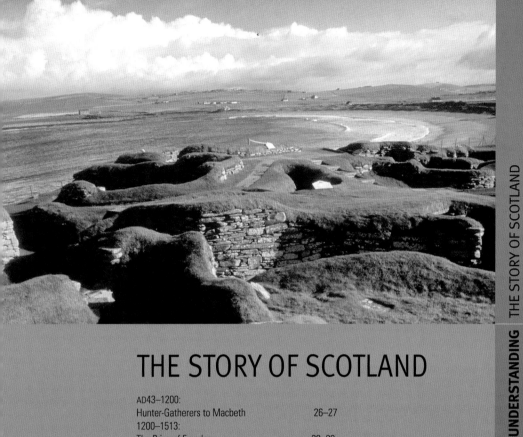

THE STORY OF SCOTLAND

As history has retreated from the landscape, it has regrouped in museums—Scotland has around 400 of them. Most notable is the National Museum of Scotland in Edinburgh (▷ 72–75). Here it's immediately apparent just how complex the Scottish past has been. It's not, for a start, that of an ethnically homogeneous nation. Human settlement goes back to the retreat of the ice-cap after 10,000BC, when hunter-gatherer communities foraged here in summer. The absence of trees over much of northern Scotland meant the extensive use of stone, and elaborate buildings—settlements, temples, passage graves—testify to a sophisticated culture, in touch with Europe, contemporary with the pyramids. This was followed, in the Bronze and Iron Ages, by farming communities.

Scotland was only temporarily held by the Romans, and on their departure in the fifth century the land was divided between the Britons in the southwest, the Scots (who straddled the Irish Sea) and the Picts in the Grampian region. The Angles pressed north along the east coast, and in the eighth century came Vikings from Scandinavia. They ravaged and looted, then settled in Orkney and Shetland and along the west coast. Remarkably, by the 11th century there was something like national unity, first under the MacAlpins and ultimately under the MacMalcolms. After 1066 this unified kingdom faced the power of the Norman kings of England. Yet they managed to coexist for almost 250 years before a formal struggle for independence began.

THE NORMAN-SCOTS
There was no Norman conquest of Scotland, but after 1066 Scottish monarchs increased their own power, and their chance of good relations with England (which then had huge French possessions) by encouraging the immigration of Norman, Flemish and Breton knights, merchants and monks. Names like Fraser, Bruce and Stewart stem from this period, and many Norman-Scots had big estates in England for which they paid homage to the English king.

Above clockwise from left to right *Beneath the grassy mound of Maes Howe lies a huge burial chamber; Scottish king Macbeth (1005–1057); reconstruction of an Iron Age longhouse at Bosta, on Lewis*

RECORDING HISTORY

The Scots were bad at this in the early days: documentation really only dates from the 1400s. Up to that time, the records kept in abbeys were the basis for medieval history—monks had to be meticulous in recording dates, as they wanted hard facts about when land was taken over or benefactors died. The Wars of Independence (▷ 28–29) would later impose a national framework on these records, in the accounts of chroniclers Walter Bower (1385–1449) and Andrew of Wyntoun (c1350–1420), and Archdeacon Barbour's *The Bru* (c1375). Many of the records on which they were based were lost at sea in 1652, as Oliver Cromwell tried to move them south.

THE CASE FOR MACBETH

William Shakespeare, writing in 1606, got the story for his play from Wyntoun, via the translated Chronicles of Wyntoun's French contemporary Jean Froissart. The real Macbeth was Mormaer (Great Steward) of Moray at a time when Scottish kings had to be acceptable to these regional magnates. He became king in 1040 by defeating and killing Duncan I (his junior) in battle, and ruled with some success, even feeling secure enough to visit Rome in 1050. In 1057 he was in turn challenged and killed by Malcolm Canmore, Duncan's son, who became Malcolm III. History is always written by the victors.

ROME'S SPECIAL DAUGHTER

In AD663 Oswiu, King of Northumbria, rejected Celtic forms of Christianity for the Roman version. The Scottish kingdoms followed suit. David I (c1080–1153) radically expanded the number of bishoprics from three to nine and invited in the monastic orders, encouraged by the papacy, which was then greatly reviving in its strength. In this he was influenced, like all of Northern Europe, by Pope Urban's preaching of the First Crusade in 1095. Popes and kings soon fought over Church autonomy. In 1175 the bishopric of Glasgow was taken from the authority of the Archbishop of York, to become a 'special daughter' of Rome, with a direct reporting line. The rest of the Church in Scotland soon followed.

PICTISH CROSSES

You'll find the frozen eloquence of these in the Perth area and around the Moray Firth. The greatest, such as Hilton of Cadboll, have pre-Christian symbols and scenes on one side—discs, broken lances, lively hunting scenes, battles and feasts—and Christian symbols on the other. The Picts, dominant here in the seventh century, left few records other than these. In the eighth century they submitted to a takeover by the Scots, driven eastward by Viking raids.

F. Hall sculp.

The so-called Wars of Independence were as much a struggle for mastery in Scotland between several great Norman-Scots families as against the English. The background to this was the stand-off in Europe between an increasingly powerful Plantagenet monarch in England, and the rulers of France who were out to evict him from his French possessions.

Edward I was the most formidable English king: legalistic, reforming, but also the ruthless conqueror of Wales. He attempted to secure overlordship on his terms. Scots noblemen were not in principle hostile, but they resented being taxed to support Edward's French wars. Between 1295 and his death in 1307, Edward invaded Scotland four times. He was opposed by a minor noble, William Wallace (c1274–1305), who raised a force and defeated Edward's army at Stirling Bridge in 1297. Wallace intrigued with possible allies abroad, and was ultimately captured, hanged and dismembered at Smithfield, London in 1305. This was the signal for an ambitious campaign by Robert Bruce, Earl of Carrick (1274–1329), to take over the Scots throne and provide the focus for an increasingly national resistance. Edward II's Scots allies were steadily swept aside by Bruce. In 1314 Edward suffered a crushing defeat at Bannockburn, and Bruce's recognition within Scotland as Robert I was confirmed. England finally accepted Scottish independence in 1328.

LORDS OF THE ISLES

Relations between MacDonald and Campbell are, even today, cool. In the Middle Ages half the Scots people lived in the Highlands, and were dominated by Clan Donald, whose power ran from Donegal in Ireland to Inverness and Lewis. As Lords of the Isles they conducted their own diplomacy for their own ends. Post-reformation kings gave preference to the Protestant Clan Campbell, based at Inveraray. Despite a setback stemming from the Massacre at Glencoe, 1692, the Argathelians (as the followers of the Campbell Duke of Argyll were known) dominated politics until population shifts moved authority into the hands of Edinburgh lawyers.

A DECLARATION

In 1320 the nobility, bishops and 'community of the realm' petitioned Pope John XXII to support their right to independence. Their words made up one of the finest pieces of political rhetoric of all time: *We are bound to him (King Robert) for the maintaining of our freedom both by his right and his merits, as to him by whose salvation has been wrought unto our people, and by him… we mean to stand. Yet if he should give up what he has begun, seeking to make us or our kingdom subject to the king of England or the English, we would strive at once to drive him out as our enemy… For, as long as a hundred of us remain alive, we will never on any conditions be subjected to the lordship of the English. For we fight not for glory, or riches, or honour, but for freedom alone…*

Opposite clockwise from left to right Duart Castle, ancient seat of the McLeans; Edward III at the gates of Berwick, taken from Froissart's Chronicles; The Declaration of Arbroath, 1320; William Wallace at the Battle of Stirling Bridge

THE AULD ALLIANCE

Scotland's special relationship with France lasted from 1295 to 1560—more lasting was the Scots taste for French wine, architecture, philosophy and culture, which still continues. Most Scottish attempts to invade England, at the request of their French allies, were disastrous, and there was only one significant use of French troops in Scotland, in James III's reign (1460–88): They were not popular. Clerics and chroniclers portrayed the alliance as a national cause, perhaps to stifle popular discontent. Meanwhile the Anglo-Scottish split widened. Scotland was hit less severely than England by the Black Death (1349-50), but from parity with the pound sterling the currency began to sink into the cellar, and trade was menaced by English piracy.

THE STEWARTS…

…(later Stuarts) were a Breton family who became Stewards to the Bruces, until one married Robert I's daughter and their son became Robert II in 1371. Stewart monarchs, provided they lived to grow up, were intelligent, determined, and, given a chance, greedy. They defeated the great nobles, most dramatically the Douglases of the southwest, and their most successful king, James IV (1488–1513), played the Renaissance monarch, extorting greater autonomy for the Scottish Church, which he and his son then looted. It's from this period that Scotland's oldest intact secular stone buildings date. Most castles and halls built before this time were of timber, plaster and wattle.

BORDER BALLADS

The Scots ballads have been compared to the Greek epics. Sung or declaimed in the halls of the Border towers and carried by gypsies and tinkers, they retold the battles, loves and tragedies of the 'debatable land'. Their language could vary in the same ballad from the plodding to the sublime. Some were set down by Allan Ramsay in the 1720s, and later by Sir Walter Scott and James Hogg, although Hogg's mother complained, 'If you write them down, folk winnae sing them nae mair'. This seemed to be the case, yet folklorist Hamish Henderson encountered the remarkable Jeannie Robertson in 1946—an illiterate gypsy woman, who still knew more than 100 of the great ballads off by heart.

UNDERSTANDING THE STORY OF SCOTLAND

The Auld Alliance was wearing thin by 1513, and there was a mounting crisis as Church property declined, leading to weakness and corruption. Reform was delayed until it was too late. France was backing the Counter-Reformation (the radical reform movement within the Roman Catholic Church), while Scots intellectuals embraced the Protestantism associated with John Calvin (1509–64) and Geneva.

Again the fulcrum was an active and insensitive English monarch, Henry VIII. Following his defeat of James IV at Flodden in 1513, Henry drove repeatedly into Scotland, leaving a trail of burned towns and abbeys behind him, but also an increasingly resistant Scots population. The French continued to use their advantage to effect, but eventually their great hope, Mary of Guise (widow of James V and mother of Mary Stewart), a fervent Counter-Reformer, drove the Scots away. John Knox led Protestant riots at Perth in 1559 and, when the French left in 1560, founded the Protestant Church of Scotland (the Kirk). A year later Mary Stewart arrived.

Catholic Mary (1542–87), Queen of Scotland at one week old, had married the Dauphin in France. The accidental death of the French King in 1559 made her Queen of both France and Scotland. Her husband died when she was 18, and in 1561 she returned to a Scotland which had become radically Protestant. The contrast between the splendour of the French court and 'black Genevan' kirk was stark.

THE TROUBLE WITH MARY

Mary, backed by the might of France, was handsome, intelligent and athletic; she was also impulsive and uncalculating. She wed her cousin Henry Stewart, Lord Darnley, whom she called King Henry I. Unstable and probably syphilitic, a Catholic, then a waverer, he alienated his wife by murdering her secret lover David Rizzio. Mary avenged herself through her new love, the Earl of Bothwell, who had Darnley murdered in 1567. She married Bothwell, but he lacked a power base. The two were opposed by the Protestant nobility, and overthrown at a skirmish east of Edinburgh. Mary was forced to abdicate, and her baby son was crowned James VI at Stirling in 1567. She was finally executed for treason by Elizabeth I.

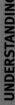

Opposite clockwise from left to right *The Massacre of Glencoe by James Hamilton; the River Garry runs through Killicrankie, site of a momentous battle in 1689; the Darien Scheme promised much but left the coffers empty*

THE WISEST FOOL…

…was a great survivor. James VI (1566–1625) reigned for nearly 60 years. His early years were marked by intrigue and unstable regencies, until he was formally made Elizabeth of England's heir in 1583. He resumed the Stewart drive to power, subordinating the Kirk and the nobility and even trying to take on the Highlands. He was successful and conceited, with a tendency to lecture. As an enlightened patron he grasped at the wealth he encountered after reaching the English—or 'Great British' as he preferred—throne in 1603 as James I. However, he overestimated both his control over Scotland, and the permanency of his management of English politics, for he failed to confront the Puritans in the English Parliament.

KIRK AND COVENANT

Scots Calvinists had a fairly political attitude to religion, which was framed by covenants: contracts between man and God, and man and his rulers. James VI/I had outmanoeuvred them, but his successor was proud, obstinate and not very clever. In 1638 Charles I's attempts to impose Anglican forms on the Kirk led to the National Covenant and military confrontation. Charles lost these Bishops' Wars (1639–40) and, bankrupt, conceded power to the London Parliament. He reneged and the Civil War broke out in 1642. The Scots initially co-operated with the Parliamentarians, but when leader Oliver Cromwell didn't play along with their attempt to impose Presbyterianism throughout Britain, they again courted the King, and failed.

THE KILLING TIME

The monarchy was restored to the joint Crown in 1660, and with it the Edinburgh parliament. While most ministers made their peace with the new regime, a minority in the southwest did not and were expelled from their parishes. Their supporters, the Covenanters, started an intermittent rebellion of risings and guerrilla attacks, which was met with force—the Killing Time—by Charles II's commissioners. Casualties were low, but martyrdom and repression created a lasting culture of popular resistance. In 1688 Catholic King James VII and II was overthrown and exiled. A Jacobite campaign to restore him failed when its leader, Viscount Dundee, was killed at Killiecrankie (▷ 198). New monarchs William and Mary restored the rights of Kirk and parliament, though with bad grace.

DARIEN, FAMINE AND UNION

In the 1690s there were years of severe famine, with many deaths. About a quarter of the country's wealth vanished when the ill-fated attempt to create a Scottish trading post on the isthmus of Darien, in Panama, failed due to fever, and English and Spanish interference. The Westminster Parliament worried what would happen when Anne, last of the Stuart monarchs, died, while the Scots Parliament threatened an independent foreign policy. This led to an extended political crisis (1701–07), in which the Scots nobility, merchants and Kirk were bribed into a formal union with England.

ENLIGHTENMENT AND PROGRESS 1707–1815

The Union was undertaken for reasons of short-term expediency. Its boasted advantages took over 20 years to materialize, but this was a period of relative calm, and the Jacobites (followers of the exiled Stewarts) got little support on the three occasions they attempted invasion. The cultural foundations of later social revolution were laid, notably among lawyers, in the Kirk and in the universities. England needed Scotland: Its trade routes were free from French raiding, and Glasgow's dominance of the tobacco trade was an economic breakthrough.

Society started to adopt the new opportunities, and classical architecture and art flourished. Intellectually Scotland overtook England, with William Robertson (1721–93) and David Hume (1711–76) emerging as leading historians. Law, science, agricultural improvement: These were rapidly disseminated by clubs and societies, along with road building, land enclosure and efforts to create a Scottish militia. By the 1780s a French visitor said he could stand at Edinburgh's toll booth and 'within half an hour take fifty men of genius by the hand'. The Enlightenment was typified by economist Adam Smith (1723–90) and philosophers Thomas Reid (1710–96) and Adam Ferguson (1723–1816), scientifically radical but socially conservative thinkers who feared the social impact of the new commercialism. By the 1780s, Scotland rivalled England in industrial and urban growth. The downside was the clearance in the Highlands after 1745 of tenant crofters (farmers) to make way for huge-scale sheep farming.

THE LAST BATTLE ON BRITISH SOIL

In 1745 Prince Charles Edward Stewart (1720–88), son of the Old Pretender to the throne, James III, raised an army at Glenfinnan. Supposedly backed by the French, this turned into a move that menaced the government in London. The Jacobites took Edinburgh before swinging southward. But though people joined the cause in England, the French didn't invade, and the dispirited army retreated to Culloden (▷ 241), where it was crushed by an army of (predominantly Scots) soldiers under George II's son, the Duke of Cumberland. The prince fled.

NEW TOWN, NEW VILLAGE

New Pitsligo, Gavinton, Helensburgh: Some 120 such villages were built by 'improving' lairds, as a means of easing their people away from the self-governing townships to the rationally structured 'muckle farm' (great farm), the linen industry or the first factories. The new villages were designed to keep people on the land, as the cultured classes were worried about the social dangers posed by the growth of large towns. They contained the amenities—schools, church, dispensary, library—which 17th-century Scotland had so conspicuously lacked, and were laid out in symmetrical rectangles with well-proportioned houses and gardens. Edinburgh's New Town (▷ 77) would follow the same principle on a grander scale.

'OSSIAN' (1762)

Poet James Macpherson (1736–96) was of Gaelic origins and claimed to have discovered manuscripts of a lost third-century Celtic epic poem about the legendary hero Fingal, as told to his son Ossian. Its impact was like that of *The Lord of the Rings* two centuries later—but could it be a fake? This question divided the literary pundits of Edinburgh and London. English lexicographer Dr. Samuel Johnson's doubts led to his journey north in 1773, with his friend James Boswell in attendance, as recounted in his classic *A Journey to the Western Isles of Scotland*. Johnson was right, as Macpherson failed to produce his 'original' manuscripts. Yet for a generation of European writers, on the eve of the romantic movement, 'Ossian' provided a powerful cultural input.

BROTHERS IN ARMS

The Union and southern wealth gave access for Scots professionals to wealthy English patrons, and opened up the Grand Tour of Europe to the local nobility. Clever Scots, travelling with aristocrats on the Grand Tour, codified the rules of classical architecture. By the mid-18th century the Scots laird's (landowner's) house was Palladian in style, and his architects—including Sir William Chambers (1726–96) and the Adam brothers, Robert (1728–92) and James (1730–94), who left their mark on London as architects of the king's works—were among the best in the world.

PORTRAIT OF AN AGE

The great portrait painter Sir Henry Raeburn (1754–1823) was an Edinburgh orphan, raised in a charity school. He studied under Sir Joshua Reynolds, but forewent the grand style for intimate, psychologically profound studies of the lairds, clergy, lawyers and professors of 'improving' Scotland. He became the visual counterpart to literary giant Sir Walter Scott, although doubt has recently been cast on whether the celebrated portrait of Reverend Robert Walker is one of his works.

Opposite clockwise from left to right *Glenfinnan Monument, where Bonnie Prince Charlie raised the standard in 1745;* Prince Charles Edward Stewart, *by Antonio David (1732); fine crewelwork in the National Museum of Scotland, Edinburgh*

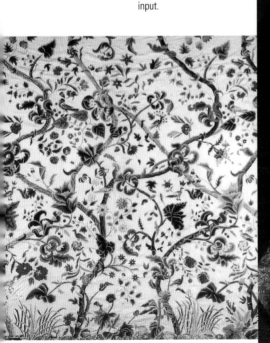

THE WORLD'S WORKSHOP 1815–1922

The needs created by the Napoleonic Wars (1800–15) had boosted the cotton, wool, linen and iron industries. Scotland's real breakthrough came in 1828, however, when J. B. Neilson (1792–1865) devised a means of smelting the high-grade mixture of iron and coal called blackband, found in the Monkland district of Glasgow: It gave a very pure form of iron, which could be cast or turned with great accuracy. This changed the pace of industrialization, attracting engineers and industrialists to Clydeside like a magnet. Steam engines were built, first for textile manufacture, then for ships and sugar-cane crushers. By 1848 Scotland was connected to England by two railway lines, and locomotive-building was starting. By 1900, Glasgow had the world's greatest railway engineering complex outside Philadelphia.

The new industrial Scotland was not a safe place to live. Houses were tiny and sanitation rudimentary. Cholera killed thousands between 1832 and 1866. In 1871 three-quarters of Glasgow families lived in houses of two rooms or fewer. A primitive poor law couldn't cope with industrial unemployment. The school system—advanced by English standards, with most of the population literate—buckled under the strain and had to be radically reformed in 1872.

WEE FREES
Disruption was the word of the year in 1843. The Kirk split and lost control of the poor law and education. Failure to end the intrusion (imposition) of clergy by landowners resulted in a third of the clergy leaving to form the Free Church of Scotland. Religion was a vital part of the social fabric. Social life revolved around the churches, and the hundreds of thousands of poorly paid, ill-treated Irish immigrants—the workforce behind Scotland's economic miracle—depended on their priests. From the initiative of one such priest, Father Walfrid, in Glasgow's poverty-racked East End, came in 1888 a young men's soccer team, the now legendary Glasgow Celtic.

Above clockwise from left to right *Arrol and Fowler's iconic Forth Rail Bridge cost 57 lives during its construction; poster for Glasgow's underground railway, which opened in 1896; photographic portrait of Sandy Linton and his family by Hill and Adamson (1845)*

IRON BRIDGES, NORTHERN LIGHTS

Scottish roads were primitive. In 1720 it took two weeks to get from Edinburgh to London. The great civil engineers like Thomas Telford (1757–1834) made fortunes by building roads and canals throughout Britain and Europe, and training the generation who would build the railways. Telford's bridges at Dean and Craigellachie were the forerunners of masterpieces like Arrol and Fowler's Forth Bridge (1883–90) and Robert 'Concrete Bob' MacAlpine's West Highland Railway (1894–1901). Robert Stevenson (1772–1850), grandfather of writer Robert Louis Stevenson (▷ 82), understood the importance of rail, but his lasting achievement was the chain of 23 powerful lighthouses, including the Bell Rock, constructed in often hellish weather, to protect the shipping on which Scotland's trade depended.

SUN PICTURES

Portrait photography was taken to new heights by two young Scottish pioneers. David Octavius Hill (1802–70) was a keen recorder, and painted a portrait of the first steam train to arrive in Glasgow in 1831. In 1843 he was commissioned to paint the heroes of the Disruption of the Kirk (see Wee Frees, left). To make the job easier, along with his friend and chemist Robert Adamson (1821–48), he set out to record the men first by taking photographs, using the calotype method invented by William Henry Fox Talbot only two years before. The pair revealed a remarkable talent for the new art form, and opened a studio on Calton Hill for portraits, as well as recording landscapes and scenes such as the fishermen of Newhaven. Their work is now in the Scottish National Portrait Gallery (▷ 82).

STEAM AT SEA

The first successful steamboat in the world sailed on the Forth and Clyde Canal in 1802. In 1812, Henry Bell of Helensburgh put Europe's first commercial steamer, *Comet*, into service on the Clyde, and by 1840 there were regular transatlantic services. But the engines used sea water, which kept efficiency low and fuel consumption high. In the 1850s and 1860s Glasgow engineers Randolph and Elder, along with the scientist James Thomson (brother of William, Lord Kelvin) devised a combination of compound cylinders and condensers which drastically cut fuel consumption. Within three decades the cargo steamer had taken over from the sailing clipper. The world's first commercial turbine steamer, *King Edward VII* (1901) carried Glasgow holiday-makers as part of a huge fleet.

DOCTORS AS HEROES

The Scottish universities gave Britain its medical élite, notably the Medical Officers of Health in the 1850s—Edinburgh's Henry Littlejohn and Glasgow's William Russell—who ensured that the cities were adequately drained and supplied with clean water, in great projects such as Glasgow's Loch Katrine pipeline (1859). Medical missionaries like David Livingstone (1813–73) and researchers like Ronald Ross (1857–1932), who conquered the mystery of the malaria-bearing mosquito, and Robert Philip (1857–1939), who did the same for tuberculosis, became role models. Robert Knox, the surgeon who notoriously employed body-snatchers William Burke and William Hare in the 1820s to supply corpses for his Edinburgh dissection room (turning a blind eye to their murderous acts), and preached 'scientific' racism, did not.

Scots had always sought careers and fortunes abroad, from the medieval philosopher Duns Scotus to John Paul Jones (1747–92) and Samuel Greig (1735–88), founders respectively of the US and Russian navies. The enormous expansion of the Scots economy in the 19th century accelerated this involvement, and nearly every family saw up to a third of its members emigrate.

The country is marked by this experience, from tangible signs like Madras College in St. Andrews, founded out of Indian trade profits, to an absorption with overseas commerce and missionary work. Alexander Duff (1806–78) created the English-language educational system in India. David Livingstone's reputation crowned a golden age of missionary effort. He was succeeded by many others. New Zealand was partly settled by Free Church migrants under the Rev. Norman MacLeod. Many politicians were of Scots origins. The first Australian federal prime minister, Andrew Fisher (1862–1928), was a former miner from Ayrshire.

Meanwhile, Thomas Blake Glover (1838–1911), builder of the first Japanese railway, and Richard Henry Brunton (1841–1901), who gave Japan a lighthouse system, helped build up a formidable trade competitor.

NEW SCOTLAND

The largest number of Scots emigrants headed for Canada, where they effectively became the ruling élite. The great agitator for self-government in the 1830s was William Lyon Mackenzie from Dundee, and the first federal prime minister after 1867 was Sir John A. MacDonald from Glasgow. The Maritimes saw considerable Gaelic settlement, preserved in local Mods (festivals) and music, notably in Cape Breton. The great romancer John Buchan was a popular Governor General (1935–40), and his last novel, *Sick Heart River* (1941), expresses an inclusive Canadian nationalism.

Opposite clockwise from left to right David Livingstone (1813–73), explorer and missionary, born in Low Blantyre, Lanarkshire; loading a locomotive for export at Glasgow docks; Thomas Lipton (1850–1931) founded a tea and grocery empire; emigration poster from 1920

NABOBS

Scots made a lot of money out of India, by sheer rapacity as well as trade. Returning home (if they survived) they bought estates and lived well, creating an early Scots taste for fiery curries which continues to this day. Jute from Calcutta brought wealth to Dundee (▷ 193). British administration was reformed, and a later generation immersed themselves in the culture of the East. In 1885 the Indian Congress was founded by a Scot, Allan Hume; a later supporter was Sir Patrick Geddes (1854–1932), the friend of Gandhi and Nehru, whose legacy of humane town-planning is being rediscovered in Scotland, not least with a proposal to make the whole central belt into a linear park focused on the reopened Forth and Clyde Canal.

DRUG BARONS

On a hillside overlooking the village of Lairg in Sutherland is an Indian temple commemorating Sir John Matheson, a tacksman's son from the shores of Loch Shin. In the 1830s Matheson, with his partner Robert Jardine, broke into the oriental trade previously monopolized by London's East India Company. They sold opium to the Chinese and claimed they were advancing Christianity and Western civilization, despite provoking two wars (1839–42 and 1856–60). There were few voices raised against them in their home country, where they were regarded as better landlords than most. Until very recently their descendants, known as Taipans, dominated the Royal Bank of Scotland.

TOURISTS

Dr. Johnson was followed in his Highland tour by many English artists of the Romantic era—including poets William Wordsworth and Samuel Taylor Coleridge, painter J. M. W. Turner and philosopher John Ruskin. Another visitor, teenage Mary Shelley, brought Scotland into her horror masterpiece *Frankenstein* (1818). German composer Felix Mendelssohn got to Staffa and Fingal's Cave in 1829 and wrote his *Hebrides* overture; US poet Ralph Waldo Emerson visited essayist Thomas Carlyle at Craigenputtoch in 1833, the start of a life-long correspondence; and English pioneer of tourism Thomas Cook followed hard on the heels of Queen Victoria's residence at Balmoral (1848).

A SELF-MADE MAN

A weaver's son who left Dunfermline in 1848 for the US, Andrew Carnegie (1835–1919) became a telegraph operator on the railroads. From there he moved into steel, founding a company which became the largest iron and steel works in the country. He bought out the opposition and crushed the trade unions, and eventually sold out for £89 million in 1901. He returned to Scotland and built a castle at Dornoch. Carnegie gave subsidies to Scots students, funded some superb libraries and endowed an international peace institution.

A DIFFICULT COUNTRY 1914–1973

Scots casualties in World War I were huge, as much as 40 per cent over the overall British level, and by concentrating industry on munitions production (who would buy them in peacetime?) and selling shipping, banking and railways to London bodies, the war damaged Scotland's ability to compete. In 1921 unemployment rose to over 20 per cent, and stayed there for 20 years. For the first time, the Scots began to question both the capitalist system and the Union.

One result was 'Red Clydeside'. Before 1914 the Labour movement was little represented here outside the coalfields, but the huge munitions drive of the war radicalized the engineers, the women and the unskilled workers of Glasgow. It was led by charismatic men including John Wheatley (1869–1930), architect of social housing, and James Maxton (1885–1946). Their shadow lay long over the whole of the 20th century, inspiring communist, Labour and nationalist alike.

Another result was the remarkable intellectual movement—the Scottish Renaissance, headed by fire-eating nationalist Hugh MacDiarmid (1892–1978). The manifesto was his long, witty and lyrical poem 'A Drunk Man looks at the Thistle', written during the General Strike of 1926. The renaissance was probably less about nationalism than about struggling free from the religious inhibitions that remained from the 19th century—and about giving a voice to women—but it fundamentally altered Scots' perceptions of themselves. They were no longer the lieutenants of Empire.

WOMEN IN POLITICS
In the 1900s the Scots were ardent suffragettes, with notable stars including World War I heroine Dr. Elsie Inglis, who was a nurse in the Balkans, birth-control pioneer Marie Stopes (1880–1958) and writers Naomi Mitchison (1897–1999) and Rebecca West (1892–1983). The vote came in 1918, but only a handful of women were actually elected to Parliament, perhaps because of the élitist 'grouse moor' image of the Tories on the right and the legacy of male-dominated trade unionism on the left. This situation changed dramatically with the establishment of the Scottish Parliament in 1999. It now has the second highest female representation in Europe.

NEW ART

In the later 19th century, Scottish painters had rejected the Victorian stag-and-glen sentimentalism for the sharpness of the French Barbizon school and, later, the Post-Impressionists. They were never very interested in urban subjects, despite the fact that 75 per cent of Scots lived in big towns. This tradition lasted; Scots art in the 1970s was as conservative, or as exciting, as it had been a century earlier. One major difference from English painting is that the Scots have always preferred representational art. They feel closer to German expressionism than to French or American abstraction. This applies to a recent, talented generation: Elizabeth Blackadder (1931–), John Bellany (1942–), Stephen Conroy (1964–) and Peter Howson (1958–).

AMERICAN FACTORIES…

…weren't new in Scotland. But after 1945 US firms, worried about being excluded from Europe—not least by communist-dominated regimes—set up satellite factories to assemble mainly consumer goods in designated development areas. This brought Caterpillar tractors and Hoover cleaners to the Glasgow area, Westclox to Dundee (Scotland produced more clocks than Switzerland for a time) and most notably IBM to Greenock, the first settlement in Silicon Glen. The jobs were welcome, even to trade unionists who were often excluded from the factories, and their 'all workers together' spirit was a far cry from the rigidities of old-style heavy industry..

AXEMAN BEECHING

Railway building occurred in Scotland between 1840 and 1880, when about 50 per cent of the people still lived on the land; by the 1900s trains were coming under pressure from trams and buses in the central belt. By the 1950s about a third of the railway system was hopelessly insolvent, and when Prime Minister Harold Macmillan appointed Dr. Richard Beeching from ICI to reorganize it, Scotland was going to be hard hit. Huge swathes of the country—the Borders, Buchan, Galloway—lost their lines. A fierce political resistance saved the Highland lines to Wick, Kyle of Lochalsh, Oban and Mallaig, routes that are now kept alive partly by their scenic appeal for visitors.

NEW TOWNS

The Labour government of 1945–51 tackled the appalling overcrowding of the old city centres with an agenda of building New Towns. East Kilbride and Glenrothes were started in the late 1940s, followed by Cumbernauld, Livingston and Irvine in the 1960s and 1970s. They were well equipped with schools, shops and sports facilities, unlike so many city housing schemes, and found it easy to attract new industries, notably the technology manufacturing of Silicon Glen, but this overspill hit the older cities badly. Glasgow had over a million people in 1945, and scarcely 600,000 in 2001.

Opposite clockwise from left to right *Shipyards on the River Clyde in Glasgow; Marie Stopes, reformer and pioneer of birth control; Tulips and Fruit, by Samuel John Peploe (c1919)*

In 1945 the Scottish National Party (SNP) returned its first MP to Westminster—and its last for over 20 years. Although a Covenant in support of home rule got over 2 million signatures, and some young nationalists 'liberated' the Stone of Scone (▷ 69, 200) from Westminster Abbey, home rule was really a non-topic. The economic downturn of the 1960s stirred things up, and the SNP did so well in later polls that Prime Minister Harold Wilson set up a Royal Commission to investigate the possibility of change for Scotland. When this reported in 1973, things had shifted radically.

In the mid-1960s the government had allocated sections of the North Sea for oil exploration, without much confidence that it would prove economic. In November 1973 the Yom Kippur War and Arab pressure on the US pushed up the price of crude oil by a factor of four. This made North Sea oil exploitable and focused international attention on Scotland, where support for the SNP soared. A moderate measure of devolution was rejected at a referendum in 1979, just when the black stuff, and the profits, were coming ashore, but the issue of home rule did not go away.

A SCOTTISH PARLIAMENT

In 1977 the people of Scotland voted in favour of a new Scottish parliament. It met for the first time in July 1999. That year First Minister Donald Dewar (1937–2000) commissioned a new parliament building opposite Holyrood Palace. It was to cost £70 million. By the time it was completed in July 2004, the cost had soared to £430 million, and a lot of criticism was directed at MSPs. But the Executive and Parliament has generally performed well. Problems over school exams were resolved, foot-and-mouth disease was met with a co-ordinated policy, and steps have been made towards bettering Scotland's poor record on pollution and recycling. But there is still much work to do.

Above *The Beryl Alpha oil platform in the North Sea*

ON THE MOVE

On the Move gives you detailed advice and information about the various options for travelling to Scotland before explaining the best ways to get around the country once you are there. Handy tips help you with everything from buying tickets to renting a car.

ARRIVING

ARRIVING BY AIR

There are non-stop flights from leading European cities to Edinburgh, Glasgow (International and Prestwick) and Aberdeen airports. From the US, there are regular flights from New York (Newark) and Los Angeles to Glasgow (Continental Airlines) and Philadelphia (summer only) to Glasgow (US Airways). There are also flights from New York (JFK) to Edinburgh (Delta Airlines), and a variety of regular flights from Canada to Glasgow. Visitors from Australia and New Zealand fly to a London airport and then take a domestic flight to Scotland.

London's Heathrow and Gatwick airports are served by all major cities worldwide, and both destinations are connected to Edinburgh, Glasgow, Inverness and Aberdeen by regular daily flights. London's three other airports—Stansted, Luton and London City—also connect with Scotland, and are mainly associated with low-cost airlines such as Ryanair and easyJet. Other airports in the UK and Ireland also serve international

flights with connections to Scotland, including Birmingham International, Manchester and Leeds Bradford.

Glasgow, Edinburgh and Aberdeen airports have information desks, a small number of chain stores and souvenir shops (including a pharmacy), bureaux de change, restaurants, car-rental firms and left-luggage facilities.

Travellers arriving from destinations outside the UK will have to go through customs and passport controls in the normal way. Airlines require proof of identity on check-in, such as a passport, for internal flights in the UK.

Contacts:
» British Airways, tel 0844 493 0787; www.britishairways.com
» bmibaby, tel 0871 224 0224; www.bmibaby.com
» easyJet, tel 0905 821 0905; www.easyjet.com

TIP
» You'll find World Duty Free stores in the main airports.
» If you're flying within the European Union (EU), you can save money on the liquor and tobacco brands in the blue sector of the store; the green sector offers bigger discounts for passengers flying outside the EU.

GETTING TO THE CITY FROM THE AIRPORT

DESTINATION	BUS
Edinburgh to city centre	Frequent Airlink service to Waverley train station in city centre 25 min, £3 single, £5 return
Glasgow to city centre	Frequent Arriva or Fairline service 905 (bus stop 1) to Buchanan Street bus station, 20 min, £3.95 single, £5.95 return
Glasgow Prestwick International to city centre	Regular bus service to Glasgow Central train station, 50 min, £7
Aberdeen to city centre	Regular service with First Aberdeen into the city centre, £2

» Flybe, tel 0871 700 2000;
www.flybe.com
» Ryanair, tel 0871 246 0000;
www.ryanair.com

EDINBURGH AIRPORT

Edinburgh's international airport is located at Ingliston, 6 miles (9.6km) west of the city, off the A8.

All public buses depart from the arrivals area in front of the terminal building. Airlink runs services into the middle of Edinburgh every 10 minutes on weekdays, slightly less often on weekends, and every 30 minutes in the evening; buy tickets at the tourist information point inside the airport, from the ticket booth, or on the bus (Airlink 100). The bus route brings you in past the zoo and Murrayfield sports stadium, and goes all the way along Princes Street to Waverley Bridge and the railway station, right in the city centre (some alterations may be made during construction of the city centre tram). A map showing the location of stops is available from the information desk, and there is a map of the route inside the bus.

The airport has a small selection of high street and souvenir shops, including a pharmacy (Boots). Cash machines are located by the bureaux de change in the departure lounge.
» Edinburgh EH12 9DN, tel 0870 040 0007 (general enquiries);
www.baa.com

GLASGOW INTERNATIONAL AIRPORT

The main airport is located at Paisley, 8 miles (13km) northwest of Glasgow city centre.

All buses depart from the front of the terminal building. Arriva and Fairline Coaches run services into the middle of Glasgow every 10 minutes on weekdays, slightly less often on weekends, and every 30 minutes in the evening, from bus stop 2. Buy your ticket at the Travel Centre information desk or on the bus. Buses go through to Glasgow's Buchanan Street bus station. A map showing stops is available from the transport information desk. Coach (long-distance bus) services collect and drop off on Bute Road, by International Arrivals.

The airport is linked into the National Cycle Network via a route which runs into Paisley, to join up with National Route 7 (Inverness to Carlisle) and National Route 75 (Leith to Gourock). For information, contact Sustrans, tel 0845 113 0065.

The airport has a small selection of high street and souvenir shops, including a pharmacy (Boots). Cash machines are located by Travelex on the first floor, and similarly in the International Departures lounge. Bureaux de change are open at all hours. There is a children's play area on the first floor and in the International Departures lounge. There is also an area providing work spaces with pay phone and modem points.
» Paisley PA3 2ST, tel 0870 040 0008; www.baa.com

TIP
» Departing from Glasgow: Check-in desks 1–38 are in the main terminal building, but 40–64 are in the nearby T2 Building, signposted.

Opposite *Outside Glasgow International Airport's main terminal*
Below *The Edinburgh Airport bus link is a great introduction to the city*

CAR	TRAIN	TAXI
At Ingliston, west of city centre off A8; 30 min–1 hour	No direct rail link	From arrivals area in front of the main terminal, around £20 upward
In Paisley, 8 miles (13km) northwest of the city centre via M8, exit 28; 30 min	Bus to Paisley Gilmour Street station, for frequent connections to Glasgow Central, 11 min, £2.50	From outside door 5, Domestic Arrivals, 20 min, around £17 upward
At Prestwick 45 miles (72km) southwest of Glasgow via A77; 40 min	Regular train service to Glasgow Central train station, 44 min, £5.85	20 min, around £14 upward
By Dyce, 7 miles (11.3km) northwest of the city centre via the A96; 15 min	No direct rail link	15 min, around £14 upward

GLASGOW PRESTWICK INTERNATIONAL AIRPORT

Glasgow's second airport is a long way southwest of the city centre, but has a direct train link to the city. Prestwick deals mainly with charter holiday flights, plus low-cost flights with Ryanair from London (Stansted), Brussels, Dublin, Frankfurt, Oslo and Paris. Facilities include a small selection of shops, a café, cash machines and a bureau de change.

» Prestwick KA9 2PL, tel 0871 282 0669; www.gpia.co.uk

ABERDEEN AIRPORT

Aberdeen airport is known as the world's largest commercial heliport, thanks to its status as the main transport hub for North Sea oil workers, and lies 7 miles (11.3km) northwest of the city. It caters for flights from mainland Europe and Scandinavia, as well as domestic flights.

Internet access is available in the departure lounge. The bureau de change is opposite the information desk. Dyce, the nearest train station, is a short taxi ride away.

» Dyce, Aberdeen AB21 7DU, tel 0870 040 0006; www.aberdeenairport.com

ARRIVING BY TRAIN

In theory, it is possible to travel from one end of Britain to the other by train in a day. Intercity trains on major routes travel at 140mph (225kph), so journeys from London to Edinburgh can take just over four hours. Connecting trains to smaller destinations are likely to be slower and less frequent.

Virgin trains from England follow the east coast route to Edinburgh and the west coast route to Glasgow. National Express trains travel up the eastern side to Edinburgh, and go on to Glasgow, Inverness and Aberdeen. Tickets for both companies can be bought at any main line station, but note that your ticket will specify which train you can catch, and that tickets are not generally transferable between the different companies.

High-speed Eurostar trains from France (Paris and Lille) and Belgium (Brussels) reach St. Pancras station in London in less than three hours.

Passports are required for travel and, on arrival, you must also pass through customs, before continuing your journey to Scotland.

Both Edinburgh Waverley and Glasgow Central train stations are main hubs for onward travel within Scotland, and both are well served with tourist information desks (including accommodation information), cafés, shops and banking services. Electronic screens indicate from which platform you need to catch your train.

» National Rail Enquiry Service, tel 08457 484950 (daily, 24 hours); www.nationalrail.co.uk

ARRIVING BY COACH

If you travel to Britain by long-distance bus you will probably arrive at London's Victoria Coach Station. The main coach company for connections from England and Wales to Scotland is National Express. Coaches arrive at the main hubs of St. Andrews Square bus station in Edinburgh, and Buchanan Street bus station in Glasgow.

» National Express, tel 0871 781 8181; www.nationalexpress.com

ARRIVING BY FERRY

There are two direct routes by
vehicle and passenger ferry from
Northern Ireland: Belfast to Stranraer,
and from Larne to Cairnryan or
Troon. For onward travel, Stranraer
is served by a rail and coach link.
Cairnryan is linked to Stranraer by
public bus service. Troon is also on
the rail network.
» Stena Line, tel 08705 707070
(reservations); www.stenaline.co.uk
» P&O Irish Ferries, tel 0870 2424
777; www.poirishsea.com
   Overnight vehicle and passenger
ferries from Zeebrugge in Belgium
arrive at Rosyth, 13 miles (21km)
east of Edinburgh.
» Superfast Ferries, tel 0870 234
0870 (reservations) or 01383 608003;
www.superfast.com
» A weekly car and passenger ferry
in summer links Shetland with
Denmark, Iceland, Norway and the
Faroes.
» Smyril Line, Holmsgarth Terminal,
Lerwick, Shetland; www.smyril-line.
com

ARRIVING BY CAR

Driving into Scotland from England,
the two major routes are the A1(M)/
M1/A1 on the eastern side of the
country, and the M6/A74(M) up
the western side. Both routes can
become very congested around
urban areas at peak times of the
day and around holiday weekends
(▷ 315).
   If you are planning to drive
to Britain from the Continent,
Eurotunnel operates the train service
for cars, caravans and motorcycles
through the Channel Tunnel to
southern England. On your arrival
at Folkestone leave the terminal on
the M20 northbound, joining it at
junction (intersection) 11a, for major
connecting routes north to Scotland.

Above *The distinctive Zeebrugge ferry on*
the Firth of Forth
Below *Three Sisters, Glencoe Pass Road*
Opposite *Edinburgh's Waverley railway*
station, a major hub for travel in Scotland

ON THE MOVE | GETTING AROUND

For all public transport timetable enquiries within Britain, call Traveline, tel 0871 200 2233 (daily, 8am–8pm); www.traveline.org.uk. If you're planning to explore widely using public transport, then look out for deals such as the Freedom of Scotland Travelpass, which can be bought at any train station, travel agent, Britrail outlet in North America and Europe, or by phone from First Scotrail, tel 08457 550033. The Travelpass covers you for 8 days, or 15 days, and costs £105 or £140 (adult rates). This gives either 4 or 8 days of free travel within that period on the entire network of First Scotrail trains, Strathclyde Passenger Transport Service trains, National Express and Virgin trains within Scotland, and all Caledonian MacBrayne (CalMac) ferries. It also covers some CityLink, Stagecoach and Highland Bus services, and allows for discounted travel on other services such as the Orkney ferry.

GETTING AROUND IN EDINBURGH

Lothian Buses are the main public bus operators in the city, identifiable by their maroon and white livery, or red and white. Bus stops are labelled with the name of the stop (eg Waverley Bridge), then a list of the bus companies that stop there, then night services, then regular services with bus numbers.

There are lots of different tickets, but an exact-fare system operates, so you need to have correct money as no change is given. The standard adult fare is £1.10; concessions pay a 70p flat rate; child (5–15) 60p, for one journey, any distance. When you get on the bus, put the exact fare into the slot in front of the driver, then tear off your ticket from the machine behind the driver.

» Lothian bus information, tel 0131 555 6363.

» Get timetables and tickets at the Travel Shop, 27 Hanover Street (Mon–Sat 8.15–6), and at Waverley Bridge station (Mon–Sat 8.15–6, Sun 9.30–5).

» An enlarged route map and timetable on the bridge outside Waverley Station has additional information about the night bus service into the suburbs.

» Driving here is dogged by narrow streets, one-way systems, 'red' routes, residents-only parking and dedicated bus routes. On-street parking is generally pay-and-display between 8.30am and 6.30pm Mon–Sat.

There are plenty of signed parking areas, mostly to the south of Princes Street. The biggest is at Greenside Place, off Leith Street.

GETTING AROUND IN GLASGOW

For information about buses, local trains and the underground network within the city, contact the Strathclyde Passenger Transport (SPT) centre at Buchanan Street bus station on Killermont Street (Mon–Sat 6.30am–10.30pm, Sun 7am–10.30pm; tel 0141 333 3708; www.spt.co.uk). The SPT can also provide information about the ferry services to Kilcreggan and Helensburgh.

Glasgow's underground (the 'clockwork orange') forms a 6-mile (9.7km) loop from the west of the city into the centre and Buchanan Street bus station and is particularly useful for access to the Museum of Transport, Kelvingrove Art Gallery and Museum (Kelvinhall), the Hunterian Museum (Hillhead), Rangers' stadium (Ibrox) and St. Enoch shopping centre (St. Enoch). Trains operate from around 6.30am Mon–Sat, 11am Sun, and stop around 11.15pm Mon–Sat, 5.30pm Sun. You can buy tickets from the station booking offices, or from the automatic ticket machines available in many stations. A single ticket (one-way ticket) costs £1.10, a return ticket £2.20, with reductions for children. The Discovery ticket allows a day's unlimited travel for just £2.50, if travelling after 9.30am.

Glasgow is bisected by a motorway, and its streets follow a more regular grid pattern than Edinburgh's. But driving is still complicated, and you'd do best to park in one of the public parking areas such as Mitchell Street (NCP) or Albion Street (Universal Parking).

The underground network also makes 'park and ride' a more attractive option: Park at Kelvinbridge, to the north of the centre (£2), or Shields Road, to the south (£2), and catch a train into the city. All-day parking at Shields Road £4.20.

Above *The CalMac ferry is a familiar sight in the islands*
Opposite *Getting around Glasgow on the underground is easy*

On vehicle ferries the price includes the vehicle and a number of passengers (usually up to five). Some fares may be paid on the ferry, by cash or cheque only. Tickets will be either one-way or return, and usually specify the time of the ferry you should catch. Many factors affect the ticket price, such as length of stay, size and type of vehicle, so discuss your needs with the operator before booking.

If you want to explore several islands, an Island Rover ticket from Caledonian MacBrayne (CalMac)) lasts 8 or 15 days and offers a significant saving. An 8-day pass for two people with a car costs £359; for a foot passenger, or a bicyclist, it is just £53.

Island Hopscotch tickets are tailored to 26 of the most popular routes through the islands, and offer better value than tickets bought individually. For example, the cost of a car and two people on the route from Mallaig to Skye, the Uists, Harris and Lewis and back to Ullapool is £215.

If travelling with a vehicle, you should usually check in at the ferry terminal 30 minutes before departure. Foot passengers need check in only 10 minutes before.

FERRIES

In addition to the ferry ports of Rosyth, Stranraer, Cairnryan and Lerwick for overseas arrivals and departures, there are also many domestic terminals serving the islands of Scotland. The ferries may carry foot passengers, bicycles, cars, caravans and local freight, and vary in size, facilities and frequency according to the route. Some services may be disrupted by tides and bad weather conditions, so always check sailings in advance.

BUYING TICKETS

Information about timetables and fares is available direct from the ferry companies, or from tourist information centres. Tickets can be reserved in advance from the ferry operator, through travel agents and tourist information offices. When reserving you will be asked for details such as the make or size of the vehicle and number of passengers. Reserving in advance is recommended, especially at holiday times.

INDEPENDENT FERRY ROUTES

DESTINATION	TIME TAKEN	RESTRICTIONS	CONTACT
Greenock—Kilcreggan/Helensburgh	10/40 min	Foot passengers only	Clyde Marine Services Ltd, tel 01475 721281 www.clyde-marine.co.uk
Ardgour—Corran	2 min		Tec Services, Highland Council, tel 01397 709000 or 01855 841243
Oban—Kerrara	5 min	Foot passengers only	D. McEachan, tel 01631 563665
Islay—Jura	5 min		Serco Denholm, tel 01496 840681
Iona—Staffa	50 min (3-hour round trip)	Foot passengers only; Apr–end Oct	David Kirkpatrick, tel 01681 700358
Mull—Staffa	30 min	Foot passengers only; Apr–end Oct	Gordon Grant, tel 01681 700338
Mull—Staffa/Treshnish	1 hour	Foot passengers only; Apr–end Oct	Turus Mara, tel 01688 400242/ 08000 858786 www.turusmara.com
Port Appin—Lismore	10 min	Foot passengers only	Argyll & Bute Council, tel 01631 730686
Seil—Easdale	5 min	Foot passengers only	Argyll & Bute Council, tel 01631 562125
Seil—Luing	5 min	Mon–Sat	Argyll & Bute Council, tel 01631 562125
Glenelg—Skye	5 min	Easter–end Oct	Isle of Skye Ferry; www.skyeferry.co.uk

ON BOARD

Larger ferries are generally comfortable, with refreshments, toilets and TVs, and cabins can be booked for longer journeys. Boarding may involve steep ramps, so take care with strollers (pushchairs). On passenger ferries larger luggage may be stored out on the deck to leave the inside clear. Smoking is allowed in designated areas only.

Vehicles can be driven straight into the back of the ferries. You can then go up to the decks, or may be able to stay in your car.

Western Isles

The access ferry ports are Stornoway on Lewis (from Ullapool), Tarbert on Harris (from Uig and Lochmaddy), Lochmaddy on North Uist (from Uig on Skye), Lochboisdale on South Uist (from Oban and Castlebay) and Castlebay on Barra (from Oban).

At the time of printing, the main inter-island ferries for the Western Isles are operated by Caledonian MacBrayne Ltd, known familiarly as CalMac, but this may change in the future as routes are put out to competitive tender. The vessels currently take in islands which include Skye, Arran, Bute, Islay, Mull, Lewis and Harris, and North and South Uist.

» CalMac, The Ferry Terminal, Gourock PA19 1QP, tel 01475 650100/0800 066 5000; www.calmac.co.uk

The islands are served by a network of regular but infrequent buses linked in to the ferry services, Mon–Sat. For example, in summer there are four to five buses a day between Stornoway and Leverburgh, on route W10.

» For timetables and ticket prices, contact the tourist office at 26 Cromwell Street, Stornoway, Isle of Lewis HS1 2DD, tel 01851 703088 or 0845 225 5121.

Orkney and Shetland

NorthLink Orkney and Shetland Ferries operates overnight ferries from Aberdeen to Orkney and Shetland, from Scrabster (by Thurso) to Orkney, and between Lerwick in Shetland and Kirkwall in Orkney. Reclining seats or cabins can be booked for the longer crossings. The cost for a foot passenger to Lerwick starts at £21.40.

» NorthLink Orkney and Shetland Ferries Ltd, Kiln Corner, Ayre Road, Kirkwall, Orkney KW15 1QX, tel 0845 600 0449; www.northlinkferries. co.uk

From May to September, a foot passengers only ferry operates between John o'Groats and Burwick on Orkney. It takes 40 minutes and there is a 45-minute connecting coach service to Kirkwall for every crossing.

» John o'Groats Ferries Ltd, The Ferry Office, John O'Groats, Caithness KW1 4YR; tel 01955 611353 or 01955 611342; www.jogferry.co.uk

Below *The CalMac ferry from Oban to Mull*
Opposite *Taking off from Barra Airport in the Western Isles*

DOMESTIC FLIGHTS

Domestic air travel is relatively expensive in Britain but, with an increasing number of low-cost airlines competing for passengers, prices are coming down. If you are flexible about travelling dates and times, some real bargains can be had. However, check carefully what the price includes, such as taxes, credit-card reservation fees and other charges, and be aware that some advertised fares are one-way only.

All domestic flights and those to destinations within the European Union (EU) carry a £10 departure tax (usually included in the price). For flights to other destinations the charge is £40.

REGIONAL AIRPORTS

For details of Edinburgh, Glasgow and Aberdeen airports, ▷ 43–44.

The 11 main regional airports are Campbeltown, Islay, Tiree, Barra, Benbecula, Stornoway (Lewis), Sumburgh (Shetland), Kirkwall (Orkney), Wick, Dundee and Inverness. These are all operated by Highlands and Islands Airports Ltd (HIAL), and their website gives useful information on each one.
» HIAL, tel 01667 462445; www.hial.co.uk

Smaller additional airports include the remote Fair Isle.

INVERNESS AIRPORT

Inverness (Dalcross) Airport serves as the main hub for access to the Highlands and Islands (as well as offering some holiday charter flights to Zurich and Mediterranean destinations). It is located 10 miles (16km) east of Inverness, off the A96 via the B9039.

There is a regular bus service into Inverness every 30 minutes. There is no direct train link, with Inverness and Nairn offering the nearest train stations.

BUYING A TICKET

You can reserve tickets direct from the airlines by phone or online, or through travel agents. If reserving online the tickets will be posted to you or an electronic e-ticket will be sent by email.

If you have reserved far enough in advance you may be able to amend or cancel tickets, but a fee will be charged.

ON BOARD

» For security reasons no fluids or sharp objects (including scissors and cutlery) are allowed in hand luggage. Lists of prohibited items are displayed throughout the airports. Any items found will be confiscated.
» These are relatively short flights with few frills, but simple refreshments will be available on longer journeys.
» Smoking is not allowed anywhere on the planes or in the airports.

TIP

Useful websites for flights and information include:
www.cheapflights.co.uk
www.thisistravel.co.uk
www.ba.com
www.worldairportguide.com

COACHES AND BUSES

Coaches (long-distance buses) run from Edinburgh's St. Andrews Square bus station and Glasgow's Buchanan Street bus station to all parts of the country and are a slower but less expensive alternative to train travel, reaching many more destinations. Journey times can be long (with some changes necessary) but the vehicles are comfortable, with air-conditioning, toilets and sometimes refreshments for longer trips.

Citylink is the main coach operator for destinations across Scotland, linking Edinburgh, Glasgow, Aberdeen, Dundee, Perth, Inverness, Scrabster (for Orkney), Ullapool, Skye, Fort William, Oban, Campbeltown, Stranraer, Dumfries and many stops in between. They can be identified by the blue and yellow livery.

» Scottish Citylink Coaches, Buchanan Street Bus Station, Killermont Street, Glasgow G2 3NP, tel 08705 505050 (8am–9pm); www.citylink.co.uk

A wide variety of guided coach tours is available—contact travel agents and tourist information offices for more information.

BUYING TICKETS

Ticket types include standard singles or returns, plus various saver tickets which are reservable in advance. Look for deals such as the Citylink Explorer Pass, which gives unlimited travel over 3, 5 or 8 days (adult £35, £59 or £79), plus discounts on ferry travel. National Express Brit Xplorer cards are available for 7, 14 or 28 days (adult £79, £139 or £219).

Discount cards are also available for passengers over the age of 60, for students and for young people.

Baggage allowances are up to two medium-size suitcases and one item of hand luggage per person, with no guarantee that any excess will be carried. Folded and covered bicycles are acceptable.

» It is cheaper to reserve in advance and travel midweek. For example, the single adult Apex fare (reserved at least 5 days before travel) between Edinburgh and Inverness is around £17, and between Glasgow and Skye around £25. Pre-paid tickets can be sent to you, sent to key locations for personal collection or even sent to you by SMS text message.

BUSES

Local buses are reasonably comfortable and often make a pleasant alternative to trains. Major towns and cities usually have frequent buses, but services can be erratic elsewhere, notably in very rural areas, with perhaps only one or two buses a week. Some night services (denoted by an 'N' prefix) are available in major towns and cities.

Tourist information offices can provide information and timetables. Timetables can look daunting, so check them carefully for services that run only on school days or are otherwise restricted.

Several bus companies may compete in urban areas. In some cases their services may overlap, but tickets will be company-specific. Stagecoach is the main operator in southwest, east central and northeast Scotland. Rapsons operates local buses in the Highland region, and Orkney and Shetland.

The Royal Mail Postbus service (tel 08457 740740; www.postbus. royalmail.com) also carries passengers around remoter parts of the country in minibuses. Fares are inexpensive, but note that buses are scheduled to serve the mail first and passengers second, so they may set off very early in the morning.

BUS STOPS

Urban bus stops are usually denoted by a sign on a pole giving the number(s) of the buses serving that stop, its location and the destination (direction of travel), sometimes accompanied by sheltered seats. In contrast, rural bus stops may be difficult to spot and are unlikely to have much information.

» Buses will stop at main bus stops if passengers are waiting to get on or off. At a 'request stop' (usually intermediate stops and rural stops), hold out your arm to hail the bus you want.

» Check the number and destination on the front before you get on, or check with the driver, as the stop will probably serve many different routes. At night treat all stops as request stops.

ON BOARD

Keep your ticket until the end of the journey because inspectors regularly board the buses to check tickets and catch fare-dodgers.

» Tickets are usually bought from the driver as you board.

» Children under 5 travel free, and those aged 5–15 travel for half fare. Card concessions for students and seniors are also available.

» Some driver-only buses have two doors: one at the front, where you board, and one midway, where you get off.

» Show your pass or have your change ready to pay the driver when you board. Drivers and conductors prefer the exact fare but they will give change. Tell the driver or conductor where you want to go and he or she will tell you the fare.

» On all buses press the red button once and the bus will call at the next scheduled stop.

TAXIS

Taxis are generally an expensive way of getting around in Britain, but very convenient for shorter trips. If you are planning a longer trip by taxi, agree on a fee in advance. There are basically two types of taxi: the traditional black London-style cab (found in major cities) and the minicab. The black cabs are world famous and, despite the fact that they now feature advertising and come in shades other than black, the design remains distinctive. All private taxis are licensed and regulated and should have meters. Vehicles can range from ordinary saloon (sedan) and estate cars (station wagons) to seven-seater 'people carriers'. A notice confirming that a vehicle is licensed to carry passengers should be displayed on the back of the vehicle.

FINDING A TAXI

You'll find designated taxi stands outside train stations and large hotels, near shopping malls and at other major points within cities. Taxi cabs can also be hailed in the street: Look for an illuminated orange TAXI light on the top and hold out your arm to attract the driver's attention.

Private taxis and minicabs can be reserved by phone; look in the *Yellow Pages* phone book for local companies, or ask at your hotel.

Taxis can be scarce to find at busy times, especially on Friday and Saturday nights in the city, so reserve a ride home in advance if you're going out on the town.

» Avoid minicab drivers touting at airports and stations as they may overcharge and may be unlicensed or uninsured. Take licensed cabs from taxi stands or reserve with a recommended minicab firm in advance.

» Unlike black cabs, it is acceptable to sit in the front passenger seat of ordinary taxis.

» A tip of around 10 per cent of the total fare is expected and customary, but not compulsory.

TIP

» www.traintaxi.co.uk lists all taxi stands and operators that serve all train, tram, metro and underground stations in Britain. This is also available as a publication, *Traintaxi Guide*.

Opposite *Rural bus services are limited across the country*
Below *Taxi in Edinburgh*

TRAINS

Train services across Britain generally work efficiently and are not too crowded outside peak periods. More than 20 different companies now operate the country's railway. This can lead to differing facilities and some curious price anomalies as each company determines its own fare structure.

Train services are subject to delays, so allow plenty of time for your journey, especially if you have to change trains.

Essential engineering work is usually carried out on weekends and public holidays, and can severely disrupt services. Details are displayed at relevant stations, or check in advance with National Rail (www.nationalrail.co.uk).

FIRST SCOTRAIL

First Scotrail operates the majority of train services within Scotland, between 335 stations, as well as the overnight sleeper services that link Edinburgh, Glasgow, Fort William, Aberdeen and Inverness with London. For planning ahead, their website (www.firstscotrail.com) has a useful table, which shows the resources available at every station, including parking, buffet services and access for travellers with disabilities.

The Railbus scheme offers scheduled onward bus links to non-rail destinations such as Callander, St. Andrews and Ullapool, tel 08457 550033.

» National Rail Enquiry Service, tel 08457 484950 (daily, 24 hours); www.nationalrail.co.uk

Detailed information for the whole network, including operating companies, timetables, fares and engineering works, is available from National Rail Enquiries (see above). Their useful free leaflet *Map and Guide to Using the National Rail Network* is available from stations.

Staffed stations usually have free timetables of local services, and almost all stations display timetables. Note that service is generally more limited on Saturday and Sunday.

» There are two classes of train travel: first and standard. First is more expensive but guarantees you a seat on crowded trains as well as complimentary drinks and newspapers. Otherwise standard class is perfectly acceptable and you can reserve a seat if you reserve in advance.

» Sleeping compartments can be reserved with First Scotrail on some overnight services to and from Scotland (tel 08457 550033).

Above *Steam train in Aviemore station in the Cairngorms National Park*
Opposite *Boat of Garten ticket office*

Avoid weekday rush hours (7–9.30am and 4–7pm) if possible. Note that the evening rush hour often starts earlier on Friday, especially before public holidays. Allow plenty of time, especially to make connections.

If you are planning to continue your journey via England and the Eurostar train into continental Europe, ask about discounted fares to London International.

» Eurostar, tel 08705 186186; www. eurostar.com

TIPS

» The West Highland Line is a spectacular scenic route between Glasgow and Mallaig; vintage steam trains sometimes travel it in the summer. First Scotrail, tel 08457 550033; www.firstscotrail.com

» The Royal Scotsman is a luxury train that takes passengers on tours of 1–4 nights; tel 0845 077 2222; www.royalscotsman.com

BUYING TICKETS

You must always have a valid ticket for your journey in advance or you may be liable to a fine. Your ticket or rail pass must be available for inspection on any train, along with any relevant documentation. You can buy a ticket in person for any destination run by any company from any train station, either from the ticket office or from automated machines (usually for shorter journeys). Most travel agents also sell train tickets.

You can also buy tickets online through www.thetrainline.com or www.qjump.co.uk, which give prices and fast reservation for different types of ticket for any journey. If there is no means of purchasing a ticket in advance, you will be sold one on the train.

» Seat reservations are not usually necessary, but are advisable at peak times and are compulsory for certain services, in which case there is no extra charge involved.

TYPES OF TICKET

The variety of ticket types, pricing and restrictions offered by different rail companies can be bewildering. For example, National Express, which runs trains between London and Scotland, offers return fares from London to Edinburgh from around £39 to £296. Broadly, the earlier you reserve your ticket in advance (up to 10 weeks) and the more flexible you can be about which days and times you travel, the less money you are likely to have to pay. There may also be significant reductions for up to four people travelling together.

» A cheap-day return is best for a day out, but you can buy and use it only after 9.30am.
» Except for certain 'rover' or 'open' tickets your journey(s) must be on the date(s) shown on the ticket and you cannot break the journey (that is, get off en route and join a later train).

OTHER DISCOUNTS

» Children under 5 travel free and 5 to 15-year-olds pay half price for most tickets, but check as there are exceptions.
» Britrail Pass: Unlimited rail travel in Britain and Northern Ireland for non-UK residents only, but it can only be purchased abroad.

Britrail passes also come in family and group forms, offering considerable savings to accompanying passengers. In addition to regional passes for Scotland, there are passes for London and Wales and combinations with Irish and European passes. For information: www.britrail.com
» Railcard: A young person's railcard (age 16–25 and mature students in full-time education) costs £24 and is valid across the country. You'll need a passport-size photograph and proof of eligibility to buy a railcard.
» Freedom of Scotland Travelpass, ▷ 46.

AT THE STATION

Most train stations have electronic information displays showing departure times, station stops, platform numbers and estimated time of arrival. Departures and arrivals for each platform may be shown at larger stations. Smaller country stations may have few facilities.
» Some urban stations have automatic barriers. Put your ticket into the slot on one side to open the barrier: It will pop out at the top. If you need help, go to the staffed gate at the side of the
barrier. The barriers retain used tickets at the end of a journey.
» Major stations have facilities in varying degrees, ranging from basic newsagents and cafés to specialist shops, minimarkets, travel offices, restaurants, dry-cleaners, bureaux de change and pubs. Small or rural stations are usually pretty spartan.
» Smoking is not allowed in public places.
» Few stations have left-luggage facilities for security reasons. Larger stations have information desks where you can report lost property.

ON THE TRAIN

Facilities and conditions on board trains vary, depending on the route. Generally, all trains have toilet facilities, ranging from the basic to larger, wheelchair-accessible booths with baby-changing facilities. Many trains have at-seat trolley service for refreshments, and some longer routes also have buffet cars where you can buy drinks and snacks.
» Smoking is banned on trains.

MAIN TICKET OPTIONS

In approximately descending order of price.

TICKET	RESTRICTIONS	VALIDITY
Open one-way	None	On the date shown, or on either of the two following days.
Day one-way/day return	None	Date shown; return same day.
Saver return	Peak travel restrictions	Return within one calendar month.
SuperSaver return	Not available for travel before 9.30am, on Fri, summer Sat and peak holidays	Return within one calendar month.
Cheap-day return	Not before 9.30am	Return the same day.

Left *Enjoying a drive on the open road in Glen Affric*

DRIVING

The most flexible way to get around Scotland is by car. On the whole, motorists drive safely, roads are good and signposting is efficient. Note that the wearing of seatbelts is compulsory. Major routes are well served with rest stop areas and petrol (gas) stations, but on rural routes these may be few and far between. Drink driving laws are strictly enforced—the best advice is not to drive after drinking alcohol.

DRIVING ON THE LEFT

Vehicles drive on the left side of the road. Remember this particularly when: first moving off from the side of the road; turning from one road into another road; driving on a road with few other cars or at night; approaching a roundabout/traffic circle (keep to the left, go clockwise, see also tips below); and meeting another vehicle on a single-track road. Do not overtake on the left.

SPEED LIMITS

The speed limit in built-up areas is generally 30mph (48kph). Outside built-up areas it is generally 60mph (97kph) on single carriageways and 70mph (113kph) on two-lane carriageways and motorways (highways).

FUEL

Most garages are self-service. Higher octane unleaded petrol (gas), unleaded 95 octane petrol and diesel are sold.

CLAMPING AND TOWING AWAY

If your car is parked illegally it may be clamped; the notice posted on your windscreen explains how to get it released. Vehicles are usually released within one hour of payment. If your vehicle is removed it will cost at least £125 to get it back. Vehicles must be collected in person and you must produce identification.

BREAKDOWN AND ACCIDENTS

Several organizations in the UK can assist you in the event of breakdown, inluding the Automobile Association (AA). Check whether membership in your home country entitles you to reciprocal assistance.

AT THE SCENE OF AN ACCIDENT

If you are involved in a road-traffic accident, stop and remain at the scene for a reasonable period and give your vehicle registration number, your name and address, and that of the vehicle owner (if different), to anyone with reasonable grounds for asking for those details. If you do not exchange those details at the scene, you must report the accident at a police station or to a police constable within 24 hours.

CAR RENTAL

Arranging a rental car through your travel agent before arriving saves money and allows you to find out about deposits, drop-off charges, cancellation penalties and insurance costs in advance. Established car rental firms have offices throughout Britain; smaller, local firms and online agents may offer better deals; check the *Yellow Pages*. For further information and contact details, ▷ 318.

» You must have a valid driver's licence (an international driver's licence is not required).

» Most rental firms require the driver to be at least 23 years old and have at least 12 months of driving experience.

TIPS:
SINGLE-TRACK ROADS

Many of the minor country roads in Scotland are single track (lane) for all or some of their length.

» Passing places are marked with a post, usually topped by a square or diamond-shaped white sign. Don't park in a passing place.

» Keep your speed down. Visibility is often limited, and you need time to slow down and pull in to let approaching vehicles pass.

» If the nearest passing place is on the right side of the road, wait opposite to allow approaching traffic to pass you.

» If the driver behind you is in a hurry, pull into a passing place and let them pass. An impatient driver on your tail is a liability.

» When passing a vehicle that has pulled into a passing place, check ahead first for approaching vehicles or pedestrians.

» If you meet another vehicle and there is no passing place in sight, be prepared to reverse back to a space.

» Watch out for livestock on the road. Slow down and be prepared to give way to cattle and particularly sheep, who can wait until the last second before bolting in front of you. Deer can also be a hazard at night.

» Be courteous—if somebody has pulled in for you to pass, give them a wave of thanks.

» Towing a caravan (trailer) on single-track roads demands extra vigilance; be prepared to pull in to let following traffic pass.

MAKING IT EASY AT ROUNDABOUTS/TRAFFIC CIRCLES

When reaching a roundabout give priority to traffic on your right, unless directed otherwise by signs, road markings or traffic lights. Pause before moving to make sure traffic in front has moved. Watch out for vehicles already on the roundabout; be aware they may not be signalling correctly or at all.

Approach mini roundabouts in the same way. Vehicles MUST pass around the central markings.

Use the chart below to work out the distance in km (green) and estimated duration in hours and minutes (blue) of a car journey

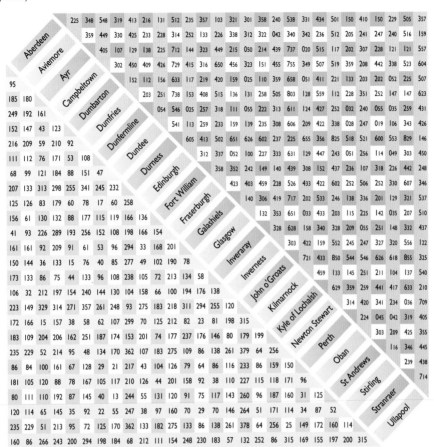

ROAD SIGNS

Give way to traffic on major road

Stop and give way

Crossroads

Roundabout

Mini roundabout (roundabout circulation)

No through road

No stopping (clearway)

National speed limit applies

Maximum speed limit applies

One-way traffic

No overtaking

No entry for vehicular traffic

Two lanes merge into one

Double bend

Two-way traffic ahead

Cycle route ahead

Road works

Slippery road

VISITORS WITH A DISABILITY

VisitScotland's publication *Practical Information for Visitors with Disabilities* is available directly from the tourist board or from tourist offices (▷ 321).

DPTAC
The Disabled Persons Transport Advisory Committee (DPTAC) offers travel advice and information for people with mobility problems. Their website has advice on travel by rail, air, bus and sea and links to other sources of information. For information tel 020 7944 8012; www.dptac.gov.uk

AIR TRAVEL
Most airlines have departments dedicated to answering inquiries and making the arrangements for people who have special requirements. Some budget airlines may charge for providing assistance. The travel agent or airline should be given prior notice of what is needed.

BUSES AND COACHES
Scheduled coach and bus travel in the UK is not widely accessible for wheelchair users, or for anyone with a severe walking problem. The vehicles currently used on scheduled coach (long-distance bus) services have high, steep steps which are difficult to negotiate, though these are being replaced with modern low-floor buses with ramps. People with sufficient mobility can use scheduled coach services, but the staff are not allowed to lift or give any other physical assistance with boarding.

TRAINS
While wheelchairs up to a maximum width of 67cm (26in) can be accommodated on trains, large powered wheelchairs, strollers (pushchairs) and scooters are excluded from most passenger rail services because of their size. Many trains carry lightweight portable ramps for use at unstaffed stations.

Be aware that many smaller stations are either unstaffed or only staffed at peak times. Information about both these and alternative, more accessible stations, can be obtained when reserving assistance from the disabled passengers' assistance telephone line provided by each rail company.

For discounted rail fares, the Disabled Persons Railcard is available to people with a range of disabilities, and is also valid for their carers.
» Further information can be found in the booklet *Rail Travel for Disabled Passengers*, available from train stations.

DRIVING
Everyone travelling in a motor vehicle is required by law to wear a seatbelt when the vehicle is fitted with them. This applies to people with disabilities, with few exceptions. If you have been directed not to wear a seatbelt for medical reasons, a doctor's certificate will be required.

Vehicle rental
Some of the major rental companies in the UK have vehicles with hand controls. Similarly, wheelchairs, scooters and other mobility and medical aids can be rented both in the UK and abroad. The Automobile Association (AA) helpline (tel 0800 262050) can supply contact details.

Roadside stops and accommodation
All motorway service stations are required to provide full access to all their facilities, including toilets, rest rooms, restaurants and shops.

Most of the lodge type hotels, such as Travelodge, Travelinn and Premier, have at least one, and usually several, accessible rooms on the ground floor.

Holiday Care is a charity that specializes in information about access to serviced accommodation.

It can assist with details of hotels, bed-and-breakfast accommodation and guest houses that can accommodate people with disabilities.
» Holiday Care, 7th floor, Sunley House, 4 Bedford Park, Croydon CR0 2AP, tel 08451 249974, textphone 08451 249976, fax 08451 249972; www.holidaycare.org.uk

Motorway breakdown
All emergency motorway phones have an inductive coupler for use with the 'T' switch on hearing aids. For people who are profoundly deaf or without access to such hearing aids, when using a standard motorway phone, repeat twice the name, car registration number, disability and the nature of the emergency to enable the operator to deal with the call.

Parking
For many years, motorists with disabilities in the UK used to have the Orange Badge to assist with parking. It has now been superseded by a European Union (EU) scheme using an identical Blue Badge in all member states; however, UK regulations may differ from those of other countries. The AA has a multi-lingual booklet that outlines the details.
» AA Disability Helpline, tel 0800 262 050.

TOURIST ATTRACTIONS
Places of interest such as stately homes, museums and theme parks are required to make their attractions accessible to people with disabilities, but the degree to which this is possible with older buildings may vary. Most major attractions have already taken considerable steps to provide or improve access, and both the National Trust for Scotland (NTS) and Historic Scotland (HS) include access information in their standard guides (▷ 322).

REGIONS

This chapter is divided ino the six regions of Scotland (▷ 8–9). Places of interest are listed alphabetically within each region.

Scotland's Regions

SIGHTS 62
WALKS 84
WHAT TO DO 88
EATING 98
STAYING 104

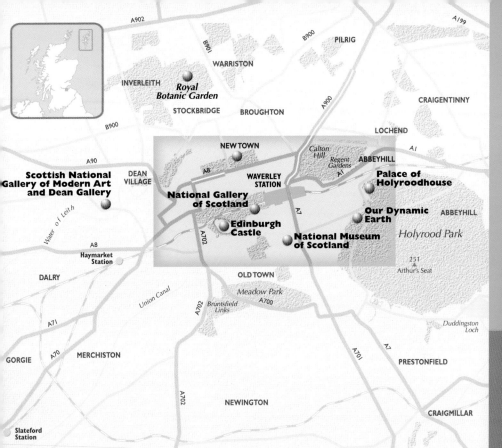

EDINBURGH

Scotland's capital city has a genteel, cultured outlook reflected in the magnificent 18th century architecture of its so-called New Town. Some of the country's major visitor attractions are found here, including national museums, galleries and the city's famous castle on top of a rocky crag overlooking the city.

Central Edinburgh is relatively compact, and divides into two halves: the narrow, steep, curving streets of the Old Town to the south of Princes Street Gardens, and the neat grid, broad boulevards and crescents of the New Town to the north of Princes Street. The Old Town is built along a ridge of rock that stretches from the castle for around a mile eastwards to Holyrood Palace, which lies in the shadow of the tilted volcanic hill of Arthur's Seat. All the main streets run parallel to this line—Queen Street, George Street (for boutique shopping) and Princes Street (high street shopping) to the north; Castle Hill, Lawnmarket, High Street and Canongate (which together form the famous 'Royal Mile') on the top of the ridge; and Grassmarket, Cowgate and Chambers Street (with the Royal Museum and Museum of Scotland) to the south. The best places to get your bearings are from the top of Calton Hill, at the east end of Princes Street, or from the castle esplanade. Views extend north to the Firth of Forth, the Forth bridges and the hills of central Scotland, south to the Pentland Hills and east to the conical mound of Berwick Law.

Edinburgh grew up in medieval times as a warren of narrow streets around the castle (▷ 66–69). Wealth led to expansion in the 18th century and the development of the gracious New Town (▷ 77). Today it is the home of the Scottish Parliament (join a guided tour, tel 0131 348 5200), and is the financial, legal and tourism hub of Scotland. Its annual arts festivals are world renowned, and in 2005 it was declared the first ever literary capital of Europe for its numerous connections with esteemed writers over the centuries, from Sir Walter Scott and Robert Louis Stevenson to J. K. Rowling and Alexander McCall Smith (▷ 24).

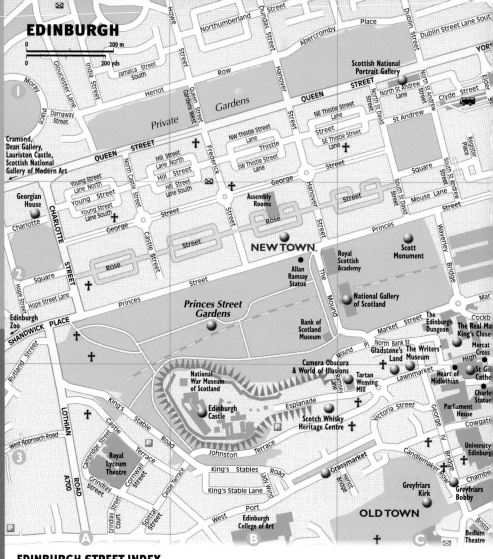

EDINBURGH STREET INDEX

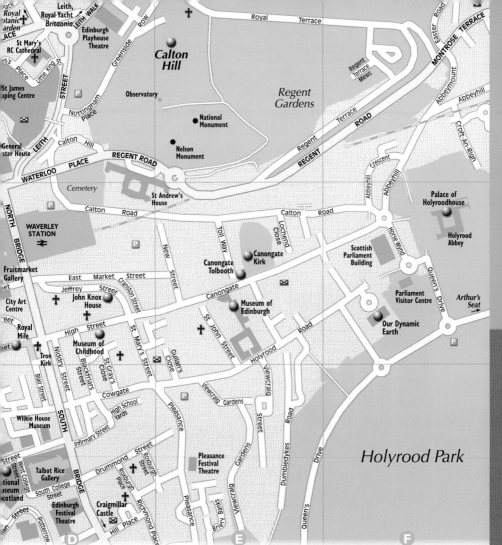

ARTHUR'S SEAT

The bare green hill of Arthur's Seat is a great landmark in the city, 251m (823ft) high and visible for miles around. It's the remains of a volcano 325 million years old, with seven smaller hills around it and the high cliffs of Salisbury Crags, tilted in a later ice age. It forms the bottom of the Old Town ridge which leads up to the castle Mound. There is open access to the hills and four small lochs, part of the Royal Park of Holyrood, with walks and views down over Holyrood Palace itself.

✚ 61 off E2 🚌 24, 25 🚉 Edinburgh Waverley

CALTON HILL

In the 18th century Edinburgh was known as the Athens of the North; this reached absurd proportions when a reproduction of the Parthenon was planned. Apparently the money ran out in 1829, but the remaining folly is part of the distinctive skyline of Calton Hill, at the east end of Princes Street. It shares the spot with the City Observatory, founded in 1776, the 1807 tower of the Nelson Monument (Apr–end Sep Mon 1–6, Tue–Sat 10–6; rest of year Mon–Sat 10–3) and other monuments. It's worth the climb to the park at the top for views over the city.

✚ 61 E1 ℹ Edinburgh Lothian Tourist Information Centre, 3 Princes Street EH2 2QP, tel 0845 225 5121 🚌 40 🚉 Edinburgh Waverley

Left *The Stewart Monument, Calton Hill*
Below *Edinburgh's museum of everyday life*
Right *The view towards Salisbury Crags*

CAMERA OBSCURA AND WORLD OF ILLUSIONS

www.camera-obscura.co.uk
The Camera Obscura is lodged at the top of the Royal Mile in a castellated building known as the Outlook Tower. It started life in 1853 as Short's Popular Observatory, and grew into the Victorian equivalent of today's hands-on science centres.

The camera obscura is like a giant pin-hole camera, with no film involved: It projects on to a viewing table a fascinating panorama of the city outside, which changes minute by minute. There are also great views, a Magic Gallery of optical illusions, holograms and live viewcams.

✚ 60 C3 ✉ Castlehill, The Royal Mile EH1 2ND ☎ 0131 226 3709 🕐 Apr–end Jun, Sep–end Oct daily 9.30–6; Jul–end Aug daily 9.30–7.30; rest of year daily 10–5 💷 Adult £7.95, child (5–15) £5.50 🚌 23, 27, 41, 42, 45 🚉 Edinburgh Waverley ♿

CANONGATE KIRK

www.canongatekirk.org.uk
When James VII converted the abbey church at Holyrood (▷ 79) to a chapel for the Knights of the Thistle in 1688, the Canongate district needed a new church. It was built up the hill, next to the Tolbooth (▷ right), the following year, its Dutch gable and plain interior reflecting the Canongate's trading links with the Low Countries. At the gable top, note the gilded stag's head, traditionally a gift of the monarch. Some of Edinburgh's finest are buried in the graveyard. Robert Burns paid for a headstone for fellow poet Robert Fergusson (1750–74), but his vernacular poetry about the city gave it one of its nicknames, Auld Reekie.

✚ 61E2 ✉ Canongate EH8 8BR ☎ 0131 556 3515 🕐 Jun–end Sep Mon–Sat 10.30–4, Sun 10–12.30; rest of year Sun 10–12.30 💷 Free 🚌 35 🚉 Edinburgh Waverley

CANONGATE TOLBOOTH/ THE PEOPLE'S STORY MUSEUM

www.cac.org.uk
Up the hill from the Canongate Kirk, the French-style old Tolbooth dates from 1591 and served as the council chamber for the independent burgh of Canongate until its incorporation into the city in 1856. It also served as a prison.

The building is now the home of The People's Story, a museum dedicated to everyday life and times in Edinburgh from the 18th century to the present day. Tableaux and objects, sounds and smells evoke life in a prison cell, a draper's shop, of a servant at work and a tramcar conductor (a 'clippie', who clipped the tickets). With a host of other everyday details, it portrays the struggle for better conditions, better health, and better ways to enjoy what little leisure the citizens had.

✚ 61 E2 ✉ 163 Canongate EH8 8BN ☎ 0131 529 4057 🕐 Mon–Sat 10–5; Aug also Sun 12–5 💷 Free 🚌 35 🚉 Edinburgh Waverley ♿

CRAIGMILLAR CASTLE

www.historic-scotland.gov.uk

Lying 2.5 miles (4km) southeast of the city centre off the A7, this splendid medieval castle is often forgotten, in the shadow of its more famous Edinburgh neighbour. Craigmillar fell into ruin after its abandonment in the mid-18th century. At its core is a stout 15th-century L-plan tower house with walls up to 2.7m (9ft) thick, constructed on the site of an older fortification by the Preston family.

The main defensive features include massive doors, a spiral turnpike stair, narrow passageways and two outer walls to fend off English attackers. Mary, Queen of Scots, fled here on several occasions when the pressures of life at Holyroodhouse became too great, notably after the murder of her secretary David Rizzio in 1566, and the tiny chamber where she slept bears her name.

In the mid-19th century Queen Victoria made plans to restore the by-now derelict castle to use as her Scottish home, but this never happened and she discovered Balmoral instead. From the top of Craigmillar's tower there are excellent views towards Edinburgh, with Edinburgh Castle, Arthur's Seat and Holyrood Park all clearly visible. In the grounds, one of the unusual features is a fishpond in the shape of the letter P, for the Preston family, who owned the castle when Mary Queen of Scots visited.

🕂 61 off D3 ✉ Craigmillar Castle Road EH16 4SY ☎ 0131 661 4445 🕐 Apr–end Sep daily 9.30–5.30; Oct–end Mar Sat–Wed 9.30–4.30 🖑 (HS) adult £4.20, child (5–16) £2.10 🚌 33 🖴 🎁

CRAMOND

Edinburgh is made up of many villages, some of which retain their own identity and appeal. One such is Cramond, to the west of the centre, near Queensferry: It was a hive of water-powered industry in the 18th century thanks to its location at the mouth of the River Almond. All sorts of useful items were manufactured here, with four separate iron works, and later a papermill, but all is peaceful today on the secluded tree-lined walk by the stream, which leads up to a 17th-century bridge.

The Romans built a port here in the second century to supply troops stationed along the Antonine Wall. A ferry used to transport passengers across to Dalmeny: there is talk of a small bridge being built soon.

On a summer's evening, join local people on the riverside stroll, followed by a drink at the popular Cramond Inn. Or visit nearby Lauriston Castle (▷ 70).

🕂 60 off A1 ⓘ VisitScotland Edinburgh Information Centre, 3 Princes Street EH2 2QP, tel 0845 225 5121 🚌 41, 42

EDINBURGH CASTLE

▷ 66–69.

EDINBURGH ZOO

www.edinburghzoo.org.uk

In an era when zoos have to work hard to justify themselves, Edinburgh remains a better example of its type, allowing close access to many animals while at the same time promoting conservation and education. The site is at Corstorphine, 3 miles (4.8km) west of the city centre, on the side of a steep hill, covering an area of some 33ha (82 acres). Highlights include the swinging-gibbon enclosure, the hilltop safari to the African Plains exhibit (admire zebras and antelopes against the distinctly Scottish backdrop of Edinburgh Castle!), and the ever-popular penguins who stroll outside their enclosure (daily 2.15, Apr–end Sep) weather permitting. The zoo has a history of successful penguin breeding. Look for special events such as night tours.

With over 600,000 visitors a year, it is second only to Edinburgh Castle as one of the city's major paying visitor attractions.

🕂 60 off A2 ✉ 134 Corstorphine Road EH12 6TS ☎ 0131 334 9171 🕐 Apr–end Sep daily 9–6; Oct, Mar daily 9–5; Nov–end Feb daily 9–4.30 🖑 Adult £11.50, child (3–14) £8, under 3 free, family £35–£40; special events extra 🚌 12, 26, 31; Airport Bus 🖴 🎁

Left *The penguins are a very popular attraction at Edinburgh Zoo*
Below *A trip out to Craigmillar Castle makes a pleasant change from the city bustle*

Top left *A gilded hawk adorns the entrance to Gladstone's Land*
Above *Fine 18th-century furnishings in the Georgian House*

FRUITMARKET GALLERY

www.fruitmarket.co.uk

As the name tells you, this contemporary art gallery, found behind Waverley Station, is built in the original fruit market. With the separate and more populist City Art Centre just opposite (Mon–Sat 10–5), it forms part of a chic artistic enclave at the heart of the city. The wide expanse of glass frontage on this handsome old building reveals a minimum of its exhibits to the street, but entices with its excellent and buzzing café. Inside, changing exhibitions showcase the work of new Scottish artists and also international work in a Scottish context. The bookshop has a good selection of art books.

✚ 61 D2 ✉ 45 Market Street EH1 1DF ☎ 0131 225 2383 ⏰ Mon–Sat 11–6, Sun 12–5 🎫 Free 🚋 Edinburgh Waverley ☕ 🏛

GEORGIAN HOUSE

www.nts.org.uk

The north side of Charlotte Square is the epitome of 18th-century New Town elegance (▷ 77), designed by architect Robert Adam (1728–92) as a single, palace-fronted block. With its symmetrical stonework, rusticated base and ornamented upper levels, it is an outstanding example of the style.

For a feel of gracious Edinburgh living in 1800, visit the Georgian House, a preserved residence right in the middle. It is a typically meticulous recreation by the National Trust for Scotland, reflecting all the fashionable details of the day. The NTS also owns No. 28, which has exhibition space, a café and shop.

✚ 60 A2 ✉ 7 Charlotte Square EH2 4DR ☎ 0844 493 2118 ⏰ Mar daily 11–4; Nov daily 11–3; Apr–end Jun, Sep–end Oct daily 10–5; Jul–end Aug daily 10–6 🎫 (NTS) adult £5, child (5–16) £4, under 5 free, family £14 🚌 36 🚋 Edinburgh Waverley 🏛

GLADSTONE'S LAND

www.nts.org.uk

This fascinating example of 17th-century tenement housing is a highlight of the Old Town. Its narrowness was typical of the cramped Old Town conditions—the only space for expansion was upwards, and its eventual height of six floors reflects the status of its merchant owner, Thomas Gledstanes, who extended the existing tenement in 1617.

The building is unique for its stone arcading, once common along the High Street but now vanished elsewhere. Inside, the National Trust for Scotland has reconstructed 17th-century shop-booths on the ground floor, and there are original painted ceilings to admire, adorned with flowers and birds. The first floor is furnished as a typical home of the period.

✚ 60 C3 ✉ 477b Lawnmarket EH1 2NT ☎ 0844 493 2120 ⏰ Easter–end Jun, Sep–end Oct daily 10–5; Jul–end Aug daily 10–7 🎫 (NTS) adult £5, child £4, under 5 free, family £10 🚌 23, 27, 41, 42, 45 🚋 Edinburgh Waverley

GRASSMARKET

The old road into the city from the west used to run (via the West Port, or gate, which survives in a street name) into this long open space below Castle Rock. The Grassmarket was used for various activities—from 1477, corn and cattle markets were held here, and it was the site of public executions until 1784.

A stone disc marks the location of the old gibbet, and commemorates the Covenanting martyrs who died here. The Grassmarket was also a haunt of the notorious 19th-century 'body-snatchers' Burke and Hare, who murdered their victims to sell on to the anatomists of the city's hospitals. Today it has good shops and eating places, and several excellent pubs, including the ancient White Hart Inn.

✚ 60 B3 ℹ VisitScotland Edinburgh Information Centre, 3 Princes Street EH2 2QP, tel 0845 225 5121 🚌 2 🚋 Edinburgh Waverley

EDINBURGH CASTLE

INTRODUCTION

One million visitors a year come to view Scotland's oldest castle. To enter, you must first cross the Esplanade, which in summer is bedecked with seating for the Military Tattoo (▷ 97). Pass through the gate and up the steep, cobbled ramp for great views over the city and various attractions. Once you step inside the thick walls, the castle feels like a complete community, remote, powerful, and cut off from the rest of Edinburgh.

Edinburgh Castle towers over the city from its perch high on a wedge of volcanic rock, a solid symbol of the Scottish nation which has withstood centuries of battering. It owes its defensive position to a volcano, which became extinct 70 million years ago. The plug of volcanic rock withstood the Ice-Age glaciers, which scoured the landscape around it, creating near-vertical faces to the north and south and leaving a descending 'tail' of rock to the east—the ridge which is occupied today by the Royal Mile.

Bronze-Age people settled on the top around 850BC, and in AD600 it was occupied by an army who called it Din Eidyn. By the Middle Ages it was a heavily fortified site and royal residence.

A key event in the castle's history was the Lang (long) Siege of 1571–73, by the regent of James VI. James had been born in the castle in 1566, and it was occupied by supporters of his mother, Mary, Queen of Scots. They held out against the forces of regent James Douglas, Earl of Morton (c1516–81) and his English back-up. Much of the castle was destroyed, and it was the victorious Morton who instigated the rebuilding, including the Half Moon Battery.

Later royalty preferred the comforts of Holyroodhouse (▷ 79), and Oliver Cromwell's army converted the 16th-century Great Hall into a barracks for his soldiers when he took the castle in 1650 (since restored, its hammerbeam roof is notable). The castle's primary function has been as a garrison fortress ever since.

WHAT TO SEE

ARGYLE BATTERY

This great terrace offers the first chance to catch your breath and enjoy the view north over the city as you wind your way up the Castle Rock. Behind you is the Lang Stairs, a steep, curved flight of steps which was the main entrance in medieval times, before the shifting of heavy guns necessitated the building of a wider, gentler approach. The cannons along the battery were a picturesque improvement suggested by Queen Victoria—in fact, they are front-loading naval guns, and totally impractical in this setting. The One o'Clock Gun, a 105mm field gun, fires from nearby Mills Mount Battery at precisely 1pm in a tradition dating from 1861.

No longer firing is the other famous cannon at Edinburgh Castle, the monumental Mons Meg. This siege gun was built in the 15th century and when it was in use it was capable of firing a 400-pound (181kg) cannon ball a distance of almost 2 miles (3km). To put that into perspective, it is just a mile (1.2km) from the Castle of Holyroodhouse at the far end of the Royal Mile. The gun was probably made for Philip III, the Duke of Burgundy, who later presented it to King James II of Scotland, Philip's nephew by marriage. Part of its name comes from that fact that it was first tested at Mons, in Belgium. Such was the ferocity of its power that it could only be used a few times each day, because of the enormous heat that the explosive force generated. It was only in operation for about a hundred years, and was last used in 1681 for the birthday celebrations of James, the Duke of Albany and York, who later became King James II of England.

INFORMATION

www.historic-scotland.gov.uk
✚ 60 B2 ✉ Castle Hill EH1 2NG
☎ 0131 225 9846 ⏱ Apr–end Sep daily 9.30–6; rest of year daily 9.30–5 ⚿ (HS) Jun–end Sep adult £12, child (5–16) £6; Oct, Mar–end May adult £11, child £5.50; Nov–end Feb adult £10, child £5 🚍 23, 27, 28, 45, 35 🚆 Edinburgh Waverley
🎧 Free guided tours every half-hour, from just inside the main gate. Hand-held audio guide in eight languages ☕ Cafés in the castle 🎁 Gift shops stock books, Scottish souvenirs and exclusive jewellery

Opposite *View of Edinburgh Castle and the National Gallery of Scotland from the Scott Monument*
Below *The Honours of Scotland*

» A courtesy minibus is available to take less mobile people to the top of the castle site — check when you buy your ticket.
» Historic Scotland members can skip the ticket queues and go straight into the castle.
» Personal audio tours slow visitors down on the route to see the crown jewels, giving the impression of a queue — move straight through if your time is limited and you don't want to see the static tableaux.

Below *Mighty Mons Meg, now silent on the ramparts of the castle, used to fire stone cannon balls*

ST. MARGARET'S CHAPEL

The oldest structure in the castle is also the simplest and most moving. It's the 12th-century chapel, dedicated to St. Margaret by her son, King David I. Margaret was the wife of Malcolm III and died here in 1093. The chapel, with its single, whitewashed chamber and tiny Norman arched windows, survived intact through several razings of the castle, and is still used for occasional weddings and baptisms. The chapel is almost overshadowed by the huge cannon on the rampart outside—Mons Meg (▷ 67). Its barrel exploded in 1681 and it has never been fired again.

SCOTTISH NATIONAL WAR MEMORIAL

One of the newest buildings on Castle Rock, the National War Memorial was designed by Sir Robert Lorimer in 1923–28 to honour the 150,000 Scottish personnel who died in World War I, and was later amended with the names of the 50,000 who died in World War II. Its impressive entrance, flanked by a stone lion and unicorn, is to your right as you enter Crown Square. Inside, the dark stone gives the building a sombre air. Each of the 12 Scottish regiments is commemorated in its own bay in the Hall of Honour, with the bays at either end dedicated to sailors and airmen respectively. In an open chamber at the heart of the building, the highest peak of the 70-million-year-old rock on which the castle stands has been polished into a shrine, on which stands a casket containing the names of the dead. The figure above is of St. Michael.

CROWN ROOM

The Crown Room is on the first floor of the Royal Palace, and comes at the end of a winding route past endless static tableaux of historical scenes. Skip these (unless you are into the audio commentary) to reach the real treasures:

the ancient Honours of Scotland, consisting of crown, sceptre and sword. The crown dates from 1540, and is made of Scottish gold, studded with semi-precious stones from the Cairngorms. It was made by James Mosman, who lived in the John Knox House (▷ 70). Both the sword and sceptre were papal gifts. The regalia were locked away after the union with England in 1707, and largely forgotten about until unearthed by Sir Walter Scott in 1818.

The Stone of Destiny shares the same display case. Originally at Scone Palace (▷ 200), it was the stone on which Scottish kings were crowned until it was pinched by Edward I and taken to Westminster Abbey in London. It was returned by the British government in 1996, and is a poignant symbol for the revival in Scottish nationalism.

Above *The Royal Apartments and Half Moon Battery*
Below *Pipe majors at the Military Tattoo*

'PRISONERS OF WAR'
This exhibition reveals the vaults where American, French, Spanish, Dutch and Irish prisoners of war were held during the 18th-century American War of Independence. French prisoners carved their names on the doors, and the graffiti can be seen in parts restored to their appearance as it was in 1781.

SCOTTISH NATIONAL WAR MUSEUM
The history of the Scottish soldier is told in this fascinating museum, in the former Ordnance Storehouse. There's a bit of everything in here, from an oath of allegiance to Charles Edward Stewart signed by Jacobite soldiers for the Duke of Perth's Regiment in 1745 (▷ 32). to a tunic worn by Earl Haig when he commanded the British army in France in 1916. On the way, there are uniforms and badges, an explanation of the phrase 'iron rations', and weapons galore. The most bizarre exhibit is three elephant's toes, which belonged to a regimental mascot who died around 1840. The creature had been a living symbol of the elephant badge worn by the 78th Highland Regiment of Foot, and lived at the castle. It shared with its keeper a deep thirst for beer, which hastened its early demise.

GREYFRIARS BOBBY

At the top of Candlemaker Row, opposite the National Museum of Scotland (▷ 72–75), stands a favourite Edinburgh landmark: a bronze statue of a little Skye terrier, which has stood here since 1873. The dog's story was memorably told by American Eleanor Atkinson in her sentimental novel of 1912, *Greyfriars Bobby*.

He was the devoted companion of a local farmer who dined regularly in Greyfriars Place. After 'Auld Jock' died, faithful Bobby slept on his grave in the nearby churchyard for 14 years, while returning to the same pie-shop for his dinner. A later version suggests he was owned by a local policeman, and taken in by local residents when his owner died. A nearby pub is named after the celebrated hound.

✚ 60 C3 ✉ At the junction with George IV Bridge 🚌 2, 23, 27, 35, 41, 42, 45 🚆 Edinburgh Waverley

GREYFRIARS KIRKYARD

The Kirk of the Grey Friars was built on the site of the garden of a former Franciscan monastery in 1620. Just 18 years later it was the scene of a pivotal event in Scottish history, when Calvinist petitioners gathered to sign the National Covenant, an act of defiance against the King (▷ 30–31). The church itself was trashed by Cromwell's troops in 1650, and later accidentally blown up. The kirkyard made a makeshift prison for hundreds of Covenanters captured after the battle of Bothwell Bridge in 1679; they were kept here for five dreadful months. Today it is full of elaborate memorials, including the grave of architect William Adam (1689–1748).

✚ 60 C3 ✉ Greyfriars Tolbooth and Highland Kirk, Greyfriars Place EH1 2QQ ☎ 0131 226 5429 🕐 Apr–end Oct Mon–Fri 10.30–4.30, Sat 10.30–2.30; rest of year Thu 1.30–3.30 ✋ Free 🚌 23, 27, 35, 41, 45 🚆 Edinburgh Waverley 📷

JOHN KNOX HOUSE

It is said that John Knox (c1505–72), the great Protestant reformer and founder of the Church of Scotland, used to preach from the front window of this handsome old corner house on the Royal Mile. Whether he actually lived here is less certain. The house, now part of the Scottish Storytelling Centre, dates back to 1490, and with its gables projecting out above the street, it gives a clear impression of how crowded the city's medieval High Street must have been. Inside and upstairs, you can admire the painted ceiling of the Oak Room, dating from 1600. There are exhibitions about Knox, a focused and surprisingly witty man, and also about goldsmith James Mossman, who lived in the house in the mid-16th century.

✚ 61 D2 ✉ 43–45 High Street EH1 1SR ☎ 0131 556 9579 🕐 Mon–Sat 10–6 (Sun 12–6 Jul, Aug only) ✋ Adult £3.50, child £1, under 7 free 🚌 8, 35 🚆 Edinburgh Waverley 📷

LAURISTON CASTLE

www.cac.org.uk

This gabled and turreted mansion, in a leafy setting overlooking the Firth of Forth near Cramond (▷ 64), offers up a slice of neatly preserved Edwardian comfort and style. Once a simple tower house, Lauriston was remodelled and extended several times, most notably in 1827 by architect William Burn (1789–1870), before it came to William Robert Reid. He was the wealthy head of a firm of cabinetmakers, and an avid collector of fine furniture and precious objects—his collection of pieces made from the fluorspar mineral called Blue John is particularly unusual. He left the castle to the City of Edinburgh in 1926, on condition that it remained just as it was, for the edification and education of the public.

✚ 60 off A1 ✉ 2A Cramond Road South EH4 5QD ☎ 0131 336 2060 🕐 Apr–end Oct Sat–Thu tours every hour 11, 12, 2, 3, 4; rest of year Sat–Sun at 12, 2, 3 ✋ Castle: adult £4.50, child (3–15) £3, under 3 free. Grounds: free 🚆 Edinburgh Waverley

Below *Greyfriars Kirkyard is the resting place of many famous Scottish people, but the Kirk authorities would not allow Greyfriars Bobby to be buried on consecrated ground*

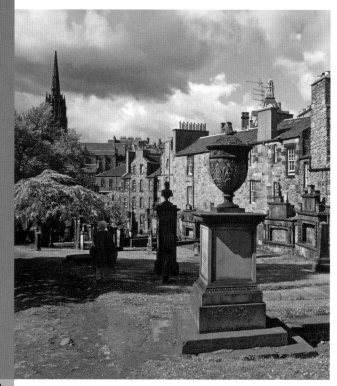

LEITH

Edinburgh's seaport is connected to the city centre by Leith Walk, and was for many years a prosperous town in its own right. As the shipbuilding industry began to wane in the 20th century the town went into decline, but in recent years it has come up in the world, and now it buzzes with fashionable eating places. Edinburgh's river, the Water of Leith, flows through the middle.

The town has witnessed its share of history—Mary, Queen of Scots, landed here from France in 1561 and stayed at Lamb House, in Water Street, and Charles I played golf on the links in the park. Where Tower Street meets The Shore, look for the Signal Tower, built in 1686 as a windmill. The Royal Yacht *Britannia* is a major draw (▷ 81).

🚻 61 off D1 🅸 VisitScotland Edinburgh Information Centre, 3 Princes Street EH2 2QP, tel 0845 225 5121 🚌 1, 7, 10, 12, 14, 16, 22, 25, 32, 32A, 34, 35, 36, 49, N22

MUSEUM OF CHILDHOOD

www.cac.org.uk
Edinburgh claims the first museum in the world dedicated to the history of childhood. It was the brainchild of bachelor Joseph Patrick Murray (d1981), a town councillor, who argued that the museum presented a specialized branch of social science, and was about children rather than for them. It opened in 1955, and is a nostalgic treasure-trove of dolls and doll's houses, train sets, tricycles, board games and teddy bears. There's even a recreated 1930s schoolroom.

🚻 61 D2 ✉ 42 High Street EH1 1TG

☎ 0131 529 4142 🕐 Mon–Sat 10–5 ✋ Free 🚌 35 🚉 Edinburgh Waverley 📅

MUSEUM OF EDINBURGH

www.cac.org.uk
Across the road from the Canongate Tolbooth (▷ 63), Edinburgh's own museum occupies Huntly House, a 16th-century dwelling much altered through the years, and at one time occupied by a trade guild, the Incorporation of Hammermen. Its three pointed gables mark it out. Inside, the museum is a treasure-house of local details which bring the history of the city to life. Items on display include maps and prints, silver, glass and old shop signs, and Greyfriars Bobby's collar. You can see the original National Covenant (▷ 31), signed in 1638.

🚻 61 E2 ✉ Huntly House, 142 Canongate, Royal Mile EH8 8DD ☎ 0131 529 4143 🕐 Mon–Sat 10–5; Aug also Sun 12–5 ✋ Free 🚌 35 🚉 Edinburgh Waverley 📅

NATIONAL GALLERY OF SCOTLAND

▷ 76.

NATIONAL MUSEUM OF SCOTLAND

▷ 72–75.

NEW TOWN

▷ 77.

OUR DYNAMIC EARTH

▷ 78.

PALACE OF HOLYROODHOUSE

▷ 79.

PRINCES STREET GARDENS

This long thin park lies at the heart of the city, in a sound-muffling dip between Castle Rock and noisy Princes Street. It's a great place to take a break, sit down and admire the backs of the Old Town tenements across the steep-sided valley. In summer there are band concerts to enjoy, and an Edinburgh institution since 1902, the floral clock—a flowerbed planted up as a clock, complete with moving hands, at the Waverley Station end.

In 1460 this valley was dammed and flooded to form the Nor' Loch, an extra defence for the castle which quickly filled up with the city's detritus. It was drained in the mid-18th century, and the public gardens first laid out in 1820. Now it is an oasis of relative peace, giving a touch of grace to one of the city's busiest shopping streets.

🚻 60 B2 ✉ Princes Street ☎ 0131 3322 368 🕐 summer 7am–10pm; winter 7–5 ✋ Free 🚉 Edinburgh Waverley 📱

THE REAL MARY KING'S CLOSE

www.realmarykingsclose.com
Mary King's Close is a narrow alleyway that once led between the tall houses of 17th-century Edinburgh, part of the rabbit warren of the Old Town. It is now preserved under the City Chambers, which were built over the top in 1753. Archaeological research has produced insights into the lives of the people who lived here. Guided tours help to create the atmosphere of what the Old Town was like—you can walk through the houses, see the cramped living conditions, and learn about the outbreak of plague in 1644. Tours run every 20 minutes; reserve ahead.

🚻 60 C2 ✉ 2 Warriston's Close, High Street EH1 1PG ☎ 08702 430160 🕐 Easter–end Jul, Sep–end Oct daily 10–9; Aug daily 9–9; rest of year Sun–Fri 10–4, Sat 10–9 💷 Adult £9.50, child (5–15) £6 (under 5 not admitted) 🚌 23, 27, 41, 42, 45 🚉 Edinburgh Waverley 📅

INFORMATION

www.nms.ac.uk

⊕ 61 D3 ⊠ Chambers Street, EH1 1JF
☎ 0131 225 7534 ⏲ Daily 10–5
⏺ Free; may be charge for some temporary exhibitions ⊟ 35 ⏹ Check at the information desk on arrival for times of free daily tours. Free audio guides available in English, Gaelic, French, Italian, Spanish and German
⛁ £4.99 🍴 The Tower Restaurant is the place to be seen, booking essential at weekends 🏷 Gift shop, shared with the Royal Museum, stocks unusual presents

INTRODUCTION

Treasures abound in this superb collection, which gives an entertaining introduction to Scottish history and culture, but the multiple levels of the fortress-like building mean it can be confusing to find your way around. However, armed with the knowledge that the floors work chronologically, you can work your way up from the basement through history from the earliest beginnings, or start at the top and work down. Alternatively, get hold of a floorplan to go straight to the things that interest you most, and explore from there. Objects are grouped according to colour-coded themes.

The structure of the building, designed by Gordon Benson and Alan Forsyth, is impressively modern. A lofty central courtyard, narrow slit windows and a round tower at the entrance contribute to the feeling of being in a fortified castle, built to protect a precious heritage

WHAT TO SEE

PICTISH SCULPTURED STONE

The chief legacy of the Pictish period is vivid relief carvings in stone, generally depicting figures and strangely intertwined beasts. The displays on level 0 contrast these nicely with more regular Roman stonework. Among the noble groups of horsemen engaged in hunting or fighting there is one less gallant figure worthy of special note. He rides alone, bearded and bare-headed. His drooping nag is ambling along at a walking pace, and no wonder—for this warrior is quaffing deeply from a drinking horn, and drunk. The stone, from Bullion in Angus, reads as a skilled stonemason's joke.

HUNTERSTON BROOCH

The Hunterston Brooch dates to around AD700, and is a potent symbol of wealth and power. No contemporary clasp in the museum's collection

Above *The striking National Museum building with its circular entrance tower*

can touch it in terms of size (about 12cm/5in high) or craftsmanship, which suggests that it was made as a gift to impress a king. A runic inscription on the back claims the brooch for Melbrigda, a Viking, but the brooch predates the Viking period and the identity of its original owner is lost in time. Although the lighting is dim, you can walk around both sides of the display case, to admire close up the detail of the gold, amber and gilded silver worked into exquisite curling, intertwined Celtic motifs. The brooch was found at Hunterston, on the Ayrshire coast, but is believed to have been made at Dunadd, in Argyll, the heart of the ancient Scots kingdom of Dalriada.

LEWIS CHESS PIECES

In 1831 a collection of 82 carved chess pieces was discovered in the sands of Uig, on Lewis (▷ 253). They had been hidden there 700 years before, possibly by a merchant, during a time of upheaval and violence when the islands were subject to an influx of Viking settlers from Denmark and Norway. Clearly treasured by their original owner, they form one of the most popular exhibits in the museum today. Find them on the street level (level 1) near the Monymusk Reliquary. The small, greyish pieces are carved from walrus ivory, and were probably made by a Scandinavian craftsman in the 12th century. They include kings and queens, pop-eyed bishops, 'berserker' warders chewing on their shields, and knights on horseback. The carving of the solemn facial expressions reflects minute attention to detail, and is carried through even to the patterns on the fabric worn by the kings.

Above *The intricate Hunterston Brooch*
Below *The tiny Monymusk Reliquary dates from the eighth century*
Bottom *Some of the famous carved chess pieces found on the Isle of Lewis*

BURNS'S PISTOLS

For an unusual view of Scotland's national bard, look out for a pair of pistols on level 3, part of an opulent display about the emergence of a monied society in the 18th century. The reputation of Robert Burns (1759–96) is as a poet and writer of songs, many with an anti-establishment bias. Poetry was a poor basis for making a living, however: Burns needed paid employment and took a job as a collector of taxes. The pair of wooden-handled and wooden-barrelled pistols which he carried with him for self-protection—tax collectors were no more popular then than now—give further insight into this well-loved character. More regular Burns items are shown on level 5.

MINIATURE COFFINS

One of the most mysterious displays here was brought to public attention by Ian Rankin in his 2001 novel, *The Falls*. It is the group of tiny wooden coffins, each holding a body not much longer than an adult finger, that was discovered on Arthur's Seat in Edinburgh in 1836. Each body fits its own coffin precisely. The figures have been carved with some care, including facial features, feet that stick out, and moving joints, and some are clothed. Eight have survived of the original 17 coffins, but nobody knows who made this collection, or why. They may represent a mock burial for the 17 victims of murderers Burke and Hare, who provided bodies for the local medical school from 1827 to 1828.

SCOTLAND: A CHANGING NATION

To show that the story of Scotland is as much about the present and the future as it is about the past, the National Museum's latest permanent exhibition is about the Scottish people, from World War I to the present day. It allows the Scots to tell their own stories in their own words, covering five major themes and the impact these have had on ordinary lives: war, industry, daily life, social change and immigration. It's the inclusion of the controversial topic of immigration that makes the exhibition especially interesting. Another section covers five areas of life in which the Scots have made great contributions: sport, culture, medicine, science and technology.

MODERN SCULPTURE

The museum has some fine modern sculptures blending in with the older objects, most notaby the work of English sculptor Andy Goldsworthy. He is world-renowned for his work with natural objects and materials, and his most notable works are outdoors, but here he has created works specifically for inside the museum. They include *Hearth*, made from wood found on the site when the museum was being built, and *Whale Bones*, an intricate white ball of bones made from the complete skeleton of a pilot whale.

TIPS

» Don't expect to see everything in the museum in one hit. Focus first on the things that interest you most, and come back another day to enjoy the rest—entry is free.

» Only one lift stops at all levels in the museum: Find it at the far side of the building from the entrance.

Above *An 18th-century ebony and ivory quaich (drinking bowl)*
Left *These miniature coffins were found at Arthur's Seat*
Opposite *Detail from the Bullion Stone, a Pictish stone with a fine relief carving*

INFORMATION

www.nationalgalleries.org

✚ 60 C2 ✉ The Mound EH2 2EL
☎ 0131 624 6200 🕐 Fri–Wed 10–5,
Thu 10–7 💷 Free 🚌 23, 27, 41, 42,
45 🚆 Edinburgh Waverley 📖 £9.95
🎁 Shop stocks cards, books and gifts
🍴 🛈

Above *A bust by Patric Park (1811–55)*
Below *John Singer Sargent's portrait of*
Gertrude, Lady Agnew of Lochnaw

NATIONAL GALLERY OF SCOTLAND

Scotland's National Gallery, a breathtaking collection of artistic masterpieces displayed on a friendly, human scale, stands prominently on the Mound, the raised road that bisects Princes Street Gardens. Designed by New Town architect William Playfair (1789–1857), and completed in the year of his death, it is easily spotted by the huge golden stone pillars of its neoclassical flanks (and should not be confused with its linked neighbour, the Royal Scottish Academy building).

Its collection of paintings, sculptures and drawings runs to more than 20,000 items and in the UK is second only to London's National Gallery in importance, but it is smaller and feels much more accessible. At its heart are paintings by the great masters of Europe, including Vermeer, Hals, Tiepolo, Van Dyck, Raphael, Cezanne, Degas and Titian. Look for Monet's *Haystacks* (1891), Vélazquez's *Old Woman Cooking Eggs* (1618) and Botticelli's masterpiece, *Virgin Adoring the Sleeping Christ Child* (c1485). (Note: works may sometimes be on loan to other collections.) The display is boosted by loans from the Queen's collection, and from that of the Duke of Sutherland. A fabulous collection of watercolours by English landscape artist J. M. W. Turner (1775–1851), bequeathed to the gallery in 1900, is displayed each January. You might also see Canova's famous marble sculpture of *The Three Graces* (1815–17), jointly acquired with the V&A in 1994.

THE SCOTTISH COLLECTION

Not surprisingly, the gallery has an outstanding collection of works by Scottish artists, which are displayed in their own section downstairs. Favourites here include Sir Henry Raeburn's unusual 1795 portrait of *The Reverend Robert Walker Skating*; Allan Ramsay's delicate portraits of his first wife, *Anne Bayne* (c1740), and his second wife, *Margaret Lindsay* (1757); and the sweeping land- and seascapes of William McTaggart (1835–1910). Look out for the vivid scenes of everyday life among the common people, as captured on canvas by Sir David Wilkie (1785–1841), such as *Pitlessie Fair* (1804) and *Distraining for Rent* (1815), and Raeburn's over-the-top tartan clad chieftain, *Colonel Alasdair Macdonnell of Glengarry* (1812).

NEW TOWN

Edinburgh's so-called New Town covers an area of about 2.6sq km (1sq mile) to the north of Princes Street, and is characterized by broad streets of spacious terraced (row) houses with large windows and ornamental door arches. The original area comprised three residential boulevards to run parallel with the Old Town ridge: Princes Street, George Street and Queen Street.

Until the mid-18th century, Edinburgh had been contained on the narrow ridge of rock between Arthur's Seat and the castle. Conditions were overcrowded and insanitary, so the need for expansion became clear. A competition was held in 1766 to design a new city to the north. The winner was unknown architect James Craig (1744–95), and within three years the first house was ready. The first New Town was so successful that a second one was laid out in 1802, extending north.

HIGHLIGHTS

While Princes Street has lost its shine in the glare of modern commerce, the wide Charlotte Square, with its preserved Georgian House (▷ 65), is the epitome of the planners' intentions.

The North Bridge was needed to allow pedestrians to reach the new city without foundering in the muddy valley (the Nor' Loch was still being drained at the time). A second link, the Mound, came about by accident, when a clothier in the Old Town started to dump earth rubble in the marsh. The builders from the New Town joined in, as they dug out foundations for the new buildings. The causeway became the Mound, later home to the National Gallery of Scotland (▷ opposite) and the Royal Scottish Academy.

Stockbridge, a former mining village, was developed as part of the second New Town. It became a Bohemian artisans' corner, and Ann Street is now one of the city's most exclusive addresses.

INFORMATION

✚ 60 B2 🛈 Edinburgh Lothian Tourist Information Centre, 3 Princes Street EH2 2QP, tel 0845 225 5121 🚉 Edinburgh Waverley

TIP

» Comfortable shoes are essential for a walking tour of the cobblestones and pavements.

Below *It took some 2 million cartloads of rubble to create the Mound, which became home to the National Gallery of Scotland and the Royal Scottish Academy*

REGIONS EDINBURGH • SIGHTS

INFORMATION

www.dynamicearth.co.uk

⊞ 61 F2 ✉ 112 Holyrood Road EH8
8AS ☎ 0131 550 7800 🕐 Easter–end
Jun, Sep–end Oct daily 10–5;
Jul–end Aug daily 10–6; rest of year daily
Wed–Sun 10–5 💷 Adult £9.50, child
(3–15) £5.95, under 3 free, family from
£32–£55; may be additional charges for
special exhibitions 🚌 35, 64; also stop
on Edinburgh Tour and City Sightseeing
tour routes 🚉 Edinburgh Waverley
📖 £4 🍴 The Food Chain café 🎁 Well-
stocked themed gift shop ❓ Allow at
least 90 minutes to explore

Above *The futurist dome that houses
Our Dynamic Earth, on the edge of
Holyrood Park*

OUR DYNAMIC EARTH

Our Dynamic Earth offers fun science and the perfect antidote to Edinburgh's more staid attractions. The tented roof of this science park rises like a spiked white armadillo on the edge of Holyrood Park. It's like nothing else in the city, and has proved a popular and successful millennium project. It tells the story of the Earth and its changing nature, from the so-called Big Bang (as viewed from the bridge of a space ship) to the present day (exactly who lives where in the rainforest), in slick, bite-sized chunks of virtual reality science—ideal entertainment for kids with a short attention span, but it may prove a bit too whizzy for some.

The underlying message, that the world is a fascinating and ever-changing place, is unarguable. The planet is explored inside out through 11 galleries, from the effect of erupting volcanoes to the icy chill of the polar regions, and including a 'submarine' exploration of strange creatures and coral reefs along the way.

In the Restless Earth section you'll feel the tremors of a simulated earthquake while lava apparently boils below, and you may get caught (and a bit damp for real) in a rain storm in the Tropical Rainforest. You can even experience a sense of infinity in the Time Machine, where numberless stars are created using lights and mirrors.

A multi-screen flight over mountains and glaciers of Scotland and Norway in the Shaping the Surface is a dizzying highlight to any visit. Here you will dsicover how our landscape has been eroded by the power of ice to create what we see today.

PALACE OF HOLYROODHOUSE

This pepperpot-towered castle at the foot of the Royal Mile is the Queen's official residence in Scotland, which means it may be closed for odd days at short notice to make way for investitures, royal garden parties and other state occasions. It offers all the advantages of exploring a living palace steeped with history and filled with works of art from the Royal Collection. More precious artworks are on view in the stunning Queen's Gallery, by the entrance and opposite the Scottish Parliament, which is also where you'll find the well-stocked gift shop.

The palace, rich with historical associations, was probably founded in 1128 as an Augustinian monastery. In the 15th century it became a guesthouse for the neighbouring Holyrood Abbey (now a scenic ruin), and its name is said to derive from the Holy Rood, a fragment of Christ's cross belonging to David I (c1080–1153). Mary, Queen of Scots, stayed here, and a brass plate marks where her favourite, David Rizzio, was murdered in her private apartments in the west tower in 1566. Following serious fire damage in 1650 during the Civil War, major rebuilding was required. Bonnie Prince Charlie held court here in 1745, followed by George IV on his triumphant visit to the city in 1822, and later Queen Victoria on her way to Balmoral (▷ 235).

The state rooms, designed for Charles II by architect William Bruce (1630–1710) and hung with Brussels tapestries, are particularly elaborate and splendid. A large number of preposterous royal portraits painted in a hurry by the Dutch artist Jacob de Wet between 1684 and 1686 are on display in the Great Gallery.

INFORMATION
www.royal.gov.uk
🕂 61 F2 🕂 EH8 8DX ☎ 0131 556 5100 🅒 Easter–end Oct daily 9.30–6; rest of year daily 9.30–4.30. May close at short notice ✋ Adult £9.80, child (5–16) £5.80, under 5 free, family £25.40. Private guided tours available on special dates—£30 per person, tel 0207 766 7322 for information. A Royal Edinburgh ticket covers admission to Holyroodhouse, Edinburgh Castle and the Royal Yacht *Britannia*, plus two days travel on City Tour buses: adult £34, child (5–15) £13 🚌 35 🚉 Edinburgh Waverley 🎧 Free audio tour available 📖 £4.50 🛍 ♿ Gift shop stocks cards, books and commemorative china

Below *The Palace of Holyroodhouse is closely associated with Scotland's turbulent past*

INFORMATION

www.rbge.org.uk

✚ 61 off D1 ✚ 20A Inverlieth Row EH3 5LR ☎ 0131 552 7171 ◑ Mar, Oct daily 10–6; Apr–end Sep daily 10–7; rest of year daily 10–4 👜 Free; glasshouses adult £3.50, child (5–15) £1, under 5 free, family £8 🚌 8, 17, 22, 27, also on Majestic Tour route 🚇 Edinburgh Waverley 🚌 Tours lasting around 90 minutes leave the West Gate at 11 and 2, Apr–end Sep, £3 📷 £5 🍴 Terrace Café 🎁 Extensive Botanics gift shop with stationery, plants and related souvenirs

TIP

» To find your way about, pick up a map at the West or East gates (small charge).

ROYAL BOTANIC GARDEN

The Botanics, as it is known locally, a green oasis in a busy capital, with year-round interest and ten big glasshouses for wet days, boasts 15,500 plant species on display, lending weight to its claim to be one of the largest collections of living plants in the world. This total includes some 5,000 species in the rock garden alone (seen to best advantage in May). Occupying this site since 1823, it covers over 28ha (70 acres) of beautifully landscaped and wooded grounds to the north of the city centre, forming a minutely maintained green oasis.

There are ten glasshouses alone to explore, collectively called the Glasshouse Experience Windows on the World and offering the perfect escape on chilly days. They include an amazingly tall palm house dating back to 1858, and the Tropical Aquatic House, where you can enjoy an above-the-waterline view of giant waterlilies, and then go downstairs for an underwater view of fish swimming through the roots.

Outdoors, the plants of the Chinese Hillside and the Heath Garden are particularly interesting, and in summer the herbaceous border, backed by a tall beech hedge, is breathtaking. Check out the rhododendron collection and the rock garden. It's a great place for a break, and for children to let off steam and feed the inquisitive squirrels.

Exhibitions of contemporary art and photography are held in the different buildings around the site.

The West Gate, also known as the Carriage Gate, is the main entrance, but don't miss the stunning inner east side gates, designed by local architect Ben Tindall in 1996. A silvery riot of electroplated steel, they depict rhododendron foliage.

ROYAL MILE

This is the name given to the long, almost straight route linking Holyroodhouse with the castle, up the spine of rock on which the Old Town was built. About 60 narrow closes lead off between the buildings on either side, many with names indicating the trades once carried out there. The Writers' Museum (▷ 82) is in Lady Stair's Close. The route consists of four streets, each with its own identity. At the bottom, Canongate feels practical and workaday, the dressed stone of its facades giving way to rough and ready stonework on the sides of the buildings. Drop into the Museum of Edinburgh (▷ 71) for a view of the interiors of these old houses. Look for a board outside the Canongate Church, indicating celebrities buried there.

Where St. Mary's Street and Jeffrey Street cross over, you enter High Street, and sweet shops and tea rooms give way to boutiques and the postmodern pastiche of the Radisson SAS Hotel. Above the Tron Kirk the road retains its setts (cobbles) and broadens. Buildings appear more regular, with fewer baronial towers and turrets. After St. Giles' (▷ right), with the Heart of Midlothian in the cobbles marking the site of a prison, the street becomes the Lawnmarket, where linen (lawn) was manufactured. The

final stretch, Castle Hill, lies above Café Hub (a converted church), as the road narrows on the steep approach to the castle.
➕ 61 D2

ROYAL MUSEUM OF SCOTLAND

www.nms.ac.uk
This huge museum, which houses a world-class collection of international treasures, is closed until 2011 for a £46.4 million revamp.
➕ 61 D3 ➕ Chambers Street EH1 1JF
🚆 Edinburgh Waverley

ROYAL YACHT *BRITANNIA*

www.royalyachtbritannia.co.uk
It is said that many a royal tear was shed when *Britannia* was decommissioned in 1997. Since its launch at Clydebank in 1953, it had carried the Queen and her family on 968 official voyages to all parts of the world. Now it's a floating museum at Edinburgh's port of Leith (▷ 71), accessed via the Ocean Terminal shopping and leisure complex. While bigger than most 'yachts', *Britannia* is surprisingly compact, just 125.6m (412ft) long. She carried a crew of 240, including a Royal Marine band and around 45 household staff when the royal family were aboard.
➕ 61 off D1 ➕ Ocean Terminal, Leith EH6 6JJ ☎ 0131 555 5566 🕐 Apr–end Jun, Sep, Oct daily 10–4.30; Jul, Aug daily 9.30–4.30; rest of year daily 10–3.30

🖐 Adult £9.75, child (5–17) £5.75, under 5 free, family £27.75 🚌 11, 22; also on Majestic Tour route 🚆 Edinburgh Waverley
🚇

ST. GILES' CATHEDRAL

www.stgilescathedral.org.uk
The dark stonework of the High Kirk of Edinburgh, near the top of the Royal Mile, is forbidding on first sight. The columns inside, which support the 49m (160ft) tower with its distinctive crown top, are a relic of the 12th-century church which occupied the site. The tower dates from 1495, and the rest of the church from the 15th and 16th centuries. Presbyterian reformer John Knox (*c*1505–72) became minister here in 1559, arguing openly against Mary, Queen of Scots' attempts to revive the Roman Catholic cause. Inside is the exquisite Thistle Chapel by architect Robert Lorimer (1864–1929). The body of James Graham, Marquis of Montrose (1612–50) is interred here, and there is a bronze memorial to writer Robert Louis Stevenson (1850–94), who died in Samoa.
➕ 60 C3 🕐 Royal Mile EH1 1RE ☎ 0131 225 9442 🕐 May–end Sep Mon–Fri 9–7, Sat 9–5, Sun 1–5; rest of year Mon–Sat 9–5, Sun 1–5 🖐 Free 🚌 23, 27, 41, 42, 45
🚆 Edinburgh Waverley 🚇

Below *The Royal Mile stretches from the Castle to the Palace of Holyroodhouse*

SCOTCH WHISKY HERITAGE CENTRE

www.whisky-heritage.co.uk

Whisky is synonymous with Scotland and you can learn all about Scotland's national spirit at this popular attraction, at the top of the Royal Mile immediately below the castle. Tours set off every 15 minutes and last around an hour. They include a short film, a slow-moving barrel-ride through history, and a talk through the manufacturing process. With models and a 'ghost'—a master blender from 150 years ago—it's a better all-round family experience than most distillery tours. Adults get a free taste (juice is provided for children), and can explore more than 300 whiskies and liqueurs at the Amber Bar.

✚ 60 B3 ⊠ 354 Castlehill, Royal Mile EH1 2NE ☎ 0131 220 0441 ◑ Sep–end May daily 10–6; Jun–end Aug daily 9.30–6.30 🖐 Adult £9.50, child (13–17) £4.95, under 12 free, family £22 🚌 23, 27, 41, 42, 45 🚇 Edinburgh Waverley 🖥 🍴 🛍 🏛

SCOTT MONUMENT

www.cac.org.uk

This Gothic sandstone pinnacle 61m (200ft) high dominates the eastern end of Princes Street, and is well worth the drafty climb up 287 steps to the top for the magnificent views over the city. It was built between 1840 and 1846, to the design of George Meikle Kemp, as a memorial to the novelist and poet Sir Walter Scott (1771–1832), and was later encrusted with stone figures based on characters from his novels. A marble statue of Scott, with his deerhound Maida, sits at the bottom. It is by sculptor John Steell (1804–91).

✚ 60 C2 ⊠ East Princes Street Gardens EH2 2EJ ☎ 0131 529 4068 ◑ Apr–end Sep Mon–Sat 9–6, Sun 10–6; Oct–end Mar Mon–Sat 9–3, Sun 10–3 🖐 £3 (one price) 🚇 Edinburgh Waverley

SCOTTISH NATIONAL PORTRAIT GALLERY

www.nationalgalleries.org

The faces of the men and women who shaped Scotland hang here, forming a fascinating group of the great and the good, the vain and the bad, the beautiful and the long-forgotten.

Scottish artists are well represented, including locals Allan Ramsay (1713–84) and Henry Raeburn (1756–1823). This is also where you'll find the original and much copied portrait of poet Robert Burns by Alexander Nasmyth (1758–1840), as well as a host of other familiar faces.

The national photography collection is also held here, including the body of work by Edinburgh pioneers David Octavius Hill and Robert Adamson (▷ 35).

✚ 60 C1 ✚ 1 Queen Street EH2 1JD ☎ 0131 624 6200 ◑ Fri–Wed 10–5, Thu 10–7 🖐 Free, may be charges for temporary exhibitions 🚇 Edinburgh Waverley 🚌 4, 8, 15, 15A, 16, 17, 26, 44 🖥 🏛

SCOTTISH PARLIAMENT

▷ 94.

WRITERS' MUSEUM

www.cac.org.uk

Robert Burns (1759–96), Sir Walter Scott (1771–1832) and Robert Louis Stevenson (1850–94) are three of Scotland's most famous authors, and this little museum, in the narrow 17th-century Lady Stair's House, is dedicated to them. Burns wrote 'Ae Fond Kiss' while staying at the White Hart in the city's Grassmarket (▷ 65). Scott and Stevenson were both born in Edinburgh, and both studied law at the university. Displays to the former include a reconstruction of his New Town drawing room. Unlike the others, Stevenson has no museum elsewhere dedicated to him, and he died abroad, so this collection of memorabilia, including his hand-printing press, is particularly significant. Quotations by other famous Scottish writers are set into the paving slabs of Maker's Court, outside the museum.

✚ 60 C2 ⊠ Lady Stair's Close, Lawnmarket, Royal Mile EH1 2PA ☎ 0131 529 4901 ◑ Mon–Sat 10–5, Aug also Sun 12–5 🖐 Free 🚌 23, 27, 41, 42, 45 🚇 Edinburgh Waverley 🏛

Above A mosaic frieze adorns the entrance to the Scottish National Portrait Gallery
Below Burns memorabilia on display in the Writers' Museum

SCOTTISH NATIONAL GALLERY OF MODERN ART AND DEAN GALLERY

Scottish painting and sculpture flourished in the 20th century, and this is the place to view it. A sweeping, living sculpture of grassy terraces and semi-circular ponds is the first thing you see as you arrive at the main gallery, an installation called *Landform UEDA* by Charles Jencks. After that, the gallery itself feels quite small, but it has an enviable and varied collection of modern art treasures from around the world.

Temporary exhibitions occupy the ground floor, with a regularly changing display from the permanent collection on the first floor. Among these pieces, look for works by Picasso, Braque and Matisse, Hepworth and Gabo. The work of the early 20th-century group of painters known as the Scottish Colourists is particularly striking, with canvases by Samuel John Peploe (1871–1935), George Lesley Hunter (1877–1931), Francis Cadell (1883–1937) and John Duncan Fergusson (1874–1961). Also of interest are Fergusson's dramatic *Portrait of a Lady in Black* (c1921), the vibrant colours of Cadell's *Blue Fan* (c1922) and Peploe's later, more fragmentary work, such as *Iona Landscape, Rocks* (c1927). Modern artists such as Andy Warhol, Lucien Freud, Gilbert and George, Damien Hirst and Tracey Emin are also represented.

Cross the road to the Dean Gallery, an outstation of the Gallery of Modern Art. Housed in a former orphanage and surrounded by picturesque allotment gardens, the collection majors on Dada and the Surrealists, and the Scottish sculptor Eduardo Paolozzi (1924–2005). Paolozzi's striding Vulcan statue of welded stainless steel, half man and half machine, takes up an entire two-floor gallery on its own. A chamber on the ground floor gives an insight into how a sculptor works, with a re-creation of Paolozzi's London studio, including 3,000 plaster casts and moulds.

INFORMATION

www.nationalgalleries.org
✚ 60 off A1 ✚ 75 Belford Road EH4 3DR ☎ 0131 624 6200 🕐 Daily 10–5 👆 Free, but may be charges for temporary exhibitions 🚇 Edinburgh Haymarket 🚌 🏪 Shop stocks books, cards, gifts

TIP

» If you're on the free galleries bus, visit the main gallery first and return to the town centre from the Dean Gallery.

Above *The Scottish National Gallery provides the ideal setting for works by those at the forefront of modern art*

WALK

EDINBURGH'S ELEGANT NEW TOWN

A walk in the footsteps of a fistful of literary giants.

THE WALK

Distance: 3 miles (5km)
Allow: 1 hour 30 minutes
Start/end: Tourist Information Centre, Princes Street, Edinburgh
Grid reference NT 257739

★ Edinburgh's New Town (▷ 77) is an elegant, 18th-century planned development of wide streets, sweeping crescents and soft grey Georgian buildings. It became the haunt of the Scottish literati, celebrated in the paving stones around the Writers' Museum (▷ 82).

From the tourist information office, turn left and walk along Princes Street.

❶ Princes Street marks the dividing line between the medieval Old Town, on your left, and the Georgian New Town (▷ 77), to your right.

Just after you pass the Scott Monument (▷ 82) on your left, cross the road to reach Jenners, the famous Edinburgh department store. Continue along Princes Street, then take a right turn up Hanover Street.

❷ Milne's Bar on Hanover Street was a popular haunt of several of Scotland's most influential modern poets. Hugh MacDiarmid, Norman MacCaig and Sorley MacLean are just some of the figures who used to meet here in the last century. The pub walls are still covered with their memorabilia.

Take the second turning on your left and walk along George Street.

❸ English Romantic poet Percy Bysshe Shelley (1792–1822) stayed at 60 George Street with his young bride, Harriet Westbrook, in 1811.

Reach Charlotte Square and turn right and right again to go along Young Street. At the end, turn left and walk down North Castle Street to reach Queen Street.

❹ Kenneth Grahame (1859–1932), author of *The Wind in the Willows*, was born at 30 Castle Street. Sir Walter Scott (1771–1832) was also born in the city, and kept a town residence at 39 Castle Street.

Cross the road, turn left, then right down Wemyss Place and right into Heriot Row.

❺ Robert Louis Stevenson (1850–94), best known as the author of the adventure stories *Treasure Island* and *Kidnapped*, and for the macabre tale of *Dr Jeykyll and Mr Hyde*, spent his childhood at No. 17 Heriot Row.

Above *Detail of the entrance gates to the Royal Botanic Garden*
Left *Georgian facades on Heriot Row*

At Howe Street turn left and, before you reach the church in the middle of the street, turn left and walk along South East Circus Place. Walk past the sweep of Royal Circus and down into Stockbridge.

Cross the bridge, then turn left along Dean Terrace. At the end, turn right into Ann Street. At Dean Park Crescent turn right and follow the road around into Leslie Place and into Stockbridge again. Cross the road and turn left and then right at the traffic lights to walk down St. Bernard's Row (almost opposite). Follow this, then bear left into Arboretum Avenue.

Continue past the Water of Leith and down to Inverleith Terrace. Cross over and walk up Arboretum Place to reach the entrance to the Royal Botanic Garden on the right (▷ 80). Turn left after the gardens and retrace your steps to Stockbridge.

Turn left at Hectors Bar and walk uphill, then turn left along St. Stephen Street. At the church follow the road, then turn left along Great King Street. At the end, turn right, then immediately left to walk along Drummond Place, past Dublin Street and ahead into London Street.

At the roundabout turn right and walk up Broughton Street to Picardy Place. Turn left and go past the statue of Sherlock Holmes.

6 The statue of the great fictional detective is a tribute to his Edinburgh-born creator Sir Arthur Conan Doyle, who lived nearby at 11 Picardy Place (now demolished). Conan Doyle studied medicine at Edinburgh University and modelled Holmes on one of his former lecturers—Dr. Joseph Bell, who helped the police in solving several murders in the city. Many believe that Conan Doyle assisted Bell with his work in this capacity, acting as Dr. Watson to his Holmes.

Bear left towards the Playhouse Theatre. Cross over, continue left, then turn right into Leopold Place and right again into Blenheim Place. At the church turn right and walk up steps. Turn left at the meeting of paths.

Go up the steps on the right, walk over Calton Hill, then turn right to pass the cannon. Go downhill, take the steps on your left and walk down into Regent Road. Turn right and walk back into Princes Street.

WHERE TO EAT
Apart from Milne's Bar (Hanover Street, tel 0131 225 6738) there are plenty of pubs and bars to choose from in New Town. George Street has several bistros and restaurants. Down in Stockbridge you can relax in a coffee bar such as Patisserie Florentin (North Castle Street, tel 0131 220 0225), which serves great cakes, or have a light snack in Maxi's (Raeburn Place, tel 0131 343 3007) or Hectors (Deanhaugh Street, tel 0131 343 1735).

PLACE TO VISIT
ROYAL BOTANIC GARDENS
✉ 20A Inverleith Row, Edinburgh EH3 5LR ☎ 0131 552 7171 ⏰ Apr–end Sep daily 10–7; Mar, Oct daily 10–6; Nov–end Feb daily 10–4 ✋ Free, with admission charge to the glasshouses

WHEN TO GO
Edinburgh is buzzing all year round. Visit in the spring and enjoy the blossom.

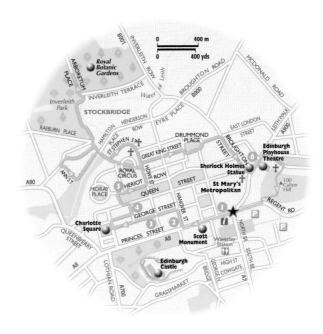

WALK

EDINBURGH'S OLD SECRETS

A stroll through the atmospheric streets of Edinburgh's Old Town to see a brooding castle.

THE WALK
Distance 2 miles (3.2km)
Allow: 1 hour
Start/end: Waverley Station, NT 256739
Suggested map AA Street by Street
Edinburgh

★Edinburgh is usually thought
to be an extremely respectable,
rather genteel city. But as you will
find out in this walk through the
city's ancient heart, the medieval
Old Town, it has a darker, more
mysterious side to its nature.

From the main entrance to Waverley
Station, turn left, go to the end of
the street, then cross over and walk
up Cockburn Street to the Royal
Mile, where you turn left and walk
downhill.

❶ The Old Town, the original city,
was enclosed by city walls, which
protected it from the ravages of
conflict, but also stopped it from
expanding. This meant that as the
population grew, the city became
increasingly overcrowded, and
was at one time the most densely

populated city in Europe. The only
solution was to build upwards.
People lived in towering tenements
known as 'lands', with the wealthy
taking the rooms at the bottom,
the poorer classes living at the top.
Its main street, the Royal Mile,
became a complicated maze of
narrow 'wynds' or alleyways, which
gradually deteriorated into a slum by
the 18th century.

Continue to the black gates of
Holyroodhouse. Turn right and walk
to face the new Parliament visitor
centre.

For the definitive view of the city,
leave the main walk by the Scottish
Parliament Visitor Centre and
head up the road to St Margaret's
Loch. From here a track leads to
St Anthony's Chapel and on up to
the summit of Arthur's Seat. After
admiring the view, drop down to
Dunsapie Loch, turn right and follow
the road beneath Salisbury Crags
back to the Scottish Parliament
Visitor Centre to resume the main
walk.

Turn left and follow the road to the
right, then turn right again past
Dynamic Earth (the building looks
like a huge white woodlouse) and
walk up into Holyrood Road. Turn
left, walk past the new buildings of
newspaper, *The Scotsman*, and walk
up to St Mary's Street, where you
turn right and rejoin the Royal Mile.
Were you to continue ahead you
would join the Cowgate, some parts
of which were devastated by fire in
December 2002.

Turn left to the main road then
left again along South Bridge. At
Chambers Street turn right and walk
past the museums. At the end of
the road, cross and then turn left.

❷ Here you will see the little statue
of Greyfriars Bobby, the dog that
refused to leave this spot after his
master died.

You can now cross the road and
make the short detour into Greyfriars
Kirk to see where Greyfriars Bobby
is buried close to his master. Or turn
right and walk down Candlemaker

Left *View of the back of the Royal Mile*

Row. At the bottom, turn left and wander into Grassmarket filled with shops and lively restaurants.

❸ There are dark secrets in the Grassmarket. Here the body-snatchers Burke and Hare used to lure their victims before murdering them. They then sold the bodies to a local surgeon who used them in his research. Deacon Brodie, the seemingly respectable town councillor, had a secret nocturnal life as a criminal and gambler—and was eventually hanged. He was the inspiration for Robert Louis Stevenson's Dr Jekyll, who turned into Mr Hyde at night.

When you've explored the Grassmarket, walk up Victoria Street (it says West Bow at the bottom). About two-thirds of the way up look for a flight of steps hidden away on the left. Climb them and, when you emerge at the top, walk ahead at the top to join the Royal Mile again. Turn left to walk up to the castle.

❹ Edinburgh Castle dominates the city. It dates back to the 12th century, although there was a hill-fort there long before that. You can see the Honours of Scotland here, the name given to the Scottish Crown Jewels, as well as the Stone of Destiny. The castle was the birthplace of Mary, Queen of Scots' son James—who became James VI of Scotland and later James I of England.

Walk down the Royal Mile again. You eventually pass St. Giles' Cathedral on your right.

❺ St. Giles' Cathedral is the main cathedral in Scotland. It was here that John Knox launched the Reformation in Scotland. Look for the plaque to Jenny Geddes, who threw a stool at the minister during a service. She was furious because he had tried to introduce the English prayer book into Scottish services.

Next on your left you pass the City Chambers (under which lies the mysterious Real Mary King's Close).

❻ In the progressive 18th century new public buildings were constructed along the steep slopes of the Royal Mile, using the walls of the old slums as foundations. As the city council chambers were extended over the next century, stories were told of cobbled lanes and long-abandoned rooms that still existed deep below in vaulted basements. It wasn't until late in the 20th century that one of these old lanes was opened to the public. Called Mary King's Close, it is full of atmosphere and, as you might expect, is said to be haunted.

Continue until you reach the junction with Cockburn Street. Turn left and walk back down this winding street. At the bottom of the street cross the road and return to the entrance to Waverley Station.

PLACE TO VISIT
ST GILES' CATHEDRAL
✉ High Street, Edinburgh EH1 1RE
☎ 0131 225 4363 🕐 May–end Sep Mon–Fri 9–7, Sat 9–5, Sun 1–5; Oct–end Apr Mon–Sat 9–5, Sun 1–5 💷 £3 donation per person

WHEN TO GO
Go at dusk if you want to feel the ghostly atmosphere in Old Town.

WHERE TO EAT
Greyfriars Bobby on Candlemaker Row (tel 0131 225 8328) is a friendly pub, named after the loyal dog.

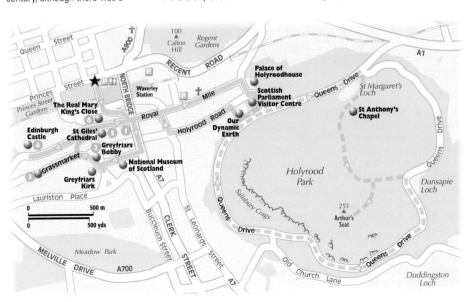

SHOPPING

ANTA
www.anta.co.uk
Upmarket independent shop selling stoneware, tiles, carpets and luggage from Scotland. Also high-quality fabrics, throws and cushions in wool and woven tweed in a variety of contemporary and classic tartans. Stylish but expensive.
✉ 93 West Row EH2 2JP ☎ 0131 225 4616 🕑 Mon–Sat 10–6

ARMSTRONGS
www.armstrongsvintageco.uk
Armstrongs is an Edinburgh institution—an Aladdin's Cave for lovers of vintage clothing. This shop, in the heart of the Old Town, sells everything from accessories to coats, from a variety of eras.
✉ 80 The Grassmarket EH1 2H3 ☎ 0131 220 5557 🕑 Mon–Thu 10–5.30, Fri–Sat 10–6, Sun 12–6

CODA MUSIC ON THE MOUND
www.codamusic.co.uk
This small shop on the Mound stocks a fabulous collection of recordings of traditional and contemporary Scottish folk music, as well as world and country music, and is a great place to find out about the Edinburgh folk scene.
✉ 12 Bank Street, The Mound EH1 2LN ☎ 0131 622 7246 🕑 Mon–Sat 9–5.30, Sun 11–5

CRUISE
www.cruiseclothing.co.uk
This is where Edinburgh's fashionistas go shopping for designer clothes, shoes and accessories, with labels such as Gucci, Prada and Paul Smith. Prices are not for the faint-hearted. Both shops are in the smart New Town area, with menswear in George Street, and the ladies' store in Castle Street. Further stores at 80 George Street and 14 St. Mary's Street.
✉ 94 George Street EH2 3DF ☎ 0131 226 3524 ✉ 31 Castle Street EH3 2DN ☎ 0131 220 4441 🕑 Mon–Wed, Fri–Sat 9.30–6, Thu 10–7, Sun 11–5.30

EDINBURGH BOOKCRAFTS
This bookshop specializes in conserving and repairing rare and antiquarian books. It also has a selection of second-hand books.
✉ 2 Summer Place ☎ 0131 556 7857 🕑 Sat 9.30–5.30, Sun 12.30–4.30

FRASERS (HOUSE OF FRASER)
www.houseoffraser.co.uk
In price terms, this popular department store falls midway between John Lewis in the St. James shopping centre and Jenners. Good selection of accessories, perfumes, clothes (including labels such as DKNY and Ralph Lauren), kitchenware and accessories. On the west corner of Princes Street.
✉ 145 Princes Street EH2 4YZ ☎ 0870 160 7239 🕑 Mon–Wed 9.30–6, Thu 9.30–7.30, Fri 9.30–6.30, Sat 9–6, Sun 11–6 🍴 Café on the fifth floor for coffee, light lunch and three-course meals

HARVEY NICHOLS
www.harveynichols.com
Perfumes, designer handbags, accessories and clothes including

Left Pipe bands celebrating the Queen's Golden Jubilee at the Military Tattoo

Gucci, Burberry, Prada, Fendi and Dior make this an exclusive but expensive shopping experience. More designer labels are to be found in next-door Multrees Walk.

✉ 30–34 St. Andrew Square EH2 3AD ☎ 0131 524 8388 🕓 Mon–Wed 10–6, Thu 10–8, Fri–Sat 10–7, Sun 11–6 🍴 Bar, brasserie and top-floor restaurant

HAWICK CASHMERE COMPANY
www.hawickcashmere.com
The 'Cashmere Made In Scotland' swing ticket indicates that the clothes in this shop at the foot of Victoria Street are of the highest quality. Sweaters and scarves in every hue. Cashmere doesn't come cheap: sweaters start from around £140.

✉ 71–81 Grassmarket EH1 2HJ ☎ 0131 225 8634 🕓 Mon–Sat 10–6, also Sun 12–4 Apr–end Nov

HECTOR RUSSELL
www.hector-russell.com
The Princes Street branch of this well-known chain of kilt shops is a good place to rent or buy a kilt or kilt outfit, whether you're looking for a sgian dubh (small knife traditionally worn inside the sock) or the full works. A complete outfit won't cost less than £500, but purchases can be mailed home. Ladies are also well catered for. Additional branch in High Street.

✉ 95 Princes Street EH2 2ER ☎ 0131 225 3315; freephone order number (UK only) 0800 980 4010 🕓 Mon–Sat 9–6, Sun 11–5

JENNERS
www.houseoffraser.co.uk
Snootier than its newest rival Harvey Nichols, Jenners is an Edinburgh institution, founded in 1838. Until it was recently bought by House of Fraser, it was the world's oldest independent department store. Inside it is a confusing rabbit warren of different levels, with a central galleried arcade reminiscent of Liberty's in London—pick up a printed store guide to help you find

the bits you want, or explore and discover. Jenners sells everything from high-quality clothes and shoes to toys, glassware, groceries and perfume, and also offers online shopping from its website. It's on the corner of St. David Street, opposite Waverley train station. There is a branch at the Loch Lomond shores.

✉ 48 Princes Street EH2 2YJ ☎ 0131 225 2442 🕓 Mon–Wed 10–6, Thu 9–8, Fri–Sat 9–6, Sun 11–6 🍴 Four cafés on different floors serve coffee, snacks and full meals

NESS
www.nessbypost.co.uk
Funky modern knitwear and accessories in vibrant tones make the most of flamboyant local design and quality Scottish wool. You'll find everything from Harris tweed handbags to long scarves in zingy shades. Also farther down the Royal Mile at 367 High Street.

✉ 336–340 Lawnmarket, Edinburgh ☎ 0131 225 8815 🕓 Daily 10–6

OCEAN TERMINAL
www.oceanterminal.com
Designed by Jasper Conran and opened in 2001, Ocean Terminal is a vast shopping and cinema complex which overlooks the Firth of Forth and the Royal Yacht *Britannia* (▷ 81). The shops are mainly the high street names that you can find in the centre of Edinburgh. However, the huge, free parking area makes shopping here an attractive option. The lofty central space is the venue for exhibitions of anything from artwork to tents.

✉ Ocean Drive, Leith EH6 6JJ ☎ 0131 555 8888 🕓 Mon–Fri 10–8, Sat 10–7, Sun 11–6 🚌 11, 22, 36 🍴 Food outlets, including Costa Coffee and Starbucks for caffeine, Ocean Kitchen for buffet food and Ocean Bar for stylish drinks

OLD TOWN BOOKSHOP
www.oldtownbookshop.co.uk
The place to come for second-hand books on poetry, music, travel, art and, of course, Scotland and Scottish writers. Also has a good selection of prints and maps.

✉ 8 Victoria Street EH1 2HG ☎ 0131 225 9237 🕓 Mon–Sat 10.30–5.45

PALENQUE
www.palenque.co.uk
This small jewellery shop, just below the junction with South Bridge, specializes in contemporary and silver rings, necklaces and bracelets and hand crafted accessories, all reasonably priced. There is a second shop on Rose Street.

✉ 56 High Street, Royal Mile EH1 1TB ☎ 0131 557 9553 🕓 Mon–Sat 9.30–5.30, Sun 11–5

PRINCES MALL
www.princesmall-edinburgh.co.uk
This surprisingly light and spacious subterranean shopping centre next to Waverley train station has many of the usual high street names in fashion and gifts. Look out for handmade chocolates at Maxwell & Kennedy and Orkney jewellery at Ortak.

✉ Princes Street EH1 1BQ ☎ 0131 557 3759 🕓 Mon–Sat 9–6, Sun 11–5 🍴 Food court in the lower mall with McDonald's, Costa Coffee and Spud-U-Like (baked potatoes)

RAGAMUFFIN
Eye-catching displays in the large windows of this shop on the corner of St. Mary's Street show brightly hued, handmade chunky knitwear, clothes, scarves and toys from all over England and Scotland.

✉ 276 Canongate EH8 8AA ☎ 0131 557 6007 🕓 Mon–Sat 10–6, Sun 12–5

ROYAL MILE WHISKIES
www.royalmilewhiskies.com
This specialist whisky shop opposite St. Giles Cathedral stocks a vast range of malt whiskies, some of which are 100 years old. It's the best place to buy rare whiskies if you want them shipped home—order by phone or online for delivery within the UK or overseas.

✉ 379 High Street, Royal Mile EH1 1PW ☎ 0131 225 3383 🕓 Mon–Sat 10–6, Sun 12.30–6 (open longer in Aug)

ST. JAMES CENTRE
www.thestjames.co.uk

High street favourites such as HMV, Boots and Accessorize dominate this modern shopping mall at the east end of Princes Street. The big draw is the John Lewis department store, which has everything for the home, clothes, a large beauty counter and a café with panoramic views. Large parking area.

✉ Leith Street EH1 3SS ☎ 0131 557 0050 🕐 Mon–Wed, Sat 7.30–6.30, Thu–Fri 7.30–8.30, Sun 11–5 Z

TARTAN WEAVING MILL AND EXHIBITION
www.tartanweavingmill.co.uk

Walk down the floors of this massive tartan and tartanalia shop at the top of the Royal Mile to discover the source of all that clacking and burring of machinery—the weaving looms in the basement. On the way you can have your photo taken in full Highland rig, and consult the Clans and Tartans Bureau for information about your own clan history. The shop and exhibition make imaginative use of a building which once housed the Old Town's water reservoir.

✉ 555 Castlehill, The Royal Mile EH1 2ND ☎ 0131 226 4162 (shop)/0131 226 1555 (mill) 🕐 Apr–end Sep Mon–Sat 9–6.30, Sun 10–6.30; rest of year Mon–Sat 9–5.30, Sun 10–5.30 🖐 Free ▢

TISO
www.tiso.com

The best outdoor clothing and equipment shop in Edinburgh. Helpful and knowledgeable staff can give you advice on everything you need for walking, climbing, camping or skiing. There's also an excellent travel and mountaineering book section. Rose Street is in the heart of the city.

✉ 123–125 Rose Street EH2 3DT ☎ 0131 225 9486 🕐 Mon, Wed, Fri–Sat 9.30–5.30, Tue 10–5.30, Thu 9.30–7.30, Sun 11–5

WATERSTONE'S
www.waterstones.co.uk

One of the leading bookshop chains in Britain, Waterstone's has several branches in Edinburgh. The shop at the west end of Princes Street is on several floors, with large windows and a café on the top level which gives great views to the castle. The branch at the east end of Princes Street has a well-stocked Scottish travel and literature section. Further branches on George Street and at Ocean Terminal.

✉ 128 Princes Street EH2 4AD (west end branch) ☎ 0131 226 2666 🕐 Mon 8.30–8, Tue 9–8, Wed–Sat 8.30–8, Sun 10–7 ▢

ENTERTAINMENT AND NIGHTLIFE

BAILIE BAR
This basement pub has an unusual, triangular-shaped bar, low ceilings and sumptuous dark-red decor. There's plenty of space, and a lounge area where you can enjoy the real ales. On the corner of St. Stephen Street and North West Circus Place, in Stockbridge.

✉ 2 St. Stephen Street, New Town EH3 5AL ☎ 0131 225 4673 🕐 Mon–Thu 11am–12am, Fri–Sat 11am–1am, Sun 12.30pm–11pm

BLUE MOON
Everybody is welcome at this gay bar, noted for serving the best food in the area all day. Alongside the substantial range of beers and a wine list, try Mexican food or even vegetarian haggis, neeps and tatties. Deep red-painted walls, a coal fire and relaxing fish tanks. Off Broughton Street, a few minutes' walk from the east end of Princes Street.

✉ 1 Barony Street, New Town EH1 3SB ☎ 0131 557 0911 🕐 Mon–Fri 10am–midnight, Sat–Sun 10am–1am

BONGO CLUB
www.thebongoclub.co.uk

The Bongo nightclub's club nights are diverse and cover different styles of live music, from hip hop to reggae and breakdancing. In the daytime, it's a café, with free internet access and exhibition space.

✉ Moray House, 37 Holyrood Road EH8 8AQ ☎ 0131 558 7604 🕐 Variable; café open Mon–Fri 1–7 🖐 Up to £10

BOW BAR
Painted blue and located halfway down Victoria Street, this is the best bar in the city for whisky, with over 140 to choose from and usually several on special offer. Good selection of real ales too. Wood panelling and old brewery mirrors.

✉ 80 The West Bow, Victoria Street, Old Town EH1 2HH ☎ 0131 226 7667 🕐 Mon–Sat 12–11.30, Sun 12.30–11

CABARET VOLTAIRE
www.thecabaretvoltaire.com

These caverns in the Old Town host club events every night. Diverse styles of dance music, big-name DJs and live music—with performances by national and international acts.

✉ 36–38 Blair Street EH1 1QR ☎ 0131 220 6176 🕐 Check website for hours and prices

CAFÉ ROYAL CIRCLE BAR
This traditional pub in a grade 'A' listed building is almost 150 years old, and boasts the most impressive pub interior in Edinburgh. It's well worth having a drink here to admire the Victorian interior with Doulton tile portraits, stained glass, ornate ceiling and comfy leather sofas. Find it down an alley behind Burger King at the east end of Princes Street.

✉ 19 West Register Street EH2 2AA ☎ 0131 556 1884 🕐 Mon–Wed and Sun 11–11, Thu 11am–midnight, Fri–Sat 11am–1am

CAMEO
www.picturehouses.co.uk

Small, friendly independent cinema showing low-key Hollywood, international and independent films. Near the King's Theatre. Ask for a plastic glass and you can take your drink into the cinema with you.

✉ 38 Home Street EH3 9LZ ☎ 0870 755 1231; 0131 228 2800 (24-hour recorded information) 🖐 £5.90; all tickets £4 Mon except bank holidays 🔲 Extended bar hosts exhibitions by local artists

CASK AND BARREL
An unpretentious, traditional pub with plenty of constantly changing real ales served by staff who know their stuff. The Cask is well known

as a soccer pub, and on the day of an important match it's shoulder-to-shoulder in here, with standing room only as locals pile in to watch the game on the TVs around the bar. At the foot of Broughton Street.
✉ 115 Broughton Street, New Town EH1 3RZ ☎ 0131 556 3132 🕐 Mon–Wed 11am–12.30am, Thu–Sat 11am–1am, Sun 12.30pm–12.30am

CORN EXCHANGE
www.ece.uk.com
This pop and rock music venue is 2 miles (3.2km) southwest of the city centre. Opened in 1999 by Blur, and acts have included Blur, Travis, Pulp, Fun Lovin' Criminals and Coldplay.
✉ 11 New Market Road, Gorgie EH14 1RH ☎ 0131 477 3500 🕐 All year 👋 From £12 🍸

DOMINION
www.dominioncinema.net
This small, family-run, independent cinema in the southern suburb of Morningside is the perfect antidote to the plethora of giant multiplex cinemas. It shows independent and mainstream movies, and has traditional leather Pullman seats. The Gold Class service even offers leather sofas along with the

complimentary wine or beer and nibbles. Look out for the collection of photos of famous faces that have visited the cinema over the years.
✉ 18 Newbattle Terrace, Morningside EH10 4RT ☎ 0131 447 4771 (box office) 👋 From £5.80 🍸 🚌 11, 15, 16, 23

DORIC TAVERN
There's a warm atmosphere in this traditional pub, and the smell of good food. Now into its fourth century, it's a very old pub indeed, but the facade is unassuming and easy to miss. A wine bar and bistro are upstairs. Market Street is behind Waverley train station.
✉ 15–16 Market Street, Old Town ☎ 0131 225 1084 🕐 Daily 12pm–1am. Food 12–10.30

EDINBURGH FESTIVAL THEATRE
www.eft.co.uk
Prestigious concert venue close to the city's east end hosts a variety of international and British touring productions of dance, theatre, musicals and comedy, from contemporary ballet to Scottish Opera. It has a distinctive all-glass facade and the largest stage in Britain.
✉ 13–29 Nicolson Street EH8 9FT ☎ 0131 529 6000 🕐 All year 👋 From £8.50

Above *Outside the Festival Theatre, with its distinctive glass facade*

🍴 Café Lucia in the foyer 🍸 Three further bars

EDINBURGH PLAYHOUSE
www.edinburghplayhouse.org.uk
The best venue in town for touring productions of big-budget musicals and dance. Located a five-minute walk away from the east end of Princes Street, next door to the huge Vue cinema.
✉ 18–22 Greenside Place EH1 3AA ☎ 0870 606 3424 (Ticketmaster, 24 hours) 🕐 All year 👋 From £15 🍸

ESPIONAGE
www.espionage007.com
It's late, it's free and you can dance the night away at this bar/club—small wonder it's popular with young people looking to extend their evening. Four themed bars and two dance floors spread over five floors make this an easy place to lose your friends and find new ones. At the top of Victoria Street, near George IV Bridge.
✉ 4 India Buildings, Victoria Street, Old Town EH1 1EX ☎ 0131 477 7007 🕐 Nightly 7pm–3am (to 5am during Festival) 👋 Free entry

FILMHOUSE

www.filmhousecinema.com

This three-screen art house cinema opposite the Usher Hall has the best range of independent and international cinema in Edinburgh and hosts local film festivals.

✉ 88 Lothian Road EH3 9BZ ☎ 0131 228 2688 (box office); 0131 228 2689 (recorded information) 🍴 Relaxed Filmhouse Café Bar is great for a coffee or for a full pre-film meal, 10am–10pm 💷 From £6

GRAPE

A smart and stylish city centre wine bar on George Street. There's an extensive selection of wines, but Grape is equally good for a coffee break while you're out shopping. Comfy sofas and a dramatic painted ceiling.

✉ The Capital Building, 13 St. Andrew's Square EH2 2BH ☎ 0131 557 4522 🕐 Mon–Sat from 11; closing times vary

GREYFRIARS BOBBY

Behind its traditional wooden facade there is a friendly pub, named after the famously loyal dog. Popular with students and visitors alike. Located in front of Greyfriars kirk.

✉ 34 Candlemaker Row EH1 2QE ☎ 0131 225 8328 🕐 Mon–Thu 11am–12am, Fri–Sat 11am–1am, Sun 11am–12am 🚌 23, 27, 103

HENRY'S JAZZ CELLAR

www.henrysvenue.com

The best place in Edinburgh for contemporary jazz, with something to suit all tastes, including Latin, free and Jamaican jazz. There's a bar, but no food is served. Morrison Street is a short walk from the West End.

✉ 78 Morrison Street EH3 8BJ ☎ 0131 538 7385 🕐 All year 💷 From £5

JOLLY JUDGE

www.jollyjudge.co.uk

It's not easy to find this pub, but it's well worth seeking out for its genuine 17th-century character complete with painted, low-beamed ceiling and for its wide choice of malt whiskies. At the top of the Royal Mile look out for the sign; go down East Entry into James Court, and the pub is down some steps on the left.

✉ 7 James Court, Old Town EH1 2PB ☎ 0131 225 2669 🕐 Sun–Thu 12–11, Fri–Sat 12–12

KING'S THEATRE

www.eft.co.uk

This grand old Edwardian building is one of Edinburgh's oldest theatres. The King's is great for family entertainment, majoring on shows and musicals, pantomime, comedy and plays. Also drama, including Shakespeare.

✉ 2 Leven Street EH3 9LQ ☎ 0131 529 6000 🕐 All year 💷 From £5 🍷 Two, for interval drinks

THE LIQUID ROOM

www.liquidroom.com

Nightclub and live music venue in a basement in Edinburgh's Old Town. Club nights cover everything from Indie music to chart hits, while performers have included Travis, Coldplay, the Kaiser Chiefs and Red Hot Chilli Peppers.

✉ 9c Victoria Street EH1 2HE ☎ 0131 225 2564 🕐 Club nights: Wed–Sat from 10.30pm. Check website for live acts and prices

NETHERBOW CENTRE

www.scottishstorytellingcentre.co.uk

A small, intimate venue with an innovative programme of Scottish

and children's theatre, and traditional stories and poetry readings.
✉ 43–45 High Street EH1 1SR ☎ 0131 556 9579 ⊕ Phone for details ⏺ ⏹

ODEON
www.odeon.co.uk
The Odeon is a five-screen cinema off the west end of Princes Street, showing mostly mainstream movies.
✉ 118 Lothian Road EH3 8BG ☎ 0871 224 4007 ⏹ Light bar

OPAL LOUNGE
www.opallounge.co.uk
Stylish New Town basement cocktail bar and fusion restaurant where the beautiful and famous hang out. Reputedly a favourite haunt of Prince William.
✉ 51a George Street EH2 2HT ☎ 0131 226 2275 ⊕ Daily 12pm–3am

PO NA NA
www.eclecticbars.co.uk
A popular city centre bar/nightclub, if you fancy a dance after the pubs have closed. Moroccan themed interior, with dance floors and secluded alcoves. The queues start forming at around 10pm. Just down from George Street, below Café Rouge.
✉ 43B Frederick Street EH2 1EP ☎ 0131 226 2224 ⊕ Mon–Sat 10pm–3am ✋ From £2

QUEEN'S HALL
www.thequeenshall.net
A more intimate venue than the Usher Hall, the Queen's Hall, in a converted church, is a very popular hot spot for jazz, blues, rock and soul, as well as for classical music and comedy, attracting top names such as Courtney Pine and Ruby Turner.
✉ Clerk Street EH8 9JG ☎ 0131 668 2019 ⊕ All year ✋ From £8 ⏺ Café on two floors, good for coffee and filled rolls (only on performance days) ⏹ Stocks good selection of real ales and malt whiskies

RICK'S
Trendy, minimalist basement bar in the heart of the city, with over 20 types of vodka as well as a list of bar snacks. Rick's serves as restaurant, cocktail bar, breakfast café and boutique hotel, all in one. Just off Princes Street.
✉ 55a Frederick Street, New Town EH2 1LH ☎ 0131 622 7800 ⊕ Daily 7am–1am

ROYAL LYCEUM THEATRE
www.lyceum.org.uk
One of the leading production theatres in Scotland, the magnificent Victorian Lyceum creates all its own shows. Contemporary and classic theatre predominate, including Shakespeare productions. Off Lothian Road near the West End of the city.
✉ Grindlay Street EH3 9AX ☎ 0131 248 4848 ⊕ All year; closed Sun ✋ From £11 ⏹

STAND COMEDY CLUB
www.thestand.co.uk
Enjoy live comedy from new and well-known Scottish comedians, seven nights a week, at this dark and intimate basement bar. Weekend shows often sell out, so advance booking is advised.
✉ 5 York Place EH1 3EB ☎ 0131 558 7272 ⊕ Mon–Thu, Sun 7.30pm–midnight, Fri–Sat 7pm–1am ✋ £5–£12

TRAVERSE THEATRE
www.traverse.co.uk
The Traverse is famous for its productions of experimental theatre and dance, and is a good place to catch hot new work by Scottish playwrights. Located next to the Usher Hall, near the city's West End.
✉ 10 Cambridge Street EH1 2ED ☎ 0131 228 1404 ⊕ All year ✋ From £9 ⏹ Traverse Bar Café downstairs warm and intimate, with a wide selection of exotic and draught lagers ⏺ Bar Café, upstairs, is one of the best restaurants in Edinburgh, tel 0131 228 5383

USHER HALL
www.usherhall.co.uk
Edinburgh's most prestigious concert hall attracts high-quality performers such as the English Chamber Orchestra and the Moscow Philharmonic Orchestra. A distinctive circular building towards the West End, its high dome can be seen from many parts of the city.
✉ Lothian Road EH1 2EA ☎ 0131 228 1155 ⊕ All year ✋ From £10 ⏹ Three bars

VUE EDINBURGH
www.myvue.com
A huge glass-fronted building opposite John Lewis, this multiplex cinema has stadium seating and the latest in digital surround sound. The Gold Class ticket gives you luxury leather seats, waiter bar service during the film and a wall-to-wall screen. Don't miss the remarkable giraffe sculpture by Helen Denerley outside.
✉ Omni Leisure Building, Greenside Place, Leith Street EH1 3EN ☎ 08712 240240 ⊕ Screenings from lunchtime Mon–Fri; also morning screenings Sat–Sun ✋ From £5.60

VUE EDINBURGH OCEAN TERMINAL
www.myvue.com
This 12-screen, state-of-the-art cinema shows mainstream films on the largest multiplex screen in Scotland, with the latest in digital surround sound. The ergonomically designed seats are particularly comfortable, and give extra leg room. Free parking, and possibly the best view of Edinburgh from the top of the escalator.
✉ Ocean Terminal, Ocean Drive, Leith EH6 7DZ ☎ 08712 240240 ✋ From £5 ⏹ Trendy Ocean Bar

SPORTS AND ACTIVITIES
ADRIAN'S EDINBURGH CITY CYCLE TOUR
www.edinburghcycletour.com
Enjoy a 3-hour guided bicycle tour, taking in Edinburgh's history, design, Holyrood and other top attractions. All equipment, including bicycles, helmets and waterproofs are supplied. No age restrictions, but not recommended for children under 10. Meet by Holyrood Palace gates, at Abbey Sanctuary. Advance reservations required.
☎ 07966 447 206 ⊕ Daily at 10 and 2.30 (Jul–end Sep) ✋ Adult £15

BIKE TRAX
www.biketrax.co.uk
Rent a bicycle to explore the city for yourself. Bike Trax rents mountain and hybrid bicycles, kids' bicycles, trailer bicycles and child seats, and is found to the south of the city centre, near the King's Theatre.
✉ 7–11 Lochrin Place, Tollcross EH3 9QX ☎ 0131 228 6633 ① Apr–end Oct Mon–Fri 9.30–6, Sat 9.30–5.30, Sun 12–5; Oct–end Apr Mon–Sat 9.30–5.30 ✋ Mountain bicycle hire from £12 a day

CITY OF THE DEAD WALKING TOUR
www.blackhart.uk.com
Enjoy a night-time guided walk through the mysterious dark lanes of the Old Town, ending up in a haunted mausoleum in Greyfriars graveyard. Meet up at St. Giles Cathedral. Advance reservations recommended. Not suitable for younger children.
✉ 40 Candlemaker Row EH1 2QE ☎ 0131 225 9044 /0771 542 2750 ① Tours nightly 8.30, 9.15 and 10 Easter–Halloween ✋ Adult £8.50, child (under 16) £6.50

EDINBURGH BUS TOURS
www.edinburghtour.com
A guided open-top bus tour is a great way to see the city and, as your ticket is valid all day, you can get off to see the attractions and catch the next bus. The live tour is in English, or there is a recorded multi-lingual version. You can join the tour at Waverley Bridge, Lothian Road, Grassmarket, Royal Mile, Princes Street or George Street. Buy tickets on the bus itself or at the tourist information office. There is also a wide range of other tours available.
✉ Waverley Bridge EH1 1BQ ☎ 0131 220 0770 ① Tours leave daily every 10–15 minutes from 9.30am; last tour Easter–end Oct 6.30pm, Nov–Easter 3.30pm ✋ Adult £3, child (5–15) accompanied by adult £5, under 5 free, family £31

THE EDINBURGH LITERARY PUB TOUR
www.edinburghliterarypubtour.co.uk
A 2-hour walking (and drinking) tour of pubs with literary associations, in the company of knowledgeable actors. Advance reservations are recommended. Meet at the Beehive Inn in the Grassmarket. Minimum age 18.
☎ 0800 169 7410 ① Tours start at 7.30pm: nightly May–end Sep; Thu–Sun Mar, Apr, Oct; Fri only Nov–end Feb ✋ £8

HEART OF MIDLOTHIAN FOOTBALL CLUB
www.heartsfc.premiumtv.co.uk
The Hearts ground lies 1 mile (1.6km) southwest of the city centre.
✉ Tynecastle Stadium, Gorgie Road EH11 2NL ☎ 0871 663 1874 ✋ Adult £35, child £5–£15 🚌 1, 2, 3, 3a, 25, 33

HIBERNIAN FOOTBALL CLUB
www.premiumtv.co.uk
The Hibs ground is off Easter Road, towards Leith, 1 mile (1.6km) from the centre.
✉ Easter Road Stadium, 12 Albion Place EH7 5QG ☎ 0871 663 1874 ① Adult £21–£27, child (under 18) £11 🚌 1

MANSFIELD TRAQUAIR CENTRE
www.mansfieldtraquair.org.uk
One of Edinburgh's most extraordinary hidden treasures is accessed via free guided tours, and not to be missed. It's a former church of 1885, remarkable for its decoration from floor to ceiling with murals by the Arts and Crafts artist Phoebe Anna Traquair (1852–1936). The impact of the freshly restored paintings is stunning.
✉ 15 Mansfield Place EH3 6BB ① 2nd Sun of each month, extra dates during Festival ✋ Free

MERCAT TOURS
www.mercattours.com
Take an hour-long guided tour of Edinburgh's haunted underground city, through the vaults at South Bridge, or perhaps a late-night stroll on the Ghosthunter Trail. Reservations are essential. Meet at the Mercat Cross on the Royal Mile.
✉ Niddry Street South EH1 1NS ☎ 0131 225 5445 ① Daily, times vary ✋ Adult from £8.50, child £5, family £22

MURRAYFIELD STADIUM
www.scottishrugby.org
Rugby is arguably Edinburgh's favourite sport, and games throughout the year are well supported, so advance reservations are essential. It has a seating capacity of 67,500 and still holds the world record for the largest attendance at a rugby game. An enormous crowd of just over 104,000 packed into the statium to watch Scotland play Wales in 1975. Located in the Murrayfield district, 1 mile (1.5km) from the city centre. No age restrictions.
✉ Off Roseburn Terrace, Murrayfield EH12 5PJ ☎ 0131 346 5000 ✋ £20–£50 (for Scotland matches) 🚌 12, 31, 36

ROYAL COMMONWEALTH POOL
www.edinburghleisure.co.uk
This Olympic-size indoor swimming pool below Arthur's Seat has water slides, a diving pool and a children's pool as well as a gym, sauna and Clambers—a soft, safe play area for younger children.
✉ 21 Dalkeith Road EH16 5BB ☎ 0131 667 7211 ① Mon–Tue, Thu–Fri 6am–9.30pm, Wed 6am–9am, 8.45am–9.30am, Sat 6am–7pm, Sun 10–7 ✋ Adult £4.30, child (under 18) £1.90, family £9; cheaper rates Mon–Fri before 4pm 🚌 14, 21, 33 🅿

SCOTTISH PARLIAMENT
www.scottish.parliament.uk
Take a tour of Scotland's most talked-about modern building, and get an insight into Scottish democracy at work. Guided tours take in the Debating Chamber, the Garden Lobby and views to the MSP Building—advance reservations are essential. And if you just want to see what all the fuss was about, access to the Main Hall and a peep inside the Chamber (on non-business days) will cost you nothing. The public entrance is tucked around a corner, opposite Holyrood Palace.
✉ Edinburgh EH99 1SP ☎ 0131 348 5200 ① Tours: Mon –Fri when in session 10.20–2.40; Apr–end Oct 10.20–4; public hols Apr–end Oct 11.20–4 ✋ Adult £6, child (5–16) £3.60 🅿 🅿

THE WITCHERY TOUR

www.witcherytours.com

For a glimpse of the Old Town's murkier side, including tales of witchcraft, torture and plague, join a guided walking tour. Witchery tours last 1 hour 15 minutes, and meet outside the Witchery restaurant on Castlehill. Not suitable for the very nervous. Advance reservations are essential.

✉ 84 West Bow, EH1 2HH ☎ 0131 225 6745 ☻ Ghosts and Gore tour nightly May–end Aug 7, 7.30; Murder and Mystery tour nightly all year 9, 9.30, according to demand ✋ Adult £7.50, child £5 (price includes Witchery Tales book)

HEALTH AND BEAUTY
ANTHYLLIS

www.anthyllis.co.uk

Organic beauty parlour specializing in luxurious Dr. Hauschka products and treatments—the celebrities' choice. Treatments range from facials to foot care, as well as facial gymnastics, massage and reflexology.

✉ 30 Haymarket Terrace EH12 5JZ ☎ 0131 313 2001 ✋ Prices vary: a 2-hour Dr. Hauschka facial £80, 1-hour massage £55 🚌 Haymarket Station

EDINBURGH FLOATARIUM

Massage and alternative therapies are the order here. Enjoy the float tank, reflexology, therapeutic massage, aromatherapy massage and facials. Make reservations well in advance.

✉ 29 North West Circus Place, Stockbridge EH3 6TP ☎ 0131 225 3350 ☻ Mon–Fri 9–7, Sat 9–6, Sun 9.30–4 ✋ 1-hour float £30; 1-hour aromatherapy massage £35; 2-hour Sheer Bliss £70 🚌 24, 29,36, 42 🏧 Sells pure essential oils, candles, incense, books, CDs, crystals, crystal jewellery and homeopathic remedies

ONE SPA AT THE SHERATON GRAND

www.one-spa.com

This luxurious spa is equipped with an extensive range of treatments including massage, facials, body wraps and Ayurvedic treatments. Facilities include a 19m (62ft) ozone friendly pool, a gym with mood-enhancing lighting, a thermal suite and a mud room. The rooftop hydropool provides spectacular views of Edinburgh's skyline. Advance reservations are recommended.

✉ 8 Conference Square EH3 9SR ☎ 0131 221 7777 ☻ Mon–Fri 6.30am–10pm, Sat–Sun 6.30am–9pm; children's hours daily 3–5, and Sat–Sun 8.30–9.30am and 3–5pm ✋ Day spa break from £65; overnight residential spa package for two from £300 🚌 10, 11, 16, 17 🍴 Spa Café

EDINBURGH FESTIVAL SURVIVAL GUIDE

Millions throng to the capital every year for the world's biggest arts festival and its spin-offs. Here is information and insider tips to help you plan and get the most out of your visit.

EDINBURGH INTERNATIONAL ARTS FESTIVAL

www.eif.co.uk

This three-week festival offers the highest quality opera, dance, classical music and theatre, and is held in August every year. The programme, which is free and available from the Edinburgh Festival Office, is published at the end of March and you can book tickets from the middle of April. Many events sell out quickly, so it's advisable to book as far ahead as possible to secure tickets. Festival performances are held in Edinburgh's larger and more prestigious venues such as the Usher Hall.
✉ Edinburgh Festival Office, The Hub, Castlehill EH1 2NE ☎ 0131 473 2000

EDINBURGH FRINGE FESTIVAL

www.edfringe.com

The ever-expanding Fringe is host to hundreds of different productions of varying quality. Performances of theatre, comedy, music and dance are held in every venue imaginable.

Availability of tickets hinges on positive or negative reviews, so get in there quickly if you hear good things about a production. The Fringe programme, which you can get from the Fringe office on the Royal Mile, comes out in June. Give yourself enough time to sift through the thousands of entries.
✉ Festival Fringe Office, 180 High Street EH1 1QS ☎ 0131 226 5257

EDINBURGH INTERNATIONAL BOOK FESTIVAL

www.edbookfest.co.uk

The two-week bookfest, held in the green calm of Charlotte Square Gardens, is near to, but separated from, the madness of the Fringe. You can hear talks and readings, join in question and answer sessions with famous writers and of course, meet your favourite authors and buy books at signing sessions. The Book Festival is particularly child friendly with many events specifically for children.
☎ 0845 373 5888

EDINBURGH INTERNATIONAL FILM FESTIVAL

www.filmhousecinema.com

The Film Festival has been going for more than 50 years, showing international and independent films in Edinburgh's art house cinemas. Highlights include screenings followed by question and answer sessions with the director. Just don't expect anything from Hollywood.
✉ Filmhouse Cinema, 88 Lothian Road EH3 9BZ ☎ 0131 228 2688

EDINBURGH INTERNATIONAL JAZZ AND BLUES FESTIVAL

www.edinburghjazzfestival.co.uk

Lasting ten days, the Jazz Festival hosts musicians from all over the world who play in pubs and clubs throughout the city. Check the website for dates, as the 2003 Festival had finished before the official Jazz Festival began.
☎ 0131 473 2000

Left *Fireworks during the Edinburgh Festival*
Bottom left *Mime artist at the Fringe*
Bottom right *The Military Tattoo*

EDINBURGH MILITARY TATTOO

www.edintattoo.co.uk

The Tattoo—the annual outdoor military spectacle on the castle esplanade—runs for three weeks in August. Pipe bands, soldiers in kilts—they're all here. The show sells out most nights so buy your ticket as early as possible.

✉ Tattoo Office, 32–34 Market Street EH1 1QB ☎ 0131 225 1188

EDINBURGH ART FESTIVAL

www.edinburghartfestival.org

Held for the first time in 2004, this is the newest of the city's festivals, with art, crafts and photography highlighted in galleries and other venues throughout August.

HOW TO ENJOY THE FESTIVAL WITHOUT SPENDING A FORTUNE

» On the first Sunday of the Fringe in Queen's Park is the aptly named Fringe Sunday. Theatre groups, musicians and comedians showcase their acts in the shadow of Arthur's Seat for free.

» The Festival Cavalcade along Princes Street is another opportunity for acts to advertise their shows and for you to pick up the free goodies they throw to the crowd.

» Street theatre happens every day of the Festival on the Royal Mile and outside the National Gallery of Scotland.

» The Bank of Scotland Fireworks from Edinburgh Castle takes place on the last day of the Festival. Princes Street and Calton Hill are good viewing points.

» Buy unsold tickets for Official Festival productions for half price on the day of the performance. Available 1–5 from The Hub, or from the venue an hour before curtain-up.

» *The Scotsman* newspaper offers free tickets to Fringe shows every day, to the first person bearing a copy of their paper to present him/herself at the Fringe Office.

» Bigger venues tend to have more established, well-known acts. For 'more established' read 'more expensive'. Ergo, smaller venue, smaller price.

» Not officially part of the Festival, but the charming Cameo independent cinema has every film for £4.50 on a Monday.

» Edinburgh's art galleries often start new exhibitions at this time of year. Entrance is free.

TOP FESTIVAL TIPS

» When in the queue at the Fringe office, note the acts which have sold out for that day (usually written on a blackboard). Book tickets for that show for the next night. With so many acts to choose from, a sell-out show is going to be good.

» If going to the Tattoo take as many of the following as you can find: binoculars, hip flask, waterproof, cushion and rug. It may be summer but this is still Scotland.

» The best venues for that 'I'm sure I've seen him on TV' moment are the Pleasance and the Assembly Rooms on George Street.

» Give yourself enough time to have a good look at the Fringe programme. It may be the size of a telephone book but it's free and lists every show in the Fringe.

» Try to see a play performed in the Royal Botanic Gardens. It's rare to be allowed into the gardens at night and it's a wonderfully atmospheric location for theatre. Also, dress warmly and bring a rug to sit on.

» Take a punt. The Mongolian throat singers were the surprise hit of 2000, while a rap version of Chaucer's *Canterbury Tales* won an award in 2007.

» Book your accommodation before you arrive. It's not unheard of for every hotel, B&B and hostel in the city to be fully booked on certain days in August.

REGIONS ● EDINBURGH ● WHAT TO DO

EATING

PRICES AND SYMBOLS
The restaurants are listed alphabetically. The prices are for a two-course lunch (L) and a three-course à la carte dinner (D). Prices in pubs are for a two-course lunchtime bar meal and a two-course dinner in the restaurant, unless specified otherwise. The wine price is for the least expensive bottle.

For a key to the symbols, ▷ 2.

AGUA
www.apexhotels.co.uk
The stylish bistro at the Apex City Hotel offers an eye-catching menu that plays to the gallery with something for everyone; dishes allow for some mixing and matching and prices are competitively priced. Quality ingredients and light, clear flavours deliver in dishes such as sea bream with fragrant rice and sweet-and-sour salsa, and a classic crème brûlée to finish.
✉ Apex City Hotel, 61 Grassmarket EH1 2JF ☎ 0131 243 3456 ⊙ 12–2, 4–10; closed

20–28 Dec 🍴 L £8.50, D £19.95, Wine £12.95 🚌 Continue towards west end of Princes Street, at main junction turn into Lothian Road, then turn left into King Stables Road, which leads into Grassmarket

ATRIUM
www.atriumrestaurant.co.uk
White bean soup with confit duck garnish characterizes the starters, while roast chicken with chive mash and roasted root vegetables is a typically robust main course; desserts include chocolate orange tart with crème fraîche. There is an extensive wine list.
✉ 10 Cambridge Street EH1 2ED ☎ 0131 228 8882 ⊙ 12–2, 6–10; closed Sun, L Sat except Aug; 25–26 Dec, 1–2 Jan 🍴 L £15.50, D £27, Wine £18.50 🚌 From Princes Street turn into Lothian Road, 2nd left and 1st right, by the Traverse Theatre

BELLINI
Enjoy regional Italian cuisine in a Georgian dining room in the heart

of New Town, where you'll find a relaxed and friendly atmosphere. The finest Scottish produce is used. Starters could include *zuppa paste e faggioli* (traditional bean soup from Abruzzi) or a variety of fresh mushrooms simply pan-fried, followed by main courses such as risotto Bellini, made with lobster and tiger prawns, or *filetto al Barolo* (Scottish beef fillet in a red wine jus enriched with onions and rosemary.
✉ 8b Abercromby Place EH3 6LB ☎ 0131 476 2602 ⊙ Daily Tue–Sun 6–11pm. L by arrangement 🍴 D £19.95, Wine 15.90

BENNETS BAR
Popular with actors from the nearby Kings Theatre, Bennets prides itself on its straightforward home-made food at a reasonable price. Typical menu features steak pie and breaded fresh haddock fillet.
✉ 8 Leven Street EH3 9LG ☎ 0131 229 5143 ⊙ Mon–Wed 11am–12.30am,

Thu–Sat 11am–1am, Sun 12.30–11.30. Bar meals: Mon–Sat 12–2, 5–8.30, Sun 12.30–5 🖐 L £8, D £11, Wine £10

BLUE
www.bluescotland.co.uk

This trendy modern brasserie and bar goes from strength to strength with a menu that is flexible, good value and imaginative. Lunch could be as simple as a crayfish sandwich or a bowl of white bean and chorizo soup. A more substantial meal would be red wine poached pear and Roquefort tart or carpaccio of beef with parmesan, followed by mushroom and barley risotto with rocket or corn-fed chicken with aromatic risotto and bacon dressing. Desserts include chocolate tart with caramelized oranges.

✉ Cambridge Street EH1 2ED ☎ 0131 221 1222 🕐 12–2.30, 6–11; closed Sun, 25–26 Dec 🖐 L £15, D £24, Wine £14.50 🚍 From Princes Street turn into Lothian Road, 2nd left, 1st right, above the Traverse Theatre

THE BOW BAR
The huge selection of whiskies in the bar features 160 malts on tap, and eight cask ales. Bar snacks only, and there are no gaming machines or music to distract from good conversation.

✉ 80 The West Bow EH1 2HH ☎ 0131 226 7667 🕐 Mon–Sat 12–11.30, Sun 12.30–11; closed 25–26 Dec, 1–2 Jan 🖐 L £2.80, Wine £2.95 (glass), £10.95 (bottle)

THE BRIDGE INN
www.bridgeinn.com

Dating back to around 1750, the Bridge Inn is famous for its fleet of restaurant boats and sightseeing launches. Local produce is freshly prepared and served, and top-quality Scottish meat has been a speciality for over 30 years. Typical dishes include shank of Lothian lamb, roast Barbary duck breast, Thai green curry, and salmon and asparagus pie. Principal beers on offer include Bellhaven 80/-.

✉ 27 Baird Road, Ratho EH28 8RA ☎ 0131 333 1320 🕐 Mon–Fri 12–11, Sat 11am–

12am, Sun 12.30–11pm; closed 26 Dec, 1–2 Jan. Bar meals: daily 12–9. Restaurant: daily 12–2.30, 6.30–9.30 🖐 L £10, D £22, Wine £11.25 🚍 From Newbridge B7030 junction (intersection) follow signs for Ratho

LE CAFÉ ST. HONORÉ
You will find intimate, chilled-out dining at this bistro, set in a quiet cobbled side street five minutes from Princes Street. Plenty of fine Scottish produce, majoring on fish, in tempting combinations like warm salad of scallops, monkfish, chorizo and cashew nuts, mixed with some sublime French classics, such as boeuf bourguignon with mash. To finish try the hot plum crumble with cinnamon ice cream. The wine list is extensive.

✉ 34 NW Thistle Street Lane EH2 1EA ☎ 0131 226 2211 🕐 L Mon–Sat 12–2.15; D Mon–Fri 7–10, Sat 6–10; closed 24–26 Dec, 3 days New Year 🖐 L £15, D £30, Wine £14 🚍 City centre, between Hanover Street and Frederick Street

CHANNINGS BAR AND RESTAURANT
www.chanings.co.uk

The basement restaurant at this traditional town-house property, former home of the polar explorer Ernest Shackleton, has a refreshingly simple approach to cooking quality local produce. The style is modern brasserie—pan-fried sea bream with olive oil mash and salsa verde, or leek chervil and tarragon risotto with a parmesan tuile.

✉ 15 South Learmonth Gardens EH4 1EZ ☎ 0131 315 2225 🕐 12–2.30, 610 🖐 L £12, D £19.50, Wine £15.50 🚍 From Princes Street follow signs to Forth Bridge (A90), cross Dean Bridge and take 4th right into South Learmonth Avenue. Follow road to bottom of hill

REGIONS EDINBURGH • EATING

DORIC TAVERN

A bustling bistro, pub and wine bar, built in 1710. Classics and innovative modern dishes include fillet of venison, steaks and pastas, and sweet potato pie, with traditional pub snacks like sausage and mash, hamburger and bruschetta.
✉ 15–16 Market Street EH1 1DE ☎ 0131 225 1084 🕐 12–1am; closed 25–26 Dec, 1 Jan. Bar meals: daily 12–7. Restaurant: daily 12–4, 5–11 ✋ L £12, D £15, Wine £12 🚇 Close to south entrance of Waverley Station

DUCK'S AT LE MARCHÉ NOIR

www.ducks.co.uk
Well-established Edinburgh staple offering pleasingly direct cooking in a relaxed setting. Mains might include slow-roast belly of pork and sour apple, or chargrilled veal rump with truffled pecorino; imaginative vegetarian options might include rosemary scone with roasted Jerusalem artichokes and ceps. Sugared doughnuts with chocolate and Pedro Ximenez sherry are among the desserts.
✉ 2–4 Eyre Place EH3 5EP ☎ 0131 558 1608 🕐 12–2.30, 6–10; closed L Sat–Mon, 25–26 Dec ✋ L £15, D £28, Wine £14.50 🚇 Follow the Mound across Princes Street, George Street, Queen Street to bottom of Dundas Street

LA GARRIGUE

www.lagarrigue.co.uk
La Garrigue is named after an area of the Languedoc in France, and is an authentic showcase for the region's food. Chef Jean Michel Gauffre combines hearty no-frills Gallic cooking with presentation that's full of finesse but never fussy. Mains might include boneless leg of rabbit filled with juniper berries and thyme flavoured stuffing or the famous cassoulet, and both wines and cheeses are sourced from the region.
✉ 31 Jeffrey Street EH1 1DH ☎ 0131 557 3032 🕐 12–2.30, 6.30–9.30; closed 25–26 Dec, 1–2 Jan ✋ L £13.50, D £30, Wine £13.50 🚇 Halfway down Royal Mile towards Holyrood Palace, turn left at lights into Jeffrey Street

HADRIANS

www.thebalmoralhotel.com
Chic informal brasserie on the ground floor of the Balmoral Hotel serving good-quality Scottish cuisine with a European influence. Choose from seared scallops served with creamy mash and sauce vièrge or Scottish lamb cutlets with roasted tomatoes and a feta and mint salad. Or try the Dover sole or rib-eye from the grill, with a choice of sauces— from peppercorn to tartare.
✉ Balmoral Hotel, 1 Princes Street EH2 2EQ ☎ 0131 557 5000 🕐 12–2.30, 6.30–10.30 ✋ L £25, D £27.50, Wine £22 🚇 At the east end of Princes Street, by Waverley Station

HALDANES

www.haldanesrestaurant.com
The finest seasonal Scottish produce features on a monthly-changing menu of modern dishes, simply prepared. For starters, try a warm salad of west coast king scallops with sautéed charlotte potatoes and Parma ham, or cullen skink soup and follow it with a grillet fillet of halibut

with a panaché of sweet potatoes and purple sprouting broccoli, served with cherry tomato confit and red pepper dressing. Coffee is served with home-made truffles and creamy fudge.

✉ 13B Dundas Street EH3 6QG ☎ 0131 556 8407 🕐 L Tue–Fri, D Tue–Sat; closed Sun and Mon ✋ L £12, D £32, Wine £15 🚌 At top end of Dundas Street, just after turn-offs for Abercromby Place and Heriot Row

IGGS

A convivial, modern, glass-fronted restaurant in the heart of Edinburgh's Old Town, near the Royal Mile where the food is Mediterranean/Spanish, with a choice of four dishes at each course. The best Scottish produce stars in starters of king scallops with pea and mint purée and a main course of fish stew or turmeric-coated sole fillets. Other options include roast ballotine of goose or, for vegetarians, Mediterranean vegetable cake. There's also an excellent selection of Spanish wines to choose from to accompany your meal.

✉ 15 Jeffrey Street EH1 1DR ☎ 0131 557 8184 🕐 12–2.30, 6–10.30; closed Sun ✋ L £15, D £29, Wine £18 🚌 Just off the Royal Mile, 0.5 miles (0.8km) from the Castle

THE KITCHIN

www.thekitchin.com

Tom Kitchin's eponymous restaurant is on Leith's rejuvenated waterfront. Expect slick, modern cooking, a successful marriage of fresh, seasonal Scottish produce and classical French technique. Impressive presentation creates a focal point on every plate; take hare cooked à la royale and served with soft polenta, celeriac purée and tomato chutney.

✉ 78 Commercial Quay, Leith EH6 6LX ☎ 0131 555 1755 🕐 Tue–Thu 12.30–1.45, 6.45–10, Fri–Sat 12.30–2, 6.45–10.30, closed Sun, Mon, Christmas, New Year, 1st week Jul ✋ L £21, D £46.50, Wine £30 🚌 Opposite Scottish Executive building, short drive from city centre

MALMAISON HOTEL & BRASSERIE

www.malmaison.com

A chic hotel priding itself on simple French-style brasserie food and memorable wine selections. Cod brandade with paprika aïoli and cucumber salsa, lamb cutlets and clapshot rosti with red wine jus, pork medallions with Agen prunes and grain mustard and grilled halibut with warm squid and caper sauce.

✉ One Tower Place, Leith EH6 7DB ☎ 0131 468 5000 🕐 12–2.30, 6–10.30; closed D 25 Dec ✋ L £13.50, D £24, Wine £14.95 🚌 From the city centre follow Leith Docklands signs through 3 sets of traffic lights and left into Tower Street

Below Looking out over the New Town from Edinburgh Castle's Argyle Battery

REGIONS EDINBURGH • EATING

MELVILLE CASTLE HOTEL

www.melvillecastle.com

At this candle-lit brasserie restaurant local produce dominates the menu, with favourites such as seasonal game casserole, or perhaps roast halibut with bacon and cabbage, followed by a delicious sticky toffee pudding.

✉ Melville Gate, Gilmerton Road EH18 1AP ☎ 0131 654 0088 🕐 12–2.30, 6.30–9.30 ✋ L £10.50, D £24, Wine £16.95 🚌 2 minutes from city bypass (A720) via Sheriffhall roundabout

NORTON HOUSE

www.handpicked.co.uk/nortonhouse

Choose from lighter meals at the brasserie or a real treat in the stylish Ushers Restaurant, where top-quality food is simply and brilliantly prepared. You might start with lobster ravioli, or twice-baked Scottish crab soufflé with langoustines and a soy and lime dressing, followed by fillet of Buccleuch beef, and round off with rosewater crème brûlée and poached pear in ginger wine.

✉ Ingliston EH28 8LX ☎ 0131 333 1275 🕐 Dinner only, 7–9.30; closed Sun–Mon, 1 Jan ✋ D £38, Wine £23 🚌 M8 junction 2, off A8, 0.5 miles (1km) past Edinburgh airport

NUMBER ONE

www.thebalmoralhotel.com

The stylish modern restaurant specializes in luxurious simple dishes created from top-quality, local ingredients. The menu has a range of meats and seafood (braised oxtail, Barbary duck, organic salmon) with a list of accompaniments such as sautéed spinach or creamed cabbage. Begin with a starter of peanut-encrusted scallops served with curried oxtail and parsnip purée, followed by a deliciously tender fillet of beef with truffle mash. Desserts include chocolate and orange tart with five differing styles of orange, and prune d'Agen soufflé with Armagnac ice cream.

✉ Balmoral Hotel, 1 Princes Street EH2 2EQ ☎ 0131 557 6727 🕐 6.30–10 dinner (starts earlier in summer); 1–7 Jan

✋ D £55, Wine £25 🚌 At the east end of Princes Street, by Waverley Station

OFF THE WALL RESTAURANT

www.off-the-wall.co.uk

An uncomplicated approach to cuisine, with no fussiness and unnecessary flourishes. Expect modern cooking: beef fillet, perhaps, with red cabbage, port sauce and buttery truffle mash; venison with celeriac and a chocolate sauce; saddle of Scottish lamb served with baby spinach and ragout of carrots, dauphinoise potatoes and a port sauce; or the odd surprise, such as squab pigeon with black pudding and orange sauce. Finish with a chocolate torte with chocolate sauce and mint ice cream

✉ 105 High Street, Royal Mile EH1 1SG ☎ 0131 558 1497 🕐 12–2, 7–10; closed Sun, Dec, 1–2 Jan ✋ L £16.50, D £38, Wine £13.95 🚌 On Royal Mile near John Knox House. Entrance via stairway next to Baillie Fyfes Close

PLUMED HORSE RESTAURANT

www.plumedhorse.co.uk

This restaurant was originally in tiny Crossmichael, Castle Douglas, but relocated here. Starters may include tian of marinated salmon, sour cream, two caviars and dill oil; meat dishes might include chicken and fresh herb sausage. Vegetarian menu on request.

✉ 50–54 Henderson Street EH6 6DE ☎ 0131 554 5556 🕐 12.30–1, 7–9; closed D Sun–Mon, 25–26 Dec, 2 weeks Jan, 2 weeks Sep ✋ L £17.50, D £39, Wine £17.50 🚌 Off Great Junction Street in Leith, Edinburgh

THE RESTAURANT AT THE BONHAM

www.thebonham.com

Stylish dining is on offer at this fashionable boutique hotel. Main courses are simple contemporary dishes with well-matched flavours (Scottish beef with seared foie gras and porcini sauce, or herb gnocchi and roasted ceps with truffle sauce). Desserts like orange blossom pannacotta with lavender tuile are (almost) too pretty to eat.

✉ 35 Drumsheugh Gardens EH3 7RN ☎ 0131 274 7444 🕐 Mon–Sat 12–2.30, Sun 12.30–3, daily 6.30–10 ✋ L £13.50, D £33, Wine £15.50 🚌 West end of Princes Street

RESTAURANT MARTIN WISHART

www.martin-wishart.co.uk

At this tiny, minimalist restaurant the short menus change daily, with lunch a more low-key affair than dinner. Your evening meal might begin with duck consommé or ravioli of lobster, followed by braised shin of beef with celeriac purée and glazed vegetables or succulent roast squab pigeon. In season, warm apricot tart with crème anglaise is hard to beat. The wine list is extensive.

✉ 54 The Shore, Leith EH6 6RA ☎ 0131 553 3557 🕐 12–2, 7–10; closed Sun, Mon, 25 Dec, public holidays ✋ L £22.50, D £50, Wine £19.50

RHUBARB, THE RESTAURANT AT PRESTONFIELD

www.prestonfield.com

Rhubarb makes a frequent appearance at this theatrical restaurant. A meal here might start with shank of garlic-crusted cod on pea purée, followed by roast saddle of rabbit, and perhaps a rhubarb and gingerbread crème brûlée, or warm chocolate fondant with basil anglaise and Greek yoghurt.

✉ Prestonfield, Priestfield Road EH16 5UT ☎ 0131 225 1333 🕐 Mon–Sat 12–2, 6.30–10, Sun 1–3 ✋ L £16.95, D £42, Wine £20 🚌 Leave city centre on Nicholson Street, join Dalkeith Road. At traffic lights turn left into Priestfield Road, hotel is on left

SANTINI

Santini's first restaurant in the UK outside London is situated at Edinburgh's city spa, a relaxed contemporary restaurant serving pizza, pasta and lighter dishes. Dishes are authentic Italian, such as creamy porcini mushroom risotto or osso buco-braised veal shank, plus more modern options such as sea bass with rosemary and balsamic vinegar sauce.

✉ 8 Conference Square EH3 8AN ☎ 0131 221 7788 🕐 12–2.30, 6.30–10.30; closed

Sun, L Sat, New Year 🖐 L £17, D £28, Wine £17

THE SCOTSMAN

www.thescotsmanhotel.co.uk
This magnificent Victorian building as formerly the headquarters of *The Scotsman* newspaper and the restaurant combines the best of the original features with cutting-edge design. The chef offers a modern take on classic ingredients. Typical dishes could be fillet of beef with oxtail bread pudding, dressed crab with breaded langoustines and tomato and herb salad, with vanilla custard tart and poached rhubarb to finish.

✉ 20 North Bridge EH1 1YT ☎ 0131 556 5565 🕐 D only 7–10; closed Mon, Tue 🖐 D £23, Wine £17.50 🚌 Town centre, next to railway station

STAC POLLY

www.stacpolly.com
Modern Scottish cuisine dominates the menu—for example, baked supreme of Scottish salmon served with braised leeks, bacon dumplings and a lemon butter sauce, or sliced crown of Scottish lamb with Parma ham, tomato farci and balsamic and red wine reduction. Appealing desserts and an interesting wine list. A second restaurant is at 29–33 Dublin Street EH3 6NL (tel 0131 556 2231).

✉ 8–10 Grindlay Street EH3 9AS ☎ 0131 229 5405 🕐 12–2, 6–9.30; closed L Sat–Sun 🖐 L £15, D £34, Wine £17.95 🚌 Beneath the castle near Lyceum Theatre

THE STARBANK INN

The bar menu typically offers roast lamb with mint sauce, poached salmon, a vegetarian dish of the day, and chicken with tarragon cream sauce. Principal beers include Bellhaven 80/- and Timothy Taylor Landlord.

✉ 64 Laverockbank Road EH5 3BZ ☎ 0131 552 4141 🕐 Mon–Wed 11–11, Thu–Sat 11–12am, Sun 12.30–11 (food served weekends 12–9.30). Bar meals: daily 12–2.30, 6–9.30. Restaurant: daily 12–2.30, 6–9.30 🖐 L £9, D £11, Wine £8

Above *The Witchery by the Castle uses the very best of Scottish produce*

TOWER RESTAURANT & TERRACE

www.tower-restaurant.com
Chic and elegant, the Tower aims for a classic and contemporary take on quality Scottish ingredients. The menu is an interesting mix: from oysters to prawn cocktail to sushi, and from seared yellowfin tuna to fish and chips (French fries). A top recommendation is the fillet of Angus beef.

✉ Museum of Scotland, Chambers Street EH1 1J ☎ 0131 225 3003 🕐 12–11; closed 25–26 Dec 🖐 L £12.95, D £34, Wine £16.95 🚌 Museum of Scotland at corner of George IV Bridge and Chambers Street

THE VINTNERS ROOMS

www.thevintnersroom.com
The romantic restaurant in this former warehouse dating from the 15th century serves modern French dishes created from quality Scottish produce—Aberdeen Angus fillet with a Périgord truffle sauce, or steamed wild halibut with a mussel broth. This is rustic cuisine presented with great artistry and complemented by an extensive wine list.

✉ The Vaults, 87 Giles Street, Leith EH6 6BZ ☎ 0131 554 6767 🕐 12–2, 7–10; closed 1–16 Jan, Sun, Mon 🖐 L £16,

D £28.50, Wine £18.50 🚌 At end of Leith Walk, left into Great Junction Street, right into Henderson Street. Restaurant is in old warehouse on right

THE WITCHERY BY THE CASTLE

www.thewitchery.com
Heavy with theatrical, Gothic charm, the entire restaurant is candlelit and is *the* place to come for a special night out. The sumptuous menu provides a contemporary spin on modern classics—typically, game, fish and shellfish feature highly. Scottish lobster and rock oysters sit alongside Witchery classics like hot smoked salmon with leeks and hollandaise, while main courses might includes the likes of Angus beef fillet with smoked garlic broth, or a jambonette of Borders guinea fowl served with a blanquette of baby vegetables, caramelized apples and smoked garlic. And there is an extensive global wine list.

✉ Castlehill, Royal Mile EH1 2NF ☎ 0131 225 5613 🕐 12–4, 5.30–11.30; closed 25–26 Dec 🖐 L £12.95, D £43, Wine £15.95 🚌 At the gates of Edinburgh Castle, at the top of the Royal Mile

PRICES AND SYMBOLS

Prices are the starting price for a double room for one night, unless otherwise stated. Breakfast is included unless noted otherwise. All the hotels listed accept credit cards unless otherwise stated. Note that rates vary widely throughout the year.

For a key to the symbols, ▷ 2.

ABBOTSFORD GUEST HOUSE

www.abbotsfordguesthouse.co.uk
Within walking distance of the city centre, this guest house offers individually decorated and thoughtfully equipped bedrooms. Breakfast is taken at individual tables in the elegant dining room.
✉ 36 Pilrig Street EH6 5AL ☎ 0131 554 2706 💷 £70 🛈 8

ALLISON HOUSE

www.allisonhousehotel.com
Part of a Victorian terrace, Allison House offers modern comforts in a splendid building. It's convenient for the city centre, theatres, tourist attractions and is on the main bus route. The attractive bedrooms are

generally spacious and very well equipped. Breakfast is served at individual tables in the ground-floor dining room. Off-road parking is available.
✉ 17 Mayfield Gardens EH9 2AX ☎ 0131 667 8049 💷 £60 🛈 11

APEX INTERNATIONAL GRASSMARKET HOTEL

www.apexhotels.co.uk
This hotel stands in Edinburgh's historic Old Town. It has an excellent fitness centre with a stainless steel ozone pool, while the bedrooms are extremely well equipped and contemporary in style. There is a rooftop restaurant, plus a relaxed bar and brasserie.
✉ 31–35 Grassmarket EH1 2HS ☎ 0845 365 0000 or 0131 300 3456 💷 £120; breakfast £9.50 per person (continental), £12.50 per person (cooked) 🛈 171 🚘 Into Lothian Road at west end of Princes Street, then 1st left into King Stables Road, which leads into Grassmarket

ARDEN GUEST HOUSE

www.ardenedinburgh.co.uk
Colourful flowering baskets adorn the front of this welcoming, personally run guest house on the south side of the city, convenient for leisure and business travellers. The modern bedrooms offer good overall freedom of space. Traditional Scottish breakfasts are served at individual tables in the conservatory-dining room. Off-road car parking is a bonus.
✉ 126 Old Dalkeith Road EH16 4SD ☎ 0131 664 3985 💷 £50 🛈 11
🚘 2 miles (3km) southeast of city centre near Craigmillar Castle. On A7 just west of hospital

ASHLYN GUEST HOUSE

www.ashlyn-edinburgh.co.uk
The Ashlyn Guest House is a warm and friendly Georgian home, ideally located to take advantage of Edinburgh's attractions. The city centre is within walking distance and the Royal Botanical Gardens are minutes away. Bedrooms are all individually decorated and furnished

Left Edinburgh Castle, with St. Cuthbert's Church in the foreground

to a high standard. A generous and hearty breakfast gives a great start to the day.

✉ 42 Inverleith Row EH3 5PY ☎ 0131 552 2954 🌐 Closed 23–28 Dec 🖐 £60 🛈 8 🚌 Adjacent to Royal Botanic Garden

BEST WESTERN BRAID HILLS
www.braidhillshotel.co.uk
This long-established hotel enjoys panoramic views. Bedrooms are smart, stylish and well equipped, and there's a choice of the restaurant or brasserie and bar. Two rooms have four-poster beds.

✉ 134 Braid Road EH10 6JD ☎ 0131 447 8888 🖐 £100 🛈 67 🚌 2.5 miles (4.8km) south on A702, opposite Braidburn Park

BEST WESTERN BRUNTSFIELD
www.thebruntsfield.co.uk
Overlooking Bruntsfield Links, this smart hotel has stylish public rooms including lounge areas and a lively pub. Dinner and hearty Scottish breakfasts are served in the conservatory restaurant. Bedrooms come in a variety of sizes.

✉ 69–74 Bruntsfield Place EH10 4HH ☎ 0131 229 1393 🖐 £110 🛈 67 🚌 From the south enter Edinburgh on A702. The hotel is 1 mile (1.6km) south of the west end of Princes Street

BEST WESTERN EDINBURGH CITY
www.bestwesternedinburghcity.co.uk
Occupying the site of the old maternity hospital, this tasteful conversion is close to the city centre. Spacious rooms are smartly modern, and equipped with fridges. There's a bright contemporary restaurant.

✉ 79 Lauriston Place EH3 9HZ ☎ 0131 622 7979 🖐 £180 🛈 52 🚌 Follow signs for city centre, A8. Get on to the A702, take 3rd exit on left, hotel is on right

THE BONHAM
www.thebonham.com
This stylish, contemporary hotel sets high standards of luxury. Comfortable day rooms and

bedrooms combine Victorian architecture with 21st-century technology. Imaginative dinners highlight good use of local fresh produce.

✉ 35 Drumsheugh Gardens EH3 7RN ☎ 0131 274 7400 🖐 £110 🛈 48 🚌 Close to West End and Princes Street

BONNINGTON GUEST HOUSE
www.thebonningtonguesthouse.com
This delightful Georgian house offers individually furnished bedrooms that retain many of their original features. The comfortable lounge has a grand piano. The kilted proprietor serves a fine Scottish breakfast.

✉ 202 Ferry Road EH6 4NW ☎ 0131 554 7610 🖐 £60 🛈 7 🚌 On A902

CHANNINGS
www.channings.co.uk
Classical elegance and contemporary style define this friendly town-house hotel, with sumptuous day rooms and Channings Restaurant. The bedrooms vary in size but are all well equipped and individually designed.

✉ South Learmonth Gardens EH4 1EZ ☎ 0131 274 7401 🖐 £125 🛈 41 🚌 Approach from A90 from Forth Road Bridge, follow signs for city centre

DALHOUSIE CASTLE & AQUEOUS SPA
www.dalhousiecastle.co.uk
Bedrooms in this 13th-century castle include opulently decorated themed rooms. Dinner is served in the Dungeon restaurant, while the less formal Orangery open all day. Facilities include a hydro spa, fishing and falconry by arrangement.

✉ Bonnyrigg EH19 3JB ☎ 01875 820153 🖐 £195 🛈 36 🚌 Take A7 south through Lasswade and Newtongrange. Turn right at Shell garage on to the B704, the hotel is 0.5 miles (800m) from intersection

DUNSTANE HOUSE
www.dunstane-hotel-edinburgh.co.uk
This splendid hotel combines architectural grandeur with an intimate country-house atmosphere.

The Skerries restaurant serves fish with lighter meals and a selection of malt whisky in the bar.

✉ 4 West Coates, Haymarket EH12 5JQ ☎ 0131 337 6169 🖐 £98 🛈 16 🚌 On A8 between Murrayfield Stadium and Haymarket train station

ELMVIEW
www.elmview.co.uk
Bedrooms and attractive bathrooms are comfortable and equipped with thoughtful extras. No children under 15.

✉ 15 Glengyle Terrace EH3 9LN ☎ 0131 228 1973 🌐 Closed end Oct–1 Apr 🖐 £80 🛈 3 🚌 Take A702 south up Lothian Road, turn first left past King's Theatre into Valley Field Street one-way system leading to Glengyle Terrace

HERIOTT PARK GUEST HOUSE
www.heriottpark.co.uk
A conversion of two adjoining properties, which retain many original features. This guest house is on the north side of the city and has lovely panoramic views of the Edinburgh skyline, including Edinburgh Castle and Arthur's Seat. The attractive bedrooms are well equipped and have excellent en-suite bathrooms.

✉ 256 Ferry Road, Goldenacre EH5 3AN ☎ 0131 552 3456 🖐 £60 🛈 15 🚌 1.5 miles (2km) north of city centre on A902

Left Edinburgh offers every type of accommodation, from luxury hotels to simple guest houses

MACDONALD HOLYROOD HOTEL
www.macdonaldhotels.co.uk
Air-conditioned bedrooms are comfortably furnished, and the Club floor also boasts full butler service and a private lounge. There is also a spa.
✉ Holyrood Road EH8 6AE ☎ 0844 879 9028 🖐 £113 🛈 156 🅿 Parallel to the Royal Mile, near Our Dynamic Earth

MALMAISON EDINBURGH
www.malmaison.com
The trendy Port of Leith is home to this stylish hotel. Inside, bold contemporary designs make for a striking effect. Bedrooms are comprehensively equipped with CD players, mini-bars and loads of individual touches. Ask for one of the stunning superior rooms for a really memorable stay. The smart brasserie and a café bar are popular with the local clientele.
✉ One Tower Place EH6 7DB ☎ 0131 468 5000 🖐 £99, excluding breakfast 🛈 100 🅿 A900 from city centre towards Leith at end of Leith Walk and through three lights; left into Tower Street. Hotel on right at end of road

MARRIOTT DALMAHOY HOTEL & COUNTRY CLUB
This imposing Georgian mansion offers two 18-hole golf courses (one championship) and a health and beauty club. Bedrooms are spacious and most have wonderful views. Public rooms offer both formal and informal drinking and dining options.
✉ Kirknewton EH27 8EB ☎ 0131 333 1845 🖐 £110 🛈 203 🅿 7 miles (11.3km) west of Edinburgh on A71

MERCURE POINT HOTEL
www.mercure.com
This stylish hotel is situated close to Edinburgh Castle and all the city centre shops. The contemporary rooms have WiFi access, while the Point restaurant has a daily changing menu of local produce. There is also a hotel bar.

THE HOWARD
www.thehoward.com
There are some suites and well-proportioned rooms in this quietly elegant hotel. The rooms have bathrooms with claw-foot baths and the elegant day rooms are decked out with chandeliers. The Atholl Dining Room contains hand-painted murals from the 1800s.
✉ 34 Great King Street EH3 6QH ☎ 0131 557 3500 🖐 Double from £165–£365 🛈 18 🅿 Travelling east on Queen Street take the 2nd left, Dundas Street. Continue through three sets of traffic lights, turn right and the hotel is on the left

THE INTERNATIONAL GUEST HOUSE
www.accomodation-edinburgh.com
Guests are assured of a warm and friendly welcome at this attractive Victorian terraced house situated to the south of the city centre. The smartly presented bedrooms are thoughtfully decorated, comfortably furnished and well equipped. Hearty Scottish breakfasts are served at individual tables in the traditionally styled dining room, which boasts a beautiful ornate ceiling.
✉ 37 Mayfield Gardens EH9 2BX ☎ 0131 667 2511 🖐 £60 🛈 9 🅿 On A701, 1.5 miles (2.5km) south of Princes Street

KEW HOUSE
www.kewhouse.com
Meticulously maintained, the attractive bedrooms at this Victorian hotel suit both business and tourist guests. The lounge offers a supper and snack menu.
✉ 1 Kew Terrace, Murrayfield EH12 5JE ☎ 0131 313 0700 🖐 £95 🛈 6 🅿 On A8 Glasgow road, 1 mile (1.6km) west of city centre

KILDONAN LODGE
www.kildonanlodgehotel.co.uk
This is a carefully restored Victorian house. Bedrooms are beautifully decorated and well appointed; some have four-poster beds. Dinner is served in the Fine Dining Restaurant, while pre-dinner drinks are available from the honesty bar in the lounge.
✉ 27 Craigmillar Park EH16 5PE ☎ 0131 667 2793 🖐 £78 🛈 12 🕐 Closed Christmas 🅿 From city bypass (A720) exit A701 to city centre. Continue for 2.75 miles (4.4km) to large roundabout, go straight on, hotel located six buildings along on right-hand side

THE LODGE
www.thelodgehotel.co.uk
This charming Georgian house is within easy walking distance of the city centre and is also on the main bus route. The bedrooms are beautifully decorated and presented. There is a comfortable lounge and a bar; evening meals are available by prior arrangement. No children under 14.
✉ 6 Hampton Terrace, West Coates EH12 5JD ☎ 0131 337 3682 🖐 £75 🛈 10 🅿 On the A8, 0.75 miles (1.2km) west of Princes Street

34 Bread Street EH3 9AF ☎ 0131 221 5555 ✋ £85; continental breakfast £10 ① 139

NORTON HOUSE HOTEL
www.handpicked.co.uk
This Victorian mansion is set in extensive grounds just 6 miles (10km) outside the city centre. It is convenient for the airport and is also close to sights such as the Forth rail bridge. Rooms in the original house are furnished in the style of a grand country house, while those in the newer extension have a more contemporary style. A sleek new spa has an 18m swimming pool, sauna and steam room.
✉ Ingliston EH28 8LX ☎ 0131 333 1275 or 0845 072 7468 ✋ £180 ① 83

OLD WAVERLEY HOTEL
www.oldwaverley.co.uk
Opposite Sir Walter Scott's famous monument on Princes Street, this hotel lies right in the heart of the city close to the station. The comfortable public rooms are all on first-floor level and along with front-facing bedrooms enjoy fine views.
✉ 43 Princes Street EH2 2BY ☎ 0131 556 4648 ✋ £90, excluding breakfast ① 85

🚌 In city centre, opposite Scott Monument, Waverley Station and Jenners store

PARKLANDS
A friendly, long-established guest house, south of the centre, on a main bus route. Comfortable bedrooms are well equipped, and hearty breakfasts are served.
✉ 20 Mayfield Gardens EH9 2BZ ☎ 0131 667 7184 ✋ £50 ① 6 🚌 1.5 miles (2km) south of Princes Street on A7/A701

PRESTONFIELD
www.prestonfield.com
A centuries-old landmark, this hotel has been restored and enhanced to provide comfortable and dramatically furnished bedrooms. There is a tapestry lounge and a whisky room. Meals are served in the Rhubarb restaurant (▷ 102).
✉ Priestfield Road EH16 5UT ☎ 0131 225 7800 ✋ £225 ① 23 🚌 Off A7, Priestfield Road is 200m (200 yards) beyond the Royal Commonwealth Pool

THE SCOTSMAN
www.thescotsmanhotel.co.uk
This architectural Victorian icon was previously the head office for *The Scotsman* newspaper. The building

has since been transformed into a state-of-the-art boutique hotel. Bedrooms vary in size and style. There are a number of luxurious suites. The North Bridge Brasserie offers an informal dining option. The leisure club has a unique stainless steel swimming pool.
✉ 20 North Bridge EH1 1YT ☎ 0131 556 5565 ✋ £200 ① 69 🚗 📺 🚌 A8 to city centre, left on to Charlotte Street. Right on to Queen Street, right at roundabout on to Leith Street. Keep straight on, left on to North Bridge, hotel on right

TEN HILL PLACE HOTEL
www.tenhillplace.com
This hotel, in a Georgian terrace, is a stylish new arrival on the Edinburgh hotel scene. It has contemporary, light airy rooms, with plasma screen TVs and WiFi. There is a range of allergy-free duvets and pillows available. Although there is no restaurant, there is a bar, and a bar snack menu. Breakfast is a buffet.
✉ 10 Hill Place EH8 9DS ☎ 0131 662 2080 ✋ £122 ① 78 🚌 Turn into Hill Place, opposite Festival Theatre. Hotel is at the end

Below *The Malmaison Edinburgh*

SOUTHERN SCOTLAND

From the English border in the south, to Scotland's two major cities of Edinburgh and Glasgow in the north, Southern Scotland is a gently scenic region of hills and valleys, of rivers and market towns. Just over the English border in the west is one of the best-known towns of all, Gretna Green, and west of here is the Solway Firth, and the regions of Dumfries and Galloway. It's a part of Scotland that's less varied than the Scottish Borders, but it's a delightful part of the country, boasting the beautiful Solway coast, and some fine walking in its deserted hills.

The Scottish Border region is busier and draws more visitors, with its thriving and attractive towns such as Melrose, Hawick, Galashiels, Jedburgh, Kelso and Peebles. North of the Borders in the Lothians stands one of Southern Scotland's best-known buildings, Rosslyn Chapel, even more famous now after featuring in Dan Brown's book and film, *The Da Vinci Code*.

North of Dumfries and Galloway lies Ayrshire, home of Scotland's national poet, Robert Burns. The cottage where he was born in Alloway, near Ayr, is a major draw and forms part of the Burns National Heritage Park. Across the Firth of Clyde from here is the most southerly of Scotland's main islands, the Isle of Arran. It has been called 'Scotland in miniature', as it's divided into the northerly Highlands and the southerly Lowlands by the same Highland Boundary Fault that splits the country. With its peaks, cliffs, wildlife and beaches, Arran is one of the loveliest places in Southern Scotland.

ABBOTSFORD

www.scottsabbotsford.co.uk
This overblown, turreted grey mansion is a must for an insight into the eclectic mind of the writer Sir Walter Scott (1771–1832), best known for epic romantic poems such as *The Lady of the Lake*, and novels including *Ivanhoe*, *Kenilworth* and *Redgauntlet*. Abbotsford was the home he built for himself in 1812 on the banks of the River Tweed, 2 miles (3km) west of Melrose, and it is filled with historical curiosities, some of which—like the condemned criminals' door from the old Tolbooth in Edinburgh (▷ 63)—are built into the fabric of the house. View his library, the gracious dining room with windows looking down to the river, and a bristling armoury, its walls covered with guns (including Rob Roy's) and other paraphernalia. There's even a collection of knick-knacks of the famous, including Rob Roy's purse, James IV's hunting bottle, a pocket book worked by Flora Macdonald, a cup which Bonnie Prince Charlie carried around with him, and many more. The overall effect is one of mock, almost theatrical antiquity—a distillation of his novels.
🚌 357 K11 🚏 Melrose TD6 9BQ
☎ 01896 752043 🕐 Mid-Mar to end Oct daily 9.30–5; also Mar–end May, Oct Sun 2–5 ✋ Adult £6.20, child £3.10, under 5 free. Garden only: adult £3, under 12 free
📷 ♿

BIGGAR

Equidistant from Glasgow and Edinburgh, the bustling Borders town of Biggar has retained its character, with a broad main street and wide central square surrounded by shops and tea rooms. The town's heritage is preserved in a range of interesting museums, well signed from the centre. These include Gladstone Court (Easter to mid-Oct Mon–Sat 11–4.30, Sun 2–4.30), off High Street, with its recreation of an indoor 'street' of shops, and the Greenhill Farmhouse Museum (Easter to mid-Oct Sat, Sun 2–4.30), linked to the 17th-century

persecution of the Covenanters (▷ 30–31).
🚌 356 H11 ℹ 115 High Street ML12 6DL, tel 01899 221066, seasonal

BURNS NATIONAL HERITAGE PARK

▷ 112–113.

CAERLAVEROCK CASTLE

www.historic-scotland.gov.uk
The remains of three huge round towers mark out the corners of this ruined, triangular castle of pink sandstone, once the fortress home of the Maxwell family. It is set close to the Solway shore some 8 miles (12.8km) southeast of Dumfries; two sides were protected by an arm of the sea, while the third had a moat, earthworks and a mighty gatehouse to ward off attack. The castle dates from the 13th century, and saw plenty of action before extensive rebuilding in the 15th. In the 1630s it was remodelled for more comfortable living, and an outstanding feature from this time is the ornately carved facade within.
🚌 359 H14 🚏 Glencaple, Dumfries DG1 4RU ☎ 01387 770244 🕐 Easter–end Sep daily 9.30–5.30; Oct–end Mar daily 9.30–4.30 💷 (HS) adult £5.20, child (5–16) £2.60, under 5 free 📷 ♿

CULZEAN CASTLE AND COUNTRY PARK

▷ 114.

DRUMLANRIG CASTLE, GARDENS AND COUNTRY PARK

www.drumlanrig.com
This imposing 17th-century mansion, 18 miles (29km) north of Dumfries, is one of several homes of the Duke of Buccleuch, one of the wealthiest landowners in Scotland. Four square towers guard the corners, each topped by little turrets that give this castle its unmistakable skyline; the famous view is the one up the straight avenue as you approach. Inside, admire the wooden panelling and carved oak staircase; the art collection is internationally famous.

Outside you can wander through the formal gardens, visit the plant centre, forge and even rent a bicycle to explore the grounds.
🚌 359 H12 🚏 Thornhill DG3 4AQ
☎ 01848 330248 🕐 Castle: Easter–end Aug daily 11–4. Gardens and country park: Easter–end Sep daily 12–5 ✋ Adult £7, child (3–16) £4, under 3 free, family £19. Park and gardens only, adult £4, child £3, family £10.50 📷 ♿

Opposite *Moated Caerlaverock Castle*
Below *Privately owned Drumlanrig Castle*

INFORMATION

www.burnsheritagepark.com

358 F12 ✉ Murdoch's Lone KA7 4PQ
☎ 01292 443700 ⓘ Museum: Apr–end
Sep daily 10–5.30; Oct–end Mar daily
10–5 👆 Adult £5, child £2.50, under 5
free, family £13 📖 £2 🍴 At museum
and Tam o' Shanter Experience
🏛 At museum and Tam o' Shanter
Experience

INTRODUCTION

Robert 'Rabbie' Burns (1759–96) is Scotland's most famous poet and
songwriter, his birthday (25 January) celebrated worldwide at haggis suppers.
He was born into poverty in a tiny cottage in Alloway. With the nearby museum
and other buildings in the park opposite, it is the focus of the Heritage Park.

Burns's weaknesses were many: Attempts at farming failed, and his loves
and illegitimate children were the stuff of legend—he married Jean Armour in
1788, but only via liaisons with Elizabeth Paton, Mary Campbell and others.
Yet his love of life, and celebration of humanity with all its foibles, was
extraordinary, and is why his poetry is still enjoyed. Burns's writings ranged
from shrewd and witty observations about everyday life and his beliefs in a
universal brotherhood, to the deeply romantic and the downright bawdy. Songs
like 'Ae Fond Kiss' and 'Auld Lang Syne' are integral to Scottish culture. Burns
died in Dumfries, where you can see his house (Apr–end Sep Mon–Sat 10–5,
Sun 2–5; Oct–end Mar Tue–Sat 10–1, 2–5; free) and visit his grave.

WHAT TO SEE

STATUE HOUSE

Tam o'Shanter is a ballad telling the story of drunken Tam, making his way
home on his mare, and spying on a party of witches. They chase him, and the
mare loses its tail in the flight (hence the naming of many Scottish waterfalls,
▷ 115). Sculptor James Thom created vivid statues that bring the ballad
characters to life. Now in the Statue House, they originally toured the country
to raise funds for a permanent memorial to Burns.

BURNS MONUMENT

The Burns cult sprang up quickly after he died, with public subscription funding the first stones of the Burns Monument in 1820. At the opposite end of the park, it is a venue for events, and there are views over his beloved Alloway from the roof. There's an audio-visual presentation at the Tam o' Shanter Experience, and you can see the stone bridge, the Auld Brig o' Doon, which featured in his poetry.

BURNS COTTAGE AND MUSEUM

The cottage where Burns was born on 25 January 1759 was built by his father, William Burnes, in 1757. His father also sometimes spelled the family name as Burness, and it was Robert and one of his brothers who later simplified it to Burns.

Robert was the first of seven children, and as the two-room cottage was also where the family's animals lived, it was soon a very crowded place. Burns lived here for the first seven years of his life, before the family moved to a larger house outside Alloway. The cottage was a simple building of clay and thatch, with whitewashed walls. Not surprisingy, it's been altered over the centuries, but its restoration does give a good impression of what it must have been like for the young Robert Burns growing up here. Models are used to show the family inside the simple interior,

The museum houses the finest collection of Burns manuscripts in the world, and at the time of printing it is hoped that the museum itself (which was built in 1900), will be renovated in time for the 250th anniversary of the birth of Burns, being celebrated in 2009.

Opposite *The Burns Memorial (right) dominates the Heritage Park*
Left *Burns' parents are buried at Alloway's Auld Kirk*
Below *The original manuscript of 'Auld Lang Syne'*

INFORMATION

www.culzeanexperience.org

🔢 358 F12 ✉ Maybole KA19 8LE
☎ 0844 493 2149 🕐 Castle:
Easter–end Oct daily 10.30–5; country
park: all year daily ✋ (NTS) Castle and
country park: adult £12, child (5–18) £8,
under 5 free, family £30. Park only: adult
£8, child £5, family £20 📖 Guidebook
£3.95 🍴 Home Farm Restaurant ☕ Old
Stables Coffee House 🏛 Country Park
shop and plant centre

CULZEAN CASTLE AND COUNTRY PARK

Culzean (pronounced 'Cullane') is the National Trust for Scotland's most popular property. That's partly thanks to the surrounding country park, 228 lush green hectares (563 acres) of wild gardens and leafy woodland riddled with trails. You can discover a walled garden, a herb garden, a deer park and lots of follies dotted around.

The golden stone castle, romantically set right at the edge of the cliffs, is handsome rather than beautiful, with its baronial towers and castellated roofline. It is reached via a bridge, and rises high above a terraced garden. Inside, it is an 18th-century show home, the masterpiece of Scottish architect Robert Adam, who worked on it from 1777 to 1792 for the powerful Kennedy family, who had dominated this part of Ayrshire since the 12th century.

Highlights include the graceful oval staircase and the circular Saloon, with lofty sea views to the craggy island of Ailsa Craig. The top floor was granted to General Eisenhower in 1945, for his lifetime, as a thanks from the people of Scotland for American help during World War II; there are photographs and mementoes of his visits, and for an exclusive thrill, you can even stay in the Eisenhower apartment. You can also see the original castle kitchens.

From the castle courtyard there are views across to the Isle of Arran, and the park has several miles of coastline with some remarkable and steep cliffs. Among the many highlights in the grounds are the walled gardens, which were designed both to provide food for the kitchens and to be an attractive place for guests and visitors to wander around. There are exotic birds in the aviary, an orangery and numerous outbuildings, follies and fountains. Here you'll also find the vinery in one of the greenhouses, which were built deliberately close to a heated wall in order to allow some quite exotic plants to grow.

Below *Terraced gardens on the south side of Culzean Castle*

GLEN TROOL
www.forestry.gov.uk

The Galloway Forest Park covers around 76,000ha (187,720 acres) of wild moorland and loch. While much of it is given over to commercial conifer forestry, Glen Trool remains an area of outstanding natural scenic beauty, with semi-ancient oak woodland that is seen at its best in the autumn.

From the visitor centre east of Glentrool village, walking and bicycling routes lead through the park, and the Southern Upland Way long distance path also passes nearby. Bruce's Stone, at the end of the road by the loch, commemorates a victory by Robert the Bruce against an English force in 1307 (▷ 128–129).

➕ 358 F13 ℹ️ Glentrool Visitor Centre, Newton Stewart, tel 01671 840302 or 0845 225 5121 🕐 Park: open access all year. Visitor centre: early Sep–late Oct, Easter–early Jul daily 10.30–4.30; early Jul–early Sep daily 10.30–5.30 🖥️

GRETNA GREEN

Gretna Green's fame rests on its location on the border, and its historical association with runaway lovers from England. Several sites claim to be the original location where, under Scottish law, marriages could simply be declared in front of witnesses—and that was that. You can pay a fee and relive a version of the ceremony at the World Famous Old Blacksmith's Shop Centre (Easter–end Jun, Sep daily 9–6; Oct, Nov daily 9–6), a fairly tacky tourist trap. Despite some attractive corners, Gretna itself is unlovely. It became a boom town during World War I, when a huge munitions factory was built here: The Devil's Porridge at nearby Eastriggs (mid-May to end Oct Mon–Sat 10–4, Sun 12–4) tells the story. The town has a designer outlet shopping complex.

➕ 359 J13 ✋ 14 ℹ️ The World Famous Old Blacksmith's Shop Centre DG16 5EA, tel 01461 338224; seasonal 🚂 Gretna Green

GREY MARE'S TAIL
www.nts.org.uk

A spectacular waterfall is the focus of an unexpected Highland scene in the Borders, just off the A708, 10 miles (16km) northeast of Moffat. The waterfall tumbles straight down for 61m (200ft), over the lip of a hanging valley, its source Loch Skene, invisible from below. Steep paths lead to the top of the falls (stout footwear essential), with a view of wild loch and upland scenery that makes the climb worthwhile. Peregrine falcons nest nearby; you can watch them in the visitor centre, via a live television link. If you'd like to venture farther, there's are guided walks on offer—check with the senior ranger or the tourist information office at Moffat.

➕ 359 J12 ✋ 13 ℹ️ Unit 1, Ladyknowe, Moffat DG10 9DY, tel 01683 220620 🕐 Visitor centre: Jun–end Aug Thu–Mon 11–5 🖥️ Free, donations requested 🖥️ ❓ For information about guided walks, tel 0844 493 2249

HADDINGTON

This handsome, businesslike market town is set in prime agricultural country on the River Tyne, 18 miles (29km) east of Edinburgh. It was granted the status of a royal burgh in the 12th century (the nearby port of Aberlady, now silted up, was its gateway to trade with continental Europe), and later became the county town for East Lothian. Protestant reformer John Knox was born here in c.1505. The original medieval town was laid out to a triangular street plan which can still be traced along High Street, Market Street and Hardgate. Painted in bright, warm colours, the 18th-century Georgian buildings of the High Street create a pleasing and harmonious facade. The graciously proportioned Town House was built by William Adam in 1748. St. Mary's Church dates from the 15th century.

➕ 357 K10 ℹ️ Quality Street, North Berwick EH39 4HJ, tel 01620 892197

Left *Haddington's 16th-century Nungate Bridge*
Below *The Grey Mare's Tail waterfall*

INFORMATION

www.ayrshire-arran.com

355 E11 The Pier, Brodick KA27 8AU, tel 01770 303774 Ferry from Ardrossan to Brodick or Claonaig to Lochranza (summer)

ISLE OF ARRAN

Often described as "Scotland in miniature', this scenically attractive island caught between the Ayrshire coast and the Kintyre Peninsula has been a popular holiday resort for generations of Clydesiders. The mountain of Goat Fell (874m/2,867ft) dominates the skyline to the north, and the opportunities for outdoor activities include walking, golf and horseback riding around the island. The red sandstone Brodick Castle (NTS, castle: Easter–end Oct daily 11–4; country park: all year daily 9.30–dusk) is the single biggest attraction, with its extensive collection of porcelain and silver, 19th-century sporting pictures and trophies, and wooded country park. Most of the present buildings date from the 19th century, when the castle was hugely expanded, but it has a history going back over 1,600 years and is the only island country park in Britain. The gardens include three national collections of rhododendrons, and some of these are usually in flower almost all year round. There are almost 16km (10 miles) of marked trails to explore in the grounds, with extensive woodland walks. If Brodick Castle seems familiar then that's because it appears on the reverse side of Scottish £20 notes. Today it belongs to the National Trust.

The town of Brodick is the main settlement on Arran, and is a pleasant holiday resort with a beautiful setting on a big sandy bay. Here you'll also find the Arran Heritage Museum, the Arran Visitor Centre and the Arran Brewery. The beers here have won many awards including 'Best Bottled Beer in Scotland' for their Arran Dark Ale and 'Best British Beer' for the Arran Blonde.

An interesting side trip from Arran is to the offshore Holy Island, which is now owned by a group of Tibetan Buddhists who have turned the lighthouse into a Peace Centre. They share the island with a number of longer-established residents: Eriskay ponies, Soay sheep and Saanen goats. The ponies are the last surviving animals from the breed that originally came from the island of Eriskay in the Hebrides.

Above *View of Goat Fell from Brodick*

HERMITAGE CASTLE

The dark sandstone walls of this lonely Border fortress loom high above the marshy ground beside the river known as Hermitage Water, 15 miles (24km) south of Hawick. The lack of windows indicates that this was never a homey castle, rather a grim place for fighting and foul deeds. The Douglas family took over a simple rectangular building in the 14th century and remodelled it to the massive and forbidding structure seen today. It's easy to imagine the wooden fighting platform which once ran around the outside, near the top of the walls. One owner was boiled alive for his crimes of murder and witchcraft, and another, who starved a rival to death in the dungeon, was murdered in a nearby wood. Mary, Queen of Scots, made a flying visit in 1566 on a gruelling 80-mile (129km) round trip to visit her lover Bothwell, who was lying wounded in the castle. It's a place steeped in atmosphere and history.

➕ 359 K13 ✉ Newcastleton TD9 0LU
☎ 01387 376222 🕐 Easter–end Sep daily 9.30–5.30 ♿ (HS) Adult £3.70, child (5–16) £1.85, under 5 free 📷

ISLE OF ARRAN

▷ opposite.

JEDBURGH

Jedburgh has witnessed many conflicts. In fact, so frequently was the town's castle attacked, rebuilt and attacked again that it was finally demolished in 1409. In its place is the former county jail, now Jedburgh Castle Jail and Museum (Easter–end Oct Mon–Sat 10–4.30, Sun 1–4).

The broken brown and red sandstone walls of ruined Jedburgh Abbey (HS, Apr–end Sep daily 9.30–5.30; rest of year 9.30–4.30) still dominate the town centre. This was one of the great medieval Border abbeys, and the shepherding skills of the monks were the basis on which the town's weaving industry and wealth grew.

Mary, Queen of Scots, stayed in a fortified, crow-step gabled house (Mar–end Nov Mon–Sat 10–4.30,

Sun 11–4.30) in 1566, famously leaving it briefly to visit her lover Bothwell, who lay wounded after a scrap at Hermitage Castle. You can see her death mask here.

➕ 357 K12 ℹ 13 LMurray's Green TD8 6BE, tel 0870 608 0404

JOHN MUIR COUNTRY PARK

www.eastlothian.org
John Muir (1838–1914) was a native of Dunbar, who emigrated in 1849 and became the founder of the National Parks system in the US. He is recalled by the 733ha (1,810-acre) country park that stretches along the coast to the west of Dunbar. The park offers walkers and birdwatchers a good variety of habitats, and all within easy reach of Edinburgh. The overall impression here is one of openness and space, a landscape of horizontals with long beaches and salt marsh, as well as cliffs and rocky shores, backed by woodlands. There's a splendid view of the Bass Rock, known for its huge gannet colony, from the rocky headland at the far west of the park.

➕ 357 K10 ℹ 143A High Street, Dunbar EH42 1ES, tel 01368 863353 🚉 Dunbar

KELSO

One of the most elegant of the Borders towns, Kelso has a wide cobbled square at its heart. A poignant fragment is all that remains of Kelso Abbey, once the largest of the Border abbeys, destroyed by the English in 1545. Nearby is the handsome five-arched bridge over the River Tweed built by John Rennie in 1803. From the parapet there is a fine view across to Floors Castle (Easter, May–end Oct daily 11–5). This is the largest inhabited house in Scotland, a monument to the wealth and privilege of the dukes of Roxburghe. It was started in 1721, and remodelled by William Playfair from 1837 to 1847. Fine art, tapestries and French furniture, porcelain and paintings are all on view.

➕ 357 K11 ℹ Town House, The Square TD5 7HF, tel 0870 608 0404

Top *Hermitage Castle, a Border fortress*
Above *The ruins of Kelso Abbey*

KIRKCUDBRIGHT

This pretty harbour town (the name is pronounced Kirkoobree) lies southwest of Castle Douglas on the road to nowhere, which is perhaps why it has retained so much character. The street plan is medieval, the gap-toothed castle ruin at its heart 16th-century, and its fame as a centre for painters dates from 1901, when artist and 'Glasgow Boy' E. A. Hornel (1864–1933) settled here, among others.

Broughton House, on the High Street, where he lived and worked, is now a gallery and museum (NTS, House and garden: Easter–end Jun, Sep–end Oct Thu–Mon 12–5; Jul–end Aug daily 12–5. Garden only: Feb to mid-Mar 11–4). It is said that local residents approached Hornel and his friends for their advice whenever their house frontages needed repainting—and this is the explanation for the harmonious shades seen in the High Street today. You can also see his Japanese garden here.

More paintings by Kirkcudbright artists, including Jessie M. King, S. J. Peploe and Charles Oppenheimer, can be seen in the Tolbooth Art Centre (Jun–end Sep Mon–Sat 11–5, also Sun 2–5). Other items, including book illustrations and pottery, are on show at the Stewartry Museum on St. Mary Street (open as Tolbooth). There is also a section on American naval hero John Paul Jones (1747–92) who was born near Kirkcudbright. He joined the Union navy and fought against the British during the American War of Independence. And for 21st-century art that you can buy, don't miss the tiny Harbour Cottage Gallery, down by the old harbour.

Nearby Kirkcudbright Wildlife Park has a wide collection of animals, including pygmy goats, wildcats and Arctic foxes.

🚌 358 G14 ⓘ Harbour Square DG6 4HY, tel 01557 330494

LOGAN BOTANIC GARDEN

www.rbge.org.uk

This frost-free corner of the Rhinns of Galloway, in the far southwest, serves as an annexe for tender plants from the Royal Botanic Garden in Edinburgh (▷ 80), and is a plant-lover's delight. Exotic species from the southern hemisphere thrive on the acid soil, including palm-like cordyline, trachycarpus and the ever-popular tree-ferns (Dicksonia). Feature plants include Himalayan poppies and South African proteas, and there are bright floral displays throughout summer in the walled garden. The rhododendrons and primulas of the woodland garden are perhaps more familiar to local gardeners.

🚌 358 E14 ✉ Port Logan, Stranraer DG9 9ND ☎ 01776 860231 🕐 Mar–end Oct daily 10–6; rest of year daily 10–5 👤 Adult £4, child (5–16) £1, family £9 🎧 Self-guiding audio tour. Free guided walks Apr–end Sep every second Tue 📷 🏛

MELLERSTAIN HOUSE

www.mellerstain.com

A superb 18th-century mansion northwest of Kelso, this great house is famous for its Adam architecture and elegant interiors, and is still the family home of the Earl of Haddington. Architect William Adam started work on the house in 1725. The large central block was completed in 1778 by his son Robert (1728–92), who went on to design the interior. The delicate plasterwork throughout—but especially in the music room, library and drawing room—is outstanding.

The Italian terraced gardens were designed in 1910 by Sir Reginald Blomfield. They stretch out at the rear of the house, leading down to a lake beyond from where there are wonderful views of the Cheviot Hills.

🚌 357 K11 ✉ Gordon TD3 6LG ☎ 01573 410225 🕐 Easter, May–end Jun, Sep Sun, Wed, Bank Holiday Mon; Jul–end Aug Sun, Mon, Wed, Thu; Oct Sun only. House: 12.30–5; grounds: 11.30–5.30 👤 House and garden: adult £6, under 16 free. Garden only: £3.50 📷 🏛

MELROSE

The Romans built a massive fort here, by a bridge over the River Tweed, and called it Trimontium after the three peaks of the nearby Eildon Hills. It was used to subdue the local tribe known as the Selgovae, who lived to the west. There's little left to see, but the Three Hills Roman Heritage Centre in the middle of this compact Borders town sets it all in context (Mar–end Oct daily 11.30–4.30).

The more visible history of Melrose dates from 1136, when David I founded the pink sandstone abbey, which lies just below the town centre (HS, Easter–end Sep daily 9.30–5.30; rest of year daily 9.30–4.30). Severely battered by the English in the 14th century, it was later rebuilt, and then robbed of its stones by the Douglases, who used them to build a house. Repairs in the 19th century were at the instigation of novelist Sir Walter Scott; the ruins are majestic, and the stone carving outstanding—take time to look upward to identify saints, dragons, flowers and a pig playing the bagpipes. The burial spot of Robert the Bruce's heart in the abbey is marked by an engraved inscription. The heart was known to have been embalmed and then buried at the Abbey, at Robert the Bruce's request, in a sealed casket. No one knew for sure where it was, but an excavation took place in 1921 and the casket, still sealed, was discovered by schoolchildren taking part in the search. The casket was not opened, but was further sealed and reburied in its present location. It's also said that King Arthur is buried in the Eildon Hills just outside Melrose.

Melrose is also well known to rugby fans, for the Melrose Sevens. The town is transformed during the second week of April each year when teams from all over the world arrive to compete in this tournament, which has been going since 1883.

Otherwise, it's a genteel town to explore, with delicatessens, an excellent bookshop, and Priorwood Gardens, dedicated to growing flowers which can be dried (NTS, Easter–end Dec Mon–Sat 10–5, Sun 1–5; shop all year).

INFORMATION

www.visitscottishborders.com

⊞ 357 K11 ⓘ Abbey House TD6 9LG, tel 0870 608 0404; seasonal

Opposite *View across the water to the harbour of Kirkcudbright*
Below *The Gothic buttresses and pinnacles of Melrose Abbey's roof*

REGIONS • SOUTHERN SCOTLAND • SIGHTS

MUSEUM OF FLIGHT

www.nms.ac.uk/flight

Lying 3 miles (5km) north of Haddington, this is Scotland's national collection of historic aircraft, with more than 50 aircraft offering everything from a Glasgow-built flying machine that inspired the Wright brothers, to the majestic Concorde-G-BOAA. A number of planes from the World War II era are also on display, including a Messerschmitt Komet and a Vickers Supermarine Spitfire. The museum site itself captures a fascinating picture of another age, with original hangars and other buildings forming the most complete record of a World War II airbase in Britain. It was also the site of the launch of the famous airship, R34, for the first ever east-to-west Atlantic crossing in 1919. Percy Pilcher's Hawk glider, built in 1896, is said to have inspired American aviation pioneers Orville and Wilbur Wright.

➕ 357 K10 ✉ East Fortune Airfield, East Fortune EH39 5LF ☎ 01620 897240 🕒 Apr–end Oct daily 10–5; Nov–end Mar Sat–Sun 10–4 💷 Adult £5.50, child under 12 free; additional charges for special exhibitions 🎫 ♿

MUSEUM OF LEAD MINING

www.leadminingmuseum.co.uk

Drive up to Wanlockhead, Scotland's highest village (468m/1,535ft) set amid the windswept, heathery domes of the Lowther Hills, and you arrive in a different world. A heritage trail from the visitor centre around the settlement shows you the workings of a community where generations of miners toiled to extract lead. You can wander into Straitsteps Cottages for a taste of family life here in 1740 and 1890, and discover the little lending library, founded in 1756 and thought to be the second-oldest in Europe. Best of all, you can follow a miner into the hillside, down the workings of an old lead mine, to see how the men really worked.

➕ 359 H12 ✉ Wanlockhead, by Biggar ML12 6UT ☎ 01659 74387 🕒 Mar–end Oct daily 11–4.30; Jul–end Aug daily 10–5 💷 Adult £6.25, child £4.50, family £19 🎫 ♿

NEW ABBEY

Sweetheart Abbey is a most romantic name, and indeed the picturesque ruins which dominate this unassuming little Galloway community, south of Dumfries, tell a sad tale of devotion. The Cistercian abbey (HS, Apr–end Sep daily 9.30–5.30; Oct–end Mar Sat–Wed 9.30–4.30) was founded in the 13th century by Devorgilla, Lady of Galloway and wife of John Balliol. After he died she carried his heart in a casket with her for the next 20 years, and then was buried with it before the high altar of the abbey church here.

Nearby New Abbey Corn Mill (HS, open as abbey) is an 18th-century water-powered mill for grinding oatmeal, preserved in full working order.

Shambellie House Museum of Costume (Easter–end Oct daily 10–5) is set in a mid-19th-century house, typical of its period. Rooms are brought to life by tableaux of clothed figures, covering different periods. The main location for the National Museum of Scotland's costume collection, the museum is a must for fashion enthusiasts.

➕ 359 H14 ♿ 64 Whitesands, Dumfries DG1 2RS, tel 01387 245555

NEW LANARK WORLD HERITAGE SITE

▷ opposite.

PEEBLES

The broad main street of this bustling Borders town, 35 miles (56km) south of Edinburgh, always seems busy, its small shops and family businesses (few high street multiples here) doing a brisk trade. Visitors come here to shop and enjoy the feel of a pleasant country town. Walks, trails and cycleways lead into the wooded countryside, starting with the gentle walk upstream from the park along the River Tweed to Neidpath Castle (Easter and May–end Sep Wed–Sat 10.30–5, Sun 12.30–5), a 14th-century tower set high above the river. (You can continue the walk past the castle and return on the other bank via a disused railway bridge.)

➕ 357 J11 ♿ High Street, Peebles EH45 8AG, tel 0870 608 0404

NEW LANARK WORLD HERITAGE SITE

Glasgow philanthropist David Dale (1739–1806) first developed a cotton manufacturing plant and settlement in this steep-sided valley in 1786, harnessing the power of the River Clyde as it roars over spectacular waterfalls. However, it is his son-in-law, the Welshman Robert Owen (1771–1858), who is most clearly identified with the village, which he purchased in 1799. A benevolent idealist and pioneer of social reform, over the next two decades he established a Utopian society here—a model community with improved conditions for the workers and their families, complete with school (it is claimed, with the first day nursery and playground in the world), institute for adult education and co-operative village store. The site later declined; in 1973 the New Lanark Conservation Trust started to restore the site, with the stunning results seen today.

The workers' houses are lived in once more, though the mill no longer manufactures cotton. Understand it through the curious Millennium Experience 'dark ride', complete with tableaux and sound effects. You can also explore a millworker's cottage, Owen's house and the school. A Roof Garden is now being created on top of Mill Number Two. You can even stay here, in the 3-star New Lanark Mill hotel or self-catering cottages.

Restoration work was carried out so well that in 2001 New Lanark was included on UNESCO's list of World Heritage Sites. It is one of only four in Scotland, the others being in Edinburgh, Orkney and St. Kilda.

The walk to the three waterfalls that lie upstream is recommended, particularly after rainfall when they are at their best. It was the existence of these waterfalls, known as the Falls of Clyde, and of the fast-flowing River Clyde, that brought David Dale here in the first place. The deep gorge was inaccessible before he saw the potential of the area, and the natural power that the water could provide. It's a testimony to his vision and energy that New Lanark existed at all, let alone that it has survived and helped to preserve the landscape in which it is set for over 200 years.

INFORMATION

www.newlanark.org

☩ 356 H11 ✉ New Lanark Mills, Lanark ML11 9DB ☎ 01555 661345 🕓 Visitor centre: daily 11–5; Jun–end Aug 10.30–5 💷 Adult £5.95, child £4.95, under 3 free, family £17.95–£21.95 🚆 Lanark (1 mile/1.6km) 🅿 £1.75 🍴 The Mill Pantry, open all day for snacks and lunches 🎁 Gift shop in Owen's Warehouse, also branch of the Edinburgh Woollen Mill

TIP

» The free leaflet 'Discover New Lanark World Heritage Site', available to download from the internet and from tourist information offices, includes a simple site map, which is invaluable for planning your exploration.

Opposite top left *The parish church of Peebles overlooks the River Tweed*
Opposite top right *The village of Wanlockhead has been a lead-mining town since Roman times*
Below *New Lanark provided improved living conditions for the millworkers*

INFORMATION
www.rosslynchapel.org.uk
✚ 357 J10 ✉ Roslin EH25 9PU
☎ 0131 440 2159 ⏰ Apr–end Sep
Mon–Sat 9.30–6, Sun noon–4.45;
Oct–end Mar closes 5 Mon–Sat 👐 Adult
£7.50, child (under 16) free 📷 🏛

Above *Rosslyn Chapel contains some of
the finest medieval carving in Scotland*
Below *The deeply carved Prentice Pillar*

ROSSLYN CHAPEL

In a mining village 6 miles (10km) south of Edinburgh, this is the most mysterious building in Scotland. A church was founded here in 1446 by William St. Clair, Third Earl of Orkney. It was to be a large cruciform structure, but only the choir was ever built, along with parts of the east transept walls. It is linked with the Knights Templar and other secretive societies, and believed by some to be the hiding place of the Holy Grail, a role publicized in Dan Brown's novel *The Da Vinci Code*. Inside is a riot of medieval stone carving. Every part of roof rib, arch, corbel and pillar is encrusted with decorative work—mouldings, foliage and figures of all kinds, including representations of Green Men, the Seven Deadly Sins and other religious themes.

It is from the chapel's crypt that the Holy Grail legend arose. The crypt has been sealed and inaccessible for many years, and this has naturally led to many stories and suppositions as to what it might contain. Some say it's sealed to prevent people discovering that it leads to an even larger underground vault, and this is where Rosslyn's secret really lies. It may be the Holy Grail, the Ark of the Covenant, a piece of the True Cross, or even the mummified head of Jesus Christ. It could hide the treasures of the Knights Templar, or Scotland's original crown jewels, preceding those that are now on show in Edinburgh Castle. It seems more likely that it contains the remains of some of the Barons of Rosslyn, buried in their full armour. Before the 2nd earl of Rosslyn died in 1837, he asked to be buried in the vault where his ancestors lay, but no one could find any signs of an entrance to the vault. Instead the Earl was buried in the Lady Chapel.

Look for the famous Prentice Pillar with its spiralling strands of foliage and winged serpents, necks intertwined, biting their own tails. It was carved by a young apprentice and, the story goes, when his master saw how beautiful it was he struck the lad in a jealous rage. The master is said to have hit the apprentice with a mallet, cutting his head and killing him. In the northwest corner of the chapel and set into the ceiling is the figure of a man with a cut forehead. This is said to be the apprentice, secretly commemorated, while on the opposite side of the chapel is another head—that of the murderer.

ST. ABB'S HEAD NATIONAL NATURE RESERVE
www.nts.org.uk

Seabirds nest in their thousands here. It's a wild and beautiful landscape at any time of year, with the spectacular cliffs of soft red sandstone, sculpted by wind and waves, reaching 100m (300ft) above sea-level. Fulmars, kittiwakes, guillemots, puffins and razorbills are the most prominent breeding species, and when they are in residence in late spring, the cliffs become an astonishing vertical city.

A circular walk to the lighthouse brings you past Mire Loch, where little grebes and tufted duck may be seen.

🕂 355 F11 ✉ St. Abbs, Eyemouth TD14 5QF ☎ 0844 493 2256 🕐 Open access all year. Visitor centre: Easter–end Oct daily 10–5 👋 Donations; parking £2 🖵

SCOTTISH MARITIME MUSEUM
www.scottishmaritimemuseum.org

Though much of Irvine is modern, the town has some interesting old buildings by the waterfront and one of these houses the Scottish Maritime Museum. As well as scale models there are a number of real boats to see—the *Spartan* (under restoration on the slipway) is a Clyde puffer (steamboat), which

plied its trade up and down the west coast connecting the remote communities; the Garnock is a tug, used on the Clyde. There are some fascinating displays about Scotland's seafaring past, many housed in the impressive Linthouse Engine Shop, a restored structure from the Alexander Stephens yard in Govan. Dubbed the 'cathedral to Scottish engineering', this is where some of Scottish shipbuilding's greatest products had their massive engines fitted. Also restored in the complex is a tenement apartment, now depicting life as it would have been experienced by a shipyard worker in the early part of the 20th century.

🕂 357 K10 ✉ Harbourside, Irvine KA12 8QE ☎ 01294 278283 🕐 Apr–end Oct daily 10–5 👋 Adult £3, child (5–16) £2, family £7 🖵 🏛

SCOTTISH SEABIRD CENTRE
www.seabird.org

Perched on the edge of the sea, the Seabird Centre is the key to the birdlife of the Firth of Forth, and in particular the famous gannet colony that inhabits the Bass Rock (Jan–end Oct). Interactive displays and wildlife films inform. Panoramic views to the islands are excellent—enjoy them from the café with its outdoor terrace, or follow the spring nesting

activity of puffins and other seabirds in close-up on a television link. In winter, fluffy white seal pups can be observed on the Isle of May, home to Britain's largest grey seal colony.

🕂 357 L10 ✉ The Harbour, North Berwick EH39 4SS ☎ 01620 890202 🕐 Apr–end Sep daily 10–6; Nov–end Jan Mon–Fri 10–4, Sat–Sun 10–5.30; Feb–end Mar, Oct Mon–Fri 10–5, Sat–Sun 10–5.30 👋 Adult £6.95, family £13.95–£21.95. Joint admission and train tickets available from Edinburgh 🚇 North Berwick 🖵 🏛

TANTALLON CASTLE
www.historic-scotland.gov.uk

Twenty days of blasting from King James V's cannons in 1528 could not destroy this mighty fortress, 3 miles (4.8km) east of North Berwick. Set high on a clifftop promontory, and protected by the sea on three sides, it was almost impregnable. From the 14th century grim Tantallon was the stronghold of the Red Douglases, Earls of Angus; it was wiped out in 1651, in the Civil War, by General Monk.

🕂 357 K10 ✉ Near North Berwick ☎ 01620 892727 🕐 Easter–end Sep daily 9.30–5.30; rest of year Sat–Wed 9.30–4.30 👋 (HS) adult £4.70, child (5–16) £2.35 🏛

Above *The ill-fated Lifeboat T.G.B. capsized in 1969 with the loss of eight crew*

THIRLESTANE CASTLE

www.thirlestanecastle.co.uk

Thirlestane is one of the most sumptuously decorated great houses in Scotland. A simple pink sandstone tower house just east of Lauder was transformed from 1670 to 1676 for the Duke of Lauderdale, Secretary of State, by architect William Bruce and master craftsman Robert Mylne. Curious semi-circular stair-towers punctuate the outer walls, but it is the plasterwork of the ceilings that is the remarkable feature, created by Dutch masters. Deep garlands of flowers are adorned with gilded highlights.
🚩 357 K11 ✉ Lauder TD∪ 6RU ☎ 01578 722430 ⚙ Easter, Jul–end Aug Sun–Thu; end Apr, Jun, Sep Wed, Thu, Sun 10–3 (last admission) ✋ Adult £7.50, child £5.50, under 5 free. Grounds only: adult £3, child £1.50 🅿

THREAVE GARDEN AND ESTATE

www.nts.org.uk

Threave is a teaching garden, where horticulturalists come to learn and try out new ideas. Glorious in its own right, it offers a mixture of established splendours such as a vast walled garden, alongside less formal, more experimental areas, early spring daffodils and herbaceous summer borders. Threave House dates from 1872.
🚩 359 G14 ✉ Castle Douglas DG7 1RX ☎ 0844 493 2245 ⚙ Garden and estate: all year daily. Visitor centre and countryside centre: Easter–end Oct daily 9.30–5.30;

Mar, Nov, Dec 10–4. House: Mar–end Oct Wed–Fri and Sun, 11–3.30 (guided tours only, admission by timed ticket) ✋ House and garden: adult £10, child £7, family £25; garden only: adult £6, child £5, family £15 🅿 🎫

VIKINGAR!

www.naleisure.co.uk

This lively centre tells of the Vikings in Scotland from the early invasions to final defeat at the Battle of Largs in 1263, using models, impressive audio-visual effects and actors. Take in the Homestead, with its Viking smells, and the Hall of the Gods. There's an entertaining film show with shouting and sword-clanging, then the Hall of Knowledge with replica carvings, information boards and touch-screen computer.
🚩 355 F11 ✉ Greenock Road, Largs KA30 8QL ☎ 01475 689777 ⚙ Vikingar! Experience: Apr–end Sep daily 10.30–5.30; Oct, Mar 10.30–3.30; Nov, Feb Sat, Sun 10.30–3.30; Dec, Jan closed ✋ Adult £4.70, child (5–16) £3.10, under 5 free, family £13 🚻 Largs 🅿 🎫

THE WHITHORN STORY

www.whithorn.com

It took an Act of Parliament in 1581 to stop the pilgrims from flocking to Whithorn. Royals and commoners were drawn to the shrine of St.

Top left Theave Castle and its garden
Above Wigtown is a book-lover's delight

Ninian, Scotland's first Christian missionary, who built a stone church here in AD397. He followed it with a priory, but the existing ruins are from a later, 12th-century construction. Excavations have turned up stone carvings and smaller, more personal treasures left by the pilgrims; ongoing archaeological work is uncovering the remains of a 5th-century village. The centre includes audio-visual presentations and access to the main sites.
🚩 358 F14 ✉ 45–47 George Street, Whithorn DG8 8NS ☎ 01988 500508 ⚙ Apr–end Oct daily 10.30–5 ✋ Adult £2.70, child £1.50, under 5 free, family £7.50 🅿 🎫

WIGTOWN

www.wigtownbookfestival.com

Wigtown is Scotland's Book Town. Nearly 20 specialist and antiquarian booksellers and many other related outlets offer a wide choice for literary browsers. An annual Book Festival takes place end Sep–early Oct, tel 01988 402036).
🚩 358 F14 ℹ Machars Information Office, 26 South Main Street DG8 9EH, tel 01988 402633

TRAQUAIR

An air of romance and ancient secrecy surrounds Traquair, a beautiful old castle buried in the trees 6 miles (9.7km) southeast of Peebles. It started out as a royal hunting lodge at the time of Alexander I of Scotland—its 'modern' extensions were made way back in the 17th century, and today it presents a serene, grey-harled face to visitors. Once the Tweed ran so close that the laird could fish from his windows. That changed when the river was re-routed by Sir William Stuart, who also built most of what we see now, in 1566.

Part of Traquair's sense of mystery comes from its connections with the doomed Stewart cause: Mary, Queen of Scots, stayed here in 1566 (her bed is now in the King's Room), and the famous wrought-iron Bear Gates have not been opened since 1745, when Bonnie Prince Charlie last rode through. The 5th earl vowed they would remain closed until another Stuart king was on the British throne. There are secret stairs to the hidden Priest's Room, and touching relics of a time when Catholics were persecuted in Scotland.

All of this history means that Traquair can declare itself the oldest continually inhabited house in Scotland, and another feature which must make it unique is that it claims after all these years not to be haunted.

Outside, features include attractive gardens with a maze. It's a sizeable puzzle and even if you were to go straight to the centre, it would involve a walk of about a quarter mile (0.4km). There is also the 1745 Cottage Restaurant, which serves excellent food and is well worth a visit.

An impressive modern venture has been the revival of a brewery at Traquair. Re-established in 1965, it has proved highly successful, and now produces three rich, dark ales which you can sample in the brewery shop.

INFORMATION

www.traquair.co.uk

✚ 357 J11 ✉ Innerleithen EH44 6PW
☎ 01896 830323 🕐 Easter, Jun–end Aug daily 10.30–5.00; Apr–end May, Sep daily 12–5; Oct, Nov daily 11–3
🏰 House and grounds: adult £6.50, child (5–16) £3.50, family £18. Grounds only: adult £5.80, child £2.80 📖 £3.75
🍴 Home-baking at the 1745 Cottage Restaurant in the Old Walled Garden 🎁

Below *This former fortified Border castle is now a stately mansion*
Bottom *Traquair's ancient library*

DRIVE

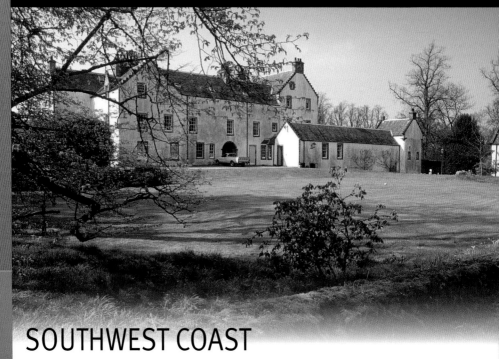

REGIONS SOUTHERN SCOTLAND • DRIVE

SOUTHWEST COAST

This scenic drive from the ancient city of Dumfries takes in some of the prettiest townships along the southwest coast, returning inland via the Galloway Forest Park.

THE DRIVE
Distance: 118 miles (193km)
Allow: 1–2 days
Start/end: Dumfries

★ Dumfries is worth exploring for its connections with Robert Burns (1759–96), who lies buried in St. Michael's kirkyard. Learn more at the Robert Burns Centre (Apr–end Sep daily 10–5.30; rest of year 10–5).

Leave Dumfries by the A710 (the Solway Coast road) and follow it south for 7 miles (11km) to New Abbey (▷ 120). Continue along the A710 beside the northern shore of the Solway Firth. After 19 miles (31km) reach Dalbeattie.

❶ The mudflats and salt marshes of the shallow Solway Firth are famous for their birdlife. Sandyhills Bay has a particularly good sandy beach.

❷ Dalbeattie is a quarrying town noted for its world-famous sparkling grey granite.

Leave the town via the A711, then turn right on to the A745. After 6 miles (10km) reach Castle Douglas.

❸ Castle Douglas is a pleasant old market town, with a broad high, and some interesting little shops to explore. The town's prosperity was built on a limey clay called marl, which was extracted from Carlingwark Loch for use as fertilizer.

❹ The National Trust for Scotland's Threave Garden (▷ 124) is on the outskirts.

Leave the town on the B736, and turn left when the A75 is met. Turn left at the A711 and follow this towards Kirkcudbright.

❺ Pass Tongland Hydroelectric Power Station, part of the Galloway Hydroelectric Scheme. Tongland Bridge lies downstream.

Reach Kirkcudbright (▷ 118). Leave by the A755 and turn left at the A75. Turn right at the B796 to reach Gatehouse of Fleet.

❻ Kirkcudbright was a planned spinning and weaving village.

Return along the B796 and turn right at the A75, passing Cardoness Castle on the right at the junction.

❼ Cardoness overlooks Fleet Bay and was a prominent 15th-century stronghold of the McCullochs.

Follow this road towards Creetown. After 8 miles (13km) turn right on to a road, signposted to Cairn Holy.

8 There are two ancient burial sites at Cairn Holy (free access) more than 3,000 years old. The main site, Cairn Holy I, is 52m (170ft) long. It has a pillared facade and two tombs which would originally have been covered by a huge mound of stones.

Return to the A75 and turn right. Leave the A75 on the right at the signposted road to Creetown.

9 The ruined tower house of Carsluith Castle is on the left before entering the town. Creetown's best attraction is the Gem Rock Museum (Easter–end Sep daily 9.30–5.30; Oct, Nov, Feb–Easter 10–4; Dec, Sat–Sun 10–4), with a fascinating collection of minerals, fossils and other exhibits from all over the world.

10 To the north of the town lies the lonely hill of Cairnsmore of Fleet (710m/2,331ft), a prominent landmark associated with Richard Hannay's flight in John Buchan's novel *The Thirty-nine Steps* (1915).

Rejoin the A75 and turn right. Turn right at the A712, and continue to

the artificial Clatteringshaws Loch and the Forest and Wildlife Centre.

11 The loch is part of the Galloway Forest Park, and surrounded by moorland and conifer plantations, home to herds of wild deer and wild goats. A memorial stone to Robert the Bruce (1274–1329) recalls a battle here in 1307, when the Scots soldiers outwitted their English foe by burying them in a landslide. This is also the start point of the Raiders' Road, a scenic forest track which follows an old cattle rustlers' route. It takes its name from a novel by S. R. Crockett (1860–1914).

Continue on the A712 for 6 miles (10km) to the quiet village of New Galloway, which stands above the 9-mile (15km) long Loch Ken. Leave by the A712, then turn left at the A713 to reach St. John's Town of Dalry.

12 Dalry has a main street of whitewashed houses. At the top stands an unusual stone seat, known as St. John the Baptist's Chair, and placed here by an acquaintance of Sir Walter Scott.

Above *The Neolithic chambered tomb, Cairn Holy I*
Opposite *Maxwelton House is still owned by the Laurie family*

The Southern Upland Way long-distance footpath passes through here on its long route from Portpatrick, on the west coast, to Cockburnspath on the east (▷ 334).

Leave the village via the A702, and follow this for 11 miles (18km) to Moniaive.

13 Moniaive is notable as the birthplace of the last Covenanter to be hanged, James Renwick, executed in 1688 at the age of 26. A monument to him stands at the edge of the village. Maxwelton House, to the east, dates from 1370 (private). It was the home of Annie Laurie, born in 1682, about whom a famous ballad was composed.

Continue on the A702, then turn right at the B729. Turn right at the A76 to return to Dumfries.

PLACE TO VISIT
THE NATIONAL TRUST FOR SCOTLAND'S THREAVE GARDEN
✉ Threave, Castle Douglas, Dumfries & Galloway DG7 1RX ☎ 0844 493 2245
🕐 Daily Thu–Sun 9.30–5, Fri 9.30–4.30
🖐 Adult £10, family £25

WHEN TO GO
Choose a fine, dry weekend as there are plenty of interesting places to explore on this tour.

GLEN TROOL—WHERE A BATTLE
MARKED THE ROAD TO INDEPENDENCE

Forest trails lead to the site of Robert the Bruce's turning point during the bitter Wars of Independence.

THE WALK

Distance: 5 miles (8km)
Allow: 2 hours
Start/end: Parking area at entrance to Caldons Campsite, Loch Trool
OS explorer 318 Galloway Forest Park
Grid reference NX 396791

★ Robert the Bruce's famous victory over the English forces at Bannockburn (▷ 28) in 1314 is regarded as the culmination of the Wars of Independence. But Bannockburn was not the end of the conflict—an earlier skirmish, when the two nations clashed at Glen Trool, was a far more important step on the road to independence.

Scotland was an independent country before these wars, but had been left without a monarch following the death of Alexander II in 1286. The Guardians of Scotland asked Edward I of England to adjudicate on the claimants to the succession. He agreed but used it as an excuse to re-assert his claim as overlord of Scotland, and the country was run by English officials.

Armed resistance to English occupation was led by Sir William Wallace, about whom little was known prior to his uprising. He was in turn appointed Guardian of Scotland by the nobility and then betrayed by them in 1305, taken to London and executed there.

Meanwhile Robert the Bruce was advancing his claim to the Scottish throne. He murdered his rival claimant, John, the Red Comyn, in Greyfriars church at Dumfries

and launched a series of attacks on the English in the southwest. He was crowned King of Scots at Scone on 25 March 1306 (▷ 200). Following a series of defeats, Bruce fled to Rathlin Island, off the coast of Antrim, Ireland, where he regrouped before returning to Scotland early in 1307.

After the attack on English forces in Galloway, an army was dispatched to capture him. But this wild part of Scotland was Bruce's home territory and he set up an ambush in Glen Trool that was successful. It marked the turning point in Bruce's fortunes and he went from here to further victories, culminating in the Battle of Bannockburn.

Edward I counterattacked between 1317 and 1319, seizing

Berwick on the Scottish–English border. In 1322 the Scottish nobility appealed to the Pope to support independence in the Declaration of Arbroath (▷ 29). Support was granted in 1324, and in 1328 England finally recognized Scotland as an independent nation in the Treaty of Edinburgh.

Leave the car park and follow the Southern Upland Way markers. Cross the bridge over the Water of Trool. Cross another bridge over the Caldons Burn. Take a left turn on to a footpath that runs along the banks of the river. Cross over a bridge.

Follow this trail and at a fork by a waymarker turn right, and then head uphill and into the forest.

Keep on the path uphill and through a clearing. Go through a kissing gate and re-enter the woodland. Continue along the southern side of Loch Trool until you reach an interpretation board near the loch end.

This marks the spot where Robert the Bruce and his army lured the superior English forces to a well-planned ambush and routed them. Using part of his force to lure the

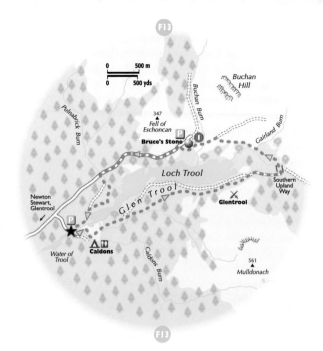

English on to the southern shores of Loch Trool, Bruce concealed the bulk of his men on the slopes above the loch. The English were forced to follow in single file, while the Scots blocked the path and hurled heavy boulders down on them.

Follow the path from here, leaving the woodland and heading downhill and to the left, before leaving the Southern Upland Way. Turn left, go through two gates and over a wooden bridge. Cross the bridge over Gairland Burn and continue. Eventually reaching the bridge over the Buchan Burn, cross over and take the path to the left, branching off uphill. Follow this to the top of the hill.

❶ At the top, Bruce's Stone was raised to commemorate the victory at the Battle of Glentrool, the first victory in the Independence Wars. From here, across the clear waters of the loch to the tree-clad hills opposite, is one of the finest views in Scotland.

Follow the track past the stone then turn left on to the narrow road. Head through the car park and keep going until you reach a marker on the left which leads to a forest trail, and take this to return to the start of the walk.

WHERE TO EAT
Eating places are few and far between but you'll find lots of suitable picnic spots on the walk, so come prepared.
 The nearest tea room is a few miles back on the road to Glen Trool at the Stroan Bridge visitor centre (tel 01671 840302). With friendly staff serving a variety of snacks, light meals and delicious hot soup, it's a popular place to stop.

PLACE TO VISIT
THE BLADNOCH DISTILLERY
✉ Bladnoch, Wigtown DG8 9AB ☎ 01988 402605

WHEN TO GO
A fine, dry day will give you the best walking conditions for this walk.

Opposite *The Galloway Forest Park at Glen Trool is owned by the Forestry Commission*
Left *Tumbling waters at Glen Trool, an area of outstanding natural beauty*

DRIVE

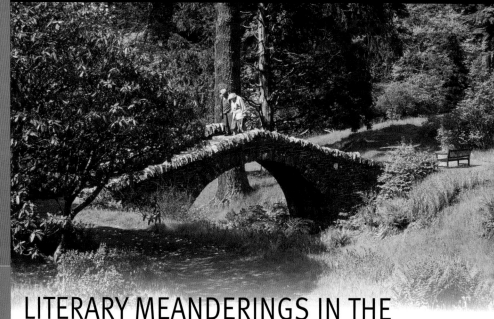

LITERARY MEANDERINGS IN THE BORDERS

This circular tour from Moffat takes in some of the loveliest landscapes of the Scottish Borders, chasing literary connections with novelists John Buchan (1875–1940) and Sir Walter Scott (1771–1832), and poets William Wordsworth (1770–1850) and James Hogg (1770–1835).

THE DRIVE

Distance: 120 miles (193km)
Allow: 1–2 days
Start/end: Moffat

★ Leave the attractive 17th-century spa village of Moffat by the A701, which follows the course of the Tweed Valley.

Turn right at the B712 to Dawyck Botanic Garden.

❶ This is an outpost of the Royal Botanic Garden, Edinburgh. Established over 300 years ago, it is noted for its trees, with spectacular autumnal displays from the magnificent beeches and maples (Apr–end Sep daily 10–6; Mar, Oct daily 10–5; Nov, Feb daily 10–4; closed Dec, Jan).

Return along the B712, turn right at the A701, and follow this to Broughton.

❷ In a converted church in Broughton, the John Buchan Centre (May to mid-Oct daily 2–5) details the history of the master storyteller whose best-known novel is *The Thirty-nine Steps*. Buchan also wrote notable biographies of Sir Walter Scott and the Marquis of Montrose. He took the title Lord Tweedsmuir when he became Governor-General of Canada in 1935. Don't miss Broughton Gallery, set in a fairy-tale castle up the hill.

Continue on the A701 and turn right at the A72. Turn left at the A721 and right at the A702. Follow this into the narrow streets of West Linton.

❸ In the 17th century West Linton became famous for its stonemasons, who were the chief gravestone carvers in the area. Gifford's Stone, a well-worn bas relief on a wall in the main street, is by James Gifford. Opposite it is another of his works, the Lady Gifford Well, which was carved in 1666. The Cauld Stane Slap, an ancient drove road across the Pentland Hills, passes nearby.

Leave the village by the B7059. Turn right at the A701 and left at the B7059. Turn left at the A72 for Peebles.

❹ Pass the solid tower of Neidpath Castle on the right, above the River Tweed, as you enter the town of Peebles (▷ 120).

Leave the town on the A72, passing the Kailzie Gardens. After 6 miles (10km) reach Innerleithen.

❺ This is the oldest spa in Scotland. It boomed in the 19th century when Sir Walter Scott named one of his novels, *St. Ronan's Well* (1823), after the mineral wells in the town. In the High Street, Robert Smail's Printing Works is a tiny print shop started in 1840 (NTS, Easter–end Oct Thu–Mon 12–5, Sun 1–5). Historic Traquair House (▷ 125) lies just over 1 mile (2km) to the south.

Stay on the A72 for 12 miles (19km) to reach Galashiels.

❻ Galashiels is famous for its weaving. The story of the mills and the process of tartan manufacture is told in the Lochcarron of Scotland Cashmere Wool Visitor Centre (Mon–Sat 9–5, Sun 11–4). Look for Old Gala House, founded around 1583. The nearby mercat (market) cross, which marks the centre of the old town, dates from 1695. It features in the Braw Lads Gathering, an annual festival dating from 1599,

during which the boundaries of the town are confirmed by being ridden on horseback.

Leave by the A7, signposted to Selkirk. Turn right at the B7060, then left at the A707 at Yair Bridge. Continue on this road, which becomes the A708 near Selkirk. Follow Ettrick Water and then Yarrow Water on the A708 to Yarrowford, a distance of 13 miles (21km).

❼ This scattered village on the Yarrow Water river inspired William Wordsworth to compose no fewer than three poems in its praise. The former 1423 royal hunting lodge of Newark Tower lies downstream.

❽ The ruins of Foulshiels House, birthplace of explorer Mungo Park (1771–1806), who died in his search for the source of the River Niger in Africa (▷ 132–133), lie this way. Bowhill House is a 19th-century mansion with a good collection of paintings, surrounded by a country park (house: Jul daily 11–5; park: mid-Apr to end Jun Sat–Sun 10–5; Jul– end Aug daily 10–5).

Above *Broughton Gallery is in a mansion designed in 1937 by Sir Basil Spence*
Opposite *Dawyck Botanic Garden*

Continue on the A708, passing along the northwestern shore of St. Mary's Loch.

❾ At around 3 miles (5km) long, this is one of the best places in southern Scotland for sailing. At the southern end of the loch, on a spit of land which separates it from the smaller Loch of the Lowes, a red sandstone monument recalls local poet James Hogg, known as the Ettrick Shepherd, who spent many an evening in the nearby Tibbie Shiels Inn with his friend Sir Walter Scott.

Continue on the A708 for 9 miles (15km) and follow signs to the parking at the Grey Mare's Tail waterfall (▷ 115). Continue on the A708 for 10 miles (16km) to return to Moffat.

PLACE TO VISIT
DAWYCK BOTANIC GARDEN
✉ Stobo EH45 9JU ☎ 01721 760254
🕐 Apr–end Sep daily 10–6; Mar, Oct 10–5; rest of year 10–4 💷 Adult £3.30, child £1, family £8

WHEN TO GO
A fine day or two in autumn or spring day will give you the perfect conditions to enjoy the many delights of this car tour.

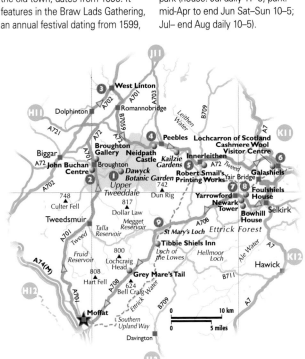

FROM SELKIRK TO THE WILDS OF AFRICA

A gentle walk by Ettrick Water, laced with memories of the great explorer Mungo Park (1771–1806).

THE WALK
Distance: 3 miles (4.8km)
Allow: 1 hour 40 min
Start/end: West Port Car Park, Selkirk

★ It is hard to imagine that the sleepy town of Selkirk has any connection with the wilds of Africa. But look carefully at the statue in the High Street and you'll see that it commemorates Mungo Park, the noted surgeon and explorer, who was born nearby at Foulshiels.

From Park's statue in the High Street walk to the Market Place, go right down Ettrick Terrace, left at the church, then sharp right down Forest Road. Follow this downhill, cutting off the corners using the steps, after No. 109, to Mill Street. Go right, then left on to Buccleuch Road. Turn right following the signs for the riverside walk and walk across Victoria Park to join a tarmac track.

❶ Park was educated at Selkirk Grammar School, trained as a doctor and then took a post as surgeon's mate on a ship bound for the East Indies. He returned from the voyage and promptly set off again, this time heading for Africa to map the River Niger. Park's journey lasted more than two and a half years. When Park returned to Scotland he published an account of his explorations, *Travels in the Interior Districts of Africa* (1799), which became a bestseller. He disappeared during a second expedition in 1806. Tragedy struck when his son followed in his footsteps some 20 years later, and also disappeared without trace.

Turn left, walk by the river, then join the road and turn right to cross the bridge. Turn left along Ettrickhaugh Road, passing a row of cottages on your left. Just past them turn left, cross a tiny footbridge, then turn left down some steps and follow the path to the riverbank and turn right.

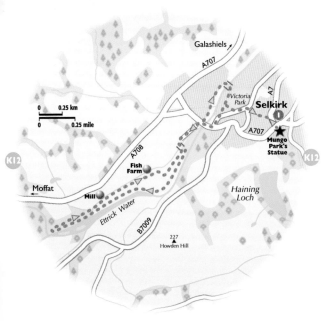

Galashiels

A707

Victoria Park

Selkirk

A7

A707

Mungo Park's Statue

A708

Fish Farm

K12

Moffat

Mill

Ettrick Water

Haining Loch

B7009

227 Howden Hill

K12

0   0.25 km
0   0.25 mile

left. Where the path splits, take the track on the left to follow a straight, concrete path beside the water to reach an abandoned fish farm; you may smell it before you see it.

Walk around the buildings, then bear left to continue following the mill lade. Go left over the footbridge, then right, passing the cottages again. At the main road go right to reach the bridge. Don't cross the bridge but join the footpath on the left.

Follow this footpath as it goes past a sports ground, then skirts a housing estate. Continue walking until you reach the pedestrian footbridge on your right-hand side, where you cross over the river, bear right, then retrace your footsteps back over Victoria Park and uphill to the Market Place at the start of the walk.

WHERE TO EAT

There are several places to try in the centre of Selkirk. Among the hotels offering bar meals is the Cross Keys by the Market Place (tel 01750 20121), which serves toasted sandwiches and light snacks. There's also a small tea room. Look out for the famous Selkirk bannock on sale in the town bakeries.

PLACE TO VISIT
SIR WALTER SCOTT'S COURTROOM
✉ Market Place, Selkirk TD7 4BT
☎ 01750 20761 🕒 Easter–end Sep
Mon–Sat 10–4; Jun–end Aug Sun 10–2;
Oct Mon–Sat 1–4 ♿ Free

WHEN TO VISIT
In spring and summer the waterside route are sprinkled with wild flowers.

Follow the path along the river margin; it's eroded in places so watch your feet. Eventually join a wider track and bear left. Follow this to reach a weir (small dam) and a salmon ladder. Turn right to cross the tiny bridge. Immediately after this go left and continue walking alongside the river until you reach a point at which Yarrow Water joins the Ettrick Water. Retrace your steps for about

90m (100 yards), then turn left at a crossing of tracks.

Your route now takes you through the woods, until you cross over the little bridge by the weir again. Take the footpath to the left and follow the cinder/gravel track around the meadow to the mill buildings. Bear right (but don't cross the bridge) and continue, walking with the mill lade (small canal) on your

Opposite *Sir Walter Scott was a sheriff of Selkirk; his statue stands in the town square*
Left *A baronial tower adds distinctive Scottish character to an old house in Selkirk*

ANNAN
LONSDALE CINEMA
www.lonsdalecitycinemas.co.uk
Mainstream cinema with twin screens, reasonably priced, in the centre of Annan. Shows mostly popular movies, but also some independent films. Snacks available. Free parking.
✉ Moat Road ☎ 01461 206901 ◎ Daily, with screenings nightly and afternoon matinees at weekends and school holidays

WESTLANDS ACTIVITIES
www.westlands-activities.co.uk
Go-carting, quad biking and paintballing are top of the list at this activity centre, which is located 4 miles (6.4km) east of Annan. Try a

cross-country ride, with guide, on a quad bike (older children only), have a go on the go-carts for adults and children, and enjoy the mayhem of paintballing. Equipment and clothing are all supplied. Trout fishing and clay pigeon shooting are also available.
✉ Westlands, Near Hollee ☎ 01461 800274 ◎ Daily 9–5 ✋ Paintball from £3; go-carts from £6; quad bikes from £5

ARRAN (ISLE OF)
ARRAN AROMATICS
www.arranaromatics.com
Natural bath and beauty products are handmade on the farm, signposted from Brodick Pier. As well as the Arran Aromatics shop, there is a gift shop on site.

✉ The Home Farm, Brodick KA27 8DD ☎ 01770 302595 ◎ Mon–Sat 9–5.30

ISLE OF ARRAN BREWERY COMPANY
www.arranbrewery.com
If beer is your tipple, come and see it being brewed at Cladach, near Brodick. The entry fee includes a taste of the beer.
✉ Cladach, Brodick KA27 8DE ☎ 01770 302353 ◎ Easter–end Oct Mon–Sat 10–5, Sun 12.30–5. Closed Tue, Sun in winter
✋ £2 🏛

ISLE OF ARRAN DISTILLERS
www.arranwhisky.com
The distillery in the north of the island produces Arran's own single

malt whisky. Take the guided tour, enjoy the exhibition and buy a gift or bottle of Arran whisky in the shop. Tours include a taste of the whisky.
✉ Distillery and Visitor Centre, Lochranza KA27 8HJ ☎ 01770 830264 🕐 Mid-Mar to end Oct daily 10-6; Nov to mid-Mar check ahead ♿ Adult £4, child £2.50, under 12 free 🍴 Restaurant serves good local food, Italian coffee and home baking 🎁

AYR
GAIETY THEATRE
www.gaietytheatre.co.uk
This busy venue in the heart of Ayr hosts a wide variety of touring productions throughout the year, including comedy, jazz, drama, pop and ballet.
✉ Carrick Street KA7 1NU ☎ 01292 611222 🕐 Box office Mon–Sat 10–5 ♿ From £8 ☕ Popplewell's café bar Mon–Sat 9.30–4

HOURSTON'S
www.hourstons.co.uk
You can't miss the window displays for this large independent department store on Alloway Street, at the top of the High Street. Hourston's sells fashion, accessories, household goods, china, glass and gifts including china by Royal Doulton and glassware by Edinburgh Crystal.
✉ 22–30 Alloway Street KA7 1SH ☎ 01292 267811 🕐 Mon–Fri 9.30–5.30, Sat 9–5.30, Sun 12–4.30 🍴 Restaurant on the top floor serves soup, sandwiches, teas and hot meals

ODEON
www.odeon.co.uk
This cinema, showing mainstream movies, is found at the top of the town, opposite the train station.
✉ 10 Burns Statue Square KA7 1UP ☎ 0871 224 4007 🕐 Daily from 12.30 ♿ From £5

TAM O'SHANTER INN
Small traditional pub with a thatched roof, dating back to 1749, on the main street of Ayr. The snug interior has a log fire and Burns poetry painted directly on to the walls.
✉ 230 High Street KA7 1RQ ☎ 01292

611684 🕐 Daily 10am–12.30am. Food daily 10–8

BIGGAR
ATKINSON-PRYCE BOOKS
A small shop front at the bottom of the High Street conceals this charming bookshop, tightly packed with goodies. It has a particularly wide range of Scottish titles including travel, poetry and literature. There's also a good selection of children's books, and classical and folk CDs. Gift wrapping service and popular second-hand section.
✉ 27 High Street ML12 6DA ☎ 01899 221225 🕐 Mon–Sat 9.30–5

PURVES WORLD OF PUPPETS
www.purvespuppets.com
This puppet theatre troupe has been going for over 35 years, and tours the world. Catch them at the puppet theatre in Biggar (clearly signposted from the main road), which has weekly shows for all the family and backstage tours. The whole attraction is designed to delight children. Check locally for show dates and times; book in advance.
✉ Puppet Tree House, Broughton Road ML12 6HA ☎ 01899 220631 🕐 Tue–Sat 10–4.30 ♿ Backstage tour £3, show £7, museum £3 ☕

BLADNOCH
BLADNOCH DISTILLERY AND VISITOR CENTRE
www.bladnoch.co.uk
Scotland's most southerly distillery, lying 2 miles (3.2km) south of Wigtown, dates from 1817. Enjoy a guided tour, see a video of how the whisky is produced and then taste a dram yourself. There's a picnic area, and nearby Cotland Wood has rare orchids and is a pleasant place for a walk.
✉ DG8 9AB ☎ 01988 402605 ♿ Adult £3 (under 18 free) 🎁 Gift shop Mon–Fri 9–5; also Jul, Aug Sat 11–5, Sun 12–5

BROUGHTON
BROUGHTON GALLERY
www.broughtongallery.co.uk
High-quality paintings, etchings and crafts are displayed in the superb

setting of a Border castle, reached via a steep private road. Includes work by local and British artists.
✉ Broughton Place ML12 6HJ ☎ 01899 830234 🕐 Apr–end Sep, mid-Nov to Christmas Thu–Sun 11–5

CAERLAVEROCK
CAERLAVEROCK WILDFOWL AND WETLANDS TRUST CENTRE
www.wwt.org.uk
This 560ha (1,400-acre) nature reserve is off the B725, 9 miles (14km) southeast of Dumfries. In autumn, winter and spring, thousands of wild geese and other birds can be seen from observation towers. In summer, wander along the nature trails or join one of the free wildlife safaris, at 11 and 2.
✉ East Park Farm DG1 4RS ☎ 01387 770200 🕐 Daily 10–5 ♿ Adult £5.39, child (5–12) £2.68, family £14.50 ☕ Small tea room

CASTLE DOUGLAS
CLOG AND SHOE WORKSHOP
www.clogandshoe.co.uk
Shoes and clogs are made at this unusual workshop, 13 miles (21km) north of Castle Douglas. In the showroom, admire the small museum collection of footwear from around the world. Shoes can be made to order.
✉ Balmaclellan DG7 3QE ☎ 01644 420465 🕐 Easter–end Oct Mon–Fri 10–5

DESIGNS GALLERY & CAFÉ
www.designsgallery.co.uk
This crafts shop and gallery on the main street of Castle Douglas specializes in contemporary art and design led crafts, and is well worth seeking out for the top quality designer jewellery, ceramics, sculpture, glass and paintings. There's also an excellent café downstairs, with conservatory and walled garden.
✉ 179 King Street DG7 1DZ ☎ 01556 504552 🕐 Mon–Sat 9.30–5.30

LOCHSIDE THEATRE
www.lochsidetheatre.co.uk
Local volunteers staff this theatre in a converted church. It's home to the

Above The historic Globe Inn is one of Dumfries' finest

Lochside Theatre Company and a venue for touring productions.
✉ Lochside Road DG7 1EU ☎ 01556 504506 🕐 All year; box office Mon, Wed, Fri–Sat 12–2 🖐 From £4

SULWATH BREWERY
www.sulwathbrewers.co.uk
Six beers are brewed in this small, family-run micro-brewery. Sample the product on a guided tour.
✉ 209 King Street DG7 1DT ☎ 01556 504525 🕐 Mon–Sat 10–4 🖐 Guided tour £3.50. Cost includes a pint of beer or, if you're driving, a bottle to take away. Tours start at 1pm

DALTON
DALTON POTTERY ART CAFÉ
www.daltonpottery.co.uk
See the clocks, vases, napkin rings and cat-and-fish-themed ceramics being made at this working pottery and café, or make your own. Fun, safe activity for children as young as four. Signposted from Carrutherstown, off the A75.
✉ Meikle Dyke, Dalton DG11 1DU ☎ 01387 840236 🕐 Easter–end Oct daily 10–5; rest of year Tue–Sun 10–5 🖐 From £3 to paint a pot 🍴 Daily 10–5; serves home baking, including children's meals 🏧 Daily 10–5

DRUMMORE
MULL OF GALLOWAY
www.mull-of-galloway.co.uk
This nature reserve, famous for its seabirds, is 22 miles (35.4km) south of Stranraer. Enjoy a circular walk around the reserve. There's usually a warden on hand to answer your questions.
✉ Visitor Centre, near Drummore ☎ 01776 830682 🕐 Apr–end Oct daily 10–4 🖐 Free

DUMFRIES
THE GLOBE INN
www.globeinndumfries.co.uk
This 400-year-old pub is an absolute must if you are in Dumfries, even if it is just to have a look at the place that was Robert Burns's local. It's full of character, with little oak-panelled rooms and crooked door lintels. The poet's favourite room is preserved as it was in the 1730s, and you can see his chair by the fire. You'll find the pub down an alley near the foot of the High Street. It serves home cooking, real ale and lots of malt whiskies.
✉ 56 High Street DG1 2JA ☎ 01387 252335 🕐 Mon–Wed 10am-11pm, Thu–Sun 10am–midnight. Food daily 12–3

GRACEFIELD ARTS CENTRE
www.web-link.co.uk/gracefield
A 10-minute walk from the centre of town, the arts centre offers a changing series of contemporary visual art and craft exhibitions and activities. There is also a permanent collection of Scottish paintings, which are shown at different times throughout the year.
✉ 28 Edinburgh Road DG1 1NW ☎ 01387 262084 🕐 Tue–Sat 10–5 🖐 Most exhibitions free 🍴 Café serves light lunches and home baking 🏧 Shop (Tue–Fri 11–3, Sat 10–3) sells locally made crafts, jewellery, cards and postcards

ODEON
www.odeon.co.uk
A single-screen cinema showing mainstream films. Found in the town centre, near the Theatre Royal. Snacks available.
✉ Shakespeare Street DG1 2JJ ☎ 0871 224 4007 🕐 Daily 🖐 Adult £5.40

ROBERT BURNS FILM THEATRE
www.rbcft.co.uk
This single-screen cinema is in the Robert Burns Centre. It shows mainstream, foreign and art-house films.
✉ Robert Burns Centre, Mill Road DG2 7BE ☎ 01387 264808 🕐 Tue–Sat. Often evening screenings only, so check beforehand 🖐 £4.70 🍴 Hullabaloo Restaurant upstairs, Mon–Sat 11–4, 6–10 (not Mon eve), Sun 11–3

THEATRE ROYAL
www.theatreroyaldumfries.co.uk
The Theatre Royal is Scotland's oldest working theatre. In the town centre, it offers plays and pantomimes performed by the theatre's resident amateur Guild of Players, and touring productions of music and drama, including Scottish Opera.
✉ Shakespeare Street DG1 2JH ☎ 01387 254209 🕐 All year 🖐 From £6 ♿

GATEHOUSE OF FLEET
CREAM O'GALLOWAY VISITOR CENTRE
www.creamogalloway.co.uk
Watch ice cream being made at this organic farm dairy, in a converted 17th-century farmstead, then choose your favourite in the shop. There are nature trails through the surrounding woodland, a dry-stone dyking exhibition and playground. From the A75, take the road to Sandgreen; after 7.5 miles (12.4km), turn left at the sign for Carrick.
✉ Dairy Co Ltd, Rainton, Gatehouse of Fleet, Castle Douglas DG7 2DR ☎ 01557 814040 🕐 Mid-Mar to end Oct daily 10–5 🖐 Free; charge for playground 🍴 🏧

MILL ON THE FLEET VISITOR CENTRE
www.millonthefleet.co.uk
At the top end of Gatehouse of Fleet, this beautifully converted 18th-century mill has two working watermills and is now a visitor centre incorporating a café, bookshop, craft shop, art gallery and wildlife exhibition. It is in grounds with picnic tables and wooden sculptures.

✉ High Street DG7 2HS ☎ 01557 814099
◉ Easter–end Oct daily 10–5 ☕ Café on a veranda overlooking the river 📖 Bookshop sells new and second-hand titles

GRETNA
GRETNA GATEWAY OUTLET VILLAGE
www.gretnagateway.com
This shopping complex in Gretna itself has a pedestrianized street with designer outlet stores on either side. Permanent discounts in stores such as Polo Ralph Lauren, Reebok, Van Heusen and Marks & Spencer.
✉ Glasgow Road DG16 5GG ☎ 01461 339100 ◉ Daily 10–6 ☕ Café Vienna and Café Thorntons for tea, coffee and light lunches

THE WORLD FAMOUS OLD BLACKSMITH'S SHOP CENTRE
www.gretnagreen.com
Although Gretna Green has a romantic history, there's nothing romantic about the rampant commercialism that exists in this low, whitewashed complex today. Shops sell knitwear, Scottish food, whisky, golf wear, china, jewellery and wood carvings. Quality varies from excellent (Johnston's of Elgin cashmere and Wedgwood china) to poor (plastic, kilted dolls). There's tax-free shopping for visitors from outside the European Union (EU), and post-it-home service for UK and overseas.
✉ Gretna Green DG16 5EA ☎ 01461 338224 ◉ Daily from 9am, all year ☕ Large café sells snacks and lunches

JEDBURGH
HARESTANES COUNTRYSIDE VISITOR CENTRE
www.scotborders.gov.uk/harestanes
Just 3 miles (4.8km) north of Jedburgh, Harestanes Countryside Visitor Centre offers beautiful woodland walks, an outdoor play area and exhibitions. Adjacent craft workshops selling leather goods, tiles and wooden objects may operate different opening hours. There are also various activities for children.
✉ Ancrum, Jedburgh TD8 6UQ ☎ 01835 830306 ◉ 1 Apr or Easter (if earlier)–end Oct daily 10–5 💷 Free ☕ Tea room serves home baking, light lunches and local ice cream in a relaxed, child-friendly atmosphere

JEDFOREST DEER AND FARM PARK
www.aboutscotland.com/jedforest
Birds of prey and deer are to be found on this working farm, 5 miles (8km) south of Jedburgh. Eagles, owls and hawks display daily. Look for ranger-led activities and talks on farming and the environment. For children there are indoor and outdoor play areas and special activities. Picnic and barbecue area.
✉ Camptown, Jedburgh TD8 6PL ☎ 01835 840364 ◉ May–end Aug daily 10–5.30; Sep–end Oct daily 11–4.30 💷 Adult £4.50, child £2.50, under 5 free ☕ 📖

R & M TURNER
A huge antiques shop behind a traditional facade on the main street of Jedburgh, this is an Aladdin's cave filled with old silver, furniture, pictures, thimbles and china, spread over three floors. They can arrange for your purchases to be sent overseas.
✉ 34–36 High Street TD8 6AG ☎ 01835 863445 ◉ Tue–Fri 9.30–5, Sat 10–4

KELSO
BORDER GALLERY
This little art gallery just off the main square sells affordable modern oil paintings, watercolours, glass, jewellery, sculptures and textiles.
✉ 6 Bowmont Street TD5 7JH ☎ 01573 226002 ◉ Mon, Tue, Thu, Fri 10–5, Wed 10–12.30, Sat 10–4

THE HORSESHOE GALLERY
www.scottishbordersartsandcrafts.co.uk
The historic oil and watercolour paintings on offer are reasonably priced, along with sporting prints and etchings, teddy bears and a variety of other gifts.
✉ 22 Horsemarket TD5 7HD ☎ 01573 224542 ◉ Mon–Sat 10–5

SPRINGWOOD PARK
www.buas.org
This 16ha (40-acre) park, close to Kelso town centre, has lovely views of Floors Castle, the largest inhabited house in Scotland. The park hosts a variety of events throughout the year, from dog shows to antiques fairs.
✉ TD5 8LS ☎ 01573 224188 ◉ Check website for upcoming events

Below *Floors Castle, near Kelso*

KIPPFORD
KIPPFORD HOLIDAY PARK
www.kippfordholidaypark.co.uk
Activities at this award-winning nature conservation park include nature walks, bicycle rental, a mountain bike track and fishing. The park has private woodland and has won awards for conservation, with views to the English Lake District 40 miles (64km) away. There's a play area and an assault course for children.
✉ Kippford, Dalbeattie DG5 4LF ☎ 01556 620636 🕐 Open all year 💷 Various prices, depending on activities 🍴 Food shop open Easter–end Sep

KIRKCUDBRIGHT
THE CORNER GALLERY
A designer knitwear shop with a wide choice of hats, sweaters, scarves and hand-knitted works of art. Almost everything is made by small, independent producers from Scotland and the islands.
✉ 1 Castle Street DG6 4JA ☎ 01557 332020 🕐 Mid-Mar to mid-Jan Mon–Sat 10–5; closed Thu from 1pm, except Jun–end Aug

GALLOWAY WILDLIFE CONSERVATION PARK
www.gallowaywildlife.co.uk
Enjoy a free guided tour of the park, which is home to nearly 150 animals in large enclosures, including pandas, lynx, Scottish wildcats, snakes, deer and llamas. Pet and snake-handling sessions, children's play area and children's quiz in the summer.
✉ Lochfergus Plantation DG6 4XX ☎ 01557 331645 🕐 Feb–end Nov Mon–Thu 10–6, Fri–Sun 10–4 💷 Adult £5, child £3

JO GALLANT
www.jogallant.co.uk
Sumptuous textiles are displayed in this traditional, stone-fronted building near the Tolbooth Art Centre. The price of the machine-embroidered and quilted wall-hangings, cushions and scarves may be high, but so is the quality.
✉ Ironstones, 70 High Street DG6 4JL

☎ 01557 331130 🕐 Mon, Wed, Fri–Sat 10–5 (call first if travelling specially)

TOLBOOTH ART CENTRE
www.dumfriesmuseum.demon.co.uk
The centre tells the story of the Kirkcudbright colony of artists through a video presentation and a permanent display of paintings. The gallery upstairs shows exhibitions of contemporary art and crafts.
✉ High Street DG6 4JL ☎ 01557 331556 🕐 Oct–end May Mon–Sat 11–4; also Jun–end Sep Sun 10–5 💷 Free 🛍 Good selection of paintings, crafts and art books in the gift shop ☕ Café on ground floor

LAGGAN O'DEE
GALLOWAY RED DEER RANGE
www.forestry.gov.uk
You can walk among the animals here. The deer range lies between New Galloway and Newton Stewart in Galloway Forest Park.
✉ Laggan o'Dee, New Galloway DG7 3SQ ☎ 01671 402420 🕐 Mid-Jun to end Sep Sun–Tue 1–2.30. Entry on guided walks only mid-Jun to end Sep Sun–Thu, starts 1pm until 2.30. To join, turn up before 1pm at car park off the A712; there are signs for the Red Deer Range 💷 Adult £3.50, child, under 16, £2.50, family £10

LIVINGSTON
MCARTHURGLEN DESIGNER OUTLET
www.mcarthurglen.com
Scotland's largest designer shopping outlet, with 100 stores under one roof, as well as a cinema and lots of eating places.
✉ Almondvale Avenue EH54 6QX ☎ 01506 423600 🕐 Mon–Wed 9–6, Thu 9–8, Fri–Sat 9–6, Sun 11–6 🚗 🍴 🚻

LOCH KEN
GALLOWAY SAILING CENTRE
www.lochken.co.uk
Activities at this watersports centre on Loch Ken include sailing, windsurfing, kayaking, canoeing, quad biking and gorge scrambling. Check availability in advance; some activities may not be suitable for younger children. You can also camp in the grounds, or take a residential course, staying in the lodge.

✉ Castle Douglas DG7 3NQ ☎ 01644 420626 🕐 Mid-Mar to end Oct 💷 Lessons from £22 ☕ Lunch, snacks and drinks

KEN-DEE MARSHES NATURE RESERVE
www.rspb.org.uk
This nature reserve has a nature trail through woods and marshes beside the loch and along the River Dee. Winter wildfowl include Greenland white-fronted geese, and in summer migrating birds such as redstarts and pied flycatchers are the stars. There are three observation hides.
☎ 01671 402861 🕐 Daily dawn–dusk 💷 Free

LOCH KEN WATER SKI SCHOOL
www.skilochken.co.uk
Learn to waterski at this watersports centre on Loch Ken. Aquatic activities to suit all ages and abilities, and all equipment and tuition is included. Advance booking is required.
✉ Loch Ken Marina, by Castle Douglas ☎ 07050 092792 🕐 Apr–end Oct daily 9am–dusk 💷 Prices vary with the activity; 15-minute waterski lesson, adult £18

MELROSE
ABBEY MILL
This large store sells knitwear, toys, clothes and Scottish food in an historic corn mill just outside town.
✉ Annay Road TD6 9LG ☎ 01896 822138 🕐 Apr–end Sep daily 9–5.30; Oct–end Mar Mon–Sat 10–5, Sun 10–4.30 ☕ Abbey Mill Tea Room serves light meals and snacks

ACTIVE SPORTS
www.activitiesinscotland.com
Choose from a half-day or full-day activity at this outdoor centre, the only one of its kind in the Borders. Rent a mountain bicycle, go quad biking or enjoy watersports. Most activities take place just outside Selkirk; some may not be suitable for younger children. Advance reservations recommended.
✉ Chain Bridge Cottage, Annay Road TD6 9LP ☎ 01896 822452 🕐 Open all year, but watersports May–end Oct only 💷 Depends on the activity

THE CRAFTERS
www.melrose.bordernet.co.uk/traders/crafters
A co-operative of local craft workers sells handmade gifts, including cards, ceramics, knitwear, silk, jewellery and woodwork.
✉ The High Street TD6 9PA ☎ 01896 823714 🕐 Mon–Sat 10–5

THE WYND THEATRE
www.thewynd.com
A small, local theatre just off the High Street, with films, concerts including blues, big band and folk music, plays and pantomime. Bar open on performance evenings.
✉ The Wynd TD6 9PA ☎ 01896 820028 🕐 All year 🖐 From £5

NEWCASTLETON
BAILEY MILL TREKKING CENTRE
www.bailey-riding-racing.com
Horseback riding and bicycling through the Scottish Borders and into Cumbria. After the day's activities, relax in the sauna and jacuzzi at this holiday complex, which also offers accommodation. Advance reservations advisable.
✉ Bailey TD9 0TR ☎ 01697 748617 🕐 All year 🖐 Trekking £15 per hour; lessons £8 per 30 minutes 🅿

STOBO
STOBO CASTLE
www.stobocastle.co.uk
Treat yourself in this luxurious health spa, which is set in a 19th-century castle, an hour's drive south of Edinburgh. State-of-the-art facilities include an ozone pool, aromatic steam room and mud room. Advance reservations essential.
✉ EH45 8NY ☎ 01721 725300 🕐 All year 🖐 Day visit from £109; overnight packages from £109 🍴

TRANENT
GLENKINCHIE DISTILLERY
www.discoveringdistilleries.com
The home of the Edinburgh Malt, southeast of the city. You can see the working distillery, an exhibition of malt whisky and taste the whisky itself. Children under 8 are welcome, but not in the production area.

✉ Pencaitland EH34 5ET ☎ 01875 342004 🕐 Easter–end Nov daily 10–5; Dec–Easter Mon–Fri 12–4 🖐 Admission (£5) includes a discount voucher for the whisky shop

TROON
ROYAL TROON
www.royaltroon.co.uk
You'll need to reserve months ahead if you want to play a round at this world-class Open Championship golf course. The facilities are excellent, and this is reflected in the prices.
✉ Craigend Road KA10 6EP ☎ 01292 311555 🕐 Daily 🖐 From £120 for two rounds on the Portland course, including lunch; £220 for one on the Portland and one on the Old Course. Available Mon–Tue and Thu only May to mid Oct 🅿 🍴 Restaurant in clubhouse 🈁

TURNBERRY
TURNBERRY
www.turnberry.co.uk
This world famous Open Championship links course is 15 miles (24km) south of Ayr. Minimum age 16 and must be accompanied by an adult. If you're with a golfing partner, the Westin Turnberry Resort has an outdoor activity centre and an award-winning spa.
✉ KA26 9LT ☎ 01655 334032 🕐 Daily 🖐 Summer green fees for the Ailsa course begin at £160 for non-residents 🅿 🍴 Clubhouse with restaurant 🈁

WIGTOWN
THE BOOK SHOP
www.the-bookshop.com
A book-lover's dream: the largest second-hand bookstore in Scotland, with over 0.5 miles (700m) of shelves for the stock of 65,000 books. Free coffee with a seat by the fire!
✉ 17 North Main Street DG8 9H ☎ 01988 402499 🕐 Mon–Sat 9–5

MING BOOKS
www.mingbooks.supanet.com
Britain's largest dealer in second-hand crime and detective books, also naval history, natural history and science fiction books. The owners will also find and mail books to you.
✉ Beechwood, Acre Place DG8 9DU or shop at Windy Mill, Unit 3, Duncan Park DG8 9JD ☎ 01988 402434 🕐 May–end Sep daily 10–6, by appointment at house

PRICES AND SYMBOLS

The restaurants are listed alphabetically within each town. The prices are for a two-course lunch (L) and a three-course à la carte dinner (D). Prices in pubs are for a two-course lunchtime bar meal and a two-course dinner in the restaurant, unless specified otherwise. The wine price is for the least expensive bottle.

For a key to the symbols, ▷ 2.

ARRAN, ISLE OF
EIGHTEEN 69 AT AUCHRANNIE COUNTRY HOUSE
www.auchrannie.co.uk
Superior local ingredients star on the short dinner menu. Try freshly caught langoustines served in a butter and coriander (cilantro) sauce or fillet of Angus beef with potatoes. Hearty desserts are popular, and the wine list is good.
✉ Brodick, KA27 8BJ ☎ 01770 302234
🕒 D, 6.30–9.30 🍴 D £32, Wine £13
🚌 From ferry terminal turn right and follow coast road through Brodick, then take 2nd left past golf club

KILMICHAEL
www.kilmichael.com
Chef Antony Butterworth delivers contemporary dishes with an often ingenious use of ingredients. You might start with roast garlic and chestnut soup, and then try lamb with a Persian sauce of walnuts and pomegranates. A concise four-course menu changes daily. No children under 12.
✉ Glen Cloy KA27 8BY ☎ 01770 302219
🕒 D only, 7–8.30; closed Tue, Nov–end Feb
🍴 D £39.50, Wine £18.95 🚌 Turn right on leaving ferry terminal through Brodick, left at golf club. Go past church and follow signs

AUCHENCAIRN
BALCARY BAY
www.balcary-bay-hotel.com
Local produce features strongly on this French and European menu. Imaginative starters include carpaccio of Galloway beef, with mains of roasted venison loin, perhaps, and a dessert of pannacotta in mulled red wine.
✉ DG7 1QZ ☎ 01556 640217 🕒 12–2, 7–8.30; L by prior booking only Mon–Sat; closed mid-Dec to mid-Feb 🍴 L £16,

D £33, Wine £13.85 🚌 On A711 between Dalbeattie and Kirkcudbright. From Auchencairn follow signs to Balcary, along Shore Road

AULDGIRTH
AULDGIRTH INN
This 500-year-old inn's typical menu includes medallions of pork fillet, beef braised in ale, pot roast supreme of guinea fowl and noisettes of Dumfriesshire lamb.
✉ DG2 0XG ☎ 01387 740250 🕒 Daily 11.30–11. Bar meals: daily 12–9pm
🍴 L £10, D £13.50, Wine £8.95
🚌 8 miles (13km) northeast of Dumfries on A76 Kilmarnock road

AYR
FAIRFIELD HOUSE
www.fairfieldhotel.co.uk
The ambitious kitchen at this friendly hotel delivers modern French dishes with plenty of flavour. Saddle of wild rabbit is served with celeriac and puy lentils; desserts may include rhubarb crumble tart with lemon thyme ice cream
✉ 12 Fairfield Road KA7 2AR ☎ 01292 267461 🕒 L 12–2, D 5–9.30 🍴 L £14,

Left *The handsome village of Kelso stands on the banks of the River Tweed*

D £35, Wine £13.95 From A77 to Ayr South. Follow signs for town centre, turn left into Miller Road. At lights turn left, then right into Fairfield Road

FOUTERS
www.fouters.co.uk
A degree of panache lifts the international, modern cooking out of the ordinary at this long-established restaurant. Expect delights such as chicken supreme with mushroom and nut mousseline.
2A Academy Street KA7 1HS 01292 261391 12–2.30, 6–9; closed Sun–Mon, 4–11 Jan L £12.50, D £26, Wine £15.50 Opposite Town Hall, down Cobblestone Lane

BALLANTRAE
GLENAPP CASTLE
www.glenappcastle.com
This is a gem of a castle, built in 1870 as a private home and now a luxury hotel set in grounds with 14.5ha (36 acres) of gardens and woodland. The castle is opulently furnished in a traditional manner, including the dining room with its elegantly set tables and views out over the garden. The kitchen team, with new head chef at the helm, deliver six-course menus based on first-class produce and demonstrating considerable craftsmanship. There are two choices of main course and dessert,

otherwise you are in the capable hands of the chef. An amuse-bouche of langoustine in tomato essence precedes seared foie gras, perfectly timed, with red pepper purée and balsamic reduction in a confident beginning. The fish course is next, perhaps seared scallops partnered with lightly spiced aubergine purée and sauce vierge. Main-course fillet of beef is served with white onion and dauphinoise and a red wine jus. Scottish cheeses are perfectly kept and there's rhubarb crumble soufflé with vanilla ice cream or tiramisù with white coffee ice cream for dessert. Service is excellent and lunch offers imaginative dishes in a three-course format.
KA26 0NZ 01465 831212
12.30–2, 7–10; closed 2 Jan-14 Mar, Christmas L £35, D £55, Wine £25
Drive south through Ballantrae, cross the bridge over the River Stinchar, turn 1st right, gates and lodge house 1 mile (1.5km)

BALLOCH
DE VERE CAMERON HOUSE HOTEL
www.devere.co.uk
Diners have a choice of two menus: a daily market menu or six courses of surprises from the tasting menu. Expect mains such as pan-fried mullet, langoustines and basil. Desserts may include strawberry soup with mint and vanilla.
Loch Lomond G83 8QZ 01389 755565
D 7–9.30; closed Sun, Mon D £45, Wine £25 M8/A82 to Dumbarton; take

road to Luss, hotel signed 1 mile (1.5km) past Balloch on right

BANKNOCK
GLENSKIRLIE HOUSE RESTAURANT
www.glenskirliehouse.com
Modern innovative Scottish cuisine is served in this elegant restaurant. Dishes may include organic chicken breast with braised chicory and a herb glaze, and Swedish-style salmon with hot buttered noodles.
Kilsyth Road FK4 1UF 01324 840201
12–2, 6–9.30; closed D Mon, 26–27 Dec, 1–3 Jan L £17.50, D £40, Wine £16.50 From Glasgow take A80 towards Stirling. At exit 4 take A803 signed Kilsyth/Bonnybridge. At T-junction (intersection) turn right. Hotel 1 mile (1.5km) on right

BIGGAR
SHIELDHILL CASTLE
www.shieldhill.co.uk
Modern European dishes display clear, rich flavours which might include ravioli with white truffle, and venison with oxtail and a wood sorrel dressing.
Shieldhill Road, Quothquan ML12 6NA 01899 220035 12–1.45, 7–8.45 L £23, D £35, Wine £18.50 From Biggar take B7016 to Carnwath. After 2.5 miles (4km) turn left on to Shieldhill Road. Castle is 1.5 miles (2.5km) on right

DALRY
BRAIDWOODS
www.braidwoods.co.uk
Keith Braidwood's unfussy restaurant delivers simply balanced food. Dine on seared hand-dived scallops with a cardamom, lentil and coriander sauce, and baked fillet of west coast turbot on a smoked salmon risotto. Follow with a truffle terrine of three types of chocolate with a Grand Marnier sauce. No children under 12 at dinner.
Drumastle Mill Cottage KA24 4LN 01294 833544 L Wed–Sun 12–1.45, D Tue–Sat 9–9; closed 1st 3 weeks Jan, 2 weeks Sep L £18, D £36, Wine £15.95 1 mile (1.5km) from Dalry on the Saltcoats road

DALRYMPLE
KIRKTON INN
Menus include roast sirloin of beef and Yorkshire pudding, steak pie, fajitas, Thai chicken, battered haddock and lasagne.
✉ 1 Main Street KA6 6DF ☎ 01292 560241 🕐 Daily 11am–midnight. Bar meals: daily 11–9. Restaurant: daily 11–9 ♨ L £7.50, D £19, Wine £9.75 🚌 Between A77 and A713, 5 miles (8km) from Ayr

DIRLETON
THE OPEN ARMS HOTEL
www.openarmshotel.com
Dishes here might include fillet of Aberdeen Angus beef stuffed with home-made parfait, served with oatmeal oyster mushrooms on Orkney Hramsa (cheese) mash, or pan-fried Barbary duck breast baked on lemon grass and served with couscous and peppercorn and black cherry coulis.
✉ EH39 5EG ☎ 01620 850241 🕐 12–2, 6–8.45 ♨ L £13.95, D £32, Wine £10.95 🚌 From A1 (south) take A198 to North Berwick then follow signs for Dirleton 2 miles (3.2km) west. From Edinburgh take A6137 leading to A198

DUMFRIES
THE LINEN ROOM
www.linenroom.com
The Linen Room's decor is striking in its simplicity—black walls and carpet setting off fresh white table linen, white cushioned captain's-style chairs and black-and-white framed prints dotting the walls. Fine dining certainly, but refreshingly unpretentious with friendly, relaxed and informed service. The innovative cuisine makes good use of local seasonal produce in well-presented modern French dishes that reveal strong flavours and a light touch. Take a starter of hand-dived scallops with white onion, rocket hot shot, crunchy mushrooms and cep vinaigrette, followed by seared sea bass with salt cod brandade, mussels and tarragon, and to finish off, 'obsession in chocolate MkII'. Two tasting menus and a comprehensive wine list complete an assured package.
✉ 53 St. Michael Street DG1 2QB ☎ 01387 255689 🕐 12.30–2.30, 10–10; closed Mon; 25–26 Dec, 1–2 Jan, 2 weeks in Jan and Oct ♨ L £12.95, D £25, Wine £18 🚌 Please telephone for directions

EDDLESTON
THE HORSESHOE INN
This converted blacksmith's house takes on a very different personality inside. This is a stylish bar-bistro and fine dining restaurant, Bardoulet's, named after the chef-director of this rejuvenated inn. The French origins of the chef are reflected in the menu and high-quality Scottish produce features large. A thin tart of Keltic crab and scallops is served as a starter with a spiced mango tartar, sweet beetroot and orange oil, while marinated foie gras is set in a rhubarb jelly and served with gingerbread. Main-course Scottish beef, fillet and shoulder, comes with creamed wild mushrooms and morel jus, and for dessert there's crème caramel with pecan cake, praline and ginger sorbet.
✉ EH45 8QP ☎ 01721 730225 🕐 12–2.30, 7–9; closed Mon, D Sun, 25 Dec, early Jan, mid-Oct ♨ L £19.50, D £31.50, Wine £11.95 🚌 On A703, 5 miles (8km) north of Peebles

ETTRICK
TUSHIELAW INN
www.tushielaw-inn.co.uk
This 18th-century inn serves wholesome meals, including steak and stout pie, deep-fried breaded haddock, Aberdeen Angus sirloin steaks, grilled lamb cutlets and local trout. Gluten-free and vegetarian options are always available.
✉ TD7 5HT ☎ 01750 62205 🕐 May–end Sep daily 12–2.30, 6.30–11. Bar meals: 12–2, 6–8.45 ♨ L £10, D £15, Wine £10 🚌 At junction (intersection) of B709 and B711, west of Hawick

GATEHOUSE OF FLEET
CALLY PALACE HOTEL
www.callypalace.co.uk
Dinner here is a formal affair (jacket and tie required). On offer is a balance between simple, traditional and adventurous, modern. Pan-fried beef fillet and steamed fillet of salmon are typical mains, followed by warm chocolate brownies.
✉ DG7 2DL ☎ 01557 814341 🕐 12–1, 6.45–9.30; closed 3 Jan–early Feb 🖐 L £16.95, D £29.50, Wine £12.90 🚗 From A74(M) take A75, at Gatehouse take B727. Hotel on left

GIFFORD
GOBLIN HA'
A patio for summer eating, a play area and dolls' house, plus a range of home-cooked dishes including pan fried herring in oatmeal, breast of chicken with herb potatoes, and pasta and pizza dishes.
✉ Main Street EH41 4QH ☎ 01620 810244 🕐 Lunch Mon–Sat 11.30–5, à la carte Mon–Sat 11.30–9.30 🖐 L £14, D £19, Wine £11.25 🚗 On A846, near village square on shore side of the road

GRANGEMOUTH
THE GRANGE MANOR
www.grangemanor.co.uk
The menu changes weekly here. Starters could include seared salmon, chilli king prawns or grilled sea bass. Roast monkfish fillet, and loin of lamb dressed with sweet herbs are possible main courses.
✉ Glensburgh Road, Glensburgh FK3 8XJ ☎ 01324 474836 🕐 Fri–Sat only 7–9pm 🖐 D £28, Wine £15.50 🚗 M9 (eastward) exit 6, 200m (220 yards) on right; M9 (west) exit 5, then A905 for 2 miles (3.2km)

GULLANE
LA POTINIÈRE
www.lapotiniere.co.uk
The four-course dinner menu is modern British. It might include warm parmesan tart, followed by roast loin of venison, and finished off with Calvados pannacotta.
✉ Main Street EH31 2AA ☎ 01620 843214 🕐 12.30–1.30, 7–8.30; closed Mon–Tue, Christmas, bank holidays 🖐 L £17.50, D £38, Wine £16 🚗 On A198

INNERLEITHEN
TRAQUAIR ARMS HOTEL
www.traquairarmshotel.co.uk
The food has a distinctive Scottish flavour with dishes of Finnan savoury, salmon with ginger and coriander (cilantro), and fillet of beef Traquair. Omelettes, salads and baked potatoes are also available.
✉ Traquair Road EH44 6PD ☎ 01896 830229 🕐 Mon–Sat 11–12am, Sun 12–12. Bar meals: daily 12–9. Restaurant: daily 12–9; closed 25–26 Dec, 1–3 Jan 🖐 L £12, D £20, Wine £10 🚗 6 miles (9.7km) east of Peebles on A72. Pub 91m (100 yards) from junction (intersection) with B709

ISLE OF WHITHORN
THE STEAM PACKET INN
The inn makes good use of seafood straight off the boats on its menu. Expect whole, locally caught lemon and Dover sole or roast breast of pheasant among the main courses.
✉ Harbour Row DG8 8LL ☎ 01988 500334 🕐 Summer daily 11–11; winter Mon–Thu 11–3, 6–11; closed 25 Dec. Bar meals and restaurant: 12–2, 7–9.30 🖐 L £12, D £25, Wine £12 🚗 From Newton Stewart take A714, then A746 to Isle of Whithorn

KELSO
THE ROXBURGHE HOTEL & GOLF COURSE
www.roxburghe.net
Owned by the Duke of Roxburghe, this impressive Jacobean country-house hotel incorporates a championship golf course. Inside, the dining room provides formal yet friendly service. The kitchen makes good use of local produce. Expect starters such as smoked salmon, cream cheese and black olive ravioli with fine bean and shallot salad dressed with lemon and olive oil, followed by grilled breast of guinea fowl wrapped in pancetta with fondant potato, creamed leeks and apple coulis. A fine choice of wines provides a fitting accompaniment.
✉ TD5 8JZ Tel 01573 450331 🕐 12–2, 7.30–9.45 🖐 L £19, D £34.95, Wine £19.50 🚗 From A68, 1 mile (1.5km) north of Jedburgh, take A698 5 miles (8km) to Heiton

KIRKBEAN
CAVENS
www.cavens.com
The intimate dining room in this charming country-house hotel has a limited number of well-spaced tables, and a daily set menu of dinner party fare offers a choice of two dishes at each course, plus alternatives on request. Impressive dishes include a classic rendition of a salmon and dill risotto; and rack of Galloway lamb with a thyme and oatmeal crust delivering all its promised flavour. Finish with an exemplary lemon crème brûlée.
✉ DG2 8AA ☎ 01387 880234 🕐 7–8.30; closed Dec–1 Mar, closed L all week 🖐 D £30, Wine £16 🚗 From Kirkbean, follow signs for Cavens

LINLITHGOW
CHAMPANY INN DD
www.champany.com
Described as a temple to beef, this inn serves Pope's eye, porterhouse, Châteaubriand or rib-eye steaks among others. The cellar contains around 25,000 wine bottles. The house starter is hot-smoked salmon with hollandaise sauce, and there's chicken, duck and lobster, too. No children under 8.
✉ EH49 7LU ☎ 01506 834532
🕐 12.30–2, 7–10; closed Sun, L Sat, 25–26 Dec ✋ L £19.50, D £65, Wine £14.50
🚗 2 miles (3.2km) northeast of Linlithgow at junction (intersection) of A904 and A803

LIVINGSTON'S RESTAURANT
www.livingstons-restaurant.co.uk
At this intimate restaurant mains include saddle of Highland venison with bramble and honey sauce, with Aberdeen angus fillet of beef. Dessert might include chocolate fondant with vanilla ice cream. No children under 8 for dinner.
✉ 52 High Street EH49 7AE ☎ 01506 846565 🕐 12–2.30, 6–9.30; closed Sun–Mon, 2 weeks Jan, 1 week Jun, 1 week Oct ✋ L £16.95, D £33.95, Wine £13.95
🚗 Opposite old post office

MELROSE
BURT'S
www.burtshotel.co.uk
The bar is popular for informal lunches and suppers. In the restaurant try avocado cheesecake to begin, while typical mains range from sea bream, venison and chicken through lamb chops and steaks to a vegetarian platter. Selkirk Bannock Pudding is served with shortbread ice cream. No children under 10.
✉ Market Square TD6 9PL ☎ 01896 822285 🕐 12–2, 7–9 ✋ L £15.50, D £31.50, Wine £13.25

MOFFAT
HARTFELL HOUSE & THE LIMETREE RESTAURANT
www.hartfellhouse.co.uk
Built in 1850, this impressive Victorian house is situated in a peaceful terrace high above the

Above *Snow-covered Linlithgow Palace in the early evening light*

town, having lovely views of the surrounding countryside. The Limetree Restaurant was previously in the high street but has moved into Hartfell House. The traditionally styled dining room has an ornate ceiling with crystal chandeliers and local art on the walls. There is a simple, intuitive approach to the traditional and modern cooking here, big on taste and flavour with great combinations. Risotto of smoked haddock, braised neck and pan-fried loin of Cumbrian blackface lamb with garlic-infused mashed potatoes and rosemary cream show the style.
✉ Hartfell Crescent, DG10 9AL ☎ 01683 220153 🕐 L Sun only, D Tue–Sat
✋ L £16.50, D25, Wine £13.50 🚗 Off High Street at War Memorial onto Well Street and Old Well Road, Hartfell Crescent on right

NEWTON STEWART
CREEBRIDGE HOUSE
www.creebridge.co.uk
Bridge's Bar and Brasserie offers a menu that might include home-made ravioli filled with local lobster in seafood broth, and steaks cut from Buccleuch beef. The Garden Restaurant offers an à la carte menu of modern Scottish cooking.
✉ Minnigaff DG8 6NP ☎ 01671 402121 🕐 Mon–Sat 12–2.30, 6–11; Sun 12–11. Bar meals: 12–2, 6–9. Restaurant: dinner only, 7–9 ✋ L £12, D £25, Wine £11.95

🚗 Take A75 into Newton Stewart, turn right over the bridge, hotel is 200m (200 yards) on left

NORTH BERWICK
MACDONALD MARINE HOTEL
www.macdonaldhotels.co.uk/marine
This recently refurbished Grade II listed Victorian property is located on East Lothian's famous championship golf course overlooking the Firth of Forth. The restaurant enjoys an equally impressive setting, its formal decor creating a regal feel. Diners enjoy canapés and pre-starters in addition to choices from the classically based menu, featuring the freshest local and seasonal ingredients. A pressing of smoked salmon with lobster, crabmeat and lime and saffron dressing shows the style, followed by a pavé of wild halibut with new potatoes and mussel vermouth, or perhaps fillet of Scottish beef with potato gratin, asparagus and Balvenie jus. Finish in style with an assiette of chocolate (warm dark chocolate tarte, white chocolate brownie cheesecake and chocolate tiramisù torte).
✉ Cromwell Road EH39 4LZ ☎ 0870 400 8129 🕐 12.30–2.30, 6.30–9.30 ✋ L £17.95, D £35, Wine £19.95 🚗 From A198 turn into Hamilton Road at lights, 2nd right into Cromwell Road

PEEBLES
CASTLE VENLAW HOTEL
www.venlaw.co.uk
The food at this romantic, family-owned castle in the Borders is traditional British cooking boosted by the occasional Mediterranean influence. Black pudding brioche might be followed by Scottish salmon with roast sweet potato and a lobster bisque. No children under 5 after 7pm.
✉ Edinburgh Road EH45 8QG ☎ 01721 720384 🕐 12–2.45, 7–9 🖐 L £13, D £30, Wine £13.95 🚗 From east end of Peebles High Street turn left at roundabout, signed A703 to Edinburgh. After 0.75 miles (1.2km) hotel is signed on right

PORTPATRICK
CROWN
The extensive menus are based on fresh local produce, with an emphasis on seafood including whitebait, langoustine, herring, lobster, crab and mussels. Selected as the AA's Seafood Pub of the Year for 2005.
✉ 9 North Crescent DG9 8SX ☎ 01776 810261 🕐 11am–12am. Bar meals: 12–9. Restaurant: 6–9 🖐 L £12.95, D £21.95, Wine £10.95

ST. MARY'S LOCH
TIBBIE SHIELS INN
www.tibbieshielsinn.com
Menus reflect the seasons with winter game and fresh fish, as well as more exotic dishes such as cashew nut loaf with tomato and herb salad. Children welcome.
✉ St. Mary's Loch TD7 5LH ☎ 01750 42231 🕐 Mon–Sat 11–11, Sun 12.30–11. Bar meals: daily 12.30–8.15. Restaurant: daily 12–8.15 🖐 L £10, D £14, Wine £8.95 🚗 From Moffat take A708. Inn is 14 miles (22.5km) on right

SORN
SORN INN DD
www.thesorninn.com
At this late 18th-century inn, chef Craig Grant provides brilliant value fixed prices. Try the warm pheasant salad or pavé of beef with wild mushroom polenta, or go for the chef's tasting menu.

✉ 35 Main Street KA5 6HU ☎ 01290 551305 🕐 Tue–Fri 12–2, 6–9, Sat 12–9, Sun 12.30–7; closed Mon 🖐 L £11.95, D £23.50, Wine £11.50 🚗 From A77 take the A76 to Mauchline, join B743, Sorn is 4 miles (6.4km) farther on

SWINTON
WHEATSHEAF RESTAURANT
The lunch menu at this country inn changes daily and offers good value; the dinner menu is equally appealing. Dishes reflect the seasons and there's a daily specials board. Look for breast of wild wood pigeon on a medallion of Scotch beef fillet with black pudding in Madeira sauce, or fillet of salmon on a crayfish, tomato and coriander (cilantro) sauce.
✉ Main Street TD11 3JJ ☎ 01890 860257 🕐 12–2, 6–9; closed D Sun, Dec–end Jan; 25, 26 Dec, 1, 2 Jan 🖐 L £16, D £28, Wine £12.95 🚗 In village centre

TROON
LOCHGREEN HOUSE
www.lochgreenhouse.co.uk
Andrew Costley has built up a solid reputation for good Scottish food and he has the ideal setting in which to showcase local dishes here. The light-and-airy formal Tapestry Restaurant comes with a high vaulted ceiling, stunning chandeliers, namesake wall-hung tapestries and furniture to match, and overlooks the fountain garden. The cooking is in the classic vein, but with a modern approach. The kitchen deals with the freshest seasonal produce and produces consistent results. Crown of quail is stuffed with Stornoway black pudding and served atop a potato and thyme blini, plus macerated grapes and apples and finished with a Calvados jus in a sophisticated and appealing starter. There is an intermediate course—spiced winter vegetable soup, perhaps—before main-course seared escalope of salmon with langoustine tempura, oriental-style vegetables and rice laced with cashew nuts. Attentive and personal service is as much a feature of the place as the fine food.

✉ Monktonhill Road, Southwood KA10 7EN ☎ 01292 313343 🕐 12–2.30, 7–9.30 🖐 L £14.95, D £39.95, Wine £17.95 🚗 From A77 follow signs for Prestwick Airport, take B749 to Troon, Lochgreen is situated on left 1 mile (1.5km) from junction

MACCALLUMS OF TROON
A former pump station has been transformed to create this spacious modern restaurant in a stunning harbourside location, where diners can watch the fishing fleet come and go. Decor in the high-raftered, wooden-floored interior is themed around America's Cup memorabilia. Expect great fish from a kitchen confident enough to take a simple approach and let the freshness of its produce shine through. Typical dishes include cullen skink, grilled langoustines with garlic butter, and baked halibut with mushy peas and lemon vinaigrette. Or look for the chargrilled tuna served with mango and chilli lime salsa. A takeaway and deli sells everything from wet fish to fish and chips.
✉ The Harbour KA10 6DH ☎ 01292 319339 🕐 12–2.30, 6.30–9.30; closed Mon, D Sun; Christmas, New Year 🖐 L £10.50, D £31, Wine £17.75 🚗 Please telephone for directions

TURNBERRY
MALIN COURT
www.malincourt.co.uk
Malin Court is situated beside the famous Turnberry golf course, with views of the Kintyre courses. Lunch here might include braised shank of Ayrshire lamb, or roasted sea bass. In the evening the menu might offer baked halibut in a herb crust with roasted celery and grain mustard sauce, seared red snapper with chive mash, or fillet of beef accompanied by herb mash and truffle jus.
✉ KA26 9PB ☎ 01655 331457 🕐 12.30–2, 7–9 🖐 L £13, D £25, Wine £10.25 🚗 On A719 1 mile (1.5km) from A77, on north side of village

STAYING

PRICES AND SYMBOLS

Prices are the starting price for a double room for one night, unless otherwise stated. Breakfast is included unless noted otherwise. All the hotels listed accept credit cards unless otherwise stated. Note that rates vary widely throughout the year.

For a key to the symbols, ▷ 2.

AYR

ENTERKINE COUNTRY HOUSE

www.enterkine.com

A gracious country mansion dating back to the 1930s, Enterkine House retains many original features, notably the luxurious bathroom suites. In keeping with country-house tradition there is no bar, drinks being served in the elegant lounge and library. Food is notably good, and many of the spacious bedrooms have lovely views over the surrounding countryside.
✉ Annbank KA6 5AL ☎ 01292 520580

⚐ £195 ⓘ 6 🚗 Follow A77 to Ayr, then B743 Mossblown/Mauchline for hotel on Coylton Road, on outskirts of Annbank

SAVOY PARK

www.savoypark.com

This friendly, traditional hotel is handy for the town's race course. There are impressive panelled walls in the public rooms, along with ornate ceilings and open fires, and the restaurant is reminiscent of a Highland shooting lodge. Superior bedrooms are large and classically elegant, while others are smart and modern.
✉ 16 Racecourse Road KA7 2UT ☎ 01292 266112 ⚐ £95 ⓘ 19 🚗 From A77 follow Holmston Road (A70) for 2 miles (3km), through Parkhouse Street, then turn left into Berresford Terrace, and take 1st right into Bellevue Road

BALLANTRAE

COSSES COUNTRY HOUSE

www.cossescountryhouse.com

A delightful country house bed-and-breakfast in 4.8ha (12 acres) of woodland and gardens. Two bedrooms have their own lounges, and all rooms are on the ground floor. Guests meet for pre-dinner drinks with hosts in the lounge, and award-winning dinners, served at an elegant communal table, include home-grown and local produce, Scottish cheese and fine wines. Breakfast offers a choice of dishes, home-made yoghurt, preserves and bread. No children under 6.
✉ Cosses KA26 0LR ☎ 01465 831363 ⚐ £80 ⓘ 3 🕐 Closed Nov–end Feb 🚗 South of Ballantrae on the A77, take the inland road at the caravan sign. House is 2 miles (3.2km) on the right

GLENAPP CASTLE

www.glenappcastle.com

Impressively restored over a six-year period, this magnificent castle lies in well-tended grounds and gardens with fine views towards Ailsa Craig and Arran. The all-inclusive price covers a set six-course dinner with matched wines (dinner for non-residents by arrangement). Afternoon tea is served in the castle's Drawing Room. Bedrooms are adorned with antiques and period pieces and there are a number of suites. Service is both attentive and welcoming.

✉ KA26 0NZ ☎ 01465 831212 👋 £375 ⓘ 17 ⊘ Closed Nov–end Mar 🚗 1 mile (1.5km) from A77, south of Ballantrae

CRAILING
CRAILING OLD SCHOOL B&B

www.crailingoldschool.co.uk

The village school until the mid-1980s, this late 19th-century property has been imaginatively converted. An open-plan lounge and dining room overlooks the garden and is the perfect setting for excellent meals (dinner by arrangement). There are three individual bedrooms in the spacious loft, while a house in the garden provides self-contained accommodation that is easily accessible for visitors with disabilities. No children under 9.

✉ TD8 6TL ☎ 01835 850382 👋 £57 ⓘ 5 ⊘ Closed 24–27 Dec and 2 weeks Feb and Nov 🚗 Off A698 Jedburgh to Kelso road on the B6400 signposted Nisbet, Harestanes Visitor Centre

DIRLETON
OPEN ARMS HOTEL

www.openarmshotel.com

This well-established hotel sits across from Dirleton's picturesque village green and 13th-century castle. There's a cosy bar, and some ground-floor rooms have a great view of the gardens. One is suitable for wheelchair users.

✉ Main Street EH39 5EG ☎ 01620 850241 👋 £130 ⓘ 12 🚗 From A1, follow signs for North Berwick, through Gullane, 2 miles (3km) on left

EAST CALDER
ASHCROFT FARMHOUSE

www.ashcroftfarmhouse.com

With nearly 40 years' experience of caring for their guests, Derek and Elizabeth Scott ensure that a stay at their farmhouse will be memorable. Their modern home is in lovely landscaped gardens, and provides attractive ground-floor bedrooms. The residents' lounge includes a video library. Breakfast, with home-made sausages, is served at individual tables. No children under 12.

✉ EH53 0ET ☎ 01506 881810 👋 £70 ⓘ 6 🚗 On the B7015, off the A71, 0.5 miles (800m) east of East Calder near to Almondell Country Park

JEDBURGH
JEDFOREST HOTEL

www.jedforesthotel.com

A tour of the central Borders would not be complete without a visit to this country house hotel in 14ha (35 acres) of woodland and pasture. Immaculately presented throughout, it offers an attractive dining room, a bright and comfortable brasserie and a relaxing lounge with open fire. The bedrooms are very smart, with the larger ones being particularly impressive. Service is very attentive, and facilities include private fishing. No children under 12.

✉ Camptown TD8 6PJ ☎ 01835 840222 👋 £100 ⓘ 12 🚗 4 miles (6.4km) south of Jedburgh, off A68

THE SPINNEY

www.thespinney-jedburgh.co.uk

Two cottages have been transformed into this attractive modern home in the foothills of the Cheviots, surrounded by landscaped gardens. Bedrooms are bright and cheerful. Breakfast is served at individual tables in the dining room, and there is a welcoming lounge. Self-catering (with kitchen) lodges are also available on site.

✉ Langlee TD8 6PB ☎ 01835 863525 👋 £56 ⓘ 3 ⊘ Closed Dec–end Feb 🚗 2 miles (3.2km) south of Jedburgh on A68

KELSO
THE ROXBURGHE HOTEL & GOLF COURSE

www.roxburghe.net

Surrounded by 202.5ha (500 acres) of mature wood and parkland, this impressive Jacobean mansion is owned by the Duke of Roxburghe. An impressive range of sporting pursuits is available for guests, including shooting, fishing, tennis and golf. Some of the bedrooms come complete with a real fire. The comfortably furnished lounges provide a perfect setting for the lavish afternoon teas, while the restaurant serves carefully prepared Scottish and other British fare.

✉ Heiton TD5 8JZ ☎ 01573 450331 👋 £185 ⓘ 22 🚗 3 miles (4.8km) southwest of Kelso off A698

KILWINNING
MONTGREENAN HOUSE

www.montgreenanhouse.co.uk

This peaceful mansion is in 19ha (48 acres) of parkland and woods. Gracious public areas retain original features such as ornate ceilings and marble fireplaces, and include a library, a tapas bar/restaurant, family restaurant and a fine dining restaurant. Bedrooms come in a variety of sizes and have been refurbished recently.

✉ Montgreenan Estate KA13 7QZ ☎ 01294 850005 👋 £150 ⓘ 16 🚗 4 miles (6.4km) north of Irvine on A736

KIRKBEAN
CAVENS

www.cavens.com

Dating back to 1752, this country house has been home to many notable figures over the years, and is in 2.4ha (6 acres) of parkland. Outdoor pursuits on offer include shooting, fishing and horseback riding. A set four-course dinner menu uses quality local produce.

✉ DG2 8AA ☎ 01387 880234 👋 £150 ⓘ 7 🚗 Hotel signed from A710 in Kirkbean

KIRKCUDBRIGHT
BAYTREE HOUSE
www.baytreekirkcudbright.co.uk
You can stay close to the centre of this appealing artists' town in this beautifully restored Georgian bed-and-breakfast. The bedrooms are thoughtfully equipped, and furnished in keeping with the style of the house. The magnificent upstairs drawing room is not to be missed. No children under 12, no credit cards.

✉ 110 High Street DG6 4JQ ☎ 01557 330824 ✋ £64 ① 3 🚗 Take A711 into middle of Kirkcudbright, turn right at crossroads into Cuthbert Street, left at Castle Street, and Baytree is facing at the end of Castle Street

SELKIRK ARMS HOTEL
www.selkirkarmshotel.co.uk
This Best Western hotel gets its name from an historical association: it was here that Robert Burns wrote the *Selkirk Grace*. Set in secluded gardens, it is a stylish hotel just outside the city centre. Rooms are furnished in an uncluttered, contemporary style. Public areas include the Aristas restaurant, bistro, air-conditioned lounge bar and the Burns lounge.

✉ Old High Street DG6 4JG ☎ 01557 330402 ✋ £52 ① 17 🚗 On A71, 5 miles (8km) south of A75

LOCHWINNOCH
EAST LOCHHEAD
www.eastlochhead.co.uk
A relaxed country-house atmosphere prevails at this former farmhouse, which dates back over 100 years and has magnificent views over Barr Loch. The stylish bedrooms are all superbly equipped, and enjoyable home-cooking is served in the dining room/lounge. A barn has been converted into four self-contained units.

✉ Largs Road PA12 4DX ☎ 01505 842610 ✋ £70 ① 3 🚗 From Glasgow take M8 exit 28a for A737 Irvine. At Roadhead roundabout turn right on to A760. Guesthouse 2 miles (3.2km) on the left

LOCKERBIE
THE DRYFESDALE
www.dryfesdalehotel.co.uk
Convenient for the M74, yet suitably screened from it, this hotel offers its guests superb care. Facilities include clay pigeon shooting and private fishing. Bedrooms, some with access to patio areas, vary in size. Dinner makes good use of local produce and is served in the airy restaurant overlooking the gardens. A warm welcome is offered by the enthusiastic young staff.

✉ Dryfebridge DG11 2SF ☎ 01576 202427 ✋ £110 ① 28 🚗 From M74 take exit 17 signed Lockerbie North. Take 3rd exit at 1st roundabout, 1st exit at next roundabout. Hotel is 183m (200 yards) on left

KINGS ARMS HOTEL
www.kingsarmshotel.co.uk
Built in the 17th century as a coaching inn, this venerable family-run hotel lies at the heart of the town, providing attractive and well-equipped bedrooms, and a choice of two homely bars serving food — one is non-smoking.

✉ High Street DG11 2JL ☎ 01576 202410 ✋ £75 ① 13 🚗 In town centre, opposite Town Hall

SOMERTON HOUSE
www.somertonhotel.co.uk
This friendly, family-run Victorian mansion has been sympathetically preserved and beautiful woodwork, particularly in the dining room, is a feature. Two attractive conservatories add a new dimension and are popular for bar meals and functions. Bedrooms are notably stylish, and well equipped.

✉ 35 Carlisle Road DG11 2DR ☎ 01576 202583 ✋ £85 ① 11 🚗 Off A74

MAYBOLE
LADYBURN
www.ladyburn.co.uk
This country house is the elegant home of the Hepburn family. It nestles in open countryside and attractive gardens. Classically styled bedrooms, two with four-poster beds, offer every comfort and are complemented by the library and

the drawing room. There's a three-course set dinner menu, discussed beforehand, served in a gracious candlelit setting. The genuine hospitality and care is a hallmark. No children under 16. Book in advance.

✉ KA19 7SG ☎ 01655 740585 ✋ £120 ① 8 🚗 Turn off A77 on to B7023, at Crosshill turn right at war memorial on to B741, signed Kilkerran. After 2 miles (3.2km) turn left, hotel is 1 mile (1.5km) farther on

MELROSE
BURT'S HOTEL
www.burtshotel.co.uk
Family-owned hotel in a small market town, offering an hospitable welcome. As well as comfortable rooms, the hotel also has a formal restaurant with daily changing menus, and a relaxed bistro bar.

✉ Market Square TD6 9PN ☎ 01896 822285 ✋ £58 ① 20 🚗 A6091, 2 miles (3km) from A68 south of Earlston

MOFFAT
MOFFAT HOUSE
www.moffathouse.co.uk
At the heart of this picturesque town, the hotel has a good level of trade from both visitors and locals. The spacious bar lounge serves a variety of lunches and dinners; the restaurant offers a more formal environment. Bedrooms are generally spacious and quiet.

✉ High Street DG10 9HL ☎ 01683 220039 ✋ £100 ① 21 🚗 From M74 exit 15, take A701 for 1 mile (1.5km). Hotel at end of High Street

NEW LANARK
NEW LANARK MILL HOTEL
www.newlanark.org
This converted 18th-century cotton mill offers the opportunity to stay in the restored model village of New Lanark, now designated a World Heritage Site (▷ 121). Bright, modern styling throughout contrasts with features from the original mill, and there are stunning views over the River Clyde. There are also eight self-catering cottages.

✉ Mill One, New Lanark Mills ML11 9DB ☎ 01555 667200 ✋ £120 ① 38

Above *New Lanark stands on the banks of the River Clyde*

🚍 Signed from all major roads, M74 exit 7 and M8

NEWTON STEWART
KIRROUGHTREE HOUSE
www.kirroughtreehouse.co.uk
This 17th-century mansion is set in 3.2ha (8 acres) of landscaped gardens, next to Galloway Forest Park. Facilities include croquet and a 9-hole pitch and putt. Sumptuous day rooms are furnished with deep, cushioned sofas and antique and period pieces. Individually styled spacious bedrooms are thoughtfully equipped. Dinners are served in the elegant dining rooms by a friendly, attentive team. No children under 10.
✉ Minnigaff DG8 6AN ☎ 01671 402141 🖐 £180 🛈 17 🕐 Closed 4 Jan–16 Feb 🚍 From A75 take A712, New Galloway road. Entrance to hotel is 274m (300 yards) on left

PEEBLES
CRINGLETIE HOUSE
www.cringletie.com
This impressive baronial mansion has a superb walled garden that provides much of the kitchen's produce. Public rooms include a cocktail lounge with adjoining conservatory, and the first floor restaurant has a fine painted ceiling. Bedrooms are all individual and several are notably spacious.
✉ Edinburgh Road EH45 8PL ☎ 01721 725750 🖐 £220 🛈 13 🚍 2 miles (3km) north on A703

PORTPATRICK
FERNHILL
www.fernhillhotel.co.uk
Splendid harbour views are the chief delight of this hotel—and you can make the most of them from the conservatory restaurant and many of the bedrooms. A modern wing offers spacious and well-appointed rooms, some with balconies. Leisure facilities are available at a sister hotel in Stranraer.
✉ Heugh Road DG9 8TD ☎ 01776 810220 🖐 £116 🛈 36 🕐 Closed mid-Jan to mid-Feb 🚍 Just past Portpatrick village sign on A77, turn right before war memorial, hotel is 1st on left

ST. BOSWELLS
DRYBURGH ABBEY
www.dryburgh.co.uk
An imposing red sandstone mansion in an attractive riverside setting next to the ruined abbey. Private fishing is available. The inviting public areas include a choice of lounges, and the elegant first floor dining room overlooks the river. There is a good choice of accommodation, with suites and many spacious rooms.
✉ TD6 0RQ ☎ 01835 822261 🖐 £150 🛈 38 🚍 From A68 at St. Boswells turn on to B6404 through village. Continue for 2 miles (3.2km), turn left on to B6356 for Scott's View. Go through Clintmains village, hotel in 2 miles (3.2km)

TROON
LOCHGREEN HOUSE
www.costley-hotels.co.uk
This impressive country house hotel offers spacious bedrooms and is peacefully in 53ha (30 acres) of immaculate grounds, including a tennis court. There is a choice of lounges with open fires. The brasserie menu includes interesting options for a light lunch, with the restaurant providing the main dining experience.
✉ Monktonhill Road, Southwood KA10 7EN ☎ 01292 313343 🖐 £175 🛈 42 🚍 From the A77 follow signs for Prestwick Airport; 0.5 miles (800m) before the airport take B749 to Troon. Hotel is 1 mile (1.5km) on left

TURNBERRY
WESTIN TURNBERRY RESORT
www.turnberry.co.uk
This world-famous hotel enjoys magnificent views over to Arran, Ailsa Craig and the Mull of Kintyre. Facilities include a superb championship golf course, the Colin Montgomerie Golf Academy, a luxurious spa and a host of outdoor and country pursuits. Elegant bedrooms and suites are located in the main hotel, while the lodges provide spacious, well-equipped accommodation. As well as the stylish main restaurant for dining, there is the Lounge, or the relaxed Clubhouse.
✉ KA26 9LT ☎ 01655 331000 🖐 £159 🛈 219 🕐 Closed 12–27 Dec 🚍 From Glasgow take the A77/M77 south. Beyond Kirkoswald, follow signs for A719 Turnberry village, hotel 500m (550 yards) on right

SIGHTS 156
WALKS 174
WHAT TO DO 178
EATING 182
STAYING 184

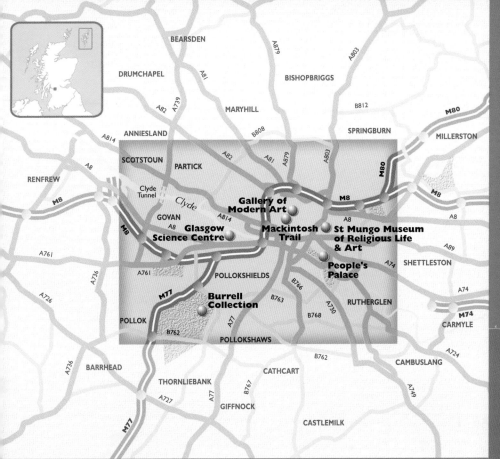

GLASGOW

It may not have the Scottish Parliament, or the Festival, but there is no doubting that Scotland's largest city is a cultural dynamo. While Glasgow lacks the obvious tourist charm of its rival on the east coast, it makes up for this in the quality of its galleries, the warmth of its people and the vitality of its nightlife. The exceptional Burrell Collection, Kelvingrove, the Hunterian and the People's Palace are world-class collections and should be taken at a leisurely pace. It can feel like a long way between some of the best sights, but if you have the time, this is a fine city to walk across. Look above the modern shop fronts and you will see the fantastic breadth of the Victorian architects' vision. Here are Venetian palaces, Egyptian temples, Gothic wonderlands and modernist gems, all cheek by jowl with the residential streets that run almost to the centre of the city. There are some excellent walking tours with guides who will explain the architectural highlights as you go. But Glasgow is also justly famous for its nightlife. Sauchiehall Street may no longer be the bawdy centre of it all, famed in music-hall song, but in the Merchant City you'll find a bar and restaurant scene to suit most tastes.

Glasgow traces its origins back to St. Mungo in the sixth century AD, who established a religious community here. A bishop was appointed in 1114 and the university came along in 1451. The Union of the Crowns in 1603 allowed seaborne trade with England to flourish, later expanding to Ireland, the Caribbean and the Americas. After the Act of Union in 1707 this trade took in the whole of the new British empire, but it was the industrial revolution which brought about the most dramatic changes. Textiles, dyeing, iron founding and shipbuilding all needed labour, and this arrived in the thousands of displaced Highlanders from the glens and Irish fleeing poverty and famine in their homeland. Glasgow's Celtic mix began to develop its own distinctive culture. By the middle of the 20th century the boom years had passed, and post-industrial Glasgow looked sorry and forlorn. But with a new spirit at the end of the century and into the 21st, Glasgow, like other British cities, has re-invented itself.

GLASGOW

0   200 m
0   200 yds

JORDANHILL

HYNDLAND

Kibble Palace and
Botanic Gardens

St Matthews
Free Church

BROOMHILL

DOWANHILL

Victoria
Park

Titan
Crane

VICTORIA PARK DRIVE SOUTH

South Street

A739

A814

CLYDESIDE EXPRESSWAY

Broomhill Drive

Thornwood Avenue

Crow Road

Dumbarton Road

PARTICK

KELVINHALL

BYRES ROAD

HILLHEAD

GREAT WESTERN ROAD

KELVINBRIDGE

Kelvin Way

Woodlands

ROAD

A81

A82

WHITEINCH

CLYDE TUNNEL

Clyde

PARTICK

PARTICK

BEITH STREET

Hunterian
Museum &
Art Gallery

Kelvingrove
Art Gallery
& Museum

Kelvingrove
Park

Argyle Street

Sauchiehall Street

SHIELDHALL

Govan Road

GOVAN

Museum of
Transport

YORKHILL

CLYDESIDE

EXPRESSWAY

EXHIBITION
CENTRE

Clydebuilt

Langlands Road

A739

A8

DRUMOYNE

GOVAN

Crossloan Road

Craigton Road

Govan Road

Summertown Road

Whitefield Road

Broomloan Road

Scottish Exhibition
& Conference Centre

Tall Ship at
Glasgow Harbour

Glasgow
Science
Centre

Clyde

Govan Road

LANCEFIELD QUAY

SHIELDHALL ROAD

Helen Street

EDMISTON DRIVE

IBROX

PAISLEY ROAD WEST

CESSNOCK

KINNING
PARK

PAISLEY RD

BERRYKNOWES RD

CARDONALD

CRAIGTON

Cemetery

M8

A761

PAISLEY ROAD WEST

SHIELDS
ROAD

Shields Road

Scotla
Str
Sch

St Andr

House for an
Art Lover

DUMBRECK

Bellahouston
Park

Dumbreck Road

M77

Maxwell Drive

Drive

DUMBRECK

Nithsdale

St Andrews St

Road

POLLOKSHIELDS

Mosspark Drive

Bellahouston Boulevard

MOSSPARK

CORKERHILL

POLLOKSHIELDS
WEST

Terregles Avenue

MAXWELL
PARK

Darnley Road

**STRAT
BUNG**

Linthaugh Road

Corkerhill Road

Mosspark Drive

M77

Pollok
Country Park

DUMBRECK ROAD

HAGGS ROAD

CROSSMYLOOF

TITWOOD ROAD

CROSSMYLOOF

Minard Road

Langside Avenue

**Queer
Park**

Braidcraft Road

Burrell
Collection

Pollok
House

B769 ROAD

SHAWLANDS

Pollokshaws Road

SHAWLANDS

LANGSIDE

POLLOKSHAWS

POLLOKSHAWS
WEST

POLLOKSHAWS
EAST

A77

Greenbank
Garden

MUIREND

A

B

C

1

2

3

4

5

152

SPRINGBURN

COWLAIRS

BARNHILL

Cemetery

Petershill Road

PETERSHILL

Keppochill Road

PORT DUNDAS

ROYSTON

GERMISTON

Royston Road

Blochairn Road

North Woodside Leisure Centre

ST GEORGE'S CROSS

17

16

M8

15

Roystonhill

14

M8

13

8

The Tenement House

COWCADDENS

BAIRD ST

KYLE STREET

TOWNHEAD

ALEXANDRA PARADE

Alexandra Park

ALEXANDRA PARK

Glasgow School of Art

McLellan Galleries

Museum of Piping

Theatre Royal

Glasgow Cathedral

Glasgow Necropolis

A8

CUMBERNAULD ROAD

King's Theatre

Buchanan Galleries & Royal Concert Hall

Provand's Lordship

Wishart Street

St Mungo Museum of Religious Life & Art

CUMBERNAULD ROAD

Vincent Street

BUCHANAN STREET

George Square

George Street

DENNISTOUN

DUKE STREET

Waterloo Street

Gallery of Modern Art

i

City Chambers

HIGH STREET

Duke Street

ANDERSTON

The Lighthouse

Italian Centre

HIGH STREET

Millerton St

A814

GLASGOW CENTRAL

Argyle Arcade

ST ENOCH

Tron Theatre

BELLGROVE

BIGGAR ST

9

BROOMIELAW

ST ENOCH

St Enoch Shopping Centre

LONDON ROAD

The Barras

GALLOWGATE

A89

Gallowgate

KINGSTON BRIDGE

GEORGE V BRIDGE

GLASGOW BRIDGE

VICTORIA BRIDGE

ALBERT BRIDGE

Glasgow Green

CALTON

Abercromby Street

Crownpoint Road

FIELDEN ST

Cook Street

BRIDGE STREET

The Green

People's Palace

BRIDGETON

LONDON ROAD

A74

WEST STREET

GORBALS ST

Citizens Theatre

BALLATER STREET

DALMARNOCK STREET

A749

Springfield Road

EGLINTON STREET

GORBALS

JAMES ST

LOKSHIELDS ST

CATHCART ROAD

HUTCHESONTOWN

CALEDONIA ROAD

KING'S DRIVE

Main Street

DUNN DALMARNOCK

DALMARNOCK

Strathclyde Street

DALMARNOCK ROAD

Victoria Road

RUTHERGLEN ROAD

SHAWFIELD DRIVE

Downiebrae Road

GOVANHILL

CALDER STREET

AIKENHEAD ROAD

B763 POLMADIE ROAD

FARMELOAN ROAD

CAMBUSLANG ROAD

A724

QUEEN'S PARK

Clyde

en's Drive

CROSSHILL

Albert Road

Cathcart Road

GLASGOW ROAD

RUTHERGLEN

RUTHERGLEN

A749

ageside Road

PROSPECTHILL ROAD

Quay Road

MOUNT FLORIDA

Scottish Football Museum

Holmwood

A728

Tramway Theatre

A730

A749

ATTLEFIELD

D

E

F

153

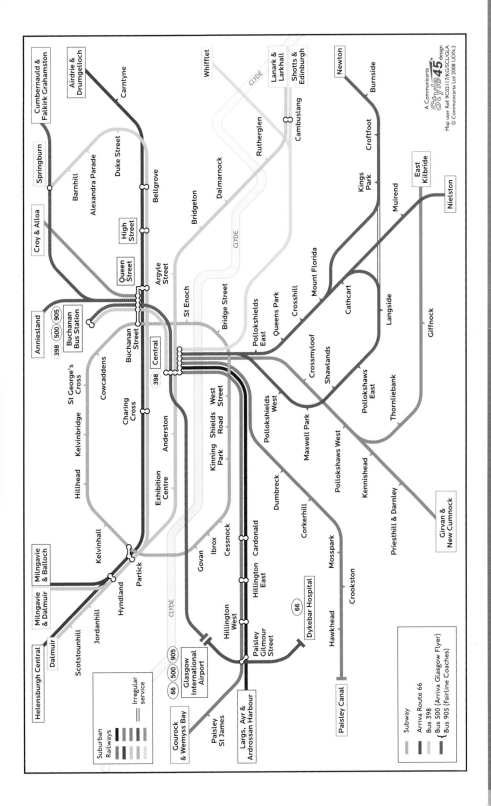

Helensburgh Central
Milngavie & Dalmuir
Milngavie & Balloch
Dalmuir

Cumbernauld & Falkirk Grahamston
Airdrie & Drumgelloch
Springburn
Croy & Alloa

Whifflet
Lanark & Larkhall
Shotts & Edinburgh
Newton
Burnside

East Kilbride
Nielston

Anniesland
398 500 905
Buchanan Bus Station
Queen Street
High Street
Argyle Street
Central
398

Carntyne
Barnhill
Alexandra Parade
Duke Street
Bellgrove
Bridgeton
Dalmarnock
Rutherglen
Cambuslang
Crofthoot
Kings Park
Muirend
Giffnock

St George's Cross
Cowcaddens
Charing Cross
Kelvinbridge
Hillhead
Kelvinhall
Jordanhill
Scotstounhill
Hyndland
Partick

St Enoch
Bridge Street
Pollokshields East
Queens Park
Crosshill
Mount Florida
Cathcart
Langside
Crossmyloof
Shawlands
Pollokshaws East
Thornliebank

Exhibition Centre
Anderston
Kinning Park
Shields Road
West Street
Pollokshields West
Maxwell Park
Pollokshaws West
Kennishead
Priesthill & Darnley

Girvan & New Cumnock

Glasgow International Airport
66 500 905

Govan
Ibrox
Cessnock
Hillington East
Hillington West
Cardonald
Dumbreck
Corkerhill
Mosspark
Crookston

Dykebar Hospital
66
Paisley Gilmour Street
Hawkhead
Paisley Canal

Gourock & Wemyss Bay
Largs, Ayr & Ardrossan Harbour
Paisley St James

CLYDE
CLYDE
CLYDE

Suburban Railways

Irregular service

Subway
Arriva Route 66
Bus 398
{ Bus 500 (Arriva Glasgow Flyer)
Bus 905 (Fairline Coaches)

A Communicarta
Style45 design
Map user Ref 9C02117KG/SCL/GLA
© Communicarta Ltd 2008 UDN.2

155

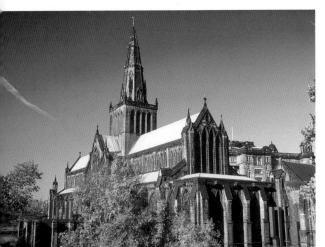
Above *Glasgow Cathedral lies to the east of the city centre*
Left *The inside of the City Chambers epitomizes full-blown Victoriana*

THE BARRAS
www.glasgow-barrowland.com
The famous flea market on the poorer east side of the city is a relic of a bygone age, a gritty, witty contrast to Glasgow's modern veneer of sleek shopping centres and debonair café society. It dates back to the 1920s, when enterprising street trader Margaret McIver raised a roof for stand-holders, who had previously sold their wares from open barrows. Today it's a sprawling hotchpotch of sheds, stands and warehouses that looks forlorn and tattered during the week, but comes to life at week-ends. You'll find everything from antique furniture to fortune-tellers and counterfeit designer clothing, plus a monthly farmers' market.
✚ 153 E3 ✉ Gallowgate and London Road, between Ross Street and Bain Street ☎ 0141 552 4601 🕐 Sat–Sun 10–5 ✋ Free 🚊 Glasgow Central, Glasgow Queen Street

BOTANIC GARDENS
Glasgow's botanic gardens grew out of a collection of plants for medical use held by the university. It moved to this site in the West End suburbs in 1842, and now covers 11ha (27 acres). Its highlight is the Kibble Palace, a 2,137sq m (23,000sq ft) glasshouse named after its donor,

who had it moved here from his own garden in 1872. Today it houses tree ferns from Australia and New Zealand, and plants from Africa, the Americas and the Far East.
✚ 152 C1 ✉ 730 Great Western Road G12 0UE ☎ 0141 276 1614 🕐 Daily 7–dusk; glasshouses: summer daily 10–4.45; winter daily 10–4.15 ✋ Free 🚇 Hillhead 🚌 G8, 11, 18, 20, 41, 66, 89, 90 🚇

BURRELL COLLECTION
▷ 158–161.

CITY CHAMBERS
www.glasgow.gov.uk
This opulent, grandiose 'palace' fills one side of George Square. The building was opened by Queen Victoria in 1888. From the outside, beneath the Venetian-style central tower, pediments and corner cupolas you can glimpse the richness of the gilded ceilings and grand entrance hall. It's worth joining one of the free tours to see the interior properly. Enjoy the murals of the vast banqueting hall, the marble staircases, and the mosaic ceiling of the loggia. The design captures the confidence of what was Britain's second city at the time, and is by architect William Young (1843–1900).
✚ 153 E2 ✉ George Square G2 1DU ☎ 0141 287 4018 🕐 Mon–Fri 9–5 ✋ Free 🚇 Buchanan Street; St. Enoch's

🚊 Glasgow Queen Street ❓ Tours at 10.30 and 2.30

CLYDEBUILT
www.scottishmaritimemuseum.org
Clydeside is synonymous with the golden age of shipbuilding in the late 19th and early 20th centuries, when the river was dredged to allow passage for huge vessels such as the *QE2*. You can catch the water bus down to Braehead, for this, one of three outlets of the Scottish Maritime Museum (the others are at Irvine and Dumbarton). Different galleries lead you through the history of shipbuilding here, from the 18th-century wooden sailing ships which were the mainstay of Glasgow's tobacco trade, to the liners of the 1940s. You can see how a liner was built, and try your hand at loading or berthing a vessel.
✚ 152 A2 ✉ Braehead Shopping Centre, Kings Inch Road G51 4BN ☎ 0141 886 1013 🕐 Mon–Sat 10–5.30, Sun 11–5 ✋ Adult £4.25, child (5–15) £2.50, under 5 free, family £10 🚌 22, 25, 55 🚇

GALLERY OF MODERN ART (GOMA)
▷ 162.

GLASGOW CATHEDRAL
www.glasgowcathedral.org.uk
With the blackness of its stonework, its modern stained glass, and its setting below the Victorian necropolis (▷ 164), you could be forgiven for assuming that Glasgow Cathedral was also 19th century. In fact it dates from the 13th to the 15th centuries. The central tower and spire are replacements dating from about 1406 The cathedral is dedicated to St. Mungo, or Kentigern, who died in AD603. His shrine, once a major pilgrimage site, is in the crypt, and the symbols of a robin, fish, bell and tree on the lampposts outside are references to miracles performed by the saint.
✚ 153 E2 ✉ Castle Street G4 0QZ ☎ 0141 552 6891 🕐 Apr–end Sep Mon–Sat 9.30–5.30, Sun 2–5.30; rest of year Mon–Sat 9.30–4, Sun 1–4 ✋ Free 🚌 213 🚊 High Street 🚇

INFORMATION

www.glasgowmuseums.com

✚ 152 B5 ✉ Pollok Country Park, 2060 Pollokshaws Road, G43 1AT ☎ 0141 287 2550 🕐 Mon–Thu, Sat 10–5, Fri, Sun 11–5 ✋ Free, but may be a charge for some special exhibitions; parking charge 🚌 45, 47, 48, 57 🚆 Pollokshaws West 🍴 Self-service café and restaurant on the lower floor with views over the parkland 🎁 Extensive gift shop at the entrance, with everything from postcards to pricey ceramics ❓ Free guided tours several times a day — check on arrival, and listen for the announcement

Above *Degas'* La Repetition *depicts a dance rehearsal*

INTRODUCTION

The Burrell Collection is housed in a modern, purpose-built museum set in leafy Pollok Country Park, south of the centre of Glasgow. Outside it appears modest and unassuming. Inside is a treasure trove of decorative arts, crafts and paintings, from all corners of the world. A changing selection of objects is shown, and the overall impression in the museum is of a few outstanding items very well displayed, so they are never overwhelming. There is always something of interest around the next corner. The museum is mainly on one level, with a small mezzanine floor, and a cafeteria downstairs. Look out for the latest temporary exhibitions, which may be more interactive.

This priceless collection of about 9,000 varied pieces of art from around the world was gifted to Glasgow in 1944 by Sir William Burrell (1861–1958) and his wife, Constance. Burrell had collected rare and precious works of art since his teens. It was 1983 before a suitable home for the collection could be made, away from city pollution in Pollok Country Park. Its huge feature walls of glass seem to pull the woodland greenery inside. Hundreds of panels from the stained-glass collection are incorporated into the windows of the South Gallery, where the natural daylight reveals their jewel-like colours.

Apart from the Burrell Collection, Pollok Country Park itself has much to offer. It was recently voted the Best Park in Britain, and has belonged to Glasgow City Council since 1966. It was given to them by Mrs. Anne Maxwell Macdonald, of the Maxwell family who had owned the estate for over 700 years. Look for the herd of Highland cattle—not something you see too often in Glasgow.

WHAT TO SEE
MEDIEVAL TAPESTRIES

Burrell loved European art of the medieval period, and while the reconstruction of rooms from his 15th-century castle form the dullest part of the museum, the objects he collected—including furnishings and stained glass—are altogether more exciting. The tapestries form the rich core of this collection, outstanding in their quality of design and workmanship, and in the preservation of their vibrant colours. The *Burgundian Peasants Hunting Rabbits with Ferrets* is a masterpiece dating from 1450–75, full of life and wit. Look for the cheeky rabbits, hiding amid the foliage while nets are prepared and ferrets released. The slightly earlier *Hercules on Mount Olympus* (c1425) shows the hero initiating the Olympic Games. While it is more formal in subject matter, there is a great vitality about the faces of both people and horses in the crowded scene, which makes this a remarkable work of art.

Above *Detail from the 15th-century tapestry* Burgundian Peasants Hunting Rabbits with Ferrets
Below *Collector William Burrell made his fortune in shipping*

RODIN'S *THE THINKER*

The light and airy Central Courtyard is dominated by the massive *Warwick Vase*, an 18th-century marble reconstruction incorporating fragments of a second-century original. Around the edge of the space are set smaller statues, including an icon of modern sculpture: Auguste Rodin's famous bronze, *The Thinker*. This was originally sculpted in 1880, one figure among hundreds in a huge commission for the entrance to a Paris museum, inspired by Dante's *Divine Comedy* and entitled *The Gates of Hell*. This brooding, muscled figure was to represent the poet himself, and reflects the inspiration of artists such as Michaelangelo and William Blake. The project was never completed, but what later became known as *The Thinker* took on its own life. Originally cast as a small bronze, the statue was scaled up between 1902 and 1904, and now exists in many different forms and sizes.

KEY

1 Dining room from Hutton Castle
2 Central Courtyard (the Warwick Vase, Rodin's *The Thinker*)
3 Doorway from Hornby Castle
4 Ancient Egypt, Greece and Rome (stone sculptures, reliefs, vessels, bronze, glass etc)
5 Drawing room from Hutton Castle
6 Chinese Art and Ceramics (earthenware, porcelain, jades, furniture)
7 Hall from Hutton Castle
8 Tapestry Galleries (tapestries are displayed in four consecutive galleries, with appropriate period furniture)
9 Arms and Armour (European, 13th to 17th century)
10 Needlework Room (embroidered textiles, lace)
11 Gothic Art (medieval religious art)
12 16th and 17th Century Room (paintings and furnishings)
13 Islamic Art (carpets, rugs, early ceramics and metalwork)
14 Burrell the Man, Burrell the Building (background to the collection)
15 Stained Glass
16 Temporary exhibitions
17 Montron Arch
18 Mezzanine floor: Paintings (generally including works by 19th-century French artists Degas, Cézanne and Boudin)

TIPS

» Allow time for your eyes to adjust to the low levels of light in the inner galleries, to really appreciate the tapestries.
» On a hot summer's day the temperature in the outer galleries can become high, so visit them early in the morning, then retreat to the cooler, windowless interior.
» The Country Park also has wildlife gardens, a ranger centre, signed woodland and riverside walks and picnic places. Pollok House (▷ 170) is worth a visit on its own.

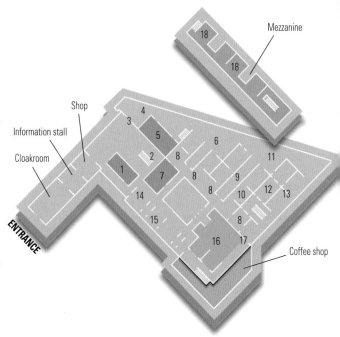

ORIENTAL ART

Although Burrell never travelled to the Far East himself, his Oriental collection is one of the best-known features of the museum, including beautiful jade carvings and magnificent porcelain figures. Rare bulbous Neolithic urns of painted earthenware date back to the Yangshao culture, which flourished more than 4,000 years ago—their survival is remarkable. Look for a comical pair of Han-dynasty earthenware bottles in the shape of startled owls. The huge Bactrian camel, glazed in brilliant orange and green, dates from slightly later; it would have been buried in the third century with its dead owner as a symbol of wealth. The soft green celadon-glazed pottery is another highlight, with delicate bowls and dishes in timeless shapes.

REMBRANDT SELF-PORTRAIT

The 16th and 17th Century Room is dominated by furniture of the period, and very British in feel. But look a little more closely, and you'll see a familiar face looking out at you from under a big, black Dutch hat. It's the face of the young Rembrandt van Rijn (1606–69), in a self-portrait of 1632, done at a time when the artist was becoming established as a portrait painter in Amsterdam, and a full ten years before he would produce his most famous work, *The Night Watch*. Rembrandt painted around 60 self-portraits during the course of his life, starting in 1629, and was the first artist to produce such a detailed autobiographical study. In the early days, he may have been saving money on models, but by the end of his life he was intrigued by the decay that he saw in his own face. A Rembrandt self-portrait of 1634 was discovered in recent years: It had been overpainted by his students, to make it anonymous and easier to sell. In its restored form, it was valued at a cool £5 million.

DEGAS PICTURES

Burrell's collection includes many paintings and pastels by the great French artists of the 19th century. He was fascinated by the work of Edgar Degas (1834–1917), best known for his images of ballet dancers, in paint and in bronze. The bright pastel *Les Jupes Rouges* is a notable example of this, portraying dancers in rehearsal. He was particularly good at capturing dancers in their private moments, in the wings at the theatre, waiting to dance, or perhaps tying on a shoe or casually stretching out a limb. Typically the women are caught in a half-light that shows up the translucence of their costume, as well as body expression, in the act of movement. Precise paintwork gave way to more impressionistic images, and pastel became his preferred medium after 1880. The artist had learned and practised his skill by drawing race horses, and his pastel *Jockeys in the Rain* (c1881) is also in the collection. It shows restless horses lining up for the start of a race, and the impatience of the animals before they set off is brilliantly captured in the flowing pastel lines.

MANET SKETCHES

Degas was influenced by fellow Parisian artist Édouard Manet (1832–83), who scandalized polite society with his bohemian image of young men picnicking with a naked woman in *Déjeuner sur l'Herbe* in 1862. In later life, Manet's painting became much looser and more impressionistic, culminating in the well-known *Un Bar aux Folies-Bergères* (1881–82). A glimpse of the work that led up to that masterpiece can be seen in Manet's sketches in the Burrell Collection, which include the delightful *Women Drinking Beer*, a free-flowing pastel of women relaxing in a Paris bar.

The Burrell Collection also includes other 19th-century French painters such as Paul Cézanne and Eugène Boudin. Not quite as famous as some of his contemporaries, Boudin was one of the first Impressionists and greatly influenced Monet, among others. The Burrell has his 1871 painting of *A Dutch Canal*, though in fact it is believed to be of the commercial dock in Brussels.

Above *Manet's* Women Drinking Beer, *a pastel dating from around 1878*
Below *The South Gallery of the Burrell*

INFORMATION

www.glasgowmuseums.com
Clunky, but useful for latest exhibitions.
🕀 153 D2 ✉ Royal Exchange Square,
Queen Street G1 3AZ ☎ 0141 229 1996
or 0845 225 5121 🕐 Mon–Wed and
Sat 10–5, Thu 10–8, Fri and Sun 11–5
🖐 Free 🚌 6, 12, 18, 20, 40, 41, 61, 62,
66, 75 🚇 Buchanan Street, St. Enoch's
🚉 Queen Street, Glasgow Central
🍴 Small café in basement 🎁 Shop
on ground floor sells good arty souvenirs
❓ Volunteer guides provide tours most
weekends (donations)

Below *GoMA is one of Scotland's major
contemporary art venues*

GALLERY OF MODERN ART (GOMA)

This exceptional contemporary art gallery at the very heart of the city never fails to provoke and inspire. GoMA occupies what was once a 1780s tobacco baron's palatial mansion. The gallery is renowned for going its own populist way, and the image it sells of itself is of the mounted statue of the Duke of Wellington outside, crowned by a traffic cone. (This icon of modern Glasgow is less frequently seen now, as the statue is better protected from the so-called vandals.)

Inside the grandiose pillored entrance, you'll find a great exhibition space, which is usually given over to some of the best contemporary works from Glasgow Museum's collection. This changes every six months or so, but it may include dramatic pieces by L. S. Lowry, the Boyle family, Sir Eduardo Paolozzi, Grayson Perry or Sir Stanley Spencer. Upstairs you can see recent acquisitions of works by Scottish artists. Look for installations by Martin Boyce, Christine Boyland and Toby Paterson.

WHAT TO LOOK FOR

Because this is an ever-changing exhibition, it's difficult to pin down even a handful of works that are likely to still be there in six months' time. However, that is what makes the Gallery of Modern Art so special, and it certainly seems to work with the public—this is the second most visited art gallery in Britain outside London.

The city's museum service has a positive acquisitions policy for contemporary Scottish art, so look out for works by artists such as Roderick Buchanan, Graham Fagen and Toby Paterson in the future. For detailed accounts of what is currently on display check the gallery's website or look for the *Preview* magazine.

GLASGOW SCIENCE CENTRE

The Science Centre lies on the south side of the River Clyde, and has three distinct elements. The first is a 24m (80ft) screen IMAX theatre housed in the silver titanium-skinned 'egg', which shows a changing schedule of films, including some in 3D. Second is a dizzying 122m (400ft) high aerofoil-shaped viewing tower, the Glasgow Tower.

The tallest tower in Scotland, it is in the *Guinness Book of Records* for its rather unusual claim to fame: it's the only building in the world that is able to rotate a full 360 degress into the prevailing wind. You have to hope that the winds aren't strong enough, however, as the Tower will close if they exceed 65kph (40mph). It takes two and a half minutes to get all the way up to the viewing cabin, which is 105m (344ft) high and gives views of up to 20 miles (32km) over the city and the surrounding countryside. The foundations giving it its stability are about 20m (66ft) deep and consist of 2,953 tons of concrete.

The main attraction is the Science Mall, with four floors containing 500 interactive exhibits. This futuristic building, with its glass wall overlooking the 'Armadillo' exhibition centre to the city beyond, was designed with a curved roof to avoid problems of wind turbulence. How do we know? It's just one of the fascinating exhibits on the second floor, in Structures, which also lets you into the engineering secrets of the Forth Rail Bridge.

The biggest laughs can be found at the distorting mirrors (floor 1). Other highlights include using computer screens to design your own dance sequence (floor 2); seeing how an artificial arm picks up signals from your body to move (floor 3); the Kinex construction sector (floor 2); and a walk-on piano for under 7s (floor 1).

It's easy for children to get overexcited and simply run through the exhibits, hitting buttons and seeing nothing. To get the best out of the experience, slow down, find something that interests them, be prepared to wait your turn, and explore in depth.

INFORMATION

www.glasgowsciencecentre.org
🛈 152 C3 🛈 50 Pacific Quay G51 1EA
☎ 0871 540 1000 🕐 Mid-Mar to end Oct daily 10–5; Nov to mid-Mar Tue–Sun 10–5 💷 Science Mall: adult £7.95, child (3–15) £5.95, under 3 free; IMAX: adult £7.95, child £5.95; Glasgow Tower: adult £6.95, child £4.95; combination tickets available 🚌 24, 89, 90 🚇 Cessnock 🚆 Exhibition Centre 🍽 Foyer restaurant seats up to 250 ☕ Two cafés and brasserie 🎁 Extensive gift shop with pocket money toys, serious scientific bits and everything in between ❓ Birdbot, an animated crane on the second floor, can answer your questions about the day's events

TIPS

» Can be overwhelming at peak holiday times, so check timed shows you want to see and plan your visit around them.
» To avoid some of the crowds, start at the top and work down.

Above *Titanium cladding gives the Science Centre a space-age look*

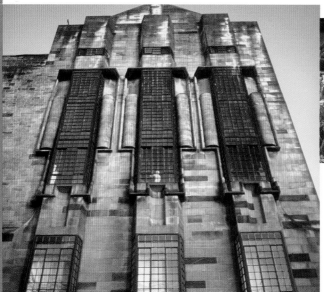

Left *The austere facade of the School of Art by Charles Rennie Mackintosh*
Above *Blooms in the Greenbank Garden*
Right *Inside the House for an Art Lover*

GLASGOW GREEN

www.glasgow.gov.uk
This green space in the East End is the oldest public park in Scotland, gifted to the people in 1450 and resonant with the city's history. For centuries it was the place where washing was dried, livestock grazed and criminals were hanged. From 1650, merchants watched the River Clyde eagerly from the top of the Steeple, to see if their ships had come in. Bonnie Prince Charlie's army received a lukewarm reception when it camped here in 1746. The obelisk of blackened brick was the first memorial anywhere to be raised to Lord Nelson (1806). The city's earliest golf club played here in the 1780s, and both Rangers and Celtic football clubs were founded on the Green.

It's the home of the People's Palace (▷ 171), and famous landmarks around the perimeter include the unlikely red and gold facade of Templeton Business Centre, a former carpet factory of 1889 by William Leiper, modelled on the Doge's Palace in Venice, and the McLennan Arch, the rescued facade of the old Assembly Rooms.
➕ 153 E3 ℹ️ 11 George Square G2 1DY, tel 0141 204 4400 🚇 Glasgow Central

GLASGOW NECROPOLIS

www.glasgownecropolis.org
This is Glasgow's fascinating city of the dead, stuffed to bursting point with ostentatious and florid monuments to Victorian worthies, the wealthy industrialists and tobacco merchants who developed the city in the 19th century. Their competitive spirit showed even after death, with extraordinary monuments commissioned from the finest architects of the day, including Alexander 'Greek' Thomson. The burial ground was set out in 1833 on a hilltop near the cathedral, where it was felt that it could be contained, thus avoiding the spread of infectious diseases such as cholera and typhus. It is said to have been based on the Père Lachaise Cemetery in Paris. There's a great view of the crowded skyline of the Necropolis from the third floor of the St. Mungo Museum (▷ 172).
➕ 153 E2 ℹ️ 11 George Square G2 1DY, tel 0141 204 4400 or 0845 225 5121 🕐 Daily 10–6 ♿ Free 🚌 213 🚇 High Street

GLASGOW SCHOOL OF ART

www.gsa.ac.uk
Glasgow's art school was founded in 1845. By 1896 it was clear that a new building was required, and a competition for a design to suit this awkward site on the side of a steep hill was announced. The winner was Charles Rennie Mackintosh (1868–1928), an innovative architect who had trained at the college and was beginning to gain a reputation in the city (▷ 168–169). The Glasgow School of Art became known as his masterpiece.

The exterior is severe, yet the stonework is adorned with a light, confident touch of wrought iron at the windows, on railings and on the roof. Inside, he designed everything down to the light fittings, creating a practical working space with a distinctive Arts and Crafts style that still, over 100 years later, looks fresh and modern. The tour includes the magnificent library, and an exhibition of artwork by Mackintosh.
➕ 153 D2 ✉️ 167 Renfrew Street G3 6RQ ☎️ 0141 353 4526 🕐 Tours Apr–end Sep daily 10, 11, 12, 1, 2, 3, 4; Oct–end Mar Mon–Sat 11, 2, 3 ♿ Adult £6.50, child £4.80, under 10 free 🚇 Cowcaddens 🚉 Queens Street 📷

GLASGOW SCIENCE CENTRE

▷ 163.

GREENBANK GARDEN

www.nts.org.uk
Some 7 miles (11.3km) south of the city centre, this garden was gifted to the National Trust for Scotland in 1976 as a demonstration piece,

to inspire suburban gardeners and show just what can be grown in a heavy clay soil.

Set in a frost pocket, with 1ha (2.5 acres) of walled garden and extensive policies (grounds) beyond, Greenbank prides itself on being very much a garden that normal people can aspire to. That may be a little optimistic, given that it contains over 3,500 different plants. As well as ideas you should be able to take away some unusual plants, available from the shop.

🕂 152 C5 ✉ Greenbank House, Flenders Road, Clarkston G76 8RB ☎ 0844 493 2201 🕙 Garden: daily 9.30–dusk. house: Easter–end Oct Sun 2–4 ✋ (NTS) adult £5, child (5–16) £4, under 5 free, family £14 🚌 44 💻 ♿

HOUSE FOR AN ART LOVER

www.houseforanartlover.co.uk
The House for an Art Lover is a fantasy, set out on paper in 1901 without limitations of budget or client's whims, by Charles Rennie Mackintosh (1868–1928) and his wife, Margaret Macdonald (1865–1933). It was for a competition set

by a German magazine for 'a grand house in a thoroughly modern style', but their entry was disqualified. The physical reality was achieved only in 1996, when artists and craftspeople were brought together by the City Council and the School of Art to build the dream in leafy Bellahouston Park. And what a dream it is, with perfect proportions, light, open spaces, a harmonious balance of straight and curved lines, and every attention to detail in the furnishings and fittings. There are recitals in the Music room on Sundays.

🕂 152 B3 ✉ Bellahouston Park, 10 Dumbreck Road G41 5BW ☎ 0141 353 4770 🕙 Apr–end Sep Mon–Wed 10–4, Thu–Sun 10–1; Oct–end Mar Sat–Sun 10–1 ✋ Adult £3.50, child £2.50, under 10 free, family £7 🚌 9, 36, 38, 54, 56 🚇 Ibrox 🚉 Dumbreck 💻 ♿

HUNTERIAN MUSEUM AND ART GALLERY

www.hunterian.gla.ac.uk
William Hunter (1718–83) was a Glasgow-trained physician, who bequeathed his scientific collections

to his old university. They were put on show in 1807, making this the oldest public museum in Scotland.

Hunter's coin collection formed the basis for one of the museum's specialities today. Other strengths are geology and archaeology (including Roman finds in Scotland). The magnificent art collection, in a separate building across University Avenue, began with Hunter's purchases of 17th-century Flemish, Dutch and Italian masters. Today it includes a range of more modern art, with works by the Scottish Colourists, the Glasgow Boys, and American James McNeill Whistler (1834–1903).

The Mackintosh House, an intriguing reconstruction, was made long after the architect's death (▷ 169).

🕂 152 C1 ✉ University of Glasgow, 82 Hillhead Street G2 8QQ ☎ 0141 330 4221/5431 🕙 Mon–Sat 9.30–5; Mackintosh House closed daily 12.30–1.30 ✋ Free. Mackintosh House £3 (free Wed after 2pm) 🚇 Hillhead 🚌 44, 59 💻 ♿

KELVINGROVE ART GALLERY AND MUSEUM

www.glasgowmuseums.com

This sprawling red-brick pile of Edwardiana dates from 1902 and houses outstanding art and objects. Its interiors have been lovingly restored and new facilities added, such as a History Discovery Centre and a Mini Museum. Since its restoration, the museum has been geared more towards children than adults and the changes divide opinion. The interpretation of its fine collection of paintings, in particular, has been criticized.

The first-floor galleries cover themes such as Scottish Identity in Art, Glasgow and the World, and Scotland's First People. Dutch, Italian and French art is also represented. The ground floor introduces themes of Life and Expression. There are Discovery Centres devoted to Art and the Environment with 'hands-on' displays. There are also galleries covering Charles Rennie Mackintosh, Scotland's Wildlife and Scottish Art.

Among the fantastic paintings on display are works by Rembrandt, Constable and Monet, as well as items by the Glasgow Boys and Scottish Colourists. The Armoury exhibits include field armour from the 15th century and the natural history display features Sir Roger the Elephant, as well as up-to-date interactive exhibts.

There is a café/restaurant on the lower ground floor.

✚ 152 C2 ✉ Argyle Street, Glasgow G3 8AG ☎ 0141 276 9599 🕙 Mon–Thu, Sat 10–5, Fri, Sun 11–5 👋 Free 🚌 9, 16, 18, 42, 62 🚇 Partick ▢

Top left *The tower that gives the Lighthouse its name*

Above *The Museum of Piping is dedicated to the history of the bagpipe*

Opposite *You could spend hours in the fascinating Kelvingrove Art Gallery and Museum*

THE LIGHTHOUSE

www.thelighthouse.co.uk

This is Glasgow's museum of architecture and design. Completed in 1895, the building was the first public commission by Charles Rennie Mackintosh (▷ 168–169), and gets its name from the tower that dominates the structure. As well as a permanent Mackintosh display, there are extensive temporary exhibitions relating to other aspects of architecture and design in the city.

A ride in the elevator to the viewing platform gives a breathtaking Glasgow panorama.

✚ 153 D2 ✉ 11 Mitchell Lane G1 3NU ☎ 0141 221 6362 🕙 Mon and Wed–Sat 10.30–5, Tue 11–5, Sun 12–5 👋 Adult £3, child (5–12) £1, under 5 free 🚌 9, 11, 12, 16, 18, 20, 23, 40, 41, 42, 44, 45, 47, 48, 54, 56, 57, 59, 61, 62, 64, 66, 75A 🚇 Buchanan Street 🚉 Glasgow Queen Street, Glasgow Central ▢ 🍴 🏛

MACKINTOSH TRAIL

▷ 168–169.

MUSEUM OF PIPING

www.thepipingcentre.co.uk

An Italianate former church of 1872 at the top of Hope Street is the home of the National Piping Centre,

Scotland's centre of excellence for the learning and performance of bagpipe music. Students from all over the world come here to study.

The building incorporates an auditorium for concerts, a sound archive and the small museum. This is an intriguing outpost of the National Museum of Scotland (▷ 72–75), dedicated to the history of the Highland bagpipe, which dates back to the 14th century.

A unique visual interpretation of the pipe music known as *piobaireachd* can be see in the three windows above the main entrance (1996), by John K. Clark.

The bagpipes are popular all over the world, and the audio-visual displays are provided in five languages, including Gaelic.

There's also a shop where you can get advice on buying bagpipes, if you're interested, and find CDs, DVDs, sheet music and accessories, if you're a piper already.

✚ 153 D2 ✉ 30–34 McPhater Street, Cowcaddens G4 0HW ☎ 0141 353 0220 🕙 Jun–end Aug daily 10–4.30; Sep–end May closed Sun 👋 Adult £3, child (5–12) £2, under 5 free, family £10 🚌 40, 61, 66, 75 🚉 Queen Street 🚇 Cowcaddens ▢ 🏛

THE MACKINTOSH TRAIL

INFORMATION

www.crmsociety.com

153 D2 11 George Square G2 1DY, tel 0141 204 4400

TIPS

» If you're a Mackintosh fan, take a trip out to Helensburgh to see the Hill House, now owned by the National Trust for Scotland (▷ 196).

» You can purchase a Mackintosh Trail Ticket (£12 per person) from the Mackintosh Society. It includes entry to the Mackintosh House, the Lighthouse, Glasgow School of Arts, House for an Art Lover, The Hill House, the Mackintosh Church and Scotland Street School.

Above *Street lamps are a modern addition to the School of Art*

INTRODUCTION

You can hardly miss the designs of Charles Rennie Mackintosh in Glasgow today—his stylized roses and trademark lettering (tall, strong capitals softened by dots and lines) stare out on endless souvenirs from mugs and tea towels to mirrors and silver jewellery. The style has become so familiar it is known affectionately as 'Mockintosh', and Glasgow, it seems, can't get enough of it. Yet Mackintosh's designs flourished for a relatively brief spell in the early 20th century, and it is only in the last 30 years or so that serious attempts have been made to preserve the major works of this remarkable and original architect. Start your tour at the Lighthouse on Mitchell Lane (map 153 D2; ▷ 166).

Charles Rennie Mackintosh was born in Glasgow in 1868, and at the age of 16 was apprenticed to a firm of architects. While attending evening classes at the School of Art he met Herbert McNair, who became a life-long friend, and Margaret Macdonald (1865–1933), whom he married in 1900. McNair married Margaret's sister Frances, and the two couples, known as 'the Four', came to dominate the emerging Glasgow Style.

Mackintosh's partnership with his wife extended into design, and her input became an acknowledged part of his work. Mackintosh's first project was in 1893, a workaday building for the *Glasgow Herald* newspaper, which is now the Lighthouse. His design for his most famous structure, the School of Art, was commissioned in 1896, and his best work was completed in the first years of the 20th century.

By 1914, his distinctive fusion of the abstracted, flowing lines of art nouveau with the simplicity of the Arts and Crafts movement had passed from fashion in Britain. Disillusioned, he moved to England and later toured Europe—delicate watercolour paintings which survive from this period can be seen at the Hunterian Gallery. He died in 1928.

WHAT TO SEE

GLASGOW SCHOOL OF ART (▷ 164)
If you only have limited time to visit Glasgow, then a glimpse of the School of Art on Renfrew Street is a must. This is authentic Mackintosh, with strong, confident lines and bold touches of unusual, stylized decoration. Guided tours show how the architect's confidence carried through into every detail of the interior design.

WILLOW TEAROOMS
The Willow Tearooms are a short walk away, above a jeweller's shop at 217 Sauchiehall Street (Mon–Sat 9–5, Sun 11–4.15, tel 0141 332 0521). They offer a magnificent restored Mackintosh interior upstairs in the Room de Luxe, complete with mirrored walls inset with purple glass, and tall-backed silver chairs. First opened in 1904, this became the most famous of local entrepreneur Kate Cranston's revolutionary tea rooms, where respectable men and women could meet up, in private or in public, without the shadow of the 'demon' drink. Mackintosh also designed interiors for Cranston at Ingram Street, Buchanan Street and Argyle Street (see surviving elements in the National Museum of Scotland ▷ 72–75).

MACKINTOSH HOUSE
Located at the university's Hunterian Museum (▷ 165), this is the exquisite re-creation of the interior of the home which the Mackintoshes made together, with original furniture, as it appeared in 1906. The fittings here show clearly the influence of Japanese style on Charles's work, and its combination with his wife's flowing, organic art nouveau patterns. More Mackintosh furniture and designs from buildings now lost are on show in the gallery itself, along with paintings of Mediterranean scenes from his later travels.

HOUSE FOR AN ART LOVER (▷ 165)
Located away from the centre in Bellahouston Park, this is a modern build (1996) of a complete dream house designed by the couple in 1901.

SCOTLAND STREET SCHOOL
For another prime example of Mackintosh's architecture completed in his lifetime, travel south of the river to admire the stunning Scotland Street School (Apr–end Sep Mon–Thu, Sat 10–5, Fri, Sun 11–5; tel 0141 287 0500). Built between 1903 and 1906, it ceased to be a school in the 1970s and is now preserved as a museum of education. The front is dominated by two tall, glazed, semicircular towers which contain the main staircases—not winding round, as you might expect from their reference to Scottish baronial style, but uncompromisingly straight and set back from the glass to create a very different light and space. The back of the building reflects a more restrained and Classical style.

THE MACKINTOSH CHURCH
Located at Queen's Cross, 870 Garscube Road, northwest of the city centre, this is Mackintosh's only complete church, designed in 1897 (Mon–Fri 10–5, also Mar–end Oct Sun 2–5). It follows a simple Gothic revival style, creating a calm interior space. Attention to detail extended to the carvings of stylized birds and foliage on the oak pulpit.

TIP
» The Mackintosh Society arranges guided tours of the best sites. Contact them at Queen's Cross Church, tel 0141 946 6600.

Above *Taking tea in the Willow Tearooms*
Below *Chair designed by Mackintosh in the School of Art*

MUSEUM OF TRANSPORT

www.glasgowmuseums.com

The spacious arena, opposite the Kelvingrove Museum (▷ 166) in the West End, is packed with historic vehicles, from steam locomotives and horse-drawn trams to early Arrol Johnson cars. The Hillman Imp car was a less enduring rival to the Mini—look for the first Imp ever to come off the production line in 1963 (blue, and driven by the Duke of Edinburgh). There are fire engines, motorbikes, model ships, the earliest pedal bicycle, prams, caravans (trailers) and other transport paraphernalia. There's even a whole reconstructed 1930s Glasgow street scene. A new riverside site for the museum is planned for 2011.

✚ 152 C2 ✉ Kelvin Hall, 1 Bunhouse Road G3 8DP ☎ 0141 287 2720 ◷ Mon–Thu and Sat 10–5, Fri and Sun 11–5 ♨ Free ➌ 9, 11, 16, 18, 42, 62, 64 ☒ Kelvinhall ☒ Partick ▣ ▥

PEOPLE'S PALACE

▷ opposite.

POLLOK HOUSE

www.nts.org.uk

Pollok House is a compact grey stone mansion 3 miles (4.8km) south of the city centre. It feels like another world, thanks to the 146ha (361 acres) of country park which surround it. The house was started for Sir John Stirling Maxwell, 2nd Baronet in 1747, and stayed in the family until 1966. The 10th Baronet was a co-founder of the National Trust for Scotland, which now maintains the house. Inside it is light and airy, with comfortably small-scale rooms including an elegant library with some 7,000 volumes, in which chamber concerts are given. El Greco's portrait of *c*1577, *Lady in a Fur Wrap*, is here, a highlight of the otherwise rather gloomy collection of Spanish paintings.

✚ 152 B5 ✉ Pollok Country Park, 2060 Pollokshaws Road G43 1AT ☎ 0141 616 6410 ◷ Daily 10–5 ♨ (NTS) adult £8, child (5–16) £5, under 5 free, family £20, Apr–Oct; free Nov–Mar ➌ 45, 47, 48, 57 ☒ Pollokshaws West ▦ ▥

PROVAND'S LORDSHIP

www.glasgowmuseums.com

The oldest house in Glasgow, Provand's Lordship lies close to the medieval cathedral (▷ 157) and opposite the St. Mungo Museum, east of the city centre. It was built around 1471 as an almshouse, and until the end of World War I was still in use as a sweet shop. Outside, it is a simple sandstone building facing a busy road junction. Inside, the thick walls and tiny windows muffle the noise of the outside world. A lack of historic atmosphere is compensated for by the collection of beautiful 15th- and 16th-century wooden furniture. The story of Rab Ha', the weighty 'Glesca Glutton', can be seen amid the amusing 19th-century illustrations of Glasgow characters on the top floor. Rab would bet his appetite on horse races and even fox hunts, and was defeated only once, by a dish of oysters with cream and sugar. A medieval herb garden has been planted at the back.

✚ 153 E2 ✉ 3 Castle Street, G4 0RB ☎ 0141 552 8819 ◷ Mon–Thu and Sat 10–5, Fri and Sun 11–5 ♨ Free ➌ 11, 12, 37, 38, 42, 51, 89, 90 ☒ High Street

PEOPLE'S PALACE

Set on Glasgow Green (▷ 164), this red sandstone building of 1898 is less a museum, more a local institution which captures the wit, eccentricity and gritty character of the city. The main exhibitions are on the first and second floors, with temporary displays and the shop at ground level. It tells the history of Glasgow through familiar objects and quotes from real people. So, a doll's house model of a prefabricated house, made by Duncan MacKenzie for his daughters, highlights the story of the post-war housing shortages, and a mock-up of a 'steamie', or communal wash-house, brings the city's social history to life.

One section asks 'what happened to Glasgow's industry?' Making It In Glasgow is a corner on the top floor devoted to famous Glaswegians, with John Byrne's portrait of comedian Billy Connolly, singer Lulu's emerald trouser suit, books by Jimmy Boyle and Iain Banks, and television scripts for Ian Pattison's *Rab C. Nesbitt* comedies. A collection of tobacco tins recalls the city's heyday, and displays of the details of everyday life bring things up to date. It's great to listen to the people around you as they recognize and reminisce.

Adjoining the palace is the Winter Gardens, a vast Victorian glasshouse which has temporary exhibitions and a café, where you can enjoy a snack or drink among the tropical plants. Outside the Palace is the Doulton Fountain, the largest terracotta fountain in the world. It was given to the City of Glasgow by Sir Henry Doulton, of the Royal Doulton pottery firm, and first erected for the 1888 Empire Exhibition in Kelvingrove Park to celebrate Queen Victoria's Golden Jubilee the previous year. In 1890 it was moved from Kelvingrove to Glasgow Green, and so was here eight years before the People's Palace was opened. It's 14m (46ft) high, some 21m (70ft) across its base, and was moved to its present position between 2003 and 2005 at cost of £4 million.

INFORMATION

www.glasgowmuseums.com

⊞ 153 E3 ✉ Glasgow Green G40 1AT
☎ 0141 271 2962 ⏱ Mon–Thu and Sat 10–5, Fri and Sun 11–5 ♿ Free 🚌 18, 61, 62, 64, M2 🚉 High Street, Argyle Street, Bellgrove 📖 Various guidebooks available ☕ Winter Gardens café
🎁 Gift shop stocks items of particular local interest

Above *The People's Palace is a museum of social and working-class history*
Opposite top *A recreation of a 1930s street in the Museum of Transport*
Left *Pollock House*

INFORMATION
www.glasgowmuseums.com
✚ 153 E2 ✉ 2 Castle Street G4 0RH
☎ 0141 553 2557 ⏰ Mon–Thu and Sat
10–5, Fri and Sun 11–5 🎫 Free 🚌 11,
36, 37, 38, 42, 89 🚉 High Street 📖 £1
🍴 Modern restaurant on ground floor
🎁 Ground-floor gift shop stocks unusual
cards, jewellery and books

ST. MUNGO MUSEUM OF RELIGIOUS LIFE AND ART

The museum is set on three floors, with an international art collection, objects relating to religious life, and a section about religion in Glasgow. In the Gallery of Religious Art on the first floor, a native American chilkat blanket woven with animal designs of whales, wolves and beavers rubs shoulders with an Australian Aboriginal Dreamtime painting and the popping figures of a Nigerian ancestral screen. There is also a statue of Shiva, one of the principal Hindu deities. European art is represented by exquisite stained-glass panels, backlit and hanging at eye level, including a Burne-Jones angel with crimson halo. The Gallery of Religious Life juxtaposes items associated with particular ceremonies from different cultures.

On the third floor, dedicated to religion in Scotland, look for the moral tale, Buy your own Cherries, a lantern slide show used by temperance preachers to show the evils of drink. A display tells the story of the Protestant/Catholic divide in Glasgow, and there is a thought-provoking exhibit about religion, society and poverty. In a hands-on section, children can learn the basics of Buddhism, Christianity, Hinduism, Islam, Judaism and Sikhism.

On the ground floor of the museum is an excellent shop, with some fascinating and very different gift ideas. Here, too, is a popular café, esepcially when the weather is fine, where you can sit out and relax at tables which surround what was the first permanent Zen garden in Britain. It's a very peaceful place, its simple shapes representing the harmony between men and nature, and it's the perfect spot to end a visit to the musuem.

Above *St. Mungo established a religious community in Glasgow in the sixth century* AD

SCOTTISH FOOTBALL MUSEUM

www.scottishfootballmuseum.org.uk
Hampden Park is the home of Scotland's oldest football (soccer) team, Queen's Park, who claim to have invented the passing style of the game as it is played today. So it's appropriate that this is also the site of the world's first national football museum. An air of vanished glory haunts the 2,500 items on display. They include part of the original Hampden dressing room as it was known to great players of the past. You can even experience the 'Hampden roar' of the 1930s, when 140,000 men would pack in here for the big games. Tours of the modern pitch take place every hour and last 45 minutes.

🕂 153 D5 ✉ The National Stadium, Hampden Park G42 9BA ☎ 0141 616 6139 🕐 Mon–Sat 10–5, Sun 11–5 👋 Museum: adult £6, child (5–15) £3, under 5 free; museum and stadium: adult £9, child £4.50. Stadium tour only: adult £6, child £3 🚌 75 🚇 Mount Florida via Glasgow Central 🚇 Bridge Street 📖 🏛

TALL SHIP AT GLASGOW HARBOUR

www.thetallship.com; www.glenlee.co.uk
The best view of this fine old steel-hulled sailing ship, moored on the River Clyde near the 'Armadillo' exhibition centre, is from the windows of the Science Centre, opposite (▷ 163). The SV *Glenlee* was built on the Clyde in 1896, and carried mixed cargoes four times around the world before serving as a training ship for the Spanish Navy. She was eventually rescued in 1993 and brought here for refurbishment. Today she's one of only five Clyde-built sailing ships left afloat. On board, you can see the huge cargo hold, the restored crew's quarters and the galley, complete with original sounds and smells. Access is through the Pumphouse Visitor Centre, with changing exhibitions, nautical gift shop and café-bar. Don't miss tales of the ship's voyages, told on board on the 'Tween Deck.

🕂 152 C2 ✉ 100 Stobcross Road G3 8QQ ☎ 0141 222 2513 🕐 Mar–end Oct daily 10–5; rest of year daily 10–4 👋 Adult £4.95, child (5–16) £3.75 (1 free per full paying adult, under 5 free) 🚌 64 🚌 Finnieston/ Exhibition Centre 🚇 Partick, Kelvinhall 📖 🏛

THE TENEMENT HOUSE

www.nts.org.uk
In the 19th and early 20th centuries, most Glaswegians lived in tenement houses, or flats, with each apartment occupying rooms on one floor level, and sharing communal facilities such as a wash-house. In poorer districts these could be horribly overcrowded, with whole families sharing one room.

This compact little house gives a clear picture of tenement life for the slightly better off. From 1911 it was the home of spinster Agnes Toward, a shorthand typist, and her mother, a seamstress. Agnes never threw anything away, and when she died in 1975, her house was found to provide a unique time capsule of social history. Remarkably, it was preserved, and is now in the care of the National Trust for Scotland.

Climb the stairs, knock at the door and you are admitted to admire the hall, with its grandfather clock and wooden Scotch chest, suggesting past family wealth; the kitchen with its curtained box bed and state-of-the-art coal-fired range, still used by Agnes in the 1960s; the parlour with its lace drapes, rosewood piano and concealed, recessed bed; the bedroom, with its pretty floral-tiled fireplace and holiday suitcases; and the bathroom, a feature of comparative luxury.

🕂 153 D2 ✉ 145 Buccleuch Street, Garnethill G3 6QN ☎ 0844 493 2197 🕐 Mar–end Oct daily 1–5 👋 (NTS) adult £5, child (5–16) £4, under 5 free, family £14 🚌 20, 66 🚇 Charing Cross 🚇 Cowcaddens 📖 £3.50, also in French, German and Italian 🏛 Small range of items at ticket desk ❓ Display about tenements in lower apartment, also owned by NTS

Left *The Tall Ship at Glasgow Harbour*
Below *Admiring a trophy at the Scottish Football Museum*

WALK

IN THE FOOTSTEPS OF ALEXANDER 'GREEK' THOMSON

Discover a Victorian city and the architect who shaped it.

THE WALK

Distance: 6.5 miles (10.4km)
Allow: 3 hours 30 minutes
Start/end: Central Station, Glasgow
OS Explorer 342 Glasgow
Grid reference NS 587653

★ Architect Alexander Thomson, with his innovative use and interpretation of Classical Greek designs, helped shape 19th-century Glasgow.

Exit Central Station and turn right. At the intersection with Union Street turn right.

❶ The structure on the opposite corner is the Ca' d'Oro building, a late 19th-century Italianate warehouse by John Honeyman,

based on the Golden House in Venice. A little way down Union Street from here and on the same side as the Ca' d'Oro is Thomson's Egyptian Halls (1871–73), a huge stone-fronted building that started life as an early form of shopping centre.

Born in 1817, Thomson was apprenticed to an architect and studied the plans, drawings and engravings of Classical architecture. Their influence on his own designs earned him the nickname 'Greek', although he never travelled abroad.

Cross over then head down Union Street, turning left into Argyle Street at the next intersection. Cross Argyle Street, then walk along to the intersection with Dunlop Street.

❷ Here you will find the Buck's Head building, named after an inn that previously stood on this spot.

Cross Argyle Street again, retrace your steps, turning right into Buchanan Street. Turn left into Mitchell Lane, pass the Lighthouse (▷ 166), then turn right.

Walk up Mitchell Street, continue along West Nile Street and then turn left into St. Vincent Street. Continue for just under 0.5 miles (800m), going uphill to the junction with Pitt Street.

❸ You are now standing in front of Thomson's St. Vincent Street Church (1857–59), one of his greatest achievements, adorned with Grecian

Above *Thomson's imposing church at the corner of Vincent Street*
Left *An engraving of Holmwood, probably Thomson's finest work*

columns and an imposing tower, built on the side of Blythswood Hill.

Cross St. Vincent Street here, then head up Pitt Street to Sauchiehall Street.

4 On the opposite corner is Thomson's Grecian Chamber (1865) and to the right along Scott Street is Rennie Mackintosh's Glasgow School of Art (▷ 164).

Much of his work was destroyed during World War II and more disappeared in the modernization of Glasgow during the 1960s and 1970s. However, the 24 buildings that have survived provide a fine cross-section of his work.

From the front of the Grecian Chamber turn left, head down Sauchiehall Street to Charing Cross, then take the pedestrian bridge over the motorway to Woodlands Road. Go along here until it ends at Park Road, turn right, then left again into Great Western Road.

Turn right into Belmont Street, left at Dounane Gardens, then continue alon Douane Quadrand and left at Queen Margaret Drive. Cross the road and head down past the

Botanic Gardens (▷ 157) to turn right, back into Great Western Road. Cross the road and continue to Great Western Terrace.

5 This is another Thomson masterpiece (1869), and known as the grandest terrace in Glasgow.

Thomson's own home was at No. 1 Moray Place, Strathbungo, a terrace that was built to his design in 1858. Like most of the houses he designed, it is privately owned.

One exception is Holmwood House in Cathcart, 4.5 miles (7km) from the city centre, now owned by the National Trust for Scotland. It is probably Thomson's finest work and is undergoing complete restoration.

Trace your steps back from here to the top of Byres Road and turn right then, near the bottom, turn left into University Avenue. Turn left into Oakfield Avenue, pass Eton Terrace on the corner with Great George Street. Turn right into Great George Street, right at Otago Street, left into Gibson Street and keep going when it becomes Eldon Street. Finally turn right into Woodlands Road and return to Sauchiehall Street.

Follow this to the intersection with Renfield Street, turn right and head downhill to Central Station.

WHERE TO EAT
On a tour of Glasgow's architecture there can be only one place to dine. The Willow Tearooms in Sauchiehall Street (▷ 169; tel 0141 332 052) were designed by Charles Rennie Mackintosh for Kate Cranston who had a string of tea rooms. Entry is through a jeweller's shop. There is always a queue for the 1904 Room de Luxe, where everything, including the chairs and tables, is by Mackintosh. It's worth the wait, and the food is good and reasonably priced.

PLACE TO VISIT
HOLMWOOD HOUSE
✉ 61–63 Netherlee Road, Glasgow G44 3YG ☎ 0844 493 204 👆 Adult £5, family £14

WHEN TO GO
Any dryish day is perfect for this walk; avoid the rain if you want to really enjoy the architecture.

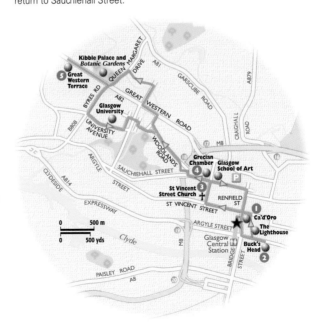

WALK

GLASGOW HARBOUR'S TALL SHIP

A pleasant walk by the last of the Clyde-built sailing ships.

THE WALK
Distance: 4.75 miles (7.7km)
Allow: 3 hours 30 min
Start/end: Scottish Exhibition and Conference Centre (SECC) car park

★ When she was towed up the Clyde in 1993 the *Glenlee* was a sorry-looking sight. Little more than a derelict hulk, she had been saved from destruction by a group of forward-thinking enthusiasts. Today, restored to her former glory, she is an important part of the regeneration of Glasgow's harbour area.

Built in 1896 by Anderson Rodger & Co of Port Glasgow, the three-masted steel barque was one of the last sailing vessels launched on the Clyde. She had a long career as a cargo vessel, circumnavigating the globe four times and sailing over a million nautical miles under a British flag. Towards the end of her cargo career, engines were fitted to help keep her on schedule. Three times

she ran aground and once almost caught fire, but on each occasion she was rescued. Then in 1921 she became a sail training ship for the Spanish Navy and remained in use until 1981. She sank at Seville, when her sea cocks were stolen to sell as scrap. With her engines drowned and rusted solid it looked like the end.

From the Scottish Exhibition and Conference Centre (SECC) car park go on to the Clyde Walkway and turn right, following signs to The Tall Ship and Museum of Transport. Leave the route along here to visit the *Glenlee*.

❶ The Clyde Maritime Trust received a letter from the Spanish Navy giving the ship's details and history and asking if the trust would like to collect the *Glenlee* and save her from being broken up. The trust had very little money but managed to raise enough to purchase, raise her and have her towed back to

Scotland. After a short spell in dry dock at Greenock, where an inspection revealed the hull to be sound, she was towed up the Clyde to Yorkhill Quay.

For the next six years volunteers and enthusiasts took on the seemingly impossible task of turning the *Glenlee* back into a sailing ship. The interior cargo holds and accommodation were lovingly re-created. Decking was fitted and Jamie White, a rigging expert from the National Maritime Museum in San Francisco, was called in to restore and reinstall the original rigging. White already looked after the rigging on the *Balclutha*, another Clyde-built sailing ship, so he knew what he was doing. When work was nearly completed in 1999, the *Glenlee* was towed back down the Clyde to Greenock for the final paint job, known as Gunport, when dark patches were painted on the side to look like gun ports. In days gone by this 'deception' was thought to increase the safety of cargo ships. Old photographs of the *Glenlee* show that she was painted in Gunport at one time. Fully restored, the *Glenlee* went on public display for the first time when the Tall Ships Race came to Greenock in 1999. Then it was a last tow up the Clyde to her permanent moorings at Yorkhill Quay.

At the roundabout with the Tall Ship on the left, go over a pedestrian bridge to cross the Clydeside Expressway. Go under a bridge into Kelvin Haugh Street. Turn west into York Hill Street, then right into Haugh Road and keep ahead, crossing Sauchiehall Street and then along Kelvin Way.

❷ Pass the recently restored Kelvingrove Art Gallery and Museum on your left. This is Scotland's number one top tourist attraction and is free.

Turn right on to the Kelvin Walkway, right again over the second bridge, then turn left at the Memorial to the Highland Light Infantry. Fork left and follow the river bank.

This eventually goes uphill. Just before the top of the hill look for a narrow path on the left. Go left here and under a bridge. Turn left at a cycle path sign to Woodside and Milngavie, go over a bridge and past a café/bar then continue along the walkway.

Cross another bridge, go left at a junction, still following the river. Go under a bridge and then go left across a humpback bridge leading to the Botanic Gardens. Head up the steps to reach the gardens. Turn right alongside the Kibble Palace.

❸ The massive glass Kibble Palace in the heart of the Botanic Gardens was not always here. Built at Coulport on Loch Long by the engineer John Kibble, it was

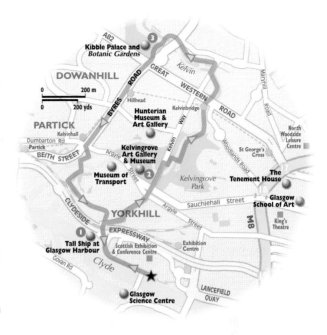

originally part of his own garden. In 1873 he gifted it to the Royal Botanic Institution, who had it dismantled, shipped up the Clyde and rebuilt at its present site where it houses plants from the temperate zones.

Turn left and follow this drive to the gates and then exit the gardens. Cross Great Western Road at the traffic lights and walk to the end of Byres Road. Cross Dumbarton Road and turn left into Partickridge Street, right into Dunaskin Street, left at a T-junction then right into Ferry Road. Just before a railway bridge turn left on to a footpath. At its junction with Sandyford Street turn right and continue under the bridge and back to the SECC.

You can do an extra leg along both banks of the River Clyde from the Scottish Exhibition and Conference Centre (SECC) car park. Cross the rive and turn left on to a riverside

pathway, which eventually leads to a suspension bridge near Glasgow Green. Cross back over the river and return to the SECC on the opposite bank, passing the *Waverley* paddle steamer.

WHERE TO EAT AND DRINK
Take your pick from the riverside café passed on this walk, coffee bars within the SECC, the restaurant in the Italianate pumping house that forms the visitor centre for the Tall Ship, any one of a number of fine restaurants in Byres Road or the famous art deco University Café on the same street.

PLACE OF INTEREST
KELVINGROVE ART GALLERY AND MUSEUM
✉ 54 Kelvingrove Street, Glasgow G3
☎ 0141 276 9599 ⏰ Daily 10–5 💷 Free

WHEN TO GO
This walk is good at any time of year.

SHOPPING

ARGYLE ARCADE
www.argyle-arcade.com
This elegant glass-covered shopping centre specializes in jewellery, with 30 shops selling modern and antique jewellery and other items in gold and silver.
✉ Buchanan Street G2 8BD ◉ Mon–Sat 10–5.30, Sun 12–5

AVALANCHE RECORDS
This large, independent music store near Queen Street station stocks a wide range of new and rare, second-hand CDs and some vinyl, with the emphasis on indie, rock and punk.
✉ 34 Dundas Street G1 2AQ ☎ 0141 332 2099 ◉ Mon–Wed, Fri–Sat 9.30–6, Thu 9–7, Sun 12–6

BARRAS
www.glasgow-barrowland.com
Glasgow's famous indoor and outdoor flea market on Gallowgate has around 150 shops inside and 1,000 traders' stands outside. Many items are second-hand, so the quality varies. The Barras is safe, but with such large crowds, beware of pickpockets (▷ 157).
✉ Gallowgate and London Road, between Ross Street and Bain Street ☎ 0141 552 4601 ◉ Sat–Sun 10–5

BORDERS
www.borders.co.uk
Overlooking Royal Exchange Square, this massive branch of the well-known chain sells all the latest books, CDs and DVDs.
✉ 98 Buchanan Street G1 3BA ☎ 0141 222 7700 ◉ Mon–Sat 8.30am–10pm, Sun 10–8 ▣ Starbucks on the first floor

BUCHANAN GALLERIES
www.buchanangalleries.co.uk
One of Glasgow's biggest shopping malls, with over 80 high-street stores on four levels. The quality of the stores, which include John Lewis, Next and Gap, is generally higher than in the St. Enoch Centre. It's at the top of Buchanan Street.
✉ 220 Buchanan Street G1 2FF ☎ 0141 333 9898 ◉ Mon–Wed, Fri–Sat 9–6, Thu 9–8, Sun 10–6 ▣ Food gallery on the second floor

FRASERS (HOUSE OF FRASER)
www.houseoffraser.co.uk
This huge department store on the corner of Buchanan Street and Argyle Street sells fashion, cosmetics, perfume, china, glassware and the best selection of menswear in the city.
✉ 45 Buchanan Street G1 3HR ☎ 0141 221 3880 ◉ Mon–Wed, Fri 9.30–6, Thu 9.30–8, Sat 9–6, Sun 12–5.30

GEOFFREY (TAILOR) KILTMAKERS & WEAVERS
www.geoffreykilts.co.uk
One of Scotland's top kilt-makers and Highland dress specialists. This big store has every kind of kilt, tartan and accessory, for sale or to rent, including the exclusive fashion range, 21st Century Kilts. Made-to-measure outfits can be sent to you. .
✉ 309 Sauchiehall Street G2 3HW ☎ 0141 331 2388 ◉ Mon–Wed, Fri–Sat 9–5.30, Thu 9–7, Sun 11–5

Left *An outdoor café in the Merchant City area of Glasgow*

GLASGOW PRINT STUDIO
www.gpsart.co.uk
The artists' studio at No. 22 is a fully equipped print-making workshop, with a shop at number 25. There are exhibitions of art by contemporary local and international artists throughout the year, much of which is for sale. Near the Tron theatre, southeast of the centre.
✉ 22 and 25 King Street G1 5QP ☎ 0141 552 0704 🕐 Tue–Sat 10–5.30

ITALIAN CENTRE
This is the place to come for famous name designer clothes and accessories. Shops are based around a stylish piazza and include Italian designer stores such as Armani and Replay.
✉ Ingram Street G1 1DN ☎ 0141 552 6368 🕐 Mon–Wed, Fri–Sat 10–6, Thu 10–8, Sun 12–5 🖥

MERCHANT SQUARE
Merchant City, east of George Square, is a small mall with a range of restaurants and bars. Come for cocktails before a night on the town.
✉ 71–73 Albion Street G1 1NY ☎ 0141 552 8908 🕐 Mon–Wed, Fri–Sat 9.30–6, Thu 9.30–7, Sun 12–5

PRINCES SQUARE
www.princessquare.co.uk
An art deco style doorway on Buchanan Street announces this indoor shopping centre. High quality shops sell clothes, shoes and gifts. .
✉ 48 Buchanan Street G1 3JX ☎ 0141 221 0324 🕐 Mon–Wed, Fri 9.30–6, Thu 9.30–8, Sat 9–6, Sun 12–5 🖥 Cafés and restaurants on the top floor, with bars and restaurants open until midnight

ST. ENOCH SHOPPING CENTRE
www.stenoch.co.uk
A huge mall on two floors with over 80 high street stores housed in the largest glass building in Europe.
✉ 55 St. Enoch Square G1 4BW ☎ 0141 204 3900 🕐 Mon–Wed and Fri–Sat 9–6, Thu 9–8, Sun 11–5.30 🚇 St. Enoch

SOLETRADER
www.soletrader.co.uk
Every type of shoe you can think of on two floors, from the latest trainers to smart, designer shoes. Labels include Hugo Boss, Paul Smith, Diesel and Adidas.
✉ 164a Buchanan Street G1 2LW ☎ 0141 353 3022 🕐 Mon–Wed, Fri–Sat 9–6, Thu 9–7.30, Sun 11–5

TISO GLASGOW OUTDOOR EXPERIENCE
www.tiso.com
A great selection of outdoor equipment, clothing, books and bicycles make this one of the top outdoor stores in Britain. The 15m (49ft) rock pinnacle, waterfall and 7m (23ft) real ice wall let you try out the equipment in the environment where you are likely to use it. .
✉ 50 Couper Street, off Kyle Street G4 0DL ☎ 0141 559 5450 🕐 Mon–Tue, Fri–Sat 9–6, Wed 9.30–6, Thu 9–7, Sun 11–5 🖥

URBAN OUTFITTERS
www.urbanoutfitters.com
This vast store on three levels specializes in fashionable, quirky clothes and accessories for the home, all with a funky, retro feel. Allow plenty of time, it's full of unusual things. There's also a music section, Carbon Records, where a live DJ plays the latest music.
✉ 157 Buchanan Street G1 2JX ☎ 0141 248 9203 🕐 Mon–Wed, Fri, Sat 9.30–6.30, Thu 9.30–8, Sun 12–6

ENTERTAINMENT AND NIGHTLIFE
ARCHES
www.thearches.co.uk
An unusual venue built under the arches of a railway bridge in the city centre, the Arches is one of Glasgow's most popular nightclubs. It has a schedule of theatre, cultural festivals and music, which might include hip-hop, house, soul or big name DJs. Over 18s only.
✉ 253 Argyle Street G2 8DL ☎ 0870 240 7528 🕐 Mon–Sat 11am–12am, Sun 12–12 ✋ From £10

BABBITY BOWSTER
This pub is known for its simple Scottish food. There's live folk music early evening on Saturdays, a good range of real ales, and it's the only pub in the city centre with a licenced beer garden. Over 18s only.
✉ 16–18 Blackfriars Street, Merchant City G1 1PE ☎ 0141 552 5055 🕐 Mon–Sat 11am–12am, Sun 12.30–12. Bar food 12–10

BACCHUS
A stylish bar with a good lunch menu, a big screen TV for soccer matches, and relaxed funk/soul DJs at the weekend. Tasteful cool, blue interior. Over 18s only after 7pm.
✉ 80 Glassford Street G1 1UR ☎ 0141 572 0080 🕐 Mon–Sat 11am–12am, Sun 12.30–12

BARFLY
www.barflyclub.com
Rock and indie venue for up-and-coming rock, punk and indie bands, on the north bank of the River Clyde.
✉ 260 Clyde Street G1 4JH ☎ 0141 204 5700 or 0844 847 2424 (ticketline) 🕐 Open on gig nights, which are most nights of the week. Bar open until 11pm weekdays, 3am weekends ✋ From £5

BARROWLAND
www.glasgow-barrowland.com
Big-name pop and rock acts play at this venue to the southeast of the city centre. Get tickets from Ticket Scotland, tel 0141 204 5151.
✉ 244 Gallowgate G4 0TS ☎ 0141 552 4601/0870 903 3444 (credit card bookings) ✋ From £6 🚇 5-minute walk from St. Enoch 🍺 Bar open on concert nights

BLACKFRIARS
A relaxed pub with an excellent selection of hand-pulled real ales, bottled beers and live jazz at weekends. Over 18s only.
✉ 36 Bell Street, Merchant City G1 1LG ☎ 0141 552 5924 🕐 Mon–Sat noon–midnight, Sun 12.30–12

BUDDHA
There's always up-to-the-minute music in this popular pre-club venue in the centre of town, with a DJ on Saturday nights. Decorated in

Turkish-cave style, the bar is dark and comfortable. Over 18s only.
✉ 142a St. Vincent Street G2 5LA ☎ 0141 248 7881 ⊕ Mon–Wed 12–12, Thu–Sat 12–late

CENTRE FOR CONTEMPORARY ARTS (CCA)
www.cca-glasgow.com
Various contemporary art forms, including music, visual art and alternative cinema are catered for at this cutting-edge centre. Everything from classics to foreign films. Worth a visit for the architecture alone.
✉ 350 Sauchiehall Street G2 3JD ☎ 0141 352 4900 (cinema tickets) ⊕ All year ✋ Cinema from £4; many exhibitions free ⊕ Cowcaddens ⊡ Café serves interesting food, 10.30–11 ⚓ Dark and stylish bar on the first floor, 12–11pm ⊞

CITIZENS THEATRE
www.citz.co.uk
The resident company at this Victorian theatre, in the Gorbals area, produces a wide range of British and European classics.
✉ 119 Gorbals Street G5 9DS ☎ 0141 429 0022 ⊕ All year ✋ Adult from £9.50, reduced rate Tue ⊟ Argyle Street Station

DELMONICAS
Cheesy tunes are the order of the day in this mainstream gay bar at the heart of Glasgow's gay village. Also offers karaoke and quizzes. Over 18s only.
✉ 68 Virginia Street G1 1TX ☎ 0141 552 4803 ⊕ Daily 12–12

GLASGOW FILM THEATRE
www.gft.org.uk
The best art house cinema in Glasgow with a retro feel to the interior. Contemporary and classic, independent and foreign films are shown on its two screens. On the corner of Rose Street and Sauchiehall Street.
✉ 12 Rose Street G3 6RB ☎ 0141 332 6535 ⊕ Daily ✋ From £5.50 ⊡ Café Cosmo serves food daily until 9pm

GLASGOW ROYAL CONCERT HALL
www.glasgowconcerthalls.com
The most prestigious venue in the city, with a programme of classical, pop and rock music. In January and February it hosts the international Celtic Connections music festival.
✉ 2 Sauchiehall Street G2 3NY ☎ 0141 353 8000 ⊕ All year ✋ From £15 ⊞ ⊪ The Green Room for a pre-show meal, tel 0141 353 8000 ⊡ Café Bar on the ground floor (Mon–Sat from 10am), plus four more bars

HORSE SHOE BAR
This city centre pub boasts the longest continuous bar in the UK, real ale, karaoke and reasonably priced food. Over 18s only.
✉ 17 Drury Street G2 5AE ☎ 0141 248 6368 ⊕ Mon–Fri 9–12, Sat 11am–12am, Sun 12.30–12

JONGLEURS
www.jongleurs.com
This city-centre venue is part of a UK-wide chain of comedy clubs, offering live comedy three nights a week. In the basement of the UGC building. Over 18s only.
✉ 11 Renfrew Street G2 3AB ☎ 0844 844 0044 ⊕ Thu–Sat; doors open 7pm, show starts at 8.30 ✋ From £7

KING'S THEATRE
www.kings-glasgow.co.uk
Big budget touring musicals dominate here, along with some comedy and lighter plays.
✉ 297 Bath Street G2 4JN ☎ 0141 240 1111; Ticketmaster (24 hours, fee) 0870 400 0680 ⊕ All year ✋ From £11.50 ⊟ 18, 42, 57 ⊡ Bar

KING TUT'S WAH WAH HUT
www.kingtuts.co.uk
The heart of the Glasgow music scene. It's an unpretentious, relaxed venue playing cutting edge indie, pop and rock. Tickets from Ticket Scotland, tel 0141 204 5151.
✉ 272a St. Vincent Street G2 5RL ☎ 0141 221 5279/0870 169 0100 (Ticketmaster) ⊕ Mon–Sat 12–12, Sun 5–12 ✋ From £5 ⚓ Modern bar or functional bar with pool table

Above *Cutting-edge exhibitions at the Centre for Contemporary Arts*

NOVEMBER
www.princessquare.co.uk
During the day shoppers come to have coffee or lunch. But at night it transforms into a smart cocktail bar: take advantage of the discounted cocktails, and dress up. A glass elevator takes you to the mahogany bar under a glass roof. Over 18s only.
✉ Rooftop, Princes Square Shopping Mall, 48 Buchanan Street G1 3JX ☎ 0141 221 0303 ⊕ Mon–Thu 10am–midnight, Fri–Sun noon–1am

PAVILION THEATRE
www.paviliontheatre.co.uk
Expect to find comedy, musicals and pantomime at this, the last bastion of Glasgow music hall tradition.
✉ 121 Renfield Street G2 3AX ☎ 0141 332 1846 ⊕ All year ✋ From £10 ⚓ Open on performance nights

QUEEN MARGARET UNION
www.qmu.org.uk
Less well-known pop, rock and indie bands and some bigger names play occasional gigs at this university venue. Get tickets from Ticket Scotland, tel 0141 204 5151.
✉ 22 University Gardens G12 8QN ☎ 0141 339 9784 ⊕ Open for 1 or 2 concerts a week. Entry with valid student card

Hillhead 🔲 Student Union bar, so the drinks are always cheap. Entry with valid student card

SCOTIA BAR

This traditional old pub serves real ale and hearty food until 3pm, seven days a week. Live music on most evenings. Patrons must be over 18.
✉ 112 Stockwell Street G1 4LW ☎ 0141 552 8681 🕐 Daily 11am–midnight

SCOTTISH EXHIBITION & CONFERENCE CENTRE (SECC)

www.secctickets.com; www.secc.co.uk
This huge venue on the north bank of the River Clyde is nicknamed the Armadillo, for its great segmented silver shell. It has big-league rock and pop concerts.
✉ G3 8YW ☎ 0870 040 4000 🖐 From £15 upwards 🚇 Exhibition Centre 🚌 Various 🍴 Various

SCOTTISH MASK AND PUPPET THEATRE

www.scottishmaskandpuppetcentre.co.uk
Puppet show for children every Saturday and accompanying mask and puppet exhibition.
✉ 8–10 Balcarres Avenue, Kelvindale G12 0QF ☎ 0141 339 6185 🕐 Shows usually Sat 2pm, and sometimes 12pm 🖐 Adult £4.75, child (under 15) £4.50 🚇

STAND COMEDY CLUB

This bar is the venue for live Scottish and international comedy, most nights. Northwest of the city centre, on the other side of the M8 motorway. Over 18s only.
✉ 333 Woodlands Road G3 6NG ☎ 0870 600 6055 www.thestand.co.uk 🕐 Check listings. Doors open at 7.30, shows start at 8.30–9 🖐 From £1 🚇 Kelvin Bridge

THEATRE ROYAL

www.theatreroyalglasgow.com
www.scottishopera.org.uk
www.scottishballet.co.uk
The best in opera, ballet, dance and theatre at the home of Scottish Opera and Scottish Ballet.
✉ 282 Hope Street G2 3QA ☎ 0141 240 1133 🕐 All year 🖐 From £10 🚇 Circle Café is good for a pre-show snack

TRAMWAY

www.tramway.org
Cutting-edge art, dance and theatre and contemporary art exhibitions, south of the River Clyde.
✉ 25 Albert Drive G41 2PE ☎ 0845 330 3501 🕐 All year, closed Mon 🖐 From £5; exhibitions free 🚌 28, M29, 38, 45, 47, 48, 57, 59 🚉 From Central station, take the train to Pollokshields East, 3 minutes 🍴 Tramway Café on ground floor

TRON THEATRE

www.tron.co.uk
Contemporary Scottish and international drama, comedy, music and dance at this theatre at the eastern end of Argyle Street.
✉ 63 Trongate G1 5HB ☎ 0141 552 4267 🕐 From 10am 🖐 From £6 🍷 Two bars serve lunch and dinner

UISGE BEATHE

www.uisgebeathebar.co.uk
There are 100 or more malt whiskies are on offer in this specialist pub. Well worth seeking out, northwest of the city centre. Over 18s only.
✉ 232–246 Woodlands Road, West End G3 6ND ☎ 0141 564 1596 🕐 Mon–Sat 12–12, Sun 12.30–12 🚇 St. George's Cross 🚌 411, 44 🚉 Charing Cross

SPORTS AND ACTIVITIES

CELTIC FOOTBALL CLUB

www.celticfc.net
Celtic enjoys passionate support both at home and worldwide. Take a tour of the stadium to the east of the city, one of Europe's largest, or go to see the team in action.
✉ Celtic Park, Glasgow G40 3RE ☎ 0870 060 1888 (tickets)/0141 551 4308 (tour) 🕐 Tours daily 🖐 Tour: adult £8.50, child (5–15) £5.50, family £20. Match: adult from £15 🏬 Superstore sells Celtic memorabilia

CLYDE TO LOCH LOMOND CYCLEWAY

www.nationalcyclenetwork.org.uk
The Clyde to Loch Lomond Cycleway is a dedicated bicycle route 20 miles (32km) long, taking in Clydebank, Dumbarton, the Vale of Leven and Balloch. The path, which is also suitable for walkers, follows forest trails, minor roads, old train tracks

and canal tow paths. Pick up a
Cycling in Scotland brochure from any tourist office.
☎ Tel 0141 287 9171 (Glasgow City Council), 0845 113 0065 (Sustrans)

GUIDE FRIDAY

www.guidefriday.com
Guided tours of the city on an open-top bus leave from George Square and take in all the main sights. Tickets are valid all day, so you can get on and off the bus as often as you like. Buy your ticket on the bus.
☎ 0141 248 7644 🕐 Daily 9.30–4.30 every 15 mins (every 30 mins Nov–end Mar) 🖐 Adult £9, child (5–14) £3, under 5 free, family £20

PURE DEAD BRILLIANT TOURS

www.puredeadbrillianttours.comk
There's a range of guided walks, such as a Merchant City tour, Charles Rennie Mackintosh's Glasgow and the city's medical heritage. Or choose a vehicle tour of the 'Sinister City', a Taggart tour (for fans of the police TV series) or a tour of Glasgow's Castles. Tours last 1–2 hours. Booking essential.
✉ 71 Coplaw Street G42 7JG ☎ 0141 585 3074 🕐 Tours: end Mar–end Sep daily, by arrangement out of season

RANGERS FOOTBALL CLUB

www.rangers.premiumtv.co.uk
Take a tour of the stadium or see a game. Tickets for an 'Old Firm' game (the Glasgow derby between Rangers and Celtic) are notoriously difficult to get hold of.
✉ Ibrox Stadium, 150 Edmiston Drive, Glasgow G51 2XD ☎ 0871 702 1972 🕐 Check website for times 🖐 Tour: adult £7, child £5. Match: adult from £22 🍴

WAVERLEY EXCURSIONS LTD

www.waverleyexcursions.co.uk
The *Waverley* is the only sea-going paddle steamer in the world. Join it for a day, afternoon or evening cruise along the River Clyde to the lochs and islands of the west coast.
✉ 33 Landsfield Quay G3 8HA ☎ 0845 130 4647 🕐 May–end Aug 🖐 From £20 🍽 Snacks, lunch and full meals available on board 🚉 Anderston, Central 🏬

EATING

PRICES AND SYMBOLS

The restaurants are listed alphabetically. The prices are for a two-course lunch (L) and a three-course à la carte dinner (D). Prices in pubs are for a two-course lunchtime bar meal and a two-course dinner in the restaurant, unless specified otherwise. The wine price is for the least expensive bottle.

For a key to the symbols, ▷ 2.

BRIAN MAULE AT CHARDON D'OR

www.brianmaule.com
Stylish classical dishes with a modern twist. Starters might feature fried ox tongue salad with capers, while mains might include roast Scottish fillet of beef with celeriac puree and truffle jus. There is a good-value short lunch menu.
✉ 176 West Regent Street G2 4RL ☎ 0141 248 3801 ⚙ L Mon–Fri 12–2.30, D Mon–Fri 6–10, Sat 6–10.30, closed L Sat and all day Sun ✋ L £16.50, D £40, Wine £20.75

GAMBA

www.gamba.co.uk
The menu has an Eastern Mediterranean feel: try crisp fried organic salmon with sweet Thai sauce, prawns and black beans. No children under 14 after 8pm.
✉ 225a West George Street G2 2ND ☎ 0141 572 0899 ⚙ 12–2.30, 5–10.30; closed 25–26 Dec, 1–2 Jan, bank holidays ✋ L £15.95, D £39.95, Wine £18.50 🚍 Near Blythswood Square

HOTEL DU VIN AT ONE DEVONSHIRE GARDENS

www.hotelduvin.com
The menu changes daily. Main courses may include roast loin of monkfish or saddle of rabbit. Desserts may feature Valrhona chocolate tart or coffee and rum soufflé, with peanut butter ice cream. Also traditional afternoon tea.
✉ 1 Devonshire Gardens G12 0UX ☎ 0141 339 2001 ⚙ L Mon–Fri 12–2.15, closed Sat, Sun 12.30–2.45 D Mon–Sun 6–10 ✋ L £21, D £41, Wine £17 🚍 In the West End of Glasgow, on the Great Western Road. Exit 17 on the M8

LUX

www.lux-stazione.co.uk
Lux serves Scottish produce cooked by adventurous chef/proprietor, Stephen Johnson, such as pan-fried fillet of Scottish beef with red Thai paste and bean sprouts with a coriander (cilantro) sour cream. No children under 12.
✉ 1051 Great Western Road G12 0XP ☎ 0141 576 7576 ⚙ D only from 6; closed Sun, 25–26 Dec, 1–2 Jan ✋ D from £35.50, Wine from £16.75 🚍 At the traffic lights signed Gartnavel Hospital

MALMAISON

www.malmaison.com
Expect accomplished French brasserie cuisine, such as venison with juniper juice and Puy lentils. Wines available by the glass. (For hotel, ▷ 185.)
✉ 278 West George Street G2 4LL ☎ 0141 572 1000 ⚙ 12–2.30, 5.30–10.30 ✋ L £13.50, D £24, Wine £15.95 🚍 From George Square take Vincent Street to Pitt Street. Hotel on corner of this and West George Street

MANNA

www.mannarestaurant.uk
A reasonably priced menu of modern Scottish food with a fusion influence provides variations on

familiar dishes. The focus is on local beef, but there are dishes such as mustard-coated fillet of pork. ✉ 104 Bath Street G2 2EN ☎ 0141 332 6678 ⏰ 12–2.30, 5–10.30; closed L Sun, 25–26 Dec, 1–2 Jan, bank holiday Mon 🖐 L £10.95, D £15, Wine £15.95 🚇 City centre at junction (intersection) of Bath Street and Hope Street

MICHAEL CAINES AT ABODE HOTEL

www.michaelcaines.com

The menus at this hotel restaurant change regularly and feature imaginative dishes. A lunchtime starter might be tea-smoked mackerel with poached quails' eggs, with tempura of vegetables and cauliflower purée to follow. Dinner might include a main of pan-fried john dory with crushed olive potatoes. There's an excellent cheese board and wine list. ✉ 129 Bath Street G2 2SZ ☎ 0141 572 6011 ⏰ Daily 12–2.30, 7–10.30 🖐 L £13, D £40, Wine £21.50

MISS CRANSTON'S

www.misscranstons.com

Miss Cranston's tea room is an outlet of Glasgow's famous local Bradford bakery, named after Kate Cranston, who commissioned Charles Rennie Mackintosh to design the interior (▷ 168–169). The tea room, with its tall windows,

Opposite *The Salon de Lux in the famous Willow Tearooms*

glass tabletops and a good view over the street, is above a ground-floor patisserie and bakery. ✉ 33 Gordon Street G1 3PF ☎ 0141 204 1122 ⏰ Mon–Sat 8–5.30

THE RESTAURANT BAR AND GRILL

www.therestaurantbarandgrill.co.uk

This relaxed restaurant is on the 2nd floor of the elegant Princes Square shopping centre. Dishes are a mix of Mediteranean, Eastern and British, such as Shetland cod fillet with spicy lentils and tomato salsa, or wild mushroom risotto with a parmesan wafer. Brunch is also served. ✉ Princes Square G1 31X ☎ 0141 225 5622 ⏰ Mon–Sat 10am–11pm, Sun 12–10.30 🖐 L £18, D £32, Wine £13.95

ROCOCO

Cuisine is modern Scottish with French and rustic Italian. Dishes include honey-roasted Barbary duck with cauliflower cream, salardaise potatoes, glazed shallots and sherry juslie. ✉ 202 West George Street G2 2NR ☎ 0141 221 5004 ⏰ 12–3, 5–9.30; closed 1 Jan 🖐 L £15, D £42, Wine £20 🚇 City centre

SHISH MAHAL

www.shishmahal.co.uk

Fast and friendly restaurant cooking meals in the classic Asian tradition: lamb favourites like Kashmiri, Rogan Josh and Bhoona; baltis in cast iron bowls; and Tarka Daal. ✉ 60–68 Park Road G4 9JF ☎ 0141 334 7899 ⏰ 12–2, 5–11; closed L Sun. Advance reservations essential 🖐 L from £5.50, D from £15.95, Wine from £14.95 🚇 Exit 8 at Charing Cross junction (intersection) and proceed down Woodland Road

STRAVAIGIN

www.stravaigin.com

On the exotic menu an Aberdeen haddie with mussel and sweetcorn veloute is a possible starter, and venison osso buco with beetroot and sweet potato dauphinoise a

main course. Puddings regularly feature chocolate. ✉ 30 Gibson Street G12 8NX ☎ 0141 334 2665 ⏰ Fri–Sun 12–11, Mon–Thu 5–11; bar daily from 11 🖐 L £20, D £30, Wine £14.45 🚇 Close to Glasgow University. 183m (200 yards) from Kelvinbridge underground

UBIQUITOUS CHIP

www.ubiquitouschip.co.uk

This city institution applies a modern slant to Scottish cuisine. Dishes include vegetarian haggis with neeps and tatties, and free-range Perthshire pork with truffle oil. ✉ 12 Ashton Lane G12 8SJ ☎ 0141 334 5007 ⏰ 12–2.30, 6.30–11; brasserie all day 12–11; closed 25 Dec, 1 Jan 🖐 L £22.80, D £39.85, Wine £15.95 🚇 In the West End of Glasgow off Byres Road. By Hillhead underground station

URBAN BAR AND BRASSERIE

www.urbanbrasserie.co.uk

This elegant brasserie is in the Bank of England's former Scottish headquarters. Dishes feature local produce and change with the seasons. You might find grilled lemon sole with citrus crème fraiche on the menu, or apple and pumpkin ravioli with parmesan. The wine and champagne bar has over 100 wines from around the world. ✉ 23–25 St Vincent Place G1 2DT ☎ 0141 248 5636 ⏰ Bar Sun–Thu 11–11, closes at 12 on Fri, Sat; L 12–4.45; D Sun–Thu 5–10, Fri, Sat 5–10.30 🖐 L £15, D £30, Wine 13.95

WILLOW TEAROOMS

www.willowtearooms.co.uk

The famous tea room, designed in white, purple and silver by Charles Rennie Mackintosh, is in a gallery above Hendersons jewellery shop. What you really want to see is the front room, the Room de Luxe, its confident design restrained and strong. The menu is extensive, and afternoon tea costs £11.95 (sandwiches, scone and cake). ✉ 217 Sauchiehall Street G2 3EX ☎ 0141 332 0521 ⏰ Mon–Sat 9–5, Sun 11–4.15

PRICES AND SYMBOLS
Prices are the starting price for a double room for one night, unless otherwise stated. Breakfast is included unless noted otherwise. All the hotels listed accept credit cards unless otherwise stated. Note that rates vary widely throughout the year.

For a key to the symbols, ▷ 2.

ABODE HOTEL
www.abodehotels.co.uk
This sleek contemporary hotel is in a converted Edwardian building in the heart of the city. Rooms are comfortable, come in a choice of sizes and have modern features such as internet access and CD players. Guests can dine at Michael Caines, the hotel's acclaimed restaurant.
✉ 129 Bath Street G2 2SZ ☎ 0141 221 6789 ✋ £79; continental breakfast £10.50, cooked £13.50 ❶ 59

CROWNE PLAZA GLASGOW
www.ichotelsgroup.com
Instantly recognizable from its mirrored glass exterior, most of the bedrooms at this modern hotel have panoramic views. There are two restaurants.
✉ Congress Road G3 8QT ☎ 0870 443 1691 ✋ £99 ❶ 283 🏊 🍴 🚗 From M8 exit 19 follow signs for SECC, hotel adjacent to centre

HOLIDAY INN
www.higlasgow.com
This hotel, close to the Theatre Royal Concert Hall and the main shopping areas, includes the Bonne Auberge restaurant, a bar area and conservatory. Some suites are available.
✉ 161 West Nile Street G1 2RL ☎ 0141 352 8300 ✋ £69 ❶ 113 🚗 M8 exit 16, follow signs for Theatre Royal Concert Hall, hotel is opposite

KELVIN PRIVATE HOTEL
www.kelvinhotel.com
Bedrooms are comfortably proportioned, attractive and well equipped. The dining room serves traditional breakfasts.
✉ 15 Buckingham Terrace, Great Western Road, Hillhead G12 8EB ☎ 0141 339 7143 ✋ £62 ❶ 21 🚗 From M8 exit 17 take A82 to Kelvinside and Dumbarton. Hotel is 1 mile (1.5km) from motorway on right, before Botanic Gardens

KELVINGROVE HOTEL
www.kelvingrove-hotel.co.uk
A private, well-maintained and friendly hotel. Bedrooms, including several family rooms, are well equipped with private bathrooms. There is a breakfast room and reception is staffed 24 hours.
✉ 944 Sauchiehall Street G3 7TH ☎ 0141 339 5011 ✋ £60 ❶ 22 🚗 0.25 miles (400m) west of Charing Cross. From M8 exit 18 follow signs for Kelvingrove Museum

Left *Bedrooms in the Malmaison exude classic contemporary design*
Right *Bridge over the River Clyde*

MALMAISON
www.malmaison.com

This smart, contemporary hotel offers impressive levels of service and hospitality. Bedrooms are spacious, with facilities such as CD players and minibars. There is also a range of split level suites. Dining is a treat here, with French brasserie-style cuisine backed by an excellent wine list, and there's a small gym.

✉ 278 West George Street G2 4LL ☎ 0141 572 1000 💧 £160; breakfast £13.95 ℹ 72 🍴 🚗 From south and east: M8 exit 18, Charing Cross; from west and north: M8, City Centre Glasgow

MENZIES GLASGOW
www.menzies-hotels.co.uk

Centrally located, this modern hotel has spacious bedrooms with internet access. Facilities include a Jacuzzi, sauna and swimming pool.

✉ 27 Washington Street G3 8AZ ☎ 0141 222 2929 💧 £70; breakfast £10 ℹ 141 🏊 🍴 50 🚗 From M8 exit 19 follow signs for SECC, then Broomielaw. Turn left at traffic lights

MERCHANT LODGE
www.merchantlodgehotel.com

This hotel is spread over five floors, and fully modernized with pleasant, understated decor. Breakfast is self-service in a lower level room.

✉ 52 Virginia Street G1 1TY ☎ 0141 552 2424 💧 £62 ℹ 40 🚗 From George Square enter North Hanover Street, head towards Ingram Street. Turn into Virginia Place, which leads into Virginia Street

MILLENNIUM HOTEL GLASGOW
www.millennium-hotels.co.uk

The whole property has a contemporary air and public areas include a glass veranda. There is a brasserie, and a separate wine bar.

✉ George Square G2 1DS ☎ 0141 332 6711 💧 £89 ℹ 117 🚗 From M8 exit 15 follow road through four sets of traffic lights, at 5th set turn left into Hanover Street. George Square is directly ahead, hotel is on the right-hand corner

NOVOTEL GLASGOW CENTRE
www.accorhotels.com

Well-equipped bedrooms include a number of larger family rooms. The all-day Brasserie and bar provide good value and are also available on room service. Facilities include a sauna. A limited amount of free parking.

✉ 181 Pitt Street G2 4DT ☎ 0141 222 2775 💧 £65 ℹ 139 🍴 🚗 Next to Strathclyde Police HQ. Close to the Scottish Conference and Exhibition Centre just off Sauchiehall Street

ONE DEVONSHIRE GARDENS
www.onedevonshiregardens.com

This famous townhouse hotel offers bedrooms—including a number of suites and four-poster rooms—that are individually designed. There are also drawing rooms, and a smart restaurant.

✉ 1 Devonshire Gardens G12 0UX ☎ 0141 339 2001 💧 £135 ℹ 36 🍴 🚗 From M8 exit 17 follow signs for A82. After 1.5 miles (2.4km) turn left into Hyndland Road, take 1st right, go right at mini-roundabout, right again at the end and continue to end of road

RADISSON SAS GLASGOW
www.glasgow.radissonsas.com

This large city-centre hotel offers contemporary design as well

as comfort and style, with two restaurants, leisure centre and bars.

✉ 301 Argyle Street G2 8DL ☎ 0141 204 3333 💧 £80; excluding breakfast ℹ 250 🏊 🍴 🚗 From M8, exit 19, take 1st right, continue to Argyle Street, 1st left. Hotel on left opposite Central train station

UPLAWMOOR HOTEL
www.uplawmoor.co.uk

At this attractive and friendly village hotel there is a formal restaurant, with cocktail bar, and the separate lounge bar serves bar meals. The bedrooms are well equipped.

✉ Neilston Road, Uplawmoor G78 4AF ☎ 01505 850565 💧 £85 ℹ 14 🚗 From M77 exit 2 take the A736 signposted to Barrhead and Irvine. Hotel is 4 miles (6.4km) beyond Barrhead

VICTORIAN HOUSE
www.thevictorian.co.uk

This raised terraced (row) house offers a range of well-equipped bedrooms, in both modern and traditional decor. The breakfast room serves buffet style meals.

✉ 212 Renfrew Street G3 6TX ☎ 0141 332 0129 💧 £60 ℹ 60 🚗 Turn left into Garnet Street at 1st set of traffic lights on Sauchiehall Street, east of Charing Cross. Go right into Renfrew Street, hotel is 90m (100 yards) on left

CENTRAL SCOTLAND

The centre of Scotland often gets overlooked by visitors, sandwiched as it is between the Highlands in the north and the southern attractions of the Borders, Glasgow and Edinburgh. It's nevertheless a fascinating and appealing part of the country, and surprisingly easy to explore on day trips from Edinburgh and especially Glasgow. In less than two hours from Glasgow you can be setting off hill-walking from the town of Pitlochry, or in about 40 minutes you can be arriving at Loch Lomond to start exploring one of Scotland's gems: Loch Lomond and the Trossachs National Park.

Here, too, in Central Scotland is the world home of golf, St. Andrews, with the equally famous Carnoustie further north, where golf is recorded as having been played even earlier than at St. Andrews. South from St. Andrews is the delightful area known as the East Neuk, a rather undefined region that includes several fishing villages and holiday resorts, with coastal walks giving you chance to perhaps spot seals in the waters here at the edge of the Firth of Forth.

Central Scotland offers several historically absorbing buildings too, such as Glamis Castle, Blair Castle and Scone Palace. Glamis Castle is where the late Queen Elizabeth the Queen Mother grew up and where her daughter Princess Margaret was born. The remarkable Blair Castle goes back to the 13th century, while Scone Palace stands on the site where the Kings of Scotland were crowned, on the Stone of Destiny.

There is also the ultra-modern Falkirk Wheel, reminding us that Scotland has always been a nation of inventors, engineers and innovators—and the Falkirk Wheel shows all those facets of the national character. North of Falkirk is the fine town of Stirling, where there's a great deal to do and see, not least visit the marvellous Stirling Castle, one of the biggest and most significant in the whole country.

Central Scotland offers man-made wonders both ancient and modern, and natural wonders too. It's largely farmland and forest, but with the Grampian Mountains in the north of the area hinting at the Highlands beyond.

ABERFELDY

www.perthshire.co.uk

Aberfeldy is a pleasant stone-built town on the River Tay in the heart of Perthshire. It has two claims to fame: a handsome hump-backed bridge with decorative obelisks, designed by architect William Adam for road-builder General Wade in 1733, which still carries the traffic, and a literary allusion by poet Robert Burns. He wrote of the 'Birks of Aberfeldie', referring to the birchwoods above the town, and signs point the way to walking trails there. Dewar's World of Whisky offers a distillery tour and visitor centre (Apr–end Oct Mon–Sat 10–6, Sun 12–4; rest of year Mon–Sat 10–4).

✚ 352 H8 🛈 The Square PH15 2DD, tel 01887 820276; seasonal

ARBROATH SIGNAL TOWER MUSEUM

www.angus.gov.uk/history

The signal tower is a significant building to the south of the town, and was the shore station for the Bell Rock Lighthouse (1811). It is a small Regency-style complex topped by a tower that was used as a signalling station. Inside, the museum tells the epic story of the lighthouse's construction on a submerged sandstone reef 12 miles (19.3km) offshore, and other aspects of Arbroath's history, including fishing and engineering, are shown in talking tableaux. On a clear day, look out to the Bell Rock Lighthouse—a pencil-thin line on the horizon. And try the local delicacy, Arbroath 'smokies'—smoked haddock, lightly grilled.

✚ 353 K8 ✉ Ladyloan DD11 1PU ☎ 01241 875598 ⚙ Mon–Sat 10–5; also Jul, Aug Sun 2–5 ✋ Free 🚉 Arbroath 🚌

CALLANDER

www.visitscotland.com

Callander is a bustling little town, the eastern gateway to the Trossachs (▷ 197). The architecture of its long main street reflects the town's heyday in the late 19th century as a holiday resort, and today it is lined with interesting shops. In the square, the former church is occupied by the tourist information office with a theatre downstairs that shows a film on Rob Roy (Mar–end May, Oct daily 10–5; Nov–end Feb 10–4; Jun–end Aug daily 10–6). Rob Roy MacGregor (1671–1734) was a folk hero and outlaw, who took refuge with his clanspeople in the Trossach hills.

Ben Ledi looms at one end of the street, and there are good walks signed to Callander Crags and Bracklinn Falls.

✚ 356 G9 🛈 Ancaster Square FK17 8ED, tel 01877 330342

CRIEFF

www.perthshire.co.uk

The old town of Crieff lies west of Perth on the very edge of the Highlands, and its shops buzz with visitors in high summer. It's a hub for activities including fishing, bicycling, watersports on nearby Loch Earn, and walking in the surrounding hills—Knock Hill, signposted from the town centre, offers the best views. Crieff Visitor Centre tells the story of ancient drovers' roads. To the west of the town, the Glenturret Distillery dates from 1775 and claims to be Scotland's oldest (Jan, Feb daily 10–4.30; Mar–end Dec daily 9.30–6). Some 2 miles (3km) south, Drummond Castle has an extensive formal garden, laid out in the 17th century, and restored in the 1950s (garden only: Easter, May–end Oct daily 1–6).

✚ 356 H9 🛈 Town Hall, High Street PH7 3HU, tel 01764 652578; seasonal

CULROSS

▷ 191.

Opposite *The restored 17th-century gardens at Drummond Castle*
Left *The wooded hills of Crieff*
Below *The Wade Bridge over the River Tay at Aberfeldy*

REGIONS | CENTRAL SCOTLAND • SIGHTS

INFORMATION
www.blair-castle.co.uk
🔲 352 H7 ✉ Blair Atholl, Pitlochry
PH18 5TL ☎ 01796 481207 🕐 Easter–
end Oct daily 9.30–4.30 🎫 House and
grounds: adult £7.90, child (5–16) £4.90,
family £20.50. Grounds only: adult £2.70,
child £1.40, family £6 🚃 Blair Atholl
Village 📖 £3.50 🍴 Café and restaurant
🎁 Gift shop includes many Blair Castle
themed items, plus other Scottish-made
souvenirs

Below *The entrance hallway of Blair
Castle is adorned with weaponry*

BLAIR CASTLE

This white-harled and turreted mansion, set against a background of dark green forestry 8 miles (13km) north of Pitlochry, seems the archetypal romantic Scottish castle, admired on shortbread tins the world over. It's been the ancestral home of the Murray and Stewart Dukes and Earls of Atholl for over 700 years, and boasts its own private army, the Atholl Highlanders, thanks to a favour granted by Queen Victoria in 1845.

The medieval castle occupied a strategic position on the main route to Inverness, so it's no surprise that in 1652 Cromwell's army seized it. The castle also played a role in the Jacobite uprisings of 1715 and 1745, when the Murray family's loyalties were tragically divided. In more peaceful times, the castle was recast as a Georgian mansion by the 2nd Duke, and with the coming of the railway in 1863, a Victorian-style remodelling took place, leaving the picturesque building seen today.

There's lots to see in the castle, from portraits and rich furnishings to an original copy of the National Covenant (▷ 31) and the small tartan-clad tower room where Bonnie Prince Charlie slept in 1745. Look for Raeburn's portrait of the legendary fiddler Neil Gow (1727–1807), and Gow's own fiddle, in the ballroom. The Treasure Room at the end, is stuffed with Jacobite relics, jewellery and intriguing personal items. Leave time to explore the mature gardens and grounds, including Diana's Grove, with conifers up to 59m (188ft) high.

CULROSS

Your first impression of this quaint little town may be one of familiarity: Culross (pronounced 'Cure-oss') looks like the paintings of very old Scottish burghs, all winding, cobbled streets and crow-stepped gables. It had an early involvement in coal-mining and salt panning, mostly through George Bruce, the town's 16th-century entrepreneur. As the local coal was gradually worked out, the emphasis on industrial activity swung to other parts of the Forth Valley and Culross became a backwater, overlooked on the muddy estuary shores. Significantly, many of the substantial merchants' and workers' houses dating from the 17th and 18th centuries were never replaced by later buildings. Paradoxically, it was Culross' poverty which created the picturesque groupings so admired today.

In the 1930s the National Trust for Scotland started buying up properties which were by that time approaching dereliction. Decades later, many of the houses, fully restored, are lived in by ordinary folk. Really exceptional buildings, such as the ochre Culross Palace (Bruce's mansion of 1597), and the Town House (1626, where suspected witches were locked in the attic), are open to the public (NTS, Palace, Study and Town House: Easter–end May Thu–Mon 12–5; Jun–end Aug daily 12–5; Sep Thu–Mon 12–5; Oct Thu–Mon 12–4. Access to Study and Town House, guided tour only).

In the centre of Culross you'll also find a statue of the town's most famous son, Admiral Thomas Cochrane, the 10th Earl of Dundonald. He is one of the country's great naval heroes, admired all the more for being a bit of a villain. He was convicted for fraud as well as being one of the the most heroic naval captains during the Napoleonic Wars.

INFORMATION

www.nts.org.uk
356 H10 ℹ Culross, Fife KY12 8JH, tel 0844 493 2189

Above *Painted cottages along Culross's Back Causeway*

Top left *The controversial state-of-the-art Falkirk Wheel*
Above *Doune Castle starred in the 1975 film* Monty Python and the Holy Grail

DEEP SEA WORLD
www.deepseaworld.com
This mega-aquarium and seal sanctuary lies just off the north side of the Forth road bridge, and is an underwater wonder-world. It has the world's longest underwater walkway (112m/360ft), where a perspex tunnel allows you to share the elements of the sharks without getting wet. You can explore tanks full of piranhas, sharks, stingrays and deadly poisonous frogs, and get your hands wet in the rock pools with safer creatures such as starfish. If you're over 16, and a certified diver, try joining a shark dive by night.
🕂 356 J10 ✉ North Queensferry KY11 1JR ☎ 01383 411880 ⏱ Mon–Fri 10–5, Sat–Sun 10–6 👆 Adult £11, child (3–15) £7.50, family £36 🚉 North Queensferry 🖥 🏛

DOUNE CASTLE
www.historic-scotland.gov.uk
The village of Doune lies 8 miles (13km) northwest of Stirling, and it would be easy to pass through and miss the castle—look for signs which lead down a narrow road to this grey ruin, hidden in the trees on a curve of the River Teith. Built in the late 14th century, it is fairly simple in construction, with a main block of buildings set with a courtyard, and contained by a great curtain wall. It is an admirable example of medieval concerns for security, with gates to secure the courtyard, further gates

to defend the buildings should the courtyard be lost, and separate stairs to the lord's hall and the retainers' hall to ensure that each could be defended in its own right. Even the Duke's bedroom has an emergency exit.
🕂 356 G9 ✉ Castle Road, Doune FK16 6EA ☎ 01786 841742 ⏱ Easter–end Sep daily 9.30–5.30; Oct–end Mar daily 9.30–4.30 👆 (HS) Adult £4.20, child (5–16) £2.10 🏛

DUNDEE
▷ opposite.

DUNKELD AND HERMITAGE
▷ 194.

EAST NEUK
▷ 195.

THE FALKIRK WHEEL
www.thefalkirkwheel.co.uk
This unique structure, 35m (115ft) high, opened in 2002 to link the canals that run across the centre of Scotland, replacing 11 locks. The wheel is a state-of-the-art means of raising and lowering boats between two very different levels of the Forth and Clyde ship canal and the Union Canal. Watch from the glass-sided visitor centre as the great beaked structure rotates, and take a 1-hour boat ride up on to the higher canal,

through a tunnel and back down again on the eerily silent Wheel.
🕂 356 H10 ✉ Lime Road, Tamfourhill, Falkirk FK1 4RS ☎ 08700 500208 ⏱ Nov–Easter Mon–Fri 10–4.30, Sat–Sun 10–6; Easter–end Jul daily 9.30–6; Aug Mon–Fri 9.30–6, Sat–Sun 9.30–7; Sep–end Oct daily 10–6 👆 Free. Boat ride: adult £8, child (3–15) £4.25, under 3 free, family £21.50 🚉 Falkirk Grahamston 🖥 🏛

FALKLAND PALACE
www.nts.org.uk
Stuart monarchs used this handsome Renaissance-fronted fortress in the heart of Fife as a hunting lodge and retreat. The palace dates to the 15th century, with major additions between 1501 and 1541. Mary, Queen of Scots, spent part of her childhood here, but when Charles II fled to exile on the Continent in 1651, it fell into ruin. In 1887 its fortunes changed when John Patrick Crichton Stuart started rebuilding and restoring, work that continued in the 20th century. A series of rooms reflects the different periods of occupation, including the Chapel Royal and the King's Room. The gardens are outstanding.
🕂 356 H10 ✉ Falkland, Cupar KY15 7BU ☎ 0844 493 2156 ⏱ Mar–end Oct Mon–Sat 10–5, Sun 1–5 👆 (NTS) adult £10, child (5–16) £7, under 5 free, family £25 🏛

DUNDEE

Dundee was founded on a 19th-century industrial base that was famously reduced to the three 'J's: jam, jute and journalism. Today it sprawls untidily along the northern shore of the Firth of Tay. Speed past on the ring road, however, and you'll miss a treat, for Dundee's waterfront has undergone a transformation. The focus is Discovery Point, centring on a famous heroine of polar exploration, the three-masted Royal Research Ship *Discovery*, which was built here in 1900–01. The story of her planning and construction is told in the museum alongside, with models, audio clips and objects that bring the city's shipbuilding to life (Apr–end Sep Mon–Sat 10–6, Sun 11–6; rest of year Mon–Sat 10–5, Sun 11–5). *Discovery*'s maiden voyage, under the command of a young Robert Falcon Scott (1868–1912), was to Antarctica, where in 1902 she became frozen in the pack ice. She was to remain there for two long winters, while scientific research was undertaken and Scott made an unsuccessful attempt to reach the South Pole. It's a fascinating story, and makes the tour of the ship all the more interesting, as you see the cramped quarters and realize the supplies needed for such an expedition.

FURTHER ATTRACTIONS

On the other side of the train station, Sensation: Dundee is a tribute to modern research (daily 10–5). It's a hands-on science centre dedicated to understanding the five senses. There's something for everybody, from an explanation of 3D technology and Roboreatic, to a climb-through nose to explain snot.

In the heart of the city is a former jute factory, the Verdant Works (Apr–end Oct Mon–Sat 10–6, Sun 11–6; rest of year Wed–Sat 10.30–4.30, Sun 11–4.30). At one time the industry employed 50,000 people in the city. This is more fun than it sounds, so allow a couple of hours for the full tour, taking in the origin of the fibre (grown in India), the manufacture and uses of jute, and its considerable impact on the people of Dundee.

INFORMATION

www.angusanddundee.co.uk
🕂 353 J8
ℹ 21 Castle Street DD1 3AA, tel 01382 527527 or 0845 225 5121
🚆 Dundee

TIPS

» At the Verdant Works, see the short Juteopolis film before starting the tour, and it will all make more sense.
» Save money by buying a joint ticket for both Discovery and the Verdant Works, or Discovery and Glamis Castle.

Above *Scott's ship* Discovery *returned to Dundee from its London berth in 1986*

INFORMATION
www.perthshire.co.uk
✚ 352 H8 🛈 The Cross, Dunkeld PH8
0AN, tel 01350 727688 or 0845 225 5121
🚉 Dunkeld and Birnham
🏛 (NTS) Ell Shop: Easter–end Oct
Mon–Sat 10–5.30, Sun 12.30–5.30;
Nov–23 Dec Mon–Sat 10–4.30, Sun
12.30–4.30

DUNKELD AND HERMITAGE

With the exception of the diminutive 13th-century cathedral, the original settlement of Dunkeld was destroyed by the Jacobites after their victory at Killiecrankie in 1689 (▷ 198). It was rebuilt, with terraced houses packed into a compact centre of just two main streets: Cathedral Street and High Street, with a neat little square, the Cross. Many of the houses are whitewashed, and its pleasing uniformity owes much to restoration by the National Trust for Scotland.

At the far end of the partly restored cathedral stands the 'Parent Larch', a tree imported from Austria in 1738 and the source of many of the trees in the surrounding forests, planted between 1738 and 1830 by the Dukes of Atholl. A walk beside the River Braan leads past the tallest Douglas fir in Britain (64.3m/211ft) to the Hermitage, an 18th-century folly. The celebrated 18th-century fiddler Neil Gow was born across the river, and his grave is at Little Dunkeld.

To the east, the Loch of the Lowes is in the care of the Scottish Wildlife Trust and noted for breeding ospreys (Apr–end Sep daily 10–5). Here you can also see otters, red squirrels, deer and, in winter, up to 3,000 migrating greylag geese.

Below The tomb of Alexander Stewart, the so-called 'Wolf of Badenoch', lies within Dunkeld Cathedral

EAST NEUK

The East Neuk is the name given to eastern Fife. It has a prosperous, well-farmed look, with rich grainfields beyond the hedgerows, but in the 15th century James II of Scotland referred to its poverty as a 'beggar's mantle, fringed with gold'. It's noted for its charming old fishing villages, along the A917.

CRAIL

The most easterly of the string, Crail has a charter dating back to 1178 and a much-photographed 16th-century harbour. Former trading links with the Low Countries show in the architecture—pantile roofs and high, stepped gables. The square-towered tolbooth even has a Dutch bell, cast in 1520. In nearby Marketgate there are some fine 17th- and 18th-century town houses, with a mercat (market) cross to complete the picture. To the southeast is a good view of the Isle of May, 6 miles (9.7km) offshore, with its lighthouse.

ANSTRUTHER

Next west is Anstruther, a larger resort town and former herring port. The Scottish Fisheries Museum is housed in historic waterfront buildings around a central courtyard, and illustrates the past and present life of Scottish fishermen and their families (Apr–end Sep Mon–Sat 10–5.30, Sun 11–5; rest of year Mon–Sat 10–4.30, Sun 12–4.30). The town also has a history of smuggling, which centred on the Dreel burn (stream) and the 16th-century Smuggler's Inn.

PITTENWEEM

Continue west to Pittenweem, the main fisheries port for the East Neuk. The town dates back to the seventh century, when St. Fillan based himself in a cave here (in Cove Wynd) while converting the local Picts to Christianity. A priory grew up here in the 13th century, and the harbour dates from the 16th century. Artists are attracted to the town, and there are lots of small galleries.

ST. MONANS AND ELIE

The tiny houses of the next village, St. Monans, crowd around its harbour, where shipbuilding as well as fish brought prosperity in the 19th century. The squat Auld Kirk (old church) standing alone at the western end dates from 1362. Elie is the most westerly of the East Neuk villages, and its golden sands made it a popular holiday resort in the late 19th century. A causeway leads to a rocky islet, with panoramic views and a busy watersports centre.

INFORMATION

✚ 357 K9

ℹ Museum and Heritage Centre, 62–64 Marketgate, Crail KY10 3TL, tel 01333 311073 or 0845 225 5121; seasonal

ℹ Tourist Information Office, Harbourhead, Anstruther KY10 3AB, tel 01333 311073; seasonal or 0845 225 5121

❓ The Fife Coastal Path (▷ 210–211) links the villages

TIPS

» These old towns have narrow streets that quickly become congested in summer, so be prepared to park your car and explore on foot.
» Although you can see all these places in one day, allow extra time to see the Fisheries Museum.

Below *The former herring port of Anstruther is home to the Scottish Fisheries Museum*

GLAMIS CASTLE

www.glamis-castle.co.uk

A grand, turreted pile 5 miles (8km) west of Forfar, Glamis (pronounced 'Glahms') has been the seat of the Earls of Strathmore and Kinghorne since 1372. It's essentially a medieval tower house extended and remodelled to palatial proportions. Visitors explore the castle on a guided tour, which lasts around 1 hour, and are then free to roam the beautiful park, landscaped in the 18th century, which includes a 0.8ha (2-acre) Italian garden. Glamis was the childhood home of Queen Elizabeth, the Queen Mother (1900–2002).

➕ 353 J8 ✉ By Forfar DD8 1RJ ☎ 01307 840393 🕐 Mid-Mar to end Oct daily 10–6; Nov–end Dec daily 11–5 ♿ Adult £10, child £5 (5–16), family £22.50 🍽 🏛

GLEN LYON

www.perthshire.co.uk

This long and beautiful hidden valley lies sandwiched in the mountains between Loch Tay and Loch Rannoch, and stretches for 34 miles (55km) to the hydroelectric dam at the eastern end of Loch Lyon. Entry is via the mountain pass at Ben Lawers (1,214m/3,982ft) or through the dramatic, steep-sided pass at Fortingall.

The road is single track and follows the route of the River Lyon, through scenery of woodland and little farms, backed by sweeping hills. In winter the valley is quickly cut off by snow; in summer it can be a sun trap, with red cattle standing in the river shallows to cool down.

The Fortingall Yew, a yew tree in the churchyard in Fortingall Village, is thought to be 5,000 years old, making it the oldest tree in Europe.

➕ 352 G8 🅿 The Square, Aberfeldy PH15 2DD, tel 01887 820276 or 0845 225 5121; seasonal

HILL HOUSE

www.nts.org.uk

Set among the 19th-century villas of Helensburgh, this 'Dwelling House' is one of architect Charles Rennie Mackintosh's (▷ 168–169) finest achievements. The house was designed with a free hand for publishing magnate Walter Blackie, and completed in 1904. Mackintosh and his wife also saw to much of the interior design, including the exquisite, calm white space of the drawing room, with its stencilled motif of roses and trellis in restrained shades of pink, green and grey. Look for domestic details such as light fittings.

Take a walk around the exterior to admire the changing pattern of shadows and rooflines.

➕ 355 F10 ✉ Upper Colquhoun Street, Helensburgh G84 9AJ ☎ 0844 493 2208 🕐 Easter–end Oct daily 1.30–5.30 ♿ (NTS) Adult £8, child (5–16) £5, under 5 free, family £20 🚉 Helensburgh Central 🍽 🏛

HILL OF TARVIT MANSIONHOUSE

www.nts.org.uk

The influence of Edinburgh-born architect Robert Lorimer (1864–1929) is seen in many of Scotland's great houses, but none more effectively than this, the Edwardian house that he remodelled in 1906 for Frederick Bower Sharp. Sharp had made his money in the Dundee jute trade, and commissioned a house that would show off his collection of fine art, including magnificent paintings, tapestries and antique furniture, much of it French. The result is grandeur without pomposity, a comfortable harmony of taste and style that reflects a golden age of Scottish craftsmanship.

If you have time, take a look at the Raeburn and Ramsay portraits in the library, the plasterwork ceiling in the dining room and the Remirol toilet in the bathroom—Lorimer spelled backwards.

➕ 357 J9 ✉ Cupar KY15 5PB ☎ 0844 493 2185 🕐 House: May, Sep–end Oct Thu–Mon 1–5; Jun–end Aug daily 1–5. Garden and grounds: all year daily ♿ (NTS) House and garden: adult £8, child (5–16) £5, under 5 free, family £20 🍽 🏛

LOCH LOMOND AND THE TROSSACHS NATIONAL PARK

The romantic beauty of the Highland landscape, epitomized by this accessible and scenic area, was first 'discovered' in the late 18th century. Novelist and poet Sir Walter Scott did much to bring it to the popular eye, with his thrilling poem *The Lady of the Lake* (1810) set in identifiable locations across the Trossachs, ending at Loch Katrine. Today, the 1,865sq km (720sq-mile) national park, Scotland's first, designated in 2002, stretches from the Argyll Forest Park in the west across to Callander (▷ 189), and from Killin (▷ 198) in the north to Balloch in the south, just 18 miles (29km) from Glasgow.

EXPLORING THE PARK

This is popular hiking country, with plenty of waymarked trails and a lovely stretch of the West Highland Way long-distance path, which runs down the eastern shore of Loch Lomond. Some 24 miles (38.6km) long, the loch is a watersports playground littered with 38 islands. It narrows to the north, where the mountains become bigger and bleaker. Ben Lomond, on the eastern shore, is a popular 'Munro' hill climb at 973m (3,192ft; ▷ 19). Luss, off the A82, is the prettiest village to explore. The Loch Lomond Shores Visitor Centre at Balloch explains the geology and history of the region (daily 10–5).

The Trossachs is the area to the east of Loch Lomond, including the wooded hills of the Queen Elizabeth Forest Park, and the peak of Ben Venue (729m/2,391ft). Some of the best scenery is around Loch Katrine, with easy walking and a steamboat ride among tree-clad islands.

The dramatic pass to the high point of Rest and Be Thankful is on the A83, west of Arrochar. After you've rested you could head along the B828, which leads to the B839 going through the strikingly named Hell's Glen, though in fine weather the scenery is positively heavenly.

INFORMATION

www.lochlomond-trossachs.org
⊞ 355 F9 ℹ National Park Gateway Centre, Loch Lomond Shores, Ben Lomond Way, Balloch G83 3QL, tel 01389 722172
🚆 Balloch, Tarbet and Ardlui on west side Loch Lomond

TIP

» Some of the best scenery is on the short but winding A821 between Aberfoyle and Loch Katrine, known as the Duke's Pass. Travel from south to north for the best views.

Above *Canoeing on Loch Lubhair, with Meall Glas in the background*
Opposite *Glamis Castle, pretty as a picture in the deep midwinter*

KILLIECRANKIE

www.nts.org.uk

This spectacular wooded gorge is worth a visit for its scenery alone. Deciduous woodland of oak and beech lines the steep sides of the valley, with the waters of the River Garry flowing through the rocks below. Wild flowers are abundant, and you may be lucky enough to see the rare native red squirrels.

Yet Killiecrankie's fame is twofold: As well as natural beauty, it is celebrated for its significance as the site of a momentous battle in 1689, when John Graham of Claverhouse, or 'Bonnie Dundee' (c1649–89), swept down here at the head of a rebel Jacobite army. The superior government force was defeated, but Dundee was mortally wounded in the conflict. The Soldier's Leap, below the visitor centre, is where a fleeing soldier, Donald McBean, jumped 5.5m (18ft) across the gorge to safety.

✚ 352 H7 ✉ Near Pitlochry PH16 5LG ☎ 0844 493 2194 ⏱ Visitor centre: Easter–end Oct daily 10–5.30 💷 Free; parking charge 🖥 🏛

KILLIN

www.incallander.co.uk

Killin lies at the western end of Loch Tay, in the ancient district of Breadalbane, and is a popular touring, walking and fishing centre for the area. It has its own attractions, notably the Falls of Dochart, which run through the middle; visitors viewing these from the old stone bridge regularly bring the holiday traffic to a standstill.

The surrounding hills abound with legends, which are brought to life at the Breadalbane Folklore Centre in St. Fillan's Mill (Apr–end Oct daily 10–5)—if you can't tell your fairies from your kelpies and urisks, this is the place to find out.

You can also visit the preserved, simple 19th-century farmhouse north of the village, Moirlanich Longhouse (NTS, May–end Sep Wed, Sun 2–5; free).

Several generations of the Robertson family have lived in this house till as recently as 1968.

✚ 352 G8 ℹ Breadalbane Folklore Centre, Falls of Dochart, Main Street FK21 8XE, tel 0845 225 5121

KIRRIEMUIR AND THE GLENS OF ANGUS

www.angusanddundee.co.uk

Kirriemuir is a proud little town built of red sandstone. It is associated with J. M. Barrie (1860–1937), whose most famous creation was Peter Pan. Barrie was born here, the son of a handloom weaver, and his birthplace on Brechin Road is now an evocative museum (NTS, Easter–end Jun, Sep–end Oct Sat, Mon, Wed 12–5, Sun 1–5; Jul–end Aug Mon–Sat 11–5, Sun 1–5).

The town's position makes it the natural gateway to the great Glens of Angus, the long valleys which stretch north into the open moorland of the Grampian Mountains. They include Glen Esk, Glen Clova and Glen Prosen, and all three offer good hill-walking, with Glen Clova giving access to the remote but beautiful Glen Doll.

The other two glens making up the famous Five Glens of Angus are Glenisla and Glen Lethnot.

✚ 353 J8 ℹ Cumberland Close, Kirriemuir ⏱ D8 4EF, tel 01575 574097 or 0845 225 5121; seasonal

LOCH LOMOND AND THE TROSSACHS NATIONAL PARK
▷ 197.

LOCHLEVEN CASTLE
www.historic-scotland.gov.uk
Near the western shore of Loch Leven, the stark grey, roofless tower of Lochleven Castle stands on a small island, accessible by boat from Kinross. This 15th-century fortress gained notoriety as the prison of Mary, Queen of Scots, after her defeat in 1567. After her forced abdication she escaped and sought refuge with Elizabeth I of England, who promptly imprisoned her again.

The castle was abandoned in the mid-18th century.

Loch Leven is a nature reserve noted for its huge over-wintering flocks of pink-footed geese, with the Royal Society for the Protection of Birds' Vane Farm Visitor Centre on its southern shore (daily 10–5).
✚ 356 J9 ✉ By Kinross KY13 7AR ☎ 07778 040483 ◑ Apr–end Sep daily 9.30–5.30 🖐 (HS) Adult £4.70, child (5–16) £2.35 ⛴ Ferry from Fisherman's Pier, Kinross 🈺

MEIGLE SCULPTURED STONE MUSEUM
www.historic-scotland.gov.uk
Our knowledge of the Picts, who lived in Scotland in the Middle Ages, is limited. Much of what we do know has been gleaned from their remarkable legacy of stone carvings, and this museum in a former schoolhouse at Meigle, northeast of Coupar Angus, is a good place to see and begin to understand. Around 26 carved stones and cross slabs are displayed, dating from the late eighth to the late tenth centuries. While salmon, dogs and horsemen can be picked out with relative ease, what can be made of the strange elephant-like creatures, camels, or birds with bulbous eyes? ✚ 353 J8 ✉ Dundee Road, Meigle, Blairgowrie PH12 8SB ☎ 01828 640612

◑ Apr–end Sep daily 9.30–12.30, 1.30–5.30 🖐 (HS) Adult £3.20, child (5–16) £1.60, under 5 free 🈺

MONTROSE
www.angusanddundee.co.uk
The harbour town of Montrose lies at the mouth of the South Esk River on Scotland's eastern seaboard, with fabulous golden sands exposed at low tide. Its comfortable prosperity was built up in the 18th century, largely on the back of trade with continental Europe, and some of its architecture echoes the style and elegance of Edinburgh's New Town (▷ 77).

A vast, shallow inland sea trapped behind the harbour, the Montrose Basin is important for migrant birds. The House of Dun, on its northern shore, is a mansion of 1730 designed by architect William Adam, and greatly restored by the National Trust for Scotland (NTS, House: Easter–end Jun, Sep–end Oct Wed–Sun 12.30–5.30; Jul–endAug daily 11.30–5.30. Garden: all year). ✚ 353 K7 🛈 Dundee tourist information office, tel 01382 527527 or 0845 225 5121; seasonal 🚉 Montrose

Above *The 18th-century House of Dun, in Montrose*
Left *Arched doorway at Lochleven Castle*
Opposite *The Falls of Dochart, Killin*

INFORMATION

www.perthshire.co.uk

✚ 356 J9 ℹ Lower City Mills, West Mill Street PH1 5QP, tel 01738 450600

🚉 Perth

Above *The city of Perth lies along the banks of the River Tay*

PERTH

The Roman settlement of Perth was founded along the banks of the sylvan River Tay in the first century; in the Middle Ages it was the capital of Scotland. Today it is a lively city at the centre of a prosperous farming community, its compact core offering great shopping and bohemian cafés that spill on to the pavements. The Perth Mart visitor centre is housed within the old cattle market—come in February or October if you want to enjoy the sights, sounds and smells of the pedigree bull sales, the biggest of their kind in all Europe.

Balhousie Castle, along the edge of the North Inch park, houses the Black Watch Regimental Museum (May–end Sep Mon–Fri 10–4.30; rest of year Mon–Fri 10–3.30).

Open-top bus tours from the train station are a good way to see the town, linking attractions such as the Art Gallery and Museum, and the 12th-century St. John's Kirk, and travelling as far as Scone Palace, 2 miles (3.2km) to the north (Easter–end Oct daily 9.30–5.30). This sumptuously furnished stately home dates mainly from the 19th century. In the grounds is a tartan maze, and the Moot Hill, the earliest crowning place of Scottish kings. The Stone of Scone, or Stone of Destiny, on which kings were crowned, was originally here, but is now held for security in Edinburgh Castle (▷ 66–69)—the one on view is a replica.

Two notable gardens on the southern outskirts are worth exploring. Branklyn Garden, covering just 0.8ha (2 acres), has plants predominantly from China, Tibet and Bhutan, with an outstanding collection of Himalayan poppies (NTS, Easter–end Oct daily 10–5). Bell's Cherrybank Gardens, sponsored by the famous whisky manufacturer, hosts the national collection of over 900 heather species (Mar–end Oct Mon–Sat 10–5, Sun 12–5; reduced hours in winter).

ST. ANDREWS

This attractive, breezy town is set on the east coast, with a sandy bay to the north (the opening scene of the 1981 movie *Chariots of Fire* was filmed here), and a narrow harbour to the south. Before the Reformation it was the ecclesiastical and scholarly centre of Scotland, and it has the country's oldest university, founded in 1413. It is also the home of the Royal and Ancient Golf Club, founded in 1754 and still the ruling authority on the game worldwide. Check out the history of the game at the British Golf Museum on Bruce Embankment (Easter–end Oct Mon–Sat 9.30–5.30, Sun 10–5; rest of year daily 10–4).

EXPLORING THE TOWN

The town received its royal charter in 1140, and the cathedral was started 20 years later. After Protestant reformer John Knox preached here in 1559, it was smashed up, and just a century later left derelict (HS visitor centre: Apr–end Sep daily 9.30–5.30; rest of year daily 9.30–4.30). Near the gaunt ruins of the cathedral stand the remains of the 12th-century St. Rule's Church (admission fee). It is dedicated to a Greek monk, who was shipwrecked here while carrying holy relics of St. Andrew in AD347. Climb the spiral stairs of the tower (33m/108ft) for great views over the town, revealing the medieval grid of its streets. The two main roads are North Street, which leads to the famous St. Andrews Links (golf course), and South Street, with the restored city gateway of 1589, the West Port, at its far end.

Northward along the shore lie the ruins of the castle, rebuilt around 1390, which was the site of a battle and siege in 1546–47 (open as cathedral visitor centre). Look for the mine and counter-mine tunnels under the walls, which date from this time. The chilling bottle-shaped dungeon in the northwest corner of the castle, 7.3m (24ft) deep, was cut from solid rock and impossible to escape from.

INFORMATION

www.standrews.co.uk

➕ 357 K9 ℹ️ 70 Market Street KY16 9NU, tel 01334 472021 or 0845 225 5121

Below *The evocative ruins of St. Andrews Castle on the shore*

REGIONS | CENTRAL SCOTLAND • SIGHTS

PITLOCHRY

www.perthshire.co.uk

This bustling town in the wooded valley of the River Tummel is based around one long main street, lined with shops and eating places. The geographical heart of Scotland, it's been a popular holiday resort since the 19th century, and boasts two distilleries: Bell's Blair Atholl Distillery (Nov–Easter, Mon–Fri 10–4; Easter–end Sep Mon–Sat 9.30–5, Sun 12–5; Oct Mon–Fri 10–5) and the tiny Edradour Distillery (Apr–end Oct Mon–Sat 9.30–5, Sun 12–5; Nov–end Mar Mon–Sat 10–4, shop only).

A footbridge leads across the river to the Festival Theatre, famous for its productions, with its Explorers' Garden, opened in 2003 to celebrate 300 years of botanical exploration and collection around the world by Scots (Apr–end Oct daily 10–5). There's a view from the footbridge to the salmon ladder, installed as part of the hydroelectric dam system along the river. Learn more about this at the Scottish Hydro Electric Visitor Centre (Apr–end Oct Mon–Fri 10–5.30; Jul–endAug also Sat–Sun), which gives free access to a fish observation window, as well as an exhibition.

➕ 352 H7 ℹ️ Atholl Road PH16 5DB, tel 01796 472215/472751 or 0845 225 5121; seasonal 🚉 Pitlochry

RUMBLING BRIDGE

It's not the bridge that rumbles at this beauty spot along the River Devon, rather the waters which thunder through the rocky gorge beneath when the river is in spate. And there's not one bridge, but two, with one built above the other. The lower bridge dates from 1713, the upper one, 36.5m (120ft) above the water, from 1816. Visitors used to flock here in such numbers that it once had its own train station. Now it's a peaceful backwater, with pleasant walks to the waterfalls of the Devil's Mill and the Cauldron Linn.

➕ 356 H9 ✉️ At junction of A823 and A977, access via nursing home gardens

ST. ANDREWS

▷ 201.

SCOTLAND'S SECRET BUNKER

www.secretbunker.co.uk

Scotland's Nuclear Command Centre, buried in a 40m (131ft) hole between St. Andrews and Anstruther, is a secret no longer. The hole was originally dug out after World War II to house a radar installation. Instead, in the 1950s it was secretly lined with 3m (10ft) of reinforced concrete, and a bomb-proof warren was built inside, with an innocuous-looking farmhouse on the top to deter the curious.

The purpose of the secret bunker was to house a self-supporting military community and seat of government in the event of the Cold War getting out of hand. Now you can explore the eerie chambers, complete with original communications equipment, and the cramped dormitories where as many as 300 personnel would have slept in rotation.

➕ 357 K9 ✉️ Crown Buildings, Troywood, near St. Andrews KY16 8QH ☎️ 01333 310301 🕐 Easter–end Oct daily 10–5 👆 Adult £8.60, child (5–15) £5.60, under 5 free, family £23.60 📷 🏪

SOUTH QUEENSFERRY

A ferry operated across the Firth of Forth from this little royal burgh, from 1129 until 1964, when the opening of the suspended road bridge made it obsolete. Lying 10 miles (16km) northeast of Edinburgh, it is a great place to come and admire the two Forth bridges on a summer's evening.

The older, cantilevered rail bridge dates from 1890, and its striking design by William Arrol (1839–1913) and partners has made it an icon of Scotland. Fifty-seven workmen died during the eight-year construction of the bridge. Its regular maintenance includes an end-to-end coating of 31,000 litres (6,817 gal) of red oxide paint (though new developments promise longer-lasting results in the future, of up to 30 years).

Hopetoun House, to the west, is a splendid early18th-century mansion built by William Bruce and William Adam, with 60ha (150 acres) of parkland giving more great views to the bridges (Easter–end Sep daily 10–5.30). Stuffed with fine paintings, original furniture, tapestries and rococo details, the house is still the home of the Marquis of Linlithgow.

Just west of South Queensferry on the way to Edinburgh is Dalmeny House, presently closed for refurbishment but due to reopen in 2009 (tel 0131 331 1888). It's been the family home of the Earls of Rosebery since it was built in 1817, though the title of the Earl of Rosebery dates back to 1703, when it was created in Queen Anne's Coronation Honours List. Dalmeny House was the first Scottish house to be designed in the Tudor style and was the work of the English architect William Wilkins, who was also responsible for London's National Gallery and University College. One of the most interesting rooms is the Library. It has lovely views over the grounds and to the sea, and is arguably where the idea for the Edinburgh Festival was born. In 1946 the 6th Earl of Rosebery was Chairman of the fairly new Scottish Tourist Board. He invited people from the city of Edinburgh to meet some music and drama producers who were friends of his wife, and who were seeking a British venue for an international arts festival. In 1944 the Earl's horse Ocean Swell had won the Epson Derby, and he offered to put his winnings forward to help back the event. And so the Edinburgh Festival came into being.

INFORMATION

www.standrews.co.uk

➕ 356 J10 ℹ️ VisitScotland Edinburgh, tel 0845 225 5121

Opposite *Pitlochry's Festival Theatre*
Below *The 19th-century Forth Rail Bridge is impressive from any angle*

REGIONS   CENTRAL SCOTLAND • SIGHTS

SCOTTISH CRANNOG CENTRE
www.crannog.co.uk

Crannogs were round, communal dwellings built on stilts above the surface of a loch, and 2,000 years ago central Scotland was apparently littered with them. One has been reconstructed near Kenmore at the eastern end of Loch Tay. Tours show some of the discoveries from the site, and take you across the uneven pier into the hut, where you can learn how the archaeologists have gleaned clues to the way of life of the original crannog dwellers. Back on land, there are demonstrations of ancient skills such as bodging and fire-making. It's essential to reserve ahead in midsummer.

✚ 352 G8 ✉ Kenmore, South Loch Tay, near Aberfeldy PH15 2HY ☎ 01887 830583 🕐 Mid-Mar to end Oct daily 10–5.30; Nov Sat–Sun 10–4 ✋ Adult £5.75, child (5–16) £4, under 5 free, family £18 📷

STIRLING

Stirling is most famous for its castle (▷ opposite), yet it has many other fascinating buildings and sites of national importance. The city was of particular importance in the wars of independence, fought against England in the 13th and 14th centuries. Notable Scottish victories included the Battle of Stirling Bridge (1297), fought at the Old Bridge just north of the town centre, when William Wallace split the opposing army in two, and the famous Battle of Bannockburn (1314), when Robert the Bruce took charge and defeated the English yet again.

Wallace is commemorated with the National Wallace Monument, a 67m (220ft) tower, on the nearby hill of Abbey Craig from where he watched the English troops gather and then despatched his men to race down to Stirling Bridge (Nov–end Feb daily 10.30–4; Mar–end May, Oct daily 10–5; Jun daily 10–6; Jul–end Aug daily 9–6; Sep daily 9.30–5.30). It was built in 1867, and if you can manage the 246 steps to the top after the lengthy walk from the car park (though there is also a shuttle bus) then the reward is some breathtaking views. Wallace's steel sword is on display, and a Hall of Heroes depicts other Scottish names of note, including Robert the Bruce, Robert Burns and Sir Walter Scott.

The story of Bruce's victory at the Battle of Bannockburn is told at the Bannockburn Heritage Centre (NTS, Mar–end Oct daily 10–5.30; grounds daily 10.30–4). There is some dispute as to whether the Heritage Centre is actually on the place where the battle took place, but accurate or not, it's still a stirring story.

Within the town there are information plaques marking notable historic buildings and features. One of the most significant is the medieval Church of the Holy Rood (May–end Sep daily 11–4), which has beautiful stained glass and a timber roof. It was rebuilt in the early 1400s after the original church was destroyed in a fire that devastated the town in 1405. Watch also for the 17th-century Argyll's Lodging mansion (Apr–end Sep daily 9.30–5; Oct–end Mar daily 9.30–4.30), the Old Town Jail (Nov–end Mar daily 10–4; Apr–end May, Oct daily 9.30–5.30; Jun–end Sep daily 9–6) and, opposite this, the Tolbooth which was the town's medieval prison before the jail was built and is now an arts centre. There are lots of other historic places in this city—the smallest city in Scotland.
www.visitscottishheartlands.com

✚ 356 H10 ℹ Stirling Visitor Centre, 41 Dumbarton Road FK8 2QQ, tel 0845 225 5121 🚆 Stirling

STIRLING CASTLE

Stirling Castle's strategic position, perched high and proud on its towering cliffs, commanding the narrow waist of land between the Forth estuary and the marshlands of the west (now drained), has given it a prominent role in Scottish history. The castle once served as a royal palace and has been remodelled many times (HS, Easter–end Sep daily 9.30–6; rest of year daily 9.30–5). Mary, Queen of Scots, spent her childhood here and was crowned in the Chapel Royal in 1543.

The castle's eventful history began in the late 11th century, when a wooden structure was raised. Edward I seized Stirling in 1296 and William Wallace took it back in 1297. Edward retrieved the castle after a furious siege in 1304, and this time held it until the English defeat at Bannockburn in 1314.

The current castle dates mainly from the 16th century and is dominated by the Great Hall. A former royal court, with fine Renaissance work, the castle was sadly misused after Scotland's James VI deserted it to become King of England as well. Much of it has been restored, including the palace of James V and the Chapel Royal of 1594.

Visitors can tour the castle with its recreated kitchens and see the exhibition in the Queen Anne Casements. The castle's main feature, however, is the spectacular view from the esplanade, which extends to the Campsie Fells in the west and the start of the Highlands to the north. You can take the Back Walk around the castle to enjoy a full panorama of the surrounding countryside.

INFORMATION

www.visitscottishheartlands.com
✚ 356 H10 ℹ Stirling Visitor Centre, 41 Dumbarton Road FK8 2QQ, tel 0845 225 5121 🚉 Stirling

Above *Stirling Castle, high on its rocky outcrop, has played a prominent part in Scottish history*
Opposite *Relive the past at the Scottish Crannog Centre, Loch Tay*

DRIVE

THE TROSSACHS TRAIL

This drive explores the varied and magnificent scenery of Scotland's first designated national park—Loch Lomond and the Trossachs (▷ 197).

THE DRIVE

Distance: 159 miles (256km)
Allow: 2 days
Start/end: Killin

★ Loch Lomond is at the heart of Scotland's first National Park, the Trossachs.

Leave the hill-walking centre of Killin (▷ 198) on the A827, and follow this northeast for 17 miles (27km) to Kenmore.

❶ As you pass Loch Tay on the right, the big, bare-looking mountain of Ben Lawers (1,214m/3,984ft) is up to your left. A National Nature Reserve, it is celebrated for its Arctic and alpine flora. Look for mountain hares on the high ground.

The National Trust for Scotland has a visitor centre, signposted from the road (Easter–end Sep daily 10.30–5; closed 30 minutes between 1 and 2pm). Glen Lyon (▷ 196) runs parallel, on the other side of the mountain ridge.

❷ Kenmore is a small resort and watersports centre, dominated by the 19th-century pile of Taymouth Castle (private).

❸ Sticking into the loch is a reconstruction of an Iron-Age roundhouse, the focus of the intriguing Scottish Crannog Centre (▷ 204).

Continue on the A827 for 6 miles (10km) to Aberfeldy (▷ 189).

❹ Pass a memorial of 1887 to the men of the Black Watch on the southern side of the bridge. The Black Watch regiment took its name from the dark tartan worn by the soldiers. The Black Watch is now a battalion within the Royal Highland Regiment.

Leave by the A826, and follow this wild road up over the high moors. Turn right at the A822, then right at the A85 and follow this into Crieff (▷ 189). Continue on the A85 for 19 miles (31km) through Comrie to Lochearnhead.

❺ Lochearnhead is a small town at the western tip of Lochearn. It grew when the railway was built through Glen Ogle, which lies to the north

Left Kenmore, at the head of Loch Tay, has
developed into a watersports centre
Right Aberfeldy's Black Watch memorial

and links up with Killin, passing to a
height of 289m (948ft).

6 Edinample Castle lies where the
Burn of Ample runs into the loch.

Leave by the A84 and follow it for 14
miles (23km) southward to Callander
(▷ 189), passing a turning right to
Balquhidder. Return along the A84,
then turn left at the A821. After
passing the former Trossachs Hotel,
follow signs (right) to Loch Katrine.

7 Leave your car in the parking area
at the end and take a walk or bicycle
ride beside the loch, whose island-
studded beauty became legendary
after Sir Walter Scott's description
in *The Lady of the Lake*. While
recreation is to the fore as visitors
come in droves to enjoy the scene
and take a ride on the steamer, the
loch also has a serious practical
function, supplying central Glasgow
with fresh water via an underground
pipeway some 35 miles (56km) long.

Return to the A821 and turn right.
Follow the A821 for 7 miles (11km)
over the hills on the Duke's Pass,
and through Achray Forest to
Aberfoyle.

8 The little town of Aberfoyle
bustles at the heart of the Trossachs.
It is surrounded by the pine trees
of the Queen Elizabeth Forest Park,
and the extensive visitor centre
1 mile (1.6km) to the north has
information about the many walking
routes in the area.

Continue on the A821 and the A81.
At the intersection with the A811,
turn right to pass Drymen, and
then go through the small village of
Gartocharn.

9 Gartocharn is best known, not for
itself, but rather for the superb view
up Loch Lomond from the hill behind
the village, Duncryne (142m/462ft).

Continue on the A811 through
Balloch and turn right at the A82.
Follow this main route north, and
after about 9 miles (15km) pass the
turning to Luss. Continue towards
the foot of the loch.

10 Lying near the foot of Loch
Lomond, Balloch received a
welcome boost in 2002 with the
opening of the visitor centre, Loch
Lomond Shores, and its companion
ultra-modern shopping centre,
which together form the National
Park Gateway Centre (daily 10–5,
extended hours in summer).

11 Pass Inverbeg, from where you
can catch a ferry across the loch to
the settlement of Rowardennan.

Rejoin the A82 and continue up the
west shore of the loch. After Ardlui,
the mountains become more rugged
as you continue up Glen Falloch to
Crianlarich. At Crianlarich, turn right
on to the A85, driving through Glen
Dochart. Pass Loch Lubhair on the
left, with Ben More looming on the
right (1,171m/3,842ft). Turn left at the
A827 to return to Killin.

PLACE TO VISIT
SCOTTISH WOOL CENTRE
✉ Aberfoyle FK8 3UQ ☎ 01877 382850
🕐 May–end Sep daily 9.30–6; rest of year
daily 10–5

WHEN TO GO
Visit in early summer when the
countryside is at its best and the
weather's perfect weather for
walking and cycling.

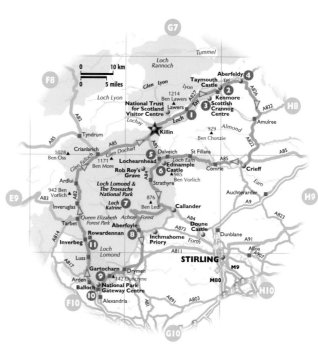

QUEEN ELIZABETH FOREST PARK

A woodland walk with spectacular views across a geological fault.

THE WALK

Distance: 4 miles (6km)
Allow: 3 hours
Start/end: Visitor Centre, Aberfoyle
Grid reference NN 519014

★ This walk crosses the Highland Boundary Fault, a geological line stretching from Arran to Stonehaven, just south of Aberdeen. It separates the Highlands from the Lowlands.

From the front of the visitor centre turn left, go down some steps on to a well-surfaced footpath and follow the blue markers of the Highland Boundary Fault Trail. Continue on this trail to reach the Waterfall of the Little Fawn with its 16.7m (55ft) drop. Shortly after this turn left

to cross a bridge, then turn right following the white arrow left again on to a forest road.

This forest road is part of the National Cycle Network (NCN), so watch out for bicyclists. Head uphill following the blue Highland Boundary Fault markers and the NCN Route 7 signs.

❶ The Highland Boundary Fault formed around 390 million years ago when the old rocks of the Highlands were forced up and the Lowland rocks pushed down. North of the fault lie Highland rocks, created over 500 million years ago. Whinstone, used extensively as a building stone, formed from extreme pressure

on mud and sand. Slate was also formed in this fashion but was compressed into layers and was valued as a roofing material. Near the walk is the Duke's Pass, one of the largest slate quarries in Scotland.

When the road forks at a junction, stay left and continue uphill until you reach a crossroads. Turn right, at the blue marker, on to a smaller and rougher road. The Boundary Fault Trail parts company with the NCN Route 7 at this point. The going is easy along this fairly level section. Keep on until you eventually reach a viewpoint on the right.

Most of the higher mountains in this area are formed from a rock

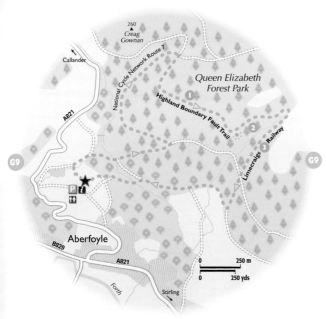

Queen Elizabeth Forest Park

260 Creag Gownan

Callander

Highland Boundary Fault Trail

Limecraigs Railway

Aberfoyle

A821

B829

Forth

Stirling

0   250 m
0   250 yds

through another barrier and once again continue to head downhill.

At the bottom of the hill is a set of steps leading to a forest road. Turn right on to the road and follow the blue markers. Stay on this road until you reach a green signpost on the left pointing to the visitor centre. Turn left on to a downhill track and head through the woods.

Eventually you'll reach a board announcing the end of the trail. From here the route is signed back to the visitor centre. When the trail forks take the right-hand turning and head uphill beside a handrail and return to the start.

WHERE TO EAT
The visitor centre at the Queen Elizabeth Forest Park (tel 01877 382258) has an excellent restaurant where you can enjoy a bowl of hot soup, hot and cold drinks and a range of sandwiches and hot meals.

PLACE TO VISIT
BLAIR DRUMMOND SAFARI PARK
✉ Blair Drummond, near Stirling PK9 4UR ☎ 01786 841456 🕐 Daily 10–5.30 🎟 Adult £10.50, child £7

WHEN TO GO
Early summer offers the best chance of sunshine. Avoid walking in poor visibility and leave plenty of time

known as Leny Gritt, which started life as sand and gravel before being moulded into shape by intense heat and pressure. Another group of rocks includes Achray Sandstone, formed when this high mountain area was under the sea.

From here the road heads uphill until it reaches a marker near a path heading uphill towards a mast. Turn right, then go through a barrier and start descending. Although this is a well-made path, it is a very steep descent through the woods, so tread carefully.

❷ A great deal of quarrying once took place here. This steep downhill path follows the line of the Limecraigs Railway, an inclined railway that was used for transporting stone from Lime Craig Quarry. The limestone was carried on wooden wagons to the lime kilns at the bottom of the hill. Heavy wooden sleepers supported the three rails of the wagon way. Full wagons went down using the centre and one outside rail, while the empties returned on the centre and other outside rail. The wagons

were attached to a wire rope, and the weight of the full wagons and gravity provided the power to return the empty ones to the top. By 1850 the quarry was depleted.

❸ This path follows the line of the Limecraigs Railway, an early 19th-century inclined railway used for transporting limestone. It continues downhill to go through another barrier where the path is intersected by a forest road. Cross this road, go

Opposite *View of the Highland Boundary Fault Trail in Queen Elizabeth Forest Park*
Below *A bench makes the most of a scenic viewpoint along the trail*

DRIVE

A CIRCUIT OF FIFE

This circular tour takes in the highlights of an east-coast peninsula with a strong tradition of farming, fishing and mining, known as the Kingdom of Fife.

THE DRIVE

Distance: 97 miles (156km)
Allow: 1 day
Start/end: St. Andrews

★ From the ancient university town of St. Andrews (▷ 201), home of golf, take the A917 southeast along the coast towards Crail, passing a turning to Scotland's Secret Bunker (▷ 202).

❶ Crail's picturesque old harbour is at the bottom of a steep lane. The town is the start of the fishing villages of the East Neuk (▷ 195), a chain of charming old fishing harbours strung out along the southeast coast of Fife. They share views out to the Isle of May, and

across the Firth of Forth to the flat lands of North Berwick. Follow the A917 for 4 miles (6km) to Anstruther, where the Scottish Fisheries Museum on the seafront is an added attraction.

Continue on the A917 for 1 mile (1.5km) to Pittenweem, the busiest of the harbours.

❷ To the north, Kellie Castle is worth a short diversion (NTS). A venerable tower house, it dates back to 1360, but most of what is visible today is from 1606. The interior was restored by the family of architect Robert Lorimer at the end of the 19th century, and has a comfortable, eccentric air, with painted panels

and some beautiful plaster ceilings upstairs. From the house there are views south towards the sea, and down the back to the beautiful walled gardens, planted with old-fashioned roses, fruit and vegetables, and herbaceous flowers.

Continue on the A917 to explore first St. Monans and then Elie, with its golden sands. Stay on the A917 to Upper Largo, then join the A915 towards Windygates, passing Largo Bay and the holiday and golfing resort of Lundin Links. Leven and Methil are also towns on the edge of the industrial and mining district which stretches towards Kirkcaldy.

3 At Windygates, join the A911 and head towards Glenrothes, a planned 'new town' established in 1949.

Turn right at a roundabout at the intersection with the A92 and head northwards. Turn left when the A912 is met and follow this to the ancient village of Falkland, which has several good eating places. Continue on the A912 and turn left at the A91 and left again at the B919. Turn left at the A911 and follow it to Scotlandwell.

4 Scotlandwell lies on the flat land to the east of Loch Leven, and records dating back to AD84 show that Roman soldiers drank from the holy well here. In medieval times, it was a place of pilgrimage. The current stone cistern marking the well is 19th century. Today the village is better known for the nearby gliding centre.

Leave by the B920 and turn right at the B9097, following the southern shore of Loch Leven, a nature reserve noted for its birdlife. Pass the Royal Society for the Protection of Birds' Vane Farm visitor centre on the left. At the intersection with the

B996, turn right and follow this road to Kinross.

5 Standing on the northwest shore of Loch Leven, Kinross is a former county town and a popular centre for anglers.

6 It is also the access point for Lochleven Castle (▷ 199). The gardens of 17th-century Kinross House are open in summer, and were designed by William Bruce (1630–1710), better known for his work on Holyrood Palace in Edinburgh.

Continue on the B996 and join the A922. After Milnathort, follow the B996 then the A91. Turn left at the A912 and right at the A913 to Abernethy.

7 Pictish carved stones discovered in the area suggest that this quiet little village was once a centre of some significance, and it is said that Malcolm II of Scotland knelt to William I of England here in 1072. Its biggest claim to fame is the curious round tower, 22.5m (74ft) high and dating from the 11th century. It is

only the second example of such an Irish Celtic church tower in Scotland (the other is at Brechin). Abernethy village, incidentally, has nothing to do with Abernethy biscuits, which were named after an English doctor. Continue on the A913 and follow it for 13 miles (21km) to the busy town of Cupar.

8 A Royal Burgh, Cupar has a charter dating back to 1363, and an unusual claim to fame in the annals of Scottish theatre. It was here, in 1535, that poet David Lyndsay's morality play, *Ane Pleasant Satire of the Three Estates*, received its first performance. As a lively attack on church corruption of the day, it was welcomed by reformers, and versions of the drama are still staged today.

9 To the south, off the A916, lies Scotstarvit Tower, a ruined tower house dating back to 1579 and part of the estate of Hill of Tarvit (▷ 196). Keys available from Hill of Tarvit mansion in the summer months (tel 01334 653127).

Leave by the A91 and follow it back into St. Andrews.

PLACES TO VISIT
KELLIE CASTLE AND GARDENS (NTS)
✉ Pittenweem, Fife Ky10 2RF ☎ 01333 720721 🕐 Open all year daily 9.30–5.30; house Easter–end Oct daily 1–5 👋 Adult £8

ROYAL SOCIETY FOR THE PROTECTION OF BIRDS VANE FARM VISITOR CENTRE
✉ Kinross ☎ 01577 862355 🕐 Daily 10–5 👋 Adult £3, child 50p, family £6.00

KINROSS HOUSE
✉ Woodside Ave, Grantown-on-Spey, Moray PH26 3JR ☎ 01479 872042 🕐 Apr–end Sep daily 10–7 👋 Adult £3, child free

WHEN TO GO
Take this tour in the summer when the gardens are in full bloom.

Opposite Red-roofed cottages face the sea at Pittenweem harbour

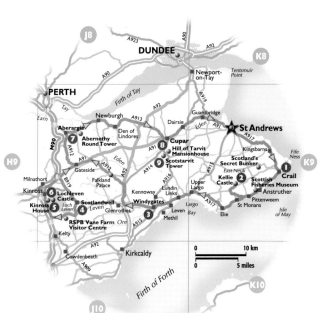

WALK

UNIVERSITY TRADITIONS AT ST. ANDREWS

An easy town trail reveals some unusual customs.

THE WALK

Distance: 4.5 miles (7.2km)
Allow: 2 hours
Start/end: Martyrs Monument, The Scores,
St. Andrews
OS Explorer 371 St. Andrews & East Fife

★ The historic town of St. Andrews
(▷ 201) is famous as the home of
golf and of an ancient university. The
university was established in 1410
and is the oldest in Scotland, and
third oldest in Britain—after Oxford
and Cambridge. The town's relatively
isolated location on the Fife coast
may be one of the reasons why
Prince William chose to study here.

The university is proud of its
traditions and you may spot students
around the town in their distinctive
scarlet gowns. First-year students

wear them over both shoulders,
gradually casting them off each year,
until in their fourth and final year the
gowns hang down, almost dragging
behind them.

Elizabeth Garrett, the first woman
in Britain to qualify as a doctor,
was allowed to matriculate at St.
Andrews in 1862 but was then
rejected after the Senate declared
her enrolment illegal. Following
this the university made efforts
to encourage the education of
women, who were finally allowed
full membership of the university
in 1892.

With the Martyrs Monument on
The Scores in front of you, walk
left past the bandstand. At the road
turn right, walk to the British Golf

Museum, then turn left. Pass the
clubhouse of the Royal and Ancient
Golf Club on your left.

❶ The Royal and Ancient Golf Club
is the governing body for the rules
of golf and overlooks the world-
famous Old Course. It's a bastion
of conservatism and the clubhouse
isn't open to visitors; women
guests are permitted to enter on
St Andrew's Day. The modern
game developed on the east coast
of Scotland. It was banned by
James II who feared that it
distracted men from their archery
practice, leaving them unable to
defend the country.

Bear right at the burn (stream) to
reach the beach.

Opposite *Before its destruction during the Reformation in the 16th century, St. Andrews Cathedral was known as the ecclesiastical heart of Scotland*

Walk along the West Sands as far as you choose, then either retrace your steps along the beach or take one of the paths through the dunes to join the road. Walk back to the Golf Museum, then turn right and walk to the main road.

Turn left and walk to St. Salvator's College.

❷ In medieval times students could enter the university at the age of 13, and a system of seniority arose among the student body. New students were initiated into the fraternity on Raisin Monday, when they were expected to produce a pound of raisins. The tradition persists today, when they are taken under the wings of older students who become their 'academic parents'. On Raisin Sunday, in November, academic 'fathers' take their charges out to get drunk. The next day, Raisin Monday, the 'mothers' dress them up in fancy dress before they congregate in St. Salvator's quad for a flour and egg fight.

Peek through the archway at the quadrangle and look at the initials PH in the cobbles outside. They commemorate Patrick Hamilton, who was martyred here in 1528—it is said that students who tread on the site will fail their exams.

Cross over and walk to the end of College Street. Turn right and walk along Market Street. At the corner turn left along Bell Street, then left again on South Street. Opposite Holy Trinity Church, turn right down Queens Gardens to reach Queens Terrace.

Turn right to reach the red-brick house, then left down steeply sloping Dempster Terrace. At the end cross the burn, turn left and walk to the main road. Cross over

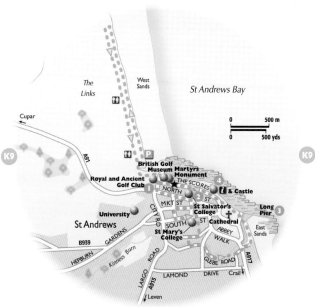

and walk along Glebe Road. At the park, take the path that bears left, walk past the play area and up to Woodburn Terrace.

Turn left to join St. Mary Street and cross over the main road to follow Woodburn Place down towards the beach.

❸ You'll get good views of the Long Pier, where students traditionally walked on Sunday mornings after church, until the pier was closed for repair. Another tradition is a mass dawn swim in the icy sea on May morning (1 May).

Just before the slipway, turn left along a tarmac path. Cross over the footbridge and join the road.

Bear right for a few paces, then ascend the steps on the left. These bring you up to the remains of a church and on to the famous ruined cathedral. A gate in the wall on the left gives access to the site.

❹ Pass the ancient castle on the right. A former royal palace

and fortress, the castle was at the forefront of the Reformation; Protestant leader John Knox preached here.

Pass the Castle Visitor Centre, then continue along The Scores to return to the car park.

WHERE TO EAT
There are plenty of pubs in St. Andrews catering for all those eternally thirsty students, as well as a choice of cafés. Fisher and Donaldson (tel 01334 472201), on Church Street, is a bakery famous for its fudge doughnuts (they're very sweet, so hang on to your fillings).

PLACE TO VISIT
ST. ANDREWS CASTLE
✉ The Scores, St. Andrews, Fife KY16 9AR ☎ 01334 477196 🕐 Apr–end Sep daily 9.30–6.30; rest of year daily 9.30–4.30 🎫 Adult £5.20, child £2.60

WHEN TO VISIT
Visit in September and see the university town in full swing.

A FISHY TRAIL IN FIFE

A linear coastal walk through the villages of Fife's East Neuk with picturesque fishing villages and extensive sea views.

THE WALK

Distance: 4 miles (6.4km)
Allow: 1 hour 30 minutes
Start: Tourist Information Centre, Crail
End: Anstruther Harbou

★ Scotland's James II described the East Neuk (nook) of Fife as 'a fringe of gold on a beggar's mantle'. This corner of the east coast is dotted with picturesque fishing villages, which nestle close together yet retain their own distinctive character.

From the tourist information centre in Crail, walk down Tolbooth Wynd. At the end turn right and, where the road divides, you bear left (a sign says 'no vehicular access to harbour').

You will now be walking beside the old castle wall to a lookout point, which gives you a grand view of the picturesque harbour. Bear right and then walk on to reach the High Street.

❶ Crail is perhaps the prettiest village, with a neat little harbour, which attracts many artists and photographers. It was once the largest fishmarket in Europe and, like all the East Neuk villages, used to trade with the Low Countries and Scandinavia; you can see the Dutch influence in the houses with their crow-stepped gables and pantiled roofs.

Fishing dominated the lives of people and each of the East

Neuk villages was a closely knit community. It was rare for people to marry outside their own village and women were as heavily involved in the work as the men. They prepared the fish, baited the hooks, mended the nets and took the fish to market for sale, carrying enormous baskets of herrings on their backs. They also used to carry their husbands out to sea on their backs so that they could board their boats without getting wet.

Turn left and walk along the road out of the village, passing the two white beacons, which help guide boats into the harbour. Turn left and walk down West Braes, following the signs for the Coastal Path. When you reach Osbourne Terrace turn left down a narrow path, then go down some steps, through a kissing gate and on to a grassy track by the shore.

From here you follow the path as it hugs the shoreline. You should soon see cormorants perched on rocks to your left and will also get views of the Isle of May. Go down some steps, over a slightly boggy area, and continue walking until you reach two derelict cottages, an area known as The Pans.

Walk past the cottages and continue along the shore, then hop over a stone stile. You'll now pass flat rocks on the left, which are covered with interesting little rock pools. Cross the burn by the footbridge—you'll now be able to see the Bass Rock and Berwick Law on your left and the village of Anstruther ahead, and will soon reach some caves.

Pass the caves then cross a little stone stile on the left-hand side and go over a footbridge. Your track is narrower now and takes you past fields on the right, then some maritime grasses on the left. Stone steps lead to another stile. Climb over it to reach Caiplie.

Go through the kissing gate to pass in front of houses, follow the wide grassy track, then go through another kissing gate to walk past a field. The path now runs past a free-range pig farm and up to a caravan park.

Continue along the shore, on a tarmac track to reach a play area and war memorial on the right. Maintain direction now as you enter the village of Cellardyke and continue to the harbour.

Pass the harbour and The Haven restaurant and continue along John Street, then James Street.

At the end of James Street maintain direction, then follow the road as it

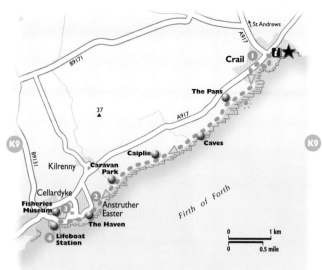

bends down to the left. You'll walk past a guiding beacon and will come into Anstruther's busy little harbour.

❷ Anstruther (known locally as 'Enster'), the largest and busiest of all the villages and home of the local lifeboat station. Fishing has always been the focus of life here. The village was the capital of the Scottish herring trade and the harbour was once so busy that you could cross it by stepping over the boats. Look at the houses as you pass and you'll see that many of them have spacious lofts with a pulley outside—designed to store fishing gear and provide an area for mending the nets.

❸ The Scottish Fisheries Museum opposite the Lifeboat Station is packed full of information on the local fishing industry and tells its story from the earliest times to the present day. There are models of fishing boats and some old vessels in the former boatyard. You can also see a reconstruction of a fisherman's cottage.

❹ The Lifeboat Station is often open to visitors. The local lifeboat, manned by RNLI volunteers, is regularly

called into service and over 300 lives have been saved since one was first established here.
You can now either walk back to Crail or take the bus, which leaves from the harbour.

PLACE TO VISIT
SCOTTISH FISHERIES MUSEUM
✉ St. Ayles, Harbourhead, Anstruther, Fife KY10 3AB ☎ 01333 310628 🕐 Apr–end Sep Mon–Sat 10–5.30, Sun 11–5; rest of year Mon–Sat 10–4.30, Sun 12–4.30 💷 Adult £5, child free

WHERE TO EAT AND DRINK
There is plenty of choice in Anstruther. Try Anstruther Fish Bar (tel 01333 310518), on Shore Street by the harbour, while the Ship Inn sells bar meals (tel 01333 310516). In Crail, the Honeypot Tearoom (tel 01333 450935) serves tasty snacks.

WHEN TO GO
A great walk for any time of year.

Opposite *Crow-stepped and pantiled houses cluster around Crail's attractive harbour, once the haunt of smugglers*

WHAT TO DO

ABERFELDY

ABERFELDY GALLERY
www.aberfeldygallery.co.uk
High quality paintings, photography, woodwork, sculpture and pottery by over 100 Scottish-based artists.
✉ 39 Kenmore Street PH15 2BL ☎ 01887 829129 🕐 Mon, Tue, Thu–Sat 10–5, Wed 10–1.30, Sun 1–4

BEYOND ADVENTURE
www.beyondadventure.co.uk
This specialist outdoor company offers a wide range of activities in and around Aberfeldy. These include full-day canoeing trips on Loch Tay, winter mountain skills course, orienteering, gorge walking and introductions to climbing and abseiling. Advance reservations recommended. Call beforehand and they will meet you at an agreed location.
✉ Alma Avenue PH15 2BL ☎ 01887 829202 🕐 All year 💷 Full day canoeing from £120 for 2 adults. Special low rates for children under 12 and families

DEWAR'S WORLD OF WHISKY
www.dewarswow.com
Just outside Aberfeldy, this distillery has an impressive visitor centre and a wide selection of whiskies for sale. Enjoy a video and tour of the production area. Hand-held audio guides are available in seven languages.
✉ PH15 2EB ☎ 01887 822010 🕐 Easter–end Oct Mon–Sat 10–6, Sun 12–4; rest of year Mon–Sat 10–4 💷 Adult £6.50, child (5–17) £4, deluxe tour £18, signature tour £30 ☕ Café serves coffee and cakes 🎁 Whisky and memorabilia

HIGHLAND ADVENTURE SAFARIS
www.highlandadventuresafaris.co.uk
Explore the high mountain country on a Land Rover tour, reaching a height of nearly 1,000m (3,300ft). Local wildlife includes grouse, mountain hares, red deer and golden eagles. Advance reservations are essential. Binoculars and telescopes provided.
✉ Drumdewan PH15 2JQ ☎ 01887 820071 🕐 All year 💷 2 hour 30 minute tour:

adult £35, child (under 12) £12.50; 1 hour 30 minute tour: adult £20, child £10; 4 hour trek: £60, including lunch

SPLASH
www.rafting.co.uk
Wide range of white-water rafting and kayaking adventures, many suitable for families. This operator also offers trips on 'duckies', a cross between a raft and a kayak, plus canyoning, abseiling and high-ropes courses. Advance reservations. Minimum age 8 for rafting, higher for other activities.
✉ Dunkeld Road PH15 2AQ ☎ 01887 829706 🕐 Rafting year round, Mon, Wed, Fri, Sat, Sun; other activities daily 💷 Adult from £40, child from £25, family of 4 £120, for half-day white-water rafting

ANSTRUTHER

EAST NEUK OUTDOORS
www.eastneukoutdoors.co.uk
This popular seaside centre offers activities for the whole family such as archery, abseiling, canoeing and orienteering. You can also rent

Left Sailing on Loch Ard, near the town of Aberfoyle

off-road bicycles and play on a putting green. Minimum age 8 for activities. Advance reservations recommended.

✉ Cellardyke Park KY10 3AX ☎ 01333 311929 🕐 Apr–end Sep daily 10–5 💷 From £20 for a half-day of different activities 🎫

ISLE OF MAY
www.isleofmayferry.com
The round trip to the national nature reserve on the tiny Isle of May takes 5 hours. The rugged island is home to seabirds including razorbills, eider ducks and puffins. Paths lead around the remains of a 12th-century monastery. Buy tickets at Anstruther harbour up to 1 hour before sailing.
✉ From Anstruther harbour ☎ 01333 310103 (24-hour recorded information line) 🕐 May–end Oct once a day 💷 Adult £15, child £7 🍴 Snack bar on board

BLAIRGOWRIE
MILLHORN FARM RIDING CENTRE
www.millhornridingcentre.co.uk
Day hacks, riding lessons and tailor-made holiday programmes can be arranged at this rural riding centre. Suitable for adults and teenagers. Advance reservations recommended.
✉ Rosemount, Blairgowrie PH13 9HT ☎ 01828 626172/07884 060648 🕐 All year 💷 Lesson from £22; 2-hour hack from £30

BO'NESS
BO'NESS & KINNEIL RAILWAY
www.srps.org.uk
Enjoy a 3.5-mile (5.6km) ride on a historic steam train from Bo'ness, west of Edinburgh, to the caverns of Birkhill Mine. At Bo'ness station, locomotives are displayed at the Scottish Railway Exhibition. At the mines you can take a guided tour to see 300-million-year-old fossils. Look for special events for children.
✉ Bo'ness Station, Union Street EH51 9AQ ☎ 01506 822298 🕐 Easter, end Mar–end Jun, Sep, Oct Sat–Sun; Jul, Aug daily 💷 Adult £5, child (5–15) £2.50. Mine

tour: adult £3, child £2, family £7 🍴 Station Coffee Shop

BRACO
PHOENIX FALCONRY SERVICES
www.scottishfalconry.co.uk
Learn about the ancient sport of falconry, and how to handle the birds yourself on half-day, full-day or evening trips. Longer trips include lunch. The Eagle Odyssey package, which involves handling birds of prey, is for those age 16 and over. Advanced reservations essential. Braco lies just off the A9.
✉ Gardeners Cottage, Braco Castle Estate FK15 9LA ☎ 01786 880539 🕐 Daily, dawn–dusk 💷 3-hour Meet the Birds experience £75

CLUNY
CLUNY CLAYS
www.clunyclays.co.uk
Try your hand at clay pigeon shooting, archery and air rifle shooting, or golf at the driving range or on the 9-hole course. Instruction and lessons are available for all activities but must be reserved in advance. Some activities are not suitable for children.
✉ Cluny Mains Farm, Cluny, by Kirkcaldy KY2 6QU ☎ 01592 720374 🕐 Apr–end Oct daily 8–8; Nov–end Mar daily 8–7 💷 Clay pigeon shooting from £19; golf from £11; archery from £19 🍴 Licensed restaurant open for lunch Mon–Thu and lunch and dinner Fri–Sun 🍴 Café serves cakes and coffee all day

COMRIE
DRUMMOND TROUT FARM AND FISHERY
www.drummondtroutfarm.co.uk
There's a choice of six pools for trout fishing at this fishery, 1 mile (1.6km) west of Comrie. An underwater camera allows fish-eye views, and food to feed the fish is free. Tuition is also free Monday to Friday and children on the beginners ponds get a badge and certificate for their first ever fish. You keep everything you catch, and pay for the fish at the end by weight. Picnic areas.
✉ PH6 2LD ☎ 01567 830400 🕐 Boat hire: Mon–Thu 9–6 (in season), Fri–Sun

dawn–dusk 💷 4 hours: £24; fishing permit per day, adult £8, child £4 🎫 Farm shop sells snacks as well as fresh trout, pâté and fishcakes

CRIEFF
CAITHNESS GLASS VISITOR CENTRE
www.caithnessglass.co.uk
Watch the famous glassware being made, then stock up on vases, whisky tumblers, decanters and paperweights at discount prices in the factory shop. Glassmaking can be seen on weekdays throughout the year. The shop offers overseas posting and engraving. There is also a glass-painting area for visitors to try their hand.
✉ Muthill Road PH7 4HQ ☎ 01764 654014 🕐 Mon–Sat 9–5, Sun 10–5 (Sun 12–5 Dec–end Feb) 💷 Free

CUPAR
GRISELDA HILL POTTERY
www.wemyssware.co.uk
This family pottery has revived the famous Wemyss Ware style of curious cats and floral pigs, popular in the 19th century. Hand-painting ensures that every piece is unique. To find it, follow signs with a grinning, pop-eyed yellow cat.
✉ Kirkbrae, Ceres KY15 5ND ☎ 01334 828273 🕐 Mon–Fri 9–5, Sat–Sun noon–5

SCOTTISH DEER CENTRE
www.tsdc.co.uk
Wolves, birds of prey and, of course, nine species of deer are the big attraction at this wildlife park, 12 miles (19km) west of St. Andrews. You can get close to all the animals. Falconry displays are given three times daily in summer, once a day in winter. There is also a playground, and picnic spots.
✉ Bow-of-Fife KY15 4NQ ☎ 01337 810391 🕐 Jul, Aug daily 10–5; rest of year daily 10–4.30 💷 Adult £6.95, child (3–15) £4.95, family £22 🍴 Café has light lunches and home baking 🎫 Several high quality shops, including outdoor clothing and golf equipment

DUNDEE

CAMPERDOWN WILDLIFE CENTRE

www.dundeecity.gov.uk/camperdown
This wildlife park just outside the city has 85 species of native Scottish and other European wildlife including lynx, bears, wolves, bats, Arctic foxes and pine martens. In the summer you can see the animals being fed. Seasonal pitch and putt and kiddie bicycles. Special events year-round include animal handling and feeding days.
✉ Camperdown Country Park, Coupar Angus Road DD2 4TF ☎ 01382 432661 ⏰ Mar–end Sep daily 10–4.30; rest of year daily 10–3.30 💷 Adult £3.30, child (3–15) £2.75, family £9.25

DUNDEE CONTEMPORARY ARTS (DCA)

www.dca.org.uk
The DCA and the Dundee Rep theatre together form the core of the arts revival in the city's cultural quarter. As well as housing exhibitions of contemporary art, the DCA is Dundee's only city-centre cinema, showing mainstream and international films.
✉ 152 Nethergate DD1 4DY ☎ 01382 909900 💷 DCA and exhibitions free; cinema from £3.50 🍴 Trendy Jute Café Bar

DUNDEE ICE ARENA

www.dundeeicearena.co.uk
A popular ice rink just outside the city, with ice skating shows, ice discos, lessons, public skating sessions and professional ice hockey games. The ice discos for children have special lighting effects.
✉ Camperdown Leisure Complex, Kingsway West DD2 3SQ ☎ 01382 889369 ⏰ Mon–Sat 10–12.30, 2.30–4.30, Sun 2.30–4.30 💷 Skating from £5, skate hire £2, under 5 £3 (includes skate hire) 🍴

DUNDEE REP

www.dundeerep.co.uk
Scotland's leading repertory theatre is set in Dundee's up-and-coming cultural quarter. As well as the summer repertory season, the theatre hosts touring productions. The building is also home to the contemporary Scottish Dance Theatre.
✉ Tay Square DD1 1PB ☎ 01382 223530 💷 From £5 🍴 Intimate café-bar with varied menu 🍷 Two bars

OLYMPIA LEISURE CENTRE

www.dundeecity.gov.uk/olympia
If you're crossing the road bridge to Dundee, you can't miss this glass-fronted sports centre with its three giant water slides, right on the waterfront. There's a 25m (75ft) training pool, a dive pool and a wave pool, as well as a gym and health suite. Opening times for different facilities vary according to age group, so check ahead.
✉ Earl Grey Place, Dundee DD1 4DF ☎ 01382 432300 ⏰ Leisure pool term time Mon–Fri 12–8.30; other times 10–8.30; Sat–Sun 10–5.30 💷 Adult from £4 🍴

OVERGATE

www.overgate.co.uk
Bright, modern shopping mall on two levels, with household name stores and more unusual ones, such as Ortak, the Orkney jewellers. Tax-free shopping widely available.
✉ DD1 1UQ ☎ 01382 314201 ⏰ Mon–Wed, Fri–Sat 9–6, Thu 9–7.30, Sun 12–5 🍴 Starbucks

SOCIAL

www.socialanimal.co.uk
The glass-walled side of this trendy bar overlooks Tay Square and the Dundee Rep theatre. Cool, contemporary decoration inside, with different events each night, including quiz nights and live music from R&B to reggae.
✉ 10 South Tay Street DD1 1PA ☎ 0845 166 6020 ⏰ Daily 12–12 🍴 Food noon–10

DUNKELD

BROUGHTON-STUART JEWELLERY LTD

www.broughton-stuartjewellery.co.uk
Craig Stuart uses an ancient technique called Mokume Gane to achieve a delicate wood-grain effect on his jewellery, combining gold, platinum and diamonds into unique miniature works of art.
✉ 25 Atholl Street, Dunkeld PH8 0AR ☎ 01350 727888 ⏰ Mon–Wed, Fri, Sat 10–4

GOING POTTIE

www.goingpottie.com
From daubing a plaster frog to decorating your own dinner service, there's something to appeal to all ages at this friendly ceramic painting centre, with expert tuition to help you make the most of your project. The perfect activity for a wet day.
✉ Cathedral Street, Dunkeld PH8 0AW ☎ 01350 728044 ⏰ Mon–Sat 10–5, Sun 10–4 💷 From £5

NAE LIMITS

www.naelimits.co.uk
This adventure sports centre offers water-, land- and snow-based activities. Try everything from whitewater rafting to cliff-jumping, according to the season. Full instruction and safety kit are included. Age restrictions apply, so check ahead.
✉ 14 The Cross, Dunkeld PH8 0AJ ☎ 0845 017 8177 ⏰ All year 💷 From £45 for half-day activity, £100 full day

ELIE

ELIE WATERSPORTS

www.eliewatersports.com
Sheltered Elie Bay is a great place to learn watersports, and this centre near the Ship Inn offers windsurfing, sailing and canoeing courses. There are also mountain bicycles to rent. Advance reservations advised.
✉ Elie Harbour ☎ 01333 330962 ⏰ May–end Sep 10–6 💷 Windsurfer rental and instruction £20 per hour; canoe rental and instruction £16 per hour; mountain bicycle rental from £8 for half-day.

FALKIRK

CINEWORLD CINEMA

www.cineworld.co.uk
Falkirk's 12-screen multiplex cinema has a policy of showing British films.
✉ Central Retail Park, Old Bison Works FK2 7AN ☎ 0871 200 2000 (reservations and information) ⏰ All year 💷 Adult from £5.70; reduced tickets Tue

GLENFARG
GLENFARG HOTEL
www.glenfarghotel.co.uk or
www.mundellmusic.com
This charming hotel, south of Perth, hosts live music every Monday. It attracts international and UK artists performing folk, country, rock, Americana and alternative country music. Acts have included Fairport Convention, the Straws and Benny Gallagher. The hotel has a bistro and restaurant too.

✉ Main Street PH2 9NU ☎ 01577 830241 🕐 Music on Mon 🎟 Tickets from £12–£30

KNOCKHILL
KNOCKHILL RACING CIRCUIT
www.knockhill.co.uk
Come and watch weekend superbike and Formula 3 racing at Scotland's National Motorsport Centre (Apr–end Oct). You can also take part in quad biking, driving racing or rally cars, 4x4s and motorcycling. Children can drive at the carting centre. Advance booking advised.

✉ By Dunfermline, Fife KY12 9TF ☎ 01383 723337 🕐 Summer and winter 9–6 🎟 Entry £5–£25 🅿

LAKE OF MENTEITH
LAKE OF MENTEITH FISHERIES
www.menteith-fisheries.co.uk
Lake Mentieth has excellent fly fishing for rainbow trout. Rent a boat through the booking office (advance reservations recommended); a qualified instructor can also be arranged.

✉ 'Ryeyards', Port of Menteith FK8 3RA ☎ 01877 385664 🕐 End Mar–end Oct Mon–Sat 9.30–5.30, Sun 12–7 🎟 Day session from £40 per boat, £50 weekends

LARBERT
BARBARA DAVIDSON DESIGNER POTTERY
www.barbara-davidson.com
The hand-thrown pottery for sale at this working pottery includes mugs, dinner sets, vases and candle-holders. Larbert is 9 miles (14.4km) south of Stirling.

✉ Muirhall Farm FK5 4EW ☎ 01324 554430 🕐 Mon–Sat 10–5

LOCH KATRINE
SS SIR WALTER SCOTT
www.lochkatrine.com
Take a steamship cruise around beautiful Loch Katrine, at the heart of the Trossachs, aboard the 100-year-old SS *Sir Walter Scott* and the SS *Lady of the Lake*. Sailing times vary, so make sure you check ahead. Can be combined with a lochside bicycle ride, contact Katrinewheelz on the same number.

✉ Trossachs Pier Complex FK17 8H2 ☎ 01877 376316 🕐 SS *Sir Walter Scott*.

May–end Oct 10.30am (3 hours adult £9.50, under 16 £7); 1.30pm (45 mins adult £8, under 16 £6); 3pm (2 hours, charges as for 10.30). SS *Lady of the Lake*: sailings at 11, 12, 1, 3.30 and 4.30 (adult £8, under 16 £6) 🍴 Restaurant and bistro 💷

LOCH LOMOND
GLENGOYNE DISTILLERY
www.glengoyne.com
Taste the whisky at this notably picturesque distillery in the reception room overlooking the loch and waterfall, enjoy a guided tour, and visit the heritage room and shop. Located 14 miles (22.5km) north of Glasgow on the A81.

✉ Dumgoyne, near Killearn, Glasgow G63 9LB ☎ 01360 550254 🕐 Mon–Sat 10–4, Sun 12–4. All tours start on the hour 🎟 Adult £5.50, under 18 free; specialized tours from £7.50

LOCH LOMOND SHORES
www.lochlomondshores.com
www.sealifeeurope.com
This pedestrianized crescent of shops has beautiful views over Loch Lomond. The main draw is Jenners, a branch of the famous Edinburgh department store, which has clothing, a food hall and a good selection of whiskies. Balloch is at the southern end of the loch. There is also a Sealife Centre/Aquarium in the Loch Lomond Shores centre, focusing on the creatures that live in the loch. In addition to the shops, you will also find the National Park Gateway centre here, and operators offering canoe hire.

✉ Ben Lomond Way, Balloch G83 8QL ☎ 0845 458 0885 (shopping centre); 01389 721500 (aquarium); 0845 345 4978 (Loch Lomond National Park Gateway) 🕐 Daily 10–6 🍴 Conservatory restaurant in Jenners 🅿 Thorntons coffee shop

LOMOND GALLERIES
www.visit-lochlomond.com
This impressive Edwardian building is now a shopping mall with clothes, sportswear, books, gifts and things for the home. Famous brands with items discounted up to 50 per cent. There are also kilt-makers and the Gallery Café. Located off the A82.

Below *The SS* Sir Walter Scott *cruising on Loch Katrine*

☒ Main Street, Alexandria G83 OUG
☎ 01389 758145 🕐 Mon–Sat 9.30–5.30,
Sun 10–5 🖥 Gallery Café serves home
baking

MAID OF THE LOCH
www.maidoftheloch.co.uk
Loch Lomond's paddle steamer,
Maid of the Loch, is docked at
Balloch. Volunteers are on hand to
answer questions about the craft,
built in 1953, as you look around.
☒ The Pier, Pier Road, Balloch G83 8QX
☎ 01389 711865 🕐 Easter–end Oct
daily 11–4; winter weekends only ✋ Free
🖥 🏛 🛈

PERTH

NOAH'S ARK FAMILY
ENTERTAINMENT CENTRE
www.noahs-ark.co.uk
Family fun, with a soft play area
for very young children, an indoor
karting track and 10-pin bowling
alley. There's also a ceramic painting
studio and a café.
☒ Western Edge, PH1 1QE ☎ 01738
445568 🕐 Daily 10.30–6.30 ✋ Call for
ticket prices

ONCE A TREE
www.onceatree.co.uk
This charming gift shop specializes
in items made from wood, including
carvings, ornaments, chess sets and
secret boxes.
☒ 255 Old High Street PH1 5QN ☎ 01738
636213 🕐 Mon–Sat 9.30–5.30

P. D. MALLOCH
www.pdmalloch.com
If you enjoy fishing, then this is
the shop for you. Everything from
permits for trout fishing on the rivers
Tay and Almond to specialist clothing
and equipment, including maggots,
worms and dead bait! Can also
advise on where to buy permits for
salmon fishing.
☒ 259 Old High Street PH1 5QN ☎ 01738
632316 🕐 Mon–Sat 9–5.15

PERTH THEATRE
www.horsecross.co.uk
Behind an art deco frontage on the
High Street lies Perth's only theatre,
home to a resident company of

actors, and visiting shows. Film star
Ewan McGregor learned his craft
here. Music and comedy as well as
drama.
☒ 185 High Street PH1 5UW ☎ 0845 612
6324 🕐 All year ✋ From £10 🍴
🖥 🛈

PERTHSHIRE VISITOR CENTRE
www.macbeth.co.uk
Lying 7 miles (11.3km) north of Perth
on the A9, this covered centre has a
collection of shops selling clothes,
Scottish food and gifts including
whisky and wines.
☒ Bankfoot PH1 4EB ☎ 01738 787696
🕐 Daily 9–7 🍴 Specializes in local
produce

PITLOCHRY

EDRADOUR DISTILLERY
www.edradour.co.uk
Scotland's smallest distillery
produces a mere 12 casks of
malt whisky a week, and is set
in a picturesque location east of
Pitlochry.
☒ Moulin PH16 5JP ☎ 01796 472095
🕐 Jan, Feb, Mon–Sat 10–4, Sun 12–4;
Mar–end Oct Mon–Sat 9.30–6, Sun 11–5;
Nov–end Dec Mon–Sat 9.30–4, Sun 12–4
✋ Free 🏛

ESCAPE ROUTE
www.escape-route.biz
Staff at this bicycle rental shop are
real enthusiasts and can give you
maps and advice about local routes.
Mountain and hybrid bicycles,
tandems, trailers and child seats are
available. A full range of walking gear
is also available.

☒ 3 Atholl Road PH16 5BX ☎ 01796
473859 🕐 Mon–Sat 9–5.30, Sun 10–5
(10–4 mid-Oct to mid-Mar)

HERITAGE JEWELLERS
www.heritage-jewellers.co.uk
This small, exclusive shop sells gold
and silver jewellery, cultured pearls,
Celtic jewellery made in Orkney, and
Scottish gold.
☒ 104 Atholl Road PH16 5BL ☎ 01796
474333 🕐 Mon–Sat 9–5, Sun 10–5;
Nov–end Mar may close Thu, Sun

PITLOCHRY FESTIVAL THEATRE
www.pitlochry.org.uk
A modern venue with lovely views
across the River Tummel to the
town, the Festival Theatre is open in
summer and autumn, with different
concerts and touring theatre
productions every night.
☒ PH16 5DR ☎ 01796 484626
🕐 May–end Oct ✋ From £13.50 🖥
🍴 Reserve in advance 🏛

THE SHEEP SHOP
www.thesheepshop.uk.com
If you love sheep, then this is
definitely the shop for you. Slippers,
mugs, T-shirts and anything you can
think of with a sheep on it.
☒ 69 Atholl Road PH16 5BL ☎ 01796
473559 🕐 Mon–Sat 10.30–5, Sun 12–4

ST. ANDREWS
BYRE THEATRE
www.byretheatre.com
The Byre Theatre hosts various
theatre productions and touring
shows, including dance, music,
comedy and poetry.

Above *Fishing in the waters of the River Tay at Aberfeldy*

☒ Abbey Street KY16 9LA ☎ 01334 475000 ✋ From £12.50 ◨ Byre bistro-bar open until midnight Mon–Sat

CENTRAL BAR
A St. Andrews institution in the town centre, popular with students and localse. Food including sandwiches and sausage and mash is served until 9pm. Located on the corner of College Street and Market Street. ☒ 79 Market Street KY16 9NU ☎ 01334 478296 🕓 Mon–Thu 11–12, Fri–Sat 11pm–1am, Sun 12.30–12

DAVID BROWN GALLERY
The gallery is worth a visit if you love antiques—but if you love antiques and golf, then it's a must. Unassuming on the outside, it's an Aladdin's cave within, crammed full of silverware, prints and vintage golfing books. Don't leave without hearing one of owner David Brown's anecdotes. Located on the corner with North Street. ☒ 9 Albany Place KY16 9HH ☎ 01334 477840 🕓 May–end Oct Mon–Sat 9–1, 2–6; Nov–end Apr Mon–Sat 10–5

DI GILPIN DESIGN STUDIO
www.digilpin.com
Unique, handmade designer jewellery, knitwear and accessories. The high quality is reflected in the prices. The shop also stocks a wide selection of knitting yarns and patterns. ☒ Hansa House, Burghers Close, 141 South Street KY16 9UN ☎ 01334 476193 🕓 Mon, Tue by appointment, Wed–Sat 10–5

NEW PICTURE HOUSE
www.nphcinema.co.uk
This cinema shows mainstream, independent and some foreign films. Drinks and snacks available. ☒ 117 North Street KY16 9AD ☎ 01334 474902/01334 473509 (recorded information line) 🕓 Daily ✋ From £4.70

ORIGINAL ST. ANDREWS WITCHES TOUR
Enjoy a thrilling night-time guided walk through the centre of St. Andrews, with spooky tales of local witches. Advance reservations recommended. ☒ 3A Drybriggs, Balgarvie Road, Cupar KY15 4AJ ☎ 01334 655057 🕓 Apr–end Oct Fri 7.30; Jun Fri, Sun 7.30; Jul, Aug Thu–Fri, Sun 7.30; rest of year Fri 7.30 ✋ Adult £7, child £5

ST. ANDREWS LINKS
www.standrews.org.uk
The largest golf complex in Europe consists of six public golf courses. The three championship courses include the legendary Old Course. There are also two clubhouses, a golf practice centre and two shops. Advance reservations are essential—the waiting list is anything from weeks to years. Check the website for rules and requirements, which vary widely according to the course. For example, to play the Old Course you need a handicap of 24 (men) or 36 (women), and must reserve at least a year ahead or enter the daily lottery early on the day on which you want to play. ☒ Pilmour House KY16 9SF ☎ 01334 466666 🕓 All year; Old Course closed Sun ✋ Strathtyrum Course £25; Old Course £130 🍴 🏌

YOUNGER HALL
www.st.andrews.ac.uk/music/home
Venue for professional and student-led classical, jazz, musicals and choir concerts. Concerts are also held in the more intimate college chapels, so check when you reserve your ticket. ☒ University of St. Andrews, North Street KY16 6YD ☎ 01334 462226 🕓 Lunchtime concerts Wed 1.15pm during term time ✋ From £2

STIRLING
BLAIR DRUMMOND SAFARI AND ADVENTURE PARK
www.safari-park.co.uk
Safari park to the west of Stirling, where you can drive among animals which roam free, including elephants, giraffes, lions and camels. The pets' farm has llamas, pigs and goats, and there are birds of prey flying demonstrations, a boat safari and a playground. Adventure and climbing area for children of all ages, plus pedal boats and 'astraglide' funfair ride. Picnic and barbecue areas. ☒ Blair Drummond, near Stirling FK9 4UR ☎ 01786 841456 🕓 End Mar–end Sep daily 10–5.30 ✋ Adult £10.50, child (3–14) £7, under 3 free ◨ Chakula Grill

CRAWFORD ARCADE
Twenty-seven independent shops lie within this covered Victorian shopping arcade in the town centre, including a well-stocked bookshop. ☒ King Street FK8 1AX ☎ 07710 086076 🕓 Mon–Sat 8–5.30 or later 🍴 ◨

TOLBOOTH
www.stirling.gov.uk/tolbooth
The Tolbooth dates from 1705 and used to be a jail and court house. It's now a lively music venue which hosts world music, ceilidhs, jazz, comedy and storytelling events. Look out for the hidden stairway outside the toilets. Opposite the old jail. ☒ Jail Wynd FK8 1DE ☎ 01786 274000 🕓 Tue–Sat 10–6 ✋ Free ◨

Above Enjoying a round of golf on the Old Course at St. Andrews

EATING

PRICES AND SYMBOLS

The restaurants are listed alphabetically within each town. The prices are for a two-course lunch (L) and a three-course à la carte dinner (D). Prices in pubs are for a two-course lunchtime bar meal and a two-course dinner in the restaurant, unless specified otherwise The wine price is for the least expensive bottle.

For a key to the symbols, ▷ 2.

ANSTRUTHER
CELLAR RESTAURANT

At this renowned seafood restaurant there is an à la carte menu, and a well-priced set lunch. Fresh local seafood includes crayfish bisque gratin, and fillet of roast cod with a pesto crust, pine nuts and bacon. No children under 8.

✉ 24 East Green KY10 3AA ☎ 01333 310378 🕐 12.30–1, 7–9.30; closed Mon in winter, L Mon, Tue, Christmas 🍴 L £18.50, D £38.50, Wine £18.50

AUCHTERARDER
ANDREW FAIRLIE AT GLENEAGLES

www.gleneagles.com
Located in Gleneagles (▷ 226–227), the Andrew Fairlie restaurant is a

dinner-only affair, with an element of theatre throughout the classical French menu. Creamy veal sweetbreads come with perfect pink slices of kidney and a fondant potato, or try assiette of apples (millefeuille, charlotte and parfait). The wine list offers a lengthy list by the glass. Advance booking recommended. No children under 12.

✉ PH3 1NF ☎ 01764 694267 or 0800 704705 🕐 Dinner only, 7–10; closed Sun, 3 weeks Jan 🍴 D £65, Wine £30 🚗 Just off A9, well signposted

STRATHEARN AT GLENEAGLES

The dining's on a grand scale at this legendary resort hotel (▷ 226–227). The Strathearn is the traditional option, offering an extensive classic menu. The wine list features the odd £2,000 gem. Expect simple, classic dishes: a terrine of goose liver infused with Sauternes wine perhaps, or braised oxtails with sauce bourguignon.

✉ PH3 1NF ☎ 01764 694270 or 0800 704705 🕐 12.30–2.30, 7–10.30; closed L Mon–Sat 🍴 L £35, D £51.50, Wine £24 🚗 Just off A9, well signposted

BALQUHIDDER
MONACHYLE MHOR

www.monachylemhor.com
Tom Lewis provides refreshingly honest cooking. Expect modern Scottish cooking with a French influence and some Asian touches. Begin with monkfish tail with artichokes, vine tomatoes, garden cress and butter sauce perhaps, then move on to guinea fowl breast, herbed pistachio farci, leek fondue, dauphines potatoes and asparagus spears. No children under 12.

✉ FK19 8PQ ☎ 01877 384622 🕐 12–1.45, 7–8.45; closed 4 Jan–14 Feb 🍴 L £25, D £46, Wine £18 🚗 On A84, 11 miles (17.7km) north of Callander turn right at Kingshouse Hotel. Continue for 6 miles (9.7km)

BRIDGEND OF LINTRATHEN
LOCHSIDE LODGE AND ROUNDHOUSE RESTAURANT

www.lochsidelodge.com
On offer here is accomplished modern British and European cuisine—tuck into a dish of cod layered with potato scale, and then indulge in chocolate fondant pudding for dessert, served with coffee ice cream, or perhaps a passion fruit

iced parfait. Hard to find, so phone ahead for directions.
✉ DD8 5JJ ☎ 01575 560340 ⏰ 12–1.30, 6.30–8.30; closed D Sun, Mon, 1–25 Jan 🖐 L £12, D £35, Wine £14.50

CALLANDER
ROMAN CAMP COUNTRY HOUSE
www.roman-camp-hotel.co.uk
Highly accomplished cooking draws on excellent Scottish produce. The four-course dinner menu changes daily; the shorter lunch menu offers good value.
✉ FK17 8BG ☎ 01877 330003 ⏰ 12.30–2, 7–8.30 🖐 L £25, D £44, Wine £18 🚗 Turn left at east end of Callander High Street, go down a 274m (300 yards) driveway into the hotel grounds

CRIEFF
THE BANK RESTAURANT
www.thebankrestaurant.co.uk
Food is simple and fresh and demonstrates good technical skills—roasted courgette (zucchini), garlic and shallot risotto; noisette of lamb with dauphinoise potato and braised red cabbage. Booking advised.
✉ 32 High Street PH7 3BS ☎ 01764 656575 ⏰ 12–1.15, 7–9.30; closed Sun–Mon, 24–26 Dec, 2 weeks mid-Jan 🖐 L £15, D £25, Wine £13.50

CUPAR
OSTLERS CLOSE RESTAURANT
www.ostlersclose.co.uk
The modern Scottish menu changes almost daily and reflects a classical

background with Mediterranean influences. Choose from a starter of pot roast breast of wood pigeon with a cassoulet of haricot beans and pancetta, or a main course of a selection of local seafood served with steamed farm seakale on a langoustine butter sauce. No children under 6 in the evening.
✉ Bonnygate KY15 4BU ☎ 01334 655574 ⏰ 12.15–1.30, 7–9.30; closed Sun, Mon, L Tue–Fri, 25–26 Dec, 1–2 Jan, 2 weeks Oct 🖐 L £19, D £35, Wine £16 🚗 In small lane off main street, A91

DRYMEN
CLACHAN INN
This is believed to be the oldest licensed pub in Scotland. Try staples such as filled baked potatoes, salads, fresh haddock in breadcrumbs and vegetable lasagne. Beers include Caledonian Deuchars IPA and Belhaven Best.
✉ 2 Main Street G63 0BG ☎ 01360 660824 ⏰ Mon–Sat 11–12am, Sun 12.30–12. Bar meals: 12–4, 6–10. Restaurant: 12–4, 6–10; closed 25 Dec, 1 Jan 🖐 L £9, D £30, Wine £11.95

DUNFERMLINE
HIDEAWAY LODGE AND RESTAURANT
The menu makes good use of local produce—you could start with grilled goats' cheese salad or Oban mussels, then move on to chargrilled tuna steak or fillet of venison, and finish with steamed ginger pudding.
✉ Kingseat Road, Halbeath KY12 0UB ☎ 01383 725474 ⏰ Tue–Sat 12–3, 5–11, Sun 12–9. Bar meals: 12–2, 6–9.

Restaurant: 12–2, 6–9 🖐 L £7.95, D £15, Wine £11.25

KEAVIL HOUSE
www.keavilhouse.co.uk
Artistic presentation is an important part of the menu, with international cooking offering temptations such as smoked haddock cheesecake wrapped in nori, and venison with turnip dauphinoise and thyme mash.
✉ Crossford KY12 8QW ☎ 01383 736258 ⏰ 12–2, 7–9.30 🖐 L £13, D £25, Wine £14.95 🚗 2 miles (3km) west of Dunfermline on A994

TOWN HOUSE RESTAURANT
www.townhouserestaurant.co.uk
The cuisine is Scottish with a hint of European—try the hot smoked duck breast with kumquat gravy, followed by mango pannacotta.
✉ 48 Eastport KY12 7JB ☎ 01383 432382 ⏰ 12–4, 6–9.30; closed 25 Dec, 1 Jan 🖐 L £7.95, D £23, Wine £13.95 🚗 200m (220 yards) from Carnegie Hall

ELIE
SANGSTERS
High-quality local produce makes the menu, from halibut with minted pea purée and chorizo to pan-seared venison with a red wine and thyme sauce. No children under 12. Dinner reservations only.
✉ 51 High Street KY9 1BZ ☎ 01333 331001 ⏰ 12.30–1.30, 7–8.30; closed L Tue and Sat, D Sun–Tue, Mon; 25–26 Dec, 1–2 Jan, 2 weeks mid-Feb and Oct 🖐 L £18.50, D £36, Wine £16

THE SHIP INN
At this lively free house, fresh fish takes pride of place on the specials board to supplement filled rolls (such as smoked salmon, prawns and cream cheese), bangers and mash in beer gravy or prime Scottish beef steaks, served plain or sauced with haggis and whisky. Alternatively, in summer, try a seafood salad that makes best use of the day's catch. There are children's choices and summer barbecues in the garden.
✉ The Toft KY9 1DT ☎ 01333 330246 ⏰ Mon–Sat 11–11, Sun 12.30–11; closed 25 Dec. Bar meals: daily 12–2, 6–9.

Restaurant: daily 12–2, 6–9 🖐 L from £14.50, D from £36.50, Wine from £11.80 🚌 Follow A915 and A917 to Elie. Follow signs from High Street to Watersport Centre to the Toft

GLAMIS
CASTLETON HOUSE
www.castletonglamis.co.uk
The menu draws on influences from all over the world—try fillet of Tamworth pig with black pudding and perhaps the Cointreau crème caramel with cardamom ice cream.
✉ Castleton of Eassie DD8 1SJ ☎ 01307 840340 🕐 12–2, 7–9 🖐 L £15.95, D £35, Wine £14 🚌 On A94 midway between Forfar and Cupar Angus, 3 miles (4.8km) west of Glamis

GLENIDEVON
TOMAUKIN HOTEL
www.anlochan.co.uk
At this 18th-century inn, lunches and suppers have a strong emphasis on fresh local produce. Try Highland beef with horseradish sauce or fillet of venison, or hand-dived scallops with black pudding and rocket. Treacle tart with clotted cream makes a tasty dessert.
✉ FK14 7JY ☎ 01259 781252 🕐 Mon–Sat 11–11, Sun 12–12; closed 25 Dec. Restaurant D only, daily 5.30–9 🖐 L £10.95, D £24.95, Wine £15.95 🚌 On A823 between M90 and A9

GLENISLA
GLENISLA HOTEL
The Glenisla specializes in hunting and fishing parties in season. Local Ales and robust meals are served—expect excellent fish and game, and local hill-farmed lamb. Aberdeen Angus steaks are a permanent feature, and puddings are generous.
✉ PH11 8PH ☎ 01575 582223 🕐 Tue–Sun 11–11. Bar meals: 12–2, 6–9. Restaurant: 12–2, 6–9.30; closed 25–26 Dec 🖐 L £17, D £18, Wine £11.50 🚌 On B954

INVERKEILOR
GORDON'S RESTAURANT
The menu is relatively traditional, although there are plenty of imaginative touches: A cappuccino of smoked tomato and roast

red pepper soup is served with Parmesan ice cream, while Angus beef is accompanied by smoked cheese soufflé, fondant potato and Pinot Noir jus. Vegetarians could try the tomato and basil polenta cake with candied fennel.
✉ Main Street DD11 5RN ☎ 01241 830364 🕐 12–1.45, 7–9; closed Mon, L Sat and Tue, first 2 weeks Jan 🖐 L £27, D £43, Wine £13.50 🚌 Just off A92, follow Inverkeilor signs

KINNESSWOOD
LOMOND COUNTRY INN
www.lomondcountryinn.co.uk
The restaurant offers sophisticated fare, such as supreme of guinea fowl on creamed mash with Calvados sauce, or chicken with a leek and Stilton sauce.
✉ Main Street KY13 9HN ☎ 01592 840253 🕐 Mon–Thu 11–11, Fri–Sat 11–12.45, Sun 12.30–11. Bar meals: 12.30–2.30, 6–9. Restaurant: 12–2.30, 6–9; closed 25 Dec 🖐 L £12.50, D £22.50, Wine £11.50 🚌 From M90, exit 5, follow signs for Glenrothes then Scotlandwell, Kinnesswood is next village

PEAT INN
THE PEAT INN
www.thepeatinn.co.uk
The Francophile owners have developed a robust Gallic menu. From a tasting menu, a fixed-price menu and a short carte select the likes of pan-fried venison liver served with kidneys, poached quails' eggs and a bitter orange sauce, and a traditional cassoulet filled with duck, pork, sausage and beans.
✉ Peat Inn KY15 5LH ☎ 01334 840206 🕐 12.30–2, 7–9.30; closed Sun–Mon, 25 Dec, 1 Jan 🖐 L £16, D £32, Wine £19 🚌 At junction (intersection) of B940/B941, 6 miles (9.7km) southwest of St. Andrews

PERTH
63 TAY STREET
www.63taystreet.com
Good food using quality ingredients is well cooked, and the simpler lunchtime menu is affordably inspiring. The three-course menu with prices fixed per course might

include herb risotto with rocket (arugula) salad and chive oil, or pan-fried halibut fillet with stir-fried greens and potato rösti. The wine list is notable.
✉ 63 Tay Street PH2 8NN ☎ 01738 441451 🕐 12–2, 6.30–9; closed Sun–Mon, 1st 2 weeks Jan, last week Jun, 1st week Jul 🖐 L £14.95, D £29.95, Wine £12.45 🚌 On the Tay River in Perth centre

DEANS@LET'S EAT
www.letseatperth.co.uk
This restaurant has built up a good reputation for its light, modern bistro food. Dishes include fillet of halibut with Skye langoustines, Glamis sea kale, asparagus and a prawn essence, and Valrhona chocolate tart with a white chocolate sorbet. Advance reservations recommended.
✉ 77–79 Kinnoull Street PH1 5EZ ☎ 01738 643377 🕐 12–2, 6.30–9.30; closed Sun–Mon, 2 weeks Jan, 2 weeks Jul 🖐 L £13.95, D £34, Wine £14.50 🚌 On corner of Kinnoull Street and Atholl Street, close to North Inch

HUNTINGTOWER HOTEL
www.huntingtowerhotel.co.uk
The restaurant of this stately hotel is a great place for formal dining. Two menus provide choice and value, with simpler specials and a more hearty contemporary menu including Scottish seafood and game. Breast of duck with plum tarte tatin, and roast loin of venison with dauphinoise potato and red cabbage are just two selections.
✉ Crieff Road PH1 3JT ☎ 01738 583771 🕐 L 12–2.30, D 6–9.30 🖐 L £12.95,

D £33, Wine £12.95 🔄 🚌 10 minutes from Perth on A85, towards Crieff

PITLOCHRY
MOULIN HOTEL
www.moulinhotel.co.uk
This hotel produces its own Braveheart beer, which appears on the food menu too, giving local venison dishes that extra flavour. ✉ 11–13 Kirkmichael Road, Moulin PH16 5EW ☎ 01796 472196 🕐 Sun–Thu 12–11, Fri–Sat 12–11.45. Bar meals: 12–9.30. Restaurant: D only, 6–9 ✋ L £10, D £23.50, Wine £11.95 🚌 From A924 at Pitlochry take A923

ST. ANDREWS
THE INN AT LATHONES
www.theinn.co.uk
Select from a menu offering modern Scottish and European cuisine: a tartare of salmon starter; rib-eye of mature beef with Yorkshire pudding and Madeira jus, and a sticky toffee pudding for dessert. ✉ Largoward KY9 1JE ☎ 01334 840494 🕐 12–2.30, 6–9.30; closed Christmas, 2 weeks Jan ✋ L £15.50, D £35, Wine £15 🚌 5 miles (8km) south of St. Andrews on A915. In 0.5 miles (800m) before Largoward on left just after hidden dip

ROAD HOLE GRILL
www.oldcoursehotel.kohler.com
Enjoy classic fine dining in sumptuous surroundings. The menu is marked out by clear flavours and quality Scottish produce, such as Highland venison with wild mushroom fricasée, and the wine list has 235 choices. There's a smart dress code. ✉ Old Course Hotel KY16 9SP ☎ 01334 474371 🕐 Dinner only, 7–10; closed 24–28 Dec ✋ D £40, Wine £33 🚌 M90 junction 8, close to A91, 5 mins from St. Andrews

SANDS BAR AND RESTAURANT
www.oldcoursehotel.kohler.com
This stylish brasserie offers a crisp, upbeat menu. Start your meal with home-cured bresaola and roasted figs, perhaps followed by a classic salad and cinnamon pannacotta. Dishes are thoughtfully marked out for healthy eating.

Above West Sands, St. Andrews' largest and best-known beach

✉ The Old Course Hotel KY16 9SP ☎ 01334 474371/468228 🕐 12–6, 6–10 ✋ L £16, D £37, Wine £17.95

SEAFOOD RESTAURANT
www.theseafoodrestaurant.com
Chosen as the AA's Restaurant of the Year for Scotland 2005, this restaurant offers a creative blend of British and European cuisine, and while there's an emphasis on seafood, other dishes such as duck with roast parsnip and fondant potato are also available. ✉ The Scores KY16 9AS ☎ 01334 479475 🕐 12–2.30, 6.30–10; closed 25–26 Dec, 1 Jan ✋ L £20, D £40, Wine £19

ST. FILLANS
THE FOUR SEASONS
www.thefourseasonshotel.co.uk
Many dishes have a modern edge. Try a trio of hill lamb cutlets with pink grapefruit salsa and mint sabayon, or pan-seared guinea fowl with an unusual mango and coriander (cilantro) salsa. ✉ Loch Earn PH6 2NF 01764 685333 🕐 12–2.30, 7–9.30; closed Jan, Feb ✋ L £12.95, D £35, Wine £17 🚌 From Perth take A85 west through Crieff and Comrie. Hotel at west end of village

ST. MONAN'S
THE SEAFOOD RESTAURANT
www.theseafoodrestaurant.com
The bar is in a 400-year-old fisherman's dwelling, and seafood specialties include grilled fillet of turbot with polenta cake and oyster mushroom ragout, or cod with spring onion colcannon and sage and anchovy beignets. ✉ 16 West End KY10 2BX ☎ 01333 730327 🕐 12–2.30, 6–9.30; closed Mon, D Sun, 25–26 Dec, 1–2 Jan ✋ L £21, D £35, Wine £19 🚌 Take A595 from St. Andrews to Anstruther, then west on A917 through Pittenweem. At St. Monans harbour turn right

STIRLING
STIRLING HIGHLAND
www.paramount-hotels.co.uk
At the Scholars Restaurant and adjoining Headmaster's Study Bar dishes include roasted spring chicken supreme with baby pak choi in a sweet and sour sauce, penne pasta with pesto, or salmon fillet on lemon risotto. ✉ Spittal Street FK8 1DU ☎ 01786 272727 🕐 6.30–9.30; L bar only daily 10–10 ✋ L £15 (bar only), D £24.50, Wine £16 🚌 On road to Stirling Castle, follow Castle signs

Above *Looking down on Loch Tummel from the Queen's View*

PRICES AND SYMBOLS

Prices are the starting price for a double room for one night, unless otherwise stated. Breakfast is included unless noted otherwise. All the hotels listed accept credit cards unless otherwise stated. Note that rates vary widely throughout the year.

For a key to the symbols, ▷ 2.

ANSTRUTHER
THE GRANGE

www.thegrangeanstruther.fsnet.com
Close to the centre of the village this Victorian house is convenient for the many golf courses in the area. Bedrooms are equipped with many thoughtful extra touches. There is a spacious, comfortable lounge, a sun lounge with sea views and a charming dining room where breakfasts are served at a large communal table. No children under 10.
✉ 45 Pittenweem Road KY10 3DT
☎ 01333 310842 ✋ £66 ① ⊟ In Anstruther go along Shore Street, then up Rodger Street to mini-roundabout. Turn left along A917, pass Craws Nest Hotel on the left and the Grange is slightly farther on

THE SPINDRIFT

www.thespindrift.co.uk
This Victorian villa is located at the western edge of the village. Bedrooms are brightly decorated and offer many extra touches. The Captain's Room, a replica of a cabin, is a particular feature. The lounge, with its honesty bar, invites relaxation, and home-cooked fare is served at individual tables in the dining room. No children under 10.
✉ Pittenweem Road KY10 3DT ☎ 01333 310573 ✋ £57 ① 8 ⊟ Approaching from the west, the hotel is the first building on left on entering town

AUCHTERARDER
CAIRN LODGE

www.cairnlodge.co.uk
This charming hotel stands in wooded grounds on the edge of the town and the friendly staff provide good levels of service. There is a choice of lounges, one with a bistro menu, and the Capercaillie Restaurant. Bedrooms include four luxury rooms providing extra quality and comfort.
✉ Orchil Road PH3 1LX ☎ 01764 662634 ✋ £140 ① 10 ⊟ From A9 take A823, pass entrance to Gleneagles Hotel and take 2nd turning towards Auchterarder on Orchil Road

GLENEAGLES HOTEL

www.gleneagles.com
With its international reputation for high standards, this grand hotel provides something for everyone. Gleneagles offers a peaceful, tranquil retreat, as well as many sporting activities, including the championship golf courses, private fishing, riding stables, shooting and off-road facilities. Afternoon tea is a treat, and cocktails are prepared

with flair and skill at the bar. You will find some inspired cooking at the two restaurants (▷ 222). Service is professional and staff are friendly.
✉ PH3 1NF ☎ 01764 662231 or 0800 389 3737 🏾 £295 🛈 232 🔄 📺 🚗 Just off A9, well signposted

BLAIR ATHOLL
ATHOLL ARMS
www.athollarmshotel.co.uk
This extensive and appealing old hotel, conveniently close to both the train station and Blair Castle, has historically styled public rooms, including a choice of bars and a splendid baronial dining room. The staff are particularly friendly, and nothing is too much trouble. Outdoor pursuits available to guests include fishing and rough shooting.
✉ Old North Road PH18 5SG ☎ 01796 481205 🏾 £75 🛈 31 🚗 In village, close to castle entrance

BLAIRGOWRIE
KINLOCH HOUSE
www.kinlochhouse.com
Idyllically amid the trees, this charming small hotel offers the highest standards of care. Inviting public areas include a choice of lounges, a conservatory bar with an impressive range of malt whiskies, and a beauty and fitness centre. Many of the spacious bedrooms have opulent bathrooms, and the restaurant serves high quality local produce cooked with skill.
✉ PH10 6SG ☎ 01250 884237 🏾 £170 🛈 18 🔄 📺 🕐 Closed 18–29 Dec 🚗 2 miles (3.2km) west of Blairgowrie on A923

CALLANDER
ARDEN HOUSE
www.ardenhouse.org.uk
This large Victorian villa lies in mature gardens in a quiet area of the town. It starred in the 1960s TV series *Dr. Finlay's Casebook* and is a friendly, welcoming house. The bedrooms are thoughtfully furnished and equipped with little extra touches. There is a stylish lounge in addition to the breakfast room. No children under 14. Two nights minimum in high season.

✉ Bracklinn Road FK17 8EQ ☎ 01877 330235 🏾 £70 🛈 6 🕐 Closed Nov–end Mar 🚗 From A84 into Callander from Stirling, turn right into Bracklinn Road signed to golf course and Bracklinn Falls. House 183m (200 yards) on left

COMRIE
ROYAL
A traditional facade gives little indication of the total refurbishment that has brought much style and elegance to this long-established hotel in the village centre. Public areas include a bar and a library, a bright modern restaurant and a conservatory brasserie. Bedrooms are furnished with smart reproduction antiques. Fishing and shooting by arrangement.
✉ Melville Square PH6 2DN ☎ 01764 679200 🏾 £140 🛈 11 🚗 Hotel in main square of Comrie, on A85

DUNBLANE
CROMLIX HOUSE
www.cromlixhouse.com
Nestling in sweeping gardens and surrounded by a 810ha (2,000-acre) estate, Cromlix House is an imposing Victorian mansion, with gracious and inviting public areas. Two dining rooms serve the creative and skilled output from the kitchen. Bedrooms are classically styled and many have a private sitting room. Facilities include private fishing, archery and clay-pigeon shooting.
✉ Kinbuck FK15 9JT ☎ 01786 822125 🏾 £195 🛈 14 🕐 Closed 2–29 Jan 🚗 Off A9 north of Dunblane. Exit B8033 to Kinbuck village, then after village cross narrow bridge, drive 183m (200 yards) on left

DUNDEE
APEX CITY QUAY HOTEL & SPA
This stylish, purpose-built modern hotel lies at the heart of Dundee's regenerated city centre. Bedrooms, including some smart suites, reflect the very latest in design, and warm hospitality and professional service are an integral part of the appeal. Open-plan public areas with panoramic windows and contemporary food options complete the package.

✉ 1 West Victoria Dock Road DD1 3JP ☎ 01382 202404 🏾 £100 🛈 152 🔄 📺 🚗 Take the A85 to Discovery Quay, exit roundabout for City Quay

DUNFERMLINE
GARVOCK HOUSE
www.gavrock.co.uk
A warm welcome is assured at this impeccably presented Georgian-house hotel, standing in beautifully landscaped gardens. Modern, stylish bedrooms include DVD players, and contemporary cuisine is served in the restaurant.
✉ St John's Drive, Transy KY12 7TU ☎ 01383 621067 🏾 £125 🛈 12 🚗 From M90 exit 3, take A907 to Dunfermline. Turn left after soccer stadium, then 1st right, hotel on right

DUNKELD
KINNAIRD
www.kinnairdestate.com
This imposing Edwardian mansion stands on a majestic estate. Public rooms are furnished with rare antiques and paintings. Sitting rooms have deep-cushioned sofas and open fires. Bedrooms are furnished with rich, luxurious fabrics, as are the marble bathrooms. Cooking is creative and imaginative, whether a breakfast using local ingredients, or lunch and dinner with produce from farther afield. Private fishing and shooting are available. No children under 12.
✉ Kinnaird Estate PH8 0LB ☎ 01796 482440 🏾 £275 🛈 9 🚗 From Perth, take the A9 north. Keep on A9 past Dunkeld and continue for 2 miles (3.2km), then take B898 left

GLENROTHES
RESCOBIE HOUSE
www.rescobie-hotel.co.uk
Hospitality and guest care are second to none at this relaxing country house, which lies in secluded gardens on the fringe of Leslie. Period architecture is enhanced by a contemporary and art deco styling—a theme which carries through to the bright, airy bedrooms. An intimate restaurant serves memorable meals.

Above Around Killiecrankie is a fine example of oak and deciduous woodland

✉ 6 Valley Drive, Leslie KY6 3BQ ☎ 01592 749555 ✋ £75 ⓘ 10 🚌 Come off A92 at Glenrothes on to A911, through Leslie. At end of High Street go straight ahead, then take 1st left. Hotel entrance 2nd on left

KILLIECRANKIE
KILLIECRANKIE HOUSE
www.killiecrankiehotel.co.uk
A long-established hotel set in mature grounds close to the historic Pass of Killiecrankie. Owner Henrietta Fergusson and her staff provide friendly and attentive service. Inviting public areas include an attractive restaurant looking on to the gardens. The bar and conservatory are popular.
✉ PH16 5LG ☎ 01796 473220 ✋ £188; including dinner ⓘ 10 🕐 Closed 3 Jan–14 Feb 🚌 Off A9 at Killiecrankie, hotel 3 miles (4.8km) along B8079 on the right

KINCLAVEN
BALLATHIE HOUSE
www.ballathiehousehotel.com
Set in extensive grounds, this splendid Scottish mansion house combines classical grandeur with modern comfort. Bedrooms range from well-proportioned master rooms to modern standard rooms and many have antique furniture and period bathrooms. For the ultimate in quality, request one of the Riverside Rooms. There is also a separate Lodge with self-catering facilities. The restaurant has views over the River Tay; private fishing is available.

✉ PH1 4QN ☎ 01250 883268 ✋ £176 ⓘ 41 🚌 From A9 2 miles (3.2km) north of Perth, take B9099 through Stanley, hotel signed; or off A93 at Beech Hedge follow signs for Ballathie 2.5 miles (4km)

KINROSS
GREEN
www.green-hotel.com
This long-established hotel offers a wide range of activities, both indoor and outdoor. There's a choice of bars and a classical restaurant, and even a well-stocked gift shop on site. The spacious bedrooms are enhanced by smart modern furnishings.
✉ 2 The Muirs KY13 8AS ☎ 01577 863467 ✋ Double from £170 ⓘ 46 🏊 ✋
🕐 Closed 23–24, 26–28 Dec 🚌 On A922 in middle of village

MARKINCH
BALBIRNIE HOUSE
www.balbirnie.co.uk
This hotel is a listed Georgian country house, and is the centrepiece of a 168ha (416-acre) estate that provides a peaceful setting in an area of breathtaking scenery. Day rooms include three luxurious lounges, one with a bar, and a conservatory restaurant. Bedrooms are spacious, and feature lovely furnishings. .
✉ Balbirnie Park KY7 6NE ☎ 01592 610066 ✋ £195 ⓘ 30 (non-smoking) 🚌 Off A92 on to B9130, entrance 0.5 miles (800m) on left

PERTH
MURRAYSHALL COUNTRY HOUSE HOTEL & GOLF COURSE
www.murrayshall.co.uk
This imposing country house is in grounds with two golf courses, one of which is of championship standard. Bedrooms come in two distinct styles; modern suites in a purpose-built building contrast with more traditional rooms in the main building. The Clubhouse bar serves meals all day, while there's more accomplished cooking can in the Old Masters Restaurant.
✉ New Scone PH2 7PH ☎ 01738 551171 ✋ £150 ⓘ 41 🏌 🚌 From Perth take A94 Coupar Angus road. After 1 mile (1.5km) turn right to Murrayshall just before New Scone

PARKLANDS HOTEL
www.theparklandshotel.com
There are great views from this hotel over the city centre park known as the South Inch. Bedrooms are furnished in a smart contemporary style. Public areas include a choice of restaurants, with fine dining offered in Acanthus.
✉ 2 St Leonards Bank PH2 8EB ☎ 01738 622451 ✋ £100 ⓘ 14 🚌 From M90 exit 10, after 1 mile (1.5km) turn left at end of park area at traffic lights, hotel is on the left

PITLOCHRY
GREEN PARK
www.thegreenpark.co.uk
This hotel is stunningly set in lovely landscaped gardens on the shore of Loch Faskally, within strolling distance of the town centre. Many of the bright, spacious bedrooms share the view, and the restaurant menu includes produce from the hotel's own kitchen garden.
✉ Clunie Bridge Road PH16 5JY ☎ 01796 473248 ✋ £152; including dinner ⓘ 51 🚌 Turn off A9 at Pitlochry, follow signs 0.25 miles (0.5km) through the town, hotel on banks of Loch Faskally

KNOCKENDARROCH HOUSE
www.knockendarroch.co.uk
This immaculate Victorian mansion overlooks the town and the Tummel Valley. There is no bar, but guests

can enjoy a drink in the lounge. Bedrooms are tastefully furnished, comfortable and well equipped. Those on the top floor are smaller but are not without character and appeal.

✉ Higher Oakfield PH16 5HT ☎ 01796 473473 🖐 £120 including dinner 🛏 12 ⊙ Closed 2nd week Nov to mid-Feb 🚗 Off A9 going north at Pitlochry sign. After railway bridge, take 1st right then 2nd left

PINE TREES
www.pinetreeshotel.co.uk
In extensive tree-studded grounds high above the town, this Victorian mansion retains many of its original features, including wood panelling, ornate ceilings and a marble staircase. Public rooms overlook the lawns, and the mood is refined and relaxing. Bedrooms come in a variety of sizes, and the staff are friendly and keen to please.

✉ Strathview Terrace PH16 5QR ☎ 01796 472121 🖐 £120 including dinner 🛏 20 🚗 From the high street (Atholl Road) turn into Larchwood Road and follow signs for the hotel

ST. ANDREWS
EDENSIDE HOUSE
www.edenside-house.co.uk
This modernized 18th-century house is family run and offers a home from home, over-looking the Eden estuary and nature reserve. Bedrooms are bright and cheerful, and are for the most part accessed externally. There is a homey lounge, and hearty breakfasts are served.

✉ Edenside KY16 9SQ ☎ 01334 838108 🖐 £56 🛏 8 🚗 Clearly visible from A91, 2 miles (3km) west of St. Andrews, directly on estuary shore

OLD COURSE HOTEL, GOLF RESORT AND SPA
A haven for golfers, this internationally renowned hotel sits right beside the 17th hole of the championship course. Bedrooms range from traditional in style to contemporary fairway rooms, with course-facing balconies. Facilities include a well-equipped spa, and a range of golf shops, as well as several excellent eating options.

✉ KY16 9SP ☎ 01334 474371 🖐 £192 🛏 144 🏊 🐶 ⊙ Closed 24–26 Dec 🚗 Close to A91 on outskirts of the city

RUFFLETS COUNTRY HOUSE
www.rufflets.co.uk
Owned and run by the same family for over 50 years, this charming country mansion lies in extensive gardens, a few minutes' drive from the town centre. The committed, friendly team ensures a memorable stay. The individually decorated bedrooms are bright and airy and many have impressive bathrooms. The Garden Room is a great setting in which to enjoy meals that utilize produce from the hotel's own gardens.

✉ Strathkinness Low Road KY16 9TX ☎ 01334 472594 🖐 £185 🛏 24 🚗 1.5 miles (2.5km) west on B939

ST. ANDREWS GOLF
www.standrews-golf.co.uk
Friendly, attentive service is a particular feature of this recently refurbished hotel, which overlooks the bay and has outstanding views of the coastline and the world-famous links. The bedrooms reflect a crisp, clean, contemporary design. The public rooms are traditional, with comfortable lounge areas and a choice of bars. The restaurant makes excellent use of local produce.

✉ 40 The Scores KY16 9AS ☎ 01334 472611 🖐 £200 🛏 22 🚗 Follow signs for Golf Course into Golf Place and after 183m (200 yards) turn right into The Scores

STRATHYRE
CREAGAN HOUSE
This delightful small hotel, originally a farmhouse, dates back to the 17th century and has been sympathetically restored and upgraded to provide comfortable accommodation. You'll find CD players, mineral water and bathrobes in the bedrooms, and the baronial-style dining room is the backdrop for memorable restaurant meals. Warm hospitality and attentive service.

✉ FK18 8ND ☎ 01877 384638 🖐 £120 🛏 5 ⊙ Closed 23 Jan–5 Mar, 6–25 Nov 🚗 North of Strathyre on A84

Left Loch Faskally was formed when the Pitlochry Dam was created

Stromness
Orkney Islands Kirkwall
Port Nis
Port of Ness Scrabster
Western Isles A857 Tongue A839 Thurso John o'Groats
Scourie A838 A9 Wick A99
Steornabhagh Altnaharra
Stornoway A894
Lewis Helmsdale
Outer Hebrides Tairbeart Ullapool Lairg Bonar
Tarbert A837 Bridge
Harris Gairloch Alness Tain
Inverewe Gardens A835 Elgin Banff Fraserburgh
Uibhist a Tuath Forres
North Uist Uig Wester Dingwall Peterhead
Lochmaddy Ross Keith A98
Beinn na Faoghla Dunvegan Portree Inverness Nairn A95 Turriff
Benbecula A90 Ellon
Uibhist a Deas Skye A87 Drumnadrochit Culloden A96
South Uist Grantown-
Loch Baghasdail Armadale Invermoriston Aviemore on-Spey Inverurie
Lochboisdale Invergarry Kingussie Cairngorms Banchory
Barraigh Rùm Mallaig Braemar & Crathes Aberdeen
Barra Eigg A830 Fort Deeside Castle A93
William Stonehaven
Inner Hebrides Coll A861 Glen Pitlochry A90
Coe Grampian Mountains Forfar Montrose
Tiree Tobermory Lochaline Blairgowrie A94
Craignure A85 Killin Dundee Arbroath
Carnoustie
Fionnphort A849 Oban Loch Lomond Perth
Mull Inveraray & The Trossachs A85 St Andrews
National Park Dunblane Glenrothes
Colonsay Helensburgh Stirling Dunfermline
Lochgilphead Loch EDINBURGH
Port Dunoon Lomond Eyemouth
Askaig A846 Dumbarton Dalkeith A1
Islay Greenock Glasgow M8
Kennacraig Paisley Motherwell Peebles A697 Coldstream
Port Ellen Ardrossan Lanark
Campbeltown Irvine Kilmarnock Biggar A708 Kelso
Prestwick Ayr Jedburgh
Arran Cumnock Hawick A68
Maybole Moffat ENGLAND

HIGHLANDS AND ISLANDS

Nowhere else in Britain can match the Scottish Highlands and Islands for sheer splendour, with their grand mountains, heather-clad hillsides and indented coastline. The Highlands fill the north and west of the country, with their snow-capped peaks, including Ben Nevis, Britain's highest mountain at 1.344m (4,406ft). Their southern boundary is the Highland Boundary Fault, the geological fault that slashes diagonally through Scotland, dividing the Highlands from the southerly Lowlands. It runs from Stonehaven, to the south of Aberdeen on the east coast, all the way across the country to the Isle of Arran in the west. It isn't an exact border, as much of the land in the east of this region is quite low-lying, but it was this monumental landslip which took place 400 to 500 million years ago that created the Highlands and the Lowlands. It's in the Highlands that you'll realize why the Scots refer to their homeland as 'God's own country'. The area is so spectacularly beautiful it's as if someone deliberately designed it to take your breath away.

Breathtaking, too, are the islands off Scotland's west coast. These range from the vast size of Lewis and Harris (so big it needs two names!) to tiny places like Muck, one of the so-called Small Isles, with a permanent population of about 30 people. On islands like this Scotland's Celtic traditions cling on the strongest, as you'll discover if you happen upon a music session one night in the local pub. And the landscape remains wonderfully unchanged too, from the beaches and cliffs to the standing stone circles—landscapes that help us escape the modern world and get in touch with ourselves again.

ABERDEEN
▷ 234.

APPLECROSS
The strung-out settlements on this remote west-coast peninsula only became fully accessible by road in the 1970s. Today this winding single-track road is the slow, scenic route between Kishorn and Shieldaig. It takes in the dramatic mountain pass of Bealach-Na-Ba, or Pass of the Cattle, to the south, and the southern shore of Loch Torridon to the north. (Note: Bealach-Na-Ba is not suitable for vehicles towing caravans (trailers). In between, acid moors and hummocks stretch to mountains inland, with the scattered remains of deserted villages along the coast, overlooking Raasay and Skye (▷ 256–259). Applecross Bay is a welcoming curve of pinkish sand, with an excellent little inn noted for its seafood (▷ 284–285).
⊞ 351 D5 ⓘ Post Office, Strathcarron, tel 0845 225 5121; seasonal

ARDNAMURCHAN
Ardnamurchan is a narrow finger of land that points west between the Small Isles and Mull. It remains one of Scotland's prettiest hidden corners, thanks to its remote location and narrow, winding roads, which lead through woodland of oak and birch to more exposed country and a lighthouse on the farthest tip of rock, the most westerly point in mainland Britain (visitor centre: Apr–end Oct daily 10–5). It's a good place for spotting seals and even otters, if you're lucky. An intriguing Natural History Centre at Glenmore explains the geological interest of this area, as well as wildlife (Easter–end Oct Mon–Sat 10.30–5.30, Sun 12–5.30).
⊞ 350 C7 ⓘ Kilchoan Community Centre, Pier Road, Kilchoan PH36 4LJ, tel 0845 225 5121 ⛴ Ferry from Tobermory on Mull to Kilchoan, summer only

BANFFSHIRE COAST
The coastline to the west and east of Banff is riddled with little fishing harbours and rocky bays, as the fertile fields give way to a wild and rugged shore. To the west, Buckie is a sprawling fishing town, with the more charming neighbours of Findochty (pronounced 'Finechty') and Portknockie. Cullen, on a magnificent sandy bay.

Portsoy is a holiday town with a little stone harbour, its prosperity built on export of the local serpentine marble (it was used for fireplaces in the French palace of Versailles). The town of Banff itself is much older than its genteel 18th-century heart, with Duff House (▷ 242) on the outskirts. To the east, the coast road continues through unlovely Macduff (but see the Marine Aquarium, ▷ 252) to the more remote villages of Gardenstown and Crovie, huddled under the red cliffs of Buchan on Gamrie Bay. The latter tiny, isolated settlement, pronounced 'Croovie', is accessible only on foot from a parking area. The road into Pennan is also steep, but worth the difficulty. Its single row of cottages backed up against the cliff, with a small hotel in the middle, will be instantly familiar to fans of the 1983 movie *Local Hero*, which was filmed here.
⊞ 349 K4 ⓘ Collie Lodge, Low Street, Banff AB45 1AU, tel 01261 812419 or 0845 225 5121; seasonal

BARRA
This island at the foot of the Outer Hebridean chain has an interest out of all proportion to its size, just 5 miles (8km) across and 8 miles (13km) long. Arriving is part of the fun—especially if you choose to come by air and land on the tidal shell beach of Traigh Mhor.

A road runs around the island but is only 12 miles (19km) long, making this a haven for bicycling and walking. In spring and summer the island is rich in wild flowers, with the machair (sea meadow) on the western side at its best. Barra survives on crofting and tourism, and the Gaelic culture flourishes.

Bagh a Chaisteil (Castlebay) is the main settlement, with Kisimul Castle, seat of the MacNeils since 1427 on a tiny island in the bay. (HS,

Above Hugh Miller's Cottage in Cromarty
Opposite Kisimul Castle, on Barra, was home to the lawless MacNeil clan

Apr–end Sep daily 9.30–5.30). The heritage centre, Dualchas, explores the history of the island (Mar, Apr, Sep Mon, Wed, Fri 10.30–4.30; May–end Aug Mon–Sat 10.30–4.30).
⊞ 350 A6 ⓘ Main Street, Castlebay, Isle of Barra HS9 5XD, tel 01871 810336; seasonal ✈ Flights from Glasgow and Benbecula ⛴ Ferry from Lochboisdale on South Uist, Eriskay and Oban to Castlebay

BLACK ISLE
Neither black nor an island, the Black Isle is the broad and fertile peninsula immediately north of Inverness, bordered by three firths or river estuaries: Cromarty, Beauly and Moray. Wild sea cliffs tip down to low-lying ground in the west, with a central wooded ridge of Ardmeanach. The harbour town of Cromarty, largely rebuilt in the late 18th century, occupies the northeast point. Its history is told in the Courthouse Museum on Church Street (Easter–end Oct daily 10–5). Cromarty's most famous son was Hugh Miller (1802–56), a geologist and fossil collector who did much to popularize natural history. His statue stands above the town, and his thatched cottage is a museum (NTS, Easter–end Sep daily 11–5; Oct Sun–Wed).
⊞ 348 G4 ⓘ North Kessock Picnic Site, North Kessock, IV1 1XB, tel 0845 225 5121; seasonal

INFORMATION
www.aberdeen-grampian.com
✚ 353 L6 ⓘ 23 Union Street AB11
5BP, tel 01224 288828 or 0845 225 5121
🚇 Aberdeen ✈ Aberdeen

ABERDEEN

Scotland's third city was once its biggest seaside resort, thanks to the miles of golden sands that stretch north from the mouth of the River Don. Today Aberdeen has a businesslike air and is better known as the oil capital of Europe (▷ 40). Its foundations as a royal burgh date back to the early 12th century, and it grew into a major port for access to the Continent, trading in wool, fish, and scholars from its two universities. The harbour is still the heart of the city.

North of the centre, in the Old Town, St. Machar's Cathedral, with its distinctive twin towers, dates from 1520. In the late 18th century the town expanded, and many of Aberdeen's finest granite buildings in the New Town date from the 19th century. Architect Archibald Simpson (1790–1847) is associated with many, including the Union Buildings and Assembly Rooms Music Hall on Union Street. Marischal College, on Broad Street, with its stunning Perpendicular frontage, was completed in 1895.

Provost Ross's House on Shiprow (1593) has the lively Aberdeen Maritime Museum (Mon–Sat 10–5, Sun 12–3), with exhibits that include an intriguing 8.5m (30ft) scale model of an oil rig.

The Aberdeen Art Gallery on Schoolhill has an outstanding collection of 18th- to 20th-century paintings (Mon–Sat 10–5, Sun 2–5). And if a cold wind is blowing off the North Sea, you can retreat to the warmth of the winter gardens in Duthie Park, one of Europe's largest covered gardens.

Below *Many of Aberdeen's buildings were made using granite, such as the Tolbooth and Town House on Castle Street*

BRAEMAR AND DEESIDE

When, in 1852, Queen Victoria and Prince Albert picked an estate between Ballater and Braemar on which to build their holiday home, the entire Dee Valley acquired a cachet that it has never quite lost. Members of the royal family, including the Queen, still spend their summer holidays at Balmoral Castle (exhibition Apr–end Jul daily 10–5), enjoying country sports in the surrounding hills and forests.

West of the busy town of Braemar, a narrow road leads upstream to the Linn of Dee, where the river plunges down between polished rocks into foaming pools. This is part of the 29,380ha (72,598-acre) Mar Lodge Estate, managed by the National Trust for Scotland, and including a number of signposted walks. The road ends near the Earl of Mar's Punchbowl, another beauty spot where, it is said, the Earl brewed punch in a natural bowl in the rocks before the Jacobite uprising of 1715.

In the village of Crathie is Crathie Church, where the royal family worship when in residence at Balmoral (Easter–end Oct daily).

EAST FROM BRAEMAR

From Braemar the A93 follows the route of the river as it flows for 60 miles (96km) to the coast at Aberdeen. Ballater is a small granite-built town, once the terminus of a branch train line. This is celebrated at the Old Royal Station, now an information centre and tea room (Jun–end Sep 9–6; Oct–end May 10–5) which recalls the days when famous guests would alight here on their way to Balmoral (www.balmoralcastle.com). Royal provisions still come from the town, as can be seen by the coats of arms everywhere from the bakery to outdoor clothing shops.

To the east lies Glen Tanar, with birch woods at the Muir of Dinnet, and good walking over the Grampian hills to the Glens of Angus. Banchory marks the shift into lower Deeside.

INFORMATION

www.braemarscotland.co.uk

⊞ 352 J6 ⓘ The Mews, Mar Road, Braemar AB35 5YL, tel 01339 741600 or 0845 225 5121; seasonal

Above *The River Dee rises in the Cairngorms before tumbling through the rocks at Braemar*

THE CAIRNGORMS

INFORMATION
www.cairngorms.co.uk
✚ 352 H6 ⓘ Grampian Road, Aviemore
PH22 1RH, tel 01479 810363 or 0845 225
5121 🚋 Aviemore

The highest massif in Britain, with alpine flora and rare wildlife, attracts
walkers, rock climbers and skiers. The Cairngorm mountains lie between
Speyside and Braemar (▷ 255, 235), dominated by the four peaks of
Ben Macdhui (1,309m/4,295ft), Braeriach (1,295m/4,249ft), Cairn Toul
(1,293m/4,242ft) and Cairn Gorm (1,245m/4,085ft). Between them runs the
ancient north–south pass of the Lairig Ghru, and around the northwest edge
the settlements of Speyside and the resort of Aviemore. The remoteness of the
Cairngorms has left them the haunt of golden eagles, ptarmigan, capercaillie
and other species that thrive in the deserted corries amid unusual alpine flora.
The area was designated Scotland's second national park in 2003.

AROUND AVIEMORE
The once-sleepy train station of Aviemore was developed in the 1960s as a ski
destination. The most brutal specimens of 1960s architecture have been razed,
and parts of the town developed as a Highland resort, with hotels and a spa.
The town is still out of place with its surroundings, but has useful shops and
services, and acts as a convenient base for exploring.

The Rothiemurchus Estate, 1.5 miles (2.4km) south, has a variety of outdoor
pursuits with beautiful mountains, lochs and Caledonian pine forest. This is the
remains of the Old Wood of Caledon which once covered much of the country,
harbouring wolves and bears. A good walk leads around Loch an Eilean.

Aviemore is linked by the preserved Strathspey Steam Railway (tel 01479
810725 for times; www.strathspeyrailway.co.uk) to Boat of Garten. The Royal
Society for the Protection of Birds (RSPB) has a visitor centre here (Apr–end
Aug daily 10–6), with a camera watching the ospreys which nest on nearby
Loch Garten. A funicular railway in the Cairngorm ski area east of Aviemore
takes visitors up the flank of Cairn Gorm itself, terminating in the highest shop

Above *Ben Macdhui, viewed from Glen
Lui in the Cairngorms National Park*

and restaurant complex in Britain (May to mid-Jun, Sep–end Nov daily 10–5.15; Jun–Sep Fri, Sat sunset dining; www.cairngormmountain.org.uk). Trains run every 15–20 minutes subject to weather conditions.

CAIRNGORMS NATIONAL PARK

When the Cairngorms National Park was created in 2003, it was twice the size of Scotland's other national park, Loch Lomond and the Trossachs, which had been estalished the previous year. Indeed, at 3,800sq km (1,467sq miles), it became the largest national park in Britain, bigger than the Lake District and North Yorkshire Moors national parks put together. It may grow bigger still, as there are plans to extend the boundaries to take in parts of Perth and Kinross.

HIGHLAND WILDLIFE PARK

Within the Cairngorms National Park, and opened back in 1972, is this very important wildlife area and visitor attraction (Apr–end Oct daily 10–5; Nov–end Mar 10–4; tel 01540 651270), run by the Royal Zoological Society of Scotland, which is also responsible for Edinburgh Zoo. While there's no doubt that seeing animals in the wild is one of the most thrilling aspects of being in the Cairngorms, there are some species that need help to survive, and others that have died out completely in the wild.

One of the big draws at the Wildlife Park is the pack of grey wolves, which live in conditions as close as possible to those they would have had when the species roamed wild in the lands around here until the 1700s. At present, there is a small pack of five wolves, and the cleverly designed, large enclosure allows visitors to watch them, both from their cars as they drive around, and on foot when they can be observed at eye-level.

The Wildlife Park is also a vital sanctuary for the Scottish wildcat, which is in serious danger of going the way of the wolves and becoming extinct in the wild in Scotland. This is one of the most endangered mammals in the British Isles, and it's not even known for sure how many remain, but their only refuge now is here.

Other native animals in the park include red deer, pine martens, otters, red squirrels and red and black grouse. There are also European animals such as European bison, European elk, lynx and wild boar, as well as animals from other mountainous areas of the world, including yaks and red pandas.

Left *Loch Avon is a fine example of a ribbon lake*
Below *Red-legged partridge*

CAPE WRATH

The far northwestern corner of Scotland feels like another country, with silvery light reflected from the grey quartzite mountains, and everywhere emptiness and space. If you want to get to Cape Wrath, prepare for a short ferry ride over the Kyle of Durness (May–end Sep), then a minibus ride across the bleak moor called The Parph. The road passes between the peaks of Sgribhisbheinn (371m/1,217ft) and Fashven (457m/1,499ft) to reach the sheer 280m (920ft) Clo Mor cliffs and the remote lighthouse, built in 1827 by the grandfather of Robert Louis Stevenson, which blinks out over the Atlantic. Durness is a scattered settlement, with Smoo Cave to the east. The main cavern here is huge—about 60m (200ft) long and 35m (115ft) wide. Just west of Durness, Balnakeil has a beautiful sandy beach and an unusual craft village, which occupies a former military installation.

✚ 347 F1 ℹ️ Durine, Durness IV27 4PN, tel 0845 225 5121; seasonal

CASTLE FRASER

www.nts.org.uk

This magnificent turreted tower house, 16 miles (25.8km) west of Aberdeen, was built between 1575 and 1636. The original structure, known as Muchalls-in-Mar, was remodelled at that time to give it the distinctive Z-plan by the addition of a square tower at one corner and a round one at the opposite corner. The changes were made by the 6th Laird, Michael Fraser, and the castle remained in that family until the 20th century. Family portraits are displayed inside, along with a rich collection of carpets and drapes. The surrounding estate is extensive, with waymarked walks and a walled garden.

✚ 353 K6 ✉️ Sauchen, Inverurie AB51 7LD ☎️ 0844 493 2164 🕐 Easter–end Jun Wed–Sun 11–5; Jul, Aug daily 11–5; Sep, Oct Wed–Sun 12–5. Gardens: daily ✋ (NTS) adult £8, child (5–16) £5, family £20 🖥️ 🎁

CAWDOR CASTLE

www.cawdorcastle.com

The name of Cawdor evokes Shakespeare's Macbeth. It stands inland, between Inverness and Nairn, with a central tower dating back to 1454, a drawbridge, and proud turrets and wings that proclaim later additions. It is the home of Angelika, the Dowager Countess of Cawdor, and the presentation of family portraits and treasures within is refreshingly relaxed and even light-hearted. The influence of the owner and her late husband is most clearly seen in the gardens, which are symbolically themed. They include a holly maze surrounded by a tunnel of golden laburnum, and the mysterious Paradise Garden with a seven-pointed star at its core.

✚ 352 H5 ✉️ Nairn IV12 5RD ☎️ 01667 404401 🕐 May to mid-Oct daily 10–5.30 ✋ Adult £7.90, child (5–15) £4.90, under 5 free, family £24. Gardens only, £4 🖥️ 🍴 🎁

Left Shakespeare's Macbeth was the thane (lord) of Cawdor Castle
Below Turret-topped Castle Fraser

COWAL AND BUTE

The Cowal peninsula points its fingers down from Arrochar, caught between Loch Long and Loch Fyne. Its top reaches are covered in forestry, and are part of the Loch Lomond national park (▷ 197). Dunoon is the only town of size, a holiday resort with a statue to Robert Burns's love, 'Highland Mary', born nearby. Benmore, 7 miles (11km) to the north, is an outpost of Edinburgh's Royal Botanic Garden, with particularly good autumn foliage (Mar–end Oct daily 10–6; Mar daily 10–5).

Elsewhere the landscape is of mountains and wild moorland intersected by sea lochs, including Holy Loch, formerly a submarine base. To the south, captured in the long fingers of Cowal, is the low-lying island of Bute, with the small town of Rothesay once a pleasure ground for steamers from Glasgow. Mount Stuart, in the southern sector, is a sumptuous Victorian mansion (Easter, May–end Sep Sun–Fri 11–5 Sat 10–2.30).

✚ 353 E10 ▮ 7 Alexandra Parade, Dunoon PA23 8AB, tel 0845 225 5121 ▮ Isle of Bute Discovery Centre, Winter Gardens, Victoria Street, Rothesay PA20 0AH, tel 01700 502151

CRAIGIEVAR CASTLE

www.nts.org.uk
The quintessential Scottish baronial tower house, Craigievar has a fairy-tale quality that makes it stand out from its fellows. It was built by merchant trader William Forbes between 1600 and 1626, and—unusually—remained unaltered in the following centuries of occupation by the Forbes and Forbes-Sempill families. The result is a six-storey pinkish-harled fantasy of turrets on a central Great Tower, a delight to the eye in the leafy setting of the Don valley. While the surrounding policies (gardens) remain open to the public, the castle itself is likely to be closed until spring 2009, when the scaffolding that restricts light inside (there is no electric lighting) is removed.

✚ 353 K6 ▮ Alford AB33 8JF ☎ 0844 493 2174 ☀ Grounds: daily 9.30–dusk ✋ Grounds only: free (restricted access)

CRARAE GARDENS

www.nts.org.uk
This hillside garden lies on the shores of Loch Fyne, between Inveraray and Lochgilphead. It was the creation of Captain George Campbell, who began the transformation of a narrow Highland glen into a Himalayan gorge in 1925. Today it is cared for by the National Trust for Scotland, and boasts over 400 species of rhododendrons and azaleas, which thrive in the mild, damp climate and acid soils. This is primarily a woodland garden, with paths winding through the eucalypts and other trees. A 20ha (50-acre) forest garden is a newish development, with fresh planting of native, broadleaved species. Look out for the Neolithic chambered cairn (c2500BC) by the picnic site.

✚ 355 E9 ▮ Inveraray PA32 8YA ☎ 0844 493 2210 ☀ Garden: daily 9.30–dusk. Visitor centre: Apr–end Sep daily 10–5 ✋ (NTS) Adult £5, child (5–16) £4, under 5 free, family £14 ▯ ▯

CRATHES CASTLE

▷ 240.

CRINAN CANAL

Winding for 9 miles (14.5km) between Ardrishaig on Loch Fyne and Crinan harbour on the Sound of Jura, the Crinan Canal is a narrow waterway through an attractive region of woodland and open marsh. It was built in 1793–1809 by the engineer John Rennie (1761–1821), when fishing craft and 'puffers', the small steam-driven boats which transported vital supplies to all parts of the Scottish coast, used it to avoid the 130-mile (209km) trip around the Kintyre peninsula. Today it is still well used by yachts and small fishing boats, which must negotiate 15 locks along its course. The towpath provides good walks from Lochgilphead, Cairnbaan and Crinan itself.

✚ 355 D10 ▮ 27 Lochnell Street, Lochgilphead PA31 8JN, tel 0845 225 5121; seasonal

CULLODEN

▷ 241.

Top left *Along the Crinan Canal*
Top right *The warm Gulf Stream encourages plant growth at Benmore*

INFORMATION

www.nts.org.uk

🞢 353 L6 ✉ Banchory AB31 5QJ
☎ 0844 493 2166 🕓 Gardens: all year
daily 9–dusk. castle and visitor centre:
Easter–end Sep daily 10.30–5.30; Oct
daily 10–4.30; Nov–Easter Wed–Sun
10.30–3.45 👤 (NTS) Adult £10, child
(5–16) £7, under 5 free, family £20
🍴 🏛

TIP

» Be prepared to wait; to contain
numbers, entry to the castle itself is by
timed tickets.

Above *High hedges around Crathes
Castle create a micro-climate in which
the gardens thrive*

CRATHES CASTLE

In 1323 Robert the Bruce gifted a parcel of land, east of Banchory, to Alexander
Burnard (Burnett) of Leys, presenting him with a carved and bejewelled ivory
horn as a symbol of tenure. In 1553 a castle was started on the site, which
took almost 50 years to complete. It is now a delightful example of a baronial-
style tower house, and famous for its Jacobean ceilings, boldly painted with
figures, designs and mottoes.

While the interior of the castle presents the comfortable setting of mellow
furnishings, oak-carved panels and family portraits you might expect, it is the
walled garden glimpsed from the windows which steals the show.

Massive hedges of Irish yew, planted up to 300 years ago, and carved into
undulating 'egg and cup' topiary sculptures, dominate the upper garden. They
frame and shelter themed 'rooms', helping to create a micro-climate in which a
rich variety of plants thrive. The deep herbaceous borders of the lower garden
are breathtaking in the colour and variety of their planting, with the June border
linking the vistas of the castle and a venerable doocote (dovecote). In their
present form, these remarkable gardens reflect a labour of love by Sir James
and Lady Sybil Burnett in the early 20th century, and their work is continued by
the National Trust for Scotland.

At the Visitor Centre you will find leaflets giving directions for walks through
some of the 240ha (595 acres) of land surrounding the castle. In the summer
Rangers lead guided walks on subjects such as birdwatching, mushrooms and
spiders, and there's a good programme for children.

CULLODEN

A boggy moor on a windy ridge 5 miles (8km) east of Inverness is the emotive scene of the final battle fought on Scottish soil, when Bonnie Prince Charlie made his last stand. The Jacobite defeat at the Battle of Culloden, fought on 16 April 1746, was the dismal outcome of a civil war that had split families and hastened the end of the already disintegrating clan system in Scotland.

Prince Charles Edward Stuart (1720–88), later known as Bonnie Prince Charlie, was raised in European exile, the heir to the Scottish throne that the Catholic Stuarts still claimed through James, the Old Pretender (Jacobus in Latin, hence Jacobite as the name for the political movement). The French were keen on stirring up political matters with the Protestant Hanoverian government in Britain, and encouraged the Prince's madcap expedition to claim the throne in 1745. Charles landed at Glenfinnan (▷ 245) and raised a mixed bag of Highland fighters, some of them coerced by their chiefs. Initially the Prince's army was successful, and reached Derby in central England before running out of steam. The Highlanders retreated northwards, but by the spring of 1746 the Hanoverian forces were closing in.

A new visitor centre opened in December 2007, which recreates the battle with special effects and interactive exhibits. It aims to clear up misconceptions that it was a battle between Scottish and English—as well as bring the events of that day to life.

AN ARMY IN RETREAT

When the two armies met at Culloden, the Prince's outnumbered and exhausted forces faced an army of regular soldiers. A tactical blunder placed his Highlanders within range of the government artillery, and the Jacobites were blown away in under an hour. More than 1,500 Jacobites and 50 Hanoverians died in the battle. Stones and flags mark the battlefield today, to show where individual clans fell.

In the aftermath, the government leader the Duke of Cumberland earned the title of 'Butcher' when he sanctioned one of the worst atrocities ever carried out by the British Army. Military looting was legalized throughout the Highlands, irrespective of loyalties, and the Highland way of life changed for ever. Jacobite propaganda retreated into sentimentality, and the romantic figure of the Prince hiding, never betrayed as he fled to exile, became legendary.

INFORMATION

www.culloden.org.uk;
www.nts.org.uk

✚ 352 G5 ✉ Culloden Moor, Inverness IV2 5EU ☎ 0844 493 2159

🕓 Site: all year daily. Visitor centre: Nov, Dec, Feb, Mar daily 10–4; Easter–end Oct daily 9–6 ✋ (NTS) Adult £10, child (5–16) £7.50, under 5 free, family £24 📖 Guidebook £5 🍴 Restaurant in visitor centre 🎦 ❓ Audio-visual programme in Gaelic

TIP

» See the stunning exhibition in the visitor centre before you explore the battlefield, to understand what you are seeing.

» There are living presentations in summer at Leanach Cottage, which survived at the heart of the battle.

Below *Memorial at the foot of a stone cairn on the site of the battlefield*

DORNOCH

A stone marks the spot near the golf course in Dornoch where, in 1727, Janet Horne was tarred, feathered and burned. Accused of changing her daughter into a pony, she was the last witch in Scotland to be executed. Today, there's no sign of such outrageous practices in the quiet streets of this east-coast town, which is better known for its world-class golf course, sandy beaches and dolphin-watching expeditions. The cathedral, once the seat of the bishops of Caithness, dates from the 13th century. Skibo Castle, 4 miles (6.4km) west, was the retreat of American philanthropist Andrew Carnegie (▷ 37). Now an exclusive golf resort, it was the centre of a maelstrom in December 2000 when pop icon Madonna held her wedding there.

➕ 348 H3 ℹ The Square IV25 3SD, tel 0845 225 5121

DUFF HOUSE

www.duffhouse.com

Tucked away in an apparently quiet corner of Banff, Duff House is the principal outstation of the National Galleries of Scotland, providing the perfect, glittering backdrop to a wealth of paintings including portraits by the Scottish painters Raeburn and Ramsay, and paintings of the Italian, Dutch and German schools of art. The house itself is a grand mansion designed by architect William Adam for the 1st Earl of Fife. It was started in 1735, but unfortunately the Earl's pride in his new house was seriously dented when a crack appeared in the structure, and he never lived there. Look for El Greco's *St. Jerome in Penitance*.

➕ 349 K4 ✉ Banff AB45 3SX ☎ 01261 818181 🕐 Apr–end Oct daily 11–5; rest of year Thu–Sun 11–4 ✋ Adult £6, child £4.50, family £16 🖥 🏛

DUNROBIN CASTLE

www.highlandescape.com

Looming above its gardens like a French château and lying just 0.5 miles (800m) north of the east-coast village of Golspie, Dunrobin Castle boasts 189 rooms, making it the largest mansion in northern Scotland. It dates back to c1275, but its outward appearance is overwhelmingly Victorian, thanks to extensions between 1845 and 1850 by Sir Charles Barry (better known as the architect of London's Houses of Parliament).

Dunrobin was the seat of the Earls and Dukes of Sutherland, censured by history for their actions during the Highland Clearances (▷ 260, Strathnaver).

Daily falconry displays take place in the French-style gardens.

➕ 348 H3 ✉ Golspie KW10 6SF ☎ 01408 633177 🕐 Apr, May, Sep, Oct to mid-Oct Mon–Sat 10.30–4.30, Sun 12–4.30; Jun–end Aug daily 10.30–5.30 ✋ Adult £7.70, child £5, family £19 🅿 Dunrobin 🖥 🏛

EILEAN DONAN CASTLE

www.eileandonancastle.com

Probably the most photographed castle in Scotland, Eilean Donan is perched on a rock near the northern shore of Loch Duich, and joined to the mainland by a bridge. There has been a fortification on the site since the 13th century, and a MacRae stronghold was destroyed here by government troops in 1719. The perfect castle as seen today, complete with stone walls up to 4.3m (14ft) thick, is the result of rebuilding between 1912 and 1932. It is said that its creator, Lt. Col. John MacRae-Gilstrap, saw an image of how it might look in a dream, and there is certainly an idealized quality to it, which has seen it star in many a calendar and in several films. Not to be missed.

➕ 351 E5 ✉ Dornie, by Kyle of Lochalsh IV40 8DX ☎ 01599 555202 🕐 Mid-May to mid-Nov daily 10–6 (opens 9am Jul, Aug) ✋ Adult £4.95, child £3.95, under 5 free, family £10.50 🖥 🏛

Left *Towering Sueno's Stone is encased in protective glass*
Above *There are great views from the cable car on Aonach Mòr*
Opposite *Eilean Donan, the epitome of a Highland castle*

FORRES

The ancient market town of Forres on the River Findhorn, 10 miles (16km) east of Nairn, was once plagued by witches. William Shakespeare made full use of this in *Macbeth* (c1606), when he set scenes with the three 'weird sisters' in the area. Three more witches are commemorated with an iron-bound stone in the town.

A huge glass box protects Sueno's Stone, on the eastern outskirts. This is a Pictish cross-slab which stands 6m (20ft) tall and is believed to date from the 9th or 10th century (free access). The sandstone is intricately carved in five sections with vivid scenes from an unidentified and bloody battle. Some think Sueno's Stone is a Pictish cenotaph. Sueno was the name of an 11th-century king of Denmark.

To the south of Forres, the Dallas Dhu Historic Distillery is preserved by Historic Scotland (Easter–end Sep daily 9.30–5.30; rest of year Sat–Wed 9.30–4.30).
🕂 348 H4 🛈 116 High Street IV36 1NP, tel 01309 672938 or 0845 225 5121; seasonal 🚆 Forres

FORT WILLIAM

Fort William's location on road and train junctions at the head of Loch Linnhe and the foot of the Great Glen (▷ 245) makes it a convenient touring base for the northwest. The town's heyday as a military outpost for subduing the Highlands is long gone—the fort, which withstood Jacobite attacks in 1715 and 1745, was knocked down in 1864 to make space for a train station. The town grew after this period, and is unappealing in itself, despite pedestrianization of the centre and other attempts to give it a clearer identity. Its strategic position makes it a popular hub for walkers and mountaineers, and shops are well stocked with outdoor gear.

Fort William's biggest attraction lies to the east: the rounded bulk of Ben Nevis. At 1,343m (4,406ft) this is Britain's highest mountain. Conditions at the top can be arctic on the best of days, and walkers should take all necessary precautions before attempting to climb it. On the first Saturday in September you may be overtaken by runners, entrants in the annual Ben Nevis Race, established in 1937. The record currently stands at 1 hour 25 minutes. There are easier walks through the more gentle landscape of Glen Nevis, west and south of the mountain, which lead to Steall Falls.

The 15-minute gondola ride takes you up Aonach Mòr (1,219m/3,998ft), the mountain beside Ben Nevis (Jul–endAug daily 9.30–6; Jan–end Jun, Sep to mid-Nov daily 10–4, weather permitting).
🕂 351 E7 🛈 Cameron Centre, Cameron Square PH33 6AJ, tel 0845 225 5121 🚆 Fort William

FYVIE CASTLE

www.nts.org.uk
This magnificent mansion, set in a landscaped park in the valley of the River Ythan, has a cream-harled frontage 46m (150ft) long, dominated by the massive gatehouse. It is said that five of Scotland's great families—the Prestons, Meldrums, Setons, Gordons and Leiths—each contributed a tower as they owned the castle in turn. The oldest part dates from the 13th century and incorporates the architectural highlight: a spiral staircase of broad, shallow stone steps known as a wheel-stair, a 16th-century addition. Opulent interiors were created in the early 20th century, making a rich backdrop to the armoury collections and portraits by Raeburn, Romney, Gainsborough and Hoppner.
🕂 353 L5 ✉ Near Turriff AB53 8JS ☎ 0844 493 2182 🕐 Castle: Easter–end Jun, Sep, Oct Sat–Wed 12–5; Jul, Aug daily 11–5. Grounds: all year daily 9.30–dusk 💷 (NTS) Adult £8, child (5–16) £5, under 5 free, family £20 🖥 🏧

INFORMATION

www.glencoe-nts.org.uk

✚ 351 E7 ℹ Ballachulish PA39 4JR, tel 0845 225 5121; seasonal

GLEN COE

Whether your first approach to Glen Coe is down from the wide, watery wasteland of Rannoch Moor, or up from the finger of sea that is Loch Leven, you cannot fail to be impressed by the majesty of this long, steep-sided valley. On a clear day you can see the tops of the Aonach Eagach ridge to the north (966m/3,169ft), with its sweeping sides of loose scree, and the peaks of the great spurs of rock known as the Three Sisters to the south, leading down from Bidean nam Bian (1,148m/3,766ft). At the eastern end the glen is guarded by the massive bulk of Buachaille Etive Mor, the 'Great Shepherd of Etive' (1,019m/3,343ft). On other days the tops are hidden in a smirr (mist) of rain clouds, the waterfalls become torrents and wind funnels up the glen at a terrific rate.

This is prime mountaineering country, and not for the unfit or unwary. In winter it becomes its own snow-filled world, offering an extra challenge to climbers and regularly claiming lives. There is a ski area on the flanks of Meall a'Bhùiridh (1,108m/ 3,635ft). Learn more at the eco-friendly visitor centre, Inverrigan (NTS, Mar daily 10–4; Apr–end Aug daily 9.30–5.30; Sep, Oct daily 10–5; Nov–end Feb Thu–Sun 10–4).

CAMPBELLS AND MACDONALDS

Memories are long in the Highlands, and there is still a frisson between Macdonalds and Campbells that dates back to a February night in 1692. At a time when clan leaders were required to swear loyalty to the monarchs William and Mary, Alastair Macdonald of Glencoe left the unsavoury task as late as possible. When he missed the deadline by a few days, Campbell of Glenlyon was sent to make an example of him. Campbell's men were billeted here for two weeks before turning on their hosts in an act of cold-blooded slaughter that left 38 dead. It was a betrayal that has never been forgotten.

Above *Springtime in Glen Coe: heading west down the valley, past the Three Sisters (left)*

Opposite *The view from the viaduct at Glenfinnan is a highlight of the West Highland Railway route*

GLEN AFFRIC

This peaceful valley, 30 miles (48km) southwest of Inverness and running parallel with the Great Glen, is one of the best-loved beauty spots in the Highlands. Its scenery combines forest and moorland, river and loch with mighty mountains such as Carn Eige (1,182m/3,878ft). A narrow road leads up from Cannich to the River Affric parking area, passing the Dog Falls and a beautiful picnic area at Loch Beinn a Mheadhoin on the way up. Footpaths are marked, and for serious hikers a trail leads through to Kintail. A 1,265ha (3,100-acre) area of native woodland, incorporating fragments of ancient Caledonian pine forest, has been established. Crested tits and crossbills may be seen year-round in the woods, with rarer golden eagles and capercaillie.
➕ 351 F5 ℹ Castle Wynd, Inverness IV2 3BJ, tel 0845 225 5121

GLENELG

This isolated spot is reached via the steep pass of Mam Ratagan from the southern shore of Loch Duich. The village is strung out along a shallow bay, with the deserted 18th-century barracks of Bernera to the north, and overlooking the narrow Sound of Sleat to Skye. A small ferry operates in summer to Kylerhea: Look out for seals in the swirling waters. The road continues south, passing above Sandaig, where Gavin Maxwell (1914–69), author of *Ring of Bright Water*, lived and is buried, and giving spectacular views to isolated Knoydart.

Dun Telve and Dun Troddan, the well-preserved remains of two Iron-Age brochs—circular stone buildings with double walls—can be found in Glen Beag.
➕ 351 D6 ⛴ Ferry to Kylerhea on Skye, Apr–end Oct daily

GLENFINNAN

On 19 August 1745 Prince Charles Edward Stewart raised the Jacobite standard here at the top of Loch Shiel, a rallying cry to supporters of his father's claim to the throne of Scotland. It was the start of the Stuarts' final campaign, which would end in disaster at Culloden (▷ 241). The occasion is recalled by a large pillar monument, topped by the statue of a kilted soldier, built here in 1815, which provides a focus for the magnificent view down the loch.

The National Trust for Scotland has an informative visitor centre nearby (Easter–end Jun, Sep, Oct daily 10–5; Jul, Aug daily 9.30–5.30).
➕ 351 E7 ℹ Cameron Centre, Cameron Square, Fort William PH33 6AJ, tel 0845 225 5121 🚂 Glenfinnan

GREAT GLEN

Slashing for 60 miles (97km) across the country from Inverness to Fort William, the Great Glen follows the line of a massive geological fault. A straight, sweeping trough between bare-topped mountains, it is strung with roads (chiefly the A82), a long-distance walking trail and bicycle route (▷ 333). Look out for the so-called Parallel Roads on the hillside at Glen Roy: in fact they are an

entirely natural feature of terracing left behind by lakes in the ice ages. The bottom of the glen is lined by a series of lochs, of which the longest and best known is Loch Ness.

Narrow and as much as 230m (754ft) deep, Loch Ness is believed by some to hide a fishy monster, with the first recorded sighting back in the sixth century AD. Find out about more recent searches and their results at Drumnadrochit's Loch Ness 2000 visitor centre (Nov–Easter daily 10–3.30; Easter–end May daily 9.30–5; Jun, Sep daily 9–6; Jul–end Aug daily 9–8; Oct daily 9.30–5.30). The long, straight nature of the loch attracts speedboat enthusiasts, and a memorial cairn at the roadside between Drumnadrochit and Invermoriston recalls racing driver John Cobb, who died here in 1952 while attempting to beat the world water speed record.

The lochs of the Great Glen are linked by the Caledonian Canal, an engineering feat planned by Thomas Telford in 1801 and completed in 1847. Loch Oich is the highest point in the chain, with a famous group of eight locks, Neptune's Staircase, at Banavie near Fort William (see also walk, ▷ 268–269).

Commando troops trained around Spean Bridge during World War II. They are commemorated in a memorial from 1952 by sculptor Scot Sutherland, off the A82.
➕ 351 F6 ℹ Castle Wynd, Inverness IV2 3BJ ℹ Cameron Centre, Cameron Square, Fort William PH33 6AJ, tel 0845 225 5121

HELMSDALE

www.helmsdale.org

Gold fever struck this little harbour on the northeast coast in 1868, when gold was discovered in the Strath of Kildonan and prospectors set up a shanty town. It was brought to a halt by local landowner, the 3rd Duke of Sutherland, who feared for the disturbances to his deer and sheep. You can try your luck at gold panning.

Helmsdale grew up in the early 19th century as a resettlement site for crofters who had been moved from farther inland to make way for large-scale sheep farming in an episode which became known as the Highland Clearances—learn more at the Timespan Heritage Centre on Dunrobin Street (Apr–end Oct Mon–Sat 10–5, Sun 12–5).
🚩 348 H2 🛈 Atrath Ullie Crafts, Shore Street, tel 01431 821402 🚏 Helmsdale

HIGHLAND FOLK MUSEUM (NEWTONMORE)

www.highlandfolk.com

This museum occupies two sites 2.5 miles (4km) apart, signed from the A9; however, the Kingussie site is now only open to pre-booked groups. Together they offer an unsanitized picture of rural life in the Highlands over the centuries, through reconstructed buildings, a working croft (small farm) and collections of everyday objects.

Kingussie is the smaller site, with more of a museum feel to it. Newtonmore has a reconstructed 18th-century village, including a tailor's workshop, a church and a school. There is also a farmsteading, dating from the 1800s and set up as it was used in 1930. You can see crops and livestock, a cottage, garage and even a little post office. Living history actors bring things to life, including traditional farming skills and crafts.
🚩 352 G6 ✉ Newtonmore PH20 1AY ☎ 01540 673551 🛈 Newtonmore: Easter–end Aug daily 10.30–5.30; Sep, Oct daily 11–4.300 🖐 Free 🖳 Newtonmore only 🏛

INNER HEBRIDES

▷ 248–249.

INVERARAY

▷ opposite.

INVEREWE GARDENS

▷ 250.

INVERNESS

The administrative capital of the Highland region, Inverness is a service town for the surrounding area. Three important roads meet here: the A96 from the northeast, the A9 from the south, and the A82 which runs up the side of the Great Glen (▷ opposite). It is also the northern end of the Caledonian Canal, where the River Ness flows into the Moray Firth.

Inverness's lack of antiquities is due, the locals will tell you, to the Highlanders' habit of burning the town down at regular intervals after English Parliamentarian leader Oliver Cromwell built a fort here in 1652. The architecture of the town is predominantly 19th century, including the red sandstone castle (closed to public) with its monument to heroine Flora Macdonald, who helped Bonnie Prince Charlie to escape in 1746 after his defeat at Culloden (▷ 241).
🚩 352 G5 🛈 Castle Wynd IV2 3BJ, tel 0845 225 5121 🚏 Inverness ✈ Inverness

INVERPOLLY

www.summer-isles.com

The road north from Ullapool leads into a sparsely populated country of peatbog and loch, heather moorland and bare, rocky mountains. This is the national nature reserve of Inverpolly, which covers around 11,000ha (27,000 acres), and the prominent lumps of rock are mountains of weathered, red Torridonian sandstone: Stac Pollaidh (612m/2,008ft), Cul Beag (769m/2,523ft) and Cul Mòr (849m/2,786ft).

The area is rich in wildlife, with otters and deer, golden eagles, and salmon. There are also sandy beaches of note at Achnahaird, Garvie, Reiff and Badentarbat.
🚩 347 F3 🛈 Argyle Street, Ullapool IV26 2UB, tel 0845 225 5121 🛥 Summer cruises twice daily from Badentarbat pier at Achiltibuie to the Summer Isles, May–end Sep Mon–Sat

INVERARAY

Spread out along a bay near the head of Loch Fyne, the handsome town of Inveraray, with its whitewashed buildings and proud history, was for centuries the capital of Argyll. The ruling family, the Campbell dukes of Argyll, had a castle nearby, and when the untidy village threatened the view from his planned new mansion in 1743, the 3rd Duke moved the lot to its present purpose-built site. This creates a harmony in the buildings, many of which were designed by Robert Mylne (1734–1811).

They include the parish church, which causes the main street to flow around it. The tall brown stone tower is that of All Saints' Episcopalian Church, famous for its peal of 10 bells and with panoramic views from the top (mid-May to Sep daily 10–1 and 2–5). The town's courthouse and jail of 1820 are now host to an entertaining and interactive exhibition about prison life (Apr–Oct daily 9.30–6; rest of year daily 10–5).

The three-masted schooner *Arctic Penguin* is moored in the small harbour (summer daily 10–6), and includes an exhibition about local-born novelist Neil Munro (1864–1930), author of the humorous Para Handy tales. (Para Handy was the roguish skipper of a 'puffer', or small steamboat, which plied the Crinan Canal.) The Para Handy stories first appeared in the *Glasgow Evening News*, and proved immensely popular. They were later published in book form, and then adapted for the television. Later still, three new stories were written for the stage, with the performances filmed and released on DVD. Inverarary is rightly proud of its famous son, who created these tales that have become classics of Scottish humour.

To the north of the town, Inveraray Castle is a splendid 18th-century mansion with pepperpot towers and a delightfully decorative interior (Apr, Oct Mon–Sat 10–5.45, Sun 12–5.45). Its leafy grounds are overlooked by the watchtower on Duniquoich Hill (255m/837ft).

The Loch Fyne Oyster Bar, at the head of Loch Fyne, is excellent for fresh and smoked seafood.

Opposite top left *The peaks of Suilven and Cul Mòr, Inverpolly*
Opposite top right *The Highland Folk Museum traces Highland life through the ages*
Below *Inveraray's whitewashed houses stretch along Loch Fyne*

INNER HEBRIDES

INFORMATION

⊞ 350, 351, 354, 355

🏠 The Pier, Craignure, Isle of Mull PA65 6AY, tel 01680 812377 or 0845 225 5121

🏠 Morrisons Court, Bowmore, Islay PA43 7JP, tel 01496 810254 or 08707 200617

🏠 Harbour Street, Tarbert PA29 6UD, tel 01880 820429

🚢 Mull: ferry from Oban, Kilchoan and Lochaline. Coll, Tiree, Colonsay: ferry from Oban. Islay and Jura: ferry from Kennacraig, near Tarbert. Gigha: ferry from Tayinloan on the Kintyre peninsula. All Caledonian MacBrayne, tel 0800 066 5000; www.calmac.co.uk

❓ Islay has its own whisky trail leaflet, detailing opening times for the distilleries, which include the famous Laphroaig, Lagavulin and Bowmore brands. (see www.islayinfo.com)

Above *Port Charlotte, Islay, in the early morning light*

INTRODUCTION

The islands of the Inner Hebrides, each with its own character and community life, hug the western shores of Scotland (for Skye, ▷ 256–259). Also marketed as Argyll's Atlantic Islands, they are accessed via scheduled ferry services, and are within reach of day excursions or longer exploration from the mainland.

WHAT TO SEE

MULL AND IONA

Mull is the largest, covering some 906sq km (350sq miles), with high mountains in the south, and the rugged inlets of Loch Scridain and Loch na Keal in the west. The main settlement is the 19th-century fishing port of Tobermory, in the northeast. The remoteness of the western seaboard makes it an ideal habitat for the reintroduced white-tailed eagle, as well as for golden eagles, buzzards, peregrines and seabirds. To see birds of prey up close, visit Wings Over Mull, a conservation centre at Craignure (Easter–end Oct daily 10.30–5.30).

Just a short ride away on the narrow-gauge railway (Apr–end Oct daily, check timetable for departures), Torosay Castle is a stately home of 1858, with 4.8ha (12 acres) of Italianate gardens (house: Easter–end Oct daily 10.30–5; gardens: summer daily 9–dusk). On the point of Duart Bay stands a much older edifice, Duart Castle, 13th-century home of the Macleans (May to mid-Oct daily 10.30–5.30; Apr Sun–Thu 11–4). West of Ben More, Mull's highest mountain, is the Ardmeanach peninsula, the tip of which is reached via an arduous 5.5-mile (8.8km) path. Its main sight is a fossilized tree, 12m (40ft) high and up to 50 million years old.

Fionnphort is the access point for Iona, a magical island known since the sixth century AD as the cradle of Christianity in Scotland. Most visitors make straight for the abbey (Easter–end Sep daily 9.30–5.30; rest of year daily

9.30–4.30), but spare time for the remains of the 13th-century priory, built for Augustinian nuns.

St. Columba founded his monastery here in AD563, and from it Christianity radiated throughout Europe. Now home to the Iona Community, the abbey welcomes pilgrims from around the world. Beside it is the ancient burial ground of Scottish kings, including Duncan and Macbeth. Excursions take in the island of Staffa, with its spectacular hexagonal basalt columns, and Fingal's Cave.

COLL, TIREE, COLONSAY AND ORONSAY

To the west of Mull, the low-lying islands of Coll and Tiree are noted for their sandy beaches, machair (sea meadow) and rare birds, including corncrakes and little terns. Colonsay and nearby Oronsay, to the south, also have fine sands and interesting birdlife.

ISLAY

By comparison, Islay is positively cosmopolitan, a working island with eight distilleries, the excellent Museum of Islay Life at Port Charlotte (Easter–end Oct Mon–Sat 10.30–4.30), and an annual festival of music and whisky. Loch Finlaggan, west of Port Askaig, was the base for the Lordship of the Isles in the 14th and 15th centuries, and is now an extensive archaeological site (Easter–end Oct Mon–Fri 10–4.30, Sat 10.30–4.30, Sun 1–4). Around 110 species of bird breed on Islay, including the chough, a black crow-like bird with startling red legs and beak. And an estimated 50,000 geese overwinter here from Greenland and Iceland.

JURA AND GIGHA

With its three high conical mountains or 'Paps', Jura is easily recognized. Standing stones and cairns date habitation here back to 7000BC. Gigha is famous for the gardens of Achamore House, noted for their camellias, azaleas and rhododendrons (all year daily).

TIPS
» Ferry services to the islands are infrequent, and may change according to local weather conditions, so plan your visit carefully and allow several days.
» Visitor accommodation on the smaller islands is limited, so reserve in advance.

Left *Baile Mòr on the Isle of Iona*
Below *Brightly painted houses are a feature of Tobermory Bay, Mull*

INFORMATION

www.nts.org.uk

➕ 347 E4 ✉ Poolewe, Achnasheen
IV22 2LG ☎ 0844 493 2225
🕐 Garden: mid-Mar–end Oct daily
9.30–8 or dusk (last entry 5); rest of year
daily 10–3. Visitor centre: May–end Aug
daily 9.30–6; mid-Mar to end Apr, Sep
daily 9.30–5; Oct daily 10–4 ♿ (NTS)
Adult £8, child (5–16) £5.25, family £16 or
£20 🚌 Private jetty in the garden allows
access by cruise boat by arrangement oly
📷 £3.50 🍴 🎒 ❓ Free guided tours
Apr–end Sep Mon–Fri at 1.30

TIPS

» Remember this is the west coast, and
receives around 152cm (60in) of rain per
year—take an umbrella!
» Dogs are not allowed in the gardens,
and there is limited shaded parking.

Above *Inverewe's lush gardens*
Opposite top *Deep-cut grave slab in*
Kilmartin churchyard
Opposite bottom *The Last House in John*
o'Groats, with its traditional roof
of Caithness flagstones

INVEREWE GARDENS

In 1862 Osgood Mackenzie (1842–1922) acquired the sporting estate of
Inverewe, and on this barren, rocky, salt-wind-blown promontory started to
plant shelter belts of trees. Soil and fertilizing seaweed had to be imported
by the back-breaking creel-load. It was the unpromising start to what would
become Scotland's best-known woodland garden.

Mackenzie had to wait patiently for another two decades before the trees
were sufficiently established for him to begin serious planting, as, with typical
enthusiasm, he set to work to collect 'every rare exotic tree and shrub which I
hear succeeds in Devon, Cornwall, and the west of Ireland'. Like these places,
Inverewe benefits from the warmth of the Gulf Stream, and rarely suffers
from serious frosts. Mackenzie's daughter Mairi Sawyer took over the garden
on her father's death, and in 1953 it was passed on to the National Trust
for Scotland.

EXPLORING THE GARDENS

Entry to the gardens is through the visitor centre and shop, leading past
the south-facing walled garden and through the rock garden. A network of
paths draws you on through the Woodland Walk, the Pond Garden and Wet
Valley, to the high viewpoint of Am Ploc Ard, the jetty on Camas Glas bay
and back around the Rhododendron and Jubilee Walks and the bamboo
garden, Bambooselem. The planting is varied and exotic, with something
flowering at almost any time of the year. Alongside great paddle-leaved
rhododendrons from the Himalayas, you'll find magnolias from the Far East,
Tasmanian eucalypts, olearias from New Zealand and even the Chilean flame
flower—flouncing its arresting red blossoms apparently effortlessly here. The
candelabra primula is an Inverewe speciality.

Whichever direction your approach, Inverewe is surrounded by some of the
most beautiful scenery in the Highlands, including Loch Maree and Gruinard
Bay, making a visit to this remote spot well worth while.

from the ninth century AD. To the south, the great rocky outcrop of Dunadd was the capital of the sixth-century Scottish kingdom of Dalriada: look for the footprint-shaped impression in the exposed stone on the top of the rock.

✚ 355 D9 ⚑ 27 Lochnell Street, Lochgilphead PA31 8JN, tel 0845 225 5121; seasonal

KINTYRE

In 1098 Norse king Magnus Barelegs hauled his ship over the narrow neck of land at Tarbert to claim the beautiful Kintyre Peninsula for an island. Despite swift, modern access down its western side provided by the A83, it still has the feeling of a world apart. The eastern road, via the holiday village of Carradale, is much slower, allowing time to enjoy the views to the island of Arran (▷ 116).

The Mull of Kintyre is the lumpy southern tip, looking across to Northern Ireland, barely 12 miles (19km) away. Tarbert, at the top, is an appealing little port, busy with yachts and small fishing boats. Campbeltown, at the southern end, remains an important service centre for the farming community of the peninsula, and the home of the Springbank distillery (advance reservations only, Easter–end Sep Mon–Fri 2pm).

✚ 355 D11 ⚑ Harbour Street, Tarbert PA29 6UD, tel 0845 225 5121; seasonal ⚑ Mackinnon House, The Pier, Campbeltown PA28 6EF, tel 0845 225 5121 ✕ Campbeltown 🚢 Ferry: Lochranza on Arran to Claonaig (summer only) and Tarbert (winter only)

JOHN O'GROATS

In popular imagination, John o'Groats is the most northerly point on the British mainland, 874 miles (1,405km) from Land's End in Cornwall. It is named after a Dutchman, Jan de Groot, who lived here in 1509, and his octagonal house overlooks the wild waters of the Pentland Firth. There are craft studios, souvenir shops and a café or two to mark the location, and never mind that the inhabitants of tiny Scarfskerry, a few miles to the northwest, have been known to take exception to the claim. There are good walks to the wind-blown cliffs of Duncansby Head.

The real most northerly point of mainland Scotland is the exposed headland of Dunnet Head, between John o'Groats and Thurso, with views to Orkney.

In 1952, Queen Elizabeth the Queen Mother (1900–2002) acquired and restored the nearby Castle of Mey as a holiday home (May–end Jul, mid-Aug to end Sep Sat–Thu 10.30–4). It contains an appealing blend of kitsch, comfort and grandeur.

✚ 349 J1 ⚑ County Road, John o'Groats KW1 4YR, tel 0845 225 5121; seasonal

KILMARTIN

The peaceful green glen which leads to the hamlet of Kilmartin, between Oban and Lochgilphead, is littered with piles of silvery boulders, the remains of burial cairns dating from around 3000BC. At the centre of each was a small tomb of stone slabs, and together with the standing stones at Ballymeanoch, the stone circle at Temple Wood, and cup-and-ring carved rocks in the surrounding hills, they form one of the most remarkable collections of early monuments in Britain. Learn more at Kilmartin House, the archaeological museum by the church (Mar–end Oct daily 10–5.30). Deeply carved grave slabs in the churchyard depicting warriors date

LANDMARK FOREST HERITAGE PARK

www.landmark-centre.co.uk

The Landmark Forest Heritage Park is a woodland-themed park, combining serious information about the natural world with activities such as a giant water slide. It lies 6 miles (9.7km) north of Aviemore.

Follow the Timber Trail to learn about the history of the logging industry, and climb the 105 steps of the creaking wooden lookout tower for magnificent views to the Cairngorms. The Ancient Forest leads you through a venerable wood of Scots pines, with a treetop walkway and wildlife feeding area favoured by red squirrels. MicroWorld is about hands-on fun with lenses, while Ant City, a playground suitable for all ages, includes a climbing wall and a giant slide.

✚ 352 H5 ✉ Carrbridge PH23 3AJ, tel 01479 841613 ⏰ Apr to mid-Jul daily 10–6; mid-Jul to end Aug daily 10–7; rest of year daily 10–5 ✋ Adult £10.05, child (4–14) £7.85, under 4 free; lower cost in winter months 🚉 Carrbridge 🖥 🏛

LEWIS AND HARRIS

▷ opposite.

LOCH AWE

A narrow loch 23 miles (37km) long, Loch Awe lies amid the dark green forested hills of Argyll surrounded by scattered small villages, castles and hotels. There are little islands and the remains of crannogs (▷ 204), and the clear waters teem with trout and pike. The Duncan Ban McIntyre Monument, signposted from Dalmally, is a good viewpoint.

At the northern end, tantalizingly surrounded by marsh, sits the picturesque ruin of Kilchurn Castle (HS, access by ferry, summer only, tel 01866 833333 to book). It dates from 1440 and was built by Colin Campbell of Breadalbane, with additions into the 17th century.

Where the northwest corner of the loch narrows into the awesome Pass of Brander, a hydroelectric power station lies on the shore below the bulk of Ben Cruachan (1,124m/3,688ft). A minibus takes you 0.5 miles (800m) into the mountain to see the mighty turbines (reserve in advance tel 01866 822618 Easter–end Oct daily 9.30–5).

✚ 355 E9 ℹ Front Street, Inveraray PA32 8UY, tel 0845 225 5121 🚉 Lochawe

MACDUFF MARINE AQUARIUM

www.macduff-aquarium.org.uk

This little gem on the northeast coast is a refreshing way to learn about the sealife of the Moray Firth. In a modern circular building by the shore, its centrepiece is a deep sea-water tank, open to the heavens and complete with wave machine, offering realistic conditions for its inhabitants. Clear sides enable you to see plants and creatures inhabiting the different levels in this naturalistic setting, from delicately fringed sea anemones and lurking conger eels, to commercial species of fish such as cod and whiting. Three times a week you can watch dive shows through the giant window in the theatre, when divers feed the fish. There are around 100 species of fish and invertebrate to see here.

✚ 349 K4 ✉ 11 High Shore, Macduff AB44 1SL ☎ 01261 833369 ⏰ Daily 10–5 ✋ Adult £5.20, child (3–15) £2.60, under 3 free, family £12.75 🏛

Left *Kilchurn Castle, Loch Awe*
Below *Display of logging at the Landmark Forest Heritage Park*

LEWIS AND HARRIS

Lewis and Harris are joined by a narrow neck of land but retain strong individual identities. They share a strong Gaelic culture and a traditional observance of the Sabbat, so plan ahead if you're here on a Sunday, as restaurants, shops and petrol stations may be closed.

Lewis, the northern part, has great undulating blanket peat moors scattered with lochs, and a surprising density of population for such an isolated place. Steornabhagh (Stornoway) is the administrative centre, a busy fishing port and the only real town on the island. Good roads lead through the crofting communities which hug the shore, and to the mountainous southwest corner, where the white sands of Uig and Reef compete with green islands to steal the view.

On a clear day, you can see the pointed peaks of St. Kilda, 41 miles (66km) away on the horizon. Harris, the southern sector, is the most beautiful of the Outer Hebrides, with high mountains and deep-cut bays. The subtle browns, greens and smoky greys of the landscape are reflected in the island's most famous export, Harris Tweed, a hand-woven wool cloth of high quality made here since the 1840s.

WHAT TO SEE

The island has many prehistoric monuments and monoliths, of which the avenue and circle of 13 stones at Calanais (Callanish), dating to around 3000BC, is outstanding (visitor centre: Apr–end Sep Mon–Sat 10–6; rest of year Wed–Sat 10–4). The stones are of the underlying rock of the island, Lewisian gneiss, some 2,900 million years old. Just up the coast, Dun Carloway Broch (HS, free access) is an excellent example of a stone-built circular Iron-Age dwelling. Set back from the beach at Bosta is a reconstructed Iron-Age house (Jun–end Aug Tue–Sat 12–6), which can be compared with the evocative 19th-century Blackhouse at Arnol (HS, Apr–end Sep Mon–Sat 9.30–5.30; Oct–end Mar 9.30–4.30). At Roghadal (Rodel), St. Clements Church dates from around 1500, and has curious sculptures on the stone tower.

There are great views to Taransay island from the luminous sands and turquoise waters of Tràigh Luskentyre.

INFORMATION

www.visitthehebrides.com

346 B3/C2

26 Cromwell Street, Stornoway, Isle of Lewis HS1 2DD, tel 01851 703088 or 0845 225 5121

Pier Road, Tarbert, Isle of Harris HS3 3DG, tel 0845 225 5121

Ferry from Uig on Skye to Tarbert, and from Ullapool to Stornoway

Flights from Glasgow and Edinburgh to Stornoway

TIPS

» If driving here, be aware that petrol (gas) stations are few and far between and may be closed on Sunday.
» Roads are good but not fast, so allow plenty of time for your journey.
» Many road signs use Gaelic spellings which can be confusing, so equip yourself with a good map.
» There is no scheduled public transport on Sundays.

Above *Gearrannan Blackhouse Village on the Isle of Lewis*

MUSEUM OF SCOTTISH LIGHTHOUSES

www.lighthousemuseum.co.uk

This is the only dedicated lighthouse museum in Britain. As well as seeing the imaginative presentation of lenses, ghostly glass prisms and working models, and an interactive map to show how the lighthouse system grew along the Scottish coastline, you can go inside a real lighthouse to see how it worked.

The Kinnaird Head lighthouse was built by Robert Stevenson in 1824, and is rather oddly placed in one corner of a square castle keep. The views from the top are windy but magnificent, overlooking the busy fishing port of Fraserburgh. Reserve your timed place on the lighthouse tour when you arrive at the museum (it's included in the entry price).
✚ 349 L4 ✉ Kinnaird Head, Fraserburgh AB43 9DU ☎ 01346 511022 🕓 Apr–end Jun, Sep, Oct Mon–Sat 10–6, Sun 12–5; Jul, Aug Mon–Sat 10–6, Sun 11–6; rest of year Mon–Sat 11–4, Sun 12–4 💷 Adult £5, child £2, under 6 free, family from £12.40 📷 🎁 Postcards and souvenirs

NORTH UIST, BENBECULA, SOUTH UIST AND ERISKAY

Part of the chain of the Outer Hebrides, these four islands are linked by a series of causeways. They are characterized by low, peaty ground glittering with a thousand trout-stocked lochans (small lakes), with big bare hills and beaches of sparkling white shell sand to the west. North Uist is rich in standing stones and other prehistoric remains, signs that these islands have been inhabited for over 4,000 years. Communities are widely scattered and surprisingly numerous, for crofting on the fertile machair (sea meadow) is still viable.

The Kildonan Museum on South Uist reveals the history and cultural heritage of the people here (Apr to mid-Oct Mon–Sat 10–5, Sun 12–5), and also has a welcoming café. The ruined croft house on South Uist that was the birthplace of Flora Macdonald (1722–90) is signed from the main road near the turning to Gearraidh Bhailteas.

The islands provide vital wetland habitat for birds such as corncrakes, red-necked phalaropes, geese and mute swans, with major reserves at Balranald and Loch Druidibeg.

The Sound of Eriskay, now crossed by a stone causeway, is where the whisky-laden SS *Politician* foundered in 1941, giving novelist Compton Mackenzie the idea for his comic tale *Whisky Galore* (1947); the classic film (released in the US as *A Tight Little Island*) was shot on neighbouring Barra (▷ 233) in the following year.
✚ 346 A4, 350 A5/6 ℹ Pier Road, Lochmaddy, Isle of North Uist HS6 5AA, tel 01876 500321 or 0845 225 5121; seasonal ℹ Pier Road, Lochboisdale, Isle of South Uist HS8 5TH, tel 01878 700286; seasonal 🚢 North Uist: ferry from Uig on Skye to Lochmaddy, from An T-ob (Leverburgh) on Harris to Otternish. South Uist: ferry to Lochboisdale from Oban and Castlebay on Barra. Ferry to Barra from Eriskay (www.calmac.co.uk)

OBAN

A busy rail-head and ferry port for the Western Isles, Oban developed as a holiday resort in the 19th century. The bustling harbour is the start point for local tours to the islands. It is on a curving bay sheltered by the low island of Kerrera, and dominated by the circular folly of stone arches on the hillside behind.

This is McCaig's Tower, erected by John Stuart McCaig, a banker and philanthropist, in 1897 as a family memorial and to relieve local unemployment. It was to have held a museum, with statues in each of the windows, but unfortunately McCaig died before it could be completed. Today it provides a superb viewpoint.

Oban is also a popular touring centre, with good shops on the main roads of Corran Esplanade and George Street. The distillery in the middle is a pleasant diversion on a wet day (Feb, Dec Mon–Fri 12.30–4; Mar–Easter, Nov 10–5; Easter–end Jun Mon–Sat 9.30–5; Jul–end Sep Mon–Fri 9.30–7.30, Sat 9.30–5, Sun 12–5; Oct Mon–Sat 9.30–5; Nov Mon–Fri 10–5; Jan closed).

Four miles (6.4km) to the north lies Dunstaffnage Castle, built in the 13th century to fight off Norsemen, and burned down in 1810 (HS, Easter–end Sep daily 9.30–5.30; Oct–end Mar Sat–Wed 9.30–4.30). In 1746, the castle was temporarily used to imprison Flora Macdonald. Beyond that, the Scottish Sea life Sanctuary at Barcaldine cares for sick and injured seals (Easter to mid-Oct daily 10–5; winter times vary).
✚ 355 E8 ℹ Argyll Square PA34 4AR, tel 01631 563122 or 0845 225 5121 🚉 Oban

Bottom left *Croft house, North Uist*
Below *McCaig's Tower, Oban*
Opposite left *Whisky barrels at Glenfiddich*
Opposite right *The abbey church at Pluscarden is the heart of the community*

PLUSCARDEN ABBEY

www.pluscardenabbey.org

This remarkable monastery is the only medieval foundation in Britain still used for its original purpose. Lying in a green valley 6 miles (10km) southwest of Elgin, it is the permanent home of 27 Benedictine monks, and a haven of spiritual retreat for both men and women. The monastery was founded in 1230 for the French Valliscaudian order by Alexander II, and during the Reformation in the 16th century was gradually abandoned.

In 1943 Benedictine monks from Prinknash Abbey in Gloucestershire started to restore it, and in 1974 it received the status of abbey. Today the white-habited monks work in the grounds and workshops and care for the abbey buildings. These focus on the massive abbey church, where ancient stonework and frescoes contrast with modern stained glass.

⊞ 348 J4 ✉ Pluscarden, Elgin IV30 8UA ⏰ Daily 9–5 ✋ Free ♿

SKYE

▷ 256–259.

SMALL ISLES

www.isleofrum.com; www.isleofmuck.com; www.isleofeigg.org

Canna, Rum, Eigg and Muck make up this island group due west of Mallaig. Each has its own distinct identity, but they share a reputation for interesting birdlife, including the rare white-tailed eagle.

Rum (or Rhum) is much the biggest, with the high mountains of Askival (810m/2,658ft) and Sgùrr nan Gillean (763m/2,503ft) to the southeast, and a reputation for particularly vicious midges. Once cleared as a private sporting island, it is now a nature reserve owned by Scottish Natural Heritage, home to red deer, feral goats and some 100,000 Manx shearwaters. About 30 people live in the small east-coast settlement around the Edwardian castle at Kinloch. Half the castle acts as a hostel, the other half is preserved in its Edwardian splendour. (Tours daily in summer; one daily tied in with ferry sailings.)

Muck is the smallest and flattest island, with by just one farm, a craft shop, tea room and limited visitor accommodation.

Canna, an early Christian settlement site, is owned by the National Trust for Scotland. Its most famous feature is Compass Hill: iron in the basalt rock can upset compasses within a radius of 3 miles (5km). Eigg, with its high spine of pitchstone porphyry called the Sgurr, has a small pierside complex with a restaurant and craft shop. In 1997 the island was bought by its occupants, in a landmark venture.

⊞ 350 C6/7 🛈 East Bay, Mallaig PH41 4QS, tel 01687 462170 or 0845 225 5121; seasonal 🚢 Reached via CalMac ferry from Mallaig (www.calmac.co.uk); cruises from Arisaig, tel 01687 450224

SPEYSIDE

www.maltwhiskytrail.com

The River Spey flows from the Cairngorms near Aviemore and winds northeast through a green landscape of gentle hills and woodland, to pour into the sea between Lossiemouth and Buckie. On the way, it flows under a magnificent iron bridge at Craigellachie by engineer Thomas Telford (1757–1834), lends its name to the historic Strathspey Railway and the town of Grantown-on-Spey, and picks up a long-distance trail, the Speyside Way, which runs north from Tomintoul to Spey Bay.

Speyside is a name associated with the area between Elgin, Keith and Grantown, and more particularly with the production of some of Scotland's most famous single malt whiskies (▷ 339–340): Signposts here can read like a well-stocked bar. Eight distilleries, mostly founded in the early 19th century, are linked by the signposted Malt Whisky Trail: Glen Grant, Cardhu, Strathisla, Glenlivet, Benromach, Dallas Dhu, Glen Moray and Glenfiddich. Each offers guided tours and whisky tastings, but opening times and admissions vary so check ahead (the tourist information office has a leaflet with all the information).

Thousands of oak barrels essential to the whisky industry are maintained at the Speyside Cooperage, Craigellachie (Mon–Fri 9–4).

⊞ 352 J5 🛈 17 High Street, Elgin IV30 1EG, tel 01343 542666 or 0845 225 5121 🛈 54 High Street, Grantown-on-Spey, tel 0845 225 5121; seasonal

SKYE

INTRODUCTION

The Isle of Skye is the largest and best known of the Inner Hebrides, its name woven into the warp of Bonnie Prince Charlie's flight after Culloden (▷ 241) in the 18th century; and into the weft of the loss of a way of island life and emigration to the New World in the 19th century. Broadford is the main hub for the south, with access to the steep, magnificently scenic road to Elgol. Portree is a more appealing township, and centre for the north of the island.

Skye is an unlikely crossroads among the Western Isles. In summer you can reach it by ferry from Mallaig or Gairloch, or by ferry across the strong currents by Glenelg, or at any time of the year by the convenient but controversial bridge from Kyle of Lochalsh (tolls were removed in December 2004). Ferries to the Outer Hebrides leave from Uig, and to little Raasay from Sconser.

Arriving in Skye, you know you've left the mainland. For a start, road signs in Gaelic as well as English quickly tell you you're in a different culture. Skye retains a strong Gaelic identity, encouraged at the college, Sabhal Mor Ostaig, in Sleat, but the economic necessity of generations of emigration have made the island outward-looking and perhaps surprisingly cosmopolitan. If your ancestors came from Skye or the western Highlands, then make sure to visit Armadale Castle, in the southwest (Easter–end Oct daily 9.30–5.30). Within it is the excellent Museum of the Isles, and a library and resource centre where you can undertake your own genealogical research.

Many people's introduction to Skye is through the romantic and well-loved melody, the 'Skye Boat Song'. It recalls the flight of Charles Edward Stewart (Bonnie Prince Charlie) after the disaster at Culloden in 1746, when the prince was smuggled to Skye from South Uist by Flora Macdonald, disguised as Betty Burke. He continued his journey in safety to Raasay and then exile in France.

While the prince escaped, Flora Macdonald was arrested and imprisoned briefly in the Tower of London. She later married a Skye man and emigrated to America; they eventually returned to live at Kingsborough, and her grave is there. There is also a memorial to the Jacobite heroine near ruined Duntulm Castle, a former Macdonald stronghold.

WHAT TO SEE

THE CUILLIN

Every view of the Isle of Skye is dominated by the Cuillin (pronounced 'Coolin'), a range of jagged mountains of dark gabbro which reaches its peak in the far south with Sgùrr Alasdair (1,009m/3,309ft). They are to be treated with respect, but Munro-baggers (▷ 19) can have a field day here, with 12 mountains reaching beyond 914.4m (3,000ft).

The southern mountains are the Black Cuillin, distinct from the scree-covered granite of the lower Red Cuillin. All are challenges for mountaineers, and the most inaccessible peaks were conquered only at the end of the 19th century. In geological terms, the Cuillin are comparatively young, formed in volcanic activity at the same time as Iceland, a mere 20 million years ago, and scoured by the ice ages.

PORTREE

The harbour town of Portree on the eastern coast is the capital of the island, and the centre of island life, its colour-washed houses around the harbour pleasing on the eye. The town was named after a royal visit in 1540 by James V—*port righ* means king's harbour—and its formal square is a miniature delight. Its Aros Experience offers an introduction to Skye's natural history with an

INFORMATION

www.skye.co.uk
🪧 350 C5 ℹ️ Bayfield House, Bayfield Road, Portree, Isle of Skye IV51 9EL, tel 0845 225 5121 🚢 Car ferry from Mallaig to Armadale (40 minutes), from Glenelg to Kylerhea (15 minutes, summer only)

Above *A fishing boat moored at Dunvegan village*
Opposite *Dunvegan Castle rises above the shores of Loch Dunvegan*

audio-visual show about the return of the white-tailed sea eagle (all year daily 9–5).

DUNVEGAN CASTLE

The MacLeod clan have owned and fought over Skye for generations, and their home in the northwest of the island, Dunvegan Castle, is well worth a visit (mid-Mar to Oct daily 10–5; Nov to mid-Mar daily 11–4; www.dunvegancastle. com). It is a fortress built on a high rock that was once completely surrounded by the sea, and has been occupied since the 13th century. Heavy restoration in the 19th century has left it impressive, if not beautiful, but the interior is full of rich treasures. The most poignant of these is the faded and tattered talisman of the Fairy Flag, said to be a gift to an early clan chief from his fairy lover, with potent powers to rescue the clan at times of peril. It is made of silk from the Middle East and dates from the 4th to 7th century AD.

Dunvegan's gardens have taken the place of the 'bare wine-dark moorland' observed by Dr. Johnson in 1773. Helped by the benign climate of the Gulf Stream, the rhododendrons planted in the 19th century have flourished alongside a surprising range of other exotics from China, the Americas, Japan, Korea and New Zealand. You can join a boat trip from Dunvegan to see the common and grey seals which loll about the rocks, or a mini-cruise on the loch to explore the history and wildlife of some of the many tiny islands.

TROTTERNISH

Trotternish is the name of the peninsula which sticks up like a long finger at the northern tip of Skye. Ancient flows of lava have produced sheer cliffs, with shearings and pinnacles down the spine created where softer rocks buckled under the weight of the lava. The most famous of these is the Old Man of Storr, a black obelisk 49m (160ft) high. The weird and mysterious stone formations of the area known as the Quiraing, 19 miles (30.4km) north of Portree, can be examined up close if you walk with care (▷ walk, 274–275). Basalt columns have formed huge cliffs on the eastern coast. Perhaps the most spectacular of these is known as the Kilt Rock, from its resemblance to the pleated garment. There's a dramatic waterfall here, too, and captivating views across to the blue hills of the mainland.

TIPS

» The voracity of Skye's midges is the stuff of legends, so be prepared with suitable insect repellent.

» The summer weather on the island is unpredictable, so be prepared for heavy rain, lowering mist and blazing sunshine — in the space of just a few hours.

» Skye looks quite small on the map, but allow several days to explore properly — the roads are slow, and the scenery big.

» Fine dining and Scottish islands don't always go together, but Skye has several excellent restaurants that make any stay here a gourmet pleasure (▷ 289). And at Carbost, the Talisker Distillery produces a fragrant, peaty single malt (Nov–end Mar Mon–Fri 2–4.30; Apr–end Oct Mon–Fri 9.30–4.30; open Sat Jul, Aug).

EILEAN BÀN

The Skye bridge sets one massive concrete foot firmly on the little 2.4ha (6-acre) island of Eilean Bàn, a nature reserve run by a charitable trust for the local community. Access is via the Bright Water Visitor Centre on the pier at Kyleakin (May–end Oct Mon–Sat 10–4, opening times can vary so tel 01599 530040), which has information about local wildlife and history, and interactive exhibits to teach children about conservation. But Eilean Bàn is more than just a wildlife reserve. The island houses a lighthouse, built in 1857 and decommissioned in 1993. Gavin Maxwell, the author best known for his tale of otter-keeping, *Ring of Bright Water* (1960), bought and refurbished the keepers' cottages in the 1960s. One of the rooms has been restored, and is now furnished with many objects that belonged to Maxwell himself.

The shapely island of Raasay, to the east of Skye, is another haven for wildlife, and benefits from fewer visitors than Skye itself. If you are unlucky enough not to spot wild otters in the coastal waters around Skye, try the hide at the Kylerhea Otter Haven (all year daily dawn–dusk).

THE SKYE MUSEUM OF ISLAND LIFE

This is one of the best attractions in the north of the island. It's located in a picturesque setting almost at the end of the Trotternish Peninsula, from where there are lovely views of the Western Isles. The difficulty of getting to the museum is part of its charm, and a reminder of how difficult travelling and communication was in pre-car days.

The museum is spread around a small group of traditional thatched cottages known as 'black houses', a few of which have survived. The ones here include the Croft House, whose cosy kitchen was a gathering place and would have had a peat fire burning constantly, even in summer, as this was where the cooking was done. There's also a Weaver's Cottage, the Old Smithy and a Ceilidh House, a community house where people would gather to tell stories and sing songs.

Above *The Cuillin Hills, looking across Loch Scavaig from Elgol*
Opposite top *The Skye Bridge at Kyle of Lochalsh*
Opposite bottom *The jagged rocky spine of the Quiraing, Trotternish*

STRATHNAVER

This remote valley is dotted with broken walls and the grassy mounds of small homesteads. Its name is resonant with the period of the Highland Clearances, and in particular with the clearing of his land by the Duke of Sutherland between 1812 and 1819, to make way for sheep farming. It was a time when the crofters were forced to leave their homes inland to eke a living on the inhospitable coast, or join the emigration to the New World. The story is well told at Strathnaver Museum near Bettyhill (Apr–end Oct Mon–Sat 10–1, 2–5).

348 G1 Clachan, Bettyhill KW14 7SS, tel 0845 225 5121; seasonal

TORRIDON

Torridon lies on the northwest coast. The 972m (3,189ft) bulk of Beinn Eighe looms above the lonely pass between Shieldaig and Kinlochewe, shedding white quartzite scree like snow. This was Scotland's first national nature reserve, with a visitor centre north of Kinlochewe, and is seen at its best from Loch Clair. To the west, Liathach (1,054m/3,456ft) is the tallest peak in the range, with seven tops along its ridge, closely followed in size by Beinn Alligin (985m/3,232ft). The mountains are for serious walkers only, but there's a more accessible path along the north shore of the loch to Redpoint.

The National Trust for Scotland has a small visitor centre on the approach to Torridon village, with video footage showing the wildlife of the area (Easter–end Sep daily 10–5).

347 E4 Auchtercairn, Gairloch IV22 2DN, tel 01445 712071 or 0845 225 5121; seasonal

ULLAPOOL

This small town stretches along a spit of land on the shore of Loch Broom. Despite its frontier feeling, Ullapool has a dignified air with its neat grid of streets, for this was a planned village, built in 1788 by the British Fisheries Society. Tourism has replaced fishing as the mainstay, and as the last settlement of size on the route up the northwest coast, it is usually busy with visitors in summer.

The MV *Summer Queen* cruises to the green bumps of the Summer Isles, 12 miles (19km) northwest at the mouth of the loch (for reservations, tel 01854 612472). The biggest island, Tanera Mhor, issues its own unique and collectable postage stamps.

The dramatic Corrieshalloch Gorge, at the head of Loch Broom, and the view from the suspension bridge below the Falls of Measach are worth seeking out.

347 E3 Argyle Street IV26 2UB, tel 0845 225 5121 Ferry to Lewis

URQUHART CASTLE

www.historic-scotland.gov.uk
The broken battlements of this castle, 2 miles (3.2km) south of Drumnadrochit, are testimony to its place in the history of the 13th to the 17th centuries. It was built on a rocky promontory sticking out into Loch Ness, offering strategic command of the Great Glen (▷ 245) to whoever could hold it. It changed hands many times between Durwards, Macdonalds and Grants, with an early spell in English hands, and in the 14th century a brief period of ownership by Robert the Bruce. It was finally blown up in 1691 to prevent its use by Jacobite rebels.

The modern visitor centre exhibits interesting medieval fragments discovered here, including an ancient harp.

352 G5 Drumnadrochit, Inverness IV63 6XJ 01456 450551 Easter–end Sep daily 9.30–6; Oct daily 9.30–5; Nov–Easter daily 9.30–4.30 (HS) Adult £6.50, child (5–16) £3.25, under 5 free

WICK HERITAGE MUSEUM

Like Ullapool in the west, Wick, in the northeast corner of the country, was built up as a fishery town in the 19th century to take advantage of the herring boom. The new development, to a design by Thomas Telford for the British Fisheries Society, was to the south of the river, complementing the older settlement on the north bank.

The Heritage Museum is a fascinating local attraction, run by volunteers. It tells of the town's heyday as one of the busiest herring ports in the world, when the harbour bristled with boats and the population was swelled by migrant workers from the west coast and Ireland. Some of the boats and whole rooms are preserved here, and you can see the old smokehouse, for curing fish, complete with its original soot.

At the core of the museum is the outstanding Johnston collection of photographs. Named after three generations of a local family, they form a vivid record of life in the town between 1863 and 1977.

349 J1 20 Bank Row, Wick KW1 5EY 01955 605393 Easter–end Oct Mon–Sat 10–5 (last entry 3.45) Adult £3, child (under 16) 50p Wick

DRIVE

CASTLES, FORTS AND BATTLEFIELDS

Legend and history come to life in this scenic Highland tour to the east of Inverness.

THE DRIVE

Distance: 106 miles (171km)
Allow: 1–2 days
Start/end: Inverness

★ Leave Inverness (▷ 246) on the A96, travelling through the flatlands south of the Moray Firth. Turn left at the B9039 to reach Ardersier, then take the B9006 to Fort George, a distance of 12 miles (19km).

❶ Fort George was built between 1748 and 1769 on a narrow spit of land which sticks out into the Moray Firth, facing Chanonry Point on the Black Isle (▷ 233). Named after George II, it was set here to protect Inverness from seaward attack, and as part of the backlash to subdue the Highlands following Culloden (▷ 241). It remains unaltered, a superb example of an artillery fort.

Return to Ardersier, then follow the B9006 and the B9090 to Cawdor Castle.

❷ This magnificent 14th-century castle is associated with Shakespeare's play *Macbeth* (▷ 238). Kilravock Castle lies to the west, the 15th-century family seat of the Roses and overshadowed by its famous neighbour.

Continue on the B9090 to Nairn.

❸ Comic actor Charlie Chaplin (1889–1977) liked to relax in this prosperous resort town. Villas and hotels spread back from the old Fishertown by the shore, where the former fishermen's houses are packed tightly together. The harbour dates from 1820, and was designed by engineer Thomas Telford.

Leave by the A96, passing Auldearn.

❹ This was the site of a major battle between Covenanters and Royalists in 1645. Continue on this road through the shady plantation of Culbin Forest.

Turn left to visit Brodie Castle.

❺ A so-called Z-plan tower house dating back to 1567, Brodie Castle is set in delightful parkland (NTS, Easter–end Apr, Jul, Aug daily 10.30–5; May, Jun, Sep, Oct Sun–Thu 10.30–5; grounds all year, daily). Remodelled into a comfortable home in the 19th century, it remained in the Brodie family until 1980, when it passed to the National Trust for Scotland. The family's collection of fine art, books and furniture is outstanding.

Regain the A96, and stay on this road into the floral town of Forres (▷ 243). Continue on the A96, then turn left at the B9011 and follow this to Findhorn.

❻ This is the third village on the site to be called Findhorn—the first was buried in 1694, the second washed away in 1701. It was once a major port, but the harbour is now given over to pleasure craft. In 1962 the Findhorn Community was founded here to find an alternative, more spiritual and sustainable way of living. It is still going strong, with an extensive holistic educational programme and an eco-village.

Return along the B9011 and A96 to Forres. Head south on the A940 and join the A939 for Grantown-on-Spey, a distance of 27 miles (43km).

7 Grantown-on-Spey lies at the edge of the Speyside whisky country (▷ 255). The village was planned in the late 18th century by Sir James Grant, and the arrival of the railway in 1863 heralded its popularity as a health resort. The railway closed in the 1960s, but the town is still popular with walkers and anglers, and in winter takes in some of the overspill of skiers from nearby Aviemore. Grantown Museum tells the story.

Leave on the A95 towards Aviemore, and at Dulnain Bridge turn on to the A938 to Carrbridge.

8 Carrbridge is noted for its picturesque old bridge of 1717, and the Landmark Forest Heritage Park (▷ 252).

Continue on the A938 and join the A9, heading towards Inverness. Just after Daviot, turn right on the B851. Turn left at the B9006.

9 Follow it to the major battle site of Culloden Moor (▷ 241).

Just east of Culloden, a minor road (B9091) passes Clava Cairns.

10 Clava Cairns are three of the most important chambered cairns in the country, dating from the Bronze Age (free access). The two outer ones are passage graves, topped with a massive flat slab. The perimeters of all three are marked by a ring of standing stones, often carved with 'cup' marks.

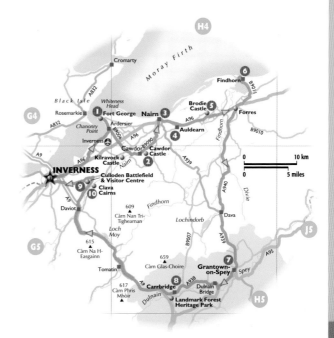

Continue along the B9006 to the A9. Join the A9 and return to Inverness.

PLACES TO VISIT
FORT GEORGE (HS)
✉ Ardersier, Grampian ☎ 01667 462777
🕐 Easter–end Sep daily 9.30–5.30; rest of year daily 9.30–4.30 ✋ Adult £5.50, child £1.50

FINDHORN COMMUNITY
✉ The Park, Forres IV36 3TZ ☎ 01309 690311 🕐 Tours Apr–end Nov Mon, Wed, Fri, Sat; also Sun May–end Sep ✋ £3

GRANTOWN MUSEUM
✉ Burnfield Avenue, Grantown-on-Spey, Moray PH26 3HH ☎ 01479 872478 🕐 Mar–end Dec Mon–Sat 10–4 ✋ Adult £2, child £1.00

WHEN TO GO
Late spring and summer are the best time for touring the Highlands.

Opposite A memorial cairn on Culloden Moor commemorates where 1,200 Jacobites died in a bloody last stand
Below Eighteenth-century Fort George

SIR JAMES GRANT'S TOWN

Explore an ancient pine wood on the banks of the Spey, and an 18th-century planned town.

THE WALK

Distance: 7 miles (11km)
Allow: 3 hours
Start/end: Grantown-on-Spey Museum
OS Explorer 419 Grantown-on-Spey
Grid reference NJ 035280

★ Around 1750, young James Grant returned to Speyside (▷ 255) from his Grand Tour of Europe. He'd seen Edinburgh New Town, just then being built, and thought Speyside could benefit from something similar. He persuaded his father, Sir Ludovic Grant, and a new town was set out above the new military bridge. Merchants, tradesmen and artisans were invited to build their own houses, to a set design, roofed with slate and walled with pale, speckled granite. The town was to be supported by a linen factory.

Go down past the museum (▷ 263).

In 1766 the market cross was moved in procession from old town to new. To persuade the townsfolk away from whisky, a brewery was set up. The Grants put up a handsome orphanage, and established a modern school. However, James Grant was obliged to subsidize the building of most of the houses, and then had to pay for the linen factory. The Industrial Revolution in England was just starting to produce cheap cloth and in 1774 the linen factory failed. By 1804 the town was threatened with economic collapse, and Grant was obliged to sell his London house to buy food for the villagers. Grantown continued as a market town, serving the barley lands of the Spey valley.

Turn left into South Street, then right into Golf Course Road. A tarred path crosses the golf course to a small gate into Anagach Wood.

The wide path ahead has a blue/ red marker. At a junction, the blue trail departs to the right; turn left, following a Spey Way marker and red-top poles. Keep following the red markers, turning left at the first intersection and bearing left at the next. When the track joins a new fence and a bend in a stream is on the left, keep ahead, following a Spey Way marker. The track emerges into open fields. After crossing a small bridge, turn right through a new hunting gate. A path with pines on its left leads to a track near the River Spey. (Bridge of Cromdale is just ahead here.)

Turn sharply right on this track, alongside the river. At a fishers' hut it re-enters forest. About 0.75 miles (1.2km) later it diminishes to a green path and slants up past the cottage of Craigroy to join its entrance track.

At Easter Anagach, a grass track on the right has red markers and runs into a birchwood. With a barrier ahead, follow marker poles to the left, on to a broad path beside a falling fence.

At the next intersection, turn right, following the red poles, over a slight rise. Descending, turn left just before a blue-top post, on to a smaller path with blue and red posts. This runs along the top of a ridge, to reach a bench above a lane.

❶ To the left down the lane is the handsome stone bridge built by Major Caulfield in the mid-18th century as part of the military road system constructed in the aftermath of the Jacobite uprising (▷ 32–33).

The path bends right, alongside the road, to meet a wide track (the

Above *View of Grantown-on-Spey from Dreggie Hill, with the Cromdale Hills beyond*
Opposite *Fishing in the River Spey at Grantown-on-Spey*

former military road). Turn right on to a path with green-top posts. At a small pool, the main path bends left for 137m (150 yards), with blue and green posts; take the path ahead, with green posts. At a five-way intersection bear left to find the next green post. At the edge of the golf course turn left to a parking area and information board.

Follow the street uphill, past the end of the golf course, to the High Street. Turn right to the Square, and the Grant Arms Hotel.

❷ In September 1860, Queen Victoria stopped off at the Grant Arms. With the arrival of the railway, middle-class visitors came in the wake of a visit by Queen Victoria. The inhabitants of Grantown moved into cottages set in their own gardens, while the middle-class families of doctors and lawyers moved in for the summer. And Sir James Grant's handsome granite town has been attracting tourists ever since.

Just past the Grant Arms Hotel, a sign points right, to return to the museum.

WHERE TO EAT
The unassuming JJ's Café (tel 01479 870100) in the High Street is open to 9pm, serving good home-cooked food. It's so popular with locals that it's often booked up. If disappointed, try a bar meal at Tyree House Hotel (tel 01479 872 615). Grantown also has two chip shops and many cafés and hotels.

PLACE TO VISIT
GRANTOWN-ON-SPEY MUSEUM
✉ Burnfield Avenue, Grantown-on-Spey PH26 3HH ☎ 01479 872478 ⏰ Mar–end Dec, Mon–Sat 10–4 💷 Adult £2, child £1.00

WHEN TO GO
September and October are superb months for walking here.

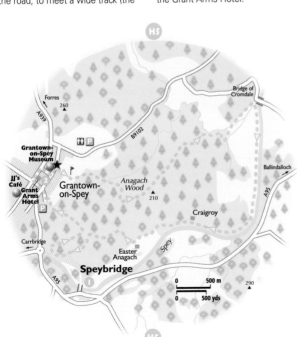

DRIVE

THE WESTERN HIGHLANDS

'The Road to the Isles', an old cattle drovers' road, leads into the western Highlands at the start of one of the most scenic routes in Scotland.

THE DRIVE
Distance: 205 miles (330km)
Allow: 2–3 days
Start/end: Fort William, map 321 E8l

★ See famous battlefields and explore Highland villages on this journey into the western Highlands.

Leave Fort William (▷ 243) on the A82 towards Inverness, then turn left at the A830, signposted to Mallaig. Turn right at the B8004 to Banavie, to admire the flight of locks on the Caledonian Canal called Neptune's Staircase (▷ 268–269). Return to the A830. Turn right and follow the road along Loch Eil to Glenfinnan.

❶ Glenfinnan, at the head of Loch Shiel, is famous for its links with the ill-fated Jacobite rebellion of 1745 (▷ 32–33). Take the short path behind the National Trust for

Scotland's visitor centre to view the 21-arch Glenfinnan viaduct, by Sir Robert MacAlpine (1847–1934), which carries the scenic West Highland Railway to Mallaig. The railway runs parallel with the road for much of the way: look for steam locomotives in summer.

Follow the A830, passing the shores of Loch nan Uamh.

❷ A cairn marks the spot from where, after defeat at Culloden in 1746 (▷ 241) and months in hiding in the Western Isles, Bonnie Prince Charlie finally fled to exile in France.

Continue on the A830, passing through woodland of beech, oak and birch to the village of Arisaig.

❸ During World War II, agents of the Special Operations Executive (SOE) trained in this area before

being dropped behind enemy lines in Europe. Their base was nearby Arisaig House, a manor house in a magnificent setting (private).

Continue on the A830 up the coast to Morar, with views out to the islands of Eigg and Skye.

❹ Morar is famous for its silvery silica sands, and for its very own monster, Morag, who is believed to live in the murky depths of Loch Morar, 310m (1,017ft) down.

Continue on the A830 to Mallaig.

❺ This fishing harbour faces the Skye across the Sound of Sleat, and is the mainland terminal for ferries to the Inner Hebrides, including Rum, Eigg, Muck and Canna, known as the Small Isles (▷ 255). Mallaig grew to prominence after the arrival of the railway in 1901,

on Mull. Silica sand is extracted here, for use in the production of high-grade optical glass.

Return on the A884 to the junction (right) with the B8043. Follow this unclassified road to meet the A861. Turn right and follow this up Loch Linnhe to Ardgour. Take the Corran ferry across the loch. At the other side turn left on to the A82 and return to Fort William.

PLACES TO VISIT
DUART CASTLE
✉ Isle of Mull, PA64 6AP ☎ 01680 812309 🕐 Apr, Mon–Sun 11–4, May to early Oct daily 10.30–5.30 👋 Adult £5, child £2.50, family £12.50

MALLAIG MARINE WORLD
✉ Mallaig Harbour PH41 4XP ☎ 01687 462292 🕐 Jun–end Aug Mon–Sat 9–6, Sun 11–6; Apr–end May, Sep–end Oct Mon–Sat 9–5, Sun 11–5; Nov–end Mar Mon–Sat 9–5 👋 Adult £2.75, child £1.50

WHEN TO GO
The summer months are the best time for exploring the Highland villages, but you will need a good mosquito repellent.

Opposite *Loch nan Uamh, where Bonnie Prince Charlie last set foot in Scotland*
Below *The Jacobite Express steam train pulling out of Glenfinnan*

which provided swift access south for fishing catches. That was during the herring boom—now prawns are a mainstay. Mallaig Heritage Centre tells the story of the settlement and its history. At the end of the road, Mallaigvaig looks across to the hills of Knoydart, one of the remotest areas of Scotland.

Return along the A830 to Lochailort. Turn right at the A861 and follow it to Kinlochmoidart and Acharacle.

❻ The village lies at the southwest tip of Loch Shiel. A detour on to the B8044 leads to the dramatic ruin of 13th-century Castle Tioram, on Loch Moidart (free access, restricted for safety reasons). It lies on a rocky islet at the end of a sandy spit. It was the seat of the Macdonalds of Clanranald, and was deliberately burned down when Allan, the 14th Chief, set off in 1715 to join the Jacobite uprising, to prevent its use by Campbell enemies.

Continue on the A861 to Salen, then turn right at the B8007, to explore the Ardnamurchan Peninsula

(▷ 233). Continue on the B8007, passing through Kilchoan, to Ardnamurchan Point.

❼ The most westerly point on the British mainland is marked with a lighthouse, and has views out to the islands of the Inner Hebrides.

Return to Salen along the B8007; turn right at the A861 to Strontian.

❽ This village gives its name to the element strontium, extracted from the mineral strontianite, discovered here in 1764. The area was extensively mined between 1722 and 1904 for lead, zinc and silver; it now supplies barytes for the lubrication of North Sea drilling rigs. There are pleasant walks through the nearby Ariundle woods.

Continue on the A861, then turn right on to the A884. Follow this to Lochaline.

❾ Lochaline stands on the Sound of Mull, with a ferry service to Fishnish, and views down to the ruins of Ardtornish Castle, and Duart Castle

DISCOVERING THE CALEDONIAN CANAL

A walk alongside—and underneath—Thomas Telford's masterpiece of civil engineering.

THE WALK
Length: 4.5 miles (7.2km)
Allow: 1 hour 45 minutes
Start/end: Kilmallie Hall, Corpach, map ref 442 D6
OS Explorer map: 392

★ The first survey for a coast-to-coast canal across Scotland, linking the lochs of the Great Glen, was made by James Watt, inventor of the steam engine, in 1767. For this great enterprise, only one name was seriously considered: Thomas Telford (1757–1834).

From Kilmallie Hall, go down past Corpach Station to the canal and cross the sea lock that separates salt water from fresh water.

❶ Each of the 29 locks on the canal was designed to accommodate the

width and length of a 40-gun frigate of Lord Nelson's navy.

Follow the canal (on your left) up past another lock, where a path on the right has a Great Glen Way marker. It passes under tall sycamores to the shore. Follow the shoreline path past a soccer pitch and then turn left, across grass to the end of a back street. A path ahead leads up a wooded bank to the towpath.

Just before the Banavie swing bridge, a path down to the right has a Great Glen Way marker.

❷ The Great Glen Way is a new National Trail that runs parallel to the tow path. It has been resurfaced as a cycleway running from the east coast to the west coast.

Follow markers on street signs to a level (train) crossing, then turn left towards the other swing bridge, the one with the road on it.

❸ The Caledonian Canal was a tremendous feat of civil engineering. Some 200 million wheelbarrow-loads of earth were shifted over the next 19 years. Four aqueducts let streams and rivers pass below the waterway, and there was a dam on Loch Lochy and diversion of the rivers Oich and Lochy. Loch Oich needed to be deepened, and for this task a steam dredger had not only to be built, but invented and designed too.

After falling into a state of neglect in the 20th century, the canal was on the verge of closure when, in 1996, the government promised £20 million for a complete refurbishment.

Just before the bridge, turn right at signs for the Great Glen Way and the Great Glen Cycle Route.

The Great Glen Way is a 75-mile (120km) coast-to-coast walking route between Fort William and Inverness. Cyclists can use the Great Glen Cycle Route which follows a similar route, sharing some of the trail.

Continue along the towpath to Neptune's Staircase.

❹ This name was given to the eight locks by Thomas Telford himself. It takes about 90 minutes for boats to work through the system. As each lock fills, slow roiling currents come up from underneath, and as each empties, water forced under pressure into the banks emerges from the masonry in little fountains. The 18m (60ft) of ascent alongside the locks is the serious uphill part of this walk.

A gate marks the top of the locks. About 183m (200 yards) later, a grey gate on the right leads to a dump

Opposite and bottom right *The Caledonian Canal and its locks at Corpach*
Below *Neptune's Staircase*

for dead cars; ignore this one. Over the next 90m (100 yards) the canal crosses a little wooded valley, with a black fence on the right. Now comes a second grey gate. Go through, to a track turning back sharply right, and descending to ford a small stream.

On the right, the stream passes right under the canal in an arched tunnel, and alongside is a second tunnel which provides a walkers' way to the other side. Water from the canal drips into the tunnel, which has a fairly spooky atmosphere. At the tunnel's end, a track runs up to join the canal's northern towpath. Turn right, back down the towpath. After passing Neptune's Staircase, cross the A830 to a level crossing without warning lights. Continue along the right-hand towpath. After a

mile (1.6km) the towpath track leads back to the Corpach double lock.

WHERE TO EAT
The Moorings Hotel at Banavie offers restaurant and bar meals. On the other side of both the A830 and canal, the unassuming Lochy family pub has picnic tables and promises 'massive portions'. At the walk start, a Spar shop sells hot pies, and Kilmallie Hall has a community garden with picnic tables to eat them at.

PLACE TO VISIT
INVERLOCHY CASTLE
✉ Fort William, Invernesshire ✋ Free

WHEN TO VISIT
An easy, enjoyable walk at any time of the year.

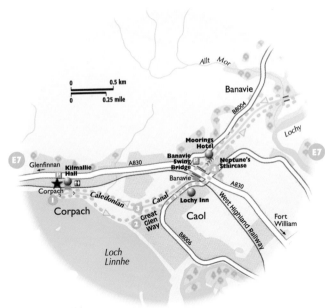

A CIRCUIT OF CASTLE COUNTRY

This circuit from the pleasant little town of Banchory takes in some of the best castles in northeast Scotland.

THE DRIVE
Distance: 143 miles (230km)
Allow: 2 days
Start/end: Banchory, map 323 K7

★ Before leaving Banchory, visit the local history museum on Bridge Street (Mon, Fri, Sat 11–1, 2–4; also Tue, Wed Jul–end Aug). It includes displays about local hero James Scott Skinner (1843–1927), known as the Strathspey King for his virtuoso fiddle playing and prolific composition of tunes.

Leave Banchory on the A93, and after 3 miles (5km) turn left to visit Crathes Castle (▷ 240). Continue on the A93 and turn left at an unclassified road to reach Drum Castle.

❶ The big, grey stone keep of Drum Castle is one of the oldest tower houses in Scotland, dating to the 13th century. Beside it is a fine Jacobean house of 1619, and the whole was embellished in the 19th century. The wooded grounds include an ancient oak forest (NTS, Easter–end Jun, Sep Wed, Thu, Sat–Mon 12.30–5; Jul–end Aug daily 11–5. Grounds: all year, daily).

Return to Crathes and turn left on the A957. Soon turn right on to a minor road and follow this along the southern bank of the River Dee to Bridge of Feugh. Turn left on to the B974 and follow this south to Fettercairn, passing over the high pass of Cairn o'Mount (465m/1,525ft).

❷ The heart of this pleasant town is dominated by an elaborate Gothic arch, erected in honour of a visit by Queen Victoria in 1861. North lies the castellated mansion of Fasque, adopted home of 19th-century prime minister William Gladstone (open to group visits only).

Leave Fettercairn, heading east, on the B966. Turn left on to the A90 and follow this to Stonehaven. On the outskirts, turn right and left on to a minor road that leads into the town.

❸ Modern Stonehaven spreads back from the harbour, where the Carron and Cowie waters flow into the sea. The Tolbooth on the wharf, with its Dutch-style crow-stepped roof, dates from the 17th century. This was a difficult period of history for the town, when it endured being burned by Montrose's army, then occupied for eight long, weary months by Cromwellian troops (who were besieging Dunnottar Castle, to the south).

Rejoin the A90 and continue for 15 miles (24km) to Aberdeen (▷ 234).

Leave Aberdeen on the A944. Turn right at the B977, then left on to an unclassified road to Castle Fraser (▷ 238). On leaving the castle grounds, turn right and follow the minor road to Craigearn. Turn left, then left again on to the B993, and continue to Monymusk. Turn right at a minor road to explore the village.

❹ Monymusk is a quiet village, with a notable Norman church dating back to 1140, making it contemporary with an Augustinian priory. The priory is long gone, its stonework absorbed into the wings of Monymusk House (private). The famous Monymusk Reliquary, believed to contain the bones of St. Columba, was held here for many years—it's now in the National Museum of Scotland in Edinburgh (▷ 72–75).

Return to the B993 and turn right by the former toll house. At the A944, turn right and follow this to Alford.

❺ This small town (pronounced Afford) has two transport museums. The Grampian Transport Museum has vintage cars, lorries, motorcycles, trams and the extraordinary Craigivar Express, a steam-powered tricycle built locally in 1895. Modern eco-friendly vehicles gather here each August for trials and competitions. Steam trains operate on the narrow-gauge Alford Valley Railway between Alford station and Haughton Country Park (Jun–end Aug daily 1–4.30; Apr, May, Sep Sat–Sun 1–4.30; also mornings in Jan).

Continue on the A944, then turn left on the A97 to Kildrummy.

❻ Kildrummy was started in around 1230 for the Earl of Mar, and grew to be one of the biggest castles in Scotland. Its structure is reminiscent of Harlech Castle in Wales. The chapel, part of the original building phase, sticks awkwardly through the walls. Besieged by the English in 1306, Kildrummy changed hands several times before its final

Opposite *Looking out over Stonehaven*
Right *The Gothic arch at Fettercairn celebrates a visit by Queen Victoria in 1861*

destruction in 1715 (HS, Easter–end Sep daily 9.30–5.30).

Continue on the A97, passing Glenbuchat Castle on the right (HS, free access), and after 18 miles (29km) turn right at the B9119 to reach the oddly named Burn o'Vat.

❼ The Burn o'Vat is a huge bottle-shaped pot-hole that was worn out of the solid rock by swirling water. It is a relic of the last ice age, and was formed between 12,000 and 15,000 years ago when melting ice washed quantities of rock debris down from the mountains.

❽ The nearby Culsh Earth-House is a well-preserved chamber and underground passage, roofed by stone slabs and believed to be 2,000 years old (free access).

Continue on the B9119 and turn left at the A93. Follow this via Kincardine O'Neil to return to Banchory.

PLACE TO VISIT
✉ Grampian Transport Museum, Alford AB33 8AE ☎ 019755 62292 ⏰ Easter–end Oct daily 10–5; Oct daily 10–4 ✋ Adult £5.50, child £2.80, under 5 free, family £14

WHEN TO GO
Plenty to see and visit indoors and out, so a good tour for when the weather is unsettled.

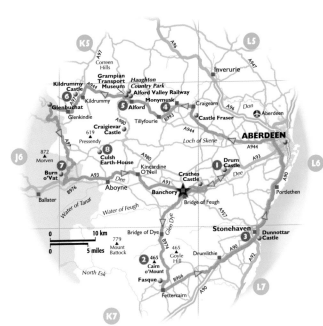

THE HIDDEN TREASURE OF STONEHAVEN

A bracing walk along the cliffs to ruined Dunnottar Castle.

THE WALK

Distance: 3.5 miles (5.7km)
Allow: 1 hour 30 minutes
Start/end: Market Square, Stonehaven
OS Explorer 273 Stonehaven
Grid reference NO 874858

★ Dunnottar Castle is a deliciously picturesque, glowering ruin perched on the edge of the cliffs and sprayed by the chilly northern seas. It was the setting for one of the most fascinating and little known episodes in Scotland's history, for Dunnottar Castle was the hiding place of the priceless Scottish regalia, or crown jewels, among the oldest in Europe. Also known as the Honours of Scotland, they comprise a crown, a sword of state and a silver sceptre. Together they are powerful symbols of Scotland's independence, and today are on display in the safety of Edinburgh Castle (▷ 68–69), along with the famous Stone of Destiny.

English Parliamentarian Oliver Cromwell invaded Scotland in 1650 and determined to destroy them, as he had done with the English crown jewels. His plan was foiled when they were spirited away from Edinburgh and taken to George Ogilvie, the King's Earl Marischal, at Dunnottar Castle for safe keeping.

Cromwell's men besieged the castle for nearly a year, but when it finally fell the jewels disappeared. They had been smuggled out by the wife of James Granger, the minister of nearby Kinneff, and her maid. The jewels remained hidden in the church at Kinneff, down the coast.

They were returned to Edinburgh after the Restoration of the Monarchy in 1660. Following the Act of Union with England in 1707, they were walled up in a sealed room in a tower in Edinburgh Castle. People eventually forgot where they were, and many believed they had been

stolen by the English. Sir Walter Scott rediscovered them, locked inside a dusty chest.

From the Market Square in Stonehaven, walk back on to Allardyce Street, turn right and cross over the road. Turn left up Market Lane and, when you come to the beach, turn right to cross over the footbridge. Turn right at a sign to Dunnottar Castle to reach the harbour. Cross here to continue down Shorehead, on the east side of the harbour. Pass the Marine Hotel, then turn right into Wallis Wynd.

Turn left into Castle Street. It becomes a steep path, to emerge at the main road, then maintain your direction walking along the road until it bends. Continue ahead, following the enclosed path, between arable fields and past a war memorial on the right-hand side. Cross the

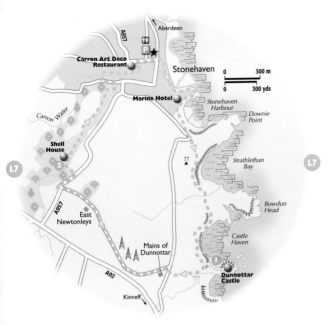

Aberdeen

A957

Carron Art Deco
Restaurant

Stonehaven

0   300 m
0   300 yds

Marine Hotel

Stonehaven
Harbour

Downie
Point

Carron Water

Shell
House

L7

2

Strathlethan
Bay

77

L7

Bowdun
Head

A957

East
Newtonleys

Mains of
Dunnottar

Castle
Haven

A92

Dunnottar
Castle

Kinneff

shells that decorate its interior. A movement sensor means it should light up as you approach close to it.

Pass the Shell House and continue along the lower path, which turns uphill to join a higher path. Bear right here, to reach the end of the woods at Carron Gate. Walk through a housing estate to join Low Wood Road and the River Carron.

Turn left, then right to cross the footbridge with the green railings. Turn right and walk by the water. You'll soon pass the striking art deco Carron Restaurant on the left-hand side, and then come to a cream-coloured iron bridge. Bear left here, then take the first right to return to the Market Square.

WHERE TO EAT
The Ship Inn (tel 01569 762617) by the harbour is a popular spot. You can get substantial dishes such as fish or pasta, as well as toasted sandwiches. The Marine Hotel (tel 01569 762155) nearby serves lunch and supper, as well as coffees.

PLACE TO VISIT
DUNNOTTAR CASTLE
✉ Dunecht Estates Office, Dunecht, Westhill AB32 7AW ☎ 01330 860223
🕐 Easter–end Oct daily 9–6; Nov–Easter Fri–Mon 9–dusk ♿ Adult £5, child (under 16) £1

WHEN TO GO
Visit on a fine day and explore Dunnottar Castle.

middle of the field, then above Strathlethan Bay.

The path turns right across the middle of a field and then over a footbridge. You now pass a path going down to Castle Haven and continue following the main path around the cliff edge. Cross another footbridge and bear uphill. Soon you'll reach steps on your left that run down to Dunnottar Castle.

❶ The ruined castle stands on a flat-topped rock stack, dominated by the remains of a 14th-century tower house. Additional buildings reflect 17th-century domestic life. Scenes from Mel Gibson's 1990 movie *Hamlet* were filmed here.

Your walk bears right here inland, past a waterfall, through a kissing gate and up to a house. Pass the house to the road into Stonehaven by the Dunnottar Mains, turn right, then take the first turn left, alongside

the farm. Follow this wide track past East Newtonleys on the left-hand side, to the main A957.

Turn right and walk downhill, then take the first road on the left, signed 'Dunnottar Church'. Follow this over the Burn of Glaslow to a path on the right signed 'Carron Gate'. Take this path into the woods but at once fork right, following the lower path that runs by the burn. Continue until you reach the Shell House on the left.

❷ The pretty little Shell House was built in the 19th century for the children of the local gentry. It gets its name from the thousands of

Opposite *Dunnottar Castle made a dramatic film location in 1990*
Right *Stonehaven's most attractive quarter is around the harbour*

REGIONS   HIGHLANDS AND ISLANDS • WALK

273

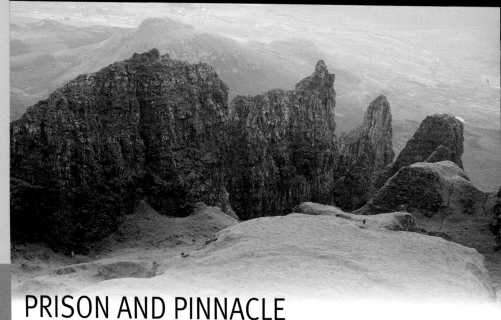

PRISON AND PINNACLE

Exploring the weird lava landscape of Skye's northern peninsula.

THE WALK

Distance: 5.25 miles (8.4km)
Allow: 3 hours
Start/end: Pull-off at the top of the pass on the Staffin–Uig road, Isle of Skye
OS Explorer 408 Skye
Grid reference NG 440679

★ The rocks of Scotland vary from ancient—about 400 million years—to a great deal older than that, but along the western edge is something quite different. The great eye of the Atlantic Ocean opened at a time that, geologically speaking, is this morning just before breakfast.

A mere 60 million years ago, the mid-Atlantic ridge lay just off the Scottish coast. And all along that ridge, new seabed emerged in exotic and interesting volcanic rocks that now form the Arran granite, the basalt of Mull and Skye, and the Skye gabbro. Basalt lava is a slippery liquid, like milk rather than treacle; it spreads in wide, shallow layers across the country.

After erosion, you get a flat-topped landscape, with long low cliffs at the edges and wide grassy plateaux.

North of Portree, the lava flowed out over older, softer rocks of Jurassic (dinosaur) age. All along the Trotternish peninsula, the sea has been steadily removing those softer rocks, and the basalt above has been breaking off in hill-sized chunks and slipping downhill and eastwards. The chunks lean over, split apart and erode: The result is some extraordinary scenery, of which the queerest is the Quiraing.

Take the well-built path that starts at a 'bendy road' sign opposite the lay-by (pull-off).

❶ The jagged tower of grass and rock on the skyline is grimly named The Prison. Some of its rock forms, with intriguing names such as the Prison, the Needle and the Fingalian Slab, have been a tourist must-see since Victorian times. As a result, a

wide, well-made path leads below these pinnacles, then back along the top.

The path crosses the steep landslip slope towards The Prison, with an awkward crossing of a small stream gully on bare rock, then passes a small waterfall high above and heads to the right rather than up into a rocky gap. It turns uphill into the wide col to the left of The Prison.

The main path does not drop, but goes forward, slightly uphill, crossing an old fence line at a crag foot. Follow as it crosses the foot of steep ground, then passes above a small peat pool. Ignore a path forking down right; the main path slants up left into a ridge where an old wall runs across.

The path descends into a landslip valley that runs across rather than down the hillside, then slants up left to a col with a stile. Cross over the

Above *Scottish primrose (Primula scotica)*
Right *Trotternish offers good hill-walking*
Left *The pinnacles of The Table*

stile and turn right for the excursion to Sron Vourlinn.

Follow the crest over a slightly rocky section with a short descent beyond, then join the main path along a grassy meadow with a very sudden edge on the right. After the highest point, continue slightly downhill to reach the north top.

2 Here at Sron Vourlinn you can see that the land is still slipping, with a crevasse beside the cliff edge where another narrow section is shortly to peel away.

Return to the col with the stile and continue uphill. The drops are now on your left, as you look down towards the pinnacles surrounding the Table, a gently undulating lawn.

After passing broken ground on the right, you come to a fallen wall, part of which appears from below as a cairn. The path continues next to the cliff edge on the left; you can fork off right, directly uphill.

3 Here you'll reach the summit trig point on Meall na Suiramach.

Follow a broad, gentle path slightly downhill to a cairn at the cliff edge.

4 You now look straight down on to the grassy feature known as The Table, 30m (100ft) below.

Turn right on the wide path. After a mile (1.6km), the path starts to descend alongside the cliff edge.

As the edge turns half right, you should turn fully right. The path is faint, but reappears ahead contouring around the fairly steep grass slope. Once above the parking area it turns straight downhill for a final steep descent.

WHERE TO EAT
The Pieces of Ate café at Brogaig (tel 01470 562787) lies at the foot of the hill road. It serves homemade snacks and soup from a small shack. Magnificently sited below the Quiraing crags, the Flodigarry Hotel (tel 01470 552203) offers evening meals and Sunday lunch at its restaurant, specializing in local lobster and other seafood. Bar meals are available in the public bar and conservatory.

WHEN TO GO
Set off early and do not attempt this walk in poor visibility.

WHAT TO DO

ABERDEEN

ALEX SCOTT AND CO (KILTMAKERS) LTD
This is the place to come to have a kilt made by hand—they'll help you determine your clan or tartan. You can also find other items of highland wear, such as sporrans.
✉ 43 Schoolhill AB10 1JT ☎ 01224 643924 💲 Mon–Wed, Fri, Sat 9–5, Thu 9–7

THE BELMONT
www.picturehouses.co.uk
Opened in 2000, this popular art house cinema shows independent, foreign and classic films. It also has French and Italian film festivals.
✉ 49 Belmont Street AB10 1JS ☎ 01224 343534 💲 Daily 💺 From £5.90 🍴 The Belmont café bar also hosts art exhibitions and has a film quiz every Tue

HIS MAJESTY'S THEATRE ABERDEEN
www.hmtheatre.com
The main theatre in Aberdeen, this is the venue for shows, plays, musicals, dance, opera and pantomimes.

✉ Rosemount Viaduct AB25 1GL ☎ 0845 270 8200/01224 641122 (box office) 💲 All year 💺 From £18 🍴 Two bars for pre-performance and interval drinks

MUSIC HALL
www.musichallaberdeen.com
Big classical concerts are held here, including performances by the Royal Scottish Orchestra and Scottish Chamber Orchestra. Also jazz, big band music, pop music and Christmas pantomime.
✉ Union Street AB10 1QS ☎ 01224 641122 (box office) 💲 All year 💺 From £8.50 🍴

🍺 OLD BLACKFRIAR'S
This pub in the city centre dates back to the time of Mary, Queen of Scots. It has a good selection of cask beers, is family-friendly and serves food. In its own words 'Centuries of history for the price of a pint.'
✉ 52 Castle Street AB11 5BB ☎ 01224 581922 💲 Mon–Sat 11am–12am, Sun 12.30–11

SLAINS CASTLE
One of the more unusual bars in the Belmont Street drag, Slains Castle occupies a former church and takes its name from the famous ruins up the coast near Cruden Bay.
✉ 14–18 Belmont Street AB10 1JE ☎ 01224 631877 💲 Fri–Sat 11am–1am, Sun–Thu 11am–midnight

ACHNASHEEN

THE STUDIO
www.studiojewellery.com
This contemporary, gallery-style shop has been in business for 25 years and stocks the largest selection of gold and silver jewellery anywhere in the Highlands. All the pieces are made in the studio. There is another branch on High Street, Fortrose.
✉ Achnasheen, by Strathconon Forest IV22 2E ☎ 01445 720227 💲 Mar–end Sep daily 9.30–5; est of year Mon–Sat 9.30–4.45 🍴 Great views from the Studio café

Opposite The Cairngorm Mountain
funicular railway
Left Making new friends at the Cairngorm
Reindeer Centre in Aviemore

CAIRNGORM REINDEER CENTRE
www.reindeer-company.demon.co.uk
Wear sensible footwear and suitable
outdoor clothes to visit the only herd
of reindeer in Britain (you can hire
wellington boots if needed). You can
get close up and even stroke the
reindeer by taking a tour out into
the hillside, where they roam freely.
Located 6 miles (10km) southeast
of Aviemore.
✉ Glenmore PH22 1QU ☎ 01479 861228
🕐 Daily 10–5; visits to the herd at
11am, all year; and at 2.30, May–end Sep
✋ Adult £9, child (6–16) £4.50, under 6
free, family £27 📅

ARDFERN
ARDFERN RIDING CENTRE
www.aboutscotland.com/argyll/appaloosa
Day rides, hacks, lessons and
cross-country jumps are all available
from this centre, overlooking Craobh
Haven yacht harbour and with
views to the Inner Hebrides. The
horses are Appaloosas. Advance
reservations advised.
✉ By Lochgilphead PA31 8QR ☎ 01852
500632 🕐 All year ✋ 1 hour £25, 2 hours
£40; tuition £30 per hour

AVIEMORE
CAIRNGORM MOUNTAIN RAILWAY
www.cairngormmountain.org
The highest in the UK, the
1.25-mile (2km) funicular Mountain
Railway is a great way for people
of all ages and physical abilities
to reach the top of Cairn Gorm to enjoy
the spectacular views. Advance
reservations advised during peak
holiday periods.
✉ CairnGorm Mountain Ltd PH22 1RB
☎ 01479 861261 🕐 May–end Oct daily
10–5.15; trains depart every 15 minutes; last
train up 4.30 ✋ Adult £9.25, child (6–16)
£5.85, under 5 free, family £27.55 🍴 The
Ptarmigan Restaurant, with a viewing
terrace, is the UK's highest restaurant, open
for lunch; dinner served Fri, Sat (Jul, Sep
only) 📅 Gift shop at the top

ELLIS BRIGHAM
www.ellis-brigham.com
This large shop on the main street
stocks ski and snowboarding clothes
and equipment, as well as mountain
and outdoor sports gear.
✉ 9–10 Grampian Road PH22 1RH
☎ 01479 810175 🕐 Daily 9–6

LOCH MORLICH WATERSPORTS
www.lochmorlich.com
This watersports centre on Loch
Morlich, in the Cairngorms National
Park, offers canoeing, kayaking,
windsurfing, mountain bicycling,
sailing and walking. Advance
reservations essential.
✉ Glenmore Forest Park, by Aviemore PH22
1QU ☎ 01479 861221 🕐 Apr–end Sep
✋ Kayak £8 per hour; rowing boat £15 per
hour; windsurfer £16 per hour 🍽 Café by
the loch

ROTHIEMURCHUS ESTATE
www.rothiemurchus.net
The 10,125ha (25,000 acre)
Rothiemurchus Estate to the south
of Aviemore has forests, rivers, lochs
and mountains, and is home to rare
native animals such as capercaillies
and red squirrels. The multi-activity
outdoor centre offers activities such
as guided walks, hill-walking, fishing,
clay pigeon shooting, bicycling and
off-road driving. Hill-walking and use

of the bicycle trails are free; phone
for prices of all other activities.
Advance reservations advised.
✉ By Aviemore PH22 1QH ☎ 01479
812345 🕐 Daily 9–5.30 📅

STRATHSPEY STEAM RAILWAY
www.strathspeyrailway.co.uk
This classic steam railway was
reopened by enthusiasts in 1978
and is still run almost entirely by
volunteers. Travel in first or third
class from the centre of Aviemore
through Boat of Garten and on to
Broomhill Station. Look for the Santa
Train in December.
✉ Aviemore Station, Dalfaber Road PH22
1PY ☎ 01479 810725 🕐 Mar–end Oct
✋ Adult from £10.50, child (5–15) £5.25,
under 5 free, family £26 🍽 Buffet car on
most services

BARCALDINE
ARGYLL POTTERY
www.argyllpottery.co.uk
Simple, high quality stoneware
pottery is hand-thrown on the
wheel at this pottery workshop
and shop on the southern shore of
Loch Creran, 8 miles (13km) north
of Oban.
✉ Barcaldine, by Oban PA37 1SQ ☎ 01631
720503 🕐 All year Mon–Fri 10–6, Sat 2–5

SCOTTISH SEA LIFE SANCTUARY
www.sealsanctuary.co.uk
This is Scotland's leading marine
animal rescue centre, caring
for seals, fish and otters. There
are feeding displays, talks, an
outdoor children's play area and an
underwater observatory.
✉ Barcaldine, by Oban PA37 1SE ☎ 01631
720386 🕐 Daily from 10am ✋ Adult
£10.50, child (3–14) £7.50, family £33
🍴 📅

BEAULY
HOUSE OF BEAUTY
www.houseofbeauty.com
This large specialist Scottish food
and gift shop sells high-quality
goods on two floors, including
crafts, knitwear, jewellery, ceramics,
furniture, food and drink. Tax-free
shopping for visitors from outside
the EU.

✉ Station Road IV4 7EH ☎ 01463 782821 ⊕ Mon–Sat 9.30–5.30, Sun 10–5 💻

BLACK ISLE
BLACK ISLE BREWERY
www.blackislebrewery.com
Located just 10 minutes from the A9 north of the Kessock Bridge, this small, independent brewery in an 18th-century house produces bottled light, dark and organic beers. Free tours every half-hour.
✉ Old Allangrange, Munlochy IV8 8NZ ☎ 01463 811871 ⊕ Mon–Sat 10–6; also Sun 11.30–5 Apr–end Sep

CARRBRIDGE
THE ARTIST STUDIO
www.carrbridgestudios.com
This gallery sells paintings and prints of local Cairngorm scenery, decorative pottery and ceramic jewellery. The pots are produced at nearby Carrbridge Studios, and by appointment you can visit the workshop. Carrbridge is 7 miles (11km) north of Aviemore.
✉ Main Street PH23 3AS ☎ 01479 8413328 ⊕ Apr–end Oct Mon–Fri 9–5, Sat 10–2, Sun 12–4; rest of year call to check times first

LANDMARK FOREST HERITAGE PARK
▷ 252.

CORPACH
SNOWGOOSE MOUNTAIN CENTRE
www.highland-mountain-guides.co.uk
This outdoor activities centre, on the A830 to Glenfinnan, offers abseiling (rappelling), hill-walking, kayaking and rock climbing in summer, with winter mountain sports and hill-walking in winter (Oct–end Apr). Suitable for age 8 and above. Advance reservations essential.
✉ The Old Smiddy, Station Road, Corpach, by Fort William PH33 7JH ☎ 01397 772467 ⊕ Daily, all year 💷 Prices depend on activities

CRAIGELLACHIE
THE MACALLAN DISTILLERY
www.themacallan.com
Enjoy a guided tour and tasting at the distillery, 13 miles (21km) from Elgin, and home of one of Scotland's favourite single malts.
✉ Easter Elchies, Craigellachie, Aberlour AB38 9RX ☎ 01340 872280 ⊕ Easter–end Sep Mon–Sat 9.30–4.30; Oct Mon–Fri 9.30–4; Nov–Easter Mon–Fri 11–3. Tours: Easter–end Sep, book first 💷 Adult £5, child (8–18) £2.50 (no children on extended tours) 💷 Adult £5, child (8–18) £2.50 (no children on extended tours)

DRUMNADROCHIT
LOCH NESS CRUISES
www.lochness-cruises.com
Join a hunt for the Loch Ness Monster on a cruise of the loch, with skippers who have studied these waters for years. The boat is equipped with Nessie-finding gear such as sonar and radar and there is an excellent photo opportunity as the cruise passes Urquhart Castle.
✉ The Original Loch Ness Visitor Centre IV3 6UR ☎ 01456 450395 ⊕ Tours Easter–end Oct, hourly in summer 💷 Adult £10, child £6. Reservations advised

DUFFTOWN
GLENFIDDICH DISTILLERY
www.glenfiddich.com
Take a tour of the famous whisky distillery and then try a dram yourself. Manufactured since 1887, it is the only Highland malt to be distilled, matured and bottled at the distillery, north of Dufftown.
✉ Dufftown, Keith AB55 4DH ☎ 01340 820373 ⊕ All year Mon–Fri 9.30–4.30; also Easter to mid-Oct Sat 9.30–4.30, Sun 12–4.30 💷 Free

EASDALE
SEA.FARI
www.seafari.co.uk
Enjoy an exhilarating adventure trip on a rigid inflatable boat to see

wildlife such as deer, wild goats, seals, seabirds, porpoises, dolphins and the occasional minke whale. Waterproof clothing provided. Minimum age 4. Advanced booking is essential. Easdale (Ellanbeich) village is on the bridge-linked island of Seil.

✉ Easdale Harbour, Seil Island, near Oban PA34 4RF ☎ 01852 300003 ⏱ Trips run all year, mainly Easter–end Oct, and are weather dependent ✋ 2-hour Corryvreckan Special: adult £33, child (under 16) £25, family £107

ELGIN

JOHNSTON'S OF ELGIN CASHMERE VISITOR CENTRE

www.johnstonscashmere.com
Take a tour of the only Scottish mill still to transform cashmere from fibre to clothes. There is an exhibition area, and a huge shop sells high quality cashmere and lambs wool clothes. Tax-free shopping for visitors from outside the EU.

✉ Newmill IV30 4AF ☎ 01343 554099 ⏱ Mon–Sat 9–5.30; Jun–end Dec also Sun 11–5 ▢

FOCHABERS

BAXTERS HIGHLAND VILLAGE

www.baxters.com
In whitewashed buildings beside the A96, this is the home of the Baxter family's food business, best known for its range of canned soups. You can enjoy cookery demonstrations and even taste new products. Several shops on the site sell food, kitchen items and Scottish gifts.

✉ IV32 7LD ☎ 01343 820666 ⏱ Jan to mid-Mar daily 10–5; mid-Mar to end Dec 9.30–5.30 🍴

WDCS WILDLIFE CENTRE

www.wdcs.org/wildlifecentre
Spey Bay and the nearby nature reserve are home to many birds, animals and plants including otters, ospreys, seals and bottlenose dolphins. Explore the dolphin exhibition with videos of the Moray Firth and farther afield. Follow the B9014 for 5 miles (8km) and head left at the Spey Bay Hotel.

✉ Tugnet, Spey Bay IV32 7PJ ☎ 01343 820339 ⏱ Apr–end Oct daily 10.30–5; call for out-of-season hours ✋ Free ▢ 🎁

FORRES

BRODIE COUNTRYFARE

www.brodiecountryfare.com
This group of shops in low, whitewashed buildings, sells high-quality Scottish gifts, outdoor clothes, kitchen and tableware, toys, games and Scottish foods. Located between Forres and Nairn.

✉ Brodie IV36 2TD ☎ 01309 641555 ⏱ Mon–Sat 9.30–5.30 (closes 5pm Oct–end Mar), Sun 10–5.30 (closes 5pm Oct–end Mar) ▢ Family restaurant serves coffee, snacks and meals

LOGIE STEADING VISITOR CENTRE

www.logie.co.uk
Shops in these converted former farm buildings, in the Findhorn Valley 6 miles (9.7km) south of Forres, sell second-hand books, antique furniture, crystal, plants and contemporary Scottish art. There's a walled garden and adventure playground. The visitor centre has information about the River Findhorn.

✉ IV36 2QN ☎ 01309 611278 ⏱ Mid-Mar to end Dec daily 10.30–5 ▢

Above *Downhill skiing is a popular winter sport*

FORT WILLIAM

BEN NEVIS

A large, friendly pub on the main street in Fort William, with comfortable leather chairs, a pool table, a real fire and real ales. Bar meals are available until 5pm and there is a restaurant upstairs (open until 10pm).

✉ 103 High Street PH33 6DG ☎ 01397 702295 ⏱ Mon–Wed 11am–midnight, Thu–Sat 11am–1am, Sun 12.30pm–11.30pm

JACOBITE STEAM TRAIN

www.steamtrain.info
The steam train (similar to the one featured as the 'Hogwarts Express' in the 2002 movie *Harry Potter and the Chamber of Secrets*) follows the scenic Road to the Isles. The train goes to Mallaig via Glenfinnan (where film scenes were shot at the great viaduct) and returns the same way.

✉ Fort William Railway Station ☎ 01524 737751 ⏱ Mid-May to early Oct Mon–Fri; late Jun–end Aug, Sat, Sun leaves Fort William 10.20 ✋ Day return: adult £29, child £16.50 ▢ 🎁 On-board souvenir shop

NEVIS RANGE

www.nevisrange.co.uk
Ski and snowboarding centre north of Fort William, with the highest skiing in Scotland. Ski runs from easy to very difficult, snowboard fun areas, off-piste skiing, a ski and

snowboard school and equipment rental. The mountain gondola takes you up Aonach Mòr.
✉ Torlundy PH33 6SW ☎ 01397 705825 🕐 Daily, closed early Dec, season usually Dec–end May; core hours 9–4, but check beforehand for times 👜 Gondola: adult £8.75, child (5–17) £5.25, family £23 🅿 🍴 Snowgoose restaurant and bar at the top gondola station

NEVISPORT
www.nevisport.com
A distinctive triangular glass atrium opposite the Alexandra Hotel holds the best outdoor clothing and equipment shop in the area. There's a huge selection to choose from, including waterproof jackets, boots, tents, books and maps, and there is also a craft shop. Staff can advise on outdoor activities in the area, and can also organize ski or mountain rental for you.
✉ High Street PH33 6EJ ☎ 01397 704921 🕐 Mon–Sat 9–5.30 (7pm in summer), Sun 9.30–5 🅿 🍴 Open from 11am

SCOTTISH CRAFTS & WHISKY CENTRE
This is the best craft shop in Fort William, with a range of very high-quality knitwear, rugs, pottery, glassware and books on offer, and a separate whisky shop.
✉ 135–139 High Street PH33 6EA ☎ 01397 704406 🕐 Jan–end Mar Mon–Sat 10–4; Apr to mid-Jun 9–5.30;

mid-Jun to end Aug 9–8; Aug–end Dec 9–5. Open Sun mid-Apr to mid-Sep Sun 10–4

INVERNESS
CASTLE GALLERY
www.castlegallery.co.uk
This outstanding contemporary art gallery has paintings, sculpture, prints, ceramics, glass, wood, textiles and jewellery by British artists. It's in an 18th-century building with vattle and daub walls.
✉ 43 Castle Street IV2 3DU ☎ 01463 729512 🕐 Mon–Sat 9–5

CLACHNAHARRY INN
There's a great view of the Moray Firth from the garden of this 17th-century coaching inn, which offers a good selection of whiskies and cask conditioned beers, and bar meals throughout the day. Over-18s only in the evening. Located 2 miles (3km) out of town on the A862, towards Beauly.
✉ 17–19 High Street, Clachnaharry IV3 8RB ☎ 01463 239806 🕐 Mon–Wed 11–11, Thu–Fri 11am–1am, Sat 11am–12.30am, Sun 12.30–midnight

EDEN COURT
www.eden-court.co.uk
The premier arts venue in the Highlands and Islands district. It continues to promote film, theatre and dance in a variety of alternative venues.

✉ Eden Court, Bishop's Road IV3 5SA ☎ 01463 234234 🕐 Daily 10–10 👜 Closed for refurbishment 🍴 Daily 10am–11pm

HOOTANANNY
A friendly town centre bar with traditional music and good food. After dinner enjoy the live music on most evenings. Over 18s only after 8pm.
✉ 67 Church Street IV1 1ES ☎ 01463 233651 🕐 Mon–Fri noon–1am, Sat noon–12.30am, Sun 7pm–12am. Food: Mon–Sat 12–3, 5–9

JOHNNY FOXES
www.johnnyfoxes.co.uk
The music is the main attraction at this welcoming riverside pub, with karaoke on a Wednesday night and live music every other night. Especially busy at weekends. The pub also offers a wide variety of food, from steak to veggie burgers. Over 18s only after 8pm.
✉ 26 Bank Street IV1 1QU ☎ 01463 236577 🕐 Mon–Sat 10am–2am, Sun noon–2am

ISLAY
ARDBEG DISTILLERY
www.ardbeg.com
Learn about this famous Islay malt in the visitor centre, then sample the whisky. The distillery was founded in 1815 and completely restored in 1997. Today it is one of eight remaining distilleries on Islay (there used to be 21!).
✉ Port Ellen PA42 7EA ☎ 01496 302244 🕐 Jun–end Aug daily 10–5; rest of year Mon–Fri 10–4; tours 10.30 and 5.30 👜 Adult £4, under 18 free 🅿 🎫

KINGUSSIE
HIGHLAND WILDLIFE PARK
www.highlandwildlifepark.org
The reserve has a viewpoint shelter where you can view red deer, Highland cattle and even some animals that are now extinct in the wild such as huge bison and ancient breeds of sheep and horses. A raised walkway takes you over the wolf enclosure. There is a children's trail and play area. Check ahead in

winter, as the park may not open in bad weather. Located 7 miles (11km) south of Aviemore.

✉ Kincraig PH21 1NL ☎ 01540 651270 🕐 Apr, May, Sep, Oct daily 10–6; Jun–end Aug 10–7; rest of year 10–4 ✋ Adult £10.50, child (3–15) £8 💻 🏫

LEWIS (ISLE OF)
HIGHLAND AIRWAYS
www.highlandairways.co.uk
For stunning views of the Hebrides from the air, join a flight from Stornoway airport on Lewis. Scenic flights take in Harris, Uist and Taransay. Flights are dependent on the weather. Advance reservations essential.

✉ Stornoway Airport HS2 0BN 0845 450 2245 ✋ From £69.99

MOSAIC CRAFTS AND GIFTS
High-quality Scottish and international ethnic crafts and jewellery, sold by friendly, Gaelic-speaking staff in this little shop by the harbour.

✉ 21 North Beach, Stornoway HS1 2XQ ☎ 01851 700155 🕐 Mon–Tue, Thu–Fri 9.30–5, Wed 10–5, Sat 10–5.30

OISEVAL GALLERY
www.oiseval.co.uk
Enjoy beautiful photographs of Hebridean landscapes by James Smith, displayed in a gallery in the photographer's house. All of the framed work on display is for sale. Brue is on the west coast.

✉ Brue HS2 0QW ☎ 01851 840240 🕐 Mon–Sat 10.30–5.30, but check times first

LOCH GARTEN
LOCH GARTEN OSPREY CENTRE
www.rspb.org.uk
Part of the RSPB's Abernethy Forest reserve, Loch Garten is famous for its ospreys, which feed on the fish here, and nest nearby. Watch the nest on a closed-circuit camera link at the RSPB centre.

✉ Tulloch, Nethy Bridge PH25 3EF ☎ 01479 831476 🕐 Easter–end Aug daily 10–6 ✋ Reserve free; Osprey Centre: adult £3, child (under 16) 50p, family £6 🏫

LOCH INSH
LOCH INSH WATERSPORTS
www.lochinsh.com
Join a half-day or full day of activities at this busy centre. Watersports include canoeing, windsurfing and sailing; try your hand at fishing, archery and skiing on the dry ski slope, or go for a mountain bicycle ride. An adventure area for children includes a climbing wall. Advance reservations essential. Loch Insh is 7 miles (11km) south of Aviemore.

✉ By Loch Insh, Kincraig PH21 1NU ☎ 01540 651272 🕐 All year daily 8.30–5.30; watersports Easter to mid-Oct ✋ Ski rental 1 day £17; sailing, 2 hours: adult £30 🍴 Boathouse bar and restaurant, open Feb–end Oct daily 10–10, rest of year daily 10–6 🏫

MONIACK CASTLE
MONIACK CASTLE WINERIES
www.moniackcastle.co.uk
Country-style wines, liquors and preserves are made from a variety of plants at this historic 16th-century castle, which lies 7 miles (11km) west of Inverness. See the wines being made and then make your choice in the shop.

✉ Moniack Castle, Inverness IV5 7PQ ☎ 01463 831283 🕐 Mar–end Oct Mon–Sat 10–5; rest of year 10–4 ✋ Tours: adult £2, child free 🏫

MULL (ISLE OF)
ISLAND ENCOUNTER
www.mullwildlife.co.uk
Join a full-day wildlife tour of the island, with a chance to see golden eagles, peregrine falcons, owls, otters, seals and porpoises. Lunch, snack and binoculars are provided. Advance reservations essential. Not suitable for very young children.

✉ Arla Beag, Aros PA72 6JS 01680 300441 🕐 All year, according to demand ✋ £34

MULL THEATRE
www.mulltheatre.com
Established in 1966, the theatre on Mull has a reputation much bigger than its size—the main theatre building used to be outside the village of Dervaig, but now a new centre has been built at Druimfin, just outside Tobermory. The resident theatre group performs original and established plays in summer, and may also tour productions around the Highlands. Advance reservations essential.

✉ Druimfin, Tobermory PA75 6QB ☎ 01688 302828/302673 🕐 May–end Sep, and some winter dates ✋ Vary from £8

Opposite Red deer at the Highland Wildlife Park in Kingussie
Below Windsurfing, one of many watersports on offer on Loch Insh

TOBERMORY CHOCOLATE COMPANY

www.tobermorychocolate.co.uk
This specialist sweet shop is above the handmade chocolate factory on the main street of Tobermory.
✉ 56–57 Main Street, Tobermory PA75 6NT ☎ 01688 302526 🕐 Mon–Sat 9.30–5; also Sun 11–5, summer school holidays only 💻

NORTH UIST
UIST OUTDOOR CENTRE

www.uistoutdoorcentre.co.uk
This outdoor activities centre offers diving, canoeing, rowing, sea kayaking, rock climbing and abseiling (rappelling), which you can do as a day visitor. Lochmaddy is noted for the richness of its birdlife. Advance reservations essential. Accommodation is also available.
✉ Cearn Dusgaidh, Lochmaddy HS6 5AE ☎ 01876 500480 🕐 All year 🖐 Full day: adult £65, child (under 12) £50; half-day: adult £32.50, child £25

OBAN
OBAN DISTILLERY

www.malts.com
There's been a distillery in the centre of Oban since 1794. Take a tour and see how the coastal location affects the taste of the whisky—it's rich and sweet, with a subtle hint of sea salt. Children are welcome, but under 8s are not admitted to production areas.
✉ Stafford Street PA34 5NH ☎ 01631 572004 🕐 Feb Mon–Fri 12–4; Mar–Easter, Nov 10–5; Easter–end Jun Mon–Sat 9.30–5; Jul–end Sep Mon–Fri 9.30–7.30, Sat 9.30–5, Sun 12–5; Oct Mon–Sat 9.30–5; Nov Mon–Fri 10–5; Jan, Dec closed 🖐 Adult £6, child (under 18) £3 🏧

OBAN INN

A large, white building on the seafront, this venerable pub dates from 1790, offers around 50 malt whiskies and a changing selection of real ales. Food is also served, with moules marinière the speciality of the house. Children welcome in the upstairs bar until 8pm.
✉ 1 Stafford Street PA34 5NJ ☎ 01631 562484 🕐 Mon–Sat 11am–12.45am, Sun 12.30pm–12.45am. Food served 12–10

O'DONNELL'S IRISH BAR

This Irish-themed pub in the town centre is popular with all ages, with live music most nights during the summer. Bar meals are available, and the restaurant is in a banqueting hall which dates from 1882. Over 18s only in the pub.
✉ Breadalbane Street PA34 5NZ ☎ 01631 566159 or 01631 565421 🕐 Sun–Wed 5pm–1am, Thu–Sat 2pm–2am

PUFFIN DIVE CENTRE

Booking office: George Street PA34 5NY Tel 01631 571190; www.puffin.org.uk
For an underwater view of Scotland's marine wildlife including fish, crabs and plants, try a shallow dive with an experienced instructor at this dive centre, 1.5 miles (2.4km) south of Oban at Port Gallanach. All equipment, including dry suits, is included. Advance reservations essential. Not suitable for children under 8.
✉ Port Gallanach PA34 4QH ☎ 01631 566088 🕐 Mon–Sat 8am–late, Sun 8–4 🖐 1.5-hour Try-a-Dive: £57.50 🏧

RAASAY
RAASAY OUTDOOR CENTRE

www.raasayoutdoorcentre.co.uk
On the little island of Raasay, off Skye (home to otters, deer, eagles and seals), the centre offers a range of activities such as fishing, walking, abseiling (rappelling), archery, canoeing and sailing. Advance reservations advised. Accommodation and camping also available. Currently closed for refurbishment.
✉ Currently closed for refurbishment

ROY BRIDGE
FISHING SCOTLAND

www.fishing-scotland.co.uk
Tuition and equipment for day and evening fly fishing excursions for wild brown trout and salmon around Lochaber. Advance reservations essential. Minimum age 8.
✉ Roy Bridge PH31 4AG ☎ 01397 712812 🕐 Fishing trips run all year, according to fish seasons 🖐 Private excursions arranged on request; price on application

SKYE (ISLE OF)
AQUAXPLORE

www.aquaxplore.co.uk
Join wildlife and watching tours on rigid hull inflatable boats, and see the isles around Skye too. Trips offer the chance to see basking sharks, dolphins, porpoises, puffins, minke whales and sea eagles. Trips can last from 1.5 hours to all day.
✉ Elgol IV49 9BJ ☎ 0800 731 3089 or 01471 866244 🕐 Easter–end Oct; times and prices vary according to trip; check website or phone for details. Booking essential

SEAPROBE ATLANTIS

www.seaprobeatlantis.com
Take a trip in a semi-submersible boat, which has underwater viewing windows. The trips are guided and give you the opportunity to see wildlife underwater, such as seals and porpoises, as well as marine kelp forests and a World War II shipwreck. Some trips go under the Skye Bridge. There is also the chance to see plenty of birdlife.
✉ Elgol IV49 9BJ ☎ 0800 731 3089 or 01471 866244 🕐 Easter–end Oct; sailing

times vary; check website or phone for details. Booking essential  1-hour trip: adult £12.50, child (4–14) £6.50, (2–3) £3, family £36; 2-hour trip: adult £24, child (4–14) £11, (2–3) £6, family £64

SKYE BATIKS
This shop sells a range of batik garments with ancient Celtic designs.
✉ The Green, Portree IV51 9BT 01478 613331 🕐 Jun–end Aug Mon–Fri 9–7, Sat 9–6, Sun 10–6; Sep–end May Mon–Fri 9.30–5.30

SKYE SILVER
www.skyesilver.com
This shop sells silver and gold jewellery, and other gifts, most with Celtic-style designs. Tax-free shopping for customers from outside the EU. It's 7 miles (11km) from Dunvegan, on the B884 to Glendale.
✉ The Old School, Colbost, Dunvegan IV55 8ZT ☎ 01470 511263 🕐 Mar–end Oct daily 10–6

SOUTH UIST
HEBRIDEAN JEWELLERY
www.hebridean-jewellery.co.uk
The distinctive jewellery in this shop comes in ancient Pictish and Celtic styles, as well as some contemporary designs. Items are made of gold and silver, and are

handmade—you can sometimes see craftspeople in the workshop here. You can also commission your own piece of jewellery. There are other branches at Portree on Skye, and on Stornoway. This branch on South Uist also has a café.
✉ Carnan, Lochdar HS8 5QX ☎ 018706 10288 🕐 Mon–Fri 9–5.30, Sat 9.30–5.30

SPEAN BRIDGE
SPEAN BRIDGE MILL
www.foreverscotland.com/mini_sites/spean_bridge
An extensive old mill has been converted to a bright Scottish goods shopping centre selling whisky, specialist foods, knitwear, cashmere, souvenirs, Harris Tweed and outdoor clothing. Regular weaving demonstrations are held during the week, and you can trace your clan history at the tartan centre. Located 10 miles (16km) north of Fort William.
✉ PH34 4EP ☎ 01397 712260 🕐 Mon–Sat 9.30–5, Sun 10–5 (closes 5.30 Apr–end Oct 🖥

STRATHDON
LECHT 2090
www.lecht.co.uk
This ski and snowboarding centre is ideal for families, and also offers tubing, quad biking and carting. A points card system means you

decide how much you want to spend and this is converted into points and loaded on to your card. Swipe the card to pay for your chosen activity. Fun carts are for age 10 and over, quad bikes for age 6 and over, kiddie karts are for age 4–10. The centre is on the A939 between Cockbridge and Tomintoul.
✉ Lecht 2090 Ski and Multi Activity Centre AB36 8YP ☎ 01975 651440 🕐 Daily 10–5; skiing daily from 8.30am, dependent on snowfall  Day ski rental: adult £15.75, child £10; 2-day package including lift pass, skis and instruction: adult £90, child (under 11) £70, child (secondary age) £80. Other activities from £4.50 🖥

ULLAPOOL
HIGHLAND STONEWARE
www.highlandstoneware.com
See this distinctive pottery being made and hand-painted by skilled craftspeople at the Ullapool factory and also on the shoreline at Lochinver. The full range of tableware is available in the shops and you can even commission your own tiles.
✉ North Road IV26 2UN ☎ 01854 612980 🕐 Mon–Fri 9–6; shop only also open Easter–end Oct Sat 9–5

Opposite *Sailing boat, Oban Bay*
Below *Portree harbour, on Skye*

EATING

PRICES AND SYMBOLS

The restaurants are listed alphabetically within each town. The prices are for a two-course lunch (L) and a three-course à la carte dinner (D). Prices in pubs are for a two-course lunchtime bar meal and a two-course dinner in the restaurant, unless specified otherwise. The wine price is for the least expensive bottle.

For a key to the symbols, ▷ 2.

ABERDEEN
MARYCULTER HOUSE
www.maryculterhousehotel.com
Enjoy a candle-lit dinner with fillet of Aberdeen Angus with potato and celeriac purée, rack of lamb on fried potatoes with wild mushroom ragout, and venison with pommes dauphinoise, red cabbage and Madeira jus. No children under 4.
✉ South Deeside Road, Maryculter AB12 5GB 01224 732124 ⏰ D only, 7.15–9.30 ✋ D £27, Wine £16.95 🚗 From Aberdeen take B9077 (South Deeside Road) for 8 miles (13km)

NORWOOD HALL
www.norwood-hall.co.uk
Dishes are classic with the odd Scottish twist: breast of pheasant is stuffed with haggis, while Grampian chicken is accompanied by black pudding mousse and a whisky sauce.
✉ Garthdee Road, Cults AB15 9FX ☎ 01224 868951 ⏰ 12–2, 7–9.30 ✋ L £23, D £29, Wine £18.50 🚗 From the south, leave the A90 at 1st roundabout, cross bridge and turn left at roundabout into Garthdee Road; continue for 1.5 miles (2.4km)

SILVER DARLING
www.silverdarlingrestaurant.co.uk
French cuisine includes locally landed seafood—try turbot, clams and mussels in a veal jus, with a starter of seared scallops served with Parmesan and balsamic syrup.
✉ Pocra Quay, North Pier AB11 5DQ ☎ 01224 576229 ⏰ 12–1.45, 7–9; closed L Sat, Sun, Christmas, New Year ✋ L £17, D £38, Wine £17

ACHILTIBUIE
THE SUMMER ISLES HOTEL
www.summerisleshotel.co.uk
The style is broadly European, the daily changing five-course menu could include goats' cheese crouton on black olive tapenade, and langoustine and spiny lobsters with hollandaise sauce. Lighter lunches are served in the bar. No children under 8 in the restaurant.
✉ By Ullapool IV26 2YG ☎ 01854 622282 ⏰ 12.30–2, D at 8; closed mid-Oct–Easter ✋ L £25, D £52, Wine £12.50 🚗 10 miles (16km) north of Ullapool. Turn left off A835 on to single-track road. 15 miles (24km) to Achiltibuie. Hotel 91m (100 yards) after post office on left

APPLECROSS
APPLECROSS INN
www.applecross.uk.com
Favourites include king scallops in garlic butter with crispy bacon on rice, and fresh monkfish and squat lobster in a rich prawn sauce on home-made tagliatelle. Or try

venison casserole with braised red cabbage on apple and wholegrain mustard mash, and raspberry cranachan or cardamom pannacotta.

✉ Shore Street IV54 8LR ☎ 01520 744262 🕐 Mon–Sat 11–11, Sun 12.30–11; closed 25 Dec, 1 Jan. Bar meals: daily 12–9 ✋ L £14, D £20, Wine £10.50 🚌 From Lochcarron to Kishorn, then left on to unclassifed road to Applecross

BALLATER
DARROCH LEARGE HOTEL

A modern approach to food at this long-established Deeside hotel. From a starter such as ravioli of smoked haddock with parmesan and chive cream, you might move on to loin of venison with creamed greens, chickpea croquette and goats'; cheese gnocchi.

✉ Braemar Road AB35 5UX ☎ 01339 755443 🕐 Daily 7–9, L Sun 12.30–2 ✋ D £45, Wine £22

BOAT OF GARTEN
BOAT HOTEL

www.boathotel.co.uk

Medallions of halibut, slices of veal and chargrilled lamb cutlets might feature as mains, with desserts like warm orange and toffee pudding on an apricot brandy sabayon. A seven-course tasting menu is also available. No children under 12.

✉ Deshar Road PH24 3BH ☎ 01479 831258 🕐 D only, 7–9; closed 3 weeks Jan ✋ D £35, Wine £13.50 🚌 Turn off A9 north of Aviemore on to A95. Follow signs to Boat of Garten

CAWDOR
CAWDOR TAVERN

Arbroath smokie and citrus mousse to start, then the traditional haggis, neeps and tatties. A daily specials menu might focus on confit of pheasant leg on a bed of clapshot, collops of Scottish beef fillet.

✉ The Lane IV12 5XP ☎ 01667 404777 🕐 May–end Oct daily 11–11; rest of year daily 11–3, 5–11; closed 25 Dec, 1 Jan. Bar meals: Mon–Sat 12–2, 5.30–9, Sun 12.30–3, 5.30–9. Restaurant: Mon– Sat 12–2, 6.30–9, Sun 12.30–3, 5.30–9 ✋ L £12, D £25, Wine £12.95 🚌 From A96, Inverness–Aberdeen road, take B9006 and follow signs for Cawdor Castle. Pub is in village centre

CLACHAN
BALINAKILL COUNTRY HOUSE HOTEL

www.balinakill.com

Sample fresh (and often organic) produce with a French twist: fillet of Kintyre sika venison in a claret reduction, and warm organic chocolate tart are two of the possibilities.

✉ PA29 6XL ☎ 01880 740206 🕐 D only, 7–9 ✋ D £28.95, Wine £14.50 🚌 10 miles (16km) south of Tarbert, on Loch Fyne, off A83

CLACHAN-SEIL
TIGH AN TRUISH INN

www.tigh-an-truish.co.uk

Seafood pie, moules marinière, salmon steaks and locally caught prawns feature, while other options might include steak and ale pie, followed by sticky toffee pudding.

✉ Oban PA34 4QZ ☎ 01852 300242 🕐 May–end Sep all day; rest of year 11–3, 5–11; closed 25 Dec, 1 Jan. Bar meals: daily 12–2, 6–8.30. Restaurant: daily 12–2, 6–8.30 ✋ L £9, D £15, Wine £8. No credit cards 🚌 14 miles (22.5km) south of Oban take A816. After 12 miles (19.3km) turn off B844 towards Atlantic Bridge

CRAIGELLACHIE
CRAIGELLACHIE HOTEL

www.craigellachie.com

A meal here could include a starter of smoked, whisky-marinated beef followed by baked fillet of sea bass on a sweet pimento and saffron salsa, with warm lemon dressing.

✉ AB38 9SR ☎ 01340 881204 🕐 12–2, 6–10 ✋ L £8.90, D £34.50, Wine £17.50 🚌 On A95 in the village centre

Opposite *Langoustines, large prawns and crawfish just landed at Mallaig*
Left *The River Spey at Boat of Garten*

DORNOCH
2 QUAIL RESTAURANT
www.2quail.com
A limited number of unfussy dishes form a set-price, four-course meal. Cheese and chive soufflé might be followed by a main of poached halibut supreme with an oyster ravioli and vermouth sauce. Advance reservations essential.
✉ Inistore House, Castle Street IV25 3SN ☎ 01862 811811 🕐 D only, 7.30–9.30; closed Sun and Mon, Christmas, 2 weeks Feb–Mar 🖐 D £39, Wine £15.50 🚗 Just before cathedral

FORT WILLIAM
INVERLOCHY CASTLE
www.inverlochycastlehotel.com
Creative, seasonal Scottish food such as roast loin of roe deer with a fig crust, and baked rice pudding with spiced pineapple. Dinner is a four-course set menu.
✉ Torlundy PH33 6SN ☎ 01397 702177 🕐 12.30–1.30, 6 for 6.30 or 9 for 9.30 for non-residents 🖐 L £28, D £65, Wine £75 🚗 Hotel is 3 miles (4.8km) north of Fort William on A82

MOORINGS
www.moorings-fortwilliam.co.uk
The menu is modern, and West Coast seafood and Highland game are regular features. Classics such as bangers and mash, or fisherman's creel pie are typical. There are several vegetarian choices.
✉ Banavie PH33 7LY ☎ 01397 772797 🕐 D only, 7–9.30 🖐 L £14, D £19, Wine £13.95 🚗 3 miles (4.8km) north, off A830. Take A830 for 1 mile (1.5km), cross the Caledonian Canal, then take 1st right

GAIRLOCH
THE OLD INN
www.theoldinn.net
Locally caught seafood is used for Mediterranean-style bouillabaisse, or home-made seafood ravioli. Highland game also features. Children welcome.
✉ IV21 2BD ☎ 01445 712006 🕐 Daily 11–12am. Bar meals: daily 12–9.30. Restaurant: daily 6–9.30 🖐 L £12, D £25, Wine £9.95 🚗 Just off A832, near harbour at southern end of village

GLENELG
GLENELG INN
Local produce is used for such dishes as fresh scallops pan-fried with organic garlic butter and roast lemon, followed by fresh West Coast collops of monkfish, prawns and smoked haddock in flaked pastry with white wine, slow roasted broccoli and dill sauce. Meat dishes include roast chicken with lime, garlic and chilli on spiced lentils. Vegetarian dishes are available.
✉ IV40 8JR ☎ 01599 522273 🕐 12–11 (bar closed lunchtimes during winter). Bar meals: daily 6–8.45 🖐 D £23, Wine £15 🚗 From Shiel Bridge (A87) take unclassified road to Glenelg

GLENFINNAN
THE PRINCE'S HOUSE
www.glenfinnan.co.uk
The restaurant offers local food, with a short menu reflecting the best of seasonal cooking.
✉ PH37 4LT ☎ 01397 722246 🕐 D only, 7–9. Closed Christmas, Jan–Feb; by reservation only in winter 🖐 D £32, Wine £12.35 🚗 On A830, 17 miles (27km) north of Fort William

GRANTOWN-ON-SPEY
THE GLASS HOUSE RESTAURANT
www.theglasshouse-grantown.co.uk
This conservatory restaurant uses fresh local ingredients in an imaginative way. Starters might include avocado with grilled black pudding and an orange and watercress salad. A typical main would be seared Morayshire beef with chestnut mushrooms, asparagus and garlic cream potatoes.
✉ Grant Road PH26 3LD ☎ 01479 872980 🕐 L 12–1.45 (Sun 12.3–2) , D Tue–Sat 7–9; closed L Tue, D Sun and all day Mon 🖐 L £9.95, D £29, Wine £14.25

THE PINES
www.thepinesgrantown.co.uk
The menu features traditional British and Scottish fare, with an emphasis on game. Local produce is used whenever possible. Pre-order during the afternoon the likes of warm pigeon salad with lentils and bacon, followed by sea bass and herb risotto.
✉ Woodside Avenue PH26 3JR ☎ 01479 872092 🕐 D only from 9.30; closed Nov–end Feb 🖐 D £35, Wine £14 🚗 Woodside Avenue is off A939 to Tomintoul, on outskirts of town

HARRIS, ISLE OF
SCARISTA HOUSE
www.scaristahouse.com
The set menu at this haven for food lovers might feature a rich and intense langoustine bisque, followed by navarin of Harris lamb with dauphinoise potatoes. Pudding might feature brown bread ice cream with glazed fresh figs and port syrup. No children under 7.
✉ Scarista HS3 3HX ☎ 01859 550238 🕐 L 12–3, D daily at 8; closed 25 Dec

L £15, D £34.50, Wine £13.50 On A859 15 miles (24km) south of Tarbert

INVERNESS

ABSTRACT RESTAURANT
www.abstractrestaurant.com
This hotel restaurant offers a range of modern French dishes, with top-quality local produce. Try a starter of scallops and asparagus in frothy fennel milk, followed by wild duck served in two sauces.
20 Ness Bank IV2 4SF 01463 223777
Tue–Sat 7–9 D £42, Wine £18
On the riverside opposite the theatre, five minutes from the town centre

BUNCHREW HOUSE
www.bunchrew-inverness.co.uk
Expect West Coast crab cake with braised scallops, roast loin of west Highland lamb, and caramelized lemon tart with an Armagnac sauce.
Bunchrew IV3 8TA 01463 234917
12–1.45, 7–9 L £21, D £39, Wine £15 2.5 miles (4.4km) from Inverness on A862 towards Beauly

RIVERHOUSE
Start with fresh oysters served with lemon, red wine and shallot dressing. Mains range from Dover sole and pan-seared scallops to Aberdeen Angus fillet steak. No children under 8.
1 Greig Street IV3 5PT 01463 222033
12–2.15, 5.30–10; closed Mon and Sun Sep–end Apr L £11.50, D £28.95, Wine £18.50 On the corner of Huntly Street and Greig Street

ROCPOOL RESERVE
www.rocpool.com
Sleek, contemporary hotel restaurant in the city centre, serving classic dishes with a modern flourish. There are two menus, one featuring modern Italian dishes. Starters might include pan-fried red mullet, or Scottish hand-dived scallops. Mains might be roast Goosnargh duck with honey and spices, or pan-fried calves' liver with smoked pancetta, polenta and a marsala sauce.
Culduthel Road 1V2 4AG 01463 240089 L £12.95, D £37, Wine £13.50

ISLAY

THE HARBOUR INN
www.harbour-inn.com
Local specialities might include pheasant, partridge and woodcock, or a special recipe fish chowder. Many dishes are paired with whiskies from local distilleries.
The Square, Bowmore PA43 7JR
01496 810330 12–2, 6–9 L £20, D £35, Wine £13.75 8 miles (13km) from the ports of Port Ellen and Port Askaig

KILBERRY

KILBERRY INN
www.kilberryinn.com
Everything served here is home-made. Menu favourites include Kilberry sausage pie, spinach and ricotta pasta and venison game pie.
PA29 6YD 01880 770223 11–3, 6.30–10.30; closed Nov–end Mar. Restaurant: Tue–Sun 12.15–2.15, 6.30–9 L £16, D £27, Wine £15 From Lochgilphead take A83 south. Take B8024 signposted Kilberry

KILCHRENAN

THE ARDANAISEIG
www.ardanaiseig.com
The classical French cuisine might feature Inverawe smoked trout with potato salad, trout caviar and herb oil, followed by herb crusted saddle of lamb with Provençale vegetables. Dinner is a set six-course tasting menu, which can be adapted for individual preferences (such as vegetarian diets) if you inform them when making the reservation. No children under 7.
PA35 1HE 01866 833333
12.30–2, 7–9; closed 2 Jan–11 Feb
L £10, D £45, Wine £16 Take A85 to Oban. At Taynuilt turn left on to B845 towards Kilchrenan. In Kilchrenan turn left by pub. Hotel in 3 miles (4.8km)

TAYCHREGGAN
www.taychregganhotel.co.uk
The five-course dinner menu is based largely on traditional recipes and fresh local ingredients: Loch Awe rainbow trout served with a bouquet of asparagus tips might be followed by monkfish with smoked haddock dauphinois and a black cauliflower fricassée.
PA35 1HQ 01866 833211
12.30–2, 7.30–8.45 L £12.50, D £40, Wine £14.95 West from Crainlarich on A85 to Taynuilt. Then on B845 to Kilchrenan and Taychreggan

Above *The Museum and Bell Tower at Grantown-on-Spey*

KINGUSSIE
THE CROSS
www.thecross.co.uk
Chef David Young's cooking is simple with an emphasis on seasonality. Scallops served with pannacotta and fennel oil might be followed by fillet of beef with red onion marmalade and chips (french fries), and the meal rounded off by lemon tart. The wine collection is notable. No children under 9.
✉ Tweed Mill Brae, Ardbroilach Road PH21 1LB ☎ 01540 661166 🕓 D only, at 7; closed Sun–Mon, Christmas and Jan ✋ D £45, Wine £18 🚗 From traffic lights in town centre go uphill along Ardbroilach Road for 330m (330 yards), turn left into Tweed Mill Brae

LOCHGILPHEAD
CAIRNBAAN
www.cairnbaan.com
The carte specializes in fresh local produce, notably langoustines, scallops and game. Loch Etive mussels, smoked salmon and smoked trout pâté for starters, while mains might include breast of pheasant with haggis en croûte, lobster and fillet of halibut. There's also a bistro-style menu.
✉ Cairnbaan PA31 8SJ ☎ 01546 603668 🕓 12–6. Bar meals: daily 12–2.30, 6–9.30. Restaurant: D only, daily 6–9.30 ✋ L £15, D £22, Wine £13.50 🚗 2 miles (3.2km) north of Lochgilphead on A816, bear left, hotel off B841

LOCHINVER
INVER LODGE HOTEL
www.inverlodgehotel.co.uk
Stunning sea views this restaurant of this hotel. Local produce features in dishes such as pan-fried sea bass with courgette spaghetti and shellfish bisque; home-smoked pigeon breast with beetroot salsa; spinach and peppercorn crepes with vegetables in Madeira sauce. No children under 10.
✉ IV27 4LU ☎ 01571 844496 🕓 Tue–Sat; closed Nov–end Mar ✋ L £6.75, D £40, Wine £16.95 🚗 Take A835 to Lochinver, left at village hall, private road for 0.5 miles (1km)

LUSS
COLQUHOUN'S
www.loch-lomond.co.uk
The cooking style is simple: A sample menu includes lobster ravioli with creamed leeks and tarragon, followed by roast wild venison with red cabbage and black pudding, rounded off by hot chocolate fondant.
✉ Lodge on Loch Lomond Hotel G83 8PA ☎ 01436 860201 🕓 L Mon–Sat 12–2.30, Sun 12.30–3.30; D 6–9.45 ✋ L £15, D £29.95, Wine £15.95 🚗 30 miles (48km) north of Glasgow on A82

NETHY BRIDGE
MOUNTVIEW HOTEL
www.mountainviewhotelnethybridge.co.uk
Imaginative dinners might include layered wild mushroom pancake with a hazelnut cream, roast monkfish with a butter bean and vanilla stew, then warm pecan nut tart with ginger sauce.
✉ Grantown Road PH25 3EB ☎ 01479 821248 🕓 D only, 6–9, Sun 12–2; closed Mon–Tue, Christmas ✋ D £28, Wine £13.95 🚗 From Aviemore follow signs for Nethy Bridge through Boat of Garten. Go through Nethy Bridge, hotel on right

OBAN
EEUSK
www.eeusk.com
All but two of the varieties of wet fish on offer are landed in the harbour here, and the fish is simply prepared. Halibut with creamed leeks and sautéed potatoes followed by clootie dumpling are bound to warm you on a breezy day. No children under 10 after 6pm.
✉ North Pier PA34 5QD ☎ 01631 565666 🕓 12–2.30, 6–9.30; closed 25–26 Dec, 1 Jan ✋ L £20, D £27, Wine £11.95

ISLE OF ERISKA
www.eriska-hotel.co.uk
There is a modern twist to classic dishes at the exclusive hotel restaurant. Fine Scottish produce and daily changing specials include mains such as roast Aberdeen Angus beef, served with horseradish sauce and Yorkshire pudding. Fresh oysters and scallops are always available. Indulgent desserts might include a hot chocolate Madeleine with rhubarb compote and gingerbread ice cream. There is a set five-course menu for dinner.
✉ Ledaig, by Oban PA37 1SD ☎ 01631 720371 🕓 12.30–1.30, 8–9 ✋ L £25, D £39, Wine 12.50 🚗 Take A85 to Oban, at Connel bridge take A828 to Bendeloch village for 4 miles (6km)

ONICH
ONICH
www.onich-fortwilliam.co.uk
The menu features traditional and more contemporary takes on Scottish specialities. The bar food offers good value for money.
✉ PH33 6RY ☎ 01855 821214 🕓 D only, 7–9 ✋ D £22, Wine £12.50. Bar meals 12–9, £10 🚗 Beside A82, 2 miles (3.2km) north of Ballachulish Bridge

Left *The Three Chimneys Restaurant and House Over-By*

Below *View over Wester Ross, Shieldaig*

PLOCKTON
PLOCKTON INN & SEAFOOD RESTAURANT
www.plocktoninn.co.uk
Local fish and shellfish are smoked locally. Lunch includes a seafood platter from the smokery and moules marinière. A more extensive dinner menu might include venison collops with bramble and port sauce.
✉ Innes Street IV52 8TW ☎ 01599 544222 ◷ Mon–Sat 11am–midnight, Sun 12.30–11. Bar meals: daily 12–2.30, 6–9. Restaurant: daily 12–2.30, 6–9 ✋ L £13, D £18, Wine £10.95

SHIELDAIG
TIGH AN EILEAN HOTEL
www.stevecarter.com
There are two excellent dining choices at this hotel. Relaxed meals can be taken in the hotel's pub, the Shieldaig Bar and Coastal Kitchen, which focuses on fresh fish dishes such as fish and chips, Shieldaig crab bisque with home-made bread, or fresh Loch Torridon langoustines with garlic mayonnaise. The hotel's restaurant offers a set three-course dinner which changes regularly. It may feature roast cannon of venison with a quince and red onion marmalade, or escalope of Scottish salmon with broccoli mousse and dill cream.

✉ IV54 ☎ 01520 755251 ◷ Bar meals 12–2.30, 6–8.30; restaurant 7–8.30 ✋ L £15, D £44, Wine £15 🚗 From Torridon take A896 5 miles (8km) to Shieldaig

SKYE, ISLE OF
CUILLIN HILLS HOTEL
www.cuillinhills-hotel-skye.co.uk
Local meat, fish and game feature largely: steamed Loch Eilort mussels might be followed by braised saddle of venison and pigeon with red wine, topped off with a dark chocolate terrine.
✉ Portree IV51 9QU ☎ 01478 612003 ◷ 12–2, 6.30–9; closed L Mon–Sat ✋ L £13, D £32.50, Wine £15 🚗 0.25 miles (0.5km) north of Portree on A855

ROSEDALE
www.rosedalehotelskye.co.uk
Emphasis is placed on fresh, local and organic produce in the imaginative set-price menu. Expect locally caught fillet of Skye cod or a cannon of Highland lamb
✉ Beaumont Crescent, Portree IV51 9DB ☎ 01478 613131 ◷ D only, 6.30–8.30; closed Nov–end Mar ✋ D £28, Wine £14.95 🚗 On harbour front

THREE CHIMNEYS RESTAURANT AND HOUSE OVER-BY
www.threechimneys.co.uk
Starters might include crab risotto cake with langoustines, while mains might include beef with caramelized onions and pommes Anna. For

dessert try brioche bread and butter pudding with Seville orange anglaise. Advance reservations recommended.
✉ Colbost IV55 8ZT ☎ 01470 511258 ◷ 12.30–2.30, 6.30–9.30; closed L Sun, 1 week Dec, 3 weeks Jan ✋ L £22.50, D £50, Wine £18.50 🚗 From Dunvegan take B884 to Glendale

STONEHAVEN
TOLBOOTH
www.tolboothrestaurant.co.uk
At this award-winning seafood restaurant, the day's catch is marked up on a blackboard, and locally sourced fish and seafood is the mainstay, although non-fish eaters are also catered for.
✉ Old Pier Road AB3 2JU ☎ 01569 762287 ◷ Tue–Sat 12–2, 6–9.30; closed 3 weeks after Christmas ✋ L £12, D £27, Wine £16.95 🚗 15 miles (24km) south of Aberdeen on A90

STRACHUR
CREGGANS INN
www.creggans-inn.co.uk
The fixed-price dinner offers three or four dishes per course, such as saddle of lamb, with bacon, mushrooms and Savoy cabbage; and roast fillet of beef with tian of black pudding.
✉ PA27 8BX ☎ 01369 860279 ◷ Bar meals 12–2.30, 6–8.30, D only 7–9 ✋ L £10, D £30, Wine £16.50 🚗 Follow A82 along Loch Lomond to Arrochar, then west on A83 and A815 to Strachur

PRICES AND SYMBOLS

Prices are the starting price for a double room for one night, unless otherwise stated. Breakfast is included unless noted otherwise. All the hotels listed accept credit cards unless otherwise stated. Note that rates vary widely throughout the year.

For a key to the symbols, ▷ 2.

ABERDEEN
THE MARCLIFFE AT PITFODELS

www.marcliffe.com

Set in attractive landscaped grounds, bedrooms are well proportioned and equipped, and there is a restaurant, and a cocktail lounge.

✉ North Deeside Road AB15 9YA
☎ 01224 861000 🖐 £215 ① 42 🚗 Turn off A90 on to A93 signposted Braemar. Hotel 1 mile (1.5km) on right after turn-off at traffic lights

ARDUAINE
LOCH MELFORT

www.lochmelfort.co.uk

This popular, family-run hotel has outstanding views; and the cuisine is based around fresh seafood. The skerry bistro serves lighter meals and afternoon teas.

✉ By Oban, PA34 4XG ☎ 01852 200233
🖐 £138 ① 23 🚗 On A816, midway between Oban and Lochgilphead

AVIEMORE
THE OLD MINISTER'S HOUSE

www.theoldministershouse.co.uk

Beautifully furnished and immaculately maintained, bedrooms are spacious. There is a lounge, and hearty breakfasts are served. No children under 12.

✉ Rothiemurchus PH22 1QH ☎ 01479 812181 🖐 £76 ① 4 🚗 From Aviemore take the B970, signed Glenmore and Coylumbridge. B&B is around 0.75 miles (1.2km) from Aviemore at Inverdruie

BALLACHULISH
BALLACHULISH HOUSE

www.ballachulishhouse.com

Bedrooms are tastefully decorated, with many thoughtful touches, and the atmosphere is friendly and welcoming. The sitting room has an open fire, and top Scottish cuisine is served in the dining room.

✉ PH49 4JX ☎ 01855 811266 🖐 £125 ① 8 🚗 Off A82 on to A825 Oban road. Guesthouse is 400m (440 yards) on left just beyond Ballachulish Hotel

BALLATER
DARROCH LEARG

www.darrochlearg.co.uk

Elegant day rooms include a drawing room and a former smoking room. The restaurant serves modern Scottish cuisine. Some bedrooms have four-poster beds.

✉ Braemar Road AB35 5UX ☎ 01339 755443 🖐 £130 including dinner ① 17
🕐 Closed Christmas and Jan (except New Year) 🚗 Hotel on the A93, at western edge of Ballater

LOCH KINORD HOTEL

www.lochkinord.com

This family-run hotel makes an excellent base for leisure and sporting activities in Deeside. The rooms are well appointed and one has a four-poster bed. There's a pleasant garden, restaurant and even a pub, in a separate building at the back of the hotel.

✉ Ballater Road, Dinnet ☎ 01339 885229 ✋ £95 🛈 22

BANCHORY
RAEMOIR HOUSE
www.raemoir.com
Public rooms include sitting rooms, a cocktail bar and a dining room. The bedrooms are individual in style and size. There are also some self-catering apartments. Facilities nearby include tennis courts, shooting, deer stalking and a 9-hole golf course.
✉ Raemoir AB31 4ED ☎ 01330 824884 ✋ £140 🛈 20 🚗 Take A93 to Banchory, turn right on to A980 to Torphins. The main drive is 2 miles (3.2km) ahead at the T-junction (intersection)

BRORA
GLENAVERON
www.glenaveron.co.uk
Two bedrooms are pine-furnished and one has lovely period pieces. There is a lounge, and breakfasts are served house-party style.
✉ Golf Road KW9 6QS ☎ 01408 621601 ✋ £68 🛈 3 🚗 From the south, cross bridge in the middle of Brora, turn right off A9 into Golf Road and take 2nd left. Second house on the right

ROYAL MARINE
www.highlandescapehotels.com
This splendid mansion has a leisure centre (with pool, spa and Jacuzzi). An 18-hole golf course and tennis court are nearby. There's a restaurant, a café-bar and a snooker room.
✉ Gold Road KW9 6QS ☎ 01408 621252 ✋ £130 🛈 22 🚗 Off A9 in village, towards beach and golf course

CARDROSS
KIRKTON HOUSE
www.kirktonhouse.co.uk
Bedrooms are individual in style with lots of extras, and home-cooked breakfasts are served in the dining room. Riding stables are nearby.
✉ Darleith Road G82 5EZ ☎ 01389 841951 ✋ £70 🛈 6 🕐 Closed Dec–end Jan 🚗 0.5 miles (800m) north of village, turn

north off A814 into Darleith Road at west end of village. Kirkton House is 0.5 miles (800m) on the right

CLACHAN-SEIL
WILLOWBURN
www.willowburn.co.uk
Friendly, attentive service and fine food. There is a homey bar with a veranda, a formal dining room and a lounge. No children under 8.
✉ PA34 4TJ ☎ 01852 300276 ✋ £170, including dinner 🛈 7 🕐 Closed Dec–end Feb 🚗 0.5 miles (800m) from Atlantic Bridge, on left

DUNDONNELL
DUNDONNELL
www.dundonnellhotel.com
A beautiful but isolated location with a range of attractive and comfortable public areas and a choice of eating options and bars. Many of the bedrooms enjoy fine views.
✉ Little Loch Broom IV23 2QR ☎ 01854 633204 ✋ £90 🛈 32 🚗 Off A835 at Braemore junction (intersection) on to A832. Hotel is 14 miles (22km) farther on

ELGIN
MANSION HOUSE
www.mansionhousehotel.co.uk
Facilities include a lounge, a bar, a leisure centre with spa, a bistro and a formal restaurant. Many bedrooms are spacious and feature four-poster beds.
✉ The Haugh IV30 1AW ☎ 01343 548811 ✋ £143 🛈 23 🏊 🍴 🚗 In Elgin turn off the A96 into Haugh Road, the hotel is at the end of the road by the river

ERISKA
ISLE OF ERISKA
www.eriska-hotel.co.uk
Situated on its own private island with beaches and walking trails, spacious bedrooms are comfortable with some antique pieces. Local produce features on the restaurant menu, as do vegetables and herbs grown in the hotel's kitchen garden. An indoor swimming pool and spa treatment rooms are available, along with private fishing and nature trails.
✉ Ledaig PA37 1SD ☎ 01631 720371 ✋ £300, including dinner 🛈 17

🕐 Closed Jan 🏊 🍴 🚗 Leave A85 at Connel, join A828; continue for 4 miles (6.4km) through Benderloch, then follow signs

FORT WILLIAM
ASHBURN HOUSE
www.highland5star.co.uk
The bedrooms are spacious, and there is a conservatory lounge and a dining room; breakfast is cooked on an Aga. No children under 12.
✉ 8 Achintore Road PH33 6RQ ☎ 01397 706000 ✋ £80 🛈 7 🚗 At the junction (intersection) of the A82 and Ashburn Lane, 457m (500 yards) from the large roundabout at the southern end of High Street; or 366m (400 yards) on the right after entering 30mph zone from the south

THE GRANGE
www.thegrange-scotland.co.uk
Two of the bedrooms have loch views. The dining room serves hearty breakfasts. No children under 13.
✉ Grange Road PH33 6JF ☎ 01397 705516 ✋ £98 🛈 4 🕐 Closed Nov–end Mar 🚗 Leave Fort William on the A82 south. 274m (300 yards) from the roundabout go left on to Ashburn Lane. The Grange is at the top on the left

LIME TREE
www.limetreefortwilliam.co.uk
The Lime Tree is a charming and contemporary small hotel, with its own art gallery. The hotel has comfortable lounges with real fires, and a restaurant serving excellent local produce. The rooms are individually designed and spacious.
✉ Achintore Road PH33 6RQ ☎ 01397 701806 ✋ £80 🛈 9

GRANTOWN-ON-SPEY
CULDEARN HOUSE
www.culdearn.com
This hotel has the atmosphere of a relaxed country house. Fresh Scottish produce is served in the restaurant. No children under 10.
✉ Woodlands Terrace PH26 3JU ☎ 01479 872106 ✋ £112 🛈 6 🕐 Closed Jan–end Feb 🚗 Enter Grantown on A95 from the southwest and turn left at 30mph sign

MUCKRACH LODGE
www.muckrach.co.uk
This hotel has recently been refurbished to a high standard. There's a bar and restaurant and some rooms have four-poster beds. There is self-contained accommodation for families. It is close to several golf courses and on the edge of the Cairngorm National Park.
✉ Dulnain Bridge PH26 3LY ☎ 01479 851257 🖐 £89 🛈 12 🕓 Closed 5–20 Jan 🚗 Leave A95 at Dulnain Bridge exit, follow A938 towards Carrbridge; hotel 500m (500 yards) on right

HARRIS, ISLE OF
SCARISTA HOUSE
www.scaristahouse.com
Food lovers will know of this restaurant with rooms. The house is run in a relaxed country house manner, so expect wellies (rubber boots) in the hall and books and CDs in one of the two lounges.
✉ Scarista HS3 3HX ☎ 01859 550238 🖐 £175 🛈 5 🕓 Closed Christmas 🚗 On A859, 15 miles (24km) south of Tarbert

INVERNESS
BALLIFEARY GUESTHOUSE
www.ballifearyhousehotel.co.uk
This house in its own grounds offers comfortable bedrooms. There is a lounge and the breakfasts use local produce. No children under 15.
✉ 10 Ballifeary Road IV3 5PJ ☎ 01463 235572 🖐 £70 🛈 6 🕓 Closed Christmas 🚗 Off A82, 0.5 miles (800m) from the town centre, turn left into Bishops Road and sharp right into Ballifeary Road

CULLODEN HOUSE
www.cullodenhouse.co.uk
Some bedrooms are located in a separate house. No children under 10.
✉ Culloden IV2 7BZ ☎ 01463 790461 🖐 £250 🛈 28 🕓 Closed 24–28 Dec 🚗 Take A96 from town and turn right for Culloden. After 1 mile (1.5km), turn left at White Church after 2nd traffic lights

GLENMORISTON TOWN HOUSE
www.glenmoriston.com
Bold contemporary designs blend seamlessly with the classical architecture. Bar and restaurant. The bedrooms are well equipped.
✉ 20 Ness Bank IV2 4SF ☎ 01463 223777 🖐 £130 🛈 30 🚗 On the riverside opposite the theatre, five minutes from the town centre

MOYNESS HOUSE
www.moyness.co.uk
This elegant villa offers beautifully decorated bedrooms and well-fitted bathrooms. There is a sitting room, a dining room where traditional Scottish breakfasts are served, and a garden.
✉ 6 Bruce Gardens IV3 5EN ☎ 01463 233836 🖐 £72 🛈 6 🚗 Off A82 Fort William road, almost opposite Highland Regional Council headquarters

ROCPOOL RESERVE
www.rocpool.com
This boutique hotel in the centre of Inverness offers a luxurious and contemporary retreat. Rooms range from 'extra decadent'—with outdoor hot tubs—to 'chic' garden rooms. The hotel has a fine dining restaurant and also a bar/brasserie for more relaxed meals.
✉ 14 Culduthel Road, IV2 4AG ☎ 01463 240089 🖐 £165 🛈 11

TRAFFORD BANK
www.traffordbankguesthouse.co.uk
Bedrooms in this impressive Victorian villa are furnished with restored traditional furniture, and thoughtful extras.
✉ 96 Fairfield Road IV3 5LL ☎ 01463 241414 🖐 £80 🛈 5 🚗 Turn off A82 at Kenneth Street, take 2nd left, Fairfield Road, Trafford Bank is 549m (600 yards) on left

KINGUSSIE
OSPREY HOTEL
www.ospreyhotel.co.uk
Dinner uses local produce, and hearty breakfasts include home-baked breads and preserves. Bedrooms vary in size and style.
✉ Ruthven Road PH21 1EN ☎ 01540 661510 🖐 £60 🛈 8 🚗 Turn off A9 into Kingussie, hotel is at the southern end of the main street

MULL, ISLE OF
HIGHLAND COTTAGE
www.highlandcottage.co.uk
Bedrooms feature antique beds and a range of extras. Public areas include a lounge, an honesty bar, and a conservatory. No children under 10.
✉ Breadalbane Street, Tobermory PA75 6PD ☎ 01688 302030 🕓 Mid-Mar to late Oct only 🖐 £150 🛈 6 🚗 A848 Craignure/Fishnish ferry terminal, pass Tobermory signs, go ahead at mini-roundabout across narrow bridge, turn right. Hotel on the right opposite the fire station

TOBERMORY HOTEL
www.thetobermoryhotel.com
Pretty pink-washed hotel on the seafront. Rooms, converted from fishermen's cottages, are simply furnished, with some individual features such as window seats. Some have sea views. The hotel's restaurant serves fresh local produce.
✉ 53 Main Street PA75 6NT ☎ 01688 302091 🖐 £90 🛈 15 🚗 On the waterfront, overlooking Tobermory Bay

NAIRN
BOATH HOUSE
www.boath-house.com
Five-course dinners are matched only by the excellence of the breakfasts. The house itself is delightful, with inviting lounges and a dining room overlooking a trout loch. Bedrooms include many fine antique pieces.
✉ Auldearn IV12 5TE ☎ 01667 454896 🖐 £190 🛈 8 🕓 Closed Christmas 🚗 2 miles (3.2km) past Nairn on A96 driving east towards Forres, signposted on main road

OBAN
GLENBURNIE HOUSE
Bedrooms include a four-poster room and a mini suite. There is a lounge and traditional breakfasts are served in the dining room. No children under 12.
✉ The Esplanade PA34 5AQ ☎ 01631 562089 🖐 £74 🛈 14 🕓 Closed Nov–end Mar 🚗 Directly on Oban waterfront, follow signs for Ganavan

Above *The CalMac ferry heading towards Oban's harbour*

MANOR HOUSE
www.manorhouseoban.com
The Georgian Manor House, built in 1780 as the dower house for the family of the Duke of Argyll, has a welcoming atmosphere. A daily-changing five-course dinner is served in the dining room. Most of the bedrooms are furnished with period pieces and many of them have views across the bay. No children under 12.
✉ Gallanach Road PA34 4LS ☎ 01631 562087 ✋ £108 ❶ 11 ⏰ Closed 25–26 Dec ⛟ Follow signs for MacBrayne Ferries, go past ferry entrance, hotel is on right

POOLEWE
POOL HOUSE HOTEL
www.poolhousehotel.com
Set on the shores of Loch Ewe where the river meets the bay, this hotel, run very much as a country house, has spacious bedrooms and stunningly romantic suites. Local produce features strongly on the menus. No children under 8.
✉ IV22 2LD ☎ 01445 781272 ✋ £255 ❶ 7 ⏰ Closed Jan–end Feb ⛟ 6 miles (10km) north of Gairloch on A832. Located in the middle of Poolewe village

PORT APPIN
AIRDS
www.airds-hotel.com
The front-facing bedrooms enjoy the views of Loch Linnhe, as do the lounges and restaurant. The well-equipped bedrooms provide style and luxury, and many of the bathrooms are fitted with marble and have power showers. Expertly prepared dishes, using the finest ingredients, are served in the elegant dining room.
✉ Appin PA38 4DF ☎ 01631 730236 ✋ £245, including dinner ❶ 11 ⏰ Closed 5–26 Jan ⛟ From Ballachulish Bridge take the A828 south for 16 miles (26km), turn right and continue for 2 miles (3.2km)

SHIELDAIG
TIGH AN EILEAN
There are three comfortable lounges and an honesty bar at this delightful small hotel, with views over the bay. The brightly decorated bedrooms are comfortable, but don't expect a television, except in one of the lounges. The dinner menu features seafood and quality local produce, with lighter snacks served at lunchtime.
✉ IV54 8XN ☎ 01520 755251 ✋ £150 ❶ 11 ⏰ Closed late Oct–end Mar ⛟ From A896 take the village road signposted Shieldaig. The hotel is in the village centre on loch front

SKYE, ISLE OF
HOTEL EILEAN IARMAIN
www.eileaniarmain.co.uk
Bedrooms are individual and traditional, and there are four suites. Public rooms are homey. Facilities include private fishing and whisky tasting.
✉ Isle Ornsay IV43 8QR ☎ 01471 833332 ✋ £100 ❶ 16 ⛟ A851, A852, right to Isle Ornsay harbour front

STRONTIAN
KILCAMB LODGE
www.kilcamblodge.co.uk
Bedrooms in this former hunting lodge are well decorated. The short choice of dishes uses local produce.
✉ PH36 4HY ☎ 01967 402257 ✋ £130 ❶ 11 ⛟ Off A861, via Corran Ferry

TAIN
GLENMORANGIE HIGHLAND HOME AT CADBOLL
www.theglenmorangiehouse.com
This highly individual hotel has bedrooms in both the main house and in converted farm cottages. Prices include afternoon tea, a four-course dinner and wines.
✉ Cadboll, Fearn IV20 1XP ☎ 01862 871671 ✋ £230, including dinner ❶ 9 ⛟ From A9 turn on to B9175 towards Nigg and follow signs

TORRIDON
LOCH TORRIDON COUNTRY HOUSE HOTEL
www.lochtorridonhotel.com
Most bedrooms enjoy Highland views, the day rooms are comfortable, and the whisky bar stocks over 300 malts. Wide range of outdoor activities include shooting, bicycling, horseback riding and walking.
✉ By Achnasheen IV22 2EY ☎ 01445 791242 ✋ £225, incuding dinner ❶ 19 ⏰ Closed 3–27 Jan ⛟ From A832 at Kinlochewe, take A896 towards Torridon; do not turn into village, instead carry on for 1 mile (1.5km). Hotel on right

ULLAPOOL
DROMNAN
www.dromnan.com
This friendly modern house offers attractive bedrooms with private facilities. The lounge/breakfast room overlooks Loch Broom. Minimum two-night stay July and August.
✉ Garve Road IV26 2SX ☎ 01854 612333 ✋ £60 ❶ 7 ⛟ From the A835 south on entering the town, turn left at 30mph sign

ORKNEY AND SHETLAND

Although the islands of Orkney are visible from the Scottish mainland, the Orcadians have a fierce independence of spirit and a culture all of their own. Orkney owes as much to Scandinavia as it does to Scotland, and the islands were only annexed to Scotland in 1468 by the future king James III; prior to this they belonged to Norway. The history of these 67 islands (17 of them inhabited) goes back even further, of course, and they are thought to have been first inhabited 5,500 years ago. Among their many attractions, which have seen parts of Orkney declared a UNESCO World heritage Site, are the prehistoric village of Skara Bare, standing stones such as the Stones of Stenness, and ancient burial tombs.

The Scandinavian links are much more emphatic in the hundred or so islands that make up Shetland. Even the name of the group comes from the Norse word, Hjaltland. These were annexed to Scotland by James III in 1469. The population today is only about 23,000, with one main settlement, Lerwick, accounting for almost 7,000. The rest are spread over the remainder of the main island, Mainland, and the 14 other islands that are also inhabited. Most people make their living from farming and fishing, although the petroleum industry is also important, as is tourism. Among the attractions that bring visitors, apart from just the magical experience of the islands themselves, are wildlife areas such as the Isle of Noss and Hermanesse, the Jarlshof Prehistoric and Norse Settlement and a range of 'most northerly in Britain' places, including the most northerly phonebox, the most northerly settlement at Skaw, the most northerly castle (Muness Castle) and the most northerly brewery, called Valhalla.

ORKNEY

This low-lying green and fertile cluster of more than 70 islands and skerries lies off the northern coast of Scotland, usually clearly within view of the mainland, and separated by the churning waters of the Pentland Firth. Approaching on the ferry from Scrabster or Aberdeen, the first view of Hoy, with its tall rock stacks and slabby red sandstone cliffs, is misleading.

Only when the boat swings towards the harbour at Stromness is a more typical view of Orkney revealed, low and green and richly fertile, with cattle grazing and crops growing on this well-farmed land, and brown trout lurking in the lochs. On a warm summer day, the scent of wild flowers in the clear air of these islands is invigorating.

Kirkwall, on the eastern side of Mainland, the largest island in the archipelago, is the capital. There is much to explore among the islands, which are linked by causeway, ferry or air, including the shortest scheduled air route in the world—just under two minutes for the 1.5-mile (2.4km) flight between Westray and Papa Westray.

Orkney, like Shetland, shares a close history with Scandinavia and tends to regard itself as a part of Britain which is separate from Scotland, having little in common with, say, the deeply religious and Gaelic culture of the Western Isles. Orkney became part of Scotland in the 15th century, part of a dowry when Margaret of Denmark married Scottish king James III. Today these islands ring with Norse-sounding placenames, although Picts and Celts pre-dated the Vikings by at least 3,500 years, leaving extraordinary signs of their presence at Maes Howe and Skara Brae.

Reminders of a more recent history are also all around, in the remains of gun emplacements and the giant concrete blocks of the Churchill Barriers, recalling a time when the sheltered bay of Scapa Flow was a vital naval base through two world wars.

INFORMATION

www.visitorkney.com

349 6 Broad Street, Kirkwall KW15 1NX, tel 01856 872856 or 0845 225 5121 From Aberdeen (6 hours) or Scrabster, by Thurso (1 hour 30 minutes), or Lerwick (8 hours); John O'Groats (40 minutes), summer only Kirkwall

Above *The old harbour of Stromness, Orkney's second town*
Opposite *A day at the beach on the Bay of Skail*

HOY

The second largest of the Orkney islands, Hoy derives its name from the Old Norse term Ha-ey, meaning 'high island'. Its best-known feature is the columnar stack of red sandstone just off the western cliffs, known as the Old Man of Hoy. Standing 137m (450ft) high, it is a challenge for climbers. The heather covered hills of Cuilags (433m/1,420ft) and Ward Hill (479m/1,570ft) offer excellent walking country.

This sheltered bay was home to the Royal Navy during two world wars, and famously the site of the scuttling of the German fleet after the end of World War I, in 1919. The remains now prove popular with divers. Learn more at the fascinating Scapa Flow Visitor Centre and Museum, in the former naval base at Lyness (Mon–Fri 9–4; also mid-May to end Sep Sat, Sun 10.30–4).

Near Rackwick, the Dwarfie Stane is a neolithic chambered cairn hollowed out of a single solid rock.

In the north of the island is an important RSPB reserve, from where you can look back and get good views of the Old Man of Hoy. In the breeding season the climbers there sometimes get dive-bombed by protective parents. Among the big attractions at the reserve are the ever-popular puffins, great skuas and raptors such as hen harriers. These are best seen in the spring, while in summer the cliffs are alive with the squabbling, nesting sea birds. You can also see whales and dolphins in the waters here during summer.

There is a poignant monument on Hoy to Betty Corrigall. In the 1770s she killed herself when her boyfriend left her, unmarried and pregnant, while he went to sea on a whaling ship. As a suicide she could not be buried in consecrated ground. For years she lay in an unmarked grave until her body was moved in 1940 to its present location and she was given a decent reburial.
✚ 349 K3 ℹ 6 Broad Street, Kirkwall KW15 1NX, tel 01856 872856 or 0845 225 5121 🚢 From Houton, on Mainland, to Lyness, and from Stromness to Moaness

ITALIAN CHAPEL

After a German U-boat successfully broke into Scapa Flow in 1939 and sank HMS *Royal Oak* with the loss of 833 lives, it became clear that further defences were needed to block access to this vital natural harbour. Italian prisoners of war were drafted in to construct massive concrete blocks, which were piled between Mainland and the eastern islands of Lamb Holm, Glimps Holm, Burray and South Ronaldsay to form impregnable causeways known as the Churchill Barriers.

The Italian workers created their own memorial, converting two Nissen huts to make a chapel. The inside is beautifully painted with frescoes and *trompe-l'oeil* on plasterboard and concrete mouldings, with even a rood screen. The result is extraordinary, and a moving tribute to the ingenuity, skill and imagination of the prisoners, so far from home, which the islanders have carefully preserved.
✚ 349 K3 ✉ Dunedin, St. Mary's, Lamb Holm KW17 2RT ☎ 01856 781268 🕐 Daily dawn–dusk 💷 Free, donations welcome

Opposite The remarkable painted interior of the Italian Chapel
Bottom left The Italian Chapel was created by Italian prisoners of war
Below Looking towards St. John's Head, Hoy

KIRKWALL

This is the main town of Orkney.
There's been a settlement here
since the 11th century, but most of
the compact buildings seen in the
narrow, paved streets of the old
harbour town today date from the
16th to the 18th centuries. The long
main street is lined with interesting
little shops, including high-quality
crafts and jewellers.

Dominating all is the red
sandstone bulk of St. Magnus
Cathedral on Broad Street, begun
by Earl Rognvald in 1137 (great-
nephew of St. Magnus, murdered
20 years before) and completed
in the 15th century (Apr–end Sep
Mon–Sat 9–6, Sun 2–6; rest of
year Mon–Sat 9–1 and 2–5). Inside,
the huge Romanesque pillars and
decorative stonework create a sense
of space and peace. One of the best
views is from the top of the ruins
of the nearby Bishop's Palace (HS,
Mar–end Sep daily 9.30–5.30).

While here, have a taste of the
local Highland Park whisky, from
Scotland's most northerly distillery
(tours every half-hour, May–end Aug
Mon–Sat 10–5, Sun 12–5; Apr, Sep,
Oct Mon–Fri 10–5; and Nov–end Mar
at 2pm only).
349 K2 6 Broad Street, Kirkwall
KW15 1NX, tel 01856 872856 or 0845 225
5121 Kirkwall

MAES HOWE

www.historic-scotland.gov.uk
A 7m (23ft) high grassy mound
in a field to the south of Loch of
Harray, on the road from Stromness
to Finstown, Maes Howe looks
unpromising at first sight. Under
the turf, however, lies a chambered
grave dating from around 2800BC
which is a treasure of World
Heritage status.

You must take your turn and bend
double to walk through the 14.5m
(47ft) entrance passageway, before
you emerge into the beautifully
formed inner chamber, which is
almost 4.5m (15ft) square. The walls
are lined with neatly fitting stone
slabs, the roof is corbelled, and
there are three small side chambers.
While the contents were looted
centuries ago and can only be
guessed at, the structure itself has
survived more or less undamaged,
barring some runic graffiti left by
passing Vikings.

The nearby Ring of Brogar is
a magnificent stone circle, with
surrounding ditch.
349 K2 By Tormiston Mill, Mainland
KW16 3HA 01856 761606 Apr–end
Sep daily 9.30–5; Oct–end Mar daily 9.30–4;
advance reservations only. Tours hourly
(HS) Adult £5.20, child (5–16) £2.60,
under 5 free

SKARA BRAE
▷ opposite.

STROMNESS

Orkney's second town, Stromness,
has a history that is closely tied to
the sea. Houses and stores on the
waterfront date from the 18th and
19th centuries, each with its own
slipway—a good view of this is from
the windows of the Pier Arts Centre
(Mon–Sat 10.30–5). The Arts Centre
is a gallery specializing in exhibitions
of modern art.

The town's winding main street is
paved with the local huge sandstone
slabs, and cobbles; follow it to
its southern end, to the maritime
delights displayed in the excellent
Stromness Museum on Alfred
Street (Apr–end Sep daily 10–5;
rest of year Mon–Sat 11.30–3.30;
closed mid-Feb to mid-Mar). It offers
a maritime history of the town.
Stromness boomed in the early 19th
century, a centre for Arctic whaling,
and a key stopping point for vessels
of the Hudson's Bay Company who
took on crew and supplies here,
and fresh water from nearby Login's
Well. Look out for the barnacle-
encrusted treasures recovered by
divers from the sunken German fleet
in Scapa Flow.
349 K2 Ferry Terminal Building,
Ferry Road, Stromness KW16 3BH, tel
01856 850777 or 0845 225 5121 From
Scrabster

*Top left St. Magnus Cathedral is Orkney's
grandest building*
*Top right The Ring of Brogar stone circle,
northeast of Stromness*

SKARA BRAE

The remains of a stone-built neolithic village, concealed for centuries under the sand, are Orkney's 'must see' sight, offering a unique window into a domestic world long gone. It is tempting to believe that our prehistoric ancestors, who left so little record of their daily existence, were not very clever and lived wretchedly in dark hovels. A visit to Skara Brae suggests otherwise, and can be an eye-opening experience. Lying 19 miles (30km) northwest of Kirkwall, it is the site of a village, inhabited between 3100 and 2500BC, probably originally some distance from the sea.

At some point the sands encroached and covered the houses, which lay undiscovered until a great storm in 1850 revealed the presence of stone structures. Subsequent excavation showed nine very similar houses linked by winding passageways, their dry-stone walls buried to the eaves by the surrounding midden pits, which probably provided some degree of insulation.

EXPLORING THE SITE

As you walk around the site today, you are looking down into the houses from above, through what would have been roofs of skin and turf laid over timber spars or whalebone. Slabs of the local flagstone were used to create central hearths, cupboards in the walls, bed surrounds, clay-lined troughs in the floor, and even a dresser, suggesting a level of sophistication that is as delightful as it is unexpected.

A reconstructed house by the visitor centre shows how animal skins and bracken would have helped to make the dwellings cosy, and fragments of jewellery, tools and pottery give further insights into the lives of these mysterious people. And although very little is known about them, it's easy to relate to the kind of people they must have been—fixing their fishing hooks, protecting themselves against the elements, occasionally putting on their finery, just as people still do today.

INFORMATION

www.historic-scotland.gov.uk
✚ 349 K2 ✉ Sandwick KW16 3LR
☎ 01856 841815 🕐 Easter–end
Sep daily 9.30–5.30; rest of year daily
9.30–4.30 👋 (HS) adult £6.50, child
(5–16) £3.25, under 5 free
🍴 On-site restaurant seats 90 people
🎁 Gift shop in visitor centre stocks local
Orkney-made products

Above *Walkways between the houses let you see straight down into them*
Below *An example of Skara Brae's unusual stone furniture*

SHETLAND

Shetland, with a population of around 24,000, is the most northerly part of Britain, lying as close to the Faroes and Bergen in Norway as it does to Aberdeen. Its place on northern trade routes has given it an unusually cosmopolitan air, and a culture that is more Viking than Scots, with a broad dialect, the January festival of Up Helly Aa, a rich heritage of skilled knitting, and a vibrant tradition of fiddle music which has been exported around the world by musicians such as Aly Bain (1945–).

The landscape of these islands is wild and rugged, with low hills, exposed rock, and peaty, waterlogged moorland. Few trees survive the wind, but the wild flowers grow large and sublime, and nowhere is farther than 5 miles (8km) from the sea. Seals and porpoises are common sights around the indented coastline, and thousands of seabirds nest here, including puffins, black guillemots and gannets.

The capital is the harbour town of Lerwick, halfway up the east side of the main island. Scalloway, west of Lerwick, was the medieval heart of the island, and is dominated by its ruined castle, built in 1600. The Scalloway Museum features a fishing boat which took part in the secret 'Shetland Bus' sea link to resistance fighters in Norway during World War II (May–end Sep Mon–Sat 10–12, 2–4.30).

Shetland's prosperity rose sharply at the end of the 20th century with the exploitation of oil and gas fields in the North Sea. The money has funded new roads, new inter-island ferries and modern community centres on many of the islands, as well as other public facilities. Sullom Voe, one of the largest oil and gas terminals in Europe, lies at the north of the main island.

Flights from the mainland come in to Sumburgh, at the southern tip. There are air and sea links to other main islands and to Fair Isle, the isolated island between Orkney and Shetland which is famous as the stopover point for more than 350 species of migrating birds (May–end Oct observatory).

INFORMATION

www.visitshetland.com

346 ℹ Market Cross, Lerwick ZE1 0LU, tel 08701 999440; seasonal

From Aberdeen (14 hours); also summer ferries from Bergen in Norway via the Faroes and Iceland ✈ Sumburgh, at the southern tip of Mainland

Above *Shetland's Viking Up Helly Aa festival takes place in January*
Opposite *Looking towards St. Magnus Bay, Mainland*

JARLSHOF PREHISTORIC AND NORSE SETTLEMENT

www.historic-scotland.gov.uk

Complex layers of history were first uncovered at this fascinating site above the sea, near the southern tip of Shetland, when a mighty storm dislodged the covering turf. The most obvious survivor is the shell of the 17th-century Laird's House, which is the only structure to stick up above ground. This overlies a prehistoric broch which, it would seem, was converted during the Iron Age into a round-house. All around the site are the remains of a Viking farm dating from the ninth century, complete with the outline of a communal longhouse that was almost 20.7m (68ft) long.

Further layers have revealed a settlement from the second century BC, a medieval farm dating from the 14th century and a 16th-century laird's house, making an intriguing record of life here over the years. Signboards clarify what you see.

Migrant whooper swans can be seen in autumn on the nearby reserve of Loch of Spiggie.

✠ 346 A3 ✉ Sumburgh ZE3 9JN ☎ 01950 460112 🕐 Apr–end Sep daily 9.30–12.30, 1.30–5.30 ✋ (HS) Adult £4.70, child (5–16) £2.35 🎁 🍴 In nearby Sumburgh Hotel

LERWICK

It was Dutch herring fishermen who made Lerwick the capital of the islands, when they started using its sheltered harbour in the 17th century. Today the compact grey town stretches out to either side, with a bustling main thoroughfare one row back, stone-flagged Commercial Street.

The old harbour is active with local ferries, fishing boats and pleasure craft. Bigger ferries, cruise ships and support vessels for the oil industry tend to use the less vibrant modern harbour 1 mile (1.5km) to the north. In the shops, knitwear produced using traditional, intricate patterns is a local speciality, and if you can't see what you want, nimble-fingered workers will soon make you a garment to your own choice of pattern or colour.

Fort Charlotte, a five-sided artillery fort originally dating from 1665, is one of the oldest buildings in Shetland, and also worth seeing (keys available locally (HS) tel 01856 841815). There are good views to the island of Bressay.

The new Shetland Museum in Lerwick (Mon–Wed, Fri, Sat 10–5, Thu 10–7, Sun 12–4) overlooks the harbour and has over 3,000 artefacts on local heritage and culture. These

Above *Multiple layers of history are revealed at Jarlshof's fascinating site*
Opposite top *Eerie Mousa Broch*
Right *Puffins on Unst*

are on display over the two floors that house the collection. Highlights include a preserved lump of butter that was found in a peat bog and was a tax payment to the King of Norway before Shetland became a part of Scotland.

✠ 346 A2 ℹ Market Cross, Lerwick ZE1 0LU, tel 08701 999440

MOUSA BROCH

www.mousaboattrips.co.uk

The double-skinned circular tower of Mousa Broch dates from 100Bc to AD300, and is the best preserved example of its kind in Scotland. The walls stand up to 13m (43ft) high, and the small gaps between the neatly placed stones now provide nesting sites for tiny storm petrels.

The broch was built on a small island, off the eastern coast of southern Shetland, which suggests it had a defensive role at some time—but nobody quite understands how people lived in and used these structures. The island has no human inhabitants today, and is a designated Site of Special Scientific Interest (so no dogs allowed). Access in summer is via a small passenger boat from Leebitton, in Sandwick. There are good views to the broch from the main road near Sandwick.

✚ 346 A2 ℹ Market Cross, Lerwick ZE1 0LU, tel 08701 999440 🚢 Boat trips on *Solan IV* Apr to mid-Sep; check times beforehand, trips dependent on weather. Adult £12, child (5–16) £6. Reservations essential, tel 01950 431367

ST. NINIAN'S ISLE

St. Ninian's Isle is a green jewel, a tiny grass-covered island off the western side of southern Shetland.

It is joined to the land by a curved tombolo of silvery shell sand, which permits access except during the highest tides of the year, and makes for lovely walking. St. Ninian came from the monastery at Whithorn in Dumfries (▷ 124), the first Christian missionary to reach Shetland, and the ruins of a church from the 12th century are on the island.

In 1958 a hoard of beautifully worked Pictish silver was discovered, buried under the nave. The treasure is now in the National Museum of Scotland in Edinburgh (▷ 72–75), but replicas can be seen in the Shetland Museum in Lerwick.

✚ 346 A2 ℹ Market Cross, Lerwick ZE1 0LU

UNST

Much of Unst's fame rests on its status as the most northerly of the

Shetland isles. In this way, it can claim the most northerly house in Britain at Skaw. The nature reserve at Hermaness is no gimmick, however, but home in summer to 100,000 screaming seabirds which nest on and around the 167.4m (558ft) cliffs (free access; visitor centre: mid-Apr to mid-Sep daily 9–5). Look out for puffins and guillemots, fulmars and large, creamy gannets. Beware the great brown Arctic skuas, which are inclined to dive-bomb visitors if they feel their moorland nest sites are threatened (local people know them as bonxies).

There are great views to the lighthouse (1858) on the exposed rock of Muckle Flugga.

✚ 346 B1 ℹ Market Cross, Lerwick ZE1 0LU, tel 08701 999440 🚢 Regular ferry service to Unst from Yell

THE GLOUP LOOP

A circular walk around the nature reserve of Mull Head.

THE WALK

Distance: 4 miles (6.4km)
Allow: 2 hours 30 minutes
Start/end: Mull Head parking area (free), Mainland Orkney
OS Explorer 461 Orkney
Grid reference HY 590079

★ The parish of Deerness is a peninsula joined to Orkney's Mainland only by a very narrow spit. Nearby archaeological excavations have turned up an Iron-Age settlement, a Pictish farm, obvious Norse remains and a hog-back gravestone in the kirkyard dating from AD1100.

Leave the parking area at the right-hand corner and follow the direction sign along the gravel path to the Gloup, where you will find two viewing platforms and an information plaque.

❶ The Gloup, from the Old Norse word gluppa, meaning chasm, is not the only collapsed cave in Orkney, but at 30m (100ft) deep, it is the most visited. The rocks which you see as you walk the headland are 350 million years old. There are two types: Eday flags, which are coarse red sandstone, and Rousay flags at the south end of the reserve.

Past the Gloup you will see a red-painted kissing gate and a directional sign pointing left; this leads you along a grassy footpath to the Brough of Deerness (pronounced 'broch'), but a more interesting route, perhaps, is straight ahead and then left along the cliff edge, also following a grassy path.

At the Brough is another information plaque. In the cliff edge, a precipitous stone staircase takes you down the cliff and, by turning right at the beach, into a sheltered stony bay, Little Burra Geo. You will see, in the edge of the Brough wall, a steep dirt path which you can climb with the help of a chain set into the rock. This leads to the top of the Brough, where you can explore the ancient site.

❷ The first people to have an impact on Mull Head were Neolithic. The ancient scrubland was grazed by animals, then Norsemen played their part, followed in their turn by folk 'paring'—stripping off the top

although still clear, taking you along the northern cliff edge. The path turns sharp left just before a wire fence, and climbs uphill through moorland to another red-painted kissing gate.

Turn right here and go down to yet another gate, visible in the fencing above the derelict farmhouse of East Denwick.

Here turn left along a wide track and climb the hill. Where the track becomes very overgrown, take the left turn downhill to a small red-painted gate on your left.

Follow the narrow grass path through the gate and between wire fences, to turn sharp right and continue back into the parking area.

WHERE TO EAT

There is nowhere in Deerness to eat and drink and you will need to take your own provisions. The nearest pub, the Quoyburray (at Tankerness), is open all year, although lunches are available only on Saturday and Sunday in the winter. It's best to book (tel 01856 861255).

WHEN TO GO

Choose a fine spring or summer day for your walk.

Opposite *The entrance to the Gloup blow hole*
Below *Beyond the Gloup you will find the Brough of Deerness*

soil for use elsewhere—during the 18th century. The result of this and continuous grazing is a mature heather heath and very impoverished soil.

Continue along the coast, and at, another red-painted kissing gate on your right shows the footpath that leads to the cairn at Mull Head.

❸ Mull Head was declared a Local Nature Reserve by Orkney Islands Council in 1993, the ninth in Scotland, and because it has been spared modern agricultural 'improvement' it is now very rich in interesting plantlife. Mull Head has never been ploughed, although Clu Ber, the first range of cliffs you will see, has been burned, cultivated and fertilized to allow grazing for stock. Even though this work was done generations ago, the heather's destruction means that grass and different herb species thrive here.

The plants which survive here are determined by the location—how close to the sea they are, how fertile the soil is where they grow, how marshy it is and how influenced by humans. Plants that have to

withstand the salt spray at the cliff edge, such as sea pink or thrift, will hug the ground. In addition to salt tolerators and salt haters, plants which prefer marshy conditions, such as grass of Parnassus, grow here. Another influence on the plants are the activities of some of the birds. Islands of lush grass have grown up on the heath where great black-backed gulls roost each night, the grasses benefiting from the natural fertilizer.

From the cairn the path turns left and becomes much narrower,

WHAT TO DO

ORKNEY

HIGHLAND PARK
www.highlandpark.co.uk
Explore the most northerly malt
whisky distillery in the world,
founded in 1798. Watch the audio-
visual presentation 'The Spirit of
Orkney' and then take a guided tour.
✉ Holm Road, Kirkwall KW15 1SU 01856
874619 🕓 Sep–end Apr Mon–Fri 10–5;
May–end Sep also Sat 10–5, Sun 12–5.
Tours: Oct–end Mar 2 and 3pm; Apr–end Sep
hourly until 4pm 🖐 Adult £5

JUDITH GLUE
www.judithglue.com
Rich hues and strong design mark
out the high quality knitwear,
designed by Judith Glue and made
in the islands. The extensive shop
also sells local crafts and jewellery,
and hampers filled with food made
in Orkney. Opposite St. Magnus
Cathedral. Mail order service, online
shopping and tax-free for visitors
from outside the EU.

✉ 25 Broad Street, Kirkwall KW15 1DH
☎ 01856 874225 🕓 Mon–Sat 9–5.30; also
Jun–end Sep Sun 10–5

NEW PHOENIX CINEMA
www.pickaquoy.com
Britain's most northerly cinema is
in the Pickaquoy leisure centre. The
centre also has a gym, sports arena
and athletics track.
✉ Muddisdale Road, Kirkwall KW15 1LR
☎ 01856 879900 🕓 Daily 🖐 Adult from
£4.40 💻 🍽

ORKNEY ARTS THEATRE
This small theatre in the town centre
hosts a variety of amateur theatre,
opera and touring productions
through the year. Check locally
for show information. Drinks are
available on performance nights.
✉ Mill Street, Kirkwall ☎ 01856 872047

ORTAK
www.ortak.co.uk
Orkney has a tradition of jewellery
making which dates back 5,000
years. This jewellery shop and visitor

centre is in the Hatston area to the
west of Kirkwall. You can watch the
silver jewellery being made, see
a permanent exhibition and then
explore the shop.
✉ Hatston, Kirkwall KW15 1RH ☎ 01856
872224 🕓 Mon–Sat 9–5 🖐 Free

PIER ARTS CENTRE
www.pierartscentre.com
Contemporary visual art from local,
Scottish and international artists,
in two converted buildings on the
harbour side. Temporary exhibitions
are shown alongside the permanent
collection of modern art, which
include works by Barbara Hepworth
and Ben Nicholson.
✉ 28–30 Victoria Street, Stromness KW16
3AA ☎ 01856 850209 🕓 Mon–Sat 10–5
🖐 Free 🏛

ROVING EYE ENTERPRISES
www.rovingeye.co.uk
Take a 3-hour boat tour to see the
wrecked German war ships that
sank in Scapa Flow. A remotely
operated vehicle is sent down

Left *Stromness harbour, Orkney*
Below *St Ninian's Sands, Shetland*

to explore the wrecks and video pictures are transmitted back to the boat. The return journey concentrates on spotting wildlife such as seals and seabirds. Advance reservations essential.
✉ Westrow Lodge, Orphir KW17 2RD ☎ 01856 811309 🕐 May–end Sep daily at 1.20 ✋ Adult £28, child (under 12) £14

SHETLAND

ANDERSON & CO
www.shetlandknitwear.com
Overlooking Lerwick harbour, this large shop is full of vibrant sweaters, scarves and hats, knitted by outworkers to traditional Shetland patterns and in many different styles. Mail order service and tax-free shopping for customers from outside the European Union (EU).
✉ 62 Commercial Street, Lerwick ZE1 0BD ☎ 01595 693714 🕐 Mon–Sat 9–5

CLICKIMIN LEISURE COMPLEX
www.srt.org.uk
One of eight well-equipped leisure complexes scattered throughout Shetland, Clickimin provides great facilities, including a 25m (82ft) pool, river ride and flumes and a toddlers' pool, as well as health and fitness suites.
✉ Lochside, Lerwick ZE1 0PJ ☎ 01595 741000 🕐 Complex: Mon–Fri 7.30am–11pm. Main pool: adult £2.90, child (5–17) £1.80 📷

GARRISON THEATRE
www.shetlandarts.org
The main performing arts venue in Shetland, with everything from touring theatre productions to dance, music and a wide variety of lively community events. Films are also shown here. Refreshments are available on performance evenings.
✉ Isleburgh Community Centre, King Harald Street, Lerwick ZE1 0EQ ☎ 01595 743843 🕐 All year ✋ Cinema £3.50, theatre from £4

HIGH LEVEL MUSIC
www.shetlandmusic.co.uk
A great place to buy toe-tapping Shetland and traditional music on CD and cassette, and also musical instruments and accessories.
✉ 1 Gardie Court, Lerwick ZE1 0GG ☎ 01595 692618 🕐 Mon–Sat 9–5

ISLAND TRAILS
www.island-trails.co.uk
Several guided walking tours are offered, including an exploration of historic Lerwick. The tour to St. Ninian's Isle, famous for its sand bar, history and tales of smuggling, takes 3 hours, including a 3-mile (5km) walk—strong shoes or boots and waterproofs are required. Advance reservations essential, via the tourist office in Lerwick.
✉ Seaview, Bigton ☎ 01950 422408 🕐 St. Ninian's Isle: all year by arrangement. Historic Lanes walking tour of Lerwick May–end Sep, call for times ✋ Historic Lanes: adult £10, child (under 16) £4. Boat trip around the isles: adult £30, child £16

SEABIRDS-AND-SEALS
www.seabirds-and-seals.com
Cruise to the Noss and Bressay national nature reserves in the company of an expert wildlife guide. The twin-engined boat has a heated cabin and underwater TV cameras to help you to spot seals and seabirds. All tours leave from the small boat harbour in Lerwick. Advance reservations essential.
☎ 01595 693434 or 07831 217042 (after hours) 🕐 Mid-Apr to mid-Sep daily 10 and 2; Jun, Jul also daily 7pm ✋ 3-hour tour: adult £40, child (under 16) £25, under 5 free

SHETLAND TIMES BOOKSHOP
This wonderful store near the market cross stocks thousands of books on Shetland, Orkney and the rest of Scotland, covering subjects as diverse as archaeology, knitting and history. There is some sheet music for traditional tunes, and CDs of Scottish music. Mail order also available.
✉ 71–79 Commercial Street, Lerwick ZE1 0AJ ☎ 01595 695531 🕐 Mon–Fri 9–6

EATING AND STAYING

EATING

PRICES AND SYMBOLS

The restaurants are listed alphabetically within each town. The prices are for a two-course lunch (L) and a three-course à la carte dinner (D). Prices in pubs are for a two-course lunchtime bar meal and a two-course dinner in the restaurant, unless specified otherwise. The wine price is for the least expensive bottle.

For a key to the symbols, ▷ 2.

ST. MARGARET'S HOPE
CREEL RESTAURANT
www.thecreel.co.uk
The Creel overlooks the lovely seafront in the village of St. Margaret's Hope. It specializes in the simple use of fresh local produce, particularly fish and seafood: velvet crab bisque or steamed lemon sole; sea scallops and roasted monkfish tails served with leeks, fresh ginger and beans; mackerel with warm beetroot relish and toasted oatmeal; or grilled chicken fillet with roasted red pepper marmalade. To finish, try the glazed baked lemon tart with marmalade ice cream.
✉ Front Road, Orkney KW17 2SL ☎ 01856 831311 🕒 D only, 7–9, closed Jan–end

Mar, Nov 🖐 D £34, Wine £14 🚍 13 miles (21km) south of Kirkwall. On A961 on waterfront in village

STAYING

PRICES AND SYMBOLS

Prices are the starting price for a double room for one night, unless otherwise stated. Breakfast is included unless noted otherwise. All the hotels listed accept credit cards unless otherwise stated. Note that rates vary widely throughout the year.

For a key to the symbols, ▷ 2.

LERWICK
GLEN ORCHY HOUSE
www.guesthouselerwick.com
This welcoming and well-presented house lies above the town with views over the Knab, and is within easy walking distance of the town centre. Bedrooms are modern in design and there is a choice of lounges with books and board games, one with an honesty bar. Substantial breakfasts are served, and the restaurant offers a delicious Thai menu.
✉ 20 Knab Road ZE1 0AX ☎ 01595 692031 🖐 £40 🛏 24 🚍 Next to coastguard station

LERWICK
www.shetlandhotels.com
Set in attractive landscaped grounds, with fine views across Breiwick Bay, this hotel appeals to tourists and businesspeople. The bedrooms are well proportioned and attractively furnished, and family accommodation is available. There is a restaurant with fine seas views, and a cocktail lounge.
✉ 15 South Road, Shetland ZE1 0RB ☎ 01595 692166 🖐 £105 🛏 35 🚍 Near the town centre, on main road southwards to/from the airport

SHETLAND HOTEL
www.shetlandhotels.com
This purpose-built hotel, situated opposite the main ferry terminal, offers spacious and comfortable bedrooms on three floors. Two dining options are available, including the informal Oasis bistro and Ninians Restaurant. Service is prompt and friendly.
✉ Holmsgarth Road ZE1 0PW ☎ 01595 695515 🖐 £99 🛏 64 🚍 Opposite ferry terminal, on main road north from town centre

Below *Lerwick is Britain's most northerly commercial port*

PRACTICALITIES

Planning gives you all the important practical information you will need during your visit from money matters to emergency phone numbers.

ESSENTIAL INFORMATION

WEATHER

CLIMATE AND WHEN TO GO

Scotland is by far the most mountainous area of Britain, so weather conditions can be extreme. Its position on the edge of the continental land mass of Europe, surrounded on three sides by sea, means that the weather is always varied.

» The eastern side of the country tends to be cool and dry, the western side milder and wetter. Conditions can change dramatically in just a short distance, and an outbreak of haar (sea mist) along the coast is often a sign of bright sunshine only a little way inland.

» At any time of year it is likely to rain, but the chances are it won't last for long. Weather fronts move in from the west across the Atlantic, low pressure bringing wind, rain and changeable conditions, and high pressure bringing more settled weather.

» The best times of the year for sunny weather are spring and early summer (Apr–Jun). In high summer (Jul and Aug) the weather is changeable. Late summer and early autumn (Sep and Oct) are usually more settled and there's a better chance of good weather, but nothing is guaranteed, and mist can settle in the glens for days at a time. Late autumn and winter, Nov–Mar, can be cold, dark and wet, but you can also have sparkling, clear, sunny days of frost, when the light is brilliant. Winter can bring severe conditions of wind and snow to the Highlands and high ground, and these should not be underestimated.

» Note that many tourist sites close in winter (October to Easter),

EDINBURGH
TEMPERATURE

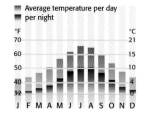

RAINFALL

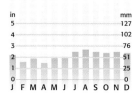

INVERNESS
TEMPERATURE

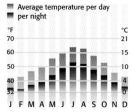

RAINFALL

GLASGOW
TEMPERATURE

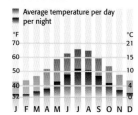

RAINFALL

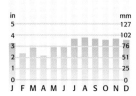

LERWICK
TEMPERATURE

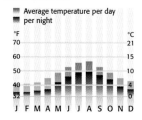

RAINFALL

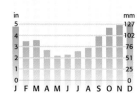

WEATHER WEBSITES

ORGANIZATION	NOTES	WEBSITE
BBC	London, UK and world weather reports and forecasts, plus many related topics. Includes satellite imagery	www.bbc.co.uk/weather/
The Met Office (UK)	Clear, professional site with good specialist links	www.metoffice.com

TIME ZONES

Scotland, like the rest of Britain, is on GMT (Greenwich Mean Time—also known as Universal Time or UTC) during winter. In summer (late March to late October) clocks go forward 1 hour to British Summer Time (BST). The chart below shows time differences from GMT.

City	Time difference	Time at 12 noon GMT
Amsterdam	+1	1pm
Auckland	+10	10pm
Berlin	+1	1pm
Brussels	+1	1pm
Chicago	-6	6am
Dublin	0	12pm
Johannesburg	+12	2pm
Madrid	+1	1pm
Montreal	-6	6am
New York	-5	7am
Paris	+1	1pm
Perth, Australia	+8	8pm
Rome	+1	1pm
San Francisco	-8	4am
Sydney	+10	10pm
Tokyo	+9	9pm

including most National Trust for Scotland properties, but major city museums stay open year round.
» Scotland's indigenous biting insect, the midge, is active from late May to mid-September, predominantly on the west coast and the islands. Though its bite is profoundly irritating, it is not life-threatening. If the widely available midge repellents don't work for you, veils can be bought at outdoor stores.

WEATHER REPORTS

Daily forecasts are given at the end of television and radio news. They are also available by phone, fax, text or on the internet (www.metoffice.gov.uk).
» Telephone 09003 444900 for regional forecasts over the phone, or fax 09060 100400 for a list of regions covered by faxed forecasts.
» For forecasts texted to a mobile phone type wthr4 followed by a UK town or city. Send this message to 8638 or dial 08700 767838 (Vodafone) or 2638 (O2).

CUSTOMS

GOODS YOU BUY IN THE EUROPEAN UNION (EU)

If you bring back large quantities of alcohol or tobacco, a Customs Officer is likely to ask about the purposes for which you have the goods. This applies particularly if you have more than the following:
» 3,200 cigarettes
» 400 cigarillos
» 200 cigars
» 3kg of smoking tobacco
» 110 litres of beer
» 10 litres of spirits
» 90 litres of wine (of which only 60 litres can be sparkling wine)
» 20 litres of fortified wine (such as port or sherry)
The EU countries are: Austria, Belgium, Cyprus, Czech Republic, Denmark, Estonia, Finland, France, Germany, Greece, Hungary, Irish Republic, Italy, Latvia, Lithuania, Luxembourg, Malta, Netherlands, Poland, Portugal, Romania, Slovakia, Slovenia, Spain, Sweden and the United Kingdom.

TRAVELLING TO THE UK FROM OUTSIDE THE EU

You are entitled to the allowances shown below only if you travel with the goods and do not plan to sell them. For further information see HM Revenue and Customs website: www.hmrc.gov.uk
» 200 cigarettes; or
» 100 cigarillos; or
» 50 cigars; or
» 250g of tobacco
» 60cc/ml of perfume
» 250cc/ml of toilet water
» 2 litres of still table wine
» 1 litre of spirits or strong liqueurs over 22 per cent volume; or
» 2 litres of fortified wine, sparkling wine or other liqueurs
» £145 worth of all other goods including gifts and souvenirs

DOCUMENTS

PASSPORTS

» Visitors from outside the UK must have a passport valid for at least six months from the date of entry into the country.

» The United Kingdom (England, Wales, Scotland and Northern Ireland), the Channel Islands, the Isle of Man and the Republic of Ireland form a common travel area. Once you have entered through immigration control into any part of it, you do not need further clearance to travel within it. However, you may be required to show photographic ID, such as a passport or a driver's licence with a photo, for internal flights.

VISAS

» Passport and visa regulations can change at short notice, so always check the current situation before you travel. For general information on visas see www.ukvisas.gov.uk
» Citizens of countries in the European Economic Area (EEA)—the EU, Switzerland, Norway and Iceland —can enter the UK for purposes of holiday or work for any length of stay, without a visa.
» Citizens of the Australia, Canada, the US or New Zealand do not need a visa for stays of up to six months.
» Those wishing to stay longer than six months and nationals of some other countries need a visa.
» You are usually allowed to enter and leave the UK as many times as you like while your visa is valid. On arrival in the UK you must be able to produce documentation establishing your identity and nationality.

TRAVEL INSURANCE

This is recommended for insuring your possessions and legal liability, and also for medical expenses.

HEALTH DOCUMENTS

» EHIC form, ▷ 316.

WHAT TO TAKE

» Your driver's licence or permit. An International Driving Permit may be useful if your licence is in a language other than English.
» Photocopies of passport and travel insurance.
» Travellers' cheques and credit cards, and a small amount of cash in sterling.

MONEY

MONEY MATTERS

You are advised to carry money in a range of forms—cash, at least one credit card, bank card/charge/Maestro card and travellers' cheques.

CASH

Britain's currency is the pound sterling. Coins are in denominations of 1p, 2p, 5p, 10p, 20p, 50p, £1 and £2. Banknotes are in denominations of £5, £10, £20 and £50.

» Scottish banks issue their own notes. These are acceptable throughout the UK, but their unfamiliarity south of the Scottish border means their validity is sometimes questioned. If this becomes a problem, they may be exchanged in any bank or post office for Bank of England notes.
» Bank of England notes are generally accepted in Scotland.
» There is no limit to the amount of cash you may import or export.
» It is worth keeping a few 10p, 20p, 50p and £1 coins handy for pay-and-display parking machines, and for parking meters.

CASHPOINTS (ATMS)

ATMs are widely available across the country. You will need a four-digit

PIN (comprising four numbers, not letters) from your bank to use an ATM. Check with your bank if you are uncertain whether you will be charged for using another bank's cash machines.

» LINK is the UK's only branded network of self-service cash machines. Use of LINK machines is free, except for credit, charge and store cards, for which you pay a cash advance fee.
» You are also charged for the use of convenience machines installed by cash machine-owners in certain private locations (such as garages); usage fees are clearly displayed, and are usually around £1.25–£2.50.

LOST/STOLEN CREDIT CARDS

American Express
01273 696933

Diners Club
0870 190 0011

MasterCard/Eurocard, Maestro, Visa/Connect
0113 277 8899 or 0800 891725

CREDIT CARDS

Credit cards are widely accepted; Visa and MasterCard are the most popular, followed by American Express, Diners Club and JCB.

» Visitors from abroad should check with their bank to make sure their card is compatible.
» Credit cards can also be used for withdrawing currency at cashpoints (ATMs) at any bank displaying the appropriate sign, for changing banknotes and cashing travellers' cheques.
» If your credit cards or travellers' cheques are stolen call the issuer immediately, then report the loss to the police.

TRAVELLERS' CHEQUES

These are the safest way to carry money, as you will be refunded in the event of loss (keep the counterfoil separate from the cheques), usually within 24 hours.

BANKS

Most banks open Monday–Friday, 9.30–4.30; some also open on Saturday morning.

» It pays to shop around for the best exchange and commission rates on currency. You do not pay commission on sterling travellers' cheques, provided you cash them at a bank affiliated with the issuing bank.
» You need to present ID (usually a passport) when cashing travellers' cheques.

POST OFFICES

Most post offices are open Monday–Friday, 9–5.30, with reduced hours on Saturday.

» Apart from the main post offices in urban centres, which offer full postal services, there are smaller sub-post offices around the country, often forming part of a newsagent or general store.
» Some post offices offer commission-free bureaux de change services (tel 08458 500900), with an online ordering service (www.postoffice.co.uk). Payment can be made in cash, or by cheque, banker's draft, Visa, MasterCard, Maestro, Delta, Solo or Electron.

BUREAUX DE CHANGE

These money-changing operations can be found at main stations and airports, and at on-street locations in the bigger cities, and are mostly open 8am–10pm. Rates of exchange may vary; it pays to shop around.

MAJOR UK BANKS

NAME	HEAD OFFICE ADDRESS	TELEPHONE
Barclays	1 Churchill Place, Canary Wharf, London E14 5HP	020 7116 1000
HSBC	8 Canada Square, London E14 5HQ	020 7991 8888
Lloyds TSB	25 Gresham Street, London EC2V 7HN	020 7626 1500
NatWest	135 Bishopsgate, London EC2M 3UR	0870 240 1155
Royal Bank of Scotland	36 St. Andrew Square, Edinburgh EH2 2YB	0131 556 8555

TIPPING

Restaurants (where service is not included)	10%
Tour guides	£1–£2
Hairdressers	10%
Taxis	10%
Chambermaids	50p–£1 per day
Porters	50p–£1 per bag

Commission rates should be clearly displayed.

DISCOUNTS

» Reduced fares on buses, underground services and trains are available for the under 16s.
» Over 60s can purchase Senior Citizens' Railcards for £24, giving a one-third reduction on off-peak rail services. See also ▷ 46.

THE EURO

It is possible to spend euros in Britain: The problem is knowing where. Generally, the bigger the city, the more places will accept euros. Ask before you shop.
» Many major chain stores, including the Body Shop, Clarks, Debenhams, Habitat, HMV, Marks & Spencer, Miss Selfridge, Topshop, Virgin and Waterstone's accept euros in some or all of their branches.
» Some pubs owned by J D Wetherspoon, Scottish & Newcastle and Shepherd Neame take euros, as do some BP and other fuel stations.
» Train tickets on Virgin trains can also be paid in euros (notes only accepted).

» One euro is made up of 100 cents. Euro notes come in denominations of 5, 10, 20, 50, 100, 200 and 500 euros. Coins come in denominations of 1 and 2 euros, and 1, 2, 5, 10, 20 and 50 cents.

WIRING MONEY

» Money wired from your home country can be expensive (agents charge fees for the service) and time consuming.
» Money can be wired from bank to bank, which takes up to two working days, or to agents such as Travelex (tel 01733 318922; www.travelex. co.uk) and Western Union (tel 0800 833833; www.westernunion.com).

VAT REFUNDS
▷ 326.

See also ▷ 46.
▷ 326.

NATIONAL HOLIDAYS

Although banks and businesses close on the public (bank) holidays listed below, major tourist attractions and some shops may open on these dates, except on 25 and 26 Dec, and 1 and 2 Jan, when almost everything shuts. If any of these days falls on a Saturday or Sunday, the next Monday is a holiday.

New Year's Day (1 January)
New Year's Holiday (2 January)
Good Friday
Easter Monday
First Monday in May
Last Monday in May
First Monday in August
Last Monday in August
Christmas Day (25 December)
Boxing Day (26 December)

EVERYDAY ITEMS AND HOW MUCH THEY COST

Take-away sandwich	£2.50
Bottle of water	£1.00
Cup of tea or coffee	£1–£2
Pint of beer	£3.00
Glass of house wine	£3.80
National daily newspaper	40p–£1.30p
Ice cream	£1.20
Litre of petrol	over £1.00

Opposite *Bank of Scotland, Edinburgh*
Above *Eating out in the Grassmarket area of Edinburgh*
Below *Loch Arklet, Lomond and the Trossachs National Park*

HEALTH

Britain's National Health Service (the NHS) provides healthcare for the country's citizens. It is funded by the taxpayer.

» While NHS care for British citizens is free, private health care can also be bought from organizations such as BUPA.

» Visitors from the European Union (EU) are entitled to free treatment on the NHS (see below), but medical insurance is still recommended.

BEFORE YOU DEPART

» It is sensible to consult your doctor at least six to eight weeks before leaving.

» Free medical treatment is available through the NHS for visitors from EU countries with reciprocal agreements. The European Health Insurance Card (EHIC) is available via post offices.

» Several countries have reciprocal healthcare agreements with the UK (▷ below). In most cases a passport is sufficient identification for hospital treatment. Most countries, however, including the US and Canada, do not have agreements with the UK, so a comprehensive travel insurance policy is advisable.

» No inoculations are required on entering Britain. However, it is advisable to have an anti-tetanus booster before travelling. Check with your doctor whether you need immunization or health advice for: meningococcal meningitis; hepatitis B; diphtheria; or measles/MMR.

COUNTRIES WITH RECIPROCAL HEALTH AGREEMENTS WITH THE UK

Anguilla, Australia, Barbados, British Virgin Islands, Bulgaria, Channel Islands, Falkland Islands, Gibraltar, Isle of Man, Montserrat, New Zealand, Romania, Russia, St. Helena, Turks and Caicos Islands, Republics of the former USSR (except Latvia, Lithuania, Estonia), Yugoslavia (i.e. Serbia and Montenegro) and successor states (Croatia, Bosnia and Herzegovina, and Macedonia).

WHAT TO TAKE WITH YOU

» Visitors from the EU should bring an EHIC card and a photocopy which should be kept in a safe place.

» Those from outside the EU should bring their travel insurance policy and a spare copy.

» Visitors with existing medical conditions and allergies, for example, to commonly used drugs, should wear a warning bracelet or tags.

IF YOU NEED TREATMENT

» If you are injured go to a hospital casualty department (emergency room).

» If you are staying at a hotel or B&B, the staff should be able to help you contact a doctor. In many cases emergency telephone numbers are posted on a noticeboard in a central area or in your room.

» If you are on your own call NHS 24 (tel 0845 424 2424) and explain the problem. Free medical advice from a qualified nurse is available to everyone over the phone through this government service or via the internet at www.nhs24.com. You do not have to give personal details.

» Non-urgent appointments can be made with any doctor listed in the Yellow Pages. Initial advice, such as whether you need to go to hospital, will be given but those visitors without a reciprocal arrangement with the UK, such as the US and Canada, will be charged to speak

to a nurse (£25) or doctor (£55) and for any prescription drugs deemed necessary. You will be given a receipt for your insurance company on your return home.

» To find the nearest doctor, dentist or pharmacy, ask at your hotel, or call NHS 24.

» Major pharmacies and large supermarkets have a wide range of medicines that you can buy over the counter, although items such as antibiotics require a prescription from a doctor.

» Pharmacists rotate after-hours duty in many areas, with times of the duty pharmacist displayed in the shop window and in the local newspaper.

» Dial 999 for an ambulance in an emergency.

WATER

Tap water is safe to drink from the main water distribution supply. Avoid drinking water that comes from a tank, for example, in a train toilet.

DENTAL TREATMENT

You will have to pay for dental treatment, either as a private patient or (slightly cheaper) as an NHS patient. It is sensible to go for a dental check-up before you depart.

» In the UK dentists are listed in telephone directories, or use the British Dental Association's online service at www.bda-findadentist.org.uk

MAJOR HIGH-STREET PHARMACIES

NAME	TELEPHONE	WEBSITE
Boots the Chemist	0115 950 6111	www.wellbeing.com
Co-op Pharmacy	0161 654 4488	www.co-oppharmacy.co.uk
Lloyds Pharmacy	024 7643 2400	www.lloydspharmacy.co.uk
Sainsbury's Pharmacy	0800 636262	www.sainsburys.co.uk
Superdrug	020 8684 7000	www.superdrug.com
Tesco Pharmacy	0800 505555	www.tesco.com

OPTICIANS

NAME	TELEPHONE	WEBSITE
Boots Opticians	0845 070 8090	www.wellbeing.com/bootsopticians
Dollond & Aitchison	0121 706 6133	www.danda.co.uk
Specsavers	01481 236000	www.specsavers.co.uk
Vision Express	0115 986 5225	www.visionexpress.com

BASICS

ELECTRICITY

Britain is on 240 or 230 volts AC, and plugs have three square pins. If you are bringing an electrical appliance from another country where the voltage is the same, a plug adaptor will suffice. If the voltage is different, as in the US — 110 volts — you need a converter.

» Small appliances such as razors and laptops can run on a 50-watt converter, while heating appliances, irons and hair-dryers require a 1,600-watt converter.

» Telephone sockets are also different and will require an adaptor if you want to access the internet.

MEASUREMENTS

Britain officially uses the metric system. Fuel is sold by the litre, and food in grams and kilograms. However, imperial measures are used widely in everyday speech, and road distances and speed limits are in miles and miles per hour respectively.

» Beer in pubs is still sold in pints (slightly less than 0.5 litres).

» Note that the British gallon (4.5460 litres) is larger than the US gallon (3.7854 litres).

PUBLIC TOILETS

Generally these are well located, plentiful and free in built-up areas. There may be a small charge to use toilets at certain large train stations. Some unpleasant facilities survive, but most are modern and well maintained.

» All major road service stations and filling stations have free toilets. In rural areas toilets can be found at some roadside pull-offs and parking areas.

» It is not acceptable for those who are not customers to use the toilets in pubs, cafés and restaurants.

SMOKING

» Smoking is banned in all public places in the UK. This includes restaurants, pubs, on public transport and places such as station concourses.

CONVERSION CHART		
From	To	Multiply by
Inches	Centimetres	2.54
Centimetres	Inches	0.3937
Feet	Metres	0.3048
Metres	Feet	3.2810
Yards	Metres	0.9144
Metres	Yards	1.0940
Miles	Kilometres	1.6090
Kilometres	Miles	0.6214
Acres	Hectares	0.4047
Hectares	Acres	2.4710
Gallons	Litres	4.5460
Litres	Gallons	0.2200
Ounces	Grams	28.35
Grams	Ounces	0.0353
Pounds	Grams	453.6
Grams	Pounds	0.0022
Pounds	Kilograms	0.4536
Kilograms	Pounds	2.205
Tons	Tonnes	1.0160
Tonnes	Tons	0.9842

LAUNDRY

» When you reserve your accommodation, ask about laundry facilities.

» Telephone directories list launderettes and dry cleaners.

» Some launderettes offer service washes, where the washing and drying is done for you (typically £5–£6 for a small bag), either within a day or with a 24–48-hour turnaround.

» Dry cleaning is widely available: a jacket or skirt individually cleaned will cost around £4. Some dry cleaners also offer clothes-mending services such as zipper replacement.

TRAVEL WITH CHILDREN

Some hotels, restaurants and pubs have a strict no-children policy or serve children only over a certain age. Some places offer excellent facilities for children, including babysitting services and baby monitors.

» Many tourist attractions offer reduced admission fees or are free for children, and some sell family tickets.

» In pubs children must be accompanied by an adult (if allowed in at all). Children under 14 are not allowed in the bar area and it is illegal for anyone under 18 to purchase alcohol. Some restaurants and pubs provide high chairs.

» Major department stores, shopping centres and public venues such as theatres have changing tables for babies, but these tend to be located in the women's toilet areas. Changing facilities are provided aboard most aircraft.

Below *Children enjoying the 'Discovery Area' at the Glasgow Science Centre*

Left *View of the Cuillin Mountains*

have at least 12 months of driving experience. If you are under 25 you may be charged an increased premium.

» Rental rates usually include unlimited mileage. A cheaper option is to opt for a limited mileage allowance, which makes an extra charge for additional mileage thereafter.

» It is important to have some form of personal insurance along with Collision Damage Waiver (CDW). Many companies also offer Damage Excess Reduction (DER) and Theft Protection for an additional premium. Expect to pay more for any additional drivers.

» Make sure you find out what equipment comes as standard (air-conditioning and automatic transmission are not always available) and check that the price quoted includes VAT, the sales tax levied on most goods and services.

» Ask about optional extras such as roof racks and child seats before collecting the car.

» Budget for about £55 per day for an economy car (such as a Ford Fiesta), £65 per day for a mid-range vehicle (such as a Ford Focus) or £80 upwards for a premium car.

» Most cars use unleaded fuel; make sure you know what's required (unleaded or diesel) before filling up.

» When the car is returned, fuel should be topped up to the level shown when you first picked it up — otherwise you will be charged extra.

VISITORS WITH A DISABILITY

Most tourist attractions and public places have facilities for visitors with disabilities, but it is always wise to check in advance. See also the information for visitors with a disability, ▷ 56.

» Any special needs should be mentioned when reserving accommodation, as many places may not be suitable for wheelchairs or for visitors with visual impairments. The Holiday Care Service (tel 08451 249971, www.tourismforall.org.uk) provides information on accommodation suitable for visitors with disabilities.

» The Royal National Institute for the Blind (tel 020 7388 2525 or 0845 766 9999) publishes a hotel guidebook.

CAR RENTAL

Arranging a rental car through your travel agent before arriving saves money and allows you to find out about deposits, drop-off charges, cancellation penalties and insurance costs well in advance. Larger, mainstream rental companies have offices in cities and major airports,

but local firms serve a wider variety of destinations, including the islands. A selection of contacts appears in the table below. More information about car rental can be supplied by the local tourist offices (▷ 321).

» Most rental cars have manual rather than automatic transmission, so ask if you want an automatic.

» You must have a driver's licence. An international driving permit may be useful if your licence is not in English.

» Most rental firms require the driver to be at least 23 years old and

CAR RENTAL CONTACTS

NAME	LOCATIONS	CONTACT
Alamo	Aberdeen, Dundee, Edinburgh, Glasgow, Prestwick, Hamilton, Inverness, Stirling	Tel 0870 400 456 www.alamo.co.uk
Avis	Aberdeen, Edinburgh, Glasgow, Inverness, Oban, Prestwick, Stirling	Tel 0844 581 0147 www.avis.co.uk
Budget	Aberdeen, Edinburgh, Glasgow, Inverness	Tel 0844 581 9998 www.budget.co.uk
Europcar BCR	Aberdeen, Edinburgh, Glasgow, Prestwick, Inverness, Orkney, Shetland	Tel 0870 607 5000 www.europcar.co.uk
Hertz	Aberdeen, Dundee, Edinburgh, Fraserburgh, Glasgow, Inverness, Perth, Prestwick, Stranraer	Tel 0870 844 8844 www.hertz.co.uk
Arnol Motors	Isle of Lewis	Tel 01851 710548

COMMUNICATION

With technology rapidly changing the way we communicate, the humble postcard is in danger of looking old-fashioned. But however you want to keep in touch with friends and family, there is a multitude of generally swift, convenient and reliable options.

TELEPHONES

The main public phone company, British Telecom (BT), operates hundreds of payphones throughout Scotland.

COUNTRY CODES FROM THE UK

Australia	00 61
Belgium	00 32
Canada	00 1
France	00 33
Germany	00 49
Ireland	00 353
Italy	00 39
Netherlands	00 31
New Zealand	00 64
Spain	00 34
Sweden	00 46
US	00 1

AREA CODES, COUNTRY CODES AND TELEPHONE DIRECTORIES

» Most area codes are four- or five-digit numbers beginning with 01.
» For Edinburgh the code is 0131 and for Glasgow it is 0141. Telephone directories (phone books) and Yellow Pages show the code in brackets for each telephone number.
» There is a full list of area codes and country codes in every phone book.
» When making a local call you can omit the area code.
» When making an international call dial the international code followed by the telephone number minus the 0 of the area code.

PUBLIC PHONES

Phone boxes (booths) are generally silver or red and are found at all major bus and train stations, on the street in town centres, and in many villages and more rural locations.

USEFUL TELEPHONE NUMBERS

Directory enquiries:

competing services from several companies: try 118500 (BT) and 118111 (One.Tel)

International directory enquiries:

competing services from several companies: try 118505 (BT) and 118211 (TalkTalk)

International operator: 155	
Operator: 100	
Time: 123	

CALL CHARGES FROM BT PAYPHONES

Minimum charge	30p (20p with BT Chargecard)
All UK calls	30p for first 15 mins, then 10p per 7 mins thereafter
Calls to mobile phones	60p per minute Mon–Fri 8–6, 40p per minute Mon–Fri after 6pm and before 8am
Italy, US and Canada	£1 per minute at all times
Belgium, France, Germany, Netherlands and Sweden	£1 per minute at all times
Australia and New Zealand	£1 per minute at all times
Call charges	These are lower after 6pm on weekdays and all day

Saturday and Sunday. Local calls are cheaper than long-distance calls within Britain, and calls to mobile phones are generally more expensive than other calls

» You can use credit and debit cards to make calls from many BT payphones (95p minimum charge; 20p per minute for all inland calls).
» Payphones accept 10p, 20p, 50p and £1 coins; some also accept £2 coins. Only unused coins are returned, so avoid using high denomination coins for short calls.
» Some establishments, such as hotels and pubs, have their own payphones, for which they set their own profit margin. These can be exorbitant and are recommended only in an emergency. Similarly, phone calls made from hotel rooms often incur higher charges.

USING A MOBILE PHONE

Britain has embraced mobile (cell) phone technology wholeheartedly, although mobiles are sometimes discouraged in some pubs and elsewhere (some trains have dedicated quiet areas). There's a proliferation of mobile phone shops in almost every shopping area.
» If you are visiting from overseas and already have a mobile phone, you can purchase a sim card for between £10 and £20, which gives you access to one of the main networks such as BT, Orange or Vodafone.
» You need to know whether your phone operates on a GSM (Global System for Mobile Communications) frequency. Single band GSM phones, which work on 900MHz frequency, can be used in more than 100 countries, but not in the US or Canada.
» Most phones sold in the US work on 1900MHz and need a new sim card for use in the UK. Dual (900 and 1900MHz) and tri band phones can

DIALLING CODE PREFIXES

00	international codes
01	area codes
02	area codes
07	calls charged at mobile rates
080	free calls
084	calls charged at local rates
087	calls charged at national rates
09	calls charged at premium rates

For details of charges, call the operator on 100.

To dial Scotland from abroad, dial 00 44 and omit the first 0 of the area code.

be used in most countries around the world without alteration. Check with your provider before you leave.
» A 'pay as you go' option allows you to top up your account at supermarkets and other shops when necessary. You are usually given a choice of accounts, depending on how much and when you are likely to make calls. A subscription-type account is more useful if you are staying in the country for a substantial period.
» Note that there are still 'black holes' across Scotland where you cannot get a mobile phone signal, and that these vary for each network.
» Remember to pack a plug adaptor for the charger.

INTERNET ACCESS

Multimedia web phones (e-payphones, or blue boxes) are being installed by BT in shopping areas, train stations, airports and road service stations across the country. These enable users to surf the internet and send emails and text messages. Internet and email access costs £1 for up to 15 minutes and 10p per 90 seconds thereafter. Text messages cost 20p a message.
» Web phones may threaten the future of the internet cafés (charges typically £1–£2 per hour) in major cities and towns.
» Some payphones allow you to send text messages and email—look for the sign that indicates this.
» Many public libraries have free internet access; for details see www.peoplesnetwork.gov.uk
» BT has introduced more than 400 wireless hot spots in locations such as airports, hotels and service stations across the UK. The hubs allow laptop and pocket PC users within a 100m (109-yard) radius broadband access to the internet using wireless technology, or WiFi. You need a laptop or pocket PC PDA running Microsoft Windows XP, 2000 or Microsoft Pocket PC 2002, and a wireless LAN card. Any WiFi approved card should work with BT Openzone.

» Note that the service remains an expensive, if convenient, way of surfing the internet.

USING A LAPTOP

If you are coming from abroad and intend to use your own laptop in the UK, remember to bring a power converter to recharge it and a plug adaptor (see Electricity, ▷ 317). A surge protector is also a good idea.
» To connect to the internet you need an adaptor for the phone socket, available (in the UK) from companies such as Teleadapt (www.teleadapt.com).
» If you use an international service provider, such as Compuserve or AOL, it's cheaper to dial up a local node rather than the number in your home country.
» Wireless technology, such as Bluetooth, allows you to connect to the internet using a mobile phone; check beforehand what the charges will be.
» Dial tone frequencies vary from country to country so set your modem to ignore dial tones.

POST/MAIL

» For all post office information, call customer services, tel 0845 722 3344.
» Post boxes are painted bright red (except some in post offices) and are either set into walls, on posts or are stand-alone circular pillar boxes. Collection times are shown on each post box.
» Stamps are available from newsagents and supermarkets as well as post offices.

» Generally airmail is preferable for mail sent outside Europe; for bulky items surface mail is substantially cheaper but typically takes around eight weeks outside Europe. Airmail to Europe takes around three days, and from five days to the rest of the world.
» Large post offices have poste restante services. This service enables mail addressed to the recipient at that address and inscribed with the words poste restante to be kept at the specified post office until collected by the addressee.
» To send items within the UK for next-day delivery, use special delivery. This service also enables you to insure the items in case of loss.

POSTAGE RATES		
First class within UK	Small letter up to 100g (usually arrives next day, but not guaranteed)	36p
Second class within UK	Small letter up to 100g (usually two days)	27p
Proof of posting		Free
Airmail Rates		
Americas, Middle East, Africa, India, Southeast Asia	Letter (100g/3.5oz)	£2.52
	Postcard	56p
Europe	Letter (100g/3.5oz)	£1.36
	Postcard	42p
Australasia	Letter (100g/3.5oz)	£2.52
	Postcard	56p

TOURIST INFORMATION

VISITSCOTLAND

The official source of information for tourists, VisitScotland (formerly the Scottish Tourist Board) supports the publication of free promotional brochures on everything from where to play golf to how to get around the Western Isles. It publishes various inspected accommodation and camping guides, and much of its information is available on www.visitScotland.com

TOURIST INFORMATION CENTRES (TICS)

There is a network of around 120 tourist information offices across the country, which are a friendly source of knowledgeable advice and free brochures, as well as official publications and maps. All can advise on places to stay, and many will reserve accommodation ahead for you. Around half of them are open only between Easter and October; standard opening hours of 9–5 may be shortened in winter. Several are located at service stations on main routes, including exit 13 off the M74, exit 6 off the M90 and exit 9 off the M9. Contact details for some of the main offices, open all year, are listed here.

EDINBURGH
Edinburgh & Scotland Information Centre,
3 Princes Street EH2 2QP
Tel 0845 225 5121

SOUTHERN SCOTLAND
AYR
22 Sandgate KA7 1BW
Tel 0845 225 5121

DUMFRIES
64 Whitesands DG1 2RS
Tel 01387 245555

MELROSE
Abbey House, Abbey Street
TD6 9LG
Tel 0870 608 0404

NORTH BERWICK
Quality Street EH39 4HJ
Tel 0845 225 5121 or 01620 892197

GLASGOW
11 George Square G2 1DY
Tel 0141 204 4400

CENTRAL SCOTLAND
ABERFOYLE
Trossachs Discovery Centre,
Main Street FK8 3UQ
Tel 0845 225 5121

DUNDEE
21 Castle Street DD1 3AA
Tel 01382 527527

PERTH
Lower City Mills, West Mill Street PH1 5QP
Tel 01738 450600

PITLOCHRY
22 Atholl Road PH16 5BX
Tel 01796 472215/472751

ST. ANDREWS
70 Market Street KY16 9NU
Tel 01334 472021

HIGHLANDS AND ISLANDS
ABERDEEN
23 Union Street AB11 5BP
Tel 01224 288828

AVIEMORE
Grampian Road PH22 1PP
Tel 0845 225 5121

FORT WILLIAM
Cameron Centre, Cameron Square PH33 6AJ
Tel 0845 225 5121

GRANTOWN-ON-SPEY
54 High Street PH26 3AS
Tel 0845 225 5121

INVERNESS
Castle Wynd IV2 3BJ
Tel 0845 225 5121

LEWIS
26 Cromwell Street, Stornoway HS1 2DD
Tel 01851 703088

LOCH LOMOND
Gateway Centre, Loch Lomond Shores,
Balloch G83 8QL
Tel 0845 345 4978

OBAN
Argyll Square PA34 4AR
Tel 01631 563122 or 0845 225 5121

SKYE
Bayfield House, Portree IV51 9EL
Tel 0845 225 5121

ULLAPOOL
Argyle Street IV26 2UB
Tel 0845 225 5121

ORKNEY AND SHETLAND
KIRKWALL
6 Broad Street, Orkney
KW15 1DH
Tel 01856 872856

LERWICK
The Market Cross, Shetland
ZE1 0LU
Tel 0870 199 9440

GUIDE TO OPENING TIMES

Banks	Mon–Fri 9.30–4.30; larger branches may open Sat am
Doctors/dentists	Mon–Fri 8.30–6.30; some may open Sat am
Pharmacies	Mon–Sat 9–5 or 5.30
Post offices	Mon–Fri 9–5.30, Sat 9–12
Pubs	Generally daily, 12–2.30pm and 6–11pm; some may stay open all afternoon
Restaurants	These vary, but are typically daily, 12–2.30pm and 6pm–11pm; many will close on one or two days in the week
Shops	Mon–Sat 9–5 or 5.30; late opening is common in larger towns and cities. Newsagents and some shops may open on a Sunday
Supermarkets/ convenience stores	Mon–Sat 8am–8pm or later and for six hours (such as 10–4) on Sunday
Visitor attractions	These vary widely, so always check ahead. Note that last admission is usually at least 30 min before closing time

USEFUL WEBSITES

TOURING INFORMATION
www.visitScotland.com
www.undiscoveredscotland.co.uk

MAPS AND GUIDES TO BUY ON LINE
www.theAA.com
www.estate-publications.co.uk
www.ordnancesurvey.co.uk
www.ukho.gov.uk
www.amazon.com

GENERAL INFORMATION ABOUT SCOTLAND
www.electricscotland.com
www.geo.ed.ac.uk/scotgaz

GAELIC INTEREST
www.cnag.org.uk
www.ambeile.org.uk
www.smo.uhi.ac.uk
www.the-mod.co.uk

HERITAGE GROUPS
www.nts.org.uk
www.historic-scotland.net

WEATHER
www.onlineweather.com
www.metoffice.com
www.bbc.co.uk/weather
www.onlineweather.com
www.sais.gov.uk/about_forecasts

TRAVEL LINKS
www.traveline.org.uk
www.citylink.co.uk

www.nationalexpress.com
www.postbus.royalmail.com
www.scotrail.co.uk
www.nationalrail.co.uk
www.britrail.com
www.eurostar.com
www.baa.com
www.gpia.co.uk
www.hial.co.uk
www.calmac.co.uk
www.seacat.co.uk
www.stenaline.co.uk
www.poirishsea.com
www.superfast.com
www.smyril-line.com
www.jogferry.co.uk

ACCOMMODATION
www.visitScotland.com
www.theAA.com
www.syha.org.uk
www.countrycottagesinscotland.com
www.forestholidays.co.uk
www.campingandcaravanningclub.
co.uk

EVENTS
www.edinburgh-festivals.co.uk
www.eif.co.uk
www.edfringe.com
www.edintattoo.co.uk
www.edinburghshogmanay.org
www.the-mod.co.uk
www.celticconnections.co.uk
www.sffs.shetland.co.uk
www.shetland-music.com/
musevent2.htm
www.spiritofspeyside.com

www.tinthepark.com
www.stmagnusfestival.com
www.scottishtraditionalboat festival.
co.uk
www.jazzfest.co.uk
www.wigtown-booktown.co.uk/
festival
www.braemargathering.com
www.cowalgathering.com

SPORTS
www.shinty.com
www.cycling.visitscotland.com
www.fish.visitscotland.com
www.scottishgolf.com
www.ridingscotland.com
www.nevis-range.co.uk
www.cairngormmountain.com
www.lecht.co.uk
www.ski-glencoe.co.uk
www.ski-glenshee.co.uk
www.heartsfc.co.uk
www.hibs.co.uk
www.celticfc.co.uk
www.rangers.co.uk
www.sru.org.uk

BANKING AND POSTAL SERVICES
www.postoffice.co.uk
www.travelex.co.uk
www.westernunion.com

EMBASSIES (LONDON)
www.australia.org.uk
www.canada.org.uk
www.nzembassy.com/uk
www.southafricahouse.com
www.usembassy.org.uk

HERITAGE ORGANIZATIONS

National Trust for Scotland (NTS) membership is excellent value if you wish to visit more than one or two NTS properties. Join at any NTS site.
» National Trust for Scotland, 28 Charlotte Square, Edinburgh EH2 4ET, tel 0844 493 2100; www.nts.org.uk

Historic Scotland (HS) also manages hundreds of historic properties, statues and monuments. Join at any HS-staffed property for free entry.
» Historic Scotland, Longmore House, Salisbury Place, Edinburgh EH9 1SH, tel 0131 668 8600; www.historic-scotland.net

VISITBRITAIN OFFICES OVERSEAS

Australia
Level 16, 1 Macquarie Place, Sydney, NSW 2000
Tel 02 9377 4400
Fax 02 9377 4499

Canada
Suite 120, 5915 Airport Road, Mississauga, Ontario L4V 1T1
Tel 0905 405 1840/1 888 VISIT UK
Fax 0905 405 1835

New Zealand
151 Queen Street, Auckland 1
Tel 09 303 1446
Fax 09 377 6965

South Africa
Lancaster Gate, Hyde Park Lane, Hyde Park, Johannesburg 2196 (visitors); PO Box 41896, Craighall 2024 (mail)
Tel 011 325 0343
Fax 011 325 0344

US
7th Floor, 551 Fifth Avenue at 45th Street, New York, NY 10176-0799
Tel (1) 212 986 2200/1 800 GO 2 BRITAIN

Website for Americans visiting Britain: www.travelbritain.org

FINDING HELP

PERSONAL SECURITY

Levels of violent crime remain relatively low, but there are hot spots to avoid in any city. In most tourist areas the main danger is petty theft.

» Be particularly wary of thieves on railway trains, in crowded public places and at busy public events.

» Avoid unlit urban areas at night, and carry bags close to you. If someone tries to grab your bag, never fight back; let go.

» If you are going out late, arrange a lift home or a taxi, and use only reputable and licensed minicab firms or black cabs.

» If you are driving alone, take a mobile phone with you if possible, but be aware that reception may be poor or limited in remoter parts of the country.

» Lock your doors when your car is stuck in stationary traffic, particularly at night. Always lock your vehicle when it is parked, and don't leave valuables in a parked car.

» Don't pick up hitchhikers.

» Sit near the driver or conductor on buses and avoid empty carriages (cars) on trains.

LOST PROPERTY

If you lose an item, contact the nearest police station and complete a lost property form. Give as much detail as possible, such as identifying marks, registration numbers and credit card numbers.

» www.lostandfound.com and www.virtualbumblebee.co.uk are free 'lost and found' services, where you can log a loss or search a database of lost and found items throughout the UK.

» At airports, dedicated offices deal with lost property within terminal buildings, but contact individual airlines if you lose belongings on board aircraft (▷ 42–43).

LOST PASSPORT

If you lose your passport, contact your embassy in the UK (see below). It helps if you have your passport number; either carry a photocopy of the opening pages or scan them and email them to yourself at an email account which you can access anywhere, such as www.hotmail.com.

SEEKING HELP

Telephone 999 or 112 in an emergency. The operator will ask you which service you require. State where you are, the number of the phone you are using, what the problem is and where it has occurred.

» If your police enquiry is not an emergency, contact the nearest police station (for directory enquiries, ▷ 319).

» If you have non-urgent health concerns, contact NHS 24 (National Health Service, tel 0845 424 2424), where trained medical staff listen to your problem, give advice and tell you where to find the nearest non-emergency doctor. This free service is available to all visitors.

» Policemen patrolling the streets on

EMERGENCY NUMBERS

Police, ambulance, fire services,
coastguard and mountain rescue
999 or 112

foot will readily give information and directions.

» The British Transport Police work on Britain's railways. Report any non-emergency crimes experienced on trains to them, tel 0800 405040.

» If you are the victim of a crime, Victim Support offers support and legal advice, tel 0845 303 0900 (0845 603 9213 in Scotland).

THE LAW

» There are serious penalties for driving while under the influence of alcohol. If you drink, don't drive.

» If you are involved in a motoring incident you are obliged to give your name and address.

» On-the-spot fixed penalty notices (traffic tickets) are given out for speeding, driving in a bus lane, driving through a red light and other motoring offences (starting at about £40).

» Even if you're not driving, you can be fined if you are found to be excessively drunk or drunk and disorderly in a public place, in licensed premises or on a highway.

» Police have the power to give on-the-spot fines for a few offences involving antisocial behaviour or wasting police time.

FOREIGN CONSULATES, EDINBURGH

COUNTRY	ADDRESS	TELEPHONE
American Embassy	3 Regent Terrace EH7 5BW	0131 556 8315
Australian Consulate	21–23 Hill Street EH2 3JP	0131 226 8161
Canadian Consulate	Burness, 50 Lothian Road, Festival Square EG3 9WJ	0131 473 6320
French Consulate	11 Randolph Crescent EH3 7TT	0131 225 7954
New Zealand Consulate	5 Rutland Square EH1 2AS	0131 222 8109

MEDIA

TELEVISION

» There are five main national terrestrial channels in Britain (see below). Scotland's mainstream television choice is essentially what is broadcast from south of the border, with local material slotted in.

» There is no advertising on the BBC channels, which are funded by a licence fee from all viewers.

» BBC1 and BBC2 are available on terrestrial television and BBC News 24 is broadcast on BBC1 throughout the night.

» BBC4, featuring cultural programming, BBC News 24, BBC Parliament and BBC Choice, which transmits extended coverage of shows featured on BBC1 and BBC2, are all available on cable networks and via digital television.

» Satellite television, dominated by Sky TV, is widely available, sometimes bringing TV to regions that had trouble with terrestrial reception in the past.

RADIO

Scotland is served by the UK's national radio stations (BBC), and has some of its own for more partisan coverage.

» BBC Radio Scotland broadcasts a broadly based mix of news, discussion, travel, magazine format and music programmes, and is useful for weather forecasts.

» Local radio stations take over the frequency at particular times—for example, on weekdays you may hear local news bulletins from the local region where you are at 7.50am, 12.54pm and 16.54pm.

» There are also several local commercial radio stations, including Radio Forth (serving Edinburgh) and Xfm 106 FM (serving Glasgow and eastwards).

NEWSPAPERS, MAGAZINES

» At the quality end of the market, *The Scotsman*, based in Edinburgh, aspires to the crown as Scotland's national newspaper, though challenged by its Glasgow-based competitor, *The Herald*.

» Both are exceeded in circulation by the unashamedly regional, if not downright parochial, Aberdeen-based *Press and Journal*, while the central region is dominated by the weekly *Dundee Courier*.

» Scotland's popular tabloid daily newspaper is the *Daily Record*.

» *The Sunday Post* is a top-selling institution peddling its own unique brand of homespun, Conservative, family-oriented journalism, and featuring two evergreen cartoon strips, 'Oor Wullie' and 'The Broons'.

» *Scotland on Sunday* is a heavyweight which vies with the *Sunday Herald* for the more serious readership.

» Scotland also has many local weekly newspapers, from the radical *West Highland Free Press* to the *Shetland Times*—worth dipping into to see what entertainment is on offer in your chosen holiday locality.

» *The List* is a lively fortnightly listings magazine, giving excellent coverage for both Edinburgh and Glasgow.

» Newspapers from around the world, including foreign language papers, can be purchased at airports, larger train stations and some newsagents such as WH Smith.

» *The Scots Magazine* is a national institution, unashamedly 'for people who love Scotland'. Its small size and thick spine set it apart on the rack. A monthly stalwart, it first appeared in 1739 and remains a rich source of Caledonian curiosities.

TERRESTRIAL TV CHANNELS

BBC1 Shows soaps, chat shows, lifestyle programmes, documentaries and drama, and children's shows. International news and national weather: 6am–9am, 1pm, 6pm, 10pm weekdays and BBC News 24 4.15am–6am. Reporting Scotland at 6.30pm is the news flagship for Scotland, with further regional broadcasts after main news programmes.

BBC2 Specializes in comedy, natural history, history and cultural programmes. News: Newsnight 10.30pm weekdays

ITV1 Shows a variety of programmes including soaps, quiz shows, children's programmes, drama and films. Commercial networks include Border Television (covering the border region), Scottish Television (central and western Scotland) and Grampian Television (covering the north and northeast). International news and national weather: 12.30pm, 6.30pm, 10pm weekdays. Regional news updates are shown after main news broadcasts. Scotland Today is the main news programme at 6pm. Saturday afternoon's Scotsport is ever popular.

Channel 4 Broadcasts include films, documentaries, comedy and quiz shows along with science and natural history programmes. News and weather: 7pm weekdays

Channel 5 Shows children's programmes, game shows, popular films and soapss. Not every area can receive it. News and weather: 6am, 11.30am, 5pm, 7pm weekdays

UK NATIONAL RADIO FREQUENCIES FOR SCOTLAND

BBC Radio 1 (98–99.5 FM): the latest pop music
BBC Radio 2 (88–90.2 FM): wide variety of popular music, plus comedy
BBC Radio 3 (90.3–92.3 FM): classical music
BBC Radio 4 (92.4–95.8 FM; 198kHz LW): topical news, current affairs, drama, travel, shipping news etc
BBC Radio Five Live (693–909 kHz/693 MW): current sport
BBC World Service (648 AM and digital; 198 kHz LW): 24-hr worldwide news and current affairs
BBC Radio Scotland (92.4–94.7 FM/585 or 810 MW): mixture of news, chat, music, weather
BBC Radio nan Gaidheal (103.5–105 FM/990 MW): Gaelic radio station
Classic FM (100–102 FM): classical music with a popular twist

BOOKS, FILMS AND MAPS

BACKGROUND READING

For a solid historical read, try the *New Penguin History of Scotland* (2001), which includes photos from the national museum collections. Christopher Harvie offers a refreshingly concise and sharply observed portrait in the pocket-size *Scotland—A Short History* (2002). Scoular Anderson's *1745 And All That: The Story of the Highlands* (2001) is an excellent cartoon introduction to Scottish history, and not just for children.

For browsing, the hefty *Collins Encyclopaedia of Scotland* by John Keay and Julia Keay (2000) is a mine of fascinating information about individuals, events and places.

PERSONAL ACCOUNTS

It seems that people can't stop writing about their experiences in Scotland—every year brings a new crop of memoirs that provide insights into special places.

Samuel Johnson and James Boswell started it all, with their *Journey to the Western Isles of Scotland* (1775), which is still in print and a surprisingly good read.

More recently, Adam Nicolson's *Sea Room* (2002) paints a memorable portrait of the Western Isles; Alison Johnson's *A House by the Shore* (1986) is an entertaining account of setting up a hotel on Harris, and Alasdair Maclean's lyrical *Night Falls on Ardnamurchan* (1984) is a powerful, melancholy account of the crofters' demise.

Muriel Gray's *The First Fifty* (1991) is an irreverant account of Munro-bagging, and an antidote to more pompous mountaineering guides.

Mairi Hedderwick has written entertaining stories of several tours, illustrated with her own watercolours; the most recent, *Sea Change* (1999), describes a six-week sailing voyage down the Caledonian Canal and around the western coast.

Archie Cameron's *Bare Feet and Tackety Boots* (1988) is a humorous account of an Edwardian boyhood on Rum. And the late poet George Mackay Brown's autobiography, *For the Islands I Sing* (1997), is a vivid memory of Orkney.

SCOTTISH FICTION

Scotland has a long history of great storytelling, and a rich literary heritage that has produced writers as varied as Sir Walter Scott (the *Waverley* novels), Robert Louis Stevenson (*Dr. Jekyll and Mr Hyde*), Neil Gunn (*The Silver Darlings*), Muriel Spark (*The Prime of Miss Jean Brodie*), Iain Crichton Smith (*Consider the Lilies*) and Irvine Welsh (*Trainspotting*). And let's not forget the doggerel rhymer William McGonagall, 1830–1902, known to some as the worst poet in the world.

Right is a selection of lighter Scottish classics and modern favourites, intended as a starting point for holiday reading.

MAP BASICS

For exploring by car, arm yourself with an up-to-date atlas such as the AA's *Great Britain Road Atlas*, widely available from bookshops, or purchase online.
» www.theAA.com
Around 20 more detailed touring maps of individual regions of Scotland, called Official Tourist Maps, are available from tourist information centres

For exploring on foot, the Ordnance Survey publishes detailed maps in the Explorer series at a scale of 1:25,000. These are available from local tourist offices and bookshops, or buy online.
» www.ordnancesurvey.co.uk
The free literature available from tourist offices includes themed maps, such as the Speyside Whisky Trail.

Standard navigational charts of the coastline are supplied by the Hydrographic Office (UKHO).
» UK Hydrographic Office, Admiralty Way, Taunton, Somerset TA1 2DN, tel 01823 337900; www.ukho.gov.uk

10 TOP SCOTTISH FILMS

The 39 Steps (1935)
Whisky Galore (1949)
The Master of Ballantrae (1953)
Local Hero (1983)
Shallow Grave (1994)
Trainspotting (1995)
Braveheart (1995)
Rob Roy (1995)
Mrs. Brown (1997)
Morvern Callar (2002)

10 BEST SCOTTISH READS

Kidnapped, by Robert Louis Stevenson (1886): Gripping 18th-century adventure, with a memorable chase across the Highlands.

Para Handy, by Neil Munro (1931): Anthology of comic tales of the skipper of a Clyde puffer (steamboat), the *Vital Spark*, and his motley crew.

A Scots Quair, by Lewis Grassic Gibbon (1934): A trilogy of novels set in the rural northeast, following the story of Chris Guthrie.

Ring of Bright Water, by Gavin Maxwell (1960): Enchanting real life story of raising otters in the idyllic but unforgiving setting of the western coast.

The Prime of Miss Jean Brodie, by Muriel Spark (1961): The fortunes of a 1930s Edinburgh schoolmistress and her talented pupils.

The Bruce Trilogy, by Nigel Tranter (1971): One of the most enduring popular histories by this evergreen historical storyteller.

The Crow Road, by Iain Banks (1992): Prentice McHoan returns to the bosom of his dysfunctional family.

Black and Blue, by Ian Rankin (1997): Crime in the oil industry for Edinburgh's Inspector Rebus—a good introduction to the Rebus series.

One Fine Day in the Middle of the Night, by Christopher Brookmyre (1999): Black humour, violent and funny, as a school reunion on an oil rig is rudely interrupted.

In Another Light, by Andrew Greig (2004): A man is haunted by his father's story, from Orkney to Penang.

WHAT TO DO

SHOPPING

Scotland's main centres of population are very well served with shopping malls full of big-name brands. Outside the bigger cities shopping takes on an altogether more small-town air, with independently owned stores geared to serving the local community. Some towns still have a market once or twice a week, or a monthly farmers' market, where you can expect to find fruit and vegetables, butchers' and fishmongers' stalls and household items.

DISTINCTIVELY SCOTTISH

Scotland is particularly good for woollen goods, which are widely available in specialist and souvenir stores. Knitted goods are found everywhere, from sweaters in the intricate designs of Shetland and Fair Isle to throws and shawls of the finest cashmere.

Woven woollen cloth in the strong shades and chequered designs of tartan is one of Scotland's best-loved exports. Tartan (also known as plaid) first appeared at the start of the 18th century. It's particularly associated with the Highlands, and its wearing was banned after the Scots' defeat at Culloden in 1746. It was not until the end of the 18th century that tartan became established as a means of identifying clans and districts.

There are many tartans today, both historic and modern. Scotland's oldest families may be associated with more than one.

The cloth known as tweed is more often associated with the weaving mills of southern Scotland, and generally carries smaller designs in more subdued hues than tartan. Harris Tweed is still hand-woven by islanders in the Outer Hebrides.

Scotland also produces some distinctive glasswear, with firms such as Edinburgh Crystal known for its fine cut-glass, and Caithness Glass for its modern designs and beautiful coloured paperweights. Pottery from Highland Stoneware, hand-painted with Scottish scenes, is also widely available.

An ornamental tin of shortbread is perhaps the ultimate Scottish souvenir, but the choice of local food available to take home has widened to embrace a wide range of goods.

TAX-FREE SHOPPING

If the goods you buy are going to be exported to a non-European Union (EU) country, you are exempt from Value Added Tax (VAT; currently 17.5 per cent), where it is applied. This can be a considerable saving (but you have to spend a minimum amount which varies from shop to shop) and it is usually reclaimed at the airport on departure rather than deducted in the shop. Most major department stores participate and will have details of their tax-free policies to help you make your claim.

OPENING TIMES
▷ 321.

The availability of evening entertainment in Scotland varies according to your location. Edinburgh and Glasgow are well served on all levels, as you would expect, with a lively night scene and top-rank entertainment. A series of great festivals, led by the Edinburgh Festival (▷ 96) helps to foster a vibrant arts scene. Live music can be heard in pubs and village halls all over the country at any time of year, and if it's advertised as a ceilidh, there's probably some dancing involved. Plays and musicals may be performed in anything from a world-class venue to the tiny theatre on Mull. While most towns have a small cinema, clubs and bars are generally confined to the larger urban centres, with pubs taking over the role in smaller communities.

CLASSICAL MUSIC, OPERA AND DANCE

Scotland has three big orchestras, led by the Royal Scottish National Orchestra (RSNO), whose main season runs from September to April. Look out also for the Scottish Chamber Orchestra (mainly touring) and the BBC Scottish Symphony Orchestra. Smaller groups such as the BT Scottish Ensemble are also worth seeking out. Scottish Opera has a wide international repertoire.

Scottish Ballet performs regularly in the main cities, and contemporary dance is led by the Scottish Dance Theatre, based in Dundee.
» For more information see www. visitscotland.com/guide/see-and-do

POPULAR MUSIC AND COMEDY

Stadiums such as Glasgow's SECC (▷ 181) are the preserve of household names and top pop acts. Jazz, blues and world music also get a look-in: Henry's Jazz Cellar in Edinburgh is just one well-known venue.

Home-grown pop and folk music thrives in clubs, festivals and more intimate venues around the country.

Meanwhile, live comedy has become increasingly evident in cities, where chains such as Stand Comedy Club provide live acts most nights.

CINEMA

Cities and larger towns are well served by huge, comfortable multiplexes showing the latest films, interspersed with fewer independent picture houses such as the Glasgow Film Theatre (▷ 180).

In the regions, cinemas may offer fewer frills and less choice.

TICKETS

The easiest ways to buy tickets are from the venue's box office, or through a ticket agency for larger events (a fee may be added).
» Agencies include Ticketmaster, tel 0870 534 4444; www.ticketmaster. co.uk

PUBS, BARS, NIGHTCLUBS

Unlike the male-dominated bastions of the past, most pubs now encourage female customers and families, and most serve food plus coffee and tea. In the countryside they may be the only option for a night out. City pubs can become very busy on Friday and Saturday evenings.

In some towns bars are taking over from pubs and nightclubs as the focal points for socializing. During the day they resemble cafés, serving food and coffee, while at night they become small nightclubs, complete with DJ and dance floor.

Most towns and cities will have at least one nightclub, but choose carefully: Smaller towns may have just one dingy venue, playing uninspiring chart music. Dress codes vary according to the location, so check before you set out. Most places accept 'smart casual', but generally not T-shirts, jeans or trainers.
» *The List* magazine appears every other Thursday (£3.50). It's a useful guide to the entertainment scenes in Edinburgh and Glasgow.

SPORTS AND ACTIVITIES

The delights of the Highlands as an outdoor venue were discovered in the 19th century, when acres of land were bought up as sporting estates for hunting, shooting and fishing. Today, influenced by the growth worldwide of adventure sports, the range of activities on offer across the country is wider than ever. It takes in white-water canoeing, diving, mountaineering, downhill skiing and other high-adrenaline pursuits, as well as more traditional activities such as hill-walking, game fishing and golf. All are a great way to see more of the countryside, and are well supported with information available at local tourist offices. Whatever you undertake, be prepared for changeable and sometimes extreme weather, and heed local advice if taking to the hills, where conditions may change rapidly.

There are plenty of opportunities to enjoy world-class spectator sports such as football (soccer) and rugby, too, and Scotland's own variations of athletic events such as hammer throwing can be seen throughout the summer at Highland games events. For information on shinty fixtures, visit www.shinty.com

BICYCLING
Forest paths, disused rail tracks and quiet rural roads make bicycling a popular holiday activity here. The National Cycle Network (Sustrans) has over 1,300 miles (2,092km) of routes marked by distinctive blue signs, including a scenic route between Glasgow and Inverness (214 miles/344km). The National Byway is a rural bicycling route in southern Scotland. The Scottish stretch of the international North Sea Cycle Route picks up in Shetland and continues down the eastern seaboard of the mainland into England.

There are many shorter bicycle trails—see local tourist offices for details and leaflets. These include KM Cycle Trail from Dumfries to Drumlanrig Castle. It is named after local hero Kirkpatrick Macmillan (1813–78), inventor of the bicycle.
» www.cycling.visitscotland. com has advice on bicycle rental.

FISHING
Scotland has an abundance of rivers, lochs and 4,000 miles (6,436km) of coastline, so you can enjoy coarse, sea and game fishing. It's essential to check the rules before fishing as many waters restrict the tackle or bait you can use. For coarse and game fishing you'll need a permit, which you can buy from the local tourist office, fishery or tackle shop.
» www.vfishisitscotland.com is a good source of information.

» www.fishing-uk-scotland.com lists a variety of fishing organizations and holiday options.

COARSE FISHING
Angling for roach, pike, carp, tench or perch lacks the cachet of game fishing, but is often more accessible on a short visit—there is no closed season for coarse fishing. Lochs Ken, Lomond and Awe are known for their pike.
» Scottish Federation for Coarse Angling; www.SFCA.co.uk

SEA ANGLING
No permit is required. Cod and pollock are favourites, caught from the southeastern shores through the summer, and off more northerly shores in winter. The southeast shores of Dumfries and Galloway produce some of the best shore fishing, with pollock and wrasse in summer and cod in winter. Porbeagle sharks, skate and halibut are more adventurous catches off the northern and western coasts. Fishing for mackerel with a long lure line is a great holiday pastime.

GAME FISHING
The brown trout season is from 15 March to 6 October. Wild brown trout are found in lochs and rivers all over the country. You can find salmon and sea trout fishing from 15 January to 30 November, although open and close season dates vary from region to region. Note that salmon fishing is prohibited on Sundays. Expect to pay a high price for a beat on the great salmon rivers—the Tweed, the Spey, the Tay and the Dee.
» Salmon and Trout Association, tel 020 7283 5838; www.salmon-trout.org

FOOTBALL (SOCCER)
The football season runs from August until May. The two big Edinburgh teams — Heart of Midlothian (Hearts) and Hibernian (Hibs) — are both worth a look. Finding tickets for the Edinburgh derby may be tricky, but for all

other games try the websites for match details and tickets. Celtic and Rangers are the great rivals in Glasgow. Advance reservations are essential.

GOLF
Golf is the national game, played by people of all ages and incomes. With more than 500 courses to choose from, you'll need advice to select a course and reserve a round. Tourist offices have information on all the main courses (▷ 321). The golf season is from April until mid-October; reserve in advance as far as possible.
» www.scottishgolf.com has a directory and reservations advice. Most regions offer a golf pass or ticket which can be used to save money: ask at any tourist office. For example, a three-day Perthshire Highland ticket gives access to 11 top courses for around £35. Some courses may have age restrictions.
» For information on individual courses, see the regional listings that follow.

HORSEBACK RIDING
Forest trails, sandy beaches and heather-covered hills make Scotland ideal for horseback riding. Find out about local facilities from the nearest tourist office. Go through a riding centre that has been approved by the British Horse Society (BHS) or the Trekking and Riding Society of Scotland (TRSS).
» www.bhsscotland.org.uk
» www.riding-in-scotland.com

RUGBY
International games have become a great spectacle even for the non-rugby fan. The home of Scottish rugby is Murrayfield, in Edinburgh.

WALKING
There is an established network of marked trails, and local tourist offices usually stock leaflets and books about walking in the area, whether you're looking for a level stroll or something more strenuous. Detailed Ordnance Survey maps

are also sold here and in most bookshops. Look for the AA's book, *100 Walks in Scotland*, which contains mapped walks for all abilities.

Access to the hills is generally open, but during the shooting season (12 August to early December) walkers should check locally for possible restrictions. On some of the most popular hills, Hillphones run by the Mountaineering Council give up-to-date information about hunting activities. Particularly during the lambing season (March–end May), dogs must be kept under strict control.

Hill walkers take a particular interest in ticking off the list of Munros, a set of 284 peaks classified as over 914.4m (3,000ft) and named after the climber who first categorized them. Corbetts and Grahams are lower level lists.

Look for the 'Walkers Welcome' symbol at accommodation sites from bothies to guesthouses, where drying facilities and early breakfasts are available.
» For information about long-distance paths ▷ 333–334.

WATERSPORTS
Scotland's inshore waters are popular with sailors of small-and medium-size craft. The seas around the Western Isles and larger lakes such as Loch Lomond are particularly good. Inland waterways like the Forth & Clyde and Union Canal offer more options for holidays afloat.

» www.sailscotland.co.uk has information on sailing courses and boat charter.

Windsurfing takes place in a number of spots around the coast, as well as on Loch Tay, Loch Lomond and other freshwater sites. Popular beaches include Elie and Lunan Bay in the east, Machrihanish in the west, Sandhead Bay in the southwest and Thurso in the north. Tiree claims to be the windsurfing capital of Scotland. Waterskiing takes place on larger lochs, including Loch Tay and Loch Lomond.

WINTER SPORTS

There are five main ski centres in Scotland. Lessons and ski rental are available at all, and day adult lift passes cost around £25. The season depends entirely on snowfall: if it

snows they open the runs. The best snowfall is usually in January and February.
» www.ski.visitscotland.com

NEVIS RANGE
Due to the altitude, this centre near Fort William is the best for snow late in the season. It is popular with skiers and snowboarders and has an excellent off-piste area, Back Corrie.
» www.nevis-range.co.uk

CAIRNGORM
The ski centre near Aviemore has a funicular railway system to take you to the top in comfort, and offers a range of runs for all ability levels.
» www.cairngormmountain.com

THE LECHT
The most easterly ski centre, family-

focused, with a snowboard fun park, snowtubing, quad bikes and deval karting.
» www.lecht.co.uk

GLENCOE
At the inland end of the pass, this is the most alpine ski centre, with dramatic, wild scenery and the steepest on-piste run in Scotland. It's also popular with snowboarders.
» www.glencoemountain.com

GLENSHEE
Close to Braemar, Glenshee is the most extensive ski and snowboard area, with 21 lifts and 36 runs.
» www.ski-glenshee.co.uk

HEALTH AND BEAUTY

Luxurious spas are a well-established feature of upmarket tourism in Scotland, with the top hotels offering wonderfully indulgent treatments in opulent surroundings.

The spectacular rooftop hydropool at Edinburgh's One-Spa at the Sheraton Grand (▷ 95), for example, has become a vital modern icon for the capital. However, the idea of self-pampering is relatively new to the Scottish spirit, and beyond the major centres you'll be lucky to find much

more than the facilities of, perhaps, a local hairdresser.

Fitness is another matter, and most towns of any size have a local gym, swimming pool and fitness centre, with training times and facilities well advertised locally.

FOR CHILDREN

From outdoor activities such as go-carting and quad biking aimed at older kids to the retelling of well-loved tales in the Scots vernacular at storytelling sessions, children are well catered for in Scotland, especially in summer.

Visitor centres offer opportunities to get involved with everything from learning how ice cream is made and hand-painting pottery to getting up close to wildlife and farm animals. Glasgow's fabulous hands-on Science Centre is the biggest of several excellent such facilities around the country, and history can be explored through steam trains, sailing ships and excellent industrial museums such as Wanlockhead and Dundee's Verdant Works.

The harbour town of Tobermory, on Mull, has become the hottest attraction for under-sixes since the advent of the BBC's storytelling programme for youngsters, Balamory—a leaflet available locally

will help them identify the real houses of characters such as Josie Jump, Miss Hoolie and Spencer the Painter.

In practical terms, many attractions are free to under-fives and offer a substantial discount to children under 16. Family discount tickets are widely available, but always check ahead as details of numbers and ages included can vary enormously according to the attraction.

It's well worth searching through the local free newspapers and tourist leaflets, too, as they often offer discount tickets (such as free child entry with one full-paying adult) on the day.

FESTIVALS AND EVENTS

Scotland has many festivals and traditions. Listed below, month by month, are the major events that take place annually. While some are free public events, most involve buying tickets which will vary in price according to the event and venue. Check for the availablility of season tickets, which may offer better value.

JANUARY
BA' GAME
Kirkwall, Orkney
www.bagame.com
An energetic game of mass soccer, when two teams from the upper and lower ends of the town (the Uppies and the Doonies) scrimmage in the streets in a tradition that dates back further than anyone can remember. The main throw-in occurs at 1pm, at the Mercat Cross, with the Doonies aiming for the harbour and the Uppies for a point near the Catholic church.
🕐 1 January

CELTIC CONNECTIONS
Glasgow, various venues
www.celticconnections.co.uk
Scotland's biggest Celtic and folk festival attracts musicians from all over the world. Concerts, workshops and ceilidhs over three weeks.
🕐 January

UP HELLY AA
Lerwick, Shetland
Tel 01595 693434
www.visitshetland.com
Viking celebrations on the last Tuesday of the month, with torchlight processions, 'guizers', a ceremonial ship burning and partying. Local Up Helly Aa festivals are held around the islands during February and March.
🕐 Late January

APRIL/MAY
SHETLAND FOLK FESTIVAL
Shetland, Lerwick and various venues
Tel 01595 694757
www.shetlandfolkfestival.com
Four days of some of the liveliest folk music around, in venues as far as Fair Isle. Attracts artists such as Aly Bain and Phil Cunningham, Frances Black and Elvis Costello as well as performers from around

the world. Join in sessions and workshops at the Isleburgh Community Centre.
🕐 End April/early May

SPIRIT OF SPEYSIDE WHISKY FESTIVAL
Speyside, various venues
Tel 07092 840566
www.spiritofspeyside.com
Four days of whisky-imbued fun all over Speyside, from vintage tastings on trains to tours of the distilleries.
🕐 End April/early May

JUNE
CAMANACHD CUP FINAL
Venues change annually
www.shinty.co.uk
The Camanachd Association is the ruling body of the predominantly Gaelic sport of shinty, and the cup final is the highlight of the year's fixtures as teams compete for the silver trophy.
🕐 Mid-June

T IN THE PARK
Balado, Fife
www.tinthepark.com
Scotland's biggest rock festival boasts a line-up of around 100 of the best local and international pop bands on seven stages over one weekend, from Idlewild and Super Furry Animals to Amy Winehouse and the Sugarbabes.
🕐 Mid-June

ROYAL HIGHLAND SHOW
Ingliston, by Edinburgh
Tel 0131 335 6200
www.royalhighlandshow.org
The biggest agricultural show in Scotland offers four days of top livestock judging, show jumping, heavy horses, crafts, trade stands and other country activities. The permanent show site is near Edinburgh airport.

ST. MAGNUS FESTIVAL
Orkney, various venues
www.stmagnusfestival.com
Prestigious summer festival of music (chiefly classical, but also folk and jazz), theatre, literature and visual arts. St. Magnus Cathedral is the main setting.
🕐 Late June

JUNE/JULY
COMMON RIDINGS
Selkirk, Hawick, Galashiels
Up to 400 horseback riders take part in these traditional Borders festivals, following the town's flag as it is borne around the edge of the common land.
🕐 June/July

JULY
GLASGOW INTERNATIONAL JAZZ FESTIVAL
Glasgow, various locations
Tel 0141 552 3552
www.jazzfest.co.uk
Eight days of the best in international jazz in venues across the city. Check out the Fringe, too.
🕐 Early July

SCOTTISH TRADITIONAL BOAT FESTIVAL
Portsoy
Tel 01261 842951
www.stbf.bizland.com
Maritime fun at this own on the Banffshire coast when, for three days, the harbour fills with wooden sailing boats reminiscent of the glory days of the fishing fleet. Racing, displays by the local Coastguard service, folk music, beer and food.
🕐 July

AUGUST
EDINBURGH FRINGE FESTIVAL
www.edfringe.com
▷ 96
🕐 August

EDINBURGH INTERNATIONAL ARTS FESTIVAL

www.eif.co.uk

▷ 96

🕓 August

MILITARY TATTOO

www.edtattoo.co.uk

▷ 97

🕓 August

WORLD PIPE BAND CHAMPIONSHIPS

Glasgow, various venues

www.rspba.org

Pipers, drummers and pipe bands from all over the world play at this prestigious annual competition.

🕓 Mid-August

COWAL HIGHLAND GATHERING

Dunoon

Tel 01369 703206

www.cowalgathering.com

The biggest Highland games boast some 3,500 competitors from as far afield as Canada and New Zealand. Highland dancing, piping and athletics over three days.

🕓 Late August

SEPTEMBER

BRAEMAR GATHERING

Braemar, Deeside

Tel 01339 755377

www.braemargathering.org

The Queen is a regular visitor to this most famous of Highland games events, augmented by teams from HM Forces.

🕓 Early September

SCOTTISH BOOK TOWN FESTIVAL

www.wigtown-booktown.co.uk/festival

▷ 124

🕓 Late September

OCTOBER

ROYAL NATIONAL MOD

Venues change annually

www.the-mod.co.uk

A major competition-based festival celebrating and helping to promote all areas of Gaelic language, arts and culture.

🕓 Early October

ACCORDION AND FIDDLE FESTIVAL

Shetland, various venues

Tel 01595 694757

www.shetland-music.com/musevnt2.htm

Dance 'til you drop at this hectic four-day festival, celebrating two of Scotland's most popular folk instruments, and held in community halls all across the islands.

🕓 Mid-October

DECEMBER/JANUARY

FLAMBEAUX

Comrie, Perthshire

www.hogmanay.net/scotland/perth

An ancient hogmanay (New Year) festival is celebrated at midnight when 3m (10ft) high flaming torches are lit in the old churchyard, then processed through the streets, to be doused in the River Earn. The torch-bearers are led by a pipe band, and followed by villagers in fancy dress.

🕓 31 December/1 January

HOGMANAY

Princes Street, Edinburgh

Tel 0131 473 3800

www.edinburghshogmanay.org

Celebrate the end of the old year and the start of the new with live music, dancing and mega-fireworks at Scotland's biggest annual party. Entry is free, but you need a pass—check for details on the website.

🕓 31 December/1 January

HIGHLAND GAMES

Highland games take place throughout the summer across Scotland. Historically trials of strength, today they generally include a number of athletic events such as hammer throwing and tossing the caber. In this event a tree trunk must be lifted and thrown end-over-end, to land as near as possible in a 'twelve o'clock' position on the ground.

They may include competitions in Highland dance and bag-piping, and there may be showjumping, tug-of-war, and livestock events such as sheepdog trials, as well as food stands and other entertainments.

Check with local tourist offices for more information.

Below *Traditional Scottish dancing at the World Pipe Band Championships in Glasgow*

Right *Looking down towards the Caledonian Canal and Loch Oich*

LONG-DISTANCE FOOTPATHS

Scotland has four officially designated national walking trails, known as Long Distance Routes: the West Highland Way, the Great Glen Way, the Speyside Way and the Southern Upland Way. Walking the full distance of any of these trails takes careful planning and a high level of fitness, but they can also be enjoyed in shorter stretches. There are many other opportunities for longer walks, which may or may not be marked, and for which leaflets and guidebooks are widely available at tourist offices. Part of the European Footpath Network, the E2, also passes through southern Scotland.

THE COWAL WAY
PORTAVADIE TO ARDGARTEN
Distance: 47 miles (75km)
Time: allow 6 days
www.colglen.co.uk
Traverses the beautiful Cowal peninsula from Portavadie on Loch Fyne to Ardgarten near Arrochar on Loch Long. On the way it passes through moorland and forestry in remote Glendaruel.

FIFE COASTAL PATH
FORTH BRIDGE TO TAY BRIDGE
Distance: 81 miles (130km)
Time: allow 4–5 days
www.fifecoastalpath.com

Relatively easy walking along the scenic coast, with extensions to St. Andrews and beyond.

GREAT GLEN WAY
FORT WILLIAM TO INVERNESS
Distance: 73 miles (117km)
Time: allow 4–6 days
www.greatglenway.com
This spectacular route is along Scotland's massive natural fault line, the Great Glen. The walking is relatively easy, on low-level woodland tracks and the tow path which runs alongside the Caledonian Canal. The start point is the Old Fort in Fort William, and highlights include Neptune's Staircase, Fort Augustus and Urquhart Castle, before it reaches Inverness Castle. A bicycle trail follows a similar route.

THE KINTYRE WAY
TARBERT TO SOUTHEND
Distance: 89 miles (142km)
Time: allow 10–12 days
www.kintyre.org
From Tarbert in the Highlands, walk the entire length of Scotland's 'mainland island' to Southend near the famous Mull of Kintyre, where the more rounded lowland scenery gives way to dramatic views across the North Channel to Ireland.

Above *Walking the West Highland Way, with the Hills of Crianlarich in the background*
Left *A walker silhouetted on a tor at Ben Avon in the Cairngorms National Park*

PILGRIMS WAY
GLENLUCE ABBEY TO THE ISLE OF WHITHORN
Distance: 25 miles 40km
Time: allow 2–3 days
A marked medieval pilgrimage route in southwest Scotland.

ROB ROY WAY
DRYMEN TO PITLOCHRY
Distance: 79 or 92 miles (127 or 148km)
Time: allow 6–7 days
www.robroyway.com
A dramatic route through the heart of Scotland, following the outlaw, Rob Roy MacGregor (1671–1743). The longer route takes a diversion into Glen Almond.

ST. CUTHBERT'S WALK
MELROSE TO LINDISFARNE
Distance: 62 miles (100km)
Time: allow 7 days
www.st-cuthberts-way.co.uk
Follow the marked trail of the seventh-century monk, St. Cuthbert, via Jedburgh to his burial place on Lindisfarne (Holy Island), Northumberland.

SOUTHERN UPLAND WAY
PORTPATRICK TO COCKBURNSPATH
Distance: 212 miles (341km)
Time: allow 10–20 days

www.dumgal.gov.uk/southernupland way;
www.sirwalterscottway.fsnet.co.uk
Britain's first official coast-to-coast footpath runs through the rolling hills and gentler farmland of southern Scotland. Highlights include industrial history at Wanlockhead, the ancient mansion of Traquair, and Melrose. The 92-mile (148km) section from Moffat to Cockburnspath overlaps with the Sir Walter Scott Way, which links places associated with the novelist.

SPEYSIDE WAY
BUCKIE TO AVIEMORE
Distance: 84 miles (135km)
Time: allow 5–7 days
www.speysideway.org
This route follows the River Spey from the Moray coast south to the edge of the Cairngorms. The route from Buckpool harbour winds via Craigellachie Forest, Cromdale, Grantown-on-Spey and Boat of Garten to the police station at Aviemore. Additional spurs divert to Dufftown and Tomintoul.

WEST HIGHLAND WAY
MILNGAVIE TO FORT WILLIAM
Distance: 95 miles (153km)
Time: allow 7–10 days
www.west-highland-way.co.uk

Opposite *The Petit Paris in Edinburgh*

This is Scotland's most popular long-distance trail, taking in some of the finest west Highland scenery, including Loch Lomond and Rannoch Moor. Usually walked from south to north, it is most taxing in its later stretches. The start is at Milngavie, on the northern outskirts of Glasgow, and it uses ancient cattle drovers' roads, military roads instituted by General Wade to help tame the country after Culloden, old coaching routes, and redundant railway as it winds its way to Fort William.

THE WEST ISLAND WAY
KILCHATTON BAY TO PORT BANNATYNE, ISLE OF BUTE
Distance: 30 miles (48km)
Time: allow 2–4 days
www.visitbute.com
This marked trail across the Isle of Bute in the Firth of Clyde offers easy walking with fantastic views of Kintyre, Arran and the Cowal Peninsula.

EATING

Scotland has a clear identity apart from the rest of the UK, which also shows in its food. In recent years, as the public has become more discerning and chefs higher profile, the country has developed clear culinary trends, traditions and undercurrents of its own based around distinctive local and seasonal ingredients.

Britain's colonial past has made it a culinary melting pot, and curry has been described as Scotland's alternative national dish. The rise of Thai cuisine, the continued popularity of Chinese food and the arrival of a host of other ethnic cuisines in the cities mean that the culinary explorer can be spoiled for choice.

Continental-style cafés have sprung up in most well-to-do towns, selling freshly prepared food, drinks and coffee. In rural areas, you are more likely to find yourself eating at a country pub or hotel. Most pubs serve food, and a new breed of so-called gastro pubs has set about catering for guests who rate good food as highly as they do a good pint of beer.

It has to be said that amid all this innovation, standards are still variable and it's not uncommon to find menus that read well but simply don't deliver. Use our list of recommended eating places to avoid disappointment and you'll find that culinary excellence exists as far afield as Ullapool, Skye and Harris. And wherever you are, you'll find the tea rooms associated with many visitor attractions a useful stand-by.

WHAT TO EAT

When it comes to cooking, Scotland's historical links with France can be seen in names such as Tartan Purry (tarte en purée) and sooty bannock (sauté bannock). While it's easy to find traditional dishes such as Cullen skink or

haggis with tatties and neeps, many modern chefs are once again looking to the classical techniques of French cookery—and to the spices of the Pacific Rim—for inspiration. 'Modern Scottish' menus combine all these influences.

Fresh, high-quality ingredients are a major feature. From the coastal waters come boatloads of fish and shellfish including herring, halibut, cod, lobsters, mussels, scallops and crabs. Treats include some of the largest langoustines you'll ever see, Loch Fyne oysters and the delicately flavoured Arbroath smokies—haddock smoked hot over oak chips for a gentle, smoky taste and a soft, cooked flesh. The Scots excel at curing fish: other specialities include Finnan haddock (salted then smoked), and smoked herring (kippers), both of which may be served at breakfast.

Scottish salmon is renowned, but beware of the difference between wild (caught) salmon and farmed varieties. Salmon farming is awash with controversy thanks to revelations about fish kept in overcrowded sea cages, the use of dye to colour the flesh, and the presence of various chemicals and pollutants. Many salmon farmers have cleaned up their acts, but wild salmon is still seen as superior to the farmed variety. Trout, both wild and farmed, is another popular option.

Other distinctive game includes grouse and venison. Aberdeen Angus beef is prized throughout Britain, and lamb is also widely available.

Oats have been grown in Scotland for centuries, and continue to thrive in the cool, damp climate. Ground into oatmeal, they are at the heart of foods such as porridge, oatcakes and haggis.

Comfort is perhaps a key word for describing Scottish food: a leisurely breakfast or an elegant high tea (served in the late afternoon or evening) can include a mouth-watering array of cakes, biscuits (especially shortbread) and scones. Spread them with local honey or the famous Dundee orange marmalade. And if that awakens your sweet tooth, you're in the right place: summer brings a supply of excellent soft fruit from the Angus glens, and all year round the country could stock a sweet shop with its crunchy toffees, buttery mints and pretty pastel sticks of rock.

Cheesemaking, another Scottish tradition, is still going strong thanks to a handful of post-war revivalists. Look out for Crowdie (a Highland soft curd cheese probably of Viking or Pictish origin) and Caboc (a soft, buttery cheese rolled in toasted oatmeal). Other classics include sharp, creamy Dunsyre Blue, and Lanark Blue — a blue-veined ewes' milk cheese.

MENU READER

Arbroath smokies: small hot-smoked haddock, with a more delicate flavour than kippers (see below)
Atholl brose: drink prepared from oatmeal and water, with whisky and honey
bannock: see oatcake, below; see also Selkirk bannock
black bun: tea-time treat made from dried fruits and spices cooked within a pastry case, served in slices
black pudding: blood sausage made from pig's blood, suet and oatmeal
butterscotch: hard golden candy made from sugar, water and butter
clapshot: a blend of cooked turnip and potato (neeps and tatties), mashed up with a little butter and milk, often served as an accompaniment to haggis
clootie dumpling: steamed sweet and spicy pudding, traditionally cooked in a cloth ('cloot'), and associated with New Year
cock-a-leekie soup: stock-based soup of chicken, leeks and other vegetables
cranachan: dessert of raspberries, cream and toasted oatmeal
crowdie: light curd cheese
Cullen skink: creamy fish broth based on 'Finnan haddie' or smoked haddock
drop scone: see Scotch pancake, below
Dundee cake: rich fruit cake, traditionally decorated with almonds on the top
Edinburgh fog: a rich, sweet dessert made with double cream, sugar, almond-flavoured biscuits, flaked almonds and Drambuie liqueur
Edinburgh rock: crumbly sweet made into round, pastel-hued sticks with flavours such as vanilla, ginger and lemon
Forfar bridie: meat pasty made with beef, onion and potato

haggis: Scotland's national dish, a sort of large mutton sausage based on the ground-up liver, lungs and heart of a sheep, mixed with oatmeal, onion and spices, and cooked up in the sheep's stomach
hot toddy: warming drink made with boiling water, a little sugar and whisky, flavoured with lemon, nutmeg and cinammon
kipper: smoked, cured herring
neeps and tatties: see clapshot, above
oatcake: thin, crumbly savoury biscuit made of oatmeal
partan bree: crab soup ('partan' means crab, 'bree' means broth)
porridge: a hot and filling breakfast dish of stewed oatmeal or rolled oats, served with milk and sugar, or salt to taste
potato scone: hot, flat, savoury cake made from potato and flour
reestit mutton: mutton preserved in salt, used as the basis of soups and stews in Shetland
Scotch broth: a hearty soup, with lamb, pearl barley and winter vegetables
Scotch pancake: small, thick pancake, eaten hot or cold with butter and syrup or jam
Scotch pie: small meat pie (traditionally using mutton) with hot-water crust pastry, and served hot or cold
Selkirk bannock: round fruit bread with sultanas
shortbread: thick, pale golden biscuit with a firm texture, made from butter, sugar and flour
stovies: a hearty, filling, hotpot-type dish with many variations, but essentially uses potatoes, onions and meat
tablet: hard fudge
Tantallon cake: named after Tantallon castle, this is not a cake as such, but another version of shortbread
Tweed kettle: a poached fish dish, sometimes called salmon hash

INTERNATIONAL DINING

Recent surveys investigating the taste of the British public have found that, while native dishes are still highly rated, they are at least matched in popularity by more ethnic menus. Most towns have an Indian or Chinese restaurant, often known in Scotland as a 'carry oot' ('carry out', or take-away). Newer international trends include Moroccan, Turkish and most notably Thai cuisine, but visit a big city and you may also find Indonesian, Caribbean, Vietnamese, Hungarian, Russian, Mongolian and Mexican. In many places you can now find exciting modern Indian restaurants that offer traditional Indian dishes, fusions of Indian and European cooking or the very latest innovations from Mumbai (Bombay).

Another long-standing favourite is Italian food, be it the genuine article or pizza chains. Large numbers of Italians immigrated to Scotland in the early 20th century, and Italian ice cream makers have become local heroes—look for Luca of Musselburgh. Italian-run cafés, restaurants and coffee bars are usually a good bet if you're looking for a decent cup of coffee.

VEGETARIAN FOOD

Dedicated wholefood vegetarian restaurants are scarce since most non-vegetarian restaurants caught on to the demand and started to offer meat-free options. These choices may be limited, so telephone in advance and check what's available, especially as some restaurants do not include a vegetarian option on the menu but are happy to prepare one if the customer requests it. The international restaurants—especially Thai, Vietnamese and Indian—generally offer a wide selection of non-meat dishes.

WHERE TO EAT

Restaurant dining reflects the diversity of British culture, and there are options to suit most tastes and pockets. The one thing many

have in common is their opening hours—between 12 and 2, and from 6 until 9—but in most larger towns and cities you can find food at any time of day. Later at night, only a few restaurants keep serving.

Many top restaurants are based in hotels, particularly in the major cities. Farther afield, hotel restaurants are mixed in quality. Some of the establishments that particularly pride themselves on their food describe themselves as 'restaurants with rooms' to indicate that the emphasis is on the dining experience.

Scotland's dining pubs are quintessentially British: bare stone walls, open fires and low beams typify the environment, so much so that modern chain pubs are often decorated in the same quaint fashion. Most (but not all) pubs welcome families and many stay open throughout the day, though food is often only available from 12 to 2 and from 6 until 9.

Pub menus traditionally include 'bar snacks'—lighter, cheaper meals including sandwiches, toasties (toasted sandwiches), filled baked potatoes and ploughmen's lunches (a cold platter of bread, meat, cheese and salad)—but these days most pubs also serve dishes such as curry, steak and ale pie, bangers and mash, and steak and chips (french fries).

Local cafés are intimate establishments selling teas and (usually fried) snacks. More recently, the word café has started to be used for the more stylish continental-style establishments (once called brasserie or bistro) found in increasing numbers in cities and towns including Glasgow, Perth and Inverness. These bridge the gap between pubs, restaurants and coffee bars by selling coffees, snacks, wines and meals.

A traditional stalwart, tea shops may be found just about anywhere and are usually open from mid-morning until 4 or 5pm. They specialize in teas, home-made cakes and light meals. Find them

in larger department stores, on the high street, at garden centres and at many tourist attractions. National Trust for Scotland tea rooms have a particularly good reputation for the high quality of their fresh home-baking.

RESTAURANT TIPS

» In some restaurants it is possible to walk in off the street and get a table, but if you have your heart set on dining in a particular place, it's always advisable to reserve a table in advance by telephone or email.
» Less formal establishments, especially pubs, may work on a 'first come, first served' basis.
» Smoking is totally banned in all public places.
» It's fairly common for a table booking to last only a couple of hours, after which time guests will be expected to move on to make way for the next sitting.
» It's also worth noting that many restaurants stop serving food earlier than elsewhere in Europe. Don't expect to turn up at 10.30pm and be fed unless you've checked in advance. The most notable exceptions are Thai, Chinese and Indian restaurants, which are often still serving food at midnight.
» In the past the British loved to dress for dinner and the more formal restaurants tended to have strict dress codes, especially where jackets and ties were concerned. These days things are more flexible, though it's unwise to turn up at a pricey restaurant wearing jeans and a T-shirt. If you're in doubt, it's quite acceptable to telephone and ask.
» You can expect excellent service in Scotland's top restaurants, but lower down the price scale things are less consistent. If you are happy with the service, it is usual to leave a tip of about 10–15 per cent at the end of the meal.
» If you pay by credit card you may find that when you sign the receipt, it includes a section in which to add an extra amount as a tip. It is acceptable to cross this section through and leave a cash tip instead.

ALCOHOL

Scotland's licensing laws are now not strictly laid down, but may vary with different establishments. Pubs traditionally serve alcohol 11am–11pm, Monday–Saturday, and 12.30–2.30, 6.30–11 on Sundays (the afternoon gap may be bridged by a license extension). Extensions to these hours may allow premises to open late. From autumn 2009, new laws allowing premises to apply for 24-hour licenses are likely to be in place.

» A bottle of wine in a restaurant usually costs significantly more than in a shop.

» Some restaurants—especially those not licensed to sell alcohol—operate a 'bring your own' system (BYO), in which case diners may pay a small corkage fee.

FAST FOOD

'Fast food' usually means take-away food, and in many cases it's possible to buy a meal for under £6. American fast-food chain outlets have reached most corners of the countrya. In remoter areas the population year-round is not large enough to support this, and you are unlikely to find anything.

Other fast food outlets are likely to be independently owned, or local chains. They include local pizza delivery shops, fish-and-chip shops (which may also sell pies, burgers and pizzas) and a wide variety of multicultural take-aways. Haggis and chips (french fries) is also found on some fast food menus, and Glaswegians are infamous for inventing the deep-fried Mars bar. In rural areas, 'fast food' may be mobile—that is, served from the back of a van.

Service stations on motorways and major trunk (long-distance) roads also supply fast food, from sandwiches and pre-packed snacks to take with you, to light restaurant meals. The quality is variable, but on a long drive it's a good excuse to stop for a break. Roadside chains include Little Chef, Granada and Welcome Break.

Above *An outdoor café in the Merchant City area of Glasgow*

QUICK GUIDE TO RESTAURANT AND FAST FOOD CHAINS

Beefeater: British steakhouse restaurants
Burger King: high-street hamburger chain
Deep Pan Pizza: winning combination of pizza, pasta and salad
Di Maggio's: chain of restaurants and tapas bars in Glasgow and west central region
Domino's Pizza: pizza to go or to your door
Harry Ramsden's: British franchise selling fried fish and chips (french fries)
Howies: Scottish chain of affordable restaurants
KFC: fried chicken, fish and fries to take away
McDonald's: ubiquitous fast food burger chain
Pizza Express: pizza restaurant chain
Pizza Hut: wide range of pizzas to eat in
Subway: the popular American chain selling filled rolls and sandwiches
T.G.I. Friday's: lively American-style restaurant chain
Wimpy: British burger restaurant chain, established in 1954

WHISKY

Scotland's landscape and history are inextricably linked with whisky, the golden distilled liquor made from malted grain, especially barley or rye, and drunk as a single malt or a blend. (In contrast, American whiskey, or bourbon, is made with rye or maize.)

The first clear written record of the production of whisky in Scotland was in 1494 during the reign of James IV, when the exchequer roll granted the right 'to friar John Cor, by order of the King, to make aqua vitae, eight bolls of malt.' Aqua vitae was the original term for spirits (alcoholic liquor made by distillation) and translates into Gaelic as uisce beatha, from which we get the word whisky.

By the 16th century whisky was being produced by everyone in Scotland from landowners to crofters. The key ingredients were close at hand: barley (which grows well in the northern climate), pure water and peat. And the tax paid on wine from continental Europe was high, making whisky an affordable alternative.

After the Battle of Culloden in 1746 the fortunes of Highland whisky changed dramatically. Legislation was introduced that made small-scale whisky production illegal. In 1774 it was legalized again, but its export beyond the Highlands was forbidden. Smuggling became rife, but by the time the final restrictions on Highland distilling were lifted in 1816, malt whisky production had been all but destroyed as a cottage industry.

In 1827 the invention of the continuous still heralded a major upturn in business. In the Lowlands large-scale whisky production had continued to flourish, although the quality of the drink, distilled from wheat, corn or unmalted barley, was considered inferior. It was now possible for the Lowland distillers to produce a better quality, and quantity, of grain whisky. When this was blended with the flavoursome Highland malts, an easy-drinking Scotch was created that would sell well both in Scotland and abroad.

The master blenders who emerged at the forefront of the new industry were men whose names are still known today, including William Teacher, Johnnie Walker and Arthur Bell.

In the later 20th century whisky's popularity took a downturn, as it went out of fashion. Then, in 1971, William Grant & Sons decided to market its single malt, Glenfiddich. A huge success, it heralded the beginning of a resurgence of interest in the single malts that had been blotted out by blends over a century earlier.

Today single malts tend to be favoured by connoisseurs. No two malt whiskies are the same—it can seem that each bottle contains the distilled essence of the place in which it was created.

WHAT'S IN A MALT?

In order to malt barley, the grain is soaked until it starts to germinate, releasing starches. It is then heated and dried out to stop germination, traditionally by burning peat, whose smoke imparts a distinctive flavour into the malt. Hot water is added to the grain and the resulting wort (into which the barley's sugars have dissolved) is drained off, cooled and pumped into fermenting vessels. Yeast is added to the wort and a bubbly fermentation begins.

Around two days later, the resulting low strength liquor is distilled in large, copper pot stills. It is distilled for a second time and 'the cut' is made to separate the 'heart' of the spirit from the volatile 'heads' (the first alcohol that condenses) and 'tails' (the heavier alcoholic compounds). The heart is transferred to a vat where it is mixed with water before being sealed into oak casks and left to mature for three years or longer.

Every detail of the manufacture affects the taste of the finished whisky, including the amount of peat used in the malting, the composition of the local water, the design of the still, the length of maturation and the type of cask in which this takes place—often used sherry casks, which lend a distinctive flavour and colour to the whisky.

Different flavours of the single malts do not fall neatly into regions, and while there are certainly patterns—the peaty flavours in the whisky of the Western Isles, for example—there are also many exceptions.

The better-known brand names are a good starting point, but investigate further and you'll quickly discover different ages and distillations of the familiar name which carry their own mystique.

REGIONAL VARIATIONS: LOWLANDS

Historically linked with large distilleries and blended whiskies, the Lowlands also produce easy-drinking malts with light peat levels.

Look for the names Auchentoshan, Springbank and Glenkinchie.

ISLAY

Some say this is the birthplace of Scotch whisky. Numerous distilleries include excellent peaty malts such as Ardbeg, Lagavulin and Laphroaig. The latter has a salty tang, as do Bruichladdich and Bunnahabhain.

SPEYSIDE

Speyside has big names and plenty of them. This is the golden triangle of malt, and there's (literally) a dizzying amount to sample, such as Cragganmore, Knockando, Glenfiddich, Glen Moray, Glenfarclas and Macallan, to name just a few. The area is often linked with a mellow sweetness, though in truth there are numerous variations.

HIGHLANDS

The reputation of Highland whisky lives on. Malts from the southern Highlands and Perthshire have a honeyed lightness and a lack of peat—Glengoyne, for example. Towards the east coast, a malty flavour comes to the fore, as in the Royal Lochnagar. West coast sea air permeates the whisky produced in Oban, while north Highland malts have a dry, fruity sweetness (as in Glenmorangie) and a hint of salt near the coast in whiskies such as Pulteney and Clynelish.

WESTERN ISLES AND NORTHERN ISLES

The distilleries may be fewer, but there are still at least five good reasons to make a pilgrimage. One of the best is Orkney's Highland Park, which takes its smoky, heathery tones from the island's peat. Another is Skye's characterful Talisker.

BLENDED WHISKY

It was blended Scotch that took over the world and it still accounts for the vast majority of worldwide whisky sales, but these days it's often overlooked by aficionados. In fact, there's a real art to the blending—probably as much as there is to making a single malt. A blender mixes grain whisky with any number of different malts (popular brands such as Famous Grouse and Bell's may have between 20 and 50 different varieties in their make-up) and has to keep the flavour consistent, even though the constituent malts may change in character or stop being produced altogether.

STAYING

Hotels and guest houses offer a wide range of accommodation, from the plushest luxury at Gleneagles to more modest retreats. While you'll have the full choice of styles and ranges in the main cities and holiday centres, the choice may be more limited and the standard more modest in the remoter areas of the country.

RESERVING ACCOMMODATION
It's worth making reservations as early as possible, particularly for the peak summer period (Jun–end Sep), and ski season (Dec–end Feb). New Year (Hogmanay), Easter and other public holidays may be busy too.

Some hotels will ask for a deposit or full payment in advance, especially for one-night reservations, and not all will take reservations for B&B or short stays. Some hotels charge half-board (bed, breakfast and dinner) whether you eat the meals or not, while others may accept only full-board reservations.

Once a reservation is confirmed, let the hotel know at if you are unable to keep your reservation. If the hotel cannot re-book your room you may be liable to pay about two-thirds of the price. In Scotland a legally binding contract is made when you accept an offer of accommodation, either in writing or by phone, and illness is not accepted as a release from this contract. You may wish to take out insurance against possible cancellation.

EN SUITE
B&B accommodation offers the opportunity to stay in somebody's home, and sometimes in some remarkable historical buildings. Be aware that en-suite facilities (with private bath) are not always available, so bathroom facilities may be shared.

BED-AND-BREAKFAST
The B&B price generally includes a full cooked breakfast, which may consist of any combination of porridge, eggs, fried bread, potato scones, sausage, bacon, mushroom and tomato. Lighter alternatives are usually available. Some places offer an evening meal, but you may need to order in advance. In Scotland, high tea is sometimes served instead of dinner—this usually consists of a savoury dish followed by bread and butter, scones and cakes. While inns and some guesthouses will have a licence to serve alcohol, few B&Bs do.

PAYING
Most hotels and restaurants accept the majority of British and international credit cards, such as Access, MasterCard, Visa, American Express and Diners Club. Debit cards and cheques are also widely accepted, but you are advised to carry some cash in case of difficulty.

Many smaller establishments, such as B&Bs, are unlikely to accept any form of credit card, so always ask about payment methods when making a reservation.

SPEAKING SCOTTISH

Standard English is the official language of Scotland, and spoken everywhere. However, like other corners of Britain, the Scottish people have their own variations of English and the way it is spoken, and dialects of their own. In Aberdeen it is known as Doric, in the Lowlands it is Lallans, Glasgow has a patter all of its own, and in Orkney and Shetland, the local dialect has Scandinavian roots.

SCOTS

The Scots language, which stems from an older form of Lowland Scots, varies across the country from a barely detectable accent on certain words and phrases, to the broad (and very individual) patois of inner-urban Glasgow and northeast Aberdeenshire.

The Scots language has its own traditions of literature, poetry (including Robert Burns) and songs (including the Border ballads), and Aberdeen University Press publishes Scots dictionaries that celebrate the richness of the language. But it was only in 1983 that the first complete translation of the New Testament into Scots was published, the work of scholar William Laughton Lorimer (1885–1967).

NORN

In Orkney and Shetland, you'll hear a completely different accent with long 'a's and many unusual words, influenced by the Nordic languages. At its thickest, among the local people, it can sound more akin to Danish than English.

GAELIC

In the Western Isles you'll hear another accent, sometimes described as soft and lilting, which is a legacy of an entirely separate language—Gaelic (pronounced Gaallic in Scotland), still spoken by around 65,000 people.

Visitors without prior knowledge of Gaelic are most likely to see it first in place names on the map— especially of mountains—and on bilingual road signs in the west. You may hear it spoken naturally as a first language between local people in the Western Isles, see a Gaelic church service advertised, or hear it sung. And if you see 'ceud mile failte', you might recognize a warm welcome.

Gaelic language and culture arrived here with the Irish around the fifth century. It was the main tongue of northern and western Scotland until the dramatic changes of the 18th century brought about by the opening up of the Highlands after the Jacobite Rebellions, and the later land clearances which uprooted whole communities.

In the 20th century, while Gaelic might be the language spoken at home, English was the imposed language of education in schools and colleges. The whole culture might have died out, but a revival of interest in the early 1970s (spurred on by the example of a more militant Welsh language revival) helped to sustain it.

With the more recent development of interest in a separate Scottish identity, led by the emergence of the Scottish parliament in the 1990s, Gaelic is firmly back in vogue. While native speakers are steadily declining in numbers, understanding is increasing as the language is taught in schools and universities, the culture celebrated in an annual festival, the Mod (▷ 332), Gaelic books and newspapers are published, and Gaelic speakers get their own air-time on radio and television (▷ 324). And as part of the wider interest in Celtic roots, Gaelic is also learned and passionately celebrated worldwide.

For more information about learning Gaelic, contact the

Gaelic college Sabhal Mór Ostaig (Sleat, Isle of Skye IV44 8RQ, tel 01471 888000; www.smo.uhi.ac.uk). Comunn na Gàighlig is a government-sponsored development agency, with useful links and information (5 Mitchell's Lane, Inverness IV2 3HQ; tel 01463 234138; www.cnag.org.uk).

The Am Baile (Gaelic Village) project is a developing website sponsored by the Highland Council offering a wide variety of resources relating to Gaelic language and culture (www.ambaile.org.uk).

PRONOUNCING SCOTTISH PLACE NAMES

Apparently complicated place names, such as Craigellachie, Wanlockhead, Clackmannan and Ecclefechan, can usually be broken down into their syllables to find the correct pronunciation. Below are some examples of Scottish place names that often cause confusion.

Ayr: Air
Breadalbane: Bred-al-bane
Cuillins: Cool-ins
Culross: Cure-oss
Culzean: Cull-ane
Edinburgh: Ed-in-burra
Eilean Donan: Ellen Donnan
Findochty: Fin-echty
Forres: Forr-es
Garioch: Geerie
Glamis: Glahms
Hawick: Hoyck
Hebrides: Heb-rid-ees
Islay: Eye-la
Kilconquhar: Kinnu-char
Kirkcudbright: Kir-coo-bree
Kyleakin: Ky-lack-in
Kylerhea: Kyle-ree
Milngavie: Mill-guy
Moray: Murr-ay
Roxburgh: Rox-burra
Scone: Scoon
Stac Pollaidh: Stack Polly
Sumburgh: Sum-burra
Tiree: Tye-ree
Wemyss: Weems

SCOTTISH WORDS IN COMMON USAGE

Auld Reekie .... nickname for Edinburgh
aye .... always/yes
bairn .... baby, child
bannock .... biscuit or scone
ben .... hill, mountain
birle .... spin, turn
bonny .... pretty
brae .... hill
braw .... fine, beautiful
burn .... stream, creek
cairn ...... stones forming a landmark
canny .... cunning, clever
ceilidh .... gathering, party, dance
coo .... cow
croft .... smallholding, small farm
doocote .... dovecot

dour .... sullen
dram .... measure of whisky
een .... eyes
factor .... estate or farm manager
fash .... bother
gae .... go
gillie .... hunting guide
glaur .... mud
glen .... valley
gloaming .... evening
greet .... weep
haver .... to talk nonsense
heavy .... dark beer
heid .... head
ken .... to know
kirk .... church
laird .... land owner

loch .... lake
machair .... coastal grassland
manse .... minister's house
messages .... shopping
nicht .... night
och .... oh
partan .... crab
piece .... sandwich
pinkie .... little finger
pirrie/peerie/peedy .... small
puffer .... antique steamboat
Sassenach .... English-speaker
sleekit .... sly
stay .... live
tattie .... potato
tattie-bogle .... scarecrow
wee .... small

GLOSSARY FOR US VISITORS

anticlockwise .... counterclockwise
aubergine .... eggplant
bank holiday .... a public holiday that falls on a Monday; there are two in May and one in August
bill .... check (at restaurant)
biscuit .... cookie
bonnet .... hood (car)
boot .... trunk (car)
busker .... street musician
car park .... parking lot
caravan .... house trailer or RV
carriage .... car (on a train)
casualty .... emergency room
chemist .... pharmacy
chips .... french fries
coach .... long-distance bus
concessions .... discount tickets
courgette .... zucchini
crèche .... day care
crisps .... potato chips
dual carriageway .... two-lane highway
en suite .... a bedroom with its own private bathroom; may also just refer to the bathroom
football .... soccer
full board .... a hotel tariff that includes all meals
garage .... gas station
garden .... yard (residential)

GP .... doctor
half board .... hotel tariff that includes breakfast and either lunch or dinner
high street .... main street
hire .... rent
inland .... within the UK
jelly .... Jello™
jumper/jersey .... sweater
junction .... intersection
lay-by .... pull-off, rest stop
level crossing .... trains crossing
licensed .... a café or restaurant that has a licence to serve alcohol (beer and wine only unless it's 'fully' licensed)
lift .... elevator
lorry .... truck
main line station ... a train station as opposed to an underground or subway station (although it may be served by the underground/subway)
nappy .... diaper
note .... paper money
off-licence .... liquor store
pants .... underpants (men's)
pavement .... sidewalk
petrol .... gas
petrol station .... gas station
plaster .... Band-Aid or bandage
post .... mail
public school .... private school

pudding .... dessert
purse .... change purse
pushchair .... stroller
return ticket .... roundtrip ticket
rocket .... arugula
roundabout .... traffic circle or rotary
self-catering .... accommodations including a kitchen
single ticket .... one-way ticket
stalls .... (in theatre) orchestra seats
subway .... underpass
surgery .... doctor's office
tailback .... traffic jam
takeaway .... takeout
taxi rank .... taxi stand
tights .... panty-hose
T-junction ...... an intersection where one road meets another at right angles (making a T shape)
toilets .... restrooms
torch .... flashlight
trolley .... cart
trousers .... pants
way out .... exit

PRACTICALITIES WORDS AND PHRASES

BRITISH FLOOR NUMBERING

In Britain the first floor of a building is called the ground floor, and the floor above it is the first floor. So a British second floor is a US third floor, and so on. This is something to watch for in museums and galleries in particular.

343

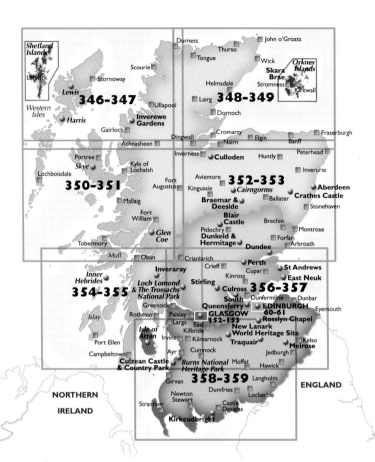

Shetland
Islands

Lerwick

Lewis

Western
Isles

Harris

346-347

Scourie

Stornoway

Ullapool

Inverewe
Gardens

Gairloch

Achnasheen

Durness

Tongue

Thurso

John o'Groats

Wick

Orkney
Islands

Skara
Brae

Stromness

Kirkwall

Helmsdale

Lairg

348-349

Dornoch

Cromarty

Dingwall

Nairn

Elgin

Fraserburgh

Banff

Portree

Skye

Lochboisdale

350-351

Kyle of
Lochalsh

Mallaig

Fort
Augustus

Fort
William

Glen
Coe

Tobermory

Inverness

Culloden

Aviemore

Kingussie

Cairngorms

Braemar &
Deeside

Blair
Castle

Pitlochry

Dunkeld &
Hermitage

Huntly

352-353

Ballater

Brechin

Forfar

Peterhead

Inverurie

Aberdeen

Crathes Castle

Stonehaven

Montrose

Arbroath

Mull

Oban

Crianlarich

Inner
Hebrides

Inveraray

354-355

Loch Lomond
& The Trossachs
National Park

Greenock

Islay

Rothesay

Isle of
Arran

Port Ellen

Campbeltown

Stirling

Crieff

Kinross

Culross

South
Queensferry

Paisley

Largs

East
Kilbride

Irvine

Kilmarnock

Cumnock

Ayr

Culzean Castle
& Country Park

Girvan

Stranraer

Newton
Stewart

Kirkcudbright

Perth

Cupar

Dunfermline

Dundee

St Andrews

East Neuk

356-357

Dunbar

Eyemouth

EDINBURGH
60-61

GLASGOW
152-153

Rosslyn Chapel

New Lanark
World Heritage Site

Traquair

Jedburgh

Melrose

Kelso

Burns National
Heritage Park

Moffat

Hawick

358-359

Dumfries

Castle
Douglas

Langholm

Lockerbie

ENGLAND

NORTHERN
IRELAND

346-359   0   15 km   0   10 miles

346-359   0   15 km   0   10 miles

346 & 349   0   20 km   0   15 miles

Motorway (Expressway)	City / Town
Motorway junction with and without number	Built-up area
National road	National Park / Area of Outstanding Natural Beauty
Regional road	Forest Park
Railway	Featured place of interest
Long distance footpath	Airport
Country boundary	Port / Ferry route
County boundary	621 Height in metres

MAPS

Map references for the sights refer to the atlas pages within this section or to the individual town plans within the regions. For example, Dundee has the reference ✚ 353 J8, indicating the page on which the map is found (353) and the grid square in which Dundee sits (J8).

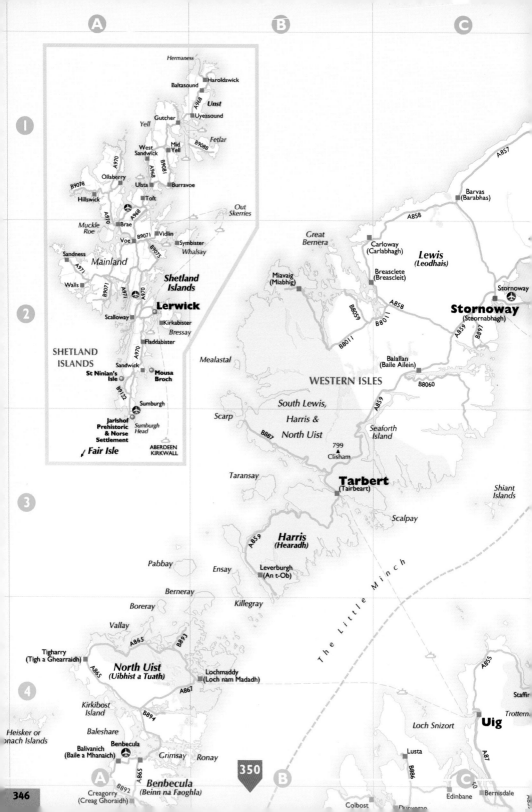

A   **B**   **C**

1

Hermaness

Haroldswick
Baltasound
Unst
Gutcher
Uyeasound
Yell
A968
West Sandwick
Mid Yell
Fetlar
B9088
B9081
Ollaberry
A968
B9078
Ulsta
Burravoe
A970
Hillswick
A968
Toft
Out Skerries
Muckle Roe
Brae
A970
Vidlin
B9071
Voe
Sandness
B9075
Symbister
Whalsay
Mainland
A971
A971
Walls
B9071
A970
Scalloway
LERWICK
Kirkabister
Bressay
Fladdabister
SHETLAND ISLANDS
A970
Sandwick
St Ninian's Isle
Mousa Broch
B9122
Sumburgh
Jarlshof Prehistoric & Norse Settlement
Sumburgh Head
Fair Isle
ABERDEEN
KIRKWALL

Shetland Islands

A857

Barvas
(Barabhas)
A858
Carloway
(Carlabhagh)
Lewis (Leodhais)
Breasclete
(Breascleit)
Stornoway
Great Bernera
B8059
A858
Stornoway
(Steornabhagh)
Miavaig
(Miabhig)
B8011
A859
B897
B8011
Balallan
(Baile Ailein)
WESTERN ISLES
B8060
Mealastal
A859
South Lewis, Harris & North Uist
Seaforth Island
Scarp
799 ▲
Clisham
Taransay
Tarbert
(Tairbeart)
Scalpay
Shiant Islands
A859
Pabbay
Ensay
Harris (Hearadh)
Taransay
Leverburgh
(An t-Ob)
Berneray
Killegray
Boreray
Vallay
The Little Minch
A865
B893
Tigharry
(Tigh a Ghearraidh)
A865
North Uist (Uibhist a Tuath)
Lochmaddy
(Loch nam Madadh)
A865
A867
A865
Kirkibost Island
B894
Staffir
Trottern
Heisker or onach Islands
Baleshare
Uig
A87
Balivanich
(Baile a Mhanaich)
Grimsay
Ronay
Loch Snizort
Lusta
B886
A865
B892
A87
Benbecula (Beinn na Faoghla)
Creagory
(Creag Ghoraidh)
Colbost
Edinbane
Bernisdale

350

2

3

4

D   E   F

Cape Wrath

1

Kinlochbervie

B801

Rhiconich

North-west
Sutherland

Scourie

A894

Achfary

A838

Drumbeg

Clashnessie

B869

Unapool

2

A894

B869   A837

Loch
Assynt

Lochinver

Inchnadamph

998
▲
Ben More
Assynt

Assynt - Coigach

A837

Knockan

348

A835   **Inverpolly**

Strathcanaird

A837

3

Butt of Lewis

Port of Ness
(Port Nis)

Cellar
Head

Tolsta
(Tolastadh)

Tiumpan
Head

A866

T h e   M i n c h

Ullapool

A835

Gruinard
Bay

Laide

A832

Cove

B8057

Melvaig

Aultbea

Dundonnell

1081
▲
Beinn
Dearg

Inverasdale

Loch na
Sealga

1062
▲
An
Teallach

B8021

Inverewe
Gardens

Poolewe

Fionn
Loch

A832

A832

Gairloch

Port
Henderson

Lochan
Fada

1109
▲
Sgurr
Mor

A833

B8056

Loch
Fannich

4

Talladale

A832

Loch
Maree

A832

Loch Torridon

Wester   *Ross*

Lower Diabaig

Kinlochewe

Achnasheen

Loch
Luichart

Gar

A832

Rona

1053
▲
Liathach

Torridon

A896

351

Shieldaig

D   E   F

A890

F   G   H

Dunnet Head

STROMNESS
TORSHAVN
(SUMMER ONLY)

Durness

Loch Eriboll

Scrabster

Thurso

Dunnet

Castletown

A9

B855

B874

1

Loch Hope

Strathnaver

Bettyhill

A836

Strathy
Point

Strathy

Melvich

A836   Reay

Loch
Calder

Halkirk

B874

Spittal

Watter

Tongue

927
Ben
Hope

Kyle of Tongue

Loch
Loyal

B871

A897

A836

B870

A9

Loch
Meadie

B873

Loch
Rimsdale

B871

Loch nan
Clar

Latheron

2

Altnaharra

Loch
Choire

Loch
Badanloch

Kinbrace

Dunbeath

347

A838

A836

Shinness

A897

A9

Berriedale

Loch
Brora

Helmsdale

Lairg

A839

Rosehall

A839

A836

B864

A837

Dunrobin
Castle

A9

Brora

A837

Inveran

Golspie

3

Bonar
Bridge

Spinningdale

Ardgay

A949

A836

Dornoch

Dornoch Firth

Edderton

Dornoch Firth

Portmahomack

Glenmorangie Distillery

Loch
Marie

Tain

Hill of
Fearn

B9165

Loch
Glass

B9176

A9

B9175

Balintore

1045
Ben
Wyvis

Alness

B817

Nigg

Lossiemouth

Hopeman

B9040

Duffus

4

A835

Garve

Invergordon

Evanton

Balblair

Cromarty

Firth

Findhorn

Burghead

B9012

A941

Loch
Luichart

Cromarty Firth

Moray

B9089

A96

Strathpeffer

A834

Dingwall

B9163

Black Isle

A832

B9160

Kinloss

Elgin

Contin

A835

A9169

A9

Rosemarkie

Fortrose

Nairn

Dyke

Forres

Rafford

Pluscarden
Abbey

Conon
Bridge

Black Isle
Brewery

A832

Avoch

352

Ardersier

Auldearn

Brodie

B9010

F   G   H

Muir
of Ord

B9161

North
Kessock

A96

Croy

Cawdor
Castle

B9090

A939

B9091

A9007

A940

Dallas

Logie Steading
Visitor Centre

348

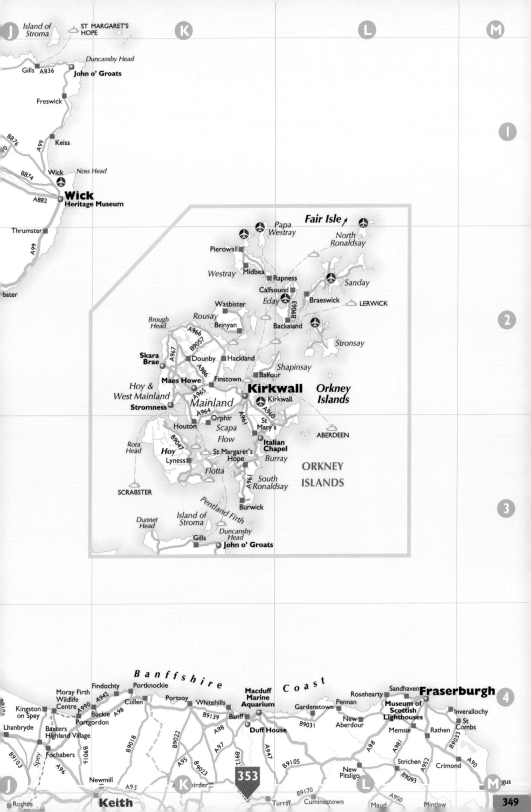

J | K | L | M

I

Island of Stroma
ST MARGARET'S HOPE

Duncansby Head

Gills A836 **John o' Groats**

Freswick

B876
A99
Keiss

B874
A99
Wick Noss Head

A882 **Wick**
Heritage Museum

Thrumster

A99

bster

Fair Isle

Papa Westray

Pierowall North Ronaldsay

Westray Midbea Rapness
Calfsound Sanday
Wasbister Eday Braeswick LERWICK
B9063
Rousay Backaland
Brough Head Brinyan Stronsay
A966
B9057 Shapinsay
Skara Brae Dounby Hackland
A967
Maes Howe Finstown Balfour
A886 **Kirkwall** **Orkney Islands**
A965 Kirkwall
Hoy & West Mainland Mainland A960
Stromness A964 Orphir ABERDEEN
Houton A961 St Mary's
Scapa **Italian Chapel**
B9047 Flow Burray
Rora Head **Hoy** Lyness St Margaret's Hope **ORKNEY**
Flotta South Ronaldsay **ISLANDS**
A961
SCRABSTER Burwick
Pentland Firth
Dunnet Head Island of Stroma Duncansby Head
Gills **John o' Groats**

2

3

4

B a n f f s h i r e C o a s t **Fraserburgh**
Findochty Portknockie Sandhaven Museum of Scottish Lighthouses
Moray Firth Wildlife Centre A942 Cullen Rosehearty Inverallochy
Kingston on Spey A990 Buckie A98 Portsoy Whitehills **Macduff Marine Aquarium** Pennan St Combs
Lhanbryde Portgordon B9139 Banff Gardenstown New Aberdour Memsie Rathen A981 E333
Baxters Highland Village B9018 B9022 A98 B9031 Strichen A90 Crimond
Fochabers B9016 B9023 A97 A947 A98 A981 A952
B9103 Spey A96 Newmill A95 ...hirder B9105 New Pitsligo B9093 gus
Rothes Keith Turriff Cuminestown Maud Mintlaw

353

J | K | L | M

349

Balivanich
(Baile a Mhanaich)
Grimsay   Ronay
Lusta

B892
Benbecula
(Beinn na Faoghla)
B886

Creagorry
(Creag Ghoraidh)
Colbost   Dunvegan   Edinbane   Bernisdale

B891
Wiay

Portree

Stilligarry
(Stadhlaigearraidh)   B890

Bracadale

5   South Uist
(Uibhist a Deas)
Skye

B8009   Drynoch
Carbost

South Uist
Machair   A865

965
Sgurr Na
Gillean

Lochboisdale
(Loch Baghasdail)

1009
Sgurr
Alasdair

B888

Soay

Eriskay

Canna

6   Barra
A888
Rùm

Barra   The
Small Isles

Castlebay
(Bagh a Chaisteil)
Vatersay

Muldoanich   Eigg

Sandray

Pabbay

Mingulay   Muck

Berneray

7

Ardnamurchan
Point
Ardnamurchan

Kilchoan

Coll   B8072

Arinagour

B8070   Tobermor

Dervaig   B8073

Calgary

B8068   Caoles
B8069

Tiree
B8073

B8065   Scarinish

8   Tiree   Loch na Kea

Ulva   Isle of Mul

Hynish

Iona   Fionnphort

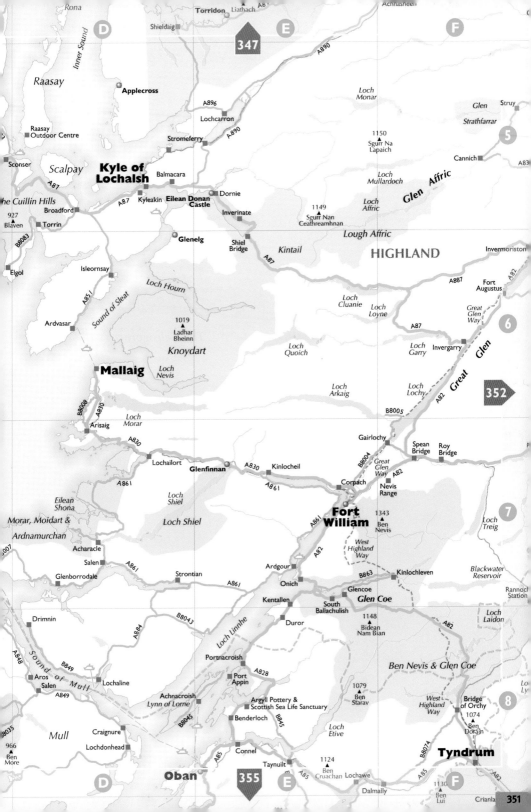

Keith

Newmill
A95
A96
Speyside
Way
A96
A95
Rothes
Craigellachie
Glenfiddich
Distillery
Aberlour
Dufftown
Ben Rinnes
A941
B9014
B9115
A920
B9022
B9024
Huntly
A97
B9117
Auchterless
Auchterless
B9001
B992
Turriff
Cuminestown
New Pitsligo
B9170
B9093
Strichen
A952
Crimond
A90
Maud
A950
Mintlaw
Longside
A950
Peterhead
New Deer
Stuartfield
B9030
A952
Clola
Boddam
A96
A97
A920
Colpy
Insch
Old Rayne
B9002
Fyvie Castle
Fyvie
B9005
Methlick
B9170
Tarves
B9005
A948
Hatton
A90
Crude Bay
A975

5

Inverurie

B9002
Lumsden
B992
Pitcaple
A920
Oldmeldrum
Pitmedden
B9000
Newburgh
Colliestone

Mossat
A944
Kildrummy
A97
Glenkindie
Alford
Monymusk
Kemnay
Kintore
B993
B994
Castle Fraser
Aberdeen
Dyce
Balmedie
B979
B977
A90
B993
A96

ABERDEENSHIRE

Strathdon
A9A4
Corgarff
A97
Tarland
A980
Craigievar Castle
B9119
B993
A944
Echt
Garlogie
Kirkton of Skene
B979
B125
B9119
Peterculter
B9077
Portlethen
A90
B979
Muchalls

ABERDEEN

CITY OF ABERDEEN
A93
A944
B977

KIRKWALL
LERWICK

6

Lumphanan
Kincardine O'Neil
Torphins
A980
B9119
A93
Aboyne
Marywell
Dee
B976
Crathes Castle
Durris
B9077

Banchory

B976
A939
A93
B976
Ballater
Crathie
Deeside
Strachan
A957

7

154 lochnagar
t
Clova
B955
a
i
n
s
B974
Fettercairn
B966
Fordoun
Kinneff
A90
A92
B967
Inverbervie

Stonehaven

ANGUS
B966
B974
Laurencekirk
Edzell
A90
A937
B9120
Marykirk
Johnshaven
St Cyrus

Brechin
A935
Tannadice
Montrose
B957
Farnell
A934
Kirriemuir & The Glens of Angus
B9134
B9113
A933
A92
Lunan
Friockheim
Inverkeilor
Forfar
A932
A928
A926
Glamis Castle
Glamis
B965
A933
B9127
B961
B9127
Meigle Sculptured Stone Museum
A928
Newtyle
B9128
B978
Arbroath Signal Tower Museum
A90

8

B951
B954
Muirhead
A923
Camperdown Wildlife Centre
A94
A926
Todhills
B961
A92
Muirdrum
Carnoustie
Monifieth
DUNDEE
CITY OF DUNDEE
Invergowrie
Dundee
Toll
Tayport
Newport-on-Tay
Wormit

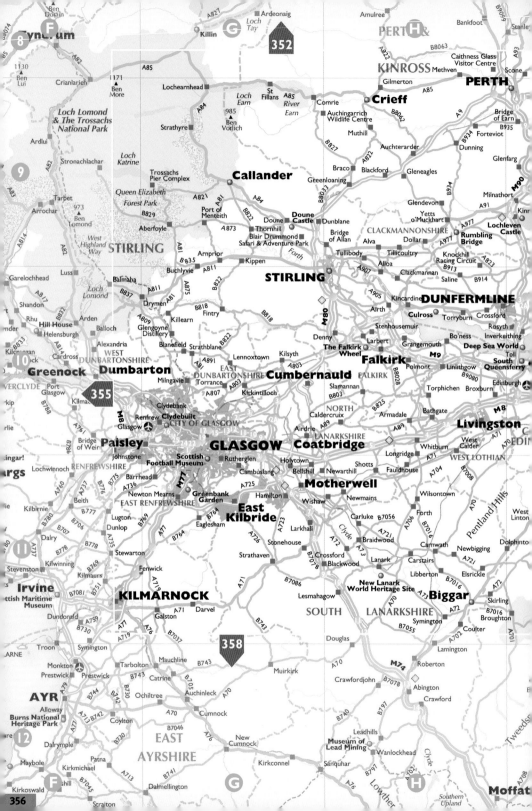

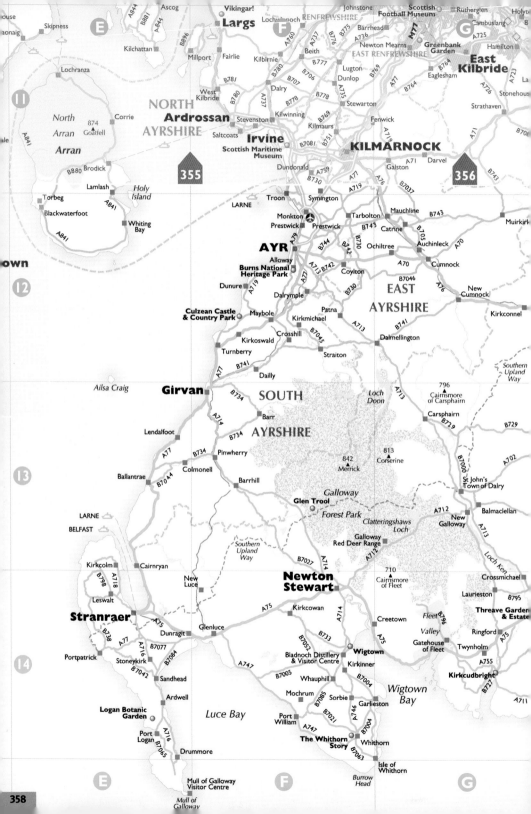

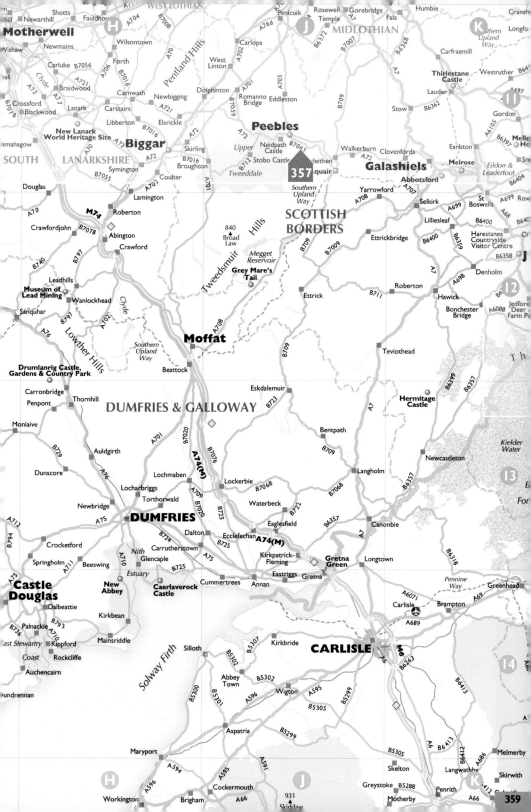

Place	Pg	Grid	Place	Pg	Grid	Place	Pg	Grid	Place	Pg	Grid
Eaglesfield	359	J13	Glasgow	356	G10	Kames	355	E10	Larkhall	356	G11
Eaglesham	356	G11	Glenbarr	354	D11	Keiss	349	J1	Latheron	348	J2
Earlston	357	K11	Glenborrodale	351	D7	Keith	353	K5	Lauder	357	K11
Easdale	355	D9	Glencaple	359	H13	Kelso	357	K11	Laurencekirk	353	K7
East Kilbride	356	G11	Glencoe	351	E7	Kemnay	353	L6	Laurieston	358	G14
East Linton	357	K10	Glendaruel	355	E10	Kenmore	352	G8	Lawers	352	G8
Eastriggs	359	J14	Glendevon	356	H9	Kennacraig	355	D10	Leadhills	359	H12
East Saltoun	357	K10	Gleneagles	356	H9	Kentallen	351	E7	Lendalfoot	358	E13
Ecclefechan	359	J13	Glenelg	351	D6	Kilberry	355	D10	Lennoxtown	356	G10
Eccles	357	L11	Glenfarg	356	J9	Kilbirnie	355	F11	Lerwick	346	A2
Echt	353	L6	Glenfinnan	351	E7	Kilchattan	355	E11	Leslie	353	K5
Edderton	348	G3	Glenkindie	353	K6	Kilchoan	350	C7	Leslie	357	J9
Eddleston	357	J11	Glenlivet	352	J5	Kilchrenan	355	E9	Lesmahagow	356	H11
Edinbane	350	C5	Glenluce	358	F14	Kilcreggan	355	F10	Leswalt	358	E14
Edinburgh	357	J10	Glenrothes	357	J9	Kildrummy	353	K6	Letham	353	K8
Ednam	357	L11	Golspie	348	H3	Kilfinan	355	E10	Leuchars	357	K9
Edzell	353	K7	Gordon	357	K11	Kilkenzie	354	D12	Leven	357	J9
Elgin	348	J4	Gorebridge	357	J11	Killearn	356	G10	Leverburgh	346	B3
Elgol	351	C6	Gourock	355	F10	Killiechronan	351	D8	Lhanbryde	349	J4
Elie	357	K9	Grangemouth	356	H10	Killiecrankie	352	H7	Libberton	356	H11
Ellon	353	L5	Grantown-on-Spey	352	H5	Killin	352	G8	Lilliesleaf	359	K12
Elsrickle	356	H11	Grantshouse	357	L10	Kilmacolm	355	F10	Linlithgow	356	H10
Embo	348	H3	Greenlaw	357	K11	Kilmany	357	J9	Linwood	356	F10
Errogie	352	G5	Greenloaning	356	H9	Kilmarnock	356	F11	Livingston	356	H10
Errol	357	J9	Greenock	355	F10	Kilmartin	355	D9	Lochailort	351	D7
Eskdalemuir	359	J13	Gretna	359	J14	Kilmaurs	355	F11	Lochaline	351	D8
Ettrick	359	J12	Gretna Green	359	J13	Kilmelford	355	E9	Locharbriggs	359	H13
Ettrickbridge	359	J12	Guardbridge	357	K9	Kilmorack	352	G5	Lochawe	355	E8
Evanton	348	G4	Gullane	357	K10	Kilninver	355	D9	Loch Baghasdail	350	A6
Eyemouth	357	L10	Gutcher	346	A1	Kilsyth	356	G10	Lochboisdale	350	A6
						Kilwinning	355	F11	Lochbuie	354	D9
Fairlie	355	F11	Hackland	349	K2	Kinbrace	348	H2	Lochcarron	351	E5
Fala	357	K11	Haddington	357	K10	Kincardine	356	H10	Lochdonhead	351	D8
Falkirk	356	H10	Halkirk	348	J1	Kincardine O'Neil	353	K6	Lochearnhead	356	G9
Falkland	357	J9	Hamilton	356	G11	Kincraig	352	H6	Lochgair	355	E10
Farnell	353	K8	Harlosh	350	C5	Kingsbarns	357	K9	Lochgilphead	355	E10
Fauldhouse	356	H11	Haroldswick	346	B1	Kingston on Spey	349	J4	Lochgoilhead	355	F9
Fearn	348	H4	Hatton	353	M5	Kingussie	352	G6	Lochinver	346	E2
Fearnan	352	G8	Hawick	359	K12	Kinlochbervie	346	F1	Lochmaben	359	H13
Fenwick	356	F11	Helensburgh	355	F10	Kinlocheil	351	E7	Lochmaddy	346	B4
Fettercairn	353	K7	Helmsdale	348	H2	Kinlochewe	346	E4	Loch nam Madadh	346	B4
Findhorn	348	H4	Hill of Fearn	348	H4	Kinloch Hourn	351	E6	Lochranza	355	E11
Findochty	349	K4	Hillswick	346	A1	Kinlochleven	351	F7	Lochwinnoch	355	F11
Finstown	349	K2	Holytown	356	G11	Kinloch Rannoch	352	G7	Lockerbie	359	J13
Fintry	356	G10	Hopeman	348	J4	Kinloss	348	H4	Longformacus	357	K11
Fionnphort	354	C9	Houton	349	K3	Kinneff	353	L7	Longniddry	357	K10
Fladdabister	346	A2	Humbie	357	K10	Kinross	356	J9	Longridge	356	H10
Fochabers	349	J4	Hume	357	K11	Kintore	353	L6	Longside	353	L5
Ford	355	E9	Hunter's Quay	355	F10	Kippen	356	G9	Lossiemouth	348	J4
Fordoun	353	L7	Huntly	353	K5	Kirkabister	346	A2	Lower Diabaig	346	D4
Forfar	353	K8	Hynish	350	B8	Kirkbean	359	H14	Lugton	355	F11
Forres	348	H4				Kirkcaldy	357	J10	Lumphanan	353	K6
Fort Augustus	352	F6	Inchnadamph	346	F2	Kirkcolm	358	E13	Lumsden	353	K5
Forteviot	356	H9	Innellan	355	E10	Kirkconnel	358	G12	Lunan	353	K8
Forth	356	H11	Innerleithen	357	J11	Kirkcowan	358	F14	Luss	355	F10
Fortingall	352	G8	Insch	353	K5	Kirkcudbright	358	G14	Lusta	346	C4
Fortrose	348	G4	Insh	352	H6	Kirkhill	352	G5	Lybster	348	J2
Fort William	351	E7	Inverallochy	349	L4	Kirkinner	358	F14	Lyness	349	K3
Foyers	352	G5	Inveran	348	G3	Kirkintilloch	356	G10			
Fraserburgh	349	L4	Inveraray	355	E9	Kirkmichael	352	H7	Macduff	349	K4
Freswick	349	J1	Inverasdale	346	D3	Kirkmichael	358	F12	Machrihanish	354	D12
Friockheim	353	K8	Inverbervie	353	L7	Kirkoswald	358	F12	Macmerry	357	K10
Furnace	355	E9	Invergarry	351	F6	Kirkpatrick-Fleming	359	J13	Mainsriddle	359	H14
Fyvie	353	L5	Invergordon	348	G4	Kirkton of Skene	353	L6	Mallaig	351	D6
			Invergowrie	353	J8	Kirkwall	349	K2	Marykirk	353	K7
Gairloch	346	D4	Inverinate	351	E5	Kirriemuir	353	J8	Marywell	353	K6
Gairlochy	351	F7	Inverkeilor	353	K8	Knockan	346	F3	Mauchline	358	G12
Galashiels	357	K11	Inverkeithing	356	J10	Kyleakin	351	D5	Maud	353	L5
Galston	356	G11	Inverkeithny	353	K5	Kyle of Lochalsh	351	D5	Maxwell Town	359	H13
Gardenstown	349	L4	Inverkip	355	F10	Kylerhea	351	D5	Maybole	358	F12
Garelochhead	355	F10	Invermoriston	352	F6				Meigle	353	J8
Garlieston	358	G14	Inverness	352	G5	Ladybank	357	J9	Melrose	357	K11
Garlogie	353	L6	Inverurie	353	L5	Laggan	352	G6	Melvaig	346	D3
Garvald	357	K10	Irvine	355	F11	Laide	346	E3	Melvich	348	H1
Garve	348	F4	Isle of Whithorn	358	G14	Lairg	348	G3	Memsie	349	L4
Gatehouse of Fleet	358	G14	Isleornsay	351	D6	Lamington	359	H11	Memus	353	K7
Gifford	357	K10				Lamlash	358	E11	Methil	357	J9
Gills	349	J1	Jedburgh	357	K12	Lanark	356	H11	Methlick	353	L5
Gilmerton	356	H9	John o' Groats	349	J1	Langholm	359	J13	Methven	356	H8
Girvan	358	F13	Johnshaven	353	L7	Largoward	357	K9	Miabhig	346	B2
Glamis	353	J8	Johnstone	356	F10	Largs	355	F11	Miavaig	346	B2

PICTURES

The Automobile Association wishes to thank the following photographers and organisations for their assistance in the preparation of this book.

Abbreviations for the picture credits are as follows (t) top;
(b) bottom;
(l) left;
(r) right;
(c) centre;
(dps) double page spread;
(AA) AA World Travel Library

COVER tbc

2 AA/Michael Taylor;
3t AA/Jonathan Smith;
3cr AA/M Alexander;
3cr AA/Jonathan Smith;
3br AA/Stephen Whitehorne;
4 AA/Jonathan Smith;
5 Edinburgh Inspiring Capital www.edinburgh-inspiringcapital.com;
6 AA/Jim Henderson;
7l Edinburgh Inspiring Capital www.edinburgh-inspiringcapital.com;
7r AA/Ronnie Weir;
9 AA/David W Robertson;
10 AA/Jim Henderson;
11l AA/Stephen Whitehorne;
11r AA/Stephen Whitehorne;
12 AA/Sue Anderson;
13 AA/Jonathan Smith;
14 Colin McPherson/Scottish Viewpoint;
15t Glasgow City Marketing Bureau;
15b John Lowrie Morrison;
16 David Robertson/Stockscotland;
17t AA/Roger Coulam;
17b John McKenna/Alamy;
18 Glasgow City Marketing Bureau;
19l AA/Stephen Gibson;
19r AA/Jonathan Smith;
20 SIME/Albanese Alessandra/4Corners;
21l James Fraser/Rex Features;
21r Chris Furlong/Getty Images;
22 Glasgow City Marketing Bureau;
23t AA/Jonathan Smith;
23b AA/Jonathan Smith;
24 P.Tomkins/VisitScotland/Scottish Viewpoint;
25 AA/Eric Ellington;
26 David Lyons/Alamy;
27l Ann Stonehouse;

27r Mary Evans Picture Library;
28l AA/Stephen Whitehorne;
28r Mary Evans Picture Library;
29t Reproduced courtesy of the National Archives of Scotland/scotlandsimages.com;
29b AA;
30 Culture and Sport Glasgow (Museums);
31l Ian Paterson/Alamy;
31r Reproduced by kind permission of the Royal Bank of Scotland Group;
32 AA/Stephen Whitehorne;
33l The Trustees of the National Museums of Scotland;
33r Scottish National Portrait Gallery;
34 AA/Jeff Beazley;
35t Glasgow Museums;
35b Scottish National Photography Collection/Scottish National Portrait Gallery;
36l Mary Evans Picture Library;
36r Reproduced courtesy of Glasgow University Archive Services;
37t Reproduced by kind permission of Unilever Bestfoods from an original in Unilever Corporate Archives;
37b Reproduced courtesy of Glasgow University Archive Services;
38 Culture and Sport Glasgow (Museums);
39l The Fine Art Society, London, UK /The Bridgeman Art Library;
39r Mary Evans Picture Library/The Women's Library;
40 Oxford Scientific/Photolibrary/Getty Images;
41 AA/Jonathan Smith;
42 www.britainonview.com;
43 Lothian Buses;
44 AA/Jonathan Smith;
45t AA/Jonathan Smith;
45b AA/Sue Anderson;
46 Iain Mclean;
47 AA/Jim Carnie;
48 Dave Wolstenholme;
49 Chris Joint/Alamy;
50 AA/Jonathan Smith;
51 AA/Jonathan Smith;
52 AA/Jonathan Smith;
53 AA/Jonathan Smith;
54 AA/Sue Anderson;
57 AA/Jonathan Smith;
58 Edinburgh Inspiring Capital www.edinburgh-inspiringcapital.com;
62 Doug Pearson/Photolibrary;

63l AA/Jonathan Smith;
63r AA/Jonathan Smith;
64l Alan R Thomson/RZSS;
64r AA/Ken Paterson;
65l AA/Jonathan Smith;
65r AA/Ken Paterson;
66 AA/Jonathan Smith;
67 Crown Copyright reproduced courtesy of Historic Scotland;
68 AA/Jonathan Smith;
69t AA/Jonathan Smith;
69b AA/Jonathan Smith;
70 AA/Douglas Corrance;
71 Colin Palmer Photography/Alamy;
72 AA/Ken Paterson;
73t The Trustees of the National Museums of Scotland;
73c The Trustees of the National Museums of Scotland;
73b The Trustees of the National Museums of Scotland;
74 The Trustees of the National Museums of Scotland;
75t The Trustees of the National Museums of Scotland;
75b The Trustees of the National Museums of Scotland;
76t AA/Ken Paterson;
76b National Gallery of Scotland;
77 StockImages/Alamy;
78 Our Dynamic Earth;
79 AA/Jonathan Smith;
80 www.britainonview.com;
81 JTB Photo/Photolibrary.com;
82t AA/Ken Paterson;
82b AA/Ken Paterson;
83 Scottish National Gallery of Modern Art;
84 Iain Masterton/Alamy;
85 AA/Isla Love;
86 AA/Jonathan Smith;
88 AA/Jonathan Smith;
91 AA/Jonathan Smith;
92 AA;
95 Image 100;
96 AA;
97l AA/Jonathan Smith;
97r AA/Jonathan Smith;
98 Edinburgh Inspiring Capital www.edinburgh-inspiringcapital.com;
99 Stockbyte Royalty Free;
100 ImageState;
101 AA/Jonathan Smith;
103 The Witchery by the Castle;
104 AA/Jonathan Smith;
105 AA/Simon McBride;
106 AA/Brent Madison;

107 Edinburgh Inspiring Capital
www.edinburgh-inspiringcapital.com;
108 AA/Jeff Beazley;
110 AA/M Alexander;
111 AA/Jeff Beazley;
112 AA/P Sharp;
113bl AA/Sue Anderson;
113br AA/Sue Anderson;
114 AA/Sue Anderson;
115l AA;
115r AA/Harry Williams;
116 Peter T Lovatt/Alamy;
117t AA/Jeff Beazley;
117c AA/Jeff Beazley;
118 AA/Sue Anderson;
119 AA/Sue Anderson;
120l AA/Jim Henderson;
120r AA/Jeff Beazley;
121 AA/Stephen Whitehorne;
122t AA/Richard Elliott;
122b AA/M Alexander;
123 AA/Sue Anderson;
124l David Robertson/National Trust for Scotland;
124r South West Images Scotland/Alamy;
125c AA/Sue Anderson;
125b AA;
126 AA/Jeff Beazley;
127 AA/Jeff Beazley;
128 AA/Sue Anderson;
129 AA/Sue Anderson;
130 AA/Cameron Lees;
131 AA/Cameron Lees;
132 AA/Cameron Lees;
133 AA/Cameron Lees;
134 AA/E A Bowness;
136 AA/M Alexander;
137 AA/Peter Sharpe;
139 AA/Jonathan Smith;
140 AA/S&O Mathews;
141 ImageState;
142 AA/Jon Wyand;
143 Photodisc;
144 AA/Ken Paterson;
146 AA/Sue Anderson;
149 AA/Stephen Gibson;
150 colinspics/Alamy;
156 Steve Hosey@DRS Graphics;
157 AA/M Alexander;
158 Culture and Sport Glasgow (Museums);
159t Culture and Sport Glasgow (Museums);
159b Culture and Sport Glasgow (Museums);
161t Culture and Sport Glasgow (Museums);
161b Culture and Sport Glasgow (Museums);
162 Culture and Sport Glasgow (Museums);
163 AA/Stephen Whitehorne;
164l AA/Stephen Gibson;
164r Glyn Satterley 1992/National Trust for Scotland;
165 AA/Stephen Whitehorne;
166l AA/Stephen Whitehorne;
166r The National Piping Centre;
167 Culture and Sport Glasgow (Museums);
168 Glasgow City Marketing Bureau;
169t AA/Stephen Gibson;
169b Glasgow City Marketing Bureau;
170t Culture and Sport Glasgow (Museums);
170b National Trust for Scotland;
171 Culture and Sport Glasgow (Museums);
172 Culture and Sport Glasgow (Museums);
173l Clyde Maritime Trust;
173r Glasgow City Marketing Bureau;
174 National Trust for Scotland;175 Doug Corrance/StillDigital Picture Library;
176 Andy Arthur/Alamy;
178 AA/Stephen Whitehorne;
180 Centre for Contemporary Arts;
182 AA/Stephen Whitehorne;
183 Photodisc;
184 Malmaison Glasgow;
185 AA/Stephen Whitehorne;
186 AA/David W Robertson;
188 AA/Stephen Whitehorne;
189l AA/Jonathan Smith;
189r AA/Steve Day;
190 AA/Jonathan Smith;
191 AA/Jonathan Smith;
192l AA/Jonathan Smith;
192r AA/Sue Anderson;
193 David Robertson/Alamy;
194 AA/Jonathan Smith;
195 AA/Michael Taylor;
196 AA/Ronnie Weir;
197 AA/D W Robertson;
198 AA/Sue Anderson;
199t AA/Jonathan Smith;
199b AA/Steve Day;
200 Navin Mistry/Alamy;
201 AA/Jonathan Smith;
202 VisitScotland/Scottish Viewpoint;
203 AA/Jonathan Smith;
204 Robert Harding Picture Library Ltd/Alamy;
205 AA/Stephen Whitehorne;
206 AA/Steve Day;
207 AA/Jim Henderson;
208 AA/Sue Anderson;
209 AA/Ken Paterson;
210 AA/Steve Day;
212 AA/Ronnie Weir;
214 AA/Michael Taylor;
216 AA/David W Robertson;
219 AA/David W Robertson;
220 AA/Steve Day;
221 AA/Jonathan Smith;
222 Gleneagles Hotel;
223 AA/David W Robertson;
224 Photodisc;
225 AA/Jonathan Smith;
226 AA/Steve Day;
228 AA/Jonathan Smith;
229 AA/Ronnie Weir;
230 AA/David W Robertson;
232 AA/Ronnie Weir;
233 AA/Michael Taylor;
234 AA/Stephen Whitehorne;
235 AA/Jonathan Smith;
236 AA/Mark Hamblin;
237l AA/Mark Hamblin;
237r AA/Jonathan Smith;
238l AA/Ronnie Weir;
238r AA;
239l AA/Dennis Hardley;
239r AA/Jim Carnie;
240 AA/Ronnie Weir;
241 Doug Houghton/Alamy;
242 AA/Stephen Whitehorne;
243l AA/Sue Anderson;
243r AA/Steve Day;
244 AA/Jim Henderson;
245 AA/Steve Day;
246l AA/Jim Henderson;
246r AA/Jim Henderson;
247 AA/Stephen Whitehorne;
248 John Macpherson/Alamy;
249l AA/Derek Forss;
249r AA/Richard Elliott;
250 AA/Jeff Beazley;
251t AA/Derek Forss;
251b AA/Ronnie Weir;
252l AA/Stephen Whitehorne;
252r AA/Michael Taylor;
253 AA/Stephen Whitehorne;
254l AA/Robert Eames;
254r AA/Derek Forss;
255l AA/Sue Anderson;
255r AA/Sue Anderson;

256 AA/Ronnie Weir;
257 AA/Stephen Whitehorne;
258t AA/Stephen Whitehorne;
258b AA/Stephen Whitehorne;
259 AA/Stephen Whitehorne;
260 AA/Stephen Whitehorne;
261 AA/Jonathan Smith;
262 AA/Jim Henderson;
263 Crown Copyright reproduced courtesy of Historic Scotland;
264 AA/Ronnie Weir;
265 AA/Mark Hamblin;
266 AA/Jim Carnie;
267 AA/Steve Day;
268 AA/Stephen Whitehorne;
269l AA/Steve Day;
269r AA/Jim Henderson;
270 AA/Ronnie Weir;
271 AA/Ken Paterson;
272 AA/Jim Henderson;
273 AA/Eric Ellington;
274 AA/Stephen Whitehorne;
275l Steve Austin/Stockscotland.com;
275r AA/A J Hopkins;
276 AA/Mark Hamblin;
277 AA/Jim Henderson;
278 AA/Sue Anderson;
279 Photodisc;
280 AA/Mark Hamblin;
281 AA/Mark Hamblin;
282 AA/Sue Anderson;
283 AA/Stephen Whitehorne;
284 AA/Jim Carnie;
285 AA/Jonathan Smith;
286 AA/Jonathan Smith;
287 AA/Mark Hamblin;
288 Three Chimneys Restaurant & House Over-By;
289 AA/Stephen Whitehorne;
290 AA/Stephen Whitehorne;
293 AA/Sue Anderson;
294 AA/Stephen Whitehorne;
296 AA/Stephen Whitehorne;
297 AA/Stephen Whitehorne;
298 AA/Stephen Whitehorne;
299l AA/Stephen Whitehorne;
299r AA/Stephen Whitehorne;
300l AA/Eric Ellington;
300r AA/Stephen Whitehorne;
301t AA/Stephen Whitehorne;
301b AA/Eric Ellington;
302 imagebroker/Alamy;
303 Scottish Viewpoint/Alamy;
304 AA/Eric Ellington;
305t Vincent Lowe/Alamy;
305b Bill Coster/NHPA/Photoshot;
306 Les Gibbon / Alamy;
307 Orkney Tourist Board, Colin Keldie;
308 AA;
309 AA/Eric Ellington;
310 AA/Eric Ellington;
311 AA/Sue Anderson;
314 AA/Jonathan Smith;
315t AA/Ken Paterson;
315b AA/David W Robertson;
317 AA/Stephen Whitehorne;
318 AA/Stephen Whitehorne;
320 AA/Jonathan Smith;
323 AA/Ken Paterson;
326 AA/Jonathan Smith;
327 AA/Sue Anderson;
328 AA/Ronnie Weir;
329 AA/Douglas Corrance;
332 AA/Jim Carnie;
333 AA/Stephen Whitehorne;
334 AA/David W Robertson;
334 AA/Mark Hamblin;
335 AA/Ken Paterson;
338 AA/Stephen Whitehorne;
339 AA/Eric Ellington;
340 AA/Jonathan Smith;
341 AA/David W Robertson;
345 AA/Mark Hamblin.

Every effort has been made to trace the copyright holders, and we apologise in advance for any unintentional omissions or errors. We would be pleased to apply any corrections in any following edition of this publication.

CREDITS

Managing editor
Sheila Hawkins

Project editor
Karen Kemp

Design
Drew Jones, pentacorbig, Nick Otway

Cover design
Chie Ushio

Picture research
Alice Earle

Image retouching and repro
Sarah Montgomery

Mapping
Maps produced by the Mapping Services
Department of AA Publishing

Main contributors
Kate Barrett, Johanna Campbell, Donna Dailey, Rebecca Ford, Mike Gerrard, David Halford, Christopher Harvie, Nicholas Lanng, Isla Love, Moira McCrossan, Jennifer Skelley, Pam Stagg, Gilbert Summers, Hugh Taylor, Ronald Turnbull, Jenny White, David Williams, Fiona Wood

Updaters
Rebecca Ford, Mike Gerrard, Donna Dailey

Indexer
Marie Lorimer

Production
Lyn Kirby, Karen Gibson

See It Scotland
ISBN 978-1-4000-0776-9
Third Edition

Published in the United States by Fodor's Travel and simultaneously in Canada by Random House of Canada Limited, Toronto.
Published in the United Kingdom by AA Publishing.
Fodor's is a registered trademark of Random House, Inc., and Fodor's See It is a trademark of Random House, Inc.
Fodor's Travel is a division of Random House, Inc.

Color separation by Keenes, Andover, UK
Printed and bound by Leo Paper Products, China
10 9 8 7 6 5 4 3 2

Special Sales: This book is available for special discounts for bulk purchases for sales promotions or premiums. Special editions, including personalized covers, excerpts of existing books, and corporate imprints, can be created in large quantities for special needs.
For more information, write to Special Markets/Premium Sales, 1745 Broadway, MD 6-2, New York, NY 10019
or e-mail specialmarkets@randomhouse.com
Important Note: Time inevitably brings changes, so always confirm prices, travel facts, and other perishable information when it matters. Although Fodor's cannot accept responsibility for errors, you can use this guide in the confidence that we have taken every care to ensure its accuracy.

A04206

This product includes mapping data licensed from Ordnance Survey® with the permission of the Controller of Her Majesty's Stationery Office. © Crown copyright 2009. All rights reserved. Licence number 100021153.
Traffic signs © Crown copyright. Reproduced with the permission of the Controller of Her Majesty's Stationery Office.
Transport map © Communicarta Ltd, UK
Weather chart statistics © Copyright 2004 Canty and Associates, LLC.

Dear Traveler,

From buying a plane ticket to booking a
room and seeing the sights, a trip goes much
more smoothly when you have a good travel
guide. Dozens of writers, editors, designers,
and cartographers have worked hard to
make the book you hold in your hands a
good one. Was it everything you expected?
Were our descriptions accurate? Were our
recommendations on target? And did you find
our tips and practical advice helpful? Your
ideas and experiences matter to us. If we have
missed or misstated something, we'd love
to hear about it. Fill out our survey at www.
fodors.com/books/feedback/, or e-mail us at
seeit@fodors.com. Or you can snail mail to the
See It Editor at Fodor's, 1745 Broadway, New
York, New York 10019. We'll look forward to
hearing from you.

Tim Jarrell
Publisher